SCRIPTURES OF THE CHURCH

BOARD OF EDITORS

SCRIPTURES OF THE CHURCH

SELECTIONS FROM THE

ENCYCLOPEDIA OF MORMONISM

EDITED BY

DANIEL H. LUDLOW

DESERET BOOK COMPANY
SALT LAKE CITY, UTAH

© 1992 by Macmillan Publishing Company, a division of Macmillan, Inc.

This collection of articles from the *Encyclopedia of Mormonism* is published by Deseret Book Company under license from Macmillan Publishing Company.

© 1995 by Deseret Book Company

Library of Congress Cataloging-in-Publication Data

Encyclopedia of Mormonism. Selections.
   Scriptures of the church : selections from the Encyclopedia of
Mormonism / edited by Daniel H. Ludlow.
      p.   cm.
   Includes bibliographical references and index.
   ISBN 0-87579-923-X
   1. Church of Jesus Christ of Latter-day Saints—Encyclopedias.
2. Mormon Church—Encyclopedias. 3. Mormons—Encyclopedias.
I. Ludlow, Daniel H. II. Title.
BX8605.5.E622   1995
289.3'03—dc20   94-24006
                                                                      CIP

Printed in the United States of America

10   9   8   7   6   5   4   3   2   1

CONTENTS

LIST OF ARTICLES

LIST OF CONTRIBUTORS

L. LaMar Adams
Brigham Young University
  Seth

William J. Adams, Jr.
Granite Community Education, Salt Lake City
  Jeremiah, Prophecies of

A. Gary Anderson
Brigham Young University
  Scripture: Words of Living Prophets

D. Brent Anderson
Business Consultant, Salt Lake City
  Book of Mormon Authorship

Richard Lloyd Anderson
Brigham Young University
  Book of Mormon Witnesses

Marilyn Arnold
Brigham Young University
  Book of Mormon: Book of Enos
  Book of Mormon: Book of Jarom
  Book of Mormon: Book of Omni

Danel W. Bachman
Church Educational System, Salt Lake City
  Anthon Transcript

Arthur A. Bailey
Church Educational System, Ephraim, Utah
  Adam: LDS Sources

Christine Purves Baker
Church Educational System, Peoria, AZ
  Helaman₃
  Ishmael

Kenneth W. Baldridge
Brigham Young University—Hawaii
  Pearl of Great Price: Contents and Publication

Terry B. Ball
Brigham Young University
  Book of Mormon: Second Book of Nephi

Glen E. Barksdale
Pleasant Grove Jr. High, Pleasant Grove, Utah
  Sunday

Norman J. Barlow
Church Educational System, Los Angeles
  David, King

Francine R. Bennion
Ricks College, Rexburg, ID
  Ruth

Steven D. Bennion
Ricks College, Rexburg, ID
  Abel

Reed A. Benson
Brigham Young University
  Sword of Laban

Allen E. Bergin
Brigham Young University
  Visions

Sue Bergin
Writer, Editor, Santa Monica, CA
  Lord's Prayer

David L. Bolliger
Church Educational System, Salt Lake City
  Israel: Lost Tribes of Israel

David F. Boone
Brigham Young University
 Signs of the Times

Donna Lee Bowen
Brigham Young University
 Women in the Book of Mormon

Walter D. Bowen
Brigham Young University
 Doctrine and Covenants: Section 107

Edward J. Brandt
Church Correlation Dept., Salt Lake City
 Aaron, Brother of Moses

Ralph A. Britsch
Brigham Young University
 Prophet: Prophets

Todd A. Britsch
Brigham Young University
 Prophet: Prophets

Bruce L. Brown
Brigham Young University
 Sin

Cheryl Brown
Brigham Young University
 Book of Mormon: Book of Alma

S. Kent Brown
Brigham Young University
 Israel: Overview
 Lehi

Victor L. Brown, Sr.
General Authority, Salt Lake City
 Doctrine and Covenants: Section 42

Glade L. Burgon
Church Educational System, Bountiful, UT
 Name of God

Marshall T. Burton
Church Educational System, Orem, UT
 Meridian of Time

C. Max Caldwell
Brigham Young University
 Doctrine and Covenants: Contents
 Doctrine and Covenants: Section 45
 Revelations, Unpublished

Beverly Campbell
Campbell Associates, Washington, DC
 Eve

Donald Q. Cannon
Brigham Young University
 Doctrine and Covenants: Section 76

Barbara R. Carter
Writer, Provo, UT
 Doctrine and Covenants: Section 88

Bruce A. Chadwick
Brigham Young University
 Native Americans

Jeffrey R. Chadwick
Church Educational System, Ogden, UT
 Daniel, Prophecies of

James H. Charlesworth
Princeton Theological Seminary
 Enoch: Ancient Sources

Lance D. Chase
Brigham Young University—Hawaii
 Spaulding Manuscript

Paul R. Cheesman [deceased]
Brigham Young University
 Book of Mormon: Book of Helaman
 Helaman$_2$

Lewis R. Church
Church Educational System, Pleasant Grove, UT
 Enoch: Book of Enoch

Carol L. Clark
Church General Relief Society Office, Salt Lake City
 Inspiration

E. Douglas Clark
Attorney, Salt Lake City
 Abraham

James R. Clark
Brigham Young University
  Joseph of Egypt: Writings of Joseph

John E. Clark
Brigham Young University
  Book of Mormon Geography

Robert A. Cloward
Church Educational System, Cedar City, UT
  Lost Scripture
  Scripture: Forthcoming Scripture

Clarissa Katherine Cole
Writer, Provo, UT
  Promised Land, Concept of a

Eleanor (Elly) Colton
Writer, Bethesda, MD
  Virgin Birth

Todd Compton
California State University, Northridge
  Organization of the Church in New
    Testament Times
  Symbolism

Lew W. Cramer
U. S. Commerce Dept., Washington, DC
  Abinadi

William J. Critchlow III
Attorney, Ogden, UT
  Manuscript, Lost 116 Pages

Larry E. Dahl
Brigham Young University
  Lectures on Faith

LeGrande Davies
Central Davis Jr. High, Layton, UT
  Isaiah: Texts in the Book of Mormon

W. D. Davies
Duke University
  Scripture: Scriptures

Franklin D. Day
Church Educational System, Orem, UT
  Elijah: LDS Sources

Ronald D. Dennis
Brigham Young University
  Gathering

Graham W. Doxey
General Authority, Salt Lake City
  Garden of Eden
  New Jerusalem

Roy W. Doxey
Church Correlation Dept., Salt Lake City
  Doctrine and Covenants: Overview

Richard D. Draper
Brigham Young University
  Hebrews, Epistle to the
  Predestination
  Sacrifice in Biblical Times

Norbert H. O. Duckwitz
Brigham Young University
  Amulek

Louise Gardiner Durham
Author, Provo, UT
  Sarah

George D. Durrant
Brigham Young University
  Doctrine and Covenants: Sections
    127–128

Rulon D. Eames
Church Educational System, West Jordan, UT
  Book of Mormon: First Book of Nephi
  Enoch: LDS Sources

Ze'ev W. Falk
Hebrew University, Jerusalem, Israel
  Law of Moses

Dennis D. Flake
Church Educational System, Fresno, CA
  Raising the Dead

Neil J. Flinders
Brigham Young University
  Voice of Warning

David Noel Freedman
University of Michigan
  Prophet: Biblical Prophets

Camille Fronk
LDS Business College, Salt Lake City

Mary, Mother of Jesus
Prophecy in the Book of Mormon

Cynthia M. Gardner
Genealogist, Provo, UT

Book of Remembrance

H. Dean Garrett
Brigham Young University

Doctrine and Covenants
Commentaries

Thomas Garrow
*Social Services, Navajo Nation,
Shiprock, NM*

Native Americans

Donald B. Gilchrist
Church Educational System, Sandy, UT

Wrath of God

David T. Giles
*Church Educational System, Salt Lake
City*

Joseph Smith—Matthew

Gary P. Gillum
Brigham Young University

Bible Dictionary

Alan Goff
Cornell University

Book of Mormon: Book of Mosiah

Paul G. Grant
Third District Court, Salt Lake City

Doctrine and Covenants: Sections
131–132

C. Wilfred Griggs
Brigham Young University

Apocalyptic Texts
Apocrypha and Pseudepigrapha
John the Beloved

John Franklin Hall
Brigham Young University

Peter

William J. Hamblin
Brigham Young University

Book of Mormon, History of
Warfare in

Ralph C. Hancock
Brigham Young University

Reason and Revelation

Grant R. Hardy
Brigham Young University

Book of Mormon Plates and Records
Gold Plates

Bruce T. Harper
Church Missionary Dept., Salt Lake City

Topical Guide

James R. Harris, Sr.
Brigham Young University

Cain

Leon R. Hartshorn
Brigham Young University

Doctrine and Covenants: Sections
137–138

Lisa Bolin Hawkins
Brigham Young University

Book of Mormon: Overview

Paul C. Hedengren
Brigham Young University

Bible: LDS Belief in the Bible
Miracles

Ray C. Hillam
Brigham Young University

Secret Combinations

George A. Horton, Jr.
Brigham Young University

Elias
Malachi, Prophecies of

Paul Y. Hoskisson
Brigham Young University

Book of Mormon Names
Oil, Consecrated
Urim and Thummim

Susan Howe
Brigham Young University
  Doctrine and Covenants: Sections
  121–123
  Parables

Glade O. Hunsaker
Brigham Young University
  Pearl of Great Price: Literature

Kent P. Jackson
Brigham Young University
  Neum
  Scripture: Authority of Scripture
  Zenock

Cardell K. Jacobson
Brigham Young University
  Doctrine and Covenants: Official
  Declaration—2

Gerald E. Jones
*Church Educational System, Concord,
  CA*
  Fate
  Man of Holiness
  Psalms, Messianic Prophecies in

L. Gary Lambert
Brigham Young University
  Allegory of Zenos
  Alma$_1$

Daniel H. Ludlow
Brigham Young University
  Zenos

Douglas Kent Ludlow
University of North Dakota
  Liahona

Victor L. Ludlow
Brigham Young University
  Bible: Bible
  David, Prophetic Figure of Last Days
  Isaiah: Authorship

Gerald N. Lund
*Church Educational System, Salt Lake
  City*
  John, Revelations of

Thomas W. Mackay
Brigham Young University
  Beatitudes
  James, Epistle of

Ann N. Madsen
*Brigham Young University Center for
  Near Eastern Studies, Jerusalem, Israel*
  Isaiah: Commentaries on Isaiah

John M. Madsen
Brigham Young University
  Hope of Israel
  Marriage Supper of the Lamb

Truman G. Madsen
*Brigham Young University Center for
  Near Eastern Studies, Jerusalem, Israel*
  Scripture: Scriptures
  Zionism

Robert L. Marrott
*Church Educational System,
  Bloomington, IN*
  Dove, Sign of the
  Witnesses, Law of

Robert J. Matthews
Brigham Young University
  Joseph Smith Translation of the Bible
  (JST)

Cory H. Maxwell
Bookcraft Publishing Co., Salt Lake City
  Angel Moroni Statue
  Restoration of All Things

Liesel C. McBride
Writer, Orem, UT
  Joseph of Egypt: Seed of Joseph

Joseph Fielding McConkie
Brigham Young University
  Joseph of Egypt: Joseph, Son of Jacob

Mark L. McConkie
*University of Colorado at Colorado
  Springs*
  Translated Beings

Daniel B. McKinlay
Writer, Provo, UT
  Strait and Narrow

Donald W. Parry
Brigham Young University
  Book of Mormon as Literature
  Washings and Anointings

Robert E. Parsons
Brigham Young University
  Book of Mormon Plates and Records
  Infant Baptism: LDS Perspective

Robert C. Patch
Brigham Young University
  Martyrs
  New Testament

Charles Randall Paul
Businessman, Pleasant Grove, UT
  Book of Mormon: Third Nephi

Erich Robert Paul
Dickinson College, Carlisle, PA
  Astronomy, Scriptural References to

Daniel C. Peterson
Brigham Young University
  Book of Mormon Economy and
    Technology

H. Donl Peterson
Brigham Young University
  Book of Abraham: Origin of the Book
    of Abraham
  Book of Abraham: Translation and
    Publication of the Book of Abraham
  Book of Mormon Commentaries
  Moroni$_2$

Paul H. Peterson
Brigham Young University
  Civil War Prophecy
  Doctrine and Covenants: Section 89

R. Douglas Phillips
Brigham Young University
  James the Apostle

Wm. Revell Phillips
Brigham Young University
  Matthew, Gospel of

Paul B. Pixton
Brigham Young University
  Sacrament: Sacrament

John P. Pratt
Ashton Research Corp., Orem, UT
  Book of Mormon Chronology

Martin Raish
State University of New York,
  Binghamton
  Tree of Life

Ellis T. Rasmussen
Brigham Young University
  Deuteronomy
  Old Testament

Tim Rathbone
Lockheed Aircraft Corp., Hesperia, CA
  Book of Mormon Translation by
    Joseph Smith

Rex C. Reeve, Jr.
Brigham Young University
  Book of Mormon: Book of Mormon
  Book of Mormon: Fourth Nephi
  Brother of Jared

Noel B. Reynolds
Brigham Young University
  Book of Mormon, Government and
    Legal History in
  Nephi$_1$

Sydney Smith Reynolds
Author, Orem, UT
  Mother in Israel

Michael D. Rhodes
Air Force Academy, Colorado Springs,
  CO
  Book of Abraham: Facsimiles from the
    Book of Abraham
  Book of Abraham: Studies about the
    Book of Abraham

Paul C. Richards
Brigham Young University
  Doctrine and Covenants: Section 124

Eldin Ricks
Brigham Young University
  Book of Mormon: Title Page from the
    Book of Mormon
  Book of Mormon: The Words of
    Mormon

Douglas A. Stewart
Church Educational System, Sandy, UT
  Israel: Scattering of Israel

Hugh G. Stocks
University of Southern California
  Book of Mormon Translations

Brian D. Stubbs
College of Eastern Utah, San Juan Campus, Blanding, UT
  Book of Mormon Language

Terrence L. Szink
Doctoral Candidate, UCLA
  Lehi
  Oaths

John S. Tanner
Brigham Young University
  Jacob, Son of Lehi
  Sacrament: Sacrament Prayers

Morgan W. Tanner
Doctoral Candidate, UCLA
  Book of Mormon: Book of Ether
  Jaredites

Charles D. Tate, Jr.
Brigham Young University
  Priestcraft

George S. Tate
Brigham Young University
  Covenants in Biblical Times

Bruce T. Taylor
Physician, Spanish Fork, UT
  Book of Moses

J. Lewis Taylor
Church Educational System, Salt Lake City
  Book of Life

M. Catherine Thomas
Brigham Young University
  Scripture, Interpretation within Scripture

Gordon C. Thomasson
School for International Training, Brattleboro, VT
  Circumcision
  Lamanites

Stephen E. Thompson
Post-Doctoral Fellowship, Brown University, Providence, RI
  Book of Abraham: Contents of the Book of Abraham

Melvin J. Thorne
F.A.R.M.S., Provo, UT
  Ezias
  Helaman$_1$
  Moroni$_1$
  Mosiah$_1$
  Nephi$_2$
  Nephi$_3$
  Nephi$_4$

Jay M. Todd
Ensign, Salt Lake City
  Papyri, Joseph Smith

Brent L. Top
Brigham Young University
  War in Heaven

Richard E. Turley, Jr.
Church Historical Dept., Salt Lake City
  Seer Stones

Rodney Turner
Brigham Young University
  Sons of Perdition
  Unpardonable Sin

Grant Underwood
Church Educational System, Pomona, CA
  Doctrine and Covenants: Sections 20–22
  Millenarianism

Robert Timothy Updegraff
Businessman, North Huntington, PA
  Sermon on the Mount

Bruce T. Verhaaren
Northeastern Illinois University, Chicago
  Ten Commandments

Klis Hale Volkening
Author and designer, Salt Lake City
  Doctrine and Covenants: Section 25

Steven C. Walker
Brigham Young University
  Doctrine and Covenants as Literature

Douglas A. Wangsgard
Church Educational System, Warrenton, VA
  Washing of Feet

John W. Welch
Brigham Young University
  Book of Mormon Religious Teachings
    and Practices
  Book of Mormon Translation by
    Joseph Smith

R. J. Zvi Werblowsky
Hebrew University, Jerusalem, Israel
  Elijah: Ancient Sources

S. Michael Wilcox
Church Educational System, Salt Lake City
  Book of Mormon: Book of Moroni
  Doctrine and Covenants: Sections
    109–110
  Samuel the Lamanite

Camille S. Williams
Brigham Young University
  Women in the Book of Mormon

Clyde J. Williams
Brigham Young University
  Book of Mormon: Book of Jacob
  Standard Works

William A. Wilson
Brigham Young University
  Three Nephites

Diane E. Wirth
Museum of Ancient Civilizations, Westford, MA
  Book of Mormon Authorship

Robert J. Woodford
Church Educational System, Salt Lake City
  Book of Commandments
  Doctrine and Covenants Editions

Dan J. Workman
Church Educational System, Orem, UT
  Doctrine and Covenants: Section 93

Dennis A. Wright
Church Educational System, Surrey, British Columbia
  Great and Abominable Church

H. Curtis Wright
Brigham Young University
  Mulek

PREFACE

This preface appears in volume 1 of the Encyclopedia of Mormonism. *Its spirit applies to all the volumes containing selections from the* Encyclopedia.

According to a standard definition, an encyclopedia is to "treat comprehensively all the various branches of knowledge" pertaining to a particular subject. The subject of this *Encyclopedia* is The Church of Jesus Christ of Latter-day Saints, widely known as the Mormon church. This is the first major encyclopedia published about the Mormons. It presents the work of hundreds of Latter-day Saint (LDS) lay scholars and others from throughout the world and provides a comprehensive reporting of Mormon history, scripture, doctrines, life, and knowledge, intended for both the non-Mormon and the LDS reader. Readers will find an article on almost any topic conceivably related to the general topic of Mormonism, and yet no article is exhaustive because of space limitations. Most articles include bibliographic references; cross-references to other articles in the *Encyclopedia* are indicated by small capital letters.

When Macmillan Publishing Company asked authorities at Brigham Young University whether they would be interested in developing an encyclopedia about The Church of Jesus Christ of Latter-day Saints, President Jeffrey R. Holland took the query to his Board of Trustees. They instructed him to proceed. Working closely with Church authorities and Macmillan, President Holland chose an editor in chief and a board of editors. Discussion of possible titles concluded that the work should be called the *Encyclopedia of Mormonism* since that is the term by which the Church is most widely known, though unofficially.

The contract called for a work of one million words in about 1,500 articles in four volumes including pictures, maps, charts, appendices, indices, and a glossary. It soon became apparent that references to what the Church calls the standard works—the Bible, the Book of Mormon, the Doctrine and Covenants, and the Pearl of Great Price—would be so frequent that readers who did not have ready access to those works would be at a serious disadvantage in using the *Encyclopedia*. A fifth volume was decided upon to include all the LDS standard works except the Bible, which is readily available everywhere.

The Church does not have a paid clergy or a battery of theologians to write the articles. It functions with a lay ministry, and all members are encouraged to become scholars of the gospel. Over 730 men and women were asked to write articles on topics assigned because of previous interest and study.

Six major articles unfold the history of the Church: (1) the background and founding period in New York; (2) the Ohio, Missouri, and Illinois period ending with the martyrdom of Joseph Smith; (3) the exodus west and the early pioneer period under Brigham Young; (4) the late pioneer Utah period ending at the turn of the century and statehood; (5) a transitional period during the early twentieth century; and (6) the post–World War II period of international growth. The history of the Church has been dramatic and moving, considering its brief span of just over 160 years. Compared to Catholicism, Judaism, ancient Far East religions, and many Protestant churches, the Church has a very short history. Nearly 250 articles explain the doctrines of the Church, with special emphasis on basic principles and ordinances of the gospel of Jesus Christ. Twenty-four articles are clustered under the title "Jesus Christ," and another sixteen include his name in the title or relate directly to his divine mission and atonement.

Over 150 articles relate the details on such topics as the First Vision, Zion's Camp, Handcart Companies, Plural Marriage, the Salt Lake Temple, Temple Square, and the Church throughout the world. Biographies cover men and women contemporary in the life of Joseph Smith, Presidents of the Church, and auxiliary founders and past presidents. The only biography of a person living at the time of publication is on the present prophet and President of the Church, Ezra Taft Benson. [Since the publication of the *Encyclopedia of Mormonism*, Howard W. Hunter was sustained as President of the Church.]

And finally, there are over a hundred articles primarily concerned with how Latter-day Saints relate to their families, the Church, and to society in general. It is said there is a "Mormon culture," and several articles explore Mormon lifestyle, folklore, folk art, artists, literature, and other facets that distinguish Latter-day Saints.

It may be that the growth of the Church in the last decades has mandated the encyclopedic account that is presented here. Yet, even as the most recent programs were set down and the latest figures listed, there is an acute awareness that the basic tenet of the Church is that its canon is open-ended. The contemporary President of the Church is sustained as a "prophet, seer, and revelator." While this makes some theological discussion moot, the basic beliefs of the Latter-day Saints, summarized in the Articles of Faith, do not change.

In several areas, the Church shares beliefs held by other Christians, and a number of scholars from other faiths were asked to present articles. However, the most distinctive tenets of the Church—those regarding the premortal and postmortal life, living prophets who receive continuous and current revelation from God, sacred ordinances for deceased ancestors, moral and health codes that provide increasingly well-documented benefits, and the potential within man for progression into an infinite future—are all treated primarily by writers selected from among Latter-day Saints.

Lest the role of the *Encyclopedia* be given more weight than it deserves, the editors make it clear that those who have written and edited have only tried to explain their understanding of Church history, doctrines, and procedures; their statements and opinions remain their own. The *Encyclopedia of Mormonism* is a joint product of Brigham Young University and Macmillan Publishing Company, and the contents do not necessarily represent the official position of The Church of Jesus Christ of Latter-day Saints. In no sense does the *Encyclopedia* have the force and authority of scripture.

ACKNOWLEDGMENTS*

The support and assistance of many persons and groups are necessary to produce a work as extensive as an encyclopedia. Special thanks are extended to the executives of Macmillan Publishing Company who introduced the idea of the the *Encyclopedia of Mormonism* to Brigham Young University. Charles E. Smith made initial contacts on the project, while Philip Friedman, President and Publisher of Macmillan Reference Division, and Elly Dickason, Editor in Chief of Macmillan Reference Division, have followed through on the multitudinous details, demonstrating skill and patience in working with us in the preparation of this five-volume work.

The editors also wish to thank the General Authorities of the Church for designating Brigham Young University as the contractual Author of the *Encyclopedia.* Two members of the Board of Trustees of the university, who are also members of the Quorum of the Twelve Apostles, were appointed by the First Presidency to serve as advisers to the project: Elder Neal A. Maxwell and Elder Dallin H. Oaks. Other General Authorities who accepted special assignments related to the project include four members of the Quorum of Seventy: Elders Dean L. Larsen, Carlos E. Asay, Marlin K. Jensen, and Jeffrey R. Holland.

Special support also came from the Administration of BYU. Jeffrey R. Holland, president of BYU at the time the project was initiated, was instrumental in appointing the Board of Editors and in developing early guidelines. Rex E. Lee, current president of BYU, has continued this support.

* The major parts of the acknowledgments appear in volume 1 of the *Encyclopedia of Mormonism.* The statement has been modified here by (1) deleting credits to individuals and institutions providing general help, illustrations, and photographs for the *Encyclopedia* and (2) adding the names of those giving special assistance to the preparation of this particular publication.

The efforts of the Board of Editors and the Project Coordinator, whose names are listed at the front of each volume, have shaped and fashioned every aspect of the project. We offer special thanks to them, and to companions and family members for graciously supporting our efforts over many months. Others who shared in final editing include Bruce B. Clark, Soren F. Cox, Marshall R. Craig, and Ellis T. Rasmussen.

Many others have provided assistance in specialized areas, including Larry E. Dahl, Michelle Eckersley, Gary R. Gillespie, Devan Jensen, Luene Ludlow, Jack M. Lyon, Robert J. Matthews, Frank O. May, Charlotte McDermott, Robert L. Millet, Don E. Norton, Monte S. Nyman, Patricia J. Parkinson, Charlotte A. Pollard, Larry C. Porter, Merle Romer, Evelyn E. Schiess, Judith Skousen, Charles D. Tate, Jr., Jay M. Todd, and John Sutton Welch. Special thanks also to Ronald Millett and Sheri Dew at Deseret Book Company for their help with this volume.

Finally, we express appreciation to the 738 authors who contributed their knowledge and insights. The hopes of all who were involved with this project will be realized if the *Encyclopedia* assists readers to come to a greater understanding and appreciation of the history, scriptures, doctrines, practices, and procedures of The Church of Jesus Christ of Latter-day Saints.

TOPICAL OUTLINE

The topical outline is designed to help the reader discover all the articles in this volume related to a particular subject. The title of every article in this volume is listed in the topical outline at least once.

The volume *Scriptures of the Church* contains selected articles from the *Encyclopedia of Mormonism* related to the general topic of scripture, including such articles as "Canon," "Lost Scripture," and all the major articles associated directly with the Bible (Old Testament, New Testament), the Book of Mormon, the Doctrine and Covenants, and the Pearl of Great Price.

A. The Bible, both Old Testament and New Testament.

    1. *Persons, places, and events of the Bible:* Aaron, Brother of Moses; Abel; Abraham; Adam*; Appendix: Joseph Smith Translation of the Bible (Selections); Armageddon; Cain; Daniel, Prophecies of; David, King; David, Prophetic Figure of Last Days; Elias; Elijah*; Elohim; Enoch*; Ephraim; Eve; Ezekiel, Prophecies of; Isaiah*; Israel*; James the Apostle; Jeremiah, Prophecies of; Jerusalem; John the Baptist; John the Beloved; Joseph of Egypt*; Malachi, Prophecies of; Mary, Mother of Jesus; Moses; Noah; Paul; Peter; Ruth; Sarah; Sermon on the Mount; Seth. [Note: The volume *Jesus Christ and His Gospel* contains numerous articles from the *Encyclopedia* under the title "Jesus Christ*."]

    2. *Selected messages and teachings related to the Bible:* Astronomy, Scriptural References to; Beatitudes; Circumcision; Covenants in Biblical Times; Creation, Creation Accounts; Daniel, Prophecies of; Enoch*;

* Indicates additional related articles are clustered under that entry title.

Ezekiel, Prophecies of; Hope of Israel; Infant Baptism*; Isaiah*; Israel*; Jeremiah, Prophecies of; Lord's Prayer; Predestination; Prophecy; Prophecy in Biblical Times; Prophet*; Psalms, Messianic Prophecies in; Restoration of All Things; Restoration of the Gospel of Jesus Christ; Reverence; Sabbath Day; Sacrament*; Sacrifice in Biblical Times; Second Coming of Jesus Christ; Sin; Sons of Perdition; Ten Commandments; Transfiguration; Unpardonable Sin.

3. *General topics related to the Bible:* Adamic Language; Apocalyptic Texts; Apocrypha and Pseudepigrapha; Armageddon; Bible*; Bible Dictionary; Bible, LDS; Bible Scholarship; Book of Remembrance; Canon; Deuteronomy; Dove, Sign of the; Fate; Garden of Eden; Gathering; Gentiles; Gentiles, Fulness of; Hebrews, Epistle to the; Inspiration; James, Epistle of; Jerusalem; Jews; John, Revelations of; Joseph Smith Translation of the Bible (JST) [Note: See also the Appendix item on this subject]; Law of Moses; Marriage Supper of the Lamb; Matthew, Gospel of; Meridian of Time; Millenarianism; Miracles; Mother in Israel; Mount of Transfiguration; New Heaven and New Earth; New Jerusalem; New Testament; Old Testament; Parables; "Peculiar" People; Promised Land, Concept of a; Raising the Dead; Revelations, Unpublished; Scripture*; Scripture, Interpretation within Scripture; Scripture Study; Seed of Abraham; Sermon on the Mount; Sign Seeking; Signs as Divine Witness; Stick of Joseph; Stick of Judah; Strait and Narrow; Symbolism; Theology; Topical Guide; Urim and Thummim; Virgin Birth; War in Heaven; Washing of Feet; Witnesses, Law of; Wrath of God.

B. **The Book of Mormon.**

1. *Persons, peoples, places, and events mentioned in the Book of Mormon:* Abinadi; Adam*; Alma$_1$; Alma$_2$; Amulek; Benjamin; Brother of Jared; Cumorah; Ephraim; Ezias; Helaman$_1$; Helaman$_2$; Helaman$_3$; Ishmael; Jacob, Son of Lehi; Jaredites; Joseph of Egypt*; Laman; Lamanites;

Lehi; Mormon; Moroni$_1$; Moroni$_2$; Moses; Mosiah$_1$; Mosiah$_2$; Mulek; Nephi$_1$; Nephi$_2$; Nephi$_3$; Nephi$_4$; Nephites; Neum; Noah; Samuel the Lamanite; Three Nephites; Zenock; Zenos; Zoram.

2. *Selected messages and teachings of the Book of Mormon:* Allegory of Zenos; Beatitudes; Gathering; Jews; Law of Moses; Lord's Prayer; New Heaven and New Earth; New Jerusalem; Oaths; Priestcraft; Prophecy in the Book of Mormon; Sign Seeking; Signs as Divine Witness; Sin; Translated Beings; Tree of Life; Unpardonable Sin; Virgin Birth; Visions. [Note: Numerous articles from the *Encyclopedia of Mormonism* related to the messages and teachings of the *Book of Mormon* are contained in the volume *Jesus Christ and His Gospel*.]

3. *General topics related to the Book of Mormon:* Angel Moroni Statue; Anthon Transcript; Astronomy, Scriptural References to; Book of Mormon*; Book of Mormon, Biblical Prophecies about; Book of Mormon, Government and Legal History in; Book of Mormon, History of Warfare in; Book of Mormon as Literature; Book of Mormon Authorship; Book of Mormon in a Biblical Culture; Book of Mormon Chronology; Book of Mormon Commentaries; Book of Mormon Economy and Technology; Book of Mormon Editions (1830–1981); Book of Mormon Geography; Book of Mormon Language; Book of Mormon Manuscripts; Book of Mormon Names; Book of Mormon Near Eastern Background; Book of Mormon Peoples; Book of Mormon Personalities; Book of Mormon Plates and Records; Book of Mormon Religious Teachings and Practices; Book of Mormon Studies; Book of Mormon Translation by Joseph Smith; Book of Mormon Translations; Book of Mormon Witnesses; Book of Remembrance; Canon; Fate; Gentiles; Gold Plates; Great and Abominable Church; Infant Baptism*; Isaiah*; Israel*; Joseph Smith—History; Liahona; Malachi, Prophecies of; Manuscript, Lost 116 Pages; Miracles; Moroni, Angel; Native Americans; Natural Man; Plates,

Metal; Predestination; Promised Land, Concept of a; Prophecy; Prophet*; Revelations, Unpublished; Scripture*; Scripture, Interpretation within Scripture; Scripture Study; Secret Combinations; Seer Stones; Spaulding Manuscript; Standard Works; Stick of Joseph; Stick of Judah; Sword of Laban; Symbolism; Ten Commandments; Urim and Thummim; *View of the Hebrews*; "Voice from the Dust"; Witnesses, Law of; Women in the Book of Mormon.

C. **The Doctrine and Covenants.**

1. *Persons, places, and events mentioned in the Doctrine and Covenants or associated with it:* Abraham; Adam*; Elias; Elijah*; Enoch*; John the Baptist; John the Beloved; Malachi, Prophecies of; Moses; New Jerusalem; Noah; Sarah; Zion. [Note: Additional articles on many persons, places, and events associated with the *Doctrine and Covenants* are in the volumes *Jesus Christ and His Gospel* and *Church History.*]

2. *Selected messages and teachings of the Doctrine and Covenants:* John, Revelations of; Man of Holiness; Name of God; New Heaven and New Earth; Oaths; Restoration of All Things; Restoration of the Gospel of Jesus Christ; Riches of Eternity; Sabbath Day; Sacrament*; Second Coming of Jesus Christ; Seed of Abraham; Sons of Perdition; Sunday; Unpardonable Sin; Washing of Feet; Washings and Anointings; Zion. [Note: Numerous articles from the *Encyclopedia of Mormonism* related to the messages and teachings of the *Doctrine and Covenants* are contained in the volume *Jesus Christ and His Gospel.*]

3. *General topics related to the Doctrine and Covenants:* Astronomy, Scriptural References to; Book of Commandments; Book of Life; Book of Remembrance; Canon; Civil War Prophecy; Doctrine and Covenants*; Doctrine and Covenants as Literature; Doctrine and Covenants Commentaries; Doctrine and Covenants Editions; Fate; Gentiles; Gentiles, Fulness of; Israel*; *Lectures on Faith;*

Law of Moses; Martyrs; Meridian of Time; Oil, Consecrated; Organization of the Church in New Testament Times; Reason and Revelation; Revelations, Unpublished; Reverence; Sabbath Day; Scripture*; Scripture, Interpretation within Scripture; Scripture Study; Sign Seeking; Signs; Signs as Divine Witness; Signs of the Times; Ten Commandments; Translated Beings; Voice of Warning; Wrath of God; Zionism.

D. The Pearl of Great Price.

1. *Persons, places, and events mentioned in the Pearl of Great Price:* Abel; Abraham; Adam*; Cain; Creation, Creation Accounts; Elijah*; Enoch*; Eve; Garden of Eden; James the Apostle; John the Baptist; John the Beloved; Malachi, Prophecies of; Moroni, Angel; Moses; Noah; Peter; Sarah; Seth.

2. *Selected messages and teachings of the Pearl of Great Price:* Creation, Creation Accounts; Second Coming of Jesus Christ; Signs as Divine Witness; Sin; Translated Beings; Visions. [Note: Many of the messages and teachings from the Pearl of Great Price associated with the Gospel of Jesus Christ are printed in the volume *Jesus Christ and His Gospel.*]

3. *General topics related to the Pearl of Great Price:* Astronomy, Scriptural References to; Book of Abraham*; Book of Moses; Book of Life; Book of Remembrance; Elohim; Garden of Eden; James, Epistle of; Joseph Smith—History; Joseph Smith—Matthew; Lost Scripture; Natural Man; Nature, Law of; New Heaven and New Earth; Papyri, Joseph Smith; Pearl of Great Price*; Restoration of the Gospel of Jesus Christ; Revelations, Unpublished; Sacrifice in Biblical Times; Scripture*; Scripture, Interpretation within Scripture; Sons of Perdition; Standard Works; War in Heaven.

KEY TO ABBREVIATIONS

AF Talmage, James E. *Articles of Faith.* Salt Lake City, 1890. (All references are to pagination in printings before 1960.)

BOM The Book of Mormon: Another Testament of Jesus Christ. Salt Lake City, 1981.

CHC *Comprehensive History of the Church,* 6 vols., ed. B. H. Roberts. Salt Lake City, 1930.

CR *Conference Reports.* Salt Lake City, 1898–.

CWHN *Collected Works of Hugh Nibley,* ed. S. Ricks, J. Welch, et al. Salt Lake City, 1985–.

Dialogue *Dialogue: A Journal of Mormon Thought,* 1965–.

D&C The Doctrine and Covenants of The Church of Jesus Christ of Latter-day Saints. Salt Lake City, 1981.

DS Smith, Joseph Fielding. *Doctrines of Salvation,* 3 vols. Salt Lake City, 1954–1956.

ER *Encyclopedia of Religion,* 16 vols., ed. M. Eliade. New York, 1987.

F.A.R.M.S. Foundation for Ancient Research and Mormon Studies. Provo, Utah.

HC *History of the Church,* 7 vols., ed. B. H. Roberts. Salt Lake City, 1st ed., 1902; 2nd ed., 1950. (All references are to pagination in the 2nd edition.)

HDC Historical Department of the Church, Salt Lake City.

IE *Improvement Era,* 1897–1970.

JC Talmage, James E. *Jesus the Christ.* Salt Lake City, 1915.

JD *Journal of Discourses,* 26 vols., ed. J. Watt. Liverpool, 1854–1886.

JST *Joseph Smith Translation of the Bible.*

MD McConkie, Bruce R. *Mormon Doctrine,* 2nd ed. Salt Lake City, 1966.

MFP *Messages of the First Presidency,* 6 vols., ed. J. Clark. Salt Lake City, 1965–1975.

PGP The Pearl of Great Price. Salt Lake City, 1981.

PJS *Papers of Joseph Smith,* ed. D. Jessee. Salt Lake City, 1989.

PWJS *The Personal Writings of Joseph Smith,* ed. D. Jessee. Salt Lake City, 1984.

T&S *Times and Seasons,* 1839–1846.

TPJS *Teachings of the Prophet Joseph Smith,* comp. Joseph Fielding Smith. Salt Lake City, 1938.

WJS *Words of Joseph Smith,* ed. A. Ehat and L. Cook. Provo, Utah, 1980.

A

AARON, BROTHER OF MOSES

Aaron was a son of Amram and Jochebed of the tribe of Levi (Ex. 6:20), and a brother of Moses and Miriam (Ex. 4:14; 15:20). God directed him to meet his brother at the "mount of God" (Ex. 4:27–28), and appointed him spokesman for Moses (Ex. 4:14–16; 7:1–2; 2 Ne. 3:17). The Aaronic Priesthood, or lesser priesthood in The Church of Jesus Christ of Latter-day Saints, takes its name from Aaron.

While the Israelites were encamped at Sinai, Aaron, two of his sons, and seventy elders accompanied Moses to the holy mountain, where they saw God (Ex. 24:1, 9–11). Aaron and his sons were called by God through the prophet Moses to serve in the priest's office (Ex. 28:1), Aaron becoming the "high," or chief, priest over the Levitical order (Num. 3:32). His call from God through a prophet is used as an example for all who receive any priesthood appointment of God (Heb. 5:4). He held the Melchizedek Priesthood, but as chief priest of the lesser priesthood he served in a lesser position equivalent to that of the modern Presiding Bishop (John Taylor, *Items on the Priesthood,* p. 5, Salt Lake City, 1881). Direct descendants of the firstborn son of Aaron have a legal right to the presidency of this priesthood (i.e., bishop; D&C 68:15–18; 107:16–17), but such an appointment requires a call from the First Presidency of the Church (D&C 68:20).

Aaron was not privileged to enter the land of promise (Num.

20:7–13). Malachi prophesied that, in the latter days, the sons of Levi—which would include Aaron's descendants—would again offer an offering in righteousness (Mal. 3:1–3; cf. D&C 13:1). Moreover, all who receive both the Aaronic and Melchizedek priesthoods and magnify their callings through sacrifice and righteous lives are spoken of as the sons of Moses and of Aaron (D&C 84:18, 27, 30–32, 34).

BIBLIOGRAPHY

Palmer, Lee A. *Aaronic Priesthood Through the Centuries.* Salt Lake City, 1964.

EDWARD J. BRANDT

ABEL

Latter-day scripture reveals much about Abel beyond what is contained in the Bible. He and CAIN had older brothers and sisters (Moses 5:2), and Abel "was a keeper of sheep" (Gen. 4:2; Moses 5:17). To his parents, the Lord had given "commandments, that they should worship the Lord their God, and should offer the firstlings of their flocks, for an offering unto the Lord" (Moses 5:5). ADAM and EVE were obedient to the Lord's commands (Moses 5:6), and Abel also "hearkened unto the voice of the Lord. . . . And the Lord had respect unto Abel, and to his offering" (Moses 5:17, 20). On the other hand, Cain specifically at Satan's behest brought an unacceptable offering (Moses 5:18–19, 21; cf. *TPJS*, pp. 58–60).

The book of Moses clarifies the Lord's differing responses to Abel and Cain, and indicates that Adam and Eve had taught their children about the things of God: "And Adam and Eve . . . made all things [of God] known unto their sons and their daughters" (Moses 5:12). Subsequently, Abel "walked in holiness before the Lord" (Moses 5:26), but Cain "loved Satan more than God" (Moses 5:18). When his offering was not accepted, Cain "rejected the greater counsel which was had from God" and "listened not any more to the voice of the Lord, neither to Abel, his brother" (Moses 5:25–26). When Satan promised Cain that "I will deliver thy brother Abel into thine hands," Cain exulted "that I may murder and get gain" (Moses 5:29–31; cf. Hel. 6:27). As a result, Cain "rose up against Abel his brother, and slew him" (Gen. 4:8; Moses 5:32), and said, "I am free; surely the flocks of my brother falleth into my hands" (Moses 5:33). The unconscionable nature of Cain's murder of Abel is underscored by the fact that thereafter "Cain was shut out from the presence of the Lord" (Moses 5:41).

The New Testament affirms Abel's faithfulness and obedience to God: "By faith Abel offered unto God a more excellent sacrifice than Cain, by which he obtained witness that he was righteous, God testifying of his gifts: and by it he being dead yet speaketh" (Heb. 11:4). Joseph Smith taught that "God spoke to [Abel]: indeed it is said that God talked with him; and if He did, would He not, seeing that Abel was righteous, deliver to him the whole plan of the Gospel? . . . How could Abel offer a sacrifice and look forward with faith on the Son of God, for a remission of his sins, and not understand the Gospel?" (*TPJS*, p. 59; cf. Moses 5:6–12). Latter-day scripture also states that the priesthood among the ancients had been passed down through Abel, who was ordained by Adam (D&C 84:6–17).

BIBLIOGRAPHY

McConkie, Bruce R. *A New Witness for the Articles of Faith*, pp. 167–68, 340, 658–59. Salt Lake City, 1985.

STEVEN D. BENNION

ABINADI

Abinadi was a courageous prophet (150 B.C.), and the best-known martyr in the Book of Mormon. His ministry and execution recounted at the heart of the book of Mosiah sharpen the contrast between righteous King BENJAMIN and wicked King Noah. ALMA₁, a converted eyewitness, recorded Abinadi's main words shortly after they were spoken (Mosiah 17:4).

Abinadi belonged to a small group of reactionary NEPHITES who had returned from Zarahemla a generation earlier to repossess from the LAMANITES the city of Nephi, the traditional Nephite capital, and its temple. When the excesses of the apostate Nephite king and priests grew intolerable, Abinadi was commanded of the Lord to denounce publicly their abominations; he prophesied their coming captivity and affliction. Abinadi was condemned to death by Noah for this, but escaped.

Where he lived in exile is unknown. Similarities between his and Benjamin's words (cf. Mosiah 16:1; 3:20; 16:5; 2:38; 16:10–11; 3:24–25) could mean that he spent some time in Zarahemla with King Benjamin and his people (W of M 1:16–17), or received similar revelation during this period.

After two years, having been commanded again by the Lord to prophesy, Abinadi reentered the city of Nephi in disguise. Before a crowd, he pronounced a curse in the name of the Lord upon the unrepentant people, their land, and their grain, with forthright predictions of destruction and humiliating bondage, reminiscent of Israel's suffering in Egypt. In a potent curse, like those used in the ancient Near East to condemn covenant breakers, he testified that Noah's life would "be valued even as a garment in a hot furnace" (Mosiah 12:3).

Abinadi was apprehended by the people, bound, delivered to Noah, and accused of lying about the king and prophesying falsely. Both accusations were violations under their law, the LAW OF MOSES (Mosiah 13:23; Ex. 20:16; Deut. 18:20–22). The dual nature of the charges appears to have complicated the ensuing trial, the king typically having jurisdiction over political charges, and the priests over religious matters.

The trial first focused on the charge of false prophecy. The priests challenged Abinadi to interpret Isaiah 52:7–10. They presumably thought this text showed that God had spoken "comfort" to their own people, who had seen the land "redeemed." They contended that whereas Isaiah extolled those who brought "good tidings," Abinadi spoke ill. Under such interpretation, Abinadi's curses conflicted with ISAIAH and were held by the priests to be false and unlawful.

Abinadi rebutted the priests in several ways. He accused them of misunderstanding and disobeying the law. He extracted from them an admission that salvation requires obedience to the law and then rehearsed to them the TEN COMMANDMENTS, the basic law of the covenant that they had not kept. He miraculously withstood the king's attempt to silence him, "and his face shone with exceeding luster, even as Moses' did while in the mount of Sinai" (Mosiah 13:5).

He then quoted Isaiah 53 and explained its relation to the coming Messiah.

Abinadi's prophetic words are among the most powerful in the Book of Mormon. He explained the "form" and coming of God mentioned in Isaiah 52:14 and 53:2 (Mosiah 13:34; 14:2) as the coming of a son in the flesh, thus "being the Father and the Son" (Mosiah 15:1–5). He also taught that God would suffer as the "sheep before her shearers" (Isa. 53:7; Mosiah 14:7). Abinadi was then in a position to answer the priests' question about Isaiah 52:7–10. He proclaimed that those "who shall declare his generation" (cf. Mosiah 15:10) and "publish peace" (Mosiah 15:14) are God's prophets and that they and all who hearken unto their words are his "seed" (Mosiah 15:11, 13). They are the ones who truly bring "good tidings" of salvation, redemption, comfort through Christ, and the reign of God at the Judgment Day.

Using Isaiah's text, Abinadi showed that God could not redeem Noah's people who had willfully rebelled against deity, and that true redemption comes only through repentance and acceptance of Christ. He also showed that his prophecies did not contradict the Isaiah text quoted by the priests.

Noah desired that Abinadi should be put to death, evidently on the charge of bearing false witness against him as the king. A young priest named Alma valiantly attested to the truthfulness of Abinadi's testimony, whereupon he was expelled and the trial recessed for three days while Abinadi was held in prison.

When the trial reconvened, Abinadi was presumably accused of blasphemy (Mosiah 17:8), another capital offense under the law of Moses (Lev. 24:10–16). Noah gave him the opportunity to recant, but Abinadi refused to change God's message, even on threats of death.

Noah was intimidated and desired to release Abinadi. The priests, however, accused Abinadi of a fourth crime, that of reviling against the king (Mosiah 17:12; Ex. 22:28). On this ground Noah condemned Abinadi, and his priestly accusers scourged and burned him. It was normal under Mosaic law for the accusers to inflict the punishment, but burning was an extraordinary form of execution. It mirrored Abinadi's alleged crime: he was burned just as he had said Noah's life would be valued as a garment in a furnace. As Abinadi died, he prophesied that the same fate would befall his accusers.

This prophecy was soon fulfilled (Mosiah 17:15–18; 19:20; Alma 25:7–12).

Abinadi was remembered by the Nephites in at least three roles:

1. To Alma, his main convert, Abinadi was a prophet of Christ. Alma taught Abinadi's words concerning the death and resurrection of Christ, the resurrection of the dead, the redemption of God's people (Mosiah 18:1–2), and the mighty change of heart through their conversion (Alma 5:12). Through Alma's descendants, Abinadi influenced the Nephites for centuries.

2. To Ammon, who beheld the martyrdom of 1,005 of his own converts (Alma 24:22), Abinadi was recalled as the prime martyr "because of his belief in God" (Alma 25:11; cf. Mosiah 17:20; see also Mosiah 7:26–28). This was recognized as the real reason for Abinadi's death, since the priests' charge of reviling proved to be a false pretext.

3. To MORMON, who witnessed the decadence and destruction of the Nephites 500 years later, Abinadi was remembered for prophesying that because of wickedness evil would come upon the land and that the wicked would be utterly destroyed (Morm. 1:19; cf. Mosiah 12:7–8).

BIBLIOGRAPHY
Welch, John W. "Judicial Process in the Trial of Abinadi." Provo, Utah, 1981.

LEW W. CRAMER

ABRAHAM

Few biblical characters figure so prominently in LDS faith as does Abraham. Belief that he was a real person is shared by others, but the LDS approach is unique: Revelations received by the Prophet Joseph Smith confirm the basic historicity of Genesis and add information echoed in ancient sources, many of which have emerged since his day.

The BOOK OF ABRAHAM as restored by Joseph Smith autobiographically recounts Abraham's early life, explaining why he was singled out as the pivotal recipient of divine promises for the blessing of mankind. Not only had he been foreordained in premortal life (Abr. 3:23; cf. *Apocalypse of Abraham* 22:1–5), but as a young man in Ur he opposed idolatry and human sacrifice, ironically turning him into an intended victim (Abr. 1:5–20; cf. *Genesis Rabbah* 38:13). The irony increases when God's last-minute rescue of Abraham foreshadowed what would transpire at Abraham's offering of Isaac.

After marrying SARAH and learning of his lineal right to the patriarchal order of the priesthood as disclosed in the "records of the fathers" (Abr. 1:2–4, 26, 31; 2:2; *Jubilees* 12:27; cf. D&C 107:40–57), Abraham traveled to Haran, where he apparently received his ordination (Abr. 2:9–11; *WJS*, pp. 245, 303). He also saw the Lord, who gave him remarkable promises: Abraham would be blessed above measure; his posterity would carry the gospel to all nations; and all who received it would bear his name, be accounted his posterity, and bless him as their father (Abr. 2:6–11; cf. Gen. 12:1–3).

Accompanied by their converts, Abraham and Sarah proceeded to Canaan (Abr. 2:15; *Genesis Rabbah* 39:14). Famine soon forced them to Egypt, but not before God commanded Abraham to ask Sarah to pose as his sister (Abr. 2:22–25; *Genesis Apocryphon* 19:14–21), and then showed him a vision of the cosmos and creation so that he could teach these things to the Egyptians (Abr. 3–5; cf. *Sefer Yetsirah*).

The book of Abraham narrative ends here, but the book's last facsimile (no. 3) depicts Pharaoh—who traditionally claimed exclusive possession of priesthood and kingship (Abr. 1:25–27)—honoring Abraham's priesthood by allowing him to occupy the throne and instruct the court in astronomy (cf. *Pseudo-Eupolemus*; Josephus, *Antiquities* 1.viii.2). Pharaoh's recognition of Abraham's priesthood was unknown in any other ancient source until the 1947 discovery of the *Genesis Apocryphon,* purporting, like the book of Abraham, to contain an autobiographical account of Abraham but continuing the narrative into Egypt (*Genesis Apocryphon* 20:8–34): When Pharaoh took Sarah to the palace, Abraham tearfully appealed to God, who immediately protected her by afflicting Pharaoh. The affliction worsened, but Pharaoh finally had a dream of Abraham healing him; the patriarch was then summoned and, laying hands on Pharaoh's head, restored him to health. This is the only known instance in the Old

Testament or related pseudepigrapha of a healing by laying on of hands, and it sets the stage for the book of Abraham scene. Together these two sources explain why the ancients considered Abraham's encounter with Pharaoh "a crucial event in the history of mankind" (Nibley, 1981 [citing Wacholder], p. 63).

But it was Sarah who had faced the most difficult dilemma in Egypt: If she honored both Abraham's request (by feigning maidenhood) and her marriage vows (by refusing Pharaoh's advances), she faced certain death. The alternative was simply to accept her new role with its dazzling wealth and influence. Sarah proved her loyalty at the peril of her life, and was—as were Abraham and Isaac—finally rescued by God. Her sacrifice demonstrated her equality with Abraham and their mutual dependence (*CWHN* 1:98; *IE* 73 [Apr. 1970]:79–95).

Later events of Abraham's life are illuminated by other LDS sources, as when Sarah, still childless after returning to Canaan, gave her maid Hagar to Abraham (Gen. 16:1–3) and thereby "administered unto Abraham according to the law" (D&C 132:65; see also verse 34)—congruent with now extant ancient Near Eastern sources describing the legal obligation of a childless wife. Sarah's action demonstrated, says one LDS Apostle, "her love and integrity to her husband" (*JD* 23:228) and was, says Philo, one of "numberless proofs" of her "wifely love. . . . Everywhere and always she was at his side, . . . his true partner in life and life's events, resolved to share alike the good and ill" (*On Abraham,* pp. xlii–xliii).

LDS sources further describe how Abraham was taught about Jesus Christ by Melchizedek (*TPJS*, pp. 322–23), who, as a prototype of Christ (JST Gen. 14:26–36; Alma 13:17–19), gave Abraham the Priesthood after the Order of the Son of God (see D&C 84:14; 107:2–4; cf. *Genesis Rabbah* 43:6) with accompanying temple ordinances foreshadowing Christ (Abr., Facsimile 2; Alma 13:2, 16; cf. *Cave of Treasures* [Budge], p. 148). Later, Abraham "looked forth and saw the days of the Son of Man, and was glad" (JST Gen. 15:9–12; Hel. 8:17; John 8:56).

Abraham's supreme test—the offering of Isaac—both recalled Abraham's prior experience and typified things to come. Centuries before Jesus, a Book of Mormon prophet pointed to Abraham's offering of Isaac as "a similitude of God and his Only Begotten Son"

(Jacob 4:4–5)—just as many Christian fathers would do retrospectively. Abraham's life thus typified and testified of his preeminent descendant Jesus, who, because he was also the Son of God, could atone for Abraham and all others.

Abraham's life also prefigured that of another descendant, Joseph Smith (D&C 132:30–31), whose prayer at age fourteen echoes young Abraham's prayer at the same age (*Jubilees* 11:16–17; JS—H 1:7–17). Both men had been foreordained; both received the priesthood, preached the gospel, and encountered formidable opposition; both spoke face to face with divine messengers and God himself; both possessed a URIM AND THUMMIM, translated ancient records, and wrote scripture; and both founded an influential community of saints.

But the connection is more direct. John Taylor reported that Abraham visited Joseph Smith (*JD* 20:174–75; 21:94), whose mission included revealing lost knowledge about Abraham (cf. 2 Ne. 3:7, 12) and whose entire ministry of restoration helped fulfill Abraham's covenant that through his seed all nations would be blessed (2 Ne. 29:14; 3 Ne. 20:27, 29). A central purpose of that restoration is to make Abraham's promises effective for his descendants, who through temple ordinances may receive the blessings of Abraham and be sealed in an ancestral chain back to Abraham and Adam (D&C 2; *TPJS*, pp. 337–38).

To achieve the glory of Abraham, Latter-day Saints are commanded to come to Christ by "do[ing] the works of Abraham," whose life constitutes a pattern (D&C 132:32; cf. Isa. 51:1–2; John 8:39; *Koran* 16:120–23). These works begin with baptism and reception of the Holy Ghost, whereupon the recipient must "press forward" (2 Ne. 31:19–20) in righteousness, as did Abraham, by obeying God, receiving the priesthood and temple ordinances, honoring covenants, building a family unit, teaching children, keeping sacred records, preaching the gospel, and proving faithful in opposition (Abr. 1–2; Gen. 12–25). Progression along this path brings increased identification with Abraham and Sarah and the blessings promised to them. For example, anyone who is not a descendant of Abraham but receives the Holy Ghost becomes the SEED OF ABRAHAM (*TPJS*, pp. 149–50; Abr. 2:10; cf. Gal. 3:29), while each man magnifying the Melchizedek Priesthood likewise becomes Abraham's seed (D&C 84:33–34). And each couple married eternally in the temple is promised the blessings of Abraham—posterity as the stars of heaven and sand of the seashore, meaning an eternal increase of posterity in the celestial kingdom (D&C 132:30; *JD* 11:151–52; 15:320).

Such blessings of innumerable posterity were promised to Abraham on several occasions (Abr. 3:13–14; Gen. 13:16; 15:5; 17:2, 6), but it was not until he demonstrated his willingness to offer Isaac as a sacrifice that the Lord guaranteed the promises (Gen. 22:16–18), showing, explains Joseph Smith, that any person who would attain eternal life "must sacrifice all things" (*TPJS*, p. 322). Accordingly, the Lord's people must be "tried, even as Abraham," to become sanctified through Abraham's descendant Christ (D&C 101:4–5; Moro. 10:33) in preparation to "sit down in the kingdom of God, with Abraham" and Sarah (Alma 5:24) on thrones of glory to inherit the same blessings of exaltation already enjoyed by that exemplary couple (D&C 132:34–37; cf. *Testament of Isaac* 2:5–7).

BIBLIOGRAPHY

Kimball, Spencer W. "The Example of Abraham." *Ensign* 6 (June 1975):3–7.

Nibley, Hugh. "A New Look at the Pearl of Great Price." *IE* 71–73 (Jan. 1968–May 1970), a series of articles covering two years.

———. *Abraham in Egypt.* Salt Lake City, 1981.

E. DOUGLAS CLARK

ADAM

[*This entry consists of two parts:*

LDS Sources

Ancient Sources

The first article discusses LDS teachings about Adam. The second one offers several apocryphal and pseudepigraphic sources as points of comparison. For further information on Adam, see Adamic Language, *and* Eve; *regarding the beginnings of earth life, see* Creation, Creation Accounts *and* Garden of Eden.]

LDS SOURCES

For Latter-day Saints, Adam stands as one of the noblest and greatest of all men. Information found in the scriptures and in declarations of latter-day apostles and prophets reveals details about Adam and his important roles in the pre-earth life, in Eden, in mortality, and in his postmortal life. They identify Adam by such names and titles as Michael (D&C 27:11; 29:26), archangel (D&C 88:112), and Ancient of Days (D&C 138:38).

The Prophet Joseph Smith taught that Michael, spoken of in the Bible (Dan. 10:13; Jude 1:9; Rev. 12:7), is Adam. In his premortal life, Adam received the priesthood (*TPJS*, p. 157), was taught the plan of God (*TPJS*, p. 167), and was appointed to be the head of the human family (*TPJS*, p. 158). He participated in the creation of the earth and occupied a position of authority next to Jesus Christ (*TPJS*, p. 158), under whose direction he at all times functions (D&C 78:16). He led the forces of righteousness against the devil "and his angels," who were overcome and expelled from heaven (*see* WAR IN HEAVEN).

Latter-day scriptures attest that Adam is a son of God, that his physical body was created by the Gods in their own image and placed in the GARDEN OF EDEN (Moses 6:9, 22; Abr. 5:7–11; *TPJS*, p. 345–53; cf. 2 Ne. 2:14–19). In this physical-spiritual state in Eden, Adam was called the "first man" (Moses 1:34) and given responsibility to dress the garden and "open the way of the world" (*TPJS*, p. 12). He was given dominion and responsibility over the earth, and he gave names to its creatures (Moses 3:19). He was joined with EVE in marriage (Abr. 5:4–19), but in their premortal condition "they would have had no children" (2 Ne. 2:23). Adam received the grand keys of the priesthood (Abr., Facsimile 2, Fig. 3), and its ordinances were confirmed upon Adam and Eve (cf. *TPJS*, p. 167).

In order to obey the command of God to multiply and people the earth, Adam and Eve transgressed the law. Their deliberate action resulted in their fall, and they were expelled from the garden. "Adam fell that men might be; and men are, that they might have joy" (2 Ne. 2:25). Thus, their action precipitated, as God had planned, the mortal phase of the plan of salvation.

In their mortal state, Adam and Eve were taught further about the plan of salvation by heavenly messengers (Moses 5:4–9; 6:50–54). They received the priesthood ordinances (Moses 5:59; 6:64–65) and all things necessary to teach their children (Moses 5:12). LDS sources indicate that with Eve, Adam had sons and daughters before Cain and Abel were born (Moses 5:2–3, 16–17). They suffered the effects of the temptations of the devil and experienced the sorrow of family dissension that led to murder and wickedness among some of their children (Moses 5:12–53).

Adam and Eve had a fully developed language and kept written records (Moses 6:5–9). They preserved their genealogical record and an account of the Creation. Three years before his death, Adam called his righteous posterity to Adam-ondi-Ahman and gave them his final blessing (D&C 107:53).

As the first on this earth to receive priesthood keys, Adam continues to dispense authority to others and to watch over priesthood administration on the earth; those to whom keys have been given must return them or account for them to Adam, and he will in turn deliver them or give an accounting of them to Christ (*TPJS*, pp. 157, 167). This will occur when the Ancient of Days (Adam) attends a council at Adam-ondi-Ahman preliminary to the second coming of Christ (Dan. 7:9–10; cf. *TPJS*, p. 122).

At the end of the Millennium, Adam as Michael will again lead the righteous in battle against the devil and his armies. Michael and the hosts of heaven will again prevail (D&C 88:111–15). When Adam then sounds the trumpet, the graves will be opened and the remainder of the dead will come forth to be judged (D&C 29:26–27). Subject to the Father and Christ, Adam will then preside eternally over his posterity (*TPJS*, p. 157).

Adam's various titles relate to particular phases of his mission. In his premortal and postmortal roles, he is known as Michael and as the archangel (D&C 29:26). In Hebrew, *michael* means one "who is like God," and in his powerful and leading role as archangel, Adam serves as the captain of the Lord's hosts in battle against the devil and his forces. Adam was the name given him for mortality (Moses 1:34). In Hebrew, *'adam* means "man" or "mankind." In LDS sources, further meanings of the word include "first man" (D&C 84:16), "many" (Moses 1:34), and "first father" (Abr. 1:3), denoting his historical role as the "grand progenitor" of the entire human family (*TPJS*, p. 167). "Ancient of Days" appears to be his title because he is "the first and oldest of all" (*TPJS*, p. 167).

Adam has been highly esteemed by all the prophets, both ancient and modern. President Brigham Young expressed the idea in

1852 and later years that Adam "is our Father and our God, and the only God with whom we have to do" (*JD* 1:50). This remark has led some to conjecture that Brigham Young meant that Adam, who was on earth as our progenitor, was in reality God the Father. However, this interpretation has been officially rejected as incorrect (Kimball, p. 77). Later in the same speech Brigham Young clearly stated "that the earth was organized by three distinct characters, namely Eloheim, Yahovah, and Michael" (*JD* 1:51). Additional information about Brigham Young's feelings on Adam can also be found in a conference speech given October 8, 1854 (*JD* 1:50), clarifying somewhat his earlier statement. It is there implied that through a process known as divine investiture, God delegates his power to his children. Adam was the first on earth to receive this authority, which includes all essential keys, titles, and dominions possessed by the Father (D&C 84:38; cf. 88:107). Thus, he had conferred upon him all things that were necessary for the accomplishment of his manifold responsibilities, and Adam is a name-title signifying that he is the first man and father of all.

BIBLIOGRAPHY
Broderick, Carl. "Another Look at Adam-God." *Dialogue* 16 (Summer 1983):4–7.
Buerger, David J. "The Adam-God Doctrine." *Dialogue* 15 (Spring 1982):14–58.
Kimball, Spencer W. "Our Own Liahona." *Ensign* 6 (Nov. 1976):77–79.
McConkie, Joseph Fielding, and Robert L. Millet, eds. *The Man Adam.* Salt Lake City, 1990.
Petersen, Mark E. *Adam: Who Is He?* Salt Lake City, 1976.

ARTHUR A. BAILEY

ANCIENT SOURCES

Adam is portrayed in ancient Jewish and Christian sources as the first human and progenitor of the race. Many apocryphal texts rework the Old Testament Adamic narrative and contain or reflect valuable ancient traditions. Some Latter-day Saints have profitably compared a few of these views with certain concepts about Adam given in Latter-day Saint sources.

In Judaism, Genesis 1–2 is used as a basis for understanding mankind's relationship to God. Adam's posterity inherited his fallen nature, yet Adam is regarded as the archetypal model for mankind—as indicated in texts that date back at least to Hellenistic times (second century B.C.) and is amplified in medieval

Jewish philosophy. Philo, following a Platonic model, saw in the two creation narratives of Genesis a distinction between a heavenly or spiritual man, created first spiritually in the image of God (Gen. 1:27; cf. Moses 3:5), and a second, earthly man, formed out of the dust (Gen. 2:7). Most early Jewish exegetes accepted the historicity of the biblical account, though Genesis 2:8–3:24 was often interpreted allegorically. The Talmud and the Aggadah supplied rich details to the Adamic story, including an impressive description of how all future generations—and their prophets—passed before Adam and were viewed by him (Sanh. 38b; Av. Zar. 5a; Gen. R. 24:2; cf. D&C 107:55–57). Adam was given the Noachian laws (Sanh. 56b) and the law of the SABBATH (Mid. Ps. to 92:6). He was the first man to offer sacrifice (Av. Zar. 8a; cf. Moses 5:5). The medieval cabalists added mystical interpretations as well, although Adam is never identified here as Michael, as in the Latter-day Saint scripture (see D&C 27:11; 107:54; 128:21).

Orthodox Christian theology, articulated during the second century by Irenaeus and others in response to the challenges posed by gnosticism, faithfully saw the Old Testament through the role of Christ. Early Christianity regarded the incarnation and atonement of Jesus Christ as the fulfillment of the work begun by Adam. While Adam was the prototype of the old, mortal man, Christ became the prototype of the new man, blessed with the promise of immortality. Jesus became the "second Adam," whose atonement enabled mankind to overcome the effects of the Fall (1 Cor. 15:22, 45).

The creation story and the Adamic narrative in Genesis were especially important in gnosticism, which interpreted the Fall as the downfall of the divine principle into the material world. This contributed to gnosticism's negative attitude toward the physical creation. Several Gnostic writings deal with Adam. One of these, the *Apocalypse of Adam*, found at Nag Hammadi, is heavily dependent upon Jewish apocalyptic traditions and contains no explicit Christian doctrines. It purports to be a revelation given to Adam after the Fall by three heavenly messengers, explaining the nature and extent of the Fall and providing the promise of a future Redeemer. This knowledge is then passed by Adam to SETH and his descendants (cf. D&C 107:41–57).

The Life of Adam and Eve is a significant apocryphal work dealing with the life and death of Adam. It was probably written in Palestine between 100 B.C. and A.D. 200. It has been preserved in Greek, Latin, and Slavonic recensions, each considerably different from the others. This work describes Adam's and EVE'S repentance after leaving the Garden of Eden at length (cf. Moses 6:50–68). No clear and central doctrine emerges, but the text stresses the ideas of final judgment and resurrection. Other eschatological features are missing. It conveys no hint of the traditional doctrine of original sin. Adam is perfect; Eve, weak but not wicked, deplores her own shortcomings while loving and obeying Adam.

A central feature of the *Cave of Treasures,* a Syriac work, is its story of a cave where Adam lived and was buried. His body was retrieved by Noah, who took it into the ark and afterward reinterred it on Golgotha. By this account, the redemptive blood of Jesus, also called the "last Adam," shed at the Crucifixion first flowed on the grave of Adam, demonstrating an inexorable link between the Fall of Adam and the atonement of Christ. Thus, in the *Gospel of Bartholomew* 1:22, Jesus says to Adam, "I was hung upon the cross for thee and for thy children's sake," and in *2 Enoch* 42, Adam in Paradise is brought out "together with the ancestors . . . so that they may be filled with joy" and eternal riches.

Many ancient texts about Adam exist, notably the Ethiopic *Book of Adam and Eve,* and the Armenian books of *Death of Adam, History of Adam's Expulsion from Paradise, History of Cain and Abel, Adam's Sons,* and *Concerning the Good Tidings of Seth.*

BIBLIOGRAPHY

Ginzberg, Louis. *Legends of the Jews,* Vol. 1, pp. 3–142. Philadelphia, 1937.

Johnson, M. D. "The Life of Adam and Eve." In *The Old Testament Pseudepigrapha,* ed. J. Charlesworth, Vol. 2, pp. 249–95. Garden City, N.Y., 1985.

Robinson, James M., ed. *The Nag Hammadi Library,* 2nd ed. New York, 1989.

Robinson, Stephen E. "The Apocalypse of Adam." *BYU Studies* 17 (Winter 1977):131–53.

————. "The Book of Adam in Judaism and Early Christianity." In *The Man Adam,* ed. J. McConkie and R. Millet, pp. 131–50, listing titles of many ancient works. Salt Lake City, 1990.

MARTIN J. PALMER

ADAMIC LANGUAGE

The concept of the Adamic language grew among Latter-day Saints out of statements from scripture, comments of early Church leaders, and subsequent tradition. It does not play a central doctrinal role, and there is no official Church position delineating its nature or status.

The scriptures state that this language, written and spoken by Adam and his children, was "pure and undefiled" (Moses 6:5–6). Brigham Young taught that it continued from Adam to Babel, at which time the Lord "caused the people to forget their own mother tongue, . . . scatter[ing] them abroad upon the face of the whole earth," except possibly for Jared and his family in the Book of Mormon (*JD* 3:100; cf. Gen. 11:1–9; Mosiah 28:17). This statement reflects the widely held Mormon belief that the founding members of the JAREDITE civilization preserved the Adamic language at their immigration to the new world (Ether 1:33–43; 3:24–28). Thus, the description by the brother of Jared of his apocalyptic vision was rendered linguistically inaccessible without divine interpretive help, since "the language which ye shall write I [God] have confounded" (Ether 3:21–28).

In the early years of the Church, some words of the Adamic language may have been revealed to Joseph Smith (*JD* 2:342), and other early Church leaders, including Brigham Young (*HC* 1:297) and Elizabeth Ann Whitney (*Woman's Exponent* 7 [Nov. 1, 1878], p. 83), who were said to have spoken it in tongues. More recently President Ezra Taft Benson alluded to its possible universal reinstatement to resolve linguistic diversity (*Teachings of Ezra Taft Benson* [Salt Lake City, 1988], p. 93; cf. Brigham Young, *JD* 3:100).

Similarly, Zephaniah 3:9, possibly referring to the future of the Adamic language, says, "I will turn to the people a pure language, that they may all call upon the name of the Lord." The word *pure* comes from the Hebrew *berurah*, from *barar*, "to cleanse" or purify; also "to choose."

Because it is generally held that a language reflects its culture, possibly the erosion of the purity of the Adamic culture after Babel led to a concomitant loss of purity of expression in its mirroring language.

JOHN S. ROBERTSON

ALLEGORY OF ZENOS

The Allegory of Zenos (Jacob 5) is a lengthy, prophetic declaration made by ZENOS, a Hebrew prophet, about the destiny of the house of ISRAEL. Evidently copied directly from the plates of brass into the Book of Mormon record by JACOB, it was intended (1) to reinforce Jacob's own teachings both about Jesus Christ ("We knew of Christ, and we had a hope of his glory many hundred years before his coming"—Jacob 4:4) and about the house of Israel's anticipated unresponsiveness toward the coming Redeemer ("I perceive . . . they will reject the stone upon which they might build and have safe foundation"—Jacob 4:15), and (2) to instruct his people about the promised future regathering of Israel, to which Jacob's people belonged.

Framed in the tradition of parables, the allegory "likens" the house of Israel to an olive tree whose owner struggles to keep it from dying. The comparison figuratively illustrates God's bond with his chosen people and with the Gentiles, and underscores the lesson that through patience and compassion God will save and preserve the compliant and obedient.

The narrative contains seventy-six verses, divisible into five parts, all tied together by an overarching theme of good winning over bad, of life triumphing over death. In the first part, an alarmed owner, recognizing threatening signs of death (age and decay) in a beloved tree of superior quality, immediately tries to nurse it back to health (verses 4–5). Even though new growth appears, his ministering does not fully heal the tree; and so, with a servant's help, he removes and destroys waning parts and in their place grafts limbs from a "wild" tree. At the same time, he detaches the old tree's "young and tender" new growth for planting in secluded areas of his property. Though disappointed, he resolves to save his beloved tree (verses 6–14).

Second, following a lengthy interval of conscientious care, the owner's labor is rewarded with a generous harvest of choice fruit, not only from the newly grafted limbs on his old tree but also from the new growth that he planted around the property. These latter trees, however, have produced unequally: the two trees with least natural advantages have the highest, positive yield; while the most advantaged tree's production is only half good, compelling removal of its unprofitable parts. Even so, the owner continues an all-out effort on every tree, even this last one (verses 15–28).

In the third part, a long time passes. The owner and the servant return again to measure and evaluate the fruit, only to learn the worst: the old tree, though healthy, has produced a completely worthless crop; and it is the same for the other trees. Distressed, the owner orders all the trees destroyed. His assistant pleads for him to forbear a little longer. In the fourth segment, the "grieved" owner, accompanied by the servant and other workers, carefully tries again in one last effort. Together they reverse the previous implantation (the "young and tender" plants are returned to the old tree) and splice other old tree limbs into the previously selected trees, appropriately pruning, cultivating, and nurturing each tree as required (verses 29–73). This particular operation of mixing and blending, mingling and merging all the trees together, meets with success in replicating the superior quality crop of "natural fruit" everywhere on his property. Elated, he promises his helpers a share ("joy") in the harvest for as long as it lasts. But he also pledges destruction of all the trees if and when their capacity for a positive yield wanes again (verses 73–77).

In the subsequent chapter Jacob renders a brief interpretation (6:1–4). Conscious that his people, the Nephites, branched from the house of Israel, he is particularly anxious to redirect their increasingly errant behavior, and therefore reads into the allegory a sober caution of repentance for these impenitent New World Israelites: "How merciful is our God unto us, for he remembereth the house of Israel, both roots and branches; and he stretches forth his hands unto them all the day long; . . . but as many as will not harden their hearts shall be saved in the kingdom of God" (6:4).

Modern interpretations of the allegory have emphasized its universality. Accordingly, readers have explored its application to the house of Israel and the stretch of covenant time, that is, beginning with God's pact with Abraham and finishing with the Millennium and the ending of the earth; its doctrinal connection to the ages of spiritual apostasy, the latter-day Restoration, Church membership, present global proselytizing, the return of the Jews, and the final judgment. Other studies have begun to explore its literary and textual correspondences with ancient documents (Hymns from Qumran) and with the Old (Genesis, Isaiah, Jeremiah) and New Testaments (Romans 11:16–24); and even its association with the known laws of botany. Some scholars have declared it one of the most demanding and engaging of all scriptural allegories, if not the most important one.

BIBLIOGRAPHY

Hess, Wilford M. "Botanical Comparisons in the Allegory of the Olive Tree." In *The Book of Mormon: Jacob Through Words of Mormon, To Learn with Joy,* ed. M. Nyman and C. Tate, pp. 87–102. Provo, Utah, 1990.

McConkie, Joseph Fielding, and Robert L. Millet. *Doctrinal Commentary on the Book of Mormon,* Vol. 2, pp. 46–77. Salt Lake City, 1988.

Nibley, Hugh. *Since Cumorah,* pp. 283–85. In *CWHN* 7.

Nyman, Monte S. *An Ensign to All People,* pp. 21–36. Salt Lake City, 1987.

L. GARY LAMBERT

ALMA₁

Alma₁ (c. 174–92 B.C.) was the first of two Almas in the Book of Mormon. He was a descendant of NEPHI₁, son of LEHI, and was the young priest in the court of King Noah who attempted a peaceful release of the prophet Abinadi. For that action, Alma incurred royal vengeance, banishment, and threats upon his life. He had been impressed by Abinadi's accusations of immorality and abuses within the government and society and by his testimony of the gospel of Jesus Christ (Mosiah 17:2). Subsequently forced underground, Alma wrote out Abinadi's teachings, then shared them with others, attracting sufficient adherents—450—to organize a society of believers, or a church. The believers assembled in a remote, undeveloped area called Mormon. Participants in the church pledged to "bear one another's burdens," "mourn with those that mourn," "comfort those that stand in need of comfort," and "stand as witnesses of God at all times and in all things" (Mosiah 18:8–9). This pledge was then sealed by baptism, which was considered "a testimony that ye have entered into a covenant to serve him [Almighty God] until you are dead as to the mortal body" (verse 13). Believers called themselves "the church of God, or the church of Christ, from that time forward" (verse 17).

Alma's leadership included ordaining lay priests—one for every fifty members—whom he instructed to labor for their own support, and to limit their sermons to his teachings and the doctrine "spoken by the mouth of the holy prophets . . . nothing save it were repentance and faith on the Lord" (Mosiah 18:19–20). Alma also required that there be faithful observance of the SABBATH, daily expressions of gratitude to God, and no contention, "having their hearts knit together in unity and in love" (18:21–23). The priests assembled with and taught the people in a worship meeting at least once weekly (18:25). Through generous donations, everyone cared for one another "according to that which he had" (18:27–28).

Eventually the believers were discovered and King Noah accused Alma of sedition, ordering his army to crush him and his followers. Forced into exile, Alma led the people deeper into the wilderness, where they thrived for twenty years in a region they named Helam (Mosiah 18:32–35; 23:1–5, 20). Alma ardently declined well-intended efforts to make him king, and successfully dissuaded his people from adopting a monarchical government, urging them to enjoy the new "liberty wherewith ye have been made free" and to "trust no man to be a king" (Mosiah 23:13). He did not oppose monarchies as such but, rather, acknowledged their fundamental limitation: "If it were possible that ye could always have just men to be your kings it would be well for you to have a king" (23:8).

Alma and his people afterward suffered oppression at the hands of Amulon, also an ex-priest and deserter from King Noah's court, who, along with the remnant of a LAMANITE army, discovered Alma's people in their wilderness refuge. During their suffering the voice of the Lord promised relief and deliverance because of their covenant with him: "I, the Lord God, do visit my people in their afflictions" (Mosiah 24:14). Once again, in Moses-like fashion, Alma guided his people out of bondage, and led them during a twelve-day journey to a new land—the land of Zarahemla—where they joined with the people of Zarahemla and exiled Nephites to form a new and stronger Nephite nation (Mosiah 24:24–25).

The king of Zarahemla, Mosiah₂, also a descendant of transplanted God-fearing NEPHITES, sanctioned and even authorized expansion of Alma's church in his kingdom; the church, however, operated separately and independently of the state. The king also assigned the reins of leadership to Alma (Mosiah 25:19; 26:8), who successfully directed the church during twenty years characterized largely by tribulations, with many confrontations between nonbelievers and church members resulting in ordeals for both him and the church (Mosiah 26:1–39). Eventually, widespread antagonism necessitated a royal injunction to lessen the tension (27:1–6). Even one of Alma's sons was among the ranks of the enemies of the church, his agitation and criticism inviting yet worse persecution for church members (27:8–10).

During his lifetime Alma watched King Mosiah dismantle the monarchy and transform it into a system of judges elected by the people (Mosiah 29:2); he also saw his own son, Alma₂—the one who earlier had brought grief to him and the church—become the first chief judge (Mosiah 29:1–44). This political transformation proved pivotal in the history of the land of Zarahemla. Directly and indirectly Alma had a hand in bringing it about; the record of his and his people's pain under oppressive rulers was widely known throughout the kingdom (25:5–6) and remained distinct in King Mosiah's mind (29:18). Alma's influence, then, can be seen as transcending the immediate spiritual boundaries of his stewardship over the church. Indeed, because of this influence the entire Nephite nation came to know unprecedented changes in almost every dimension of daily living—political, social, and economic, as well as religious. These changes—and all their connected ramifications for the social order and the populace—prepared the backdrop against which the resurrected Christ's visit to the Americas was staged. Loved by his followers for his devotion and faith, and held in esteem by his peers for his effective leadership, Alma will probably always be best known as the founder of the church in Zarahemla. His posterity became the leading Nephite family for over 400 years, down to Ammaron in A.D. 321 (4 Ne. 1:48). Alma died at age eighty-two, less than a hundred years before the birth of Jesus Christ.

L. GARY LAMBERT

ALMA₂

Few individuals have had greater influence upon a civilization than Alma₂, son of Alma₁. He was a key figure in the rise of the Nephite church and republic, serving as the first chief judge in Zarahemla, commander-in-chief of the Nephite army, and high priest (c. 90–73 B.C.). His efforts to protect his people from war, dissension, and wickedness were exceeded only by his single-minded dedication to the Savior, whom he came to know through revelation.

This crusader for righteousness first appears in the Book of Mormon as a rebellious young man. He and four of the sons of King Mosiah₂, described as "the very vilest of sinners" (Mosiah 28:4), rebelled against the teachings of their parents and sought to overthrow the church. As they went about that work (c. 100–92 B.C.), the angel of the Lord appeared to them, spoke with a voice of thunder, calling these wayward young men to repentance, and explaining that he did so because of the prayers of the people and of Alma's father. For three days and three nights Alma lay in a physically comatose state, during which time he spiritually confronted all his sins, "for which," he later said, "I was tormented with the pains of hell" (Alma 36:12–14).

In the depth of his anguish of soul, Alma remembered his father's words concerning the coming of Jesus Christ to atone for the sins of the world. As Alma cried out in his heart to Christ, pleading for mercy and deliverance from "the gall of bitterness" and "the everlasting chains of death," he stated: "I could remember my pains no more; yea, I was harrowed up by the memory of my sins no more" (Alma 36:17–19). After their conversion, Alma and the sons of Mosiah devoted their lives to preaching repentance and the joyous gospel (Alma 36:24).

For about nine years Alma served as both the high priest over the church and the chief judge or governor over a new political system of judges among the Nephites. He was well educated, the keeper of sacred and civil records, an inspiring orator, and a skillful writer. As a young civil and religious leader, he faced a number of challenges. Several religio-political factions were emerging in Nephite society, notably the Zoramites, Mulekites, members of the church, and an anti-church group, the followers of Nehor (*see* BOOK OF MORMON PEOPLES). Maintaining Nephite leadership over all these groups proved impossible. In a landmark case in his first year as chief judge, Alma held the popular Nehor guilty of enforcing priestcraft with the sword, which resulted in his execution (Alma 1:2–15). This soon led to civil war with Alma himself slaying the new rebel leader, one of Nehor's protégés, in battle (Alma 2–3). There followed a serious epidemic of pride and inequality among many in the church (Alma 4) and the secession of the arrogant Zoramites. "Seeing no way that he might reclaim [the people] save it were in bearing down in pure testimony against them" (Alma 4:19), Alma resigned his position as chief judge and devoted himself completely to the work of the ministry (Alma 4:19; 31:5). His religious work, especially in the Nephite cities of Zarahemla (Alma 5, 30) and Gideon (Alma 7), the Nehorite stronghold of Ammonihah (Alma 8–16), and the Zoramite center in Antionum (Alma 31–35), revitalized the church and set the pattern of administration for the next century down to the coming of Christ.

Alma's most enduring contributions are to be found in his sermons and his blessings upon the heads of his children. No doubt as a result of his own conversion (Mosiah 27), Alma's words frequently center on the atoning sacrifice of the Redeemer and on the necessity for men and women to be born of God, changed, and renewed through Christ. To the people of Gideon, Alma delivered a profound prophetic oracle regarding the birth of Jesus and the atonement he would make, "suffering pains and afflictions and temptations of every kind . . . that he may loose the bands of death which bind his people; and he will take upon him their infirmities, that his bowels may be filled with mercy . . . that he may know according to the flesh how to succor his people according to their infirmities" (Alma 7:11–12). In Zarahemla, Alma stressed the need for the new birth and for acquiring the image and attributes of the Master; in doing so, he provided a series of over forty questions that assess one's depth of conversion and readiness to meet one's Maker (see Alma 5).

In Ammonihah, Alma and his convert Amulek were accused of a crime, taunted, and imprisoned for several weeks without clothing or adequate food. After being forced to witness the burning of several faithful women and children, Alma and Amulek were miraculously delivered and their persecutors annihilated. The discourses of Alma and Amulek on the Creation, the Fall, and the Atonement are among the clearest and most fundamental theological statements on these subjects in scripture (see Alma 11–12, 34, 42). In explaining humility, faith, and prayer to the poor in Antionum (Alma 32–34), Alma and Amulek set forth a pattern whereby those without faith in Christ (or those within the fold who desire to strengthen their belief) would plant the seed of the word of Christ in their hearts and eventually receive the confirming impressions of testimony that come by the power of the Holy Ghost.

Some of the most penetrating doctrinal information in the Book of Mormon comes through words that Alma spoke to his sons. To HELAMAN₁, his eldest son and successor, Alma eloquently recounted the story of his own conversion, gave him loving fatherly counsel, and entrusted him with custody of the plates of brass, the plates of Nephi, the plates of Ether, and the LIAHONA (Alma 36–37). To Shiblon, he gave wise practical advice (Alma 38). To his errant youngest son, Corianton, who eventually went on to serve valiantly in the church, Alma explained the seriousness of sexual sin, that wickedness never was happiness (Alma 39, 41:10), that all spirits will be judged after death and will eventually stand before God after a perfect resurrection (Alma 40), and that the word "restoration" does not mean that God will restore a sinner to some former state of happiness (Alma 41), for divine mercy cannot rob justice when the law of God has been violated (Alma 42).

A relatively young man at the time of his conversion, Alma lived fewer than twenty years thereafter. Yet in those two decades he almost single-handedly invigorated and established the cause of truth and liberty in the Nephite church and society. Never forgetting the thunderous voice of the angel at the time of his conversion, Alma always carried with him this unchanging desire: "O that I were an angel, and could have the wish of mine heart, that I might go forth and speak with the trump of God, with a voice to shake the earth, and cry repentance unto every people! . . . that there might not be more sorrow upon all the face of the earth" (Alma 29:1–2). When he left one day and was never seen or heard again, his sons and the church supposed "that [the Lord] received Alma in the spirit, unto himself," even as Moses (Alma 45:19), drawing an apt comparison between these two great lawgivers, judges, commanders, spiritual leaders, and prophets.

For Latter-day Saints, Alma's life and lessons are rich and timeless. He serves as a hope to parents who have wandering children, and as a beacon to those who stray. He stands as a model public servant, a sterling illustration of the new life in Christ, a fearless preacher, missionary, and gifted theologian. Alma was a prophet who received a prophet's reward.

BIBLIOGRAPHY
Holland, Jeffrey R. "Alma, Son of Alma." *Ensign* 7 (March 1977):79–84.
Perry, L. Tom. "Alma the Younger." *CR* (April 1979):16–17.

ROBERT L. MILLET

AMULEK

Amulek (fl. c. 82–74 B.C.), a Nephite inhabitant of the city Ammonihah (Alma 8:20), was a wealthy man in his community (Alma 10:4). Formerly rebellious toward God, he heeded an angel of the Lord and became a missionary companion to ALMA$_2$ (Alma 10:10). An articulate defender of gospel principles, he displayed virtues of long-suffering and faith, gave up his wealth to teach the gospel, and became a special witness for Christ (see Alma 8–16; 32–34).

Amulek bore powerful testimony to his own city, which earlier had rejected Alma. He confounded opposing lawyers and called upon them to repent—particularly Zeezrom, who had plotted to tempt and destroy him (Alma 11:25). He taught about the nature of the Godhead and the role of Christ, emphasizing the Resurrection and final judgment (Alma 11:28–45). Touched by the words of Amulek and Alma, Zeezrom recognized the truth, repented, and defended the two missionaries (Alma 14:6–7).

When nonbelievers forced Alma and Amulek to witness the burning of women and children, Amulek desired to save them from the flames. He was restrained, however, by Alma (Alma 14:10–11; *see* MARTYRS). They themselves were bound, were smitten, and endured hunger as they lay naked in prison (Alma 14:14–22). At last, receiving strength according to their faith, they miraculously broke their bonds and walked out of the collapsing prison, while those who had smitten them died in its ruins (Alma 14:26–28).

Because of his faith in Christ, Amulek was rejected by his family and friends (Alma 15:16). When peace was restored after the Lamanite destruction of Ammonihah, Alma, Amulek, and others built up the church among the Nephites (Alma 16:15).

As a special witness for Christ and filled with the Holy Spirit, Amulek testified to the poor of the Zoramites that only in Christ was salvation possible (Alma 34:5–13). He stated that Christ would come into the world and make an infinite atonement for the sins of the people. "Not any man" could accomplish this act, which would be the great and last sacrifice, bringing mercy to satisfy the demands of justice and saving those who believe on his name (Alma 34:8–16). In return, Amulek said, Christ asked for faith unto repentance, charitable deeds, acceptance of the name of Christ, no contending against the Holy Ghost, no reviling of enemies, and bearing one's afflictions patiently (Alma 34: 17–41).

BIBLIOGRAPHY

Dahl, Larry E. "The Plan of Redemption—Taught and Rejected." In *Studies in Scripture*, ed. Kent P. Jackson, Vol. 8, pp. 307–320. Salt Lake City, 1987.

NORBERT H. O. DUCKWITZ

ANGEL MORONI STATUE

A monument to the angel Moroni (*see* MORONI, ANGEL) stands atop the hill Cumorah, four miles south of Palmyra, New York, where MORONI₂ gave Joseph Smith the GOLD PLATES from which he translated the Book of Mormon. Mounted on a 25-foot shaft of white granite, the ten-foot bronze figure of Moroni points toward heaven with the right hand and holds a replica of the plates with the left. Created by Norwegian sculptor Torleif S. Knaphus, the monument was dedicated by Church President Heber J. Grant on July 21, 1935.

Moroni was the last in a line of prophet-leaders in the Western Hemisphere whose history is recorded in the Book of Mormon. Latter-day Saints believe John the Revelator foretold Moroni's angelic ministry: "And I saw another angel fly in the midst of heaven, having the everlasting gospel to preach unto them that dwell on the earth, and to every nation, and kindred, and tongue, and people" (Rev. 14:6).

Because Moroni's mission was vital to the RESTORATION of the gospel of Jesus Christ and the establishment of The Church of Jesus Christ of Latter-day Saints, a statue of Moroni as a herald sounding a trumpet has been placed on several Latter-day Saint temples (e.g., Salt Lake City, Los Angeles, and Washington, D.C.).

BIBLIOGRAPHY
Giles, John D. "The Symbolism of the Angel Moroni Monument—Hill Cumorah." *Instructor* 86 (Apr. 1951):98–99.

CORY H. MAXWELL

ANTHON TRANSCRIPT

The Anthon Transcript was a sheet of paper, thought to be lost, upon which Joseph Smith copied sample "reformed Egyptian" characters from the plates of the Book of Mormon. In the winter of 1828, Martin Harris showed these characters to Dr. Charles Anthon of Columbia College (now Columbia University), and hence the name.

In February 1828, Martin Harris, a farmer from Palmyra, New York, visited the Prophet Joseph Smith, who was then residing in Harmony, Pennsylvania, where he had just begun to translate the Book of Mormon (*see* BOOK OF MORMON TRANSLATION BY JOSEPH SMITH). Smith had earlier turned to Harris for financial backing for the translation; now Harris came to Harmony to take samples of the reformed Egyptian characters from the gold plates (cf. Morm. 9:32), thereafter to obtain scholarly opinion about their authenticity. Smith gave Harris a copy of some of the characters, along with a translation, which Harris then presented to at least three scholars in the eastern United States. The most important of these, given the nature of the inquiry, was Charles Anthon, an acclaimed classicist at Columbia College.

The two men's accounts of the meeting differ. Harris said that Professor Anthon gave him a certificate verifying the authenticity of the characters but that when Anthon learned that Joseph Smith claimed to have received the plates from an angel, he took the certificate back and destroyed it. Anthon, for his part, left written accounts in 1834 and 1841 in which he contradicted himself on whether he had given Harris a written opinion about the document. In both accounts, apparently to dissociate himself from appearing to promote the book, he maintained that he told Harris that he (Harris) was a victim of a fraud. Modern research suggests that, given the state of knowledge of Egyptian in 1828, Anthon's views would have been little more than opinion. Whatever the case may be about a written statement from Anthon, Harris returned to Harmony ready to assist Joseph Smith with the translation.

The Reorganized Church of Jesus Christ of Latter Day Saints possesses a handwritten text known as the Anthon Transcript that contains seven horizontal lines of characters apparently copied from the plates. David Whitmer, who once owned the document, said it was this text that Martin Harris showed to Charles Anthon. However, this claim remains uncertain because the transcript does not correspond with Anthon's assertion that the manuscript he saw was arranged in vertical columns. Even if the document is not the original, it almost certainly represents characters either copied from the plates in Joseph Smith's possession or copied from the document carried by Harris. Twice in late 1844, after the Prophet's martyrdom, portions of these symbols were published as characters that Joseph Smith had copied from the gold plates—once as a broadside and once in the December 21 issue of the Mormon newspaper *The Prophet*. In 1980 a document surfaced that seemed to match Anthon's description and appeared to be the original Anthon Transcript. But in 1987, Mark W. Hofmann admitted that he had forged it.

Harris's visit with scholars was more than just an interesting sidelight in the history of Mormonism. By his own report, Harris returned to Harmony convinced that the characters were genuine. Thereafter, he willingly invested his time and resources to see the Book of Mormon published. Moreover, the Prophet, Harris himself, and later generations of Latter-day Saints have viewed his visit as a fulfillment of Isaiah 29:11–12, which speaks of "a book that is sealed" being delivered to "one that is learned" who could not read it (*PJS* 1:9; cf. 2 Ne. 27:6–24; *see also* BOOK OF MORMON, BIBLICAL PROPHECIES ABOUT). His efforts apparently encouraged Joseph Smith in the initial stages of the translation. The Anthon Transcript is also important to subsequent generations as an authentic sample of characters that were inscribed on the gold plates and thus one of the few tangible evidences of their existence.

[*See also* Book of Mormon Language.]

BIBLIOGRAPHY

Kimball, Stanley B. "I Cannot Read a Sealed Book." *IE* 60 (Feb. 1957):80–82, 104, 106.

———. "The Anthon Transcript: People, Primary Sources, and Problems." *BYU Studies* 10 (Spring 1970):325–52.

"Martin Harris' Visit to Charles Anthon: Collected Documents on Short-hand Egyptian." *F.A.R.M.S. Preliminary Report.* Provo, Utah, 1985.

DANEL W. BACHMAN

APOCALYPTIC TEXTS

Apocalypse is a Greek word meaning revelation, and *apocalyptic* as an adjective describes the genre of literature that contains visionary or revelatory experiences. Although such writings have been known from ancient times (examples include sections of ISAIAH, EZEKIEL, DANIEL, and the New Testament Revelation of JOHN), discoveries since the late nineteenth century of apocalyptic texts have increased scholarly interest in the subject. The apocalyptic tradition was one of those the early Christian church rejected in the third through the fifth centuries, only to be recovered in modern times through these discoveries. The importance of revelation in the RESTORATION of the gospel through the Prophet Joseph Smith makes the study of apocalyptic texts as worthwhile to Latter-day Saints as it is interesting to scholars.

The relationship between the canonical prophetic and the apocalyptic in Jewish and Christian sources is acknowledged to be very close. Some of the major characteristics of revelation literature are as follows:

1. The seer often gives a brief autobiographical account in which he recounts his initial experiences and important personal events.

2. The recipient of a vision is often, but not always, ecstatic (the spirit apparently leaving the body during the vision).

3. The prophet may be taken on a journey through the heavens.

4. Visits to the spirit world, heaven, and hell are common.

5. The teachings imparted during such experiences are secrets that the prophet is counseled to keep to himself or share only with the community of believers (the experience may be shared, but most of what is learned cannot be disclosed).

6. Usually an account of the suffering that the righteous must endure is given.

7. The descent from heaven of a new order of society in the last days is described.

8. Commonly an *angelus interpres,* a heavenly messenger, is sent to explain and interpret the vision.

9. After receiving such visions, the prophet is almost always overcome and has to wait some time before receiving back his strength or perhaps is raised up quickly by the right hand of divinity.

Although scholars have specifically identified and studied the genre of apocalyptic literature mainly since the 1950s, students of the Restoration will recognize every aspect of this ancient literary form in the life and writings of Joseph Smith before 1844. Accounts of the First Vision contain an autobiographical introduction, as do visions of NEPHI$_1$ in the Book of Mormon and of Abraham in the Pearl of Great Price. In 1 Nephi 11, Nephi is taken in the spirit to a high mountain (a very popular theme in revelation), and Moses, ALMA$_2$, Joseph Smith, and others speak of being overcome by the visions they received (Moses 1:10; Mosiah 27:19; JS—H 1:20). Enoch (Moses 7; see also 1 Enoch), Moses (Moses 1), and Joseph Smith (e.g., D&C 76) describe journeys into and through eternal realms, recording the infinite creations of God and numerous places where men may ultimately dwell. Those same prophets, and others whose accounts are found in the Book of Mormon, report visions of the last days, the wars and destructions among men, and the ultimate victory of God. In keeping with apocalyptic tradition, the details of such visions are sealed up with a promise that they will be given to the righteous in a time determined by the Lord. Angels appeared to Joseph Smith to instruct him and explain such things as how to find and recover PLATES seen in a vision and how to baptize properly and with the authority given by a messenger from God. In the Book of Mormon, Nephi saw a vision more completely through the assistance of an angel who pointed out and explained details of the apocalypse to him. These representative examples show how the apocalyptic tradition is as interwoven in the fabric of the Restoration as it was in the traditions of ancient Judaism or early Christianity.

BIBLIOGRAPHY

Hellholm, David, ed. *International Colloquium on Apocalypticism* (1979: Uppsala, Sweden). Tübingen, 1983.

Koch, Klaus. *Ratlos vor der Apokalyptik.* Gutersloh, 1970. Translated by M. Kohl as *The Rediscovery of Apocalyptic.* London, 1972.

Nibley, Hugh. "Last Call: An Apocalyptic Warning from the Book of Mormon." In *CWHN* 8:498–532.

C. WILFRED GRIGGS

APOCRYPHA AND PSEUDEPIGRAPHA

These two terms are often found together in modern scholarly writings, although they had quite different meanings in ancient times. "Apocrypha" in its various forms refers to something hidden or concealed, usually because of its special or sacred value to the one hiding it. "Pseudepigrapha" refers to writings falsely ascribed to some important or famous figure or to writings with a false title. Such writings are not considered genuine, at least in the sense of originating with the falsely ascribed name.

During the second century A.D., some Christian authors (for example, Irenaeus and Tertullian) began to use *apocryphon* (singular form) to designate a forged or false writing. Both authors, and those who followed them in this practice, were trying to discredit the secret and sacred writings of their opponents, whom they considered heretics. In time, therefore, many writings once kept hidden from the general public for reasons of their sacredness and holiness were rejected and branded as unreliable or false by church fathers who disliked them.

After Jerome translated the Bible into Latin (c. A.D. 400), the books known from the Greek version of the Old Testament but not contained in the Hebrew version became known as the Apocrypha, or writings of uncertain accuracy. This collection of writings was accepted as scripture by most Christians before the Council of Nicaea, but only by some following that council. In recent centuries, Catholics have generally accepted these books with the rest of the Old Testament, and Protestants have generally denied them scriptural status. In Joseph Smith's day, some editions of the King James Version of the Bible placed the Apocrypha between the Old and New

Testaments, and some other Protestant versions included the Apocrypha either with the Old Testament or as an appendix to the Bible.

When Joseph Smith was engaged in translating the Old Testament (*see* JOSEPH SMITH TRANSLATION OF THE BIBLE [JST]), he came to the Apocrypha and sought divine counsel on what to do with it. The revelation given in response to his prayer informed him that the Apocrypha contains both truth and error, but was "mostly translated correctly" (D&C 91:1). Although he was counseled not to translate the Apocrypha, the revelation states that any who read those writings with the Holy Spirit as a guide "shall obtain benefit therefrom"; without the Holy Ghost, a man "cannot be benefited" spiritually by reading the Apocrypha (D&C 91:5–6).

Since the nineteenth century, increased understanding of intertestamental Judaism and Hellenistic culture has shown the Apocrypha to be historically important and religiously valuable. These writings display a belief in resurrection, eternal life, and eschatological teachings concerning the last days. The fall of Adam (*see* ADAM: ANCIENT SOURCES), sin, the Jewish Law, and the need for righteousness are topics also found in the Apocrypha.

Additionally, during the past two centuries many writings have been discovered that were purportedly written by ancient prophets or apostles, or were otherwise related to biblical texts (*see* LOST SCRIPTURE). Many of these writings were considered sacred to certain groups of Jews or Christians, but were rejected in the long process of biblical canonization (primarily from the second to the fifth centuries A.D.). Scholars routinely add these discoveries to the corpus of apocryphal and pseudepigraphical writings. The application of these terms in their modern sense (i.e., writings forged or falsely ascribed to an ancient religious figure) to ancient texts displays a modern bias against their spiritual or historical authenticity, but one should also note that often modern scholars do not consider most biblical books to be inspired by God or written by the authors associated with them.

One important aspect of the expanded collection of the Apocrypha has to do with the canon itself. Centuries after it was determined which books were to be included in the Bible, people began to believe and teach that the Bible was both complete (containing all that God had given through ancient prophets and apostles) and infallible (having been transmitted without any errors). Joseph Smith received correctives to both ideas, being given additional scripture originally written by ancient prophets and being inspired to make corrections in the texts of the Bible. Among the ancient writings he restored are the BOOK OF ABRAHAM and the writings of Moses (canonized as the BOOK OF MOSES, itself including a restoration to Moses of an older Enoch writing; see Moses 6–7); quotations from ancient biblical prophets in the Book of Mormon (such as JOSEPH OF EGYPT and four otherwise unknown writers named ZENOS, ZENOCK, NEUM, and EZIAS); and writings from the New Testament apostle John (see D&C 7 and 93). Corrections to the biblical text include an expanded version of Matthew 24 and alternate readings in Isaiah.

Not only has modern revelation resulted in the restoration of ancient prophetic records and opened the canon in modern times, but the recovery of many ancient texts shows how open and diverse the canon was in earlier times. One ancient religious tradition, repeated in different settings and at different times, attests to two levels of sacred writings, one for public discourse and the other for more restricted use within the community of believers. One might note in this regard that a similar injunction to keep some writings within a restricted community is found in the Book of Moses revealed to Joseph Smith: "Show [these words] not unto any except them that believe" (Moses 1:42; cf. 4:32). Some recently found texts bear the title "Apocryphon," used in the ancient sense of secret or hidden writing. It was this "advanced" level of instruction that was rejected by the church fathers, and the negative meaning of "apocryphal" began to replace the positive or sacred sense. Because in ancient times many such writings were not made public by those who accepted them and because they were distorted and maligned by those who rejected them, scholars lack definitive methods by which to determine if these writings have been transmitted accurately.

In this large collection of writings, relating to both Old and New Testaments, many diverse subjects are discussed, and a few are found repeatedly. Revelation, in the form of APOCALYPTIC TEXTS, is perhaps the most common element: numerous apocryphal texts claim to contain the mysteries, or secrets, of heaven revealed to man. Testaments of patriarchs frequently occur in the Old Testament apocryphal writings; and instructions, eschatological warnings, ritual passages, and cosmic visions are transmitted by the resurrected Jesus to his disciples in many of the New Testament Apocrypha. The type of literature that encompasses these themes is often called Gnostic literature, and scholars generally view the gnosticism seen in apocryphal texts as a fusion of many diverse elements (Hellenism, Judaism, mystery religions, and Christianity, to name a few) into a complex and mystical religious movement. Considerable study will be necessary before all the questions relating to the origin, accuracy, meaning, and significance of apocryphal literature can be answered. Numerous versions of the fourteen books of the Old Testament Apocrypha known in Joseph Smith's time are available, either in separate publications or in modern printings of the Bible, such as the Jerusalem Bible or the New English Bible.

Joseph Smith was well in advance of modern perceptions concerning the Apocrypha when he was given the revelation warning the Saints to seek spiritual guidance when reading such works, alerting them to truths to be obtained therein.

BIBLIOGRAPHY

Charlesworth, James H., ed. *Old Testament Pseudepigrapha*, 2 vols. New York, 1983, 1985.

Cloward, Robert A. *Old Testament Apocrypha and Pseudepigrapha and the Dead Sea Scrolls: A Selected Bibliography of the Text Editions and English Translations.* F.A.R.M.S. Reports. Provo, Utah, 1988.

Griggs, C. Wilfred, ed. *Apocryphal Writings and the Latter-day Saints.* Provo, Utah, 1986.

Hennecke, Edgar, and Wilhelm Schneenelcher, eds. *New Testament Apocrypha*, 2 vols. Translated by R. McL. Wilson. Philadelphia, 1963, 1965.

C. WILFRED GRIGGS

ARMAGEDDON

The name *Armageddon* is a Greek transliteration of the Hebrew *har megiddo,* mountain of Megiddo, and is used by John the Revelator to symbolize the assembling of a vast world army in the last days (Rev. 16:16). Sixty miles north of Jerusalem, the site of the ancient city of Har Megiddo overlooks the Plain of Esdraelon or the valley of

Jezreel, forming a natural entrance to the heart of the land from the Mediterranean Sea.

Anciently the valley was the scene of violent and crucial battles. It was here, during the period of the Judges, that Deborah and Barak defeated the Canaanite general Sisera and delivered Israel from Canaanite rule (Judg. 4–5). Around 640 B.C., King Josiah of Judah was killed at Har Megiddo by the army of Pharaoh Necho, resulting in Judah's subjugation to Egypt (2 Chr. 35:20–23; 2 Kgs. 23:29).

Armageddon is destined to play a future role in world events. It is LDS belief that the prophecies of the scriptures will be fulfilled and that armies representing the nations of the earth will be gathered in the valley of Megiddo. It may be that given the extent of the conflict, Armageddon is a symbolic representation of worldwide conflict centered in this geographic area. The scriptures state that when the battle is at its zenith, Christ, the King of Kings, will appear on the Mount of Olives accompanied by dramatic upheavals. Subsequently, the armies spoken of by John will be destroyed, followed by Christ's millennial reign (cf. Zech. 11–14; Rev. 16:14–21; D&C 45:42–53; *JD* 7:189; *MD,* p. 71). How long it will take to bring about these events is not revealed. The name *Armageddon* does not occur in latter-day scripture, nor is there a known mention of it by the Prophet Joseph Smith.

V. DANIEL ROGERS

ASTRONOMY, SCRIPTURAL REFERENCES TO

Latter-day Saint scriptures indicate that both biblical and latter-day prophets and seers were shown visions of the heavenly realms to orient them to God's dominion and eternal purposes. These visions gave information about (1) the governing of systems of worlds and stellar objects; (2) a heliocentric, planetary cosmology; (3) the plurality of worlds; (4) the spiritual and physical creation of the earth and the universe; and (5) the role of Jesus Christ as creator.

The book of Abraham states that God's physical dominion (throne) is located near a star called Kolob (Abr. 3:2–3). While it might seem reasonable to suppose that this refers to some distinguishing feature of the universe, all efforts to identify it are speculative and not authoritative. Wherever Kolob is located, its purpose is to "govern" all planets that are of the same "order" as the Earth (Abr. 3:9). Since Abraham says no more than that, it is not clear whether he is speaking physically, metaphorically, or allegorically. Thus, "to govern" might mean a physical bonding as with gravity, while "order" could conceivably mean planets similar to the Earth in size, or planets in the same region of this galaxy or even in the entire Milky Way galaxy. Kolob was also said by the Egyptians to provide the light for all stars, including that for our sun (Abr. Facsimile 2). Even so, Latter-day Saints have made no definitive comment on the meaning of these passages.

In contrast to some interpretations of biblical scholars who attribute a geocentric cosmology to the words of Joshua (10:12–14), Job (9:6–7), Isaiah (38:7–8), and other Old Testament passages, the Book of Mormon affirms the sun-centered (heliocentric) view accepted by modern planetary physics. The prophets Nephi$_2$ (Hel. 12:13–15) and Alma$_2$ agree that "surely it is the earth that moveth and not the sun" (Alma 30:44).

Psalm 8:3–4 has been the classic text for discussion of the "plurality of worlds." LDS scriptures give even more direct support for modern astronomers' search for extraterrestrial intelligence. The prophets Enoch, Moses, and Joseph Smith all received revelations dealing with the existence of sentient life on other planets. Moses revealed both the spatial and temporal existence of countless worlds: that God had created "worlds without number," that "many worlds . . . have [already] passed away," and that other worlds are yet to be created (Moses 1:33–38). Joseph Smith received revelations explaining that through Jesus Christ these worlds are created and inhabited (D&C 76:22–24; 93:9–10; Moses 1:33), that all kingdoms are bound by certain laws and conditions (D&C 88:36–38, 42–47), and that resurrected beings reside on celestialized planets (D&C 130:4–7).

The various creation accounts in LDS scripture outline a spirit creation of the heavens and the earth that preceded the physical creation, thus affirming the spiritual nature of the cosmos (Moses 2–3; Abr. 4–5); spirit is indeed "matter" of a different order (D&C 131:7–8). While Moses calls creation periods "days," Abraham speaks of "times" and of thousand-year days (Abr. 3:4; 5:13), suggesting a complex physical creation process.

BIBLIOGRAPHY

Athay, R. Grant. "Worlds Without Number: The Astronomy of Enoch, Abraham, and Moses." *BYU Studies* 8 (Spring 1968):255–69.

Hansen, H. Kimball. "Astronomy and the Scriptures." In *Science and Religion: Toward a More Useful Dialogue*, ed. W. Hess and R. Matheny, Vol. 1, 181–96. Geneva, Ill., 1979.

Salisbury, Frank B. *The Creation*. Salt Lake City, 1976.

ERICH ROBERT PAUL

B

BEATITUDES

The Beatitudes, or promises of blessings in Jesus' SERMON ON THE MOUNT (Matt. 5:3–12), hold a particular significance for Latter-day Saints because the resurrected Lord gave essentially that same sermon to the Nephites and the Lamanites in the Western Hemisphere, as recorded in 3 Nephi 12–14. The words in the Beatitudes echo Isaiah 61:1–2 and Psalm 107:4–7, 9. Church members cite the setting of the Book of Mormon sermon as well as a few notable verbal differences (such as "Blessed are the poor in spirit *who come unto me*," and the phrase "for they shall be filled *with the Holy Ghost*") as examples of how the Book of Mormon complements the Bible, attesting to its message while clarifying and expanding it (cf. 1 Ne. 13 [esp. verses 39–42]; 2 Ne. 27, 29).

In the Book of Mormon, most of the sermon is addressed to baptized members of the Church (cf. 3 Ne. 11 and 12:1–2). Thus, the expectations in the sermon concern those living the law of the gospel as taught by Christ. Other parts of the sermon are directed specifically to leaders.

Some significant differences appear in the wording of the biblical and Book of Mormon versions of the Beatitudes. In the Book of Mormon, two new "beatitudes" precede those in Matthew: baptized members are blessed if they give heed to their leaders and have faith in Christ (3 Ne. 12:1), and "more blessed" are those who receive the testimony of emissaries whom Christ has called (3 Ne. 12:2). These two additional beatitudes are incorporated into the biblical sermon in the JOSEPH SMITH TRANSLATION OF THE BIBLE (JST). Matthew 5:3 is elaborated as noted above (cf. D&C 84:49–53). Matthew 5:4 is virtually unchanged at 3 Nephi 12:4 but is somewhat developed at 3 Nephi 12:19 (cf. Morm. 2:11–13). The words "shall be filled with the Holy Ghost" (3 Ne. 12:6) express on a spiritual level (cf. Ps. 17:15, Septuagint) the implicit meaning of cattle feeding upon grass (Matt. 5:6; Greek, *chortasthêsontai*; cf. the grass *[chortos]* where the disciples are miraculously fed at Matt. 14:19 and the verb "filled" at Matt. 15:33, 37). Matthew 5:5 is unchanged, as are Matthew 5:7–9; but Matthew 5:10 reads "which are persecuted for righteousness' sake," while 3 Nephi 12:10 has "who are persecuted for my name's sake," reflecting the Christ-centered theme throughout the Nephite version of the sermon. For the first two verbs of Matthew 5:12, which the KJV takes as imperatives, 3 Nephi 12:12 has "For ye shall have great joy and be exceeding glad."

Church leaders often refer to the Beatitudes as the Lord's promises of blessings and happiness to those who follow him and as the result of obedience or the "fruit of the Spirit" (Gal. 5:22–23). Those who would be obedient have the individual responsibilities of turning to the Lord and of implementing the principles inherent in the qualities described in the Beatitudes (cf. D&C 88:63–65 and 97:16, which adapt the sixth beatitude to temple worship).

BIBLIOGRAPHY

Thomas, Catherine. "The Sermon on the Mount: The Sacrifice of the Human Heart (Matt. 5–7; Luke 6:17–49)." In *Studies in Scripture*, ed. R. Millet, Vol. 5, pp. 236–50. Salt Lake City, 1986.

Welch, John W. *The Sermon at the Temple and the Sermon on the Mount.* Salt Lake City, 1990.

Wilcox, S. Michael. "The Beatitudes—Pathway to the Savior." *Ensign* 21 (Jan. 1991):19–23.

THOMAS W. MACKAY

BENJAMIN

Benjamin, son of MOSIAH₁, was an important king in Nephite history (d. c. 121 B.C.). His reign came at a crucial juncture in the history of the NEPHITES and was important both culturally and politically. His father, Mosiah₁, "being warned of the Lord," had led the Nephites out of the land of Nephi to the land of Zarahemla (Omni 1:12, 19). Thereafter, during his own reign, Benjamin fought, as was customary for kings in the ancient world (cf. Mosiah 10:10), with his "own arm" against invading LAMANITES (W of M 1:13), keeping his people "from falling into the hands of [their] enemies" (Mosiah 2:31). He succeeded in consolidating Nephite rule over the land of Zarahemla (Omni 1:19) and reigned there "in righteousness" over his people (W of M 1:17).

Benjamin, described as a "holy man" (W of M 1:17) and "a just man before the Lord," also led his people as a prophet (Omni 1:25) and was, with the assistance of other prophets and holy men, able to overcome the contentions among his people and to "once more establish peace in the land" (W of M 1:18). Accordingly, Amaleki, who was himself "without seed," entrusted Benjamin with the record on the "small plates" (Omni 1:25). Keenly interested in the preservation of sacred records, Benjamin taught his sons "in all the language of his fathers" and "concerning the records . . . on the plates of brass" (Mosiah 1:2–3).

Mosiah 2–6 records Benjamin's farewell address, designed primarily to effect a "change in heart" in his people and to bring them to Jesus Christ. He deals with man's obligations to his fellow men and to God, punishment for rebellion against God, gratitude, faith, and service. This address is as relevant now as it was when first presented. In addition, reporting the words spoken to him by an angel, Benjamin prophesied that "the Lord Omnipotent . . . shall come down from heaven among the children of men" as the Messiah, "working mighty miracles" (Mosiah 3:5). Further, Benjamin declared that the Messiah would "be called Jesus Christ, the Son of God, . . . and his mother shall be called Mary" (3:8)—the earliest mention of her name in the Book of Mormon. Moreover, Jesus would "suffer temptations, and pain of body, hunger, thirst, and fatigue, even more than man can suffer" (3:7). After being crucified, Jesus would "rise the third day from the dead; and behold, he standeth to judge the world" (3:10). Significantly, Benjamin taught that the power of the atonement of Jesus Christ was in effect for him and his people, "as though he had already come" to earth (3:13).

The impact of Benjamin's address on subsequent Nephite generations can be gauged by how much it is mentioned later in the Book of Mormon. Following Benjamin's death, his son and successor, MOSIAH$_2$, sent Ammon and fifteen other representatives from Zarahemla to the land of Nephi (Mosiah 7:1–6), where they found the Nephite king Limhi and his people in bondage to the Lamanites. After the representatives had identified themselves, Limhi caused his people to gather at the local temple, where he addressed them. Thereafter, Ammon "rehearsed unto them the last words which King Benjamin had taught them, and explained them to the people of king Limhi, so that they might understand all the words which he spake" (Mosiah 8:3). Similarly, HELAMAN$_2$ (c. 30 B.C.) admonished his sons LEHI$_4$ and NEPHI$_2$ to "remember . . . the words which King Benjamin spake unto his people; yea, remember that there is no other way nor means whereby man can be saved, only through the atoning blood of Jesus Christ" (Hel. 5:9). These words mirror one of the central themes of Benjamin's address: "Salvation was, and is, and is to come, in and through the atoning blood of Christ" (Mosiah 3:18–19; cf. Hel. 14:12).

After a long and prosperous reign, Benjamin died about 121 B.C. No higher tribute was paid to his greatness than that given by his son Mosiah$_2$. In a discourse given at the end of his own reign, in which he considers the advantages and pitfalls of various forms of government, Mosiah says, "If ye could have men for your kings who would do even as my father Benjamin did for this people, . . . then it would be expedient that ye should always have kings to rule over you" (Mosiah 29:13).

BIBLIOGRAPHY

Nibley, Hugh. *An Approach to the Book of Mormon.* In *CWHN* 4:295–310.

STEPHEN D. RICKS

BIBLE

[*The entry on the Bible is designed as an overview of the positive LDS appraisal and extensive use of this scriptural collection. Articles under this entry are:*

Bible
LDS Belief in the Bible
King James Version
LDS Publication of the Bible

The first article explains the importance of the Bible among the standard works of the Church. The second article explores the depth of belief in the Bible. The third article examines the Church's use of the King James Version of the Bible. The concluding article gives information contained in the Bible published by the Church in 1979 and details of the publication. Articles that address related issues include Old Testament *and* New Testament. *For discussions of the range of matters associated with the LDS view of scripture in general, see* Standard Works *and particularly the set of articles under the general heading* Scripture.]

BIBLE

The Bible stands at the foundation of The Church of Jesus Christ of Latter-day Saints, constitutes one of its standard works, and is accepted as the word of God. In 1820 a New Testament passage in the epistle of James prompted the young Joseph Smith to ask God about the religions of his time, and thereupon he received his first vision, in which he saw God the Father and Jesus Christ (James 1:5; JS—H 1:11–12, 17–18). Three years later, Old Testament and New Testament passages provided the principal scriptural foundation of Joseph's second major spiritual experience when the angel MORONI appeared to him and taught him from Malachi, Isaiah, Joel, Daniel, and other scriptures (JS—H 1:36–41; *JD* 24:241; *Messenger and Advocate* 1 [Apr. 1835]:109). After completing the Book of Mormon Translation and organizing the restored Church of Jesus Christ in 1830, the Prophet Joseph Smith thoroughly studied the Bible as instructed by the Lord and prepared the JOSEPH SMITH TRANSLATION OF THE BIBLE (JST).

From childhood, Latter-day Saints are introduced to the teachings of the Bible. Certain passages are emphasized in teaching children. Most children in Primary—and particularly those in families who hold family home evening and follow scripture reading programs—become familiar with the events recorded in Genesis, including stories of Adam and Eve, Noah, Abraham, Jacob, and

Joseph. Later episodes of the prophets, judges, and kings (such as Moses, Samson, Samuel, David, Solomon, Jonah, and Daniel), as well as those of New Testament personalities (e.g., Peter, Paul, and Stephen), are also favorites. The stories of Deborah, Ruth, Esther, and Mary are especially loved by girls. However, the life and teachings of Jesus Christ are the most studied and appreciated.

Richer gospel teachings come into focus in repeated study of the Bible by Latter-day Saints. In addition to Sunday School instruction, teenagers attending seminary classes spend two years of their four-year curriculum on the Bible. A similar emphasis is found in college-level religion classes in the universities and colleges of the Church Educational System and in Institute of Religion classes at other universities and colleges. LDS missionaries often refer to Bible passages as they teach investigators of the Church. One of the strongest demonstrations of the importance of Bible study to the Latter-day Saints is found in the adult Sunday School program. In the Gospel Doctrine classes, two of every four years are devoted to reading, studying, and discussing the Bible. Another strong evidence of LDS commitment to the Bible is the effort and expense incurred to produce the LDS PUBLICATION OF THE BIBLE in 1979. The General Authorities of the Church frequently quote from the Bible in their writings and general and stake conference addresses. Thus, the Bible forms an important gospel foundation for all Church members, from the newly baptized to the presiding leaders.

PREVALENT BIBLICAL TEACHINGS AND PRACTICES. Among the teachings found in the Bible, some concepts receive special emphasis. For example, Latter-day Saints readily identify with the Old Testament pattern of God speaking through living prophets (Amos 3:7), a pattern visible in the Church today. They also relate to the house of Israel through their individual patriarchal blessings, which usually identify a genealogical line back to one of the tribes of Israel. The concept of a covenant people, as taught in Genesis, Exodus, and Deuteronomy, conforms to LDS beliefs about being a covenant people today. Many laws and commandments, in particular a health code, distinguish both ancient Israel and its modern spiritual counterpart in the Church (Lev. 11; D&C 89). The wanderings of ancient Israel and the challenges in settling the PROMISED LAND also parallel early

LDS history, so much so that Brigham Young has been called a modern Moses (e.g., Arrington, 1985).

New Testament teachings that are emphasized among Latter-day Saints include the teachings of the Savior and the apostles on basic gospel principles, especially faith and repentance, and covenant ordinances, particularly baptism and the gift of the Holy Ghost. Latter-day parallels to the New Testament Church organization, priesthood offices, and missionary work have their counterparts in contemporary LDS beliefs, practices, and Church organization (*see* ORGANIZATION OF THE CHURCH IN NEW TESTAMENT TIMES).

BIBLICAL EMPHASIS WITHIN THE BOOK OF MORMON.   Among Old Testament writings, those of Moses, Isaiah, and Malachi receive special attention from Latter-day Saints because of their prominence within the Book of Mormon. The teachings of Moses as found in the Pentateuch (an expanded portion of Genesis 1–6 being available also in the PEARL OF GREAT PRICE) provide the foundation for understanding the Mosaic dispensation of the house of Israel. The Book of Mormon record, which originated with LEHI and with the people of Zarahemla (*see* MULEK), came mostly out of this Israelite setting. The record includes Adam and Eve and events in the Garden of Eden (e.g., 2 Ne. 2:15–25), and references to the flood at the time of Noah (e.g., Alma 10:22), to people divinely led to the Americas at the time of the Tower of Babel (Ether 1:3–5, 33), to events in the lives of the patriarchs (e.g., 2 Ne. 3:4–16), and to the calling, works, and words of Moses (e.g., 1 Ne. 17:23–31; 2 Ne. 3:16–17; *see also* LAW OF MOSES). The fifth chapter of 1 Nephi reviews the biblical records that Lehi's family brought out of Jerusalem (*see* BOOK OF MORMON PLATES AND RECORDS) and, along with 1 Nephi 17, highlights key biblical events, particularly the Israelite exodus from Egypt, although without the details found in the Pentateuch. The examples and teachings of Old Testament prophets, judges, and kings were also part of the biblical records of the community of Lehi. Because this group lived under the law of Moses (2 Ne. 25:24), Old Testament religious practices are continued in the Book of Mormon.

Fully one-third of the writings of Isaiah are found in the Book of Mormon, making Isaiah the most frequently quoted biblical book there. Twenty-two of the sixty-six chapters of Isaiah are quoted in whole or in part in the Book of Mormon (a total of 433 of Isaiah's

1,292 verses). Book of Mormon prophets and writers typically selected those chapters highlighting God's covenant relationships and his promises to Israel, the role and calling of the Messiah, and prophecies concerning the last days. These themes are prevalent in contemporary LDS theology as well (A of F 3, 4, 9, 10).

Malachi's teachings in the Book of Mormon are important because the resurrected Jesus quoted them and thus emphasized them (cf. 3 Ne. 24–25; Mal. 3–4; D&C 2:1–3). Malachi's words concerning a messenger sent to prepare the way for Christ's second coming, the payment of tithes and offerings, and the latter-day mission of ELIJAH thus form another important nucleus of Old Testament teachings within LDS society.

Because the main Book of Mormon colony left Jerusalem approximately six hundred years before the beginning of the New Testament period, Book of Mormon writers did not have access to New Testament records. However, they had access to two important sources of doctrines paralleling some of the New Testament: the resurrected Christ and divine revelation. The resurrected Christ delivered to his hearers in the Americas a sermon essentially the same as the one he had delivered near the Sea of Galilee. He also gave important additions and clarifications that focus on him as the Redeemer and Lord, on the fulfillment of the law of Moses, and on the latter days (3 Ne. 11–18; see also BEATITUDES; SERMON ON THE MOUNT). In addition, he amplified teachings recorded in John 10, especially verse 16, about his role as the Good Shepherd of the scattered sheep of Israel (3 Ne. 15:12–24). MORMON's important teachings about baptism and about faith, hope, and charity parallel New Testament teachings, especially those of Paul in 1 Corinthians 13.

IS THE BIBLE COMPLETE?   Latter-day Saints revere the Bible as the word of God revealed to humankind. However, Joseph Smith recognized that translations do not reflect totally and exactly the original words and intentions of the ancient prophets and other biblical writers. Thus, in the Wentworth Letter he wrote, "We believe the Bible to be the word of God as far as it is translated correctly" (A of F 8). Joseph Smith observed that "our latitude and longitude can be determined in the original Hebrew with far greater accuracy than in the English version. There is a grand distinction between the actual meaning of the prophets and the present translation" (TPJS, pp.

290–91). While Latter-day Saints accept rather explicitly what the Bible now says, they realize that more is to be accounted for than is available in the extant biblical record.

In addition to difficulties associated with translating from ancient to modern languages, other scriptures also declare that some parts of the original biblical text have been lost or corrupted (e.g., 1 Ne. 13:28–29; D&C 6:26–27; 93:6–18). Joseph Smith commented on the Bible's incompleteness: "It was apparent that many important points touching the salvation of men, had been taken from the Bible, or lost before it was compiled" (*TPJS*, pp. 10–11). He later said, "Much instruction has been given to man since the beginning which we do not possess now. . . . We have what we have, and the Bible contains what it does contain" (*TPJS*, p. 61). The Prophet Joseph further stated, "I believe the Bible as it read when it came from the pen of the original writers. Ignorant translators, careless transcribers, or designing and corrupt priests have committed many errors" (*TPJS*, p. 327). Thus, the elements of mistranslation, incompleteness, and other errors weaken the Bible; but the spirit of its messages still reveals enough of God's word to fulfill his appointed purposes. Joseph Smith summarized thus: "Through the kind providence of our Father a portion of His word which He delivered to His ancient saints, has fallen into our hands [and] is presented to us with a promise of a reward if obeyed, and with a penalty if disobeyed" (*TPJS*, p. 61). Latter-day Saints have continued to trust in the general accuracy of the biblical texts even though they know that that text may not always be correct. Thus, they study and revere the Bible, especially in the context of other scriptures and modern revelation, which have much to say about the Bible and how it is to be interpreted, and as they study they ponder and pray that they may receive inspiration from God and come to understand the Bible's messages as they need to be applied in their lives (cf. Moro. 10:3–5).

First Presidency's Endorsement of Bible Reading.   Each of the Presidents of the Church has encouraged Latter-day Saints to read the scriptures and to apply scriptural teachings in their lives, as the scriptures also admonish (cf. 2 Tim. 3:16; 1 Ne. 19:23). As a demonstration of this emphasis, in 1983, a year proclaimed as the "Year of the Bible" in the United States, the members of the First Presidency of the Church issued a strong statement in support of Bible reading and application: "We commend to all people everywhere the daily reading, pondering and heeding of the divine truths of the Holy Bible." They also declared the Church's attitude toward the Bible by saying that "the Church of Jesus Christ of Latter-day Saints accepts the Holy Bible as essential to faith and doctrine" and that the Church is committed to Bible reading and scholarship as demonstrated by the publishing of an enhanced edition of the King James Version. "Moreover," they continued, "the Holy Bible is the textbook for adult, youth and children's classes throughout the Church each year."

In the same statement, the First Presidency highlighted the role and value of the Bible in the lives of individuals. They observed that when "read reverently and prayerfully, the Holy Bible becomes a priceless volume, converting the soul to righteousness. Principal among its virtues is the declaration that Jesus is the Christ, the Son of God, through whom eternal salvation may come to all." They continued with the promise that "as we read the scripture, we avail ourselves of the better part of this world's literature" and they encouraged all to "go to the fountain of truth, searching the scriptures, reading them in our homes, and teaching our families what the Lord has said through the inspired and inspiring passages of the Holy Bible" ("Statement of the First Presidency," p. 3).

The Latter-day Saint use of the Bible differs from the Judeo-Christian norm because it is not the sole LDS source of authority (*see* SCRIPTURE: AUTHORITY OF SCRIPTURE). The Bible is interpreted and understood by Latter-day Saints through four important means: (1) other LDS scriptures, which enrich and give perspective to an understanding of biblical teachings; (2) statements of modern prophets and apostles on the meaning of some biblical passages; (3) the Joseph Smith Translation of the Bible; and (4) personal revelation through the gift of the Holy Ghost enhancing the comprehension of the scriptures. Consequently, Latter-day Saints are not left without information about the meaning of many difficult passages that have divided the entire Christian world for two millennia.

The LDS perspective on the Bible is summarized well in the statement of the seventh Church president, Heber J. Grant, who said, "All my life I have been finding additional evidences that the Bible is the Book of books, and that the Book of Mormon is the greatest witness for the truth of the Bible that has ever been published" (*IE* 39 [Nov. 1936]:660).

BIBLIOGRAPHY

Anderson, Richard L. *Understanding Paul*. Salt Lake City, 1983.

Arrington, Leonard. *Brigham Young: American Moses*. New York, 1985.

Barlow, Philip L. *Mormons and the Bible*. New York, 1990.

Harrison, Roland Kenneth. *Introduction to the Old Testament*. Grand Rapids, Mich., 1969.

Ludlow, Daniel H. *A Companion to Your Study of the Old Testament*. Salt Lake City, 1981.

Ludlow, Victor L. *Unlocking the Old Testament*. Salt Lake City, 1981.

———. *Isaiah: Prophet, Seer, and Poet*. Salt Lake City, 1982.

Matthews, Robert J. *A Bible! A Bible!* Salt Lake City, Utah, 1990.

McConkie, Bruce R. *The Mortal Messiah*. Salt Lake City, 1979.

Nyman, Monte S., ed. *Isaiah and the Prophets*. Provo, Utah, 1984.

Reynolds, Noel B. "The Brass Plates Version of Genesis." In *By Study and Also by Faith*, ed. J. Lundquist and S. Ricks, Vol. 2, pp. 136–73. Salt Lake City, 1990.

Sperry, Sidney B. *Paul's Life and Letters*. Salt Lake City, 1955.

———. *The Voice of Israel's Prophets*. Salt Lake City, 1965.

———. *The Spirit of the Old Testament*. Salt Lake City, 1970.

"Statement of the First Presidency." *Church News*, Mar. 20, 1983, p. 3.

Talmage, James E. *Jesus the Christ*. Salt Lake City, 1915.

Welch, John W. *The Sermon at the Temple and the Sermon on the Mount*. Salt Lake City, 1990.

VICTOR L. LUDLOW

LDS BELIEF IN THE BIBLE

The Church believes the word of God contained in the Bible. It accepts the Bible "as the foremost of [the Church's] standard works, first among the books which have been proclaimed as . . . written guides in faith and doctrine. In the respect and sanctity with which the Latter-day Saints regard the Bible they are of like profession with Christian denominations in general" (*AF*, 1966 ed., p. 236).

Latter-day Saints value the Bible for many reasons. The Bible presents the revelations of God in several dispensations or eras, each headed by prophets. They also read and follow the Bible for the instructional and spiritual value of the events it describes. While some of the Old Testament describes the law of Moses that Latter-day Saints believe was fulfilled with the atonement of Christ (3 Ne. 9:17), nevertheless the Old Testament stories, commandments, ordinances, proverbs, and prophetic writings still express the basic patterns of God's will toward his children and how they should act toward him.

Latter-day Saints revere the New Testament for its account of the birth, ministry, atonement, and resurrection of the Savior, Jesus Christ. The teachings of Jesus in the New Testament comprise the core of LDS doctrine, and their preeminence is evidenced by their frequent appearance in other LDS STANDARD WORKS accepted as scripture and in LDS speaking and writing.

The writings of the New Testament apostles are accepted and appreciated for their doctrine and wise and inspired counsel and for documenting the apostolic challenge of proclaiming the gospel, adhering to the original teachings of Christ, establishing the unity of the faith, and promoting the righteousness of believers in a rapidly growing Church. Latter-day Saints also find references in several letters of the early apostles of the falling away that necessitated the RESTORATION, alerting the faithful to remain fervent and active in the faith and to stay true to the love of Jesus Christ.

While Latter-day Saints devoutly regard the Bible, they do not consider it the sole authoritative source of religious instruction and personal guidance. They also study accounts of God's dealings with other ancient peoples such as those found in the Book of Mormon along with the teachings of the Prophet Joseph Smith and the latter-day prophets and apostles (*see* DOCTRINE AND COVENANTS; JOSEPH SMITH TRANSLATION OF THE BIBLE [JST]; PEARL OF GREAT PRICE). Latter-day Saints consider personal revelation the individual's ultimate source for understanding scripture and knowing God's will.

Viewed as being harmonious with each other, all these sources enhance and clarify one another, and aid modern readers in correctly comprehending and translating these texts.

Latter-day Saints believe all that God has revealed. They seek to know and do the word of God wherever it has been made known in truth and authority. They believe that salvation is in Jesus Christ and not in any combination of words or books. They believe in God and in his Son Jesus Christ, whose words and ways can be known through a lifetime of SCRIPTURE STUDY, service, and prayer, and by personal revelation through the power of the Holy Ghost.

BIBLIOGRAPHY

Matthews, Robert J. *A Bible! A Bible!* Salt Lake City, 1990.

PAUL C. HEDENGREN

KING JAMES VERSION

In various lands where The Church of Jesus Christ of Latter-day Saints has been established, it uses a translation of the Bible in the local language. In English-speaking areas, the Church uses the King James (or Authorized) Version (KJV), mainly because it was the basic English text used by the Prophet Joseph Smith and because subsequent Church leaders have approved its use. The Church does not claim that the KJV is perfect, but it is currently the preferred English version and was used in the Church's 1979 edition and later printings of the Bible.

The books of the Bible were originally written in Hebrew, Aramaic, or Greek. No original biblical manuscripts exist today, but they were copied and translated into many languages in antiquity. Many early papyri and parchments have survived. From those records, numerous modern translations have been made.

From 1604 to 1611, some fifty-four scholars worked to produce the KJV of the Bible. This was not the first English translation. In 1382, John Wycliffe translated the Bible from the Latin Vulgate; a revised edition was published in 1388. From 1523 to 1530, William Tyndale translated the Pentateuch from Hebrew and the New Testament from Greek. Still later in the 1500s, other translations appeared, including the Protestant Geneva Bible in 1560 and the Bishops' Bible in 1568. The former became popular with the laity and the latter with Protestant bishops. The Catholic Rheims-Douai Bible was finished in 1609 (1582 New Testament, 1609 Old Testament), based on the Latin Vulgate.

In an attempt to heal differences between Anglicans and Puritans, King James I appointed a body of scholars to produce a version of the Bible to be authorized for use in the English churches. They used the best texts available to them, mainly the "Received Text" of the New Testament in the multilanguage ("polyglot") editions, presenting the Old and New Testaments in Hebrew and Greek respectively, and other languages. The long and respected line of English Bibles was also diligently compared and used.

The resulting King James Version was published in 1611. Various editions of the KJV appeared throughout the 1600s, which resulted in many printing inaccuracies. The Cambridge (1762) and

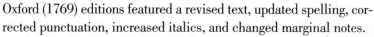

Oxford (1769) editions featured a revised text, updated spelling, corrected punctuation, increased italics, and changed marginal notes.

Many other English versions have appeared, especially in light of the discovery of additional early manuscripts, beginning with Constantin von Tischendorf's first find at St. Catherine's Monastery in the Sinai peninsula in 1844. These translations have generally endeavored to render the ancient texts into contemporary usage while reflecting the form of the oldest available manuscripts as much as possible.

Latter-day Saints have not made extensive use of these other translations. Many feel that popularization tends to dilute the sacred nature of the Bible. They also find the ancient textual variants to be relatively insignificant, usually not changing the important messages of the Bible, most of which, in any event, are corroborated elsewhere in LDS scripture.

Although the KJV was Joseph Smith's English Bible, he did not regard it as a perfect or official translation; this is why he studied Hebrew and undertook the task of producing an inspired revision of the scriptures. He commented that he preferred some aspects of the Martin Luther translation (*HC* 6:307, 364), and several other nineteenth-century Church leaders stressed the need for greater accuracy and truth in Bible translations.

Twentieth-century Church leaders have given a variety of reasons for the continued use of the KJV: it was the common translation in use in the English-speaking world at the time of the Restoration; its language prevails in all the STANDARD WORKS; a large number of passages in the Book of Mormon, which parallel the Bible, were translated into the English style of the KJV; the JOSEPH SMITH TRANSLATION OF THE BIBLE (JST) was based on the KJV, with 90 percent of the verses unchanged. All latter-day prophets have used the KJV, and using the KJV in all Church publications has made it possible to standardize annotations and indices.

The KJV is viewed by many as a masterpiece of English literature. It has been called "the noblest monument of English prose," and it is certainly the most influential; its translators "showed great sensitivity," and the result was "destined for extraordinary influence and acclaim" (Speiser, pp. lxxiii–iv). H. L. Mencken praised it as "probably the most beautiful piece of writing in all the literature of the world" (Paine, p. viii).

The KJV is a relatively conservative translation. This is generally a strength, although at times it produces obscure renderings. Moreover, some of its diction is now archaic and ungrammatical in current usage, and it is not consistent in the spelling of names in the Old and New Testaments (for example, Isaiah/Esaias and Elijah/Elias). Identical words in the synoptic Gospels are sometimes translated differently, and some misprints were never corrected (for instance, in Matt. 23:24, "strain *at* a gnat" should have been rendered "strain *out* a gnat").

After studying many modern English translations, however, President J. Reuben Clark, Jr., a counselor in the First Presidency, said in 1956 that the KJV was "the best version of any yet produced" (Clark, p. 33). For example, he felt that the KJV translators clearly portrayed Jesus as the promised Messiah and as the Son of God, and accepted the gift of prophecy, the reality of miracles, and the uniqueness of the love of Christ; whereas modern translations have tended to promote naturalistic explanations for divine action, preferred the word "sign" instead of "miracle," and used "love" in place of "charity," and "appoint" instead of "ordain." His views have been influential among most Latter-day Saints. Not all alternative translations, of course, suffer from the problems identified by President Clark.

BIBLIOGRAPHY
Barlow, Philip L. *Mormons and the Bible*, pp. 132–62. New York, 1990.
Bruce, F. F. *History of the Bible in English*, 3rd ed. New York, 1978.
Clark, J. Reuben, Jr. *Why the King James Version.* Salt Lake City, 1956.
Daiches, David. *The King James Version of the English Bible.* Chicago, 1941.
Metzger, Bruce M. *The Text of the New Testament.* New York, 1968.
Paine, G. *The Learned Men*, p. viii. New York, 1959.
Speiser, E. *Genesis*, pp. lxiii–iv. Garden City, N.Y., 1964.

D. KELLY OGDEN

LDS PUBLICATION OF THE BIBLE

An edition of the King James Version of the Bible with new Bible study aids was published by The Church of Jesus Christ of Latter-day Saints in 1979, culminating seven years' work by Church leaders and scholars. The goals were to make Bible study more meaningful for Church members by supplying maps, charts, definitions, headnotes, footnotes, and cross-references to all of the four STANDARD WORKS, and also to provide a single Bible edition for use in the Church curriculum.

This project began in 1972, about the time the study of the scriptures became the primary goal for the adult curriculum of the Church. Previously Church teachers had relied mainly on lesson manuals prepared by individuals or committees. The work was commissioned by the First Presidency, who appointed a Bible Aids committee to oversee the project. This committee (later called the Scriptures Publications Committee) consisted initially of Thomas S. Monson, Boyd K. Packer, and Marvin J. Ashton of the Quorum of the Twelve Apostles. Ashton was later given another assignment and Bruce R. McConkie was appointed.

The committee called scholars, editors, and publication specialists from Brigham Young University, the Church Educational System, and Deseret Book Company to prepare Latter-day-Saint-oriented aids to help readers better understand the King James text. Early in the project the First Presidency determined that the King James text would be used without change. This text of the Bible, along with the Book of Mormon, the Doctrine and Covenants, and the Pearl of Great Price, was entered into a computer database. Each verse was reviewed, and key topics and terms identified. Computer printouts were generated comprising long lists of possible cross-references from which useful citations were then selected. Emphasis was given to references from the Book of Mormon, Doctrine and Covenants, and Pearl of Great Price that helped clarify Bible passages along with abundant interbiblical cross-references. These now appear in the footnotes and in the TOPICAL GUIDE (an extensive subject index and modified concordance). A BIBLE DICTIONARY, 24 pages of full-color maps, and a complete gazetteer were included. The Bible Dictionary provides concise explanations of biblical items and often adds points of interest to Latter-day Saints. Brief explanations of some words or phrases from Hebrew and Greek were also included as footnotes, along with about 600 passages from the JOSEPH SMITH TRANSLATION OF THE BIBLE (JST). Unique summaries at the beginning of each chapter in this edition of the King James Bible suggest the doctrinal and historical content of each chapter from an LDS point of view.

The footnote system organizes all the aids available in this publication of the Bible. Some earlier Bible editions place cross-references in a center column on the page, but this format limits the amount of material that can be included. A flexible system of three footnote columns at the bottom of each page was designed, with "call-out" letters (*a*, *b*, *c*, etc.) allocated separately for each verse placed in the text as needed. Included in the footnotes are cross-references to other scriptures, the Topical Guide, and the Bible Dictionary; also explanatory Greek and Hebrew idioms and other clarifying information.

Once the scholarly and editorial work was completed in early 1978, typesetting began. Cambridge University Press in Cambridge, England, was selected as typesetter, because that press, one of the early printers of the King James Version after it was first issued in 1611, has been continuously involved in Bible publications since the late 1500s. Its expert staff proved invaluable to Church members who worked with them in editing the copy for typesetting and preparing the final pages. All the type was set in Monotype hot metal. Each page was prepared so that every footnote was contained on the same page as the verse to which it pertained. To serve the needs of programs in the Church Educational System, a self-imposed delivery deadline of September 1979 for the first copies of the Bible loomed over those involved in this production. The formidable task of typesetting and paginating 2,423 pages of complex text was completed in May 1979 after fifteen months of intense effort.

Printing and binding were first contracted with University Press and Publishers Book Bindery of Winchester, Massachusetts, who subcontracted some of the work to National Bible Press in Philadelphia, Pennsylvania. What at first seemed impossible production deadlines all came together, and the first copies were delivered August 8, 1979. Many Latter-day Saints acknowledged the hand of God at work in this monumental publication.

This edition of the King James Version of the Bible has stimulated further interest in Bible study throughout the Church. It has extended and deepened members' understanding of and appreciation for the Bible as the word of God. It has also demonstrated that all the Latter-day Saint books of sacred scripture are correlated in many mutually supportive and enriching ways.

BIBLIOGRAPHY

Anderson, Lavina Fielding. "Church Publishes First LDS Edition of the Bible." *Ensign* 9 (Oct. 1979):8–18.

Matthews, Robert J. "The New Publications of the Standard Works—1979, 1981." *BYU Studies* 22 (Fall 1982):387–424.

Mortimer, William James. "The Coming Forth of the LDS Editions of Scripture." *Ensign* 13 (Aug. 1983):35–41.

Packer, Boyd K. "Scriptures." *Ensign* 12 (Nov. 1982):51–53.

WILLIAM JAMES MORTIMER

BIBLE, LDS

[*The Church of Jesus Christ of Latter-day Saints reveres the Bible as the word of God given through ancient prophets and apostles, though it recognizes that the current text is not identical with the original. The Church has consistently used the King James Version (KJV) for formal classes, missionary work, and personal study among English-speaking peoples, utilizing KJV editions issued by the major Bible publishing houses. However, because latter-day revelation offers insight, interpretation, and supplemental material to thousands of biblical passages, and in order to make the message of the Bible more readily accessible to LDS readers, the Church published in 1979 an edition of the KJV with multiple study helps. These include chapter headings, cross-references to other LDS scriptural works, explanatory footnotes, clarification of Greek and Hebrew terms and idioms, a subject-matter guide, a dictionary, maps, and excerpts from an inspired translation of the Bible by the Prophet Joseph Smith.*

Articles directly related to this subject are Bible: LDS Publication of the Bible; Bible Dictionary; Joseph Smith Translation of the Bible (JST); *and* Topical Guide. *Other relevant articles are* Bible: LDS Belief in the Bible; Bible: King James Version; Scripture; Scripture Study; Standard Works.]

BIBLE DICTIONARY

In 1979 The Church of Jesus Christ of Latter-day Saints published its own edition of the King James Version of the Bible with many reader's aids, including a new Bible dictionary. This dictionary contains much information relevant to the Bible that is unique to Mormonism. Bible dictionaries have traditionally been geographic and cultural word books, dating back to works such as Langenstein's *Vocabularius Bibliae* (1476) and Heyden's *Biblisches Namen Buch* (1567), which surveyed biblical history and archaeology then known. The increase in biblical scholarship since World War II has seen both a proliferation of linguistic materials and changes in dictionaries to include doctrinal concepts as well as people and places. Many denominations have published Bible dictionaries each reflecting a unique theological stance.

Cambridge University Press granted the Church permission to use its Bible dictionary as a base, to be amended as needed. It was changed in three major ways: 1. Entries considered to be in error or of insufficient value were omitted. 2. Entries that were incomplete, because they were based on the Bible alone, were complemented by information from the BOOK OF MORMON, the DOCTRINE AND COVENANTS, the PEARL OF GREAT PRICE, and the teachings of the Prophet Joseph Smith. This affected such entries as the Fall, ZION, URIM AND THUMMIM, ADAM, CIRCUMCISION, and Temple. 3. New entries were added, including discussions on such matters as Dispensation of the Fulness of Times, Aaronic Priesthood, Melchizedek Priesthood, writing, and the family.

The dictionary provides new information in the light of such discoveries as the Dead Sea Scrolls, and explains language and cultural items, including several English words used in the Bible whose meanings have changed. Another major help is a harmony of the events in the life of Christ that includes not only the four Gospels but also 3 Nephi in the Book of Mormon and other references to latter-day revelation. The dictionary also contains an eleven-page world history chart of the major events that pertain to the Old and New Testaments and a chart of the main New Testament quotations that have Old Testament origins. The work totals 196 pages with 1,285 entries. It is not a declaration of the official position of the Church, but represents LDS perspectives as related to the products of ongoing scholarship that may be modified by further discovery and by future revelation.

BIBLIOGRAPHY

Brewster, Hoyt W., Jr. "Discovering the LDS Editions of Scripture." *Ensign* 13 (Oct. 1983):55–58.

Matthews, Robert J. "The New Publications of the Standard Works—1979, 1981." *BYU Studies* 22 (Fall 1982):387–424.

GARY P. GILLUM

BIBLE SCHOLARSHIP

Latter-day Saints recognize Bible scholarship and intellectual study of the biblical text. Joseph Smith and his associates studied Greek and Hebrew and taught that religious knowledge is to be obtained by study as well as by faith (D&C 88:118). However, Latter-day Saints prefer to use Bible scholarship rather than be driven or controlled by it.

The Prophet Joseph Smith suggested certain broad parameters for any LDS critical study of the Bible: "We believe the Bible to be the word of God as far as it is translated correctly; we also believe the Book of Mormon to be the word of God" (A of F 8). Because Latter-day Saints prefer PROPHETS to scholars as spiritual guides, and the inspiration of SCRIPTURE and the Holy Ghost to the reasoning of secondary texts, Bible scholarship plays a smaller role in LDS spirituality than it does in some denominations.

A fundamental operating principle of "revealed" religions is that all truth cannot be completely discovered through human reason alone. Without God's aid, no one can obtain the vital data, proper perspectives, and interpretive keys for knowing him (*see* REASON AND REVELATION). Because Latter-day Saints believe that their religion is revealed through living prophets of God, they subordinate human reason to revealed truth.

In this latter connection, Latter-day Saints show some affinities with contemporary conservative Roman Catholic and evangelical Bible scholarship. They accept and use most objective results of Bible scholarship, such as linguistics, history, and archaeology, while rejecting many of the discipline's naturalistic assumptions and its more subjective methods and theories. In those instances where Bible scholarship and revealed religion conflict, Latter-day Saints hold to interpretations of the Bible that appear in the other LDS scriptures and in the teachings of latter-day prophets.

These observations suggest three basic operating principles for Bible scholarship among Latter-day Saints:

1. Approaches to the Bible must accept divine inspiration and revelation in the original biblical text: it presents the word of God and is not a merely human production. Therefore, any critical methodology that implicitly or explicitly ignores or denies the significant involvement of God in the biblical text is rejected. With minor exceptions, such as the Song of Solomon, which Joseph Smith judged not to be inspired (cf. *IE* 18 [Mar. 1915]:389), the text is not to be treated in an ultimately naturalistic manner. God's participation is seen to be significant both in the events themselves and in the process of their being recorded. His activity is thus one of the effects to be reckoned with in interpreting the events and in understanding the texts that record them.

2. Despite divine inspiration, the biblical text is not uninfluenced by human language and not immune to negative influences from its human environment, and there is no guarantee that the revelations given to ancient prophets have been perfectly preserved (cf. 1 Ne. 13:20–27). Thus, critical study of the Bible is warranted to help allow for, and suggest corrections of, human errors of formulation, transmission, translation, and interpretation of the ancient records.

3. Such critical scholarship, in addition to recognizing the divine origins of the Bible, must in its conclusions take account of the teachings of the BOOK OF MORMON and the other revelations to modern prophets included in the DOCTRINE AND COVENANTS and the PEARL OF GREAT PRICE, since for Latter-day Saints such sources not only have priority over revelations recorded in antiquity (cf. D&C 5:10) but also aid in interpreting the biblical text.

Latter-day Saints insist on objective hermeneutics, that is, they maintain that the biblical text has a specific, objective meaning and that the intent of the original author is both important and largely recoverable. For this reason, LDS scholars, like other conservatives, have tended toward the more objective tools of Bible scholarship, such as linguistics, history, and archaeology—recognizing that these tools themselves have to be evaluated critically—and have generally avoided the more subjective methods of literary criticism.

The most influential LDS Bible commentators include James E.

Talmage, Bruce R. McConkie, Sidney B. Sperry, and Hugh W. Nibley, though Talmage's work was completed prior to many important discoveries, and McConkie's work is concerned less with critical exegesis than with understanding the New Testament within the overall body of LDS doctrine.

BIBLIOGRAPHY

Anderson, Richard L. *Understanding Paul*. Salt Lake City, 1983.
McConkie, Bruce R. *Doctrinal New Testament Commentary*, 3 vols. Salt Lake City, 1965–1973.
Nibley, Hugh. *CWHN*. Salt Lake City, 1986–.
Sperry, Sidney B. *Paul's Life and Letters*. Salt Lake City, 1955.
———. *The Voice of Israel's Prophets*. Salt Lake City, 1961.
———. *The Spirit of the Old Testament*. Salt Lake City, 1970.
Talmage, James E. *JC*. Salt Lake City, 1915.

STEPHEN E. ROBINSON

BOOK OF ABRAHAM

[*This entry includes five articles:*

Origin of the Book of Abraham
Translation and Publication of the Book of Abraham
Contents of the Book of Abraham
Facsimiles from the Book of Abraham
Studies about the Book of Abraham

The book of Abraham autobiographically recounts Abraham's early years and is one of the texts in the LDS scriptural collection titled Pearl of Great Price. The article Origin of the Book of Abraham *recounts the discovery and purchase of the Joseph Smith Papyri and events leading up to the publication of the book of Abraham itself. The article* Translation and Publication of the Book of Abraham *details briefly both the process by which Joseph Smith produced the text of the book of Abraham and the history of its appearance in print. The article* Contents of the Book of Abraham *surveys generally the events narrated in the book, including Abraham's miraculous rescue from death and God's covenant with him before he departed his homeland.* Facsimiles from the Book of Abraham *introduces the ancient Egyptian illustrations that are currently published with the work and assesses their relationship to the text. A review of studies published to date on the book of Abraham appears in* Studies about the Book of Abraham.]

ORIGIN OF THE BOOK OF ABRAHAM

In July 1835, while living in Kirtland, Ohio, the Prophet Joseph Smith purchased, on behalf of the Church, four Egyptian mummies and accompanying papyri from Michael H. Chandler, a traveling entrepreneur from Pennsylvania. The price was $2,400. Chandler had acquired eleven mummies in early 1833 and had sold the other seven in the eastern United States prior to meeting Joseph Smith. Shortly after obtaining the antiquities, Joseph Smith announced that the papyri contained some writings of the patriarchs ABRAHAM and JOSEPH, both of whom had lived in Egypt (Gen. 12:37, 39–50).

These antiquities had been exhumed by Antonio Lebolo on the west bank of the Nile River opposite the ancient city of Thebes (present-day Luxor), probably between 1817 and 1821. Lebolo, born in Castellamonte, Piedmont (northern Italy), had been a gendarme during Napoleon's occupation of the Italian peninsula. When Napoleon was defeated, Lebolo chose voluntary exile rather than face imprisonment under the reemerging Sardinian monarchy. He moved to Egypt, where he was employed by Bernardino Drovetti, former consul general of France in Egypt, to oversee his excavations in Upper Egypt. Drovetti also allowed Lebolo to excavate on his own. Lebolo discovered eleven well-preserved mummies in a large tomb. Because Lebolo directed several hundred men excavating at different sites, the exact location has not been identified. The mummies were shipped to Trieste, where Lebolo authorized Albano Oblasser, a shipping magnate, to sell them on his behalf. Lebolo died February 19, 1830, in Castellamonte. Oblasser forwarded the eleven mummies to two shipping companies in New York City—McLeod and Gillespie, and Maitland and Kennedy—to sell them to anybody who would pay an appropriate sum. The proceeds were to be sent to Lebolo's heirs. Chandler acquired them in the winter or early spring of 1833. He claimed that Lebolo was his uncle, but that relationship has not been confirmed.

It has become clear that some Abrahamic literature exhibits links with Egypt. For example, the *Testament of Abraham*—likely first written in Greek—almost certainly derives from Egypt.

Substituting a biblical figure such as Abraham in Egyptian hiero-glyphic scenes is a Jewish technique known from the Hellenistic period (Grobel, pp. 373–82). Thus, it is not surprising that Egyptian texts are somehow linked to the appearance of the book of Abraham.

According to some Egyptologists, the writings of Abraham acquired by Joseph Smith are to be dated to the early Christian era. Such dating is not without precedent. The *Testament of Abraham*, edited initially by M. R. James in 1892, was described by him as "a second century Jewish-Christian writing composed in Egypt" (Nibley, pp. 20–21).

The identity of the mummies is not known, since there are no primary sources that identify them.

BIBLIOGRAPHY

Grobel, K. ". . . Whose Name Was Neves." *New Testament Studies* 10 (1963–1964): 373–82.

Nibley, Hugh. *Abraham in Egypt.* Salt Lake City, 1981.

Peterson, H. Donl. *The Pearl of Great Price: A History and Commentary.* Salt Lake City, 1987.

H. DONL PETERSON

TRANSLATION AND PUBLICATION OF THE BOOK OF ABRAHAM

On October 10, 1880, in a general conference, members of The Church of Jesus Christ of Latter-day Saints voted to accept the book of Abraham as a scriptural work. Several views have been advanced concerning the process whereby the Prophet Joseph Smith produced the work. Although he and his associates began an "Egyptian Alphabet and Grammar" while they studied the papyri, the purpose of that work is obscure. It was not completed, explained, or published by Joseph Smith or any of his successors. However, it is certain that he began working in Kirtland, Ohio, on the relevant Egyptian papyri soon after purchasing them from Michael H. Chandler in 1835.

Probably no one in the United States in 1835 could interpret Egyptian hieroglyphics through ordinary translation techniques. When he translated the gold plates of the Book of Mormon from the "reformed Egyptian" text (1827–1829), the Prophet stated that he did it "by the gift and power of God." Likewise, it was principally divine inspiration rather than his knowledge of languages that produced the English text of the book of Abraham. His precise methodology remains unknown.

On July 5, 1835, the Prophet recorded, "I commenced the translation of some of the characters or hieroglyphics, and much to our joy found that one of the rolls contained the writings of Abraham. . . . Truly we can say, the Lord is beginning to reveal the abundance of peace and truth" (*HC* 2:236). After delays, Joseph Smith appointed two men on November 2, 1837, to raise funds to help translate and print the book of Abraham. But because of further difficulties, he was unable to begin publishing for four more years. The book of Abraham was first printed in three issues of the *Times and Seasons* on March 1, March 15, and May 16, 1842. These installments contained the entire current book of Abraham, including the three facsimiles. In February 1843, Joseph Smith promised that more of the book of Abraham would be published. However, continued harassment by enemies kept the Prophet from ever publishing more of the record. It did receive considerable notoriety when several prominent eastern newspapers in the United States reprinted Facsimile 1 and part of the text from the *Times and Seasons* publication.

In 1851 the writings of Abraham were published in England as a part of the Pearl of Great Price, a small compilation by Franklin D. Richards containing some of Joseph Smith's translations and revelations. It was this compilation that was canonized in 1880, in Salt Lake City, thereby placing it alongside three other sacred collections, or standard works: the Bible, the Book of Mormon, and the Doctrine and Covenants.

In 1856 the papyri were sold by Joseph's widow to Abel Combs. With the exception of a few fragments returned to the Church in 1967, the present location of the papyri is unknown.

[*See also* Papyri, Joseph Smith.]

BIBLIOGRAPHY

Nibley, Hugh. "The Meaning of the Kirtland Egyptian Papers." *BYU Studies* 11, no. 4 (Summer 1971):350–99.

Peterson, H. Donl. *The Pearl of Great Price: A History and Commentary.* Salt Lake City, 1987.

H. DONL PETERSON

CONTENTS OF THE BOOK OF ABRAHAM

The book of Abraham in the Pearl of Great Price consists of an account of Abraham's experiences with the Lord in four lands: Chaldea, Haran, Canaan, and Egypt. This observation is consistent with the work's opening phrase, "In the land of." Except for events chronicled in the first chapter, Sarai (Sarah) shared fully the vicissitudes and triumphs of her husband.

As the work opens, Abraham is living among an idolatrous people in Chaldea (Abr. 1:1, 5–7). But because of severe persecution (1:12, 15) after having preached against their wickedness, he decides to emigrate. Resulting official opposition almost costs Abraham his life, as a human sacrifice (1:12–15). When he prays for divine help, an angel rescues him, promising that he will be led to a new land and receive the priesthood (1:15–19).

When the famine prophesied by the angel comes to Chaldea (1:29–30), Abraham departs with Sarai, his nephew Lot, and his family, with his father, Terah, following the company (2:4). After they settle in Haran, the Lord commands Abraham to continue on to Canaan and reveals to him the founding elements of the Abrahamic covenant (2:6–11). Because of famine, Abraham goes to Egypt, where the Lord commands him—a feature absent from Genesis 12:11–13—to introduce Sarai as his sister so that the Egyptians will not kill him (2:21–25).

In the third chapter, Abraham describes a vision that he received through a URIM AND THUMMIM concerning the worlds created by God, the premortal spirits of people, and the Council in Heaven wherein the gods (cf. John 1:1–4, 14; Heb. 1:1–3) planned the creation of the earth and humankind. The fourth and fifth chapters recount the completion of these plans and the placing of Adam and Eve in the GARDEN OF EDEN.

By the book's account, Chaldea was under Egyptian hegemony during Abraham's lifetime. Local religion included Egyptian solar worship, the worship of Pharaoh, and human sacrifice. The discovery of the land of Egypt is attributed to Egyptus, daughter of Ham and Egyptus; her eldest son, whose name was Pharaoh, established its first government.

Doctrinal contributions of the book include a fuller explanation of Abraham's covenant and its relationship to the gospel (2:6–11), and a better understanding of premortal life (3:22–28). Concerning ASTRONOMY, it names the celestial body nearest God's abode, Kolob (3:2–4), and details the creation of the earth by a council of Gods in the fourth chapter. Abraham 1:26–27 has been interpreted by some as the scriptural basis for previously withholding the priesthood from blacks.

Concerning biblical connections, the idolatry of Terah (cf. Josh. 24:2) and the Lord's rescue of Abraham (cf. Isa. 29:22) are spelled out in the book of Abraham and in other ancient Abraham texts.

Many themes of the book appear in other ancient literatures, including Abraham's struggle against idolatry (*Jubilees* 12; Charlesworth, Vol. 2, pp. 79–80), the attempted sacrifice of Abraham (*Pseudo-Philo* 6; Charlesworth, Vol. 2, pp. 310–12), and Abraham's vision of God's dwelling place, events in the Garden of Eden, and premortal spirits (*Apocalypse of Abraham* 22–23; Charlesworth, Vol. 1, p. 700). God's instruction to Abraham to introduce Sarai as his sister is echoed in the *Genesis Apocryphon* (column 19) as having come through a dream. Abraham's teaching astronomy to Egyptians (Book of Abraham Facsimile 3) is described in *Pseudo-Eupolemus* 9.17.8 and 9.18.2 (Charlesworth, Vol. 2, pp. 881–82) and in Josephus (*Antiquities* 1.8.2).

BIBLIOGRAPHY
Charlesworth, James H., ed. *The Old Testament Pseudepigrapha*, 2 vols. Garden City, N.Y., 1983, 1985.
Millet, Robert L., and Kent P. Jackson, eds. *Studies in Scripture*, Vol. 2. Salt Lake City, 1985.
Peterson, H. Donl, and Charles D. Tate, eds. *The Pearl of Great Price: Revelations from God.* Provo, Utah, 1989.

STEPHEN E. THOMPSON

FACSIMILES FROM THE BOOK OF ABRAHAM

Three facsimiles are published with the text of the book of Abraham in the Pearl of Great Price. All are similar to Egyptian illustrations known from other sources.

FACSIMILE NUMBER 1. Representations similar to Facsimile 1 abound in Egyptian religious texts. A typical example appears in the 151st chapter of the *Book of the Dead*, showing the God Anubis embalming Osiris, who is lying on a lion couch. In some details, such as the posture of the reclining figure, Facsimile 1 differs from other Egyptian texts.

Only for Facsimile 1 is the original document known to be extant. Comparisons of the papyrus fragments as well as the hieroglyphic text accompanying this drawing demonstrate that it formed a part of an Egyptian religious text known as the *Book of Breathings*. Based on paleographic and historical evidence, this text can be reliably dated to about the first century A.D. Since reference is made to this illustration in the book of Abraham (Abr. 1:12), many have concluded that the *Book of Breathings* must be the text that the Prophet Joseph Smith used in his translation. Because the *Book of Breathings* is clearly not the book of Abraham, critics claim this is conclusive evidence that Joseph Smith was unable to translate the ancient documents.

In the historical documents currently possessed by the Church, Joseph Smith never described fully the actual process he used in translating ancient documents. In reference to the Book of Mormon, he said that it was "not expedient" for him to relate all the particulars of its coming forth (*HC* 1:220; *see* BOOK OF MORMON TRANSLATION BY JOSEPH SMITH). He did, in several instances, refer to the book of Abraham as a translation (*HC* 4:543, 548); and when the installments of the book of Abraham were published in the *Millennial Star,* it was described as being "translated by Joseph Smith" (July 1842, p. 34). Both Wilford Woodruff (in his journal) and Parley P. Pratt (in the July 1842 *Millennial Star*) maintained that the translation was done by means of the URIM AND THUMMIM, although Joseph Smith himself does not mention using this instrument anywhere in the translation.

One must consider, however, what Joseph Smith meant by translation. Section 7 of the Doctrine and Covenants offers one standard measure. Here, the Prophet, using the Urim and Thummim, translated a "record made on parchment by John the Revelator." Although it is not known whether Joseph Smith actually had this document, he provided a translation of it. Since it is not known just how Joseph Smith translated, it is reasonable to postulate that, when studying the Egyptian papyri purchased from Michael Chandler, Joseph Smith sought revelation from the Lord concerning them and received in that process the book of Abraham. He might then have searched through the papyri in his possession to find illustrations similar to those he had learned by revelation. This forms one possible explanation of how drawings done about the first century A.D. were used to illustrate the book of Abraham.

FACSIMILE NUMBER 2.   Egyptologists call Facsimile 2 a hypocephalus (Greek for "under the head"), and numerous examples are preserved in museums around the world. Their stated purpose was to keep the body warm (i.e., ready for resurrection) and to transform the deceased into a god in the hereafter. Joseph Smith explained that Facsimile 2 contained representations of God, the earth, the Holy Ghost, etc. His explanations are, in general, reasonable in light of modern Egyptological knowledge. For example, the four standing figures in the lower portion of the facsimile are said by Joseph Smith to represent "earth in its four quarters." The Egyptians called these the four sons of Horus and, among other things, they were gods of the four quarters of the earth.

FACSIMILE NUMBER 3.   Facsimile 3 presents a constantly recurring scene in Egyptian literature, best known from the 125th chapter of the *Book of the Dead.* It represents the judgment of the dead before the throne of Osiris. It is likely that it came at the end of the *Book of Breathings* text, of which Facsimile 1 formed the beginning, since other examples contain vignettes similar to this. Moreover, the name of Hor, owner of the papyrus, appears in the hieroglyphs at the bottom of this facsimile.

Joseph Smith explained that Facsimile 3 represents Abraham sitting on the pharaoh's throne teaching principles of astronomy to the Egyptian court. Critics have pointed out that the second figure, which Joseph Smith says is the king, is the goddess Hathor (or Isis). There are, however, examples in other papyri, not in the possession of Joseph Smith, in which the pharaoh is portrayed as Hathor. In fact, the whole scene is typical of Egyptian ritual drama in which costumed actors played the parts of various gods and goddesses.

In summary, Facsimile 1 formed the beginning, and Facsimile 3 the end of a document known as the *Book of Breathings,* an Egyptian religious text dated paleographically to the time of Jesus. Facsimile 2, the hypocephalus, is also a late Egyptian religious text. The association of these facsimiles with the book of Abraham might be explained as Joseph Smith's attempt to find illustrations from the papyri he owned that most closely matched what he had received in revelation when translating the book of Abraham. Moreover, the Prophet's explanations of each of the facsimiles accord with present understanding of Egyptian religious practices.

BIBLIOGRAPHY

Harris, James R. "The Book of Abraham Facsimiles." In *Studies in Scripture*, Vol. 2, ed. R. Millet and K. Jackson. Salt Lake City, 1985.

Nibley, Hugh. *Abraham in Egypt*. Salt Lake City, 1981.

Rhodes, Michael D. "A Translation and Commentary of the Joseph Smith Hypocephalus." *BYU Studies* 17 (Spring 1977):259–74.

MICHAEL D. RHODES

STUDIES ABOUT THE BOOK OF ABRAHAM

DOCTRINAL COMMENTARIES. Doctrinal studies of the book of Abraham have usually been components of general commentaries on the Pearl of Great Price without focusing on the book of Abraham in particular. George Reynolds and Janne Sjodahl's *Commentary on the Pearl of Great Price* (Salt Lake City, 1965) is a typical example. The most comprehensive study of this sort is *Doctrinal Commentary on the Pearl of Great Price* (Salt Lake City, 1969) by Hyrum Andrus.

HISTORICAL STUDIES. In 1912 the pamphlet *Joseph Smith, Jr., as a Translator* by F. S. Spaulding, Episcopal bishop of Utah, attempted the first formal non-LDS study of the book of Abraham. It contained letters from eight leading Egyptologists concerning the three book of Abraham facsimiles and commenting on the "accuracy" of their interpretation by the Prophet Joseph Smith. The scholars unanimously agreed that the Prophet was wrong. At the time, no Latter-day Saint scholar was capable of refuting their claims. It was not until 1936 that J. E. Homans, a non-Latter-day Saint writing under the pseudonym R. C. Webb, published *Joseph Smith as a Translator*, defending the Prophet's abilities as a translator, but not directly addressing the points that were made by the Egyptologists.

In 1967 eleven fragments of the Egyptian papyri once owned by Joseph Smith were rediscovered by Aziz S. Atiya and were then presented to the Church by the New York Metropolitan Museum of Art. Several pieces were determined to be from an Egyptian religious text known as the *Book of Breathings*. Three noted Egyptologists soon made translations of and commentaries on the fragments, which resulted in new attacks on Joseph Smith's "inabilities" as a translator. The critics argued that the *Book of Breathings* bore no relationship to the book of Abraham, which Joseph Smith apparently claimed to have translated from these very papyri. Indeed, the *Book of Breathings* is a late text, originating about the first century A.D., some 2,000 years after the time of Abraham. Against criticisms such as these, Hugh Nibley has consistently and ably defended Joseph Smith, maintaining that the book of Abraham should be evaluated on the basis of what it claims to be—Abraham's own account of his life. Nibley's research has shown that a significant number of links exist between the book of Abraham and ancient texts related to Abraham. These similarities seem too numerous and subtle to be attributed to mere coincidence.

In his explanation of Facsimile 2 in the book of Abraham, Joseph Smith maintained that certain information contained therein was not to be revealed to the world, "but is to be had in the Holy Temple of God." Studies of Egyptian temple ritual since the time of Joseph Smith have revealed parallels with Latter-day Saint temple celebrations and doctrine, including a portrayal of the creation and fall of mankind, washings and anointings, and the ultimate return of individuals to God's presence. Moreover, husband, wife, and children are sealed together for eternity, genealogy is taken seriously; people will be judged according to their deeds in this life, and the reward for a just life is to live in the presence of God forever with one's family. It seems unreasonable to suggest that all such parallels occurred by mere chance.

A number of pseudepigraphic texts purporting to be accounts from the life of Abraham have come to light since Joseph Smith's day, such as the *Apocalypse of Abraham* and the *Testament of Abraham,* documents that exhibit notable similarities with the book of Abraham. For example, in chapter 12 of the *Testament of Abraham* there is a description of the judgment of the dead that matches in minute detail the scene depicted in Facsimile 3 of the book of Abraham and, incidentally, chapter 125 of the Egyptian *Book of the Dead.* In fact, parallels to almost every verse in the book of Abraham can be found in the pseudepigraphical writings about Abraham.

In summary, the numerous similarities that the book of Abraham and associated Latter-day Saint doctrines share with both Egyptian religious texts and recently discovered pseudepigraphical writings may confirm further the authenticity of the Joseph Smith translation known as the book of Abraham. A major question about its authenticity continues to revolve around whether Joseph Smith translated the work from the papyrus fragments the Church now has in its possession or whether he used the URIM AND THUMMIM to receive the text of the book of Abraham by revelation, as is the case with the translation of the scroll of John the Revelator, found in Doctrine and Covenants section 7, or the book of Moses, which is excerpted from the JOSEPH SMITH TRANSLATION OF THE BIBLE and is also found in the Pearl of Great Price. From these examples, it is evident that for Joseph Smith it was not necessary to possess an original text in order to have its translation revealed to him. In his function as prophet, seer, and revelator, many channels were open to him to receive information by divine inspiration.

[See also Book of Abraham: Facsimiles from the Book of Abraham.]

BIBLIOGRAPHY
Ashment, Edward H. "The Facsimiles of the Book of Abraham: A Reappraisal." Sunstone 4, nos. 5–6 (Dec. 1979):33–48.
Baer, Klaus. "The Breathing Permit of Hor." Dialogue 3, no. 3 (1968):109–134.
Homans, J. E. Joseph Smith as a Translator. Salt Lake City, 1936.
Nibley, Hugh. The Message of the Joseph Smith Papyri. Salt Lake City, 1975.
———. Abraham in Egypt. Salt Lake City, 1981.
Parker, Richard. "The Joseph Smith Papyri: A Preliminary Report." Dialogue 3, no. 2 (1968):86–92, 98–99.
Rhodes, Michael D. "A Translation and Commentary on the Joseph Smith Hypocephalus." BYU Studies 17 (Spring 1977): 259–74.
Spaulding, F. S. Joseph Smith, Jr., as a Translator. Pamphlet. Salt Lake City, 1912.
Wilson, John. "A Summary Report." Dialogue 3, no. 2 (1968):67–85.

MICHAEL D. RHODES

BOOK OF COMMANDMENTS

The Prophet Joseph Smith and a council of high priests collected the Prophet's early revelations in November 1831, into the Book of Commandments. They originally decided to print 10,000 copies of the book at Independence, Missouri, but later reduced this number to

3,000. As editor of the Church's newspaper called *The Evening and the Morning Star* and of the Book of Commandments, William W. Phelps also printed some of the major revelations in that paper during 1832–1833.

Publication plans were frustrated when a mob destroyed the printing establishment on July 20, 1833, when Phelps had printed only five 32–page signatures. These 160 pages contained sixty-five revelations, the last of which was not completely typeset. Although fire destroyed most of these uncut pages, Church members salvaged enough to put together about a hundred copies, only a few of which survive today. The revelations in the Book of Commandments became part of a larger collection titled the Doctrine and Covenants, first printed in 1835.

BIBLIOGRAPHY

Petersen, Melvin J. "A Study of the Nature of and the Significance of the Changes in the Revelations as Found in a Comparison of the Book of Commandments and Subsequent Editions of the Doctrine and Covenants." Master's thesis, Brigham Young University, 1955.

Woodford, Robert J. "The Historical Development of the Doctrine and Covenants, Volume 1." Ph.D. diss., Brigham Young University, 1974.

ROBERT J. WOODFORD

BOOK OF LIFE

In a figurative sense, the book of life is the complete record of one's life, the sum total of thoughts, words, and deeds written in the soul, of which the Lord will take account in the day of judgment (Rev. 20:12; Alma 12:14).

The scriptures also speak of a book of life, or "the Lamb's book of life," as "the record . . . kept in heaven" (D&C 128:7) in which are written both the names and deeds of the faithful. It is also the heavenly register of those who inherit eternal life (Heb. 12:23; Alma 5:58; D&C 76:68), "the book of the names of the sanctified, even them of the celestial world" (D&C 88:2; cf. Mal. 3:16–17).

In the Bible, the phrase "book of the living" appears first in Psalm 69:28, and the notion of a heavenly ledger is alluded to often (Ex. 32:32–33; Dan. 7:10; 12:1; Isa. 4:3; 65:6; see also Phil. 4:3;

Rev. 3:5; 13:8; 21:27). Names of faithful Saints may be recorded in the book of life conditionally while they are in mortality (Luke 10:20) or "from the foundation of the world" (Rev. 17:8), but may be "blotted out" because of unrepented transgression (Rev. 3:5; 22:19; Alma 5:57; D&C 85:5, 11). Ultimately, only the names of those who qualify for eternal life remain written or "sealed" (*TPJS*, p. 9) in the Lamb's book of life.

Latter-day Saints believe that essential items written in the "books yet to be opened" are linked to proper Church records, including those of essential gospel ordinances performed by priesthood authority for individuals and attested by authorized witnesses. In ancient covenant ceremonies, the names of the righteous were solemnly recorded, thus numbering them among "the living" (e.g., Num. 1:1–46; Mosiah 6:1–2). What is properly recorded on earth is recorded in heaven (D&C 128:7–8). Final sealing in the Lamb's book requires, further, the approval of the Holy Spirit of Promise (D&C 132:19).

J. LEWIS TAYLOR

BOOK OF MORMON

[*This entry introduces the Book of Mormon, with the* Overview *describing its basic nature, contents, and purposes; a brief article follows on the* Title Page *from the Book of Mormon; and the remaining articles are devoted to a brief explanation of each book in the Book of Mormon.*

Book of Helaman
Third Nephi
Fourth Nephi
Book of Mormon
Book of Ether
Book of Moroni

The teachings of the Book of Mormon are discussed in doctrinal articles throughout the Encyclopedia; *see* Book of Mormon Religious Teachings and Practices; Prophecy; Prophecy in the Book of Mormon.

Concerning its essential relationship with the Bible and other scripture, see Bible; Book of Mormon, Biblical Prophecies about; Book of Mormon in a Biblical Culture; Isaiah; Scripture; Standard Works.

On the writing and composition of the Book of Mormon, see Book of Mormon Authorship; Book of Mormon Language; Book of Mormon as Literature; Book of Mormon Plates and Records.

For information about its origin and publication, see Book of Mormon Editions; Book of Mormon Manuscripts; Book of Mormon Translation by Joseph Smith; Book of Mormon Translations; Book of Mormon Witnesses; Manuscript, Lost 116 Pages; Moroni, Angel. *See, generally,* Book of Mormon Studies.

Separate articles can be found on Book of Mormon Peoples; Jaredites; Lamanites; Nephites; Women in the Book of Mormon; *articles on the main individuals in this scripture are listed under* Book of Mormon Personalities.

Internal aspects of Book of Mormon culture and civilization are discussed in such entries as Book of Mormon Chronology; Book of Mormon Economy and Technology; Book of Mormon Geography; Book of Mormon, Government and Legal History in; Book of Mormon, History of Warfare in; Liahona; Secret Combinations; Sword of Laban; Three Nephites; Tree of Life.]

OVERVIEW

The Prophet Joseph Smith called the Book of Mormon "the most correct of any book on earth, and the keystone of our religion" and said that a person "would get nearer to God by abiding by its precepts, than by any other book" (*TPJS*, p. 194), for it contains the fulness of the gospel of Jesus Christ (D&C 20:8–9). To members of The Church of Jesus Christ of Latter-day Saints, the Book of Mormon forms the doctrinal foundation of the Church and speaks the word of God to all the world.

The Book of Mormon both confirms and supplements the Bible: "Behold, this [the Book of Mormon] is written for the intent that ye may believe that [the Bible]; and if ye believe [the Bible] ye will believe [the Book of Mormon] also" (Morm. 7:9). The Bible is primarily a record of God's dealings with the forebears and descendants of Jacob or Israel in the ancient Near East. Latter-day Saints believe the Book of Mormon to be a record of God's dealings principally with another group of Israelites he brought to the Western Hemisphere from Jerusalem about 600 B.C. (*see* LEHI). They anticipated the birth and coming of Jesus Christ and believed in his atonement and gospel. Their complex, lengthy records were abridged by a prophet named MORMON, inscribed on plates of gold, and buried by his son, MORONI$_2$, after internecine wars destroyed all of the believers in Christ in the New World except Moroni (A.D. 385).

JOSEPH SMITH AND THE BOOK OF MORMON. In his short lifetime, Joseph Smith brought forth many scriptures (*see* DOCTRINE AND COVENANTS; PEARL OF GREAT PRICE). His first prophetic calling was to bring forth the Book of Mormon. In 1823, at age seventeen, he was shown the hidden record by Moroni, then a resurrected angelic messenger from God (JS—H 1:27–54). After several visitations during the next four years, Joseph was allowed to remove the sacred record from its resting place in the hill CUMORAH, near Palmyra, New York. Despite many interruptions and persistent persecutions (JS—H 1:57–60), Joseph Smith translated the lengthy record in about sixty working days. Latter-day Saints bear testimony that he did this "through the mercy of God, by the power of God" (D&C 1:29), "by the inspiration of heaven" (*Messenger and Advocate* [Oct. 1834]:14–16; JS—H 1:71, n.). He had the assistance of several scribes, chiefly Oliver Cowdery, who wrote what Joseph Smith dictated. The book was published in Palmyra in 1830. At least eleven witnesses, in addition to Joseph Smith, saw and/or hefted the Book of Mormon plates before he returned them to Moroni (*see* BOOK OF MORMON WITNESSES).

PURPOSES AND CONTENTS. The Book of Mormon, as its modern subtitle states, stands with the Bible as "Another Testament of Jesus

Christ." Its main purposes are summarized on its title page: to show the remnants of the Book of Mormon people what great things God did for their forefathers, to make known the covenants of the Lord, and to convince "Jew and Gentile that Jesus is the Christ, the Eternal God, manifesting himself unto all nations." The central event in the Book of Mormon is the appearance of the resurrected Christ to righteous inhabitants of the Western Hemisphere after his ascension into heaven at Jerusalem. During his visit, Christ delivered a sermon that is similar to the SERMON ON THE MOUNT recorded in the New Testament, but with certain vital clarifications and additions. He declared his doctrine, the fulness of his gospel necessary to enter the kingdom of God; and he established his Church with its essential ordinances, and ordained disciples to preside over the Church. At this time, Christ also explained the promises of God to Israel; healed the sick and disabled; blessed the children and their parents; and expressed his great love, allowing each individual to come forward and touch the wounds he had received during his crucifixion (see 3 Ne. 11–26). The record of Jesus' visit and many other passages in the Book of Mormon verify the divine sonship, ministry, atonement, resurrection, and eternal status of the Lord Jesus Christ and show that the fulness of his gospel is the same for all people, whenever and wherever they have lived.

The ancestors of these people to whom Jesus appeared had been in the Western Hemisphere for about 600 years. The Book of Mormon opens with the family of Lehi in Jerusalem at the time of the biblical prophet Jeremiah. Lehi was warned by God about 600 B.C. to take his family and flee Jerusalem before it was destroyed by Babylon (1 Ne. 1:1–2). The account, written by Lehi's son NEPHI₁, first tells of his family's departure from Jerusalem and of his dangerous return to the city with his brothers to obtain sacred records that contained their lineage, the five books of Moses, and a history of the Jews and writings of prophets down to Jeremiah's time (1 Ne. 3–5).

The group traveled in the wilderness until they reached a pleasant land by the sea where Nephi, with God's instruction, built a ship that took them to the New World (1 Ne. 17–18). Nephi's older brothers, LAMAN and Lemuel, expressed resentment at Nephi's closeness to the Lord and did not want him to rule over them (1 Ne. 16:37–39; 18:10). When the family reached the New World, this antagonism led to a schism between the NEPHITES and LAMANITES that pervades the Book of Mormon.

As the Nephite sermons, prophecies, and historical records were compiled and handed down, the writers emphasized that those who keep God's commandments prosper. Unfortunately, many who prospered became proud and persecuted others, with war as the eventual result. The desolation of war humbled the people, who began again to call upon God.

Ancient American prophets, like biblical prophets such as Moses, Isaiah, and Daniel, were shown visions of the future of various nations. For example, Nephi foresaw Christopher Columbus' discovery of America, the influx of Gentiles into the New World, and the American Revolution (1 Ne. 13:12–15, 18–19), as well as the birth and earthly ministry of Jesus Christ. Christ's birth, ministry, and death were prophesied by Lehi, Nephi, BENJAMIN, SAMUEL THE LAMANITE, and other prophets. When MOSIAH₁ discovered a people who had left Jerusalem with MULEK, a son of Zedekiah (see Jer. 52:10; Omni 1:12–15; Hel. 8:21), and King Limhi's messengers found a record of the extinct JAREDITES, the Nephites learned that they were not the only people God had brought to the Western Hemisphere.

After the appearance of Jesus Christ, the Nephites and Lamanites enjoyed peace for more than 160 years (4 Ne. 1:18–24). Then, many who had been righteous broke their covenants with God, and the Church and their civilization began to collapse. At last, in A.D. 385, the few remaining Nephites were hunted and killed by Lamanites. The book ends with Moroni₂, the last Nephite, writing to the people of modern times, admonishing them to "come unto Christ, and be perfected in him" (Moro. 10:32).

MODERN APPLICATIONS. Latter-day Saints embrace the Book of Mormon as a record for all people. In addition to instructing their contemporaries and descendants, the prophets who wrote these ancient records foresaw modern conditions and selected lessons needed to meet the challenges of this world (Morm. 8:34–35). Their book is a record of a fallen people, urging all people to live righteously and prevent a similar fall today.

The Book of Mormon has had a profound effect on the Church and its members. It is so fundamental that Joseph Smith said, "Take away the Book of Mormon and the revelations and where is our religion? We have none" (*TPJS*, p. 71).

The Book of Mormon teaches that the living God has spoken to several peoples throughout the earth who have written sacred records as he has commanded (2 Ne. 29:11–12). The Book of Mormon is one such record.

It also stands as evidence to Latter-day Saints that God restored his true and living Church through Joseph Smith. The importance of this belief for Latter-day Saints cannot be overestimated, for they are confident that God watches over the people of the earth and loves them, and that he continues to speak to them through contemporary prophets who apply unchanging gospel principles to today's challenges.

The Book of Mormon also is important to Latter-day Saints as an aid in understanding the Bible and the will of God. Nephi prophesied that many "plain and precious" truths and covenants would be taken from the gospel and the Bible after the deaths of the apostles (1 Ne. 13:26–27). Many questions that have arisen from the Bible are answered for Latter-day Saints by the Book of Mormon, such as the mode of and reasons for baptism (2 Ne. 31; 3 Ne. 11:23–26); the proper way to administer the sacrament of the Lord's Supper (Moro. 4–5); the nature of the Resurrection (Alma 40); the effects of the fall of Adam, and the reasons for evil and suffering in the world (2 Ne. 2). The Book of Mormon reinforces the LDS doctrine that the gospel of Jesus Christ existed before the Creation and has been revealed to prophets and believers throughout time.

Also sacred to Latter-day Saints is the Book of Mormon as a tutor in discerning the promptings of the Holy Ghost. Many Latter-day Saints, including those born into LDS families, trace their conversion to Jesus Christ and their commitment toward the Church to prayerful study of the Book of Mormon, and through it they learn to recognize the Holy Spirit. Thus, the book becomes a continuing symbol of personal revelation and of God's love for and attention to the needs of each person. It also declares that all mankind will be judged by its precepts and commandments (Mosiah 3:24; Moro. 10:27). It is evidence that God remembers every creature he has created (Mosiah 27:30) and every covenant he has made (1 Ne. 19:15; 3 Ne. 16:11). The Book of Mormon is the base from which millions have begun a personal journey of spiritual growth and of service to others.

For LDS children, the Book of Mormon is a source of stories and heroes to equal those of the Bible—Joseph in Egypt, Daniel in the lions' den, the faithful Ruth, and brave Queen Esther. They tell and sing with enthusiasm about the army of faithful young men led by Helaman₁ (Alma 56:41–50); of the prophet Abinadi's courage before wicked King Noah (Mosiah 11–17); of Nephi and his unwavering faithfulness (1 Ne. 3–18); of Abish, a Lamanite woman who for many years appears to have been the lone believer in Christ in King Lamoni's court until the missionary Ammon taught the gospel to the king and queen (Alma 19); and of Jesus' appearances to the Nephites (3 Ne. 11–28). There are many favorites. The book is used to teach children doctrines, provide examples of the Christlike life, and remind them of God's great love and hope for all his children.

The book is central to missionary work. It is the Church's most important missionary tool and is destined to go to every nation, kindred, tongue, and people (Rev. 14:6–7). All LDS missionaries encourage those they contact to read and pray about the book as a means of receiving their own testimony from God about the truthfulness of the Book of Mormon, a witness of Jesus Christ.

Latter-day Saints are regularly admonished to make fuller use of the Book of Mormon. In 1832, two and one-half years after the book was published, the word of the Lord warned the Saints that they had treated the revelations too lightly and had neglected to "remember the new covenant, even the Book of Mormon" (D&C 84:57). Church leaders repeatedly encourage members to make the Book of Mormon a greater part of their lives. President Ezra Taft Benson has counseled Latter-day Saints to read the book daily and to share it and the gospel message with all the world.

READING THE BOOK OF MORMON. This sacred record asks the reader to approach its words with faith and prayer. One of its teachings is that readers will "receive no witness until after the trial of [their] faith" (Ether 12:6). Therefore, although aspects of the book may seem unusual or improbable at first, it invites its readers to entertain them as possibilities until the whole picture becomes clear and other feelings are experienced and thoughts considered. Moreover, the final inscription of Moroni₂ on the title page asks readers to look beyond human weaknesses in the book: "If there are faults they are the mistakes of men; wherefore, condemn not the things of God." He closed his own book within the Book of Mormon by exhorting all who receive these things to ask God, with a sincere heart and with real intent, having faith in Christ, if they are not true, and promises that God will manifest the truth of it (Moro. 10:4).

Latter-day Saints of all ages and interests find rewards in reading the Book of Mormon. At first, people tend to focus attention on its main messages and story lines. With further reading and pondering, they discover numerous themes, meaningful nuances, interesting details, and profound spiritual expressions.

The first-time reader may find the Book of Mormon difficult at times. Its style, as translated into English, is somewhat similar to that of the King James Version of the Bible, and the reader who is not familiar with the Bible will encounter some unfamiliar word usages. The 1981 edition of the Book of Mormon is annotated with many Bible references and aids to facilitate a more detailed comparison.

Book of Mormon prophets Nephi, JACOB, and ABINADI quote extensively from Isaiah (e.g., 2 Ne. 6–8 [Isa. 49–51]; 2 Ne. 12–24 [Isa. 2–14]; Mosiah 14 [Isa. 53]), an Old Testament prophet whose poetic style and allusions have challenged readers of the Bible and also have proved difficult to many who study the Book of Mormon. Initially, some Church leaders encourage first-time readers to move through these chapters, understanding what is accessible and saving the rest for later study. In Isaiah's writings, Latter-day Saints find an important testimony of Christ and of the fulfillment of God's covenants with the house of Israel. Christ admonished his followers to "search these things diligently, for great are the words of Isaiah" (3 Ne. 23:11).

Another possible hurdle for readers is the book's nonchronological insertions. Nephi and Jacob and Jacob's descendants wrote first-person accounts from about 590 B.C. until about 150 B.C., and then Mormon (about A.D. 385) inserted a shorter chapter to explain his role as abridger of another record. Then the reader is returned via Mormon's abridgment to the history of Nephi's successors and of the descendants of ALMA$_1$. As groups of people break away from and return to the main body, parts of their records are incorporated into the book, causing the reader to jump back to earlier events. Likewise, Moroni's abridgment of the very ancient book of Ether appears out of chronological order near the end. In addition, the Book of Mormon, like the Old Testament, describes events from widely separated intervals. As an abridgment, it contains only a small part of the proceedings of these ancient peoples.

APPROACHING THE TEXT.   The arrangement of the Book of Mormon lends itself to many approaches. Three mutually supportive avenues are most often followed. First, the book serves as a source of guidance and doctrine, yielding lessons and wisdom applicable to contemporary life. This approach is recommended in the writings of Nephi, who wrote that he "did liken the scriptures unto [his people], that it might be for [their] profit and learning" (1 Ne. 19:23). Latter-day Saints find its pages rich with ennobling narratives, clear doctrines, eternal truths, memorable sayings, and principles. Knowing the conditions of the latter days, the ancient prophets periodically address the individual reader directly. Latter-day Saints emphasize the need to read the Book of Mormon prayerfully, with faith in God, to benefit personally from its teachings and to come unto Christ.

A second approach to the Book of Mormon, adding historical dimension to the first approach, is to study the book as an ancient text. The reader who accepts the Book of Mormon as an ancient Hebrew lineage history written by prophets in the New World will find the book consistent with that description and setting. The book is a repository of ancient cultures that are as far removed from modern readers as are those of the Old and New Testaments. Continuing research has found Hebrew poetic forms, rhetorical patterns, and idioms, together with many Mesoamerican symbols, traditions, and artifacts, to be implicit in the book or consistent with it.

Finally, one may enjoy the Book of Mormon as a work of literature. Although the style may seem tedious or repetitive at times, there are order, purpose, and clarity in its language. Its words are often as beautiful and as memorable as passages in the Psalms, the Gospel of John, and other notable religious works of prose and poetry.

Most faithful readers of the Book of Mormon, however, do not define or limit themselves to any single approach or methodology, for these approaches are all transcended by the overriding implications of the book's divine origins and eternal purposes. Study and faith, reflection and application, all help a person know and comprehend the messages of the Book of Mormon. But for millions of Latter-day Saints, their most important experience with the Book of Mormon has been the spiritual knowledge that they have received of its truth. It has changed and enriched their lives and has brought Jesus Christ and his teachings closer to them.

BIBLIOGRAPHY

Benson, Ezra Taft. *A Witness and a Warning*. Salt Lake City, 1988.

Downs, Robert B. *Books That Changed America*. London, 1970.

Faust, James E. "The Keystone of Our Religion." *Ensign* 13 (Nov. 1983):9.

Nibley, Hugh. "The Mormon View of the Book of Mormon." *Concilium* 10 (Dec. 1967):82–83; reprinted, *CWHN* 8:259–64.

MONTE S. NYMAN
LISA BOLIN HAWKINS

TITLE PAGE FROM THE BOOK OF MORMON

Joseph Smith once wrote, "I wish to mention here that the title-page of the Book of Mormon is a literal translation, taken from the very last leaf, on the left hand side of the collection or book of plates, which contained the record which has been translated; . . . and that said title-page is not . . . a modern composition, either of mine or of any other man who has lived or does live in this generation" (*HC* 1:71).

The title page is therefore the translation of an ancient document, at least partially written by MORONI₂, son of Mormon, in the fifth century A.D. It describes the volume as an "abridgment of the record of the people of Nephi, and also of the Lamanites" and "an abridgment taken from the Book of Ether also, which is a record of the people of Jared" (*see* BOOK OF MORMON PLATES AND RECORDS).

According to the title page, the Book of Mormon is addressed to LAMANITES, Jews, and GENTILES and is designed to inform Lamanites of promises made to their forebears and to convince "Jew and Gentile that Jesus is the Christ, the Eternal God, manifesting himself unto all nations."

The title page was used as the description of the Book of Mormon on the federal copyright application filed June 11, 1829, with R. R. Lansing, Clerk of the District Court of the United States for the Northern District of New York, at Albany.

BIBLIOGRAPHY

Ludlow, Daniel H. "The title page." In *The Book of Mormon: First Nephi, The Doctrinal Foundation*, ed. Monte S. Nyman and Charles D. Tate, pp. 19–33. Provo, Utah, 1988.

ELDIN RICKS

FIRST BOOK OF NEPHI

Written by NEPHI₁, an ancient prophet who fled Jerusalem with his father, LEHI, and Lehi's family shortly after 600 B.C., this book tells of their travels under divine guidance to the Western Hemisphere. With its detailed testimony of the mission of Jesus Christ and its panoramic view of sacred history, 1 Nephi is the doctrinal and historical foundation for all of the Book of Mormon. Its stated intent is to testify that the God of Israel can save all who repent and exercise faith in him (1 Ne. 1:20; 6:4).

Composed several years after Nephi arrived in the "promised land," the record, of which the First Book of Nephi was a part, contained prophesying and sacred preaching "for Christ's sake, and for the sake of [his] people" (Jacob 1:4). Its fundamental message is that the God of Israel is merciful and has the power to save those who obey him (1 Ne. 1:20; 6:4; 22:30–31). Nephi supports this thesis with historical and prophetic evidence. He cites Israel's exodus from Egypt twice as evidence of God's redeeming power, and saw the same power at work in his family's exodus from a doomed Jerusalem. A seer of remarkable spiritual stature, Nephi testified that greater acts of redemption lay in the future: God himself would come to earth to ransom man from death and sin (1 Ne. 11:33; 19:10), and before the end of the world, Israel would be redeemed.

The narrative of 1 Nephi is vivid and dramatic; acts of divine intervention dominate this account. It begins in the first year of the Judean King Zedekiah (1 Ne. 1:4; cf. 2 Kgs. 24:8–18; dated by Babylonian documents at 597 B.C.). Jerusalem had just capitulated after a brief Babylonian siege, and King Jehoiachin, together with many of Judah's prominent citizens, had been deported. When Jerusalem persisted in its arrogance, a host of prophets, including Jeremiah and Lehi, warned of destruction. As people conspired to kill Lehi, he was warned by the Lord and escaped south into the desert. Twice his four sons returned to the region, once to obtain a copy of the scriptures written on plates of brass and again to convince Ishmael and his family to flee with them (chaps. 3–7). Guided by a miraculous brass compass (*see* LIAHONA), Lehi's group then completed a grueling odyssey that covered eight years in the wilderness, arriving at a verdant spot on the southern coast of the Arabian Peninsula. There, Nephi was summoned by the Lord to a mountain where he was instructed to build a ship to carry the group to a land of promise. Through God's frequent inspiration and protection, the ship was finished and the treacherous voyage completed (chaps. 16–18).

Through all these events, Lehi and Nephi were opposed by the oldest sons in the family, LAMAN and Lemuel, who were not only skeptical but sometimes violent in their opposition. The record vindicates Nephi in many ways. An angel once intervened to protect Nephi from his brothers; twice he escaped from them, being filled with the power of God. Several times, by his faith, he succeeded where they failed.

Records of powerful visions are interspersed throughout the narrative. Lehi received his prophetic commission in a vision as he prayed on Jerusalem's behalf: He saw a pillar of fire dwelling upon a rock and God seated upon his throne and was given a book to read that decreed judgment upon the city (chap. 1). Soon after, Nephi heard the voice of the Lord, saying that Nephi would teach and rule over his elder brothers (chap. 2); and Lehi had a dream that centered around a magnificent tree, a river, an iron rod, and a great and spacious building (chap. 8; *see also* TREE OF LIFE). The family's escape from a proud and materialistic Jerusalem and their subsequent quest for salvation in the wilderness are vividly reflected in the imagery of this dream. Lehi also prophesied about the Babylonian captivity of the Jews, their eventual return to Palestine, and the coming of a Messiah who would redeem mankind from its lost and fallen state (chap. 10).

Inspired by Lehi's spiritual experiences and wanting to know the meaning of his father's dream, Nephi sought and received the same vision, together with its interpretation. This revelation puts the experiences of Lehi and his posterity into the context of God's redemptive plan and provides much of the historical and doctrinal framework for subsequent Book of Mormon prophecy: (1) Nephi saw the birth, ministry, and atoning sacrifice of the Son of God, and the rejection of his apostles by Israel; (2) he witnessed the division of Lehi's family, followed by the rise, decline, and destruction of his own posterity by the descendants of his brothers, and saw that the Lamb of God would visit various branches of Israel, including Nephi's posterity; (3) he saw a great and abominable church among the Gentiles, as well as a dispensation of the gospel to the Gentiles and their crucial role in gathering Israel and a remnant of Nephi's seed; and (4) he was shown the final victory of God over the powers of evil at the end of the world (chaps. 11–14).

Citing other corroborating prophecies, 1 Nephi 19–22 reinforces those four themes, the mainstays of the Nephite outlook on world history. Nephi first gives a detailed testimony of the atoning sacrifice of the God of Israel, his rejection, and the scattering of God's covenant people, quoting ZENOS, ZENOCK, and NEUM (chap. 19); he then quoted ISAIAH to show that God will defer his anger and will eventually gather his people through the assistance of gentile kings and queens (chaps. 20–21); and, finally, he exhorts all to obey God's commandments and be saved, for in the last days the wicked shall burn and the Holy One of Israel shall reign (chap. 22).

BIBLIOGRAPHY
Axelgard, Frederick W. "1 and 2 Nephi: An Inspiring Whole." *BYU Studies* 26 (Fall 1986):53–65.
Nibley, Hugh. *Lehi in the Desert.* In *CWHN* 5.
Nyman, Monte S., and Charles D. Tate, Jr., eds. *The Book of Mormon: First Nephi, the Doctrinal Foundation.* Provo, Utah, 1988.

RULON D. EAMES

SECOND BOOK OF NEPHI

The Second Book of Nephi (2 Nephi) is a work written about 550 B.C. by the same author who wrote 1 Nephi and included it on his small PLATES. The second book contains four prophetic discourses and treatises from three Book of Mormon prophets, LEHI, JACOB, and Nephi$_1$, as well as substantial excerpts of the prophecies of Isaiah from the brass plates. Additionally, 2 Nephi briefly records the difficult transition from the founding generation of Lehi's colony to the succeeding generation in their new homeland.

The first segment of the book consists of Lehi's admonitions and testament to his posterity before his death (1:1–4:11). He directed his opening words to his older sons, Laman, Lemuel, and Sam, as well as to the sons of Ishmael. He reminded them of God's mercy in leading them to a promised land, taught them concerning the covenant of righteousness that belongs to the land, warned of the loss of liberty and prosperity that will follow disobedience to God, and urged them to become reconciled to their brother Nephi as their leader (1:1–27).

Following this admonition, Lehi pronounced specific blessings on all of his descendants, either as individuals or as family groups. His blessings contain prophecies and promises concerning the future of each individual or group in the covenant land and are followed by counsel "according to the workings of the Spirit" (1:6). His instructions to his youngest sons, Jacob and Joseph, are doctrinally significant. He spoke to Jacob concerning God's plan of salvation for his children, teaching principles that are fundamental to understanding the gospel of Jesus Christ, including the doctrine of redemption through the Messiah, the necessity of opposition and agency, the role of Satan, and the importance of the fall of Adam and Eve (2:1–30). Lehi taught his son Joseph concerning the prophecies of his ancestor Joseph of Egypt, who foretold the latter-day mission of another Joseph (the Prophet Joseph Smith) and of the coming forth of the Book of Mormon (3:1–25).

Nephi₁, son of Lehi, is author of the next section, the only historical segment in the record (4:12–5:34). After recounting the death of Lehi and the subsequent rebellion of Laman, Lemuel, and the sons of Ishmael (4:12–13), Nephi noted that he was keeping two records: the large plates on which he wrote his people's secular history and the small plates on which he recorded "that which is pleasing unto God," including many excerpts from the plates of brass (4:14–15; 5:29–33).

As Nephi wrote of his delight in pondering the scriptures and "the things of the Lord," he was moved to compose a beautiful psalm (4:16–35). In these verses, much like the biblical psalmist, Nephi used inspiring imagery and poetic parallelism to praise God for his goodness, to lament his own weaknesses, and to declare his devotion to the Lord.

Nephi closed this segment by telling of the partitioning of Lehi's posterity into two distinct peoples, the NEPHITES (the believers) and the LAMANITES (the unbelievers). He described the theological, cultural, and geographical divisions that developed between the brother nations, lamenting that within forty years of separating they were at war one with another (5:1–34).

A sermon by Jacob constitutes the third entry in 2 Nephi (chaps. 6–10), followed by the fourth and final part, a long written discourse from Nephi (chaps. 11–33). Quoting substantial portions of Isaiah, both Nephi and Jacob emphasized two major themes: the history and future of God's covenant people, and the mission of the Messiah. For his discourse on these topics, Nephi first quoted the text of Isaiah 2–14 in 2 Nephi 12–24 and then commented on them in chapters 25–30, incorporating portions of Isaiah 29 in his discussion. Jacob quoted Isaiah 50:1–52:2 in chapters 7–8. Apparently, Joseph Smith put these quotations from Isaiah in King James English, but with many variant readings reflecting the Nephite source.

Citing and reflecting on Isaiah, Jacob, and Nephi focused on such events as the Babylonian captivity and return (6:8–9; 25:10–11); the apostasy, scattering, and oppression of the house of Israel; and the latter-day gathering of their descendants, their restoration by conversion to the gospel of Christ, and the establishment of Zion—themes that concerned them because of their own Israelite ancestry (6:6–18; 8:1–25; 10:1–25; 25:14–17; 26:14–30:18). They further prophesied the destruction of the wicked before the second coming of the Savior followed by the subsequent era of peace (12:1–22; 21:1–24:3).

In their discourses, Jacob and Nephi taught of the Messiah's earthly ministry, rejection, and crucifixion (6:9; 7:1–11; 9:1–54; 10:3–5; 17–19) and his gospel fundamentals of faith, repentance, baptism, and obedience (9:23–24; 31:1–21); they then prophesied his baptism, atoning sacrifice, and resurrection, followed by his ministry among the Nephites, his ultimate second coming, and the final judgment (9:5–27; 26:1–9; 31:4–12).

In chapter 29, Nephi made special mention of the Lord's desire that the Book of Mormon be used as "a standard" by his people, along with the Bible (29:2), noting that other books will come forth. In closing the record, Nephi testified that the words therein are the words of Christ, the words by which readers shall be judged (33:10–15).

BIBLIOGRAPHY

Jackson, Kent P., ed. *Studies in Scripture*, Vol. 7, pp. 86–174. Salt Lake City, 1987.

McConkie, Joseph Fielding, and Robert L. Millet. *Doctrinal Commentary on the Book of Mormon*, Vol. 1, pp. 182–376. Salt Lake City, 1987.

Nyman, Monte S., and Charles D. Tate, eds. *The Book of Mormon: Second Nephi, The Doctrinal Structure*. Provo, Utah, 1989.

TERRY B. BALL

BOOK OF JACOB

Written by JACOB, fifth son of LEHI, sometime after 545 B.C., the work follows the pattern outlined by NEPHI₁ for making entries on the small PLATES by including sacred sermons, significant revelations, prophecies, and some historical information. Jacob, a Nephite prophet, wrote to persuade all men to "come unto Christ" (Jacob 1:7).

The book appears to have been written in three stages. The first constitutes an important discourse by Jacob at the temple, in which he called his people to repent from immorality, materialism, and pride (chaps. 2–3). He counseled men and women to be generous with their possessions, promising that, if they sought the kingdom of God before seeking riches, they would be blessed with sufficient wealth to assist others (2:17–19). Jacob strongly warned his people against sins of immorality because many had transgressed the law of chastity, including practicing polygamy not authorized by the Lord (2:30). He reminded his hearers that the Lord "delight[s] in the chastity of women" and that the sins of the men had broken the hearts of their wives and children (2:22–35).

The second part contains prophecies concerning the atonement of Christ, the rejection of Jesus of Nazareth by many Jews, and the scattering and gathering of ISRAEL (chaps. 4–6). Jacob desired that later generations would "know that we knew of Christ, and we had a hope of his glory many hundred years before his coming" (4:4). The major component of this section is Jacob's quoting of the allegory of the tame and wild olive trees (chap. 5). Written by ZENOS, an Israelite prophet whose writings were preserved on the brass plates, this allegory outlines in symbolic narrative the prophetic story of the scattering and gathering of Israel, including Lehi's descendants, from the establishment of Israel to the end of the earth.

The third segment recounts Jacob's experience with an anti-Christ named Sherem, who with skill and power of language endeavored to flatter and deceive people away from belief in Christ (7:1–4). Sherem had accused Jacob of blasphemy and false prophecy and had tried to convince people that there would be no Christ. In the end, Sherem was confounded by Jacob and, after seeking for a sign, was smitten by God and died shortly thereafter (7:7–8, 13–20). Recovering from Sherem's divisive teachings through searching the scriptures, Jacob's people were able to experience anew the peace and love of God (7:23).

BIBLIOGRAPHY

Matthews, Robert J. "Jacob: Prophet, Theologian, Historian." In *The Book of Mormon: Jacob Through Words of Mormon,* ed. M. Nyman and C. Tate, Provo, Utah, 1990.

CLYDE J. WILLIAMS

BOOK OF ENOS

Following the pattern set by his father and predecessors (Jacob 1:2–4; cf. Enos 1:13–16), Enos, son of JACOB, personally recorded the testimony and prophetic promises granted to him. Enos (c. 515–417 B.C.) is a figure who touches the heart. He typifies conversion, compassion, and confidence before the Lord. While he was hunting beasts, the words of his father "concerning eternal life, and the joy of the saints, sunk deep into [his] heart," and his "soul hungered" (1:3–4). All day and into the night he "wrestle[d] . . . before God" in "mighty prayer" until he received a remission of his sins. He successively prayed for his own welfare, for the welfare of his brethren the NEPHITES, who strayed too easily from righteousness, and then for his brethren the LAMANITES, who had become increasingly ferocious and wild. Enos received a covenant declaration from the Lord that the Nephite records would be brought forth to the Lamanites. He knew with a surety that he would see his Redeemer's face with pleasure and would receive a place in the mansions of the Father (1:27).

MARILYN ARNOLD

BOOK OF JAROM

Jarom, son of ENOS, recorded a brief summary of the fortunes of the NEPHITES during his lifetime (c. 440–355 B.C.). Twice he justified the brevity of his account, pleading limited space and little new doctrine to add to the words of his predecessors. Reflecting an era of strict conservatism in the flourishing colony, Jarom recounted great Nephite efforts to observe the law of Moses and to anticipate the coming Messiah. Despite their larger numbers, the LAMANITES were unsuccessful in their frequent attacks on the prospering Nephites, and Jarom attributed the Nephite successes to the prophets, priests, and teachers who stirred them continually to repentance.

MARILYN ARNOLD

BOOK OF OMNI

This book concluded and filled the small PLATES of Nephi. It contains brief statements by a succession of record keepers who were descendants of Jacob but apparently not spiritual leaders: Omni, Amaron, Chemish, Abinadom, and Amaleki (fourth–second centuries B.C.). Amaleki, whose account is the longest of the five, described the important transition that occurred in Book of Mormon history when MOSIAH₁ led the escape of a band of faithful NEPHITES from the land of Nephi to Zarahemla (c. 200 B.C.). Here they discovered descendants of a group that had left Jerusalem with MULEK but had lost their religion and language. Amaleki connected the corruption of their language with the absence of written records, establishing the importance of record preservation. Mosiah brought with him the plates of brass containing "the record of the Jews" (Omni 1:14), including the laws that kings were required to have under the LAW OF MOSES (see Deut. 17:18–19). He was accepted as king over both these peoples and ruled for a generation. Amaleki survived Mosiah but had no heirs, so he transmitted his records to Mosiah's son, King Benjamin.

MARILYN ARNOLD

THE WORDS OF MORMON

MORMON was at work on his abridgment of the large PLATES of NEPHI₁ when he discovered the small plates of Nephi, a prophetic record from early NEPHITE history (W of M 1:3). Because he was deeply impressed with the messianic PROPHECIES that he read on the small plates, and in response to "the workings of the Spirit," Mormon included that set of plates with his digest (W of M 1:4–7). But because that record ended a few years before the book of Mosiah began (c. A.D. 130), Mormon assumed the prerogative of an editor and appended this historical postscript to the small plates to bring its conclusion into correlation with the opening of the book of Mosiah. This appendage, called the Words of Mormon, was composed about A.D. 385.

ELDIN RICKS

BOOK OF MOSIAH

The book of Mosiah is religiously rich, symbolically meaningful, chronologically complex, and politically significant. Although its disparate events range from 200 to 91 B.C., they are unified particularly by the theme of deliverance and by the reign of the Nephite king MOSIAH₂.

Several groups figure prominently in this history: (1) the main body of Nephites under King BENJAMIN and his son Mosiah₂, together with the people of Zarahemla (Mulekites), who outnumbered their Nephite rulers and neighbors; (2) the people of Zeniff, who failed in their attempt to reoccupy the Nephites' homeland, the land of Nephi; and (3) the people of ALMA₁, who broke away from the people of Zeniff and became the people of Alma, followers of the martyred prophet ABINADI. The last two groups returned to Zarahemla shortly after Mosiah became king.

The book of Mosiah is drawn from several underlying textual sources: Benjamin's speech (124 B.C.); the record of Zeniff (c. 200–120 B.C.), including Alma's record of Abinadi's trial (c. 150 B.C.) and of his people (c. 150–118 B.C.); and the annals of Mosiah (124–91 B.C.).

BENJAMIN'S SPEECH (CHAPS. 1–6). The coronation of Mosiah occurred in a setting similar to the traditional Israelite assembly at the temple, together with sacrifices, covenant renewal, confessions, pronouncements regarding Christ's atoning blood, and admonitions to serve God and help the poor. Benjamin died, and Mosiah reigned. He sponsored Ammon's expedition to find the people of Zeniff (7:1–8:21).

RECORD OF ZENIFF (CHAPS. 9–22). About seventy-five years earlier, Zeniff had established his colony; he fought two wars, and his wicked son Noah succeeded him. Twice, the prophet Abinadi delivered a condemnation of Noah; Abinadi rehearsed the Ten Commandments, quoted Isaiah 53, and discoursed on the atonement of Jesus Christ and the resurrection. As he was suffering death by fire, Abinadi prophesied that his death would prefigure Noah's. One of Noah's priests, Alma₁, believed Abinadi's preaching, fled into the wilderness, and assembled a group of converts who escaped together from Noah's soldiers. Meanwhile, a military officer named Gideon opposed Noah, the Lamanites attacked, and Noah fled and was subsequently executed by his own people in the manner that Abinadi had predicted. Noah's son, Limhi, was left to reign for many years as a vassal king in servitude to the Lamanites. At length, Limhi and his people were delivered and escaped to Zarahemla.

ALMA'S RECORD (CHAPS. 23–24).   The followers of Alma₁ practiced baptism and placed strong emphasis on unity, loving one another, and avoiding contention. In a speech that presaged Mosiah's final words establishing the reign of the judges, Alma₁ refused to become a king, wanting his people to be in bondage to no person. Nevertheless, they came under cruel bondage to the Lamanites, now led by some of Alma's former associates, the evil priests of Noah. Several years later, the people of Alma were miraculously delivered.

THE ANNALS OF MOSIAH (CHAPS. 25–29).   The Nephites, the people of Zarahemla (Mulekites), the people of Limhi, and the people of Alma₁ were unified under Mosiah as king, with Alma as high priest. Alma was given authority to organize and regulate churches, but many members apostasized and persecuted the righteous. Among the wicked were his son ALMA₂ and the four sons of Mosiah. When they were confronted by an angel of the Lord, they repented and were converted. Mosiah translated the Jaredite record, passed the Nephite records and sacred artifacts to Alma₂, and installed Alma₂ as the first chief judge according to the voice of the people.

The narratives in the book of Mosiah emphasize the theme of deliverance from bondage, whether physical or spiritual. In his address, Benjamin speaks of spiritual deliverance through the atoning blood of Christ, emphasizing mankind's dependence on God and its responsibility to the poor (both themes or typologies are similarly shaped in the Bible by the Exodus tradition). The account of the conversion of Alma₂ is a notable case of deliverance from spiritual bondage by calling upon the name of Jesus Christ (Mosiah 27; Alma 36). Two groups are delivered from physical bondage and oppression: Limhi's people and the converts of Alma after their enslavement by the Lamanites. As in the Exodus pattern, they "cried" to the Lord, who heard and delivered them from bondage. An emissary named Ammon expressly compared the deliverance of the people of Zeniff to the exodus of Israel from Egypt and of Lehi from Jerusalem (Mosiah 7:19–22, 33).

The book of Mosiah establishes several pairs of comparisons in a manner similar to a literary technique often used in the Bible: Alma₁ and Amulon are examples of good and bad priests; Benjamin and Noah are contrasting exemplars of noble and corrupt kingship. The extreme contrast between these kings is cited by Mosiah at the end of his reign to explain the wisdom in shifting the government of the Nephites from kingship to a reign of judges (Mosiah 29).

The Jaredite record is mentioned three times (Mosiah 8:9; 21:27; 28:11–19). In an attempt to get help from Mosiah's settlement, Limhi dispatched a search party; it did not find Mosiah, but found human remains, weapons of war, and twenty-four gold plates. The party returned this record to Limhi, who gave it to Mosiah, who translated it using two stones called "interpreters" (see URIM AND THUMMIM). The record told of the rise and fall of the Jaredites (see BOOK OF MORMON: BOOK OF ETHER).

BIBLIOGRAPHY

Tate, George S. "The Typology of the Exodus Pattern in the Book of Mormon." In *Literature of Belief*, ed. N. Lambert, pp. 245–66. Provo, Utah, 1981.

Thomasson, Gordon C. "Mosiah: The Complex Symbolism and the Symbolic Complex of Kingship in the Book of Mormon." *F.A.R.M.S. Paper*. Provo, Utah, 1982.

Tvedtnes, John A. "King Benjamin and the Feast of Tabernacles." In *By Study and Also by Faith*, ed. J. Lundquist and S. Ricks, Vol. 2, pp. 197–237. Salt Lake City, 1990.

ALAN GOFF

BOOK OF ALMA

The book of Alma is the longest book in the Book of Mormon. It was abridged by MORMON, principally from the records of three men, ALMA$_2$ (chaps. 1–16, 27–44), Ammon (chaps. 17–26), and Alma's son HELAMAN$_1$ (chaps. 45–62), and concludes with remarks by Mormon (chap. 63). Its broad theme is that the preaching of the word of God in pure testimony is mightier than politics or the sword in establishing peace, justice, equality, and goodness (Alma 4:19; 31:5). The book demonstrates this theme through repeated examples of individuals who were converted to faith in the anticipated Savior, Jesus Christ, and examples of people who were given victory by God over their wicked and ambitious enemies.

The book of Alma covers thirty-nine years (91–52 B.C.). The first fourteen years are covered by two concurrent accounts—one encompassing the teachings and activities of Alma$_2$, who resigned his

judgeship in order to engage in missionary work in the land of
Zarahemla (chaps. 1–16), and the other containing the words and
deeds of the sons of King MOSIAH₂ and their companions as they made
considerable personal sacrifice in their efforts to preach the gospel
among the LAMANITES (chaps. 17–26).

The first section begins with the trial of Nehor before the chief
judge Alma; Nehor was convicted and executed for the crime of
enforcing PRIESTCRAFT with the sword (chap. 1). Alma then fought a
civil war against Nehor's followers and prevailed (chaps. 2–4), but he
soon relinquished the judgeship to devote full time to the ministry.
He preached powerful sermons at the cities of Zarahemla (chaps.
5–6), Gideon (chap. 7), and Melek (chap. 8), and went to the wicked
city of Ammonihah, where he was cast out, but ordered by an angel to
return. In Ammonihah the second time, he met and was assisted by
Amulek, who was instructed by an angel to find Alma (chap. 8).
Although they were opposed by a skilled lawyer named Zeezrom,
eventually they converted many, including Zeezrom. However, their
male converts were expelled from the city, and Alma and Amulek
were imprisoned and forced to watch the wives and children of their
converts being burned to death. Eventually, Alma and Amulek were
delivered when an earthquake destroyed the prison and killed their
captors (chaps. 9–14). Shortly thereafter, this apostate city was annihilated by invading Lamanites (chap. 16).

During the same fourteen years, the sons of Mosiah and their
companions were in the land southward. Ammon went to the land of
Ishmael, and through his service to, and love of, King Lamoni, he
converted the king and many of his people (chaps. 17–19), whom he
taught to live the LAW OF MOSES in anticipation of the coming of Christ
(Alma 25:15). Ammon and Lamoni then went to the land of Middoni
to free his fellow missionaries from prison. En route they were confronted by Lamoni's father, the king of all the Lamanites, who took to
the sword. Ammon withstood his blows, gained control over the king,
and made him promise freedom for his brothers and autonomy for
Lamoni and his people (chap. 20). Once Ammon's brother, Aaron,
and his companions were free, they went to Lamoni's father, and
taught and converted him, his household, and many of his people.
These converted Lamanites, concerned about the return of prior
blood guilt, made an oath never to shed blood again (chap. 23). Other

Lamanites and dissident Nephites attacked these converts and killed 1,005, who would not defend themselves because of that oath. Many of the attacking Lamanites (but not the Nephite dissenters) felt remorse for their actions and laid down their arms and also became converted (chaps. 24–25). Eventually, Ammon led these converts, called Anti-Nephi-Lehies, to Nephite territory, where they settled in the land of Jershon (chap. 27). The Lamanites who were left behind become angry at the Nephites and then attacked and destroyed Ammonihah (Alma 25:1–2; described more fully in Alma 16:1–11).

After these developments, Korihor, an anti-Christ and advocate of blasphemous doctrines, confronted Alma as high priest in the court of the chief judge, where he asked for a sign from God, was struck dumb, and died shortly thereafter (chap. 30). Next, Alma led a delegation to preach to the Zoramites, a group that had defected from the Nephites. Many poverty-stricken Zoramites were reconverted and cast out by the other Zoramites. The unconverted promptly allied with the Lamanites, attacked the Nephites, and were defeated (chaps. 31–35, 43–44).

The chapters focusing on Alma also contain his blessings and instructions to his three sons (chaps. 36–42) and an account of his disappearance (being taken to heaven; chap. 45). The book of Alma ends with the detailed accounts by HELAMAN₁ of further wars between the Nephites and Lamanites (chaps. 43–62; *see* BOOK OF MORMON, HISTORY OF WARFARE IN). The final chapter (chap. 63) notes the deaths of Pahoran, Moroni, Helaman, and his brother Shiblon, marking the end of this era of righteous Nephite control of Zarahemla. It also tells of Hagoth, a shipbuilder who transported people to the north, but he was never heard from again after a second departure.

The book of Alma covers a critical period in Nephite history, the opening years of the Nephite judgeship (*see* BOOK OF MORMON, GOVERNMENT AND LEGAL HISTORY IN). The survival of this popularly based form of government was threatened several times in the course of the book, starting when Nehor's follower Amlici sought to become king. It was threatened again when the Zoramites (described above) defected. Further trouble arose when Amalickiah, a Zoramite, persuaded many of the lower judges to support him as king. A general named Moroni rallied the Nephite troops by raising a banner that he called the Title of Liberty; it proclaimed the need to remember and defend their God, their religion, their freedom, their peace, their wives, and their children. Amalickiah and a few of his men fled to the Lamanites, where he, through treachery and murder, established himself as king and led the Lamanites in a prolonged war against the Nephites. Amalickiah was killed after seven years of war, but the wars continued under his brother Ammoron for six more years. Those years became particularly perilous for the Nephites when "kingmen" arose in Zarahemla and expelled the Nephite government from the capital (discussed in *CWHN* 8:328–79). Moroni was forced to leave the battlefront to regain control of the capital before he could turn his full attention to defeating the Lamanites. In each case, the Nephites ultimately prevailed and gave thanks and praise to God.

In the book of Alma, the delineation of the Nephite and Lamanite nations along ancestral lines becomes blurred. Several groups of Nephites—Amlicites (chaps. 2–3), Zoramites (chaps. 31–35, 43), Amalickiahites (chaps. 46–62), and kingmen (chaps. 51, 61)—rejected Nephite religious principles and joined the Lamanites in an attempt to overthrow the Nephite government. Several groups of Lamanites—Anti-Nephi-Lehies (chaps. 17–27), converts from the army that marched against the Anti-Nephi-Lehies (chap. 25), and some Lamanite soldiers captured by Moroni (chap. 62)—embraced the gospel and Nephite way of life and went to live among the Nephites. By the end of the book, these populations are distinguished more by ideology than by lineage. Those who desired government by the "voice of the people" and embraced the teachings of the gospel are numbered among the Nephites, while those who opposed them are called Lamanites.

Many important religious teachings are found in the book of Alma. Alma chapter 5 is a speech given by Alma calling the people of the city of Zarahemla to repent and teaching all followers of Christ to judge the state of their former spiritual rebirth and present well-being. Alma chapter 7, delivered to the righteous city of Gideon, teaches believers to make the atonement of Christ a reality in their lives. Chapters 12 and 13 elucidate the mysteries of redemption, resurrection, and the Priesthood after the Order of the Son of God. Alma chapters 32 and 33 are a sermon given by Alma to the Zoramite poor, explaining the correct manner of prayer, the relationship between humility and faith in Jesus Christ, and the process of increasing faith.

Alma chapter 34 is Amulek's talk on the need for the "infinite and eternal sacrifice" made by the Son of God. In it Amulek also teaches the people how to pray and tells them how to live so that their prayers will not be vain.

Alma teaches his sons trust in God by telling of his personal conversion (chap. 36). He also gives instructions about the keeping of sacred records and explains how God's purposes are accomplished through small means (chap. 37). He teaches the evil of sexual sin (chap. 39), the nature of resurrection and restoration (chaps. 40–41), the purpose and consequences of the fall of Adam (including spiritual and temporal death), and the relationship between justice and mercy (see chap. 42).

The war chapters include instances of, and statements about, justifiable reasons for war (chap. 48), along with the example of the protective power of faith exercised by the young warriors who fought under Helaman, none of whom died in battle, for they believed their mothers' teachings that "God would deliver them" (Alma 56:47–48).

Overall, the book of Alma teaches through vivid, detailed narratives how personal ambition can lead to apostasy and war, and shows how the Lord gathers his people through the preaching of the gospel of Christ and delivers them in righteousness against aggression.

BIBLIOGRAPHY

For essays on Alma the Younger, Ammon, King Lamoni, Ammonihah, Korihor's sophistry, Amlici, several dissenters, Captain Moroni, the Nephite chief judges, and other figures in the book of Alma, see Jeffrey R. Holland, *The Book of Mormon: It Begins with a Family*, pp. 79–170. Salt Lake City, 1983.

CHERYL BROWN

BOOK OF HELAMAN

The book of Helaman chronicles one of the most tumultuous periods in the history of the NEPHITES and LAMANITES (52–1 B.C.). The narrative focuses on the unexpected difficulties (e.g., the Lamanites' invasion and unprecedented occupation of the land of Zarahemla narrated in chaps. 4 and 5) and unexpected resolutions that came from God (e.g., the withdrawal of the Lamanite occupation forces as the direct result of the missionary work of two sons of Helaman, NEPHI$_2$ and Lehi, in 5:49–52).

This book takes its name from its first author, HELAMAN$_2$, son of

HELAMAN₁. Other contributors to the record were Nephi and Lehi, sons of Helaman₂ (16:25), and MORMON, the principal editor of the Book of Mormon, who added political and religious commentary.

The account opens after Helaman had received custody of the Nephite records from his uncle Shiblon (Alma 63:11) in the fortieth year of the reign of the judges (c. 52 B.C.; Hel. 1:1). The narrative falls into six major segments: the record of Helaman (chaps. 1–3); the record of Nephi (chaps. 4–6); the prophecy of Nephi (chaps. 7–11); Mormon's editorial observations on God's power (chap. 12); the prophecy of SAMUEL THE LAMANITE (chaps. 13–15); and a brief statement about the five-year period before Jesus' birth (chap. 16). Several religious discourses are woven into the narrative, including Helaman's admonition to his sons (5:6–12), Nephi's psalm (7:7–9), Nephi's sermon from the tower in his garden (7:13–29; 8:11–28), Nephi's prayer (11:10–16), and Samuel's long speech atop the walls of Zarahemla (13:5–39; 14:2–15:17).

Perhaps the most prominent person mentioned in the book is NEPHI₂. After Nephi resigned from the office of chief judge, he and his brother Lehi devoted themselves fully to preaching the message of the gospel (5:1–4). His defense of God's providence affirmed the power of prophecy (8:11–28) and, on a practical level, led to the conviction of the murderer of the chief judge (9:21–38). The Lord entrusted him with the power to seal the heavens so that no rain would fall (10:4–11), a power that Nephi used to bring about the cessation of civil strife and wickedness (11:1–18).

The rise of the Gadianton robbers (1:9–12; 2:3–11), a hostile and secret society within the Nephite and Lamanite polities, was perhaps the most disheartening and ominous occurrence during those fifty-one years. Mormon informs readers of both the organization's character (6:17–30) and its debilitating impact on society (2:13–14; 6:38–39; 11:24–34).

In contrast to these despairing observations is one of the book's central themes: the surprising ascendancy of the Lamanites in spiritual matters. After the Nephites were overrun by a Lamanite army led by Nephite dissidents in 35 B.C. and failed to regain lost territories (4:5–10), Nephi and Lehi went among the Lamanites to preach the gospel (5:16–20). Their remarkable success in converting listeners to Christ led to their imprisonment (5:21). But in an extraordinary outpouring of the Spirit of God, all in the prison were converted, an event that led to a spiritual reversal among the Lamanites and the eventual withdrawal of Lamanite military forces from Nephite lands (5:22–52). Thereafter, Lamanites carried out the work of the Church, preaching to both their own people and the Nephites (6:1–8, 34–36).

Almost thirty years later (c. 6 B.C.), a Lamanite prophet named Samuel prophesied at Zarahemla. He condemned the decadence of Nephite society, warning of destruction of both individuals and society (13:5–39, esp. 38; 14:20–15:3). He also prophesied that signs to be seen in the Western Hemisphere would accompany both the birth and death of Jesus (14:2–25). He declared the power of the Atonement in redeeming mankind from the fall of Adam and in bringing about the Resurrection. Finally, he spoke of the Lamanites' righteousness and the promises of God to them in the latter days (15:4–16).

BIBLIOGRAPHY
Jackson, Kent P., ed. *Studies in Scripture*, Vol. 8, pp 92–124. Salt Lake City, 1988.

PAUL R. CHEESMAN

THIRD NEPHI

The book of 3 Nephi is the dramatic and spiritual climax of the Book of Mormon. It focuses on three advents of Jesus: first, as the child born in Bethlehem; second, as the resurrected Lord visiting the Nephites; and third, at his SECOND COMING as the final judge at the end of the world. Within a year of the devastating destructions at the time of his crucifixion, the resurrected Jesus descended among a group of righteous people in the Nephite city of Bountiful. He revealed himself unmistakably as the Lord and Savior of the world, expounded his gospel, and established his Church.

The book's author, NEPHI₃, was the religious leader of an ethnically mixed group of Nephites and Lamanites at the time of Christ's birth. His book covers events from that time to A.D. 34. It appears Mormon copied much of Nephi's text verbatim into his abridgment.

Nephi's record begins at the time when the fulfillment of the messianic prophecies of SAMUEL THE LAMANITE miraculously saved believers from a threatened antimessianic persecution. The signs of Jesus' birth appeared—a night of daylight and a new star—vindicating the faith of those who believed the prophecies that Jesus would be born into the world (chap. 1).

After these signs, many were converted to the Church led by Nephi. On the other hand, greed, pleasure-seeking, and pride increased drastically, and the government was soon infiltrated with organized corruption that caused complete anarchy and a breakdown of the people into family tribes and robber bands. Prolonged attacks by these bands plagued the Nephites, who finally abandoned their own properties and formed a single body with enough provisions to subsist for seven years. The Nephites eventually prevailed, but these disruptions and wickedness brought on the collapse of the central government. Although most rejected NEPHI₃'s warnings and miracles, he baptized and ordained those who would believe and follow (chaps. 2–7).

The believers began looking for the calamitous signs of Christ's death, also prophesied by Samuel. A violent storm arose and massive earthquakes occurred, demolishing many cities, killing thousands of the wicked, and leaving the more righteous survivors in a thick vapor of darkness for three days of mourning. After the tumult settled, the voice of Jesus Christ spoke out of the darkness, expressing his sadness over the unrepentant dead and his hope that those who were spared would receive him and his redemption. He announced that his sacrifice had ended the need for blood sacrifice as practiced under the law of Moses (chaps. 8–10).

Later, in radiant white, the resurrected Christ descended to show his wounds, to heal, to teach, and to ordain leaders for his Church. On the first day of several such visits, Jesus appeared to a group of 2,500 men, women, and children assembled at the temple in Bountiful. He ordained twelve disciples and gave them the power to baptize and bestow the gift of the Holy Ghost; he instructed the people in the principles, ordinances, and commandments of his gospel (*see* SERMON ON THE MOUNT); he explained that he had fulfilled the law of Moses; he healed the sick and blessed their families. He announced his plan to show himself to still other people not then known by the Jews or the Nephites. Finally, he entered into a covenant with them. The people promised to keep the commandments he had given them, and he administered to them the sacrament of bread and wine, in remembrance of his resurrected body that he had shown to them and of the blood through which he had wrought the Atonement (chaps. 11–18).

On the morning of the second day, the disciples baptized the faithful and gave them the gift of the Holy Ghost, and they were encircled by angels and fire from heaven. Jesus appeared again and offered three marvelous prayers, explained God's covenant with Israel and its promised fulfillment, reviewed and corrected some items in the Nephite scriptures, and foretold events of the future world, quoting prophesies from Isaiah, Micah, and Malachi. He inspired even babes to reveal "marvelous things" (3 Ne. 26:16). Then he explained the past and future history of the world, emphasizing that salvation will extend to all who follow him (chaps. 19–26).

A third time, Jesus appeared to the twelve Nephite disciples alone. He named his Church and explained the principles of the final judgment. Three of the disciples were transfigured and beheld heavenly visions. Jesus granted these three disciples their wish to remain on earth as special servants until the end of the world (chaps. 27–28; see also THREE NEPHITES; TRANSLATED BEINGS).

Christ revisited the Nephites over an extended period, and told them that he would also visit the lost tribes of Israel.

His Church grew having all things common, with neither rich nor poor. This peaceful condition lasted nearly 180 years, and "surely there could not be a happier people" (4 Ne. 1:16).

Mormon wrote his abridgment of 3 Nephi more than three hundred years after the actual events. By then, the descendants of the Nephites who had been so blessed had degenerated into terminal warfare. Mormon's final, sober testimony to his future readers speaks of the Lord's coming in the last days, which, like his coming to the land Bountiful, would be disastrous for the ungodly but glorious for the righteous (chaps. 29–30).

The text of 3 Nephi fits several categories. First, it is a Christian testament, a Christian gospel. It contains many direct quotations from Jesus and establishes his new covenant. Recorded in a touching personal tone by a participating eyewitness of awesomely tragic and beautiful events, the account convincingly invites the reader to believe the gospel of Jesus Christ and to feel the love he has for all people.

The text also has been compared to the pseudepigraphic forty-day literature that describes Christ's ministry to the faithful in the

Holy Land after his resurrection (see *CWHN* 8:407–34). Others have seen in chapters 11–18 a covenant ritual that profoundly expands the meaning of the Sermon on the Mount in the Gospel of Matthew (Welch, pp. 34–83). The account also resembles the apocalyptic message of the books of Enoch: From the type and purpose of the initial cataclysm, to the sublimity of its revelations to the faithful, to the creation of a righteous society, 3 Nephi is a story of theodicy, theophany, and theocracy.

The text yields practical instructions for sainthood. It is not a wishful utopian piece but a practical handbook of commandments to be accepted in covenantal ordinances and obeyed strictly, with devotion and pure dedication to God. This is not the genre of wisdom literature, not merely a book of moral suggestions for the good life. It explains Christ's gospel plainly, and makes the lofty ideals of the Sermon on the Mount livable by all who receive the Holy Ghost. Empowered by true Christian ordinances and the gifts of the Holy Spirit, the Nephites established a paradise surpassed in righteousness only by Enoch's Zion.

This Zion welcomes everyone, from every place and every time. It promises blessings to "*all* the pure in heart" who come unto Christ (3 Ne. 12:3–9, emphasis added). Thus, 3 Nephi urges all to accept and live Christ's gospel to perfect earthly society, and to join with the Zion of all the former and future righteous peoples so that, as Malachi states, the earth will not be "utterly wasted" at Christ's second coming (JS—H 1:39). This was Enoch's ancient achievement and Joseph Smith's modern hope. The text does not discuss God's millennial kingdom; nor does Christ here pray, "Thy kingdom come." For among those happy Nephites, it had come already.

BIBLIOGRAPHY

Anderson, Richard L. "Religious Validity: The Sacrament Covenant in Third Nephi." In *By Study and Also by Faith*, ed. J. Lunquist and S. Ricks, Vol. 2, pp.1–51. Salt Lake City, 1990.

Ludlow, Victor L. *Jesus' "Covenant People Discourse" in 3 Nephi.* Religious Education Lecture Series. Provo, Utah, 1988.

Stendahl, Krister. "The Sermon on the Mount and Third Nephi." In *Reflections on Mormonism*, ed. T. Madsen. Provo, Utah, 1978.

Welch, John W. *The Sermon at the Temple and the Sermon on the Mount.* Salt Lake City, 1990.

CHARLES RANDALL PAUL

FOURTH NEPHI

Abridged by MORMON, this brief work contains the writings of four Nephite prophets (A.D. 34–320): NEPHI$_4$, son of NEPHI$_3$, who was a disciple of the risen Jesus; Amos, son of Nephi$_4$; and Amos and Ammaron, two sons of Amos. The first section of 4 Nephi briefly summarizes four generations of peace, righteousness, and equality that resulted from the conversion of the people to the gospel of Jesus Christ after the visit of the resurrected Savior. In contrast, the last section foreshadows the later destruction of the Nephite nation that followed a gradual and conscious rejection of the gospel message.

Fourth Nephi narrates an unparalleled epoch in human society when all the people followed the teachings of Christ for nearly two centuries. The book is best known for its account of the social and religious power of the love of God that overcame contention and other social and political ills (4 Ne. 1:15–16). The people experienced urban renewal, stable family life, unity in the Church, and social and economic equality, as well as divine miracles (1:3–13, 15–17). "Surely there could not [have been] a happier people . . . created by the hand of God" (1:16).

The book also previews the ensuing apostasy of most of the population from the teachings of Christ, introducing a state of wickedness and chaos that eventually led to total destruction. According to the account the individual and collective decline was gradual and sequential, with the loss of social and religious order manifested in contention, pride in prosperity, class distinctions with widening social divisions, rejection of Christ and his gospel, and persecution of the Church (1:24–46).

BIBLIOGRAPHY

Skinner, Andrew C. "The Course of Peace and Apostasy." In *Studies in Scripture*, ed. K. Jackson, Vol. 8. Salt Lake City, 1988.

REX C. REEVE, JR.

BOOK OF MORMON

The short book of Mormon (A.D. 320–400/421), within the Book of Mormon, documents the extraordinary collapse of Nephite civilization, as had been foretold (1 Ne. 12:19–20; Alma 45:10–14). It consists of MORMON's abridgment of his larger and more complete history (Morm. 1–6), his final admonition both to future LAMANITES and to other remnants of the house of Israel (chap. 7), and the prophetic warnings of Mormon's son MORONI₂ to future readers of the record (chaps. 8–9). Because Nephites of Mormon's day had rejected Jesus Christ and his gospel, superstition and magic replaced divine revelation (Morm. 1:13–19). A border skirmish (1:10) escalated into a major war, driving the Nephites from their traditional lands (2:3–7, 16, 20–21). Following a ten-year negotiated peace, they repulsed a Lamanite attack, which Mormon, former commander of the Nephite army, refused to lead. As conditions worsened, Mormon reluctantly agreed to command the Nephite army at CUMORAH, where they were destroyed (chaps. 3–6). With poignant anguish, Mormon lamented over his slain people: "O ye fair ones, how could ye have rejected that Jesus, who stood with open arms to receive you!" (6:17–22).

Mormon concluded his record by inviting Lamanites and other remnants of the house of Israel to learn of their forefathers, to lay down their weapons of war, and to repent of their SINS and believe that Jesus Christ is the Son of God. His final words are, "If it so be that ye believe in Christ, and are baptized, first with water, then with fire and with the Holy Ghost, . . . it shall be well with you in the day of judgment. Amen" (7:10).

After the final battle (A.D. 385), Moroni₂—alone and unsure of his own survival—noted his father's death and concluded his father's record (8:1–5). Fifteen years later (A.D. 400), Moroni recorded that survivors of his people had been hunted from place to place until they were no more except for himself. He also observed that the Lamanites were at war with one another and that the whole country witnessed continual bloodshed. For a second time he closed the work, promising that those who would receive this record in the future and not condemn it would learn of greater spiritual matters (8:6–13).

Moroni apparently returned to the record a third time (between A.D. 400 and 421). Having seen a vision of the future (8:35), he testified that the PLATES of the Book of Mormon would come forth by the power of God in a day when people would not believe in miracles. SECRET COMBINATIONS would abound, churches be defiled, and wars, rumors of wars, earthquakes, and pollutions be upon the earth. Moroni also spoke warnings to those in the latter days who do not believe in Christ and who deny the revelations of God, thus standing against the works of the Lord (8:14–9:27). He mentioned the difficulty of keeping records, written as they were in "reformed Egyptian" (9:31–33; cf. Ether 12:23–25). Moroni closed his father's volume with a testimony of the truth of his words (9:35–37).

BIBLIOGRAPHY

Mackay, Thomas W. "Mormon and the Destruction of Nephite Civilization." In *Studies in Scripture*, ed. K. Jackson, Vol. 8. Salt Lake City, 1988.

REX C. REEVE, JR.

BOOK OF ETHER

The book of Ether is MORONI₂'s abbreviated account of the history of the JAREDITES, who came to the Western Hemisphere at the time of the "great tower" of Babel and lived in the area later known as the Nephite "land northward," much earlier than Lehi's colony. Moroni retold their account, recorded on twenty-four plates of gold found by the people of Limhi and translated by MOSIAH₂ (Mosiah 28:11–19). Ether, the last prophet of the Jaredites and a survivor of their annihilation, inscribed those plates soon after the final destruction of his people. It is not known whether Moroni relied on Mosiah's translation or retranslated the Jaredite record in whole or in part. Moroni humbly claims not to have written "the hundredth part" of the record by Ether (Ether 15:33).

The structure of the book of Ether is much like the rest of the Book of Mormon. It tells of the emigration of people by land and sea from the Near East, the Lord's prophetic guidance of these people, and their rise, prosperity, and fall, all in direct relation to their obedience to the Lord's commandments in their promised land. Moroni included the book of Ether because his father MORMON had planned to do so (Mosiah 28:19) but for some reason did not complete the project. Both knew the value of this record and could see that the Jaredite history closely paralleled certain Nephite events.

Moroni appended this history to the Nephite account as a second witness against the evils and SECRET COMBINATIONS that led to the annihilation of both the Jaredites and the Nephites. Several of its themes reinforce the messages in the Nephite section of the Book of Mormon: the necessity to follow the prophets away from persistent and pernicious wickedness, the power of faith in the Lord demonstrated by Jared and the BROTHER OF JARED, the testimony that Jesus

Christ is the eternal saving God, and the collapse of a nation when its people determinedly choose wickedness. Nevertheless, there are notable cultural differences between the Jaredite and the Nephite civilizations; for example, the Jaredites were ruled solely by kings, and they lacked Israelite law and customs, since they were pre-Mosaic.

Although condensed, the book reflects an epic style (see *CWHN* 5:153–449; 6:329–58). It begins with the emigration of the Jaredites from "the great tower" (Ether 1:33, cf. Gen. 11:9) and the valley of "Nimrod" (Ether 2:1; cf. Gen. 10:8) to a new land of promise in the Western Hemisphere. It then abridges a history of the Jaredite kings and wars, and concludes with the destruction of the Jaredite civilization. A brief outline of the book follows: Ether's royal lineage is given (chap. 1); the premortal Jesus appears to the brother of Jared in response to his prayers and touches sixteen small stones, causing them to shine to provide light as the Jaredite barges cross the sea (chaps. 2–6); the generations of Jaredite kings live, hunt, quarrel, enter into secret combinations, and Jaredite prophets warn of impending destruction (chaps. 7–11); Moroni attests that Ether was a prophet of great faith and knowledge (chaps. 12–13); Ether witnesses and records the annihilation of the Jaredite armies (chaps. 14–15).

The main figures and doctrinal statements appear mostly at the beginning and end of the book of Ether. Moroni's editing is of key importance, for he infuses the story with major insights, admonitions, and comparisons. Jared is mentioned at the outset as the founder of the Jaredite people. The revelations and faith of the brother of Jared are given special significance at the beginning and end of the book. Shiz and Coriantumr are crucial historical and symbolic figures because they become the instruments of annihilation. Ether, the author of the underlying text, was an eyewitness to the final battles, and Moroni esteemed his prophecies as "great and marvelous" (Ether 13:13). The middle of the book recounts the more mundane events associated with the reigns of the Jaredite kings.

Several doctrines taught within the book of Ether are greatly valued among Latter-day Saints, namely, that prosperity in the promised land (the Americas) is conditioned on serving "the God of the land who is Jesus Christ" (Ether 2:12), that the premortal Christ had a spirit body "like unto flesh and blood" (3:6), that God is a God of power and truth (3:4, 12), that three witnesses would verify the truth of the Book of Mormon (5:3), that the corruption and downfall of society can come because of secret combinations (8:22), that the Lord will show mankind its weakness so that through humility weak things may become strengths (12:27), and that a NEW JERUSALEM will eventually be built in the Western Hemisphere (13:3–12).

BIBLIOGRAPHY

Sperry, Sidney B. *Book of Mormon Compendium*, pp. 460–81. Salt Lake City, 1968.

Welch, John W. "Sources Behind the Book of Ether." *F.A.R.M.S. Paper*. Provo, Utah, 1986.

MORGAN W. TANNER

BOOK OF MORONI

Between A.D. 400 and 421, MORONI₂, the last custodian of the GOLD PLATES, compiled the final book in the Book of Mormon record. He wrote: "I had supposed not to have written any more; but I write a few more things, that perhaps they may be of worth unto my brethren" (Moro. 1:4). He then brought together loosely related but important items, including ordinances performed both in the church of his day and in The Church of Jesus Christ of Latter-day Saints today (chaps. 2–6), one of his father's sermons (chap. 7), and two of his father's letters (chap. 9). He concluded with his own testimony and exhortations to readers (chap. 10).

ORDINANCES (CHAPS. 2–6). Chapter 2 contains instructions given by the resurrected Jesus Christ to his twelve disciples in the Western Hemisphere at the time when he bestowed upon them the gift of the Holy Ghost. This gift is conferred in the name of Jesus Christ and by the laying on of hands from one who has received authority. Chapter 3 explains that priests and teachers were ordained in the name of Jesus Christ by the laying on of hands by one holding proper authority. The main function of priests and teachers was to teach repentance and faith in Jesus Christ. Chapters 4 and 5 contain the set prayers for blessing the sacrament of the Lord's Supper, prayers currently used in the Church. Chapter 6 outlines the requirements for baptism, which include a "broken heart," contrite spirit, and true repentance. Moroni then detailed how Church members recorded the names of all members, taught one another, met together in fasting and prayer, and partook of the sacrament often.

MORMON'S SERMON AND LETTERS (CHAPS. 7–9). Mormon's sermon (chap. 7) deals with faith, hope, and charity and includes teachings on how to distinguish between good and evil, the necessity of spiritual gifts, the nature of miracles, and instruction on how to obtain charity, "the pure love of Christ" (7:47).

The first letter (chap. 8) condemns INFANT BAPTISM. Mormon taught that children are made pure through the atonement of Christ and do not need the cleansing power of baptism until they are old enough to be accountable for their actions and can repent of their sins.

The second letter (chap. 9) recites the level of depravity to which the NEPHITES and LAMANITES had fallen (before A.D. 385), offering reasons for their prophesied destruction ("they are without principle, and past feeling"—verse 20), along with Mormon's charge to his son to remain faithful to Christ in spite of their society's wickedness.

EXHORTATION AND FAREWELL (CHAP. 10). Moroni exhorts all who read the Book of Mormon to ponder and pray for a divine witness of its truthfulness (verses 3–5) and urges his readers not to deny the gifts of the Holy Ghost, which he enumerates (verses 8–19). He bears his personal testimony of Jesus Christ and urges all to "come unto Christ, and be perfected in him, and deny yourselves of all ungodliness" (verse 32). He bids his readers farewell until he meets them on the final judgment day at "the pleasing bar of the great Jehovah" (verse 34).

BIBLIOGRAPHY
Jackson, Kent P., ed. *Studies in Scripture*, Vol. 8, pp. 282–312. Salt Lake City, 1988.

S. MICHAEL WILCOX

BOOK OF MORMON, BIBLICAL PROPHECIES ABOUT

Latter-day Saints believe that the coming forth of the Book of Mormon as an instrument in God's hand for bringing his latter-day work to fruition was revealed to biblical prophets such as ISAIAH and EZEKIEL (cf. 1 Ne. 19:21). Their prophecies about these matters, like those about the coming of Jesus Christ, are better understood when some of the historical events that surround them are known.

JOSEPH'S PROPHECY. Allusions are made to a branch that would be broken off in Jacob's blessing to Joseph, promising that he would become a fruitful bough whose "branches" would run "over the wall" and that his posterity would be heir to divine blessings (Gen. 49:22–26; 1 Ne. 19:24; cf. Deut. 33:13–17). A further prophecy in the Book of Mormon aids in interpreting Genesis 49.

According to a prophecy of Joseph in Egypt, preserved in the Book of Mormon (2 Ne. 3:4–21), two sets of records would be kept by two tribes of Israel—one (the Bible) written by the tribe of Judah and the other (Book of Mormon) kept by the tribe of Joseph (2 Ne. 3:12; cf. Ezek. 37:15–19). Those kept by the tribe of Joseph were written on PLATES of brass and largely parallel the biblical records (1 Ne. 5:10–16; 13:23). They were carried to a promised land in the Western Hemisphere by LEHI, a prophet and descendant of Joseph, who fled Jerusalem about 600 B.C. Lehi exclaimed, "Joseph truly saw our day. And he obtained a promise of the Lord, that out of the fruit of his loins the Lord God would raise up a righteous branch unto the house of Israel; not the Messiah, but a branch which was to be broken off" (2 Ne. 3:5).

VISIT OF RESURRECTED JESUS. A succession of prophets taught the gospel of Jesus Christ to Lehi's "branch" of Joseph's descendants and prophesied that after Jesus was resurrected, he would visit them (e.g., 2 Ne. 26:1). Regarding this circumstance, Jesus told his hearers in Palestine that he had "other sheep . . . which are not of this fold: them also I must bring, and they shall hear my voice; and there shall be one fold, and one shepherd" (John 10:16). When he appeared in the Western Hemisphere (c. A.D. 34), he allowed the multitude to touch the wounds in his hands and side and feet so that they would understand the reality of his resurrection (3 Ne. 11:10–15). Later, he specifically referred to his words recorded in John's gospel (3 Ne. 15:16–24; John 10:16), saying, "Ye are they of whom I said: Other sheep I have which are not of this fold" (3 Ne. 15:21). Further, he taught them his gospel, called twelve disciples, announced the fulfillment of the LAW OF MOSES, instituted the sacrament, and organized his church—causing them to become of one fold with his disciples in Palestine, having him as their common shepherd (3 Ne. 11–29).

RECORD FROM THE GROUND.   Latter-day Saints teach that Isaiah foresaw that part of this branch of Joseph's family would eventually be
destroyed. He likened it to David's city Ariel, that would also be
destroyed when hostile forces "camped against" or laid siege to it (Isa.
29:3). But despite the fact that many of the people of this branch would
be slain, both Isaiah and Nephi explained that the voice of Joseph's
descendants would be heard again as a voice "out of the ground"; their
speech would "whisper out of the dust" (Isa. 29:4; 2 Ne. 26:16). For
"the words of the faithful should speak as if it were from the dead" (2
Ne. 27:13; cf. 26:15–16; *see* "VOICE FROM THE DUST").

Perceiving how this would take place, NEPHI₁, the first writer in
the Book of Mormon, wrote about 570 B.C. to unborn generations: "My
beloved brethren, all those who are of the house of Israel, and all ye
ends of the earth, I speak unto you as the voice of one crying from the
dust" (2 Ne. 33:13). Similarly, the last writer in the Book of Mormon,
MORONI₂, wrote about A.D. 400: "I speak unto you as though I spake
from the dead; for I know that ye shall have my words" (Morm. 9:30;
cf. Moro. 10:27). As he was about to bury the records, he wrote: "No
one need say [the records] shall not come, for they surely shall, for the
Lord hath spoken it; for out of the earth shall they come, by the hand of
the Lord, and none can stay it" (Morm. 8:26; cf. *TPJS*, p. 98).

The phrase "out of the ground" is thus a metaphor for the voice
of those who have died, but it also refers to records being buried in
the earth until they come forth. The overall connection between
Isaiah, chapter 29, and the Book of Mormon people is discussed in 2
Nephi, chapters 26–29 (cf. Morm. 8:23–26).

THE RECORD APPEARS.   Parts of the GOLD PLATES were sealed when
Joseph Smith received them. Isaiah spoke of "the words of a book
that is sealed" that would be delivered to a "learned" person (Isa.
29:11). Latter-day Saints see the role of the "learned" person fulfilled
by Professor Charles Anthon of Columbia College (New York), and
these "words of a book" constitute the ANTHON TRANSCRIPT. The book
itself, however, would be delivered to another (Joseph Smith) who
would simply acknowledge, "I am not learned" (Isa. 29:12), but
would be divinely empowered to translate it.

Isaiah foresaw that when the book would appear, people would be
contending over God's word (Isa. 29:13). This circumstance would provide the context wherein God could perform his "marvelous work and

a wonder," causing the "wisdom of their wise men" to perish and the "understanding of their prudent men [to] be hid" while the meek would "increase their joy in the Lord" and the "poor among men shall rejoice in the Holy One of Israel" (Isa. 29:14, 19). Meanwhile, those who had "erred in spirit shall come to understanding, and they that murmured shall learn doctrine" (Isa. 29:22–24; cf. 2 Ne. 27:6–26).

TWO RECORDS. Ezekiel also prophesied concerning the two records—that of Joseph or Ephraim (i.e., the Book of Mormon) and that of Judah (i.e., the Bible)—that would be joined in the last days as an instrument provided by the Lord to gather his people back to himself (Ezek. 37:15–22; cf. 2 Ne. 3:11–12; *see* EZEKIEL, PROPHECIES OF; ISRAEL: GATHERING OF ISRAEL).

For Latter-day Saints, when Ezekiel spoke of "sticks" (probably waxed writing boards), he was illustrating the instruments by which God would bring peoples together in the latter days, just as he used the concept of the Resurrection to illustrate the gathering of God's people, which is the theme of chapters 34–37. Just as bodies are reconstituted in the Resurrection, so will Israel be reconstituted in the gathering; and the formerly divided nations will become one (Ezek. 37:1–14). Thus, the publication of the Book of Mormon in 1830 was a sign that the divided tribes of Israel were to become one under God and that God's latter-day work was beginning to be implemented (Ezek. 37:21–28; cf. 1 Ne. 13:34–41; 3 Ne. 20:46–21:11).

BIBLIOGRAPHY
McConkie, Bruce R. *A New Witness for the Articles of Faith*, pp. 422–58. Salt Lake City, 1985.
Meservy, Keith H. "Ezekiel's Sticks and the Gathering of Israel." *Ensign* 17 (Feb. 1987):4–13.
Robison, Parley Parker, comp. *Orson Pratt's Works on the Doctrines of the Gospel*, pp. 269–84. Salt Lake City, 1945.

KEITH H. MESERVY

BOOK OF MORMON, GOVERNMENT AND LEGAL HISTORY IN

Because the Book of Mormon focuses on religious themes, information about political and legal institutions appears only as background for the religious account. Even so, it is apparent that several different political institutions characterized NEPHITE, LAMANITE, and JAREDITE society.

The Nephites were ruled by hereditary kings from c. 550 to 91 B.C., when the rule changed to a reign of judges. After the coming of Christ, two centuries of peace under the government of his Church were followed by a breakdown of society into tribal units and finally by the destruction of the Nephites.

From the beginning, the Nephite legal system was based on the LAW OF MOSES as it was written in the scriptures, as it was possibly practiced by Israel in the seventh century B.C., and as it was modified (slightly) over the years until the coming of Jesus Christ. As the Nephite prophets had long predicted (2 Ne. 25:24), Jesus fulfilled the law of Moses. After his coming, Nephite law consisted of the commandments of Christ.

GOVERNMENT. After leading his family and a few others out of Jerusalem, Lehi established his colony in the Western Hemisphere as a branch of Israel in a new promised land, but its organization was inherently unstable, for it seems to have given no clear principle for resolving political disputes. The seven lineage groups established at Lehi's death and mentioned consistently in the Book of Mormon were Nephites, Jacobites, Josephites, Zoramites, Lamanites, Lemuelites, and Ishmaelites (Jacob 1:13; 4 Ne. 1:36–38; Morm. 1:8; Welch, 1989, p. 69). When this system proved unable to keep the peace, NEPHI₁ led away the first four of these family groups, who believed the revelations of God; established a new city; and accepted the position of Nephite king by popular acclamation. The other three groups eventually developed a monarchical system, with a Lamanite king receiving tribute from other Ishmaelite, Lamanite, and Lemuelite vassal kings.

This original split provides the basic political theme for much of Nephite and Lamanite history. Laman and Lemuel were Lehi's oldest sons, and they naturally claimed a right to rule. But a younger brother, Nephi, was chosen by the Lord to be their ruler and teacher (1 Ne. 2:22), and Nephi's account of this early history was written in part to document his calling as ruler (Reynolds). The conflict over the right to rule continued, providing much of the rhetorical base for the recurring wars between Lamanites and Nephites hundreds of years later.

Possibly because of the controversial circumstances in which Nephite kingship was established, its ideology was clear from earliest times. Nephite kings were popularly acclaimed (2 Ne. 5:18). They had a temple as their religious center (2 Ne. 5:16) and were careful to maintain venerable symbols of divinely appointed kingship in the sword of Laban, the Liahona, and ancient records (2 Ne. 5:12–14; cf. Ricks).

Only the first Nephite king (Nephi$_1$) and the last three kings (MOSIAH$_1$, BENJAMIN, and MOSIAH$_2$) are named in the Book of Mormon. These four kings served as military leaders and prophets, and worked closely with other prophets in reminding people of their obligations to God and to one another. For example, in his final address to his people, King Benjamin reported to the people a revelation from God and put them under covenant to take the name of Christ upon them and to keep God's and the king's commandments.

Some Nephite kings were unrighteous. Noah, a king of one Nephite subgroup (the people of Zeniff), exploited the weaknesses of the Nephite system, sustaining himself and his council of corrupt priests in riotous living from the labors of the people. Doubts about the institution of kingship became acute when the oppressions of Noah were reported to the main body of Nephites. King Mosiah$_2$, when his sons declined the monarchy, resolved the succession crisis by proposing to change the kingship into a system of lower and higher judges. This form of government was accepted by the people in 91 B.C. (Mosiah 29) and lasted, in spite of several crises and corruptions, for approximately a hundred years. Though the position of chief judge continued to have military and religious preeminence and was frequently passed from father to son, it differed from the kingship pattern in that the higher judges could be judged by lower judges if they broke the law or oppressed the people (Mosiah 29:29).

ALMA$_2$ became the first chief judge and served simultaneously as high priest, governor, and military chief captain. Because these offices required the approval of the people, who had rejected monarchy, critics have tended to confuse the Nephite system with the democracy of the United States. However, there was no representative legislature, the essential institution in American republican ideology. Also, the major offices were typically passed from father to son, without elections (Bushman, pp. 14–17); "the voice of the people" is reported many times as authorizing or confirming leadership appointments and other civic or political actions.

It appears that during the first two centuries after the coming of Christ, the Nephites operated under an ecclesiastical system without judges or kings, with courts constituted only of the church elders (4 Ne. 1:1–23; Moro. 6:7). With the eventual apostasy and collapse of the Nephite church, no civil institutions were in place to preserve law and order. Attempts to organize and conduct public affairs by reversion to a tribal system and, later, to military rule did not prevent the final destruction of the civilization.

The Book of Mormon also gives a brief account of the Jaredites, a much earlier civilization that began at the time of the great tower and was monarchical from beginning to end. Jaredite kings seem to have been autocrats, and succession was more often determined through political and military adventurism than through legal procedures.

LAW.   Until the coming of Christ, the Nephites and converted Lamanites strictly observed the law of Moses as they knew and understood it (2 Ne. 5:10; 25:24–26; Jarom 1:5; Jacob 4:4–5; Alma 25:15; 30:3; Hel. 13:1; 3 Ne. 1:24–25). Preserved on the brass plates, the law of Moses was the basis of their criminal and civil law, as well as of the rules of purity, temple sacrifice, and festival observances of the Nephites; they knew, however, that the law of Moses would be superseded in the future messianic age (2 Ne. 25:24–27).

Recent publications (Welch, 1984, 1987, 1988, 1989, 1990) have identified a rich array of legal information in the text of the Book of Mormon. Procedural and administrative aspects of Nephite law developed from one century to another, while the substance of the customary law changed very little. Nephite leaders seem to have viewed new legislation as presumptuous and generally evil (Mosiah 29:23) and any change of God's law without authority as blasphemous (Jacob 7:7). Their religious laws included many humanitarian provisions and protections for persons and their religious freedom and property. These rules were grounded in a strong principle of legal equality (Alma 1:32; 16:18; Hel. 4:12).

In two early incidents, Jacob, the brother of Nephi₁, was involved in controversies concerning the law. The first involved the claimed right of some Nephites to have concubines (Jacob 2:23–3:11), and the second arose when Sherem accused Jacob of desecrating the law of Moses (Jacob 7:7).

The trial of ABINADI (Mosiah 11–17) indicates that, at least in the case of Noah, the king had jurisdiction over political issues but took counsel on religious matters from a body of priests: Causes of action were brought against Abinadi for cursing the ruler, testifying falsely, giving a false prophecy, and committing blasphemy (Mosiah 12:9–10, 14; 17:7–8, 12). Legal punishments in the Book of Mormon were often fashioned so as to match the nature of the crime; thus, Abinadi was burned for reviling the king, whose life he had said would be valued as a garment in a furnace (Mosiah 12:3; 17:3).

At the time the Nephites abandoned monarchy, Mosiah$_2$ instituted a major reform of Nephite procedural law. A system of judges and other officers was instituted; lower judges were judged by a higher judge (Mosiah 29:28); judges were paid for the time spent in public service (Alma 11:3); a standardized system of weights and measures was instituted (Alma 11:4–19); slavery was formally prohibited (Alma 27:9); and defaulting debtors faced banishment (Alma 11:2). There were officers (Alma 11:2) and lawyers who assisted, but their official functions are not clear. It appears that ordinary citizens had sole power to initiate lawsuits (otherwise, the judges would have brought the action against Nephi$_2$ in Helaman 8:1).

The trial of Nehor was an important precedent, establishing the plenary and original jurisdiction of the chief judge (Alma 1:1–15). It appears that under the terms of Mosiah 29, the higher judges were intended only to judge if the lower judges judged falsely. But in the trial of Nehor, Alma$_2$ took the case directly, enhancing the power of the chief judge.

The reform also protected freedom of belief, but certain overt conduct was punished (Alma 1:17–18; 30:9–11). The case of Korihor established the rule that certain forms of speech (blasphemy, inciting people to sin) were punishable under the Nephite law even after the reform of Mosiah.

All this time, the underlying Nephite law remained the law of Moses as interpreted in light of a knowledge of the gospel. Public decrees regularly prohibited murder, plunder, theft, adultery, and all

iniquity (Mosiah 2:13; Alma 23:3). Murder was defined as "deliberately killing" (2 Ne. 9:35), which excluded cases where one did not
lie in wait (on Nephi's slaying of Laban, cf. Ex. 21:13–14 and 1 Ne.
4:6–18). Theft was typically a minor offense, but robbery was a capital crime (Hel. 11:28), usually committed by organized outsiders and
violent and politically motivated brigands, who were dealt with by
military force (as they were typically in the ancient Near East).

Evidently, technical principles of the law of Moses were consistently observed in Nephite civilization. For example, the legal resolution of an unobserved murder in the case of Seantum in Helaman 9
shows that a technical exception to the rule against self-incrimination
was recognized by the Nephites in the same way that it was by later
Jewish jurists, as when divination detected a corpus delecti (Welch,
Feb. 1990). The execution of Zemnarihah by the Nephites adum-
brated an obscure point attested in later Jewish law that required the
tree from which a criminal was hanged to be chopped down (3 Ne.
4:28; Welch, 1984). The case of the Ammonite exemption from military duty suggests that the rabbinic understanding of Deuteronomy
20 in this regard was probably the same as the Nephites' (Welch,
1990, pp. 63–65).

One may also infer from circumstantial evidence that the
Nephites observed the traditional ritual laws of Israelite festivals.
One example might be the assembly of Benjamin's people in tents
around the temple and tower from which he spoke. There are things
in the account that are similar to the New Year festivals surrounding
the Feast of Tabernacles and the Day of Atonement (Tvedtnes, in
Lundquist and Ricks, *By Study and Also by Faith,* Salt Lake City,
1990, 2:197–237).

With the coming of the resurrected Christ, recorded in 3 Nephi,
the law of Moses was fulfilled and was given new meaning. The Ten
Commandments still applied in a new form (3 Ne. 12); the "performances and ordinances" of the law became obsolete (4 Ne. 1:12), but
not the "law" or the "commandments" as Jesus had reformulated
them in 3 Nephi 12–14.

BIBLIOGRAPHY
Bushman, Richard L. "The Book of Mormon and the American Revolution." *BYU
Studies* 17 (Autumn 1976):3–20.
Reynolds, Noel B. "The Political Dimension in Nephi's Small Plates." *BYU Studies*
27 (Fall 1987):15–37.

Ricks, Stephen D. "The Ideology of Kingship in Mosiah 1–6." *F.A.R.M.S. Update*, Aug. 1987.

Welch, John W. "The Execution of Zemnarihah." *F.A.R.M.S. Update*, Nov. 1984.

———. "The Law of Mosiah." *F.A.R.M.S. Update*, Mar. 1987.

———. "Statutes, Judgments, Ordinances and Commandments." *F.A.R.M.S. Update*, June 1988.

———. "Lehi's Last Will and Testament: A Legal Approach." In *The Book of Mormon: Second Nephi, the Doctrinal Structure*, ed. M. Nyman and C. Tate, pp. 61–82. Provo, Utah, 1989.

———. "The Case of an Unobserved Murder." *F.A.R.M.S. Update*, Feb. 1990.

———. "Law and War in the Book of Mormon." In *Warfare in the Book of Mormon*, ed. S. Ricks and W. Hamblin, pp. 46–102. Salt Lake City, 1990.

NOEL B. REYNOLDS

BOOK OF MORMON, HISTORY OF WARFARE IN

Much of the Book of Mormon deals with military conflict. In diverse, informative, and morally instructive accounts, the Book of Mormon reports a wide variety of military customs, technologies, and tactics similar to those found in many premodern societies (before A.D. 1600–1700), especially some distinctive Israelite beliefs and conventions as adapted to the region of Mesoamerica.

The Book of Mormon teaches that war is a result of iniquity. Wars and destructions were brought upon the Nephites because of the contentions, murderings, idolatry, whoredoms, and abominations "which were among themselves," while those who were "faithful in keeping the commandments of the Lord were delivered at all times" from captivity, death, or unbelief (Alma 50:21–22).

The Book of Mormon implicitly condemns wars of aggression. Until their final calamity, all Nephite military objectives were strictly defensive. It was a mandatory, sacred obligation of all able-bodied Nephite men to defend their families, country, and religious freedoms (Alma 43:47; 46:12), but only as God commanded them.

WARFARE. In the Book of Mormon, aside from the Ammonite converts who swore an oath against bloodshed and a remarkable period of peace following the visitation of Christ, armed conflict at different levels of intensity was a nearly constant phenomenon. Several prophets and heroes of the Book of Mormon were military men who fought in defense of their people, reflecting the grim realities of warfare in ancient history.

Religion and warfare were closely connected in the Book of Mormon. Certain elements of the Israelite patterns of "holy war" were continued in the Book of Mormon, such as the important ancient idea that success in war was due fundamentally to the will of God and the righteousness of the people (Alma 2:28; 44:4–5; 50:21; 56:47; 57:36; 58:33; Morm. 2:26). Nephite armies consulted prophets before going to battle (Alma 16:5; 43:23–24; 3 Ne. 3:19) and entered into covenants with God before battle. On one occasion, the Nephite soldiers swore a solemn oath, covenanting to obey God's commandments and to fight valiantly for the cause of righteousness; casting their garments on the ground at the feet of their leader and inviting God to cast themselves likewise at the feet of their enemies if they should violate their oath (Alma 46:22; cf. 53:17). A purity code for warriors may be seen in the account of the stripling warriors of Helaman (Alma 56–58).

As was the case in all premodern situations, warfare in the Book of Mormon was closely bound to the natural environment and ecology: weather, altitude, terrain, food supply, seasonality, and agricultural cycles. Geography determined some of the strategy and tactics in Book of Mormon warfare (Sorenson, 1985, pp. 239–76). The favorable times for campaigns in the Book of Mormon appear to have been between the eleventh and the fourth months, which has been compared with the fact that military action often took place during the cool and dry post-harvest months from November through April in Mesoamerica (see Alma 16:1; 49:1; 52:1; 56:27; Ricks and Hamblin, pp. 445–77).

Animals, either used as beasts of burden or ridden into battle, evidently were not widely available or practical in the Nephite world: No animal is ever mentioned as being used for military purposes in the Book of Mormon.

Technologically, Nephite soldiers fought, in one way or other, with missile or melee weapons in face-to-face, hand-to-hand encounters, frequently wearing armor. They used metallurgy for making weapons and armor, and engineering for building fortifications. In the Book of Mormon, Nephi taught his people to make swords modeled after the sword of Laban (2 Ne. 5:14–15). Innovations described include a proliferation of fortifications (once thought absent in ancient America) and Nephite armor in the first century B.C. (Alma 43:19; 48), soon copied by the Lamanites (Alma 49:24). It has been pointed out that the weapons (swords, scimitars, bows, and arrows) and armor (breastplates, shields, armshields, bucklers, and head-plates) mentioned in the Book of Mormon are comparable to those found in Mesoamerica; coats of mail, helmets, battle chariots, cavalry, and sophisticated siege engines are absent from the Book of Mormon and Mesoamerica, despite their importance in biblical descriptions (Ricks and Hamblin, pp. 329–424).

The ability to recruit, equip, train, supply, and move large groups of soldiers represented a major undertaking for these societies, often pressing them beyond their limits and thereby ultimately contributing to their collapse. As the story of MORONI₁ and Pahoran illustrates, warfare exerted terrible social and economic pressure on Nephite society (Alma 58–61). Nephite army sizes coincided with general demographic growth: Armies numbered in the thousands in the first century B.C. and in the tens of thousands in the fourth century A.D.

It appears that Book of Mormon military organization was aristocratic and dominated by a highly trained hereditary elite. Thus, for example, military leaders such as Moroni₁, his son Moronihah, and MORMON each became the chief captain at a young age (Alma 43:17; 62:39; Morm. 2:1).

Book of Mormon armies were organized on a decimal system of hundreds, thousands, and ten thousands, as they typically were in ancient Israel and many other ancient military organizations.

The book of Alma chronicles the grim realities, strain, and pain of war, vividly and realistically (*CWHN* 7:291–333). Preparations for war were complex; provisioning, marching, and countermarching are frequently mentioned. Manpower was recruited from the ordinary ranks of the citizenry; soldiers had to be equipped and organized into units for marching and tactics and mobilized at central locations.

Some battles were fought at prearranged times and places, as when Mormon met the Lamanites at Cumorah (Morm. 6:2; cf. 3 Ne. 3:8). But much was typified by guerrilla warfare or surprise attacks: The Gadianton robbers typically raided towns, avoided open conflict, made terrorizing demands, and secretly assassinated government officials.

Actual battlefield operations usually represented only a small portion of a campaign. Scouts and spies reconnoitered for food, trails, and the location of enemy troops. Battle plans were generally made shortly before the enemy was encountered and frequently took the form of a council, as Moroni held in Alma 52:19.

When actual fighting began, controlling the army undoubtedly proved difficult. Soldiers generally fought in units distinguished by banners held by an officer. Moroni's banner, or "title of liberty," apparently served such functions (Alma 43:26, 30; 46:19–21, 36).

As far as one can determine, attacks typically began with an exchange of missiles to wound and demoralize the enemy; then hand-to-hand combat ensued. The battle described in Alma 49 offers a good description of archery duels preceding hand-to-hand melees. When panic began to spread in the ranks, complete collapse could be sudden and devastating. The death of the king or commander typically led to immediate defeat or surrender, as happened in Alma 49:25. The death of one Lamanite king during the night before the New Year proved particularly demoralizing (Alma 52:1–2). Most casualties occurred during the flight and pursuit after the disintegration of the main units; there are several examples in the Book of Mormon of the rout, flight, and destruction of an army (e.g., Alma 52:28; 62:31).

Laws and customary behavior also regulated military relations and diplomacy. Military oaths were taken very seriously. Oaths of loyalty from troops and oaths of surrender from prisoners are mentioned frequently in the Book of Mormon, and treaties were concluded principally with oaths of nonaggression (Alma 44:6–10, 20; 50:36; 62:16; 3 Ne. 5:4–5). Legally, robbers or brigands were considered to be military targets, not common offenders (Hel. 11:28). Further elements of martial law in the Book of Mormon included the suspension of normal judicial processes and transferral of legal authority to commanding military officers (Alma 46:34), restrictions on travel, warnings before the commencement of hostilities (3 Ne. 3; cf. Deut. 20:10–13), the extraordinary granting of military exemption on condition that those exempted supply provisions and support (Alma 27:24; cf. Deut. 20:8; Babylonian Talmud, *Sotah* 43a–44a), and requirements of humanitarian treatment for captives and women.

WARS. Eighty-five instances of armed conflict can be identified in the Book of Mormon (Ricks and Hamblin, pp. 463–74). Some were brief skirmishes; others, prolonged campaigns. Some were civil wars;

others, intersectional. Causes of war varied, and alliances shifted accordingly. The main wars include the following:

In the early tribal conflicts (c. 550–200 B.C.), social, religious, and cultural conflicts led to repeated Lamanite aggression after the Nephites separated from the Lamanites. The Nephites did not flourish under these circumstances, and to escape further attacks they eventually left the land of Nephi, moving northward to Zarahemla.

King Laman's son (c. 160–150 B.C.), envious of Nephite prosperity and angry at them for taking the records (especially the plates of brass, Mosiah 10:16), attacked both the people of Zeniff (Nephites who had returned to the land of Nephi) and the people of BENJAMIN (Nephites and Mulekites in the land of Zarahemla). As a result of these campaigns, Zeniff became a tributary to the Lamanites; Benjamin's victory more firmly united the land of Zarahemla under his rule (W of M; Mosiah 9–10).

The war of Amlici (87 B.C.) was a civil war in Zarahemla, sparked by the shift of government from a kingship to judgeship and by the execution of Nehor. Amlici, a follower of Nehor, militated in favor of returning to a kingship. This civil war was the first recorded time Nephite dissenters allied themselves with Lamanites; it resulted in an unstable peace (Alma 2–3).

The sudden destruction of Ammonihah (81 B.C.), a center of the recalcitrant followers of Nehor, was triggered by Lamanite anger toward certain Nephites who had caused some Lamanites to kill other Lamanites (Alma 16; 24–25).

The Ammonite move (77 B.C.) from Lamanite territory to the land of Jershon to join the Nephites led to a major Lamanite invasion of Nephite lands (Alma 28).

Three years later, many Zoramite poor were converted by the Nephites and moved from Antionum (the Zoramite capital) to Jershon (the land given to the Ammonites with guarantees of protection by the Nephites). The loss of these workers ignited the Zoramite attack allied with Lamanites and others against the Nephites (Alma 43–44). New forms of armor introduced by the Nephites figured prominently in this war.

During this turbulent decade, a politically ambitious man named Amalickiah, with Lamanite allies, sought to reestablish a kingship in Zarahemla after the disappearance of ALMA$_2$. Amalickiah was defeated (72 B.C.), but he swore to return and kill Moroni₁ (Alma 46–50). A seven-year campaign ensued (67–61 B.C.), fought in two arenas, one southwest of Zarahemla and the other in the seaboard north of Zarahemla. Outlying towns fell, and the capital city was plagued with civil strife. At length, a costly victory was won by the Nephites (Alma 51–62).

In the short war of Tubaloth (51 B.C.), Ammoron's son Tubaloth and Coriantumr (a descendant of King Zarahemla) captured but could not hold the land of Zarahemla during the political chaos that followed the rebellion of Paanchi after the death of the chief judge Pahoran (Hel. 1). In the aftermath, the Gadianton robbers rose to power, and some Nephites began migrating to the north.

The war of Moronihah (38, 35–30 B.C.) followed the appointment of NEPHI₂ as chief judge (Hel. 4). Nephite dissenters, together with Lamanites, occupied half of the Nephite lands, and Nephi₂ resigned the judgment seat.

The wars of Gadianton and Kishkumen (26–19 B.C.) began with the assassinations of two consecutive chief judges, Cezoram and his son; greed and struggles for power brought on conflicts with the Gadianton robbers around Zarahemla. Lamanites joined with Nephites against these robbers until a famine, called down from heaven by the prophet Nephi₂, brought a temporary Nephite victory (Hel. 6–11).

Giddianhi and Zemnarihah (A.D. 13–22) led menacing campaigns against the few righteous Nephites and Lamanites who remained and joined forces at this time (3 Ne. 2–4). Low on supplies, the Gadianton robbers became more open and aggressive; they claimed rights to Nephite lands and government. The coalition of Nephites and Lamanites eventually defeated the robbers.

The final Nephite wars (A.D. 322, 327–328, 346–350) began after heavy population growth and infestation of robbers led to a border dispute, and the Nephites were driven to a narrow neck of land. The Nephites fortified the city of Shem and managed to win a ten-year peace treaty (Morm. 1–2), but the Nephites eventually counterattacked in the south. Gross wickedness existed on both sides (Morm. 6; Moro. 9), until at a prearranged battleground the Nephites met the Lamanites and were annihilated (c. A.D. 385).

Many chapters in the Book of Mormon deal with war, and for several reasons.

1. The inevitability of war was a fundamental concern in virtually all ancient civilizations. Disposable economic resources were often largely devoted to maintaining a military force; conquest was a major factor in the transformation and development of Book of Mormon societies, as it was in the growth of most world civilizations.

2. The Book of Mormon is a religious record, and for the people of the Book of Mormon, as in nearly all ancient cultures, warfare was fundamentally sacral. It was carried out in a complex mixture of religious ritual and ideology.

3. Mormon, the compiler and abridger of the Book of Mormon, was himself a military commander. Many political and religious rulers in the Book of Mormon were closely associated with, if not the same as, their military commanders or elites.

4. Important religious messages are conveyed through these accounts. Wars in Nephite history verify the words of their prophets such as ABINADI and SAMUEL THE LAMANITE (Morm. 1:19). Wars were instruments of God's judgment (Morm. 4:5) and of God's deliverance (Alma 56:46–56). Ultimately they stand as a compelling witness to warn people today against falling victim to the same fate that the Nephites and Jaredites finally brought upon themselves (Morm. 9:31; Ether 2:11–12).

BIBLIOGRAPHY

de Vaux, Roland. *Ancient Israel.* New York, 1965.

Hillam, Ray. "The Gadianton Robbers and Protracted War." *BYU Studies* 15 (1975):215–24.

Ricks, Stephen D., and William J. Hamblin, eds. *Warfare in the Book of Mormon.* Salt Lake City, 1990. (Further bibliography is listed on pp. 22–24.)

Sorenson, John L. *An Ancient American Setting for the Book of Mormon,* pp. 239–76. Salt Lake City, 1985.

WILLIAM J. HAMBLIN

BOOK OF MORMON AS LITERATURE

Although understated as literature in its clear and plain language, the Book of Mormon exhibits a wide variety of literary forms, including intricate Hebraic poetry, memorable narratives, rhetorically effective sermons, diverse letters, allegory, figurative language, imagery, symbolic types, and wisdom literature. In recent years these aspects of Joseph Smith's 1829 English translation have been increasingly appreciated, especially when compared with biblical and other ancient forms of literature.

There are many reasons to study the Book of Mormon as literature. Rather than being "formless," as claimed by one critic (Bernard DeVoto, *American Mercury 19* [1930]:5), the Book of Mormon is both coherent and polished (although not obtrusively so). It tells "a densely compact and rapidly moving story that interweaves dozens of plots with an inexhaustible fertility of invention and an uncanny consistency that is never caught in a slip or contradiction" (*CWHN* 7:138).

Despite its small working vocabulary of about 2,225 root words in English, the book distills much human experience and contact with the divine. It presents its themes artfully through simple yet profound imagery, direct yet complex discourses, and straightforward yet intricate structures. To read the Book of Mormon as literature is to discover how such literary devices are used to convey the messages of its content. Attention to form, diction, figurative language, and rhetorical techniques increases sensitivity to the structure of the text and appreciation of the work of the various authors. The stated purpose of the Book of Mormon is to show the LAMANITES, a remnant of the House of ISRAEL, the covenants made with their fathers, and to convince Jew and Gentile that Jesus is the Christ (*see* BOOK OF MORMON: TITLE PAGE FROM THE BOOK OF MORMON). MORMON selected materials and literarily shaped the book to present these messages in a stirring and memorable way.

While the discipline of identifying and evaluating literary features in the Book of Mormon is very young and does not supplant a spiritual reading of the text, those analyzing the book from this perspective find it a work of immediacy that shows as well as tells as great literature usually does. It no longer fits Mark Twain's definition of a classic essentially as a book everyone talks about but no one reads; rather, it is a work that "wears you out before you wear it out" (J. Welch, "Study, Faith, and the Book of Mormon," *BYU 1987–88 Devotional and Fireside Speeches*, p. 148. [Provo, Utah, 1988]). It is increasingly seen as a unique work that beautifully and compellingly reveals and speaks to the essential human condition.

POETRY.   Found embedded in the narrative of the Book of Mormon, poetry provides the best examples of the essential connection between form and content in the Book of Mormon. When many inspired words of the Lord, angels, and prophets are analyzed according to ancient verse forms, their meaning can be more readily perceived. These forms include line forms, symmetry, parallelism, and chiastic patterns, as defined by Adele Berlin (*The Dynamics of Biblical Parallelism* [Bloomington, Ind., 1985]) and Wilford Watson (*Classical Hebrew Poetry* [Sheffield, 1984]). Book of Mormon texts shift smoothly from narrative to poetry, as in this intensifying passage:

> But behold, the Spirit hath said this much unto me, saying: Cry unto this people, saying—
>> Repent ye, and prepare the way of the Lord, and walk in his paths, which are straight; for behold, the kingdom of heaven is at hand, and the Son of God cometh upon the face of the earth [Alma 7:9].

The style of the Book of Mormon has been criticized by some as being verbose and redundant, but in most cases these repetitions are orderly and effective. For example, parallelisms, which abound in the Book of Mormon, serve many functions. They add emphasis to twice-repeated concepts and give definition to sharply drawn contrasts. A typical synonymous parallelism is in 2 Nephi 9:52:

> *Pray* unto him continually *by day,*
> and *give thanks* unto his holy name *by night.*

Nephi's discourse aimed at his obstinate brothers includes a sharply antithetical parallelism:

> Ye are *swift* to do *iniquity*
> But *slow* to *remember* the Lord your God. [1 Ne. 17:45.]

Several fine examples of chiasmus (an a–b–b–a pattern) are also found in the Book of Mormon. In the Psalm of Nephi (2 Ne. 4:15–35), the initial appeals to the *soul* and *heart* are accompanied by negations, while the subsequent mirror uses the *heart* and *soul* are conjoined with strong affirmations, making the contrasts literarily effective and climactic:

Awake, my *soul!* No longer droop in sin.
Rejoice, O my *heart*, and give place no more for the enemy of
my soul.
    Do not anger again because of mine enemies.
    Do not slacken my strength because of mine afflictions.
Rejoice, O my *heart*, and cry unto the Lord, and say:
O Lord, I will praise thee forever; yea, my *soul* will rejoice in
thee, my God, and the rock of my salvation. [2 Ne. 4:28–30.]

Other precise examples of extended chiasmus (a–b–c—c–b–a) are
readily discernible in Mosiah 5:10–12 and Alma 36:1–30 and
41:13–15. This literary form in Alma 36 effectively focuses attention
on the central passage of the chapter (Alma 36:17–18); in Alma 41,
it fittingly conveys the very notion of restorative justice expressed in
the passage (cf. Lev. 24:13–23, which likewise uses chiasmus to convey a similar notion of justice).

    Another figure known as *a fortiori* is used to communicate an
exaggerated sense of multitude, as in Alma 60:22, where a "number
parallelism" is chiastically enclosed by a twice-repeated phrase:

Yea, will ye sit in idleness
    while ye are surrounded with *thousands* of those,
    yea, and *tens of thousands*,
who do also sit in idleness?

    Scores of Book of Mormon passages can be analyzed as poetry.
They range from Lehi's brief desert poems (1 Ne. 2:9–10, a form
Hugh Nibley identifies as an Arabic *qasida*) [*CWHN* 6:270–75] to
extensive sermons of Jacob, Abinadi, and the risen Jesus (2 Ne.
6–10; Mosiah 12–16; and 3 Ne. 27).

NARRATIVE TEXTS.   In the Book of Mormon, narrative texts are often
given vitality by vigorous conflict and impassioned dialogue or personal narration. Nephi relates his heroic actions in obtaining the
brass plates from Laban; Jacob resists the false accusations off
Sherem, upon whom the judgment of the Lord falls; Ammon fights of
plunderers at the waters of Sebus and wins the confidence of king
Lamoni; Amulek is confronted by the smooth-tongued lawyer
Zeezrom; Alma$_2$ and Amulek are preserved while their accusers are
crushed by collapsing prison walls; Captain Moroni$_1$ engages in a

showdown with the Lamanite chieftain Zerahemnah; Amalickiah rises to power through treachery and malevolence; a later prophet named NEPHI$_2$ reveals to an unbelieving crowd the murder of their chief judge by the judge's own brother; and the last two Jaredite kings fight to the mutual destruction of their people.

Seen as a whole, the Book of Mormon is an epic account of the history of the NEPHITE nation. Extensive in scope with an eponymic hero, it presents action involving long and arduous journeys and heroic deeds, with supernatural beings taking an active part. Encapsulated within this one-thousand-year account of the establishment, development, and destruction of the Nephites is the concentrated epic of the rise and fall of the Jaredites, who preceded them in type and time. (For its epic milieu, see *CWHN* 5:285–394.) The climax of the book is the dramatic account of the visit of the resurrected Jesus to an assemblage of righteous Nephites.

SERMONS AND SPEECHES.   Prophetic discourse is a dominant literary form in the Book of Mormon. Speeches such as King BENJAMIN's address (Mosiah 1–6), Alma$_2$'s challenge to the people of Zarahemla (Alma 5), and Mormon's teachings on faith, hope, and charity (Moro. 7) are crafted artistically and have great rhetorical effectiveness in conveying their religious purposes. The public oration of SAMUEL THE LAMANITE (Hel. 13–15) is a classic prophetic judgment speech. Taking rhetorical criticism as a guide, one can see how Benjamin's ritual address first aims to persuade the audience to reaffirm a present point of view and then turns to deliberative rhetoric—"which aims at effecting a decision about future action, often the very immediate future" (Kennedy, *New Testament Interpretation Through Rhetorical Criticism* [1984], p. 36). King Benjamin's speech is also chiastic as a whole and in several of its parts (Welch, pp. 202–205).

LETTERS.   The eight epistles in the Book of Mormon are conversational in tone, revealing the diverse personalities of their writers. These letters are from Captain Moroni$_1$ (Alma 54:5–14; 60:1–36), Ammoron (Alma 54:16–24), Helaman$_1$ (Alma 56:2–58:41), Pahoran (Alma 61:2–21), Giddianhi (3 Ne. 3:2–10), and Mormon (Moro. 8:2–30; 9:1–26).

ALLEGORY, METAPHOR, IMAGERY, AND TYPOLOGY.   These forms are also prevalent in the Book of Mormon. ZENOS's allegory of the olive tree (Jacob 5) vividly incorporates dozens of horticultural details as it depicts the history of God's dealings with Israel. A striking simile curse, with Near Eastern parallels, appears in Abinadi's prophetic denunciation: The life of King Noah shall be "as a garment in a furnace of fire, . . . as a stalk, even as a dry stalk of the field, which is run over by the beasts and trodden under foot" (Mosiah 12:10–11).

An effective extended metaphor is Alma's comparison of the word of God to a seed planted in one's heart and then growing into a fruitful TREE OF LIFE (Alma 32:28–43). In developing this metaphor, Alma uses a striking example of synesthesia: As the word enlightens their minds, his listeners can know it is real—"Ye have *tasted* this *light*" (Alma 32:35).

Iteration of archetypes such as tree, river, darkness, and fire graphically confirms Lehi's understanding "that there is an opposition in all things" (2 Ne. 2:11) and that opposition will be beneficial to the righteous.

A figural interpretation of God-given words and God-directed persons or events is insisted on, although not always developed, in the Book of Mormon. "All things which have been given of God from the beginning of the world, unto man, are the typifying of [Christ]" (2 Ne. 11:4); all performances and ordinances of the law of Moses "were types of things to come" (Mosiah 13:31); and the LIAHONA, or compass, was seen as a type: "For just as surely as this director did bring our fathers, by following its course, to the promised land, shall the words of Christ, if we follow their course, carry us beyond this vale of sorrow into a far better land of promise" (Alma 37:45). In its largest typological structure, the Book of Mormon fits well the seven phases of revelation posited by Northrop Frye: creation, revolution or exodus, law, wisdom, prophecy, gospel, and apocalypse (*The Great Code: The Bible and Literature* [New York, 1982]).

WISDOM LITERATURE.   Transmitted sayings of the wise are scattered throughout the Book of Mormon, especially in counsel given by fathers to their sons. Alma counsels, "O remember, my son, and learn wisdom in thy youth; yea, learn in thy youth, to keep the commandments of God" (Alma 37:35; see also 38:9–15). Benjamin says, "I tell you these things that ye may learn wisdom; that ye may learn that when ye are in the service of your fellow beings ye are only in the service of your God" (Mosiah 2:17). A memorable aphorism is given by Lehi: "Adam fell that men might be; and men are, that they might have joy" (2 Ne. 2:25). Pithy sayings such as "fools mock, but they shall mourn" (Ether 12:26) and "wickedness never was happiness" (Alma 41:10) are often repeated by Latter-day Saints.

APOCALYPTIC LITERATURE.   The vision in 1 Nephi 11–15 (sixth century B.C.) is comparable in form with early APOCALYPTIC literature. It contains a vision, is delivered in dialogue form, has an otherworldly mediator or escort, includes a commandment to write, treats the disposition of the recipient, prophesies persecution, foretells the judgment of the wicked and of the world, contains cosmic transformations, and has an otherworldly place as its spatial axis. Later Jewish developments of complex angelology, mystic numerology, and symbolism are absent.

STYLE AND TONE.   Book of Mormon writers show an intense concern for style and tone. Alma desires to be able to "speak with the trump of God, with a voice to shake the earth," yet realizes that "I am a man, and do sin in my wish; for I ought to be content with the things which the Lord hath allotted unto me" (Alma 29:1–3). Moroni$_2$ expresses a feeling of inadequacy in writing: "Lord, the Gentiles will mock at these things, because of our weakness in writing. . . . Thou hast also made our words powerful and great, even that we cannot write them; wherefore, when we write we behold our weakness, and stumble because of the placing of our words" (Ether 12:23–25; cf. 2 Ne. 33:1). Moroni's written words, however, are not weak. In cadences of ascending strength he boldly declares:

> O ye pollutions, ye hypocrites, ye teachers, who sell yourselves for that which will canker, why have ye polluted the holy church of God? Why are ye ashamed to take upon you the name of Christ? . . . Who will despise the works of the Lord? Who will despise the children of Christ? Behold, all ye who are despisers of the works of the Lord, for ye shall wonder and perish [Morm. 8:38, 9:26].

The styles employed by the different writers in the Book of Mormon vary from the unadorned to the sublime. The tones range from Moroni's strident condemnations to Jesus' humblest pleading:

"Behold, mine arm of mercy is extended towards you, and whosoever will come, him will I receive" (3 Ne. 9:14).

A model for communication is Jesus, who, Moroni reports, "told me in plain humility, even as a man telleth another in mine own language, concerning these things; and only a few have I written, because of my weakness in writing" (Ether 12:39–40). Two concepts in this report are repeated throughout the Book of Mormon—plain speech and inability to write about some things. "I have spoken plainly unto you," Nephi says, "that ye cannot misunderstand" (2 Ne. 25:28). "My soul delighteth in plainness," he continues, "for after this manner doth the Lord God work among the children of men" (2 Ne. 31:3). Yet Nephi also delights in the words of Isaiah, which "are not plain unto you" although "they are plain unto all those that are filled with the spirit of prophecy" (2 Ne. 25:4). Containing both plain and veiled language, the Book of Mormon is a spiritually and literarily powerful book that is direct yet complex, simple yet profound.

BIBLIOGRAPHY

England, Eugene. "A Second Witness for the Logos: The Book of Mormon and Contemporary Literary Criticism." In *By Study and Also by Faith*, 2 vols., ed. J. Lundquist and S. Ricks, Vol. 2, pp. 91–125. Salt Lake City, 1990.

Jorgensen, Bruce W.; Richard Dilworth Rust; and George S. Tate. Essays on typology in *Literature of Belief*, ed. Neal E. Lambert. Provo, Utah, 1981.

Nichols, Robert E., Jr. "Beowulf and Nephi: A Literary View of the Book of Mormon." *Dialogue* 4 (Autumn 1969):40–47.

Parry, Donald W. "Hebrew Literary Patterns in the Book of Mormon." *Ensign* 19 (Oct. 1989):58–61.

Rust, Richard Dilworth. "Book of Mormon Poetry." *New Era* (Mar. 1983):46–50.

Welch, John W. "Chiasmus in the Book of Mormon." In *Chiasmus in Antiquity*, ed. J. Welch, pp. 198–210. Hildesheim, 1981.

RICHARD DILWORTH RUST
DONALD W. PARRY

BOOK OF MORMON AUTHORSHIP

Many studies have investigated Book of Mormon authorship because the book presents itself as a composite work of many ancient authors. Those who reject Joseph Smith's claim that he translated the book through divine power assume that he or one of his contemporaries wrote the book. Various claims or arguments have been advanced to support or discount these competing positions.

Disputes about the book's authorship arose as soon as its existence became public knowledge. The first general reaction was ridicule. Modern minds do not easily accept the idea that an angel can deliver ancient records to be translated by an untrained young man. Moreover, most Christians in 1830 viewed the CANON of scripture as complete with the Bible; hence, the possibility of additional scripture violated a basic assumption of their faith. Opponents of Joseph Smith, such as Alexander Campbell, also argued that the Book of Mormon was heavily plagiarized from the Bible and that it reflected themes and phraseology current in New York in the 1820s. Many critics have speculated that Sidney Rigdon or Solomon Spaulding played a role in writing the book (*see* SPAULDING MANUSCRIPT). It has also been suggested that Joseph Smith borrowed ideas from another book (*see* VIEW OF THE HEBREWS). Though these varieties of objections and theories are still defended in many quarters, they are not supported by modern authorship studies and continue to raise as many questions as they try to answer (e.g., *CWHN* 8:54–206).

Some have suggested that Joseph Smith admitted that he was the author of the Book of Mormon because the title page of the first edition lists him as "Author and Proprietor." This language, however, comes from the federal copyright statutes and legal forms in use in 1829 (1 *Stat.* 125 [1790], amended 2 *Stat.* 171 [1802]). In the preface to the same 1830 edition, Joseph Smith stated that he translated Mormon's handwriting "by the gift and power of God" (*see* BOOK OF MORMON TRANSLATION). The position of The Church of Jesus Christ of Latter-day Saints has invariably been that the truth of Joseph Smith's testimony can be validated through the witness of the Holy Ghost.

Scholarly work has produced a variety of evidence in support of the claim that the texts of the Book of Mormon were written by multiple ancient authors. These studies significantly increase the plausibility of Joseph Smith's account of the origin of the book.

The internal complexity of the Book of Mormon is often cited as a strong indication of multiple authorship. The many writings reportedly abridged by MORMON are intricately interwoven and often expressly identified (*see* BOOK OF MORMON PLATES AND RECORDS). The various books within the Book of Mormon differ from each other in historical background, style, and distinctive characteristics, yet are accurate and consistent in numerous minute details.

Historical studies have demonstrated that many things either not known or not readily knowable in 1829 about the ancient Near East are accurately reflected in the Book of Mormon. This body of historical research was expanded by the work of Hugh W. Nibley (*see* BOOK OF MORMON STUDIES), who has recently discovered that ancient communities, such as Qumran, have many characteristics parallel to those of Book of Mormon Peoples (*CWHN* 5–8). The Jews at Qumran were "sectaries," purists who left Jerusalem to avoid corruption of their covenants; they practiced ablutions (a type of baptism) before the time of Christ and wrote one of their records on a copper scroll that they sealed and hid up to come forth at a future time. One of Nibley's analyses demonstrates that King BENJAMIN's farewell speech to his people (Mosiah 2–5) is a good example of the ancient year-rite festival (*CWHN* 6:295–310). Subsequent studies have suggested that King Benjamin's people might have been celebrating the Israelite festival of Sukkoth and doing things required by Jewish laws not translated into English until after the Book of Mormon was published (Tvedtnes, 1990).

Structural studies have identified an artistic literary form, chiasmus, that appears in rich diversity in both the Bible and the Book of Mormon (*see* BOOK OF MORMON AS LITERATURE). The most significant structural studies of the Book of Mormon derive from John W. Welch's analysis (Reynolds, pp. 33–52). Little known in 1829, this literary form creates inverted parallelism such as is found in this biblical passage in Leviticus 24:17–21:

> He that killeth any man . . .
>   He that killeth a beast . . .
>   If a man cause a blemish . . .
>   Breach for breach,
>   Eye for eye
>   Tooth for tooth.
>   As he hath caused a blemish . . .
>   He that killeth a beast . . .
> He that killeth a man. . . .

And from the Book of Mormon, in Alma 41:13–14 (cf. Welch, pp. 5–22):

Good for that which is good
  Righteous for that which is righteous
    Just for that which is just
      Merciful for that which is merciful
        Therefore my son
        See that you are merciful
      Deal justly
    Judge righteously
And do good continually.

Although chiasmus can appear in almost any language or literature, it was prevalent in the biblical period around the early seventh century B.C., the time of the Book of Mormon prophets LEHI and NEPHI$_1$. The especially precise and beautiful crafting of several Book of Mormon texts further supports the idea that their authors deliberately and painstakingly followed ancient literary conventions, which is inconsistent with seeing the New England born Joseph Smith as the author of these passages.

Other stylistic studies have examined the frequency of Hebrew root words, idioms, and syntax in the Book of Mormon (Tvedtnes, 1970). Some Book of Mormon names that have no English equivalents have Hebrew cognates (Hoskisson; *CWHN* 6:281–94). There are also discernible differences between the vocabularies and abridging techniques of Mormon and his son Moroni (see Keller).

Extensive statistical studies, including stylometry (or wordprinting), have been conducted on the Book of Mormon (Reynolds, pp. 157–88; cf. Hilton). Blocks of writing were analyzed to identify the writers' near-subconscious tendencies to use noncontextual word patterns in peculiar ratios and combinations. Wordprinting has been used to ascertain the authorship of such works as twelve disputed *Federalist Papers* and a posthumously published novel by Jane Austen. When applied to the Book of Mormon, wordprinting reveals that the word patterns of the Book of Mormon differ significantly from the personal writings of Joseph Smith, Solomon Spaulding, Sidney Rigdon, and Oliver Cowdery, who served as Joseph Smith's scribe. Furthermore, patterns of Nephi$_1$ are consistent among themselves but different from those of ALMA$_2$. The results of objectively measuring these phenomena indicate an extremely low statistical probability that the Book of Mormon could have been written by one author. The introduction of new vocabulary into the text is at a low rate, which is consistent with the uniform role of Joseph Smith as translator.

BIBLIOGRAPHY

Hilton, John L. "On Verifying Wordprint Studies: Book of Mormon Authorship." *BYU Studies* 30 (Summer 1990):89–108.

Hoskisson, Paul. "An Introduction to the Relevance of and a Methodology for a Study of the Proper Names of the Book of Mormon." In *By Study and Also by Faith,* ed. J. Lundquist and S. Ricks, Vol. 2, pp. 126–35. Salt Lake City, 1990.

Keller, Roger R. "Mormon and Moroni as Authors and Abridgers." *F.A.R.M.S. Update,* Apr. 1988.

Reynolds, Noel B., ed. *Book of Mormon Authorship: New Light on Ancient Origins.* Provo, Utah, 1982.

Tvedtnes, John. "Hebraisms in the Book of Mormon: A Preliminary Survey." *BYU Studies* 2 (Autumn 1970):50–60.

———. "King Benjamin and the Feast of Tabernacles." In *By Study and Also by Faith,* ed. J. Lundquist and S. Ricks, Vol. 2, pp. 197–237. Salt Lake City, 1990.

Welch, John W. "Chiasmus in Biblical Law." In *Jewish Law Association Studies IV,* ed. B. Jackson, pp. 5–22. Atlanta, 1990.

Wirth, Diane E. *A Challenge to the Critics: Scholarly Evidences of the Book of Mormon.* Bountiful, Utah, 1986.

D. BRENT ANDERSON
DIANE E. WIRTH

BOOK OF MORMON IN A BIBLICAL CULTURE

One does not need to look beyond the prevailing revivalist sects in America to discover why the earliest Mormon elders won an immediate hearing for their sacred book. Firm calls for personal righteousness and obedience to the moral requirements of the Judeo-Christian scriptures were by 1830 the dominant motifs in all Protestant communions. Moreover, each of the American sects shared speculations about the ancient and future history of Indians and Jews.

These interests and beliefs were also predominant among Methodist, Congregational, and Baptist ministers serving congregations in and around Cheshire, in northern England. Heber C. Kimball's *Journal,* giving an account of his mission to Great Britain,

shows how the flowering of biblical study and of millennial speculation prepared the soil for early Mormon evangelization there. He
reported that even clergymen in the Church of England told their
congregations that the teachings of the Latter-day Saints reveal the
same principles taught by the apostles of old.

The Book of Mormon also gives clear direction on several matters that the Christian scriptures seem to have left unclear, including baptism by immersion and the promises that all believers, and
not just the apostles, might be "filled with the Holy Ghost"; that
Christian believers can be made pure in heart (as John Wesley had
insisted in the previous century); that the experience of salvation
received by a free response to free grace is available to all persons,
and not simply to the "elect"; and that obedience and works of righteousness are the fruit of that experience. The book also affirms the
veracity of the biblical accounts of the scattering of Israel by affirming that Native Americans originated from descendants of Joseph and
Judah.

The persuasive power of the new scriptures and of the missionaries who expounded them, therefore, lay in their testimony to beliefs
that were central to evangelical Protestant sects in both Jacksonian
America and early Victorian England. An early LDS missionary,
Parley P. Pratt, told his English hearers that two errors in interpretation of the Bible had produced widespread uncertainty. One was the
belief that direct inspiration by the Holy Ghost was not intended for
all ages of the Church; and the other was that the Jewish and
Christian scriptures contained all truth necessary to salvation and
comprised a sufficient rule of faith and practice.

Some nineteenth-century deacons and elders and a few evangelical pastors struggled with grave temptations to doubt the truth and
relevance of large portions of the book upon which they had been
taught to stake their eternal destiny. True, the details of the histories
recounted in the two sacred books were radically different. But they
fit together wondrously. And their moral structure, the story they told
of Jesus, their promise of salvation, and their description of
humankind's last days were remarkably similar. Though the new
scriptures had similarities with evangelical Arminianism, at the
expense of the Calvinist views long dominant in colonial America,
the same was true of the early nineteenth-century teachings of many

Protestants, even Presbyterians, to say nothing of Methodists and Disciples of Christ. In the voice of two witnesses, the Bible and the Book of Mormon, Latter-day Saints declared the truth confirmed, just as the prophet NEPHI₁ had predicted (cf. 2 Ne. 29:8).

In five important ways, the Book of Mormon seems to some who are not members of the Church to strengthen the authority of Holy Scripture. First in importance is the volume's affirmation that the Christian religion is grounded upon both the Old and New Testaments. The book affirms what recent biblical scholarship is now making plain: the continuity of the theology, ethics, and spirituality that the two Testaments proclaimed. In the Book of Mormon, Jesus is the Lord who gave the law to Moses, and the risen Christ is identical to the prophet Isaiah's Messiah. He delivers exactly the same message of redemption, faith, and a new life of righteousness through the Holy Spirit that the New Testament attributes to him.

Second, the Book of Mormon reinforces the unifying vision of biblical religion, grounding it in the conviction of a common humanity that the stories of creation declared, God's promise to Abraham implied, and Jesus affirmed. Puritan MILLENARIANISM may have inspired an ethnocentric view of Anglo-Saxon destiny, but the image of the future in the Book of Mormon is a wholly opposite one. It envisions a worldwide conversion of believers and their final gathering into the kingdom of God. This begins where John Wesley's "world parish" leaves off.

Third, the biblical bond linking holiness to hope for salvation, both individual and social, also finds confirmation in the Book of Mormon. Certainly, Methodists had no corner on that linkage, for Baptist preachers, Charles G. Finney's Congregationalists, Alexander Campbell's Disciples of Christ, and Unitarians like William E. Channing affirmed it. Ancient Nephites heeded the word of their prophets and looked forward to the second coming of Jesus Christ, the Son of Righteousness. When he appeared to their descendants in the New World, Jesus repeated even more understandably the words of the SERMON ON THE MOUNT that he had proclaimed in the Old.

Fourth, Joseph Smith's translation of an ancient sacred book helped bring to fruition another movement, long growing among Puritans, Pietists, Quakers, and Methodists, to restore to Christian doctrine the idea of the presence of the Holy Spirit in the lives of believers. Charles G. Finney came eventually to believe, for example, that the baptism of the Holy Spirit, or the experience of entire sanctification, would remedy the inadequacies of righteousness and love that he saw in his converts. So, of course, did almost all Methodists. Observers from both inside and outside the restored Church testified that in the early years something akin to modern pentecostal phenomena took place among at least the inner circle of the Saints. By the 1830s, evangelicals in several traditions were greatly expanding their use of the example of the Day of Pentecost to declare that God's power is at work in the world.

Fifth, the Book of Mormon shared in the restoration of some Christian expectations that in the last days biblical prophecies will be literally fulfilled. Those who by faith and baptism become Saints will be included among God's people, chosen in "the eleventh hour." They, too, should gather in ZION, a NEW JERUSALEM for the New World, and a restored Jerusalem in the Old; and Christ will indeed return.

Whatever LDS interpretations of the King James Version of the Holy Scriptures developed later, the mutually supportive role of the Bible and the Book of Mormon was central to the thinking of Joseph Smith, the early missionaries, and their converts.

BIBLIOGRAPHY

Kimball, Heber C. *Journal.* Nauvoo, Ill., 1840.

Smith, Timothy L. "The Book of Mormon in a Biblical Culture." *Journal of Mormon History* 7 (1980):3–21.

TIMOTHY L. SMITH

BOOK OF MORMON CHRONOLOGY

The Book of Mormon contains a chronology that is internally consistent over the thousand-year NEPHITE history, with precise Nephite dates for several events, including the crucifixion of Jesus Christ. However, its chronology has not been unequivocally tied to other calendars because of uncertainties in biblical dates and lack of details about the Nephite calendars. Even less information exists about JAREDITE chronology (Sorenson, 1969).

INTERNAL NEPHITE CHRONOLOGY.   Nephites kept careful track of time from at least three reference points:

1. Years were counted from the time LEHI left Jerusalem (Enos 1:25; Mosiah 6:4); not only was this an important date of origin, but also an angel had said that the Savior would come "in 600 years" from that time (1 Ne. 19:8).

2. Time was also measured from the commencement of the reign of the judges (c. 91 B.C.; cf. 3 Ne. 1:1), which marked a major political reform ending five centuries of Nephite kingship (Jacob 1:9–11; Alma 1:1), during which the years of each king's reign were probably counted according to typical ancient practices (1 Ne. 1:4; Mosiah 29:46).

3. The Nephites later reckoned time from the sign of the birth of Christ (3 Ne. 2:8).

The Book of Mormon links all three systems in several passages that are apparently consistent. Table 1 lists several events using the Nephite systems.

Most of the Nephite record pertains to three historical periods: the time of Lehi and his sons (c. 600–500 B.C.), the events preceding and following the coming of Christ (c. 150 B.C.–A.D. 34), and the destruction of the Nephites (c. A.D. 300–420). Thus, the relatively large book of Alma covers only thirty-nine years, while the much smaller books of Omni and 4 Nephi each cover more than two hundred years.

LDS editions of the Book of Mormon show dates in Nephite years, deduced from the text, at the bottom of the pages. The exact nature of the Nephite year, however, is not described. The Nephite year began with the "first day" of the "first month" (Alma 51:37–52:1; 56:1), and it probably had twelve months because the eleventh month was at "the latter end" of the year (Alma 48:2, 21; 49:1), but the lengths of the months and of the year itself are not mentioned.

Until the coming of Christ, the Nephites observed the LAW OF MOSES (2 Ne. 25:24; Alma 25:15), which generally used lunar months (new moon to new moon). The Savior was crucified on the *fourteenth* day of the first lunar month of the Jewish calendar (John 19:14; Lev. 23:5), but on the *fourth* day of the first Nephite month (3 Ne. 8:5).

TABLE 1 SELECTED EVENTS IN NEPHITE HISTORY

Nephite Years				
Lehi	Judges	Christ	*Event*	*Reference*
1		(−600)	Lehi departs from Jerusalem	1 Ne. 10:4; 19:8
9		(−592)	Lehi's group arrives in Bountiful	1 Ne. 17:4–5
56		(−545)	Jacob receives plates from Nephi	Jacob 1:1
200		(−401)	Law of Moses strictly observed	Jarom 1:5
477		(−124)	King Benjamin's speech	Mosiah 6:3–4
510	1	(−91)	Alma$_1$, Mosiah die; Alma$_2$ first judge	Mosiah 29:44–46
	9	(−83)	Nephihah becomes judge	Alma 4:20–8:2
	15	(−77)	The return of the sons of Mosiah	Alma 17:1–6
	18	(−74)	Korihor refuted	Alma 30
			Alma's mission to the Zoramites	Alma 31:6–35:12
	18	(−74)	War because of Zoramites	Alma 35:13; 43:3–4
			Moroni leads army	Alma 43:17
	37	(−55)	Nephites begin migrating northward	Alma 63:4–6
	42	(−50)	Helaman$_2$ becomes judge; Gadianton	Hel. 2:1–5
	53	(−39)	Helaman$_2$ dies; Nephi$_2$ chief judge	Hel. 3:37
	58	(−34)	Zarahemla captured	Hel. 4:5
	67	(−25)	Most Nephites join Gadianton	Hel. 6:16, 21
	73	(−19)	Nephi invokes a famine	Hel. 11:2–5
	75	(−17)	Gadianton robbers expelled	Hel. 11:6–17
	77	(−15)	Most Nephites reconverted	Hel. 11:21
	80	(−12)	Robbers return	Hel. 11:24–29
	86	(−6)	Samuel the Lamanite prophesies	Hel. 13:1–16:9
601	92	(1)	Sign of the birth of Christ	3 Ne. 1:1, 4, 19
609	100	9	Begin to reckon time from Christ	3 Ne. 2:5–8
		13	Severe war with robbers begins	3 Ne. 2:11–13
		19	Major Nephite victory	3 Ne. 4:5, 11–15
		26	Nephites prosper	3 Ne. 6:1–4
		30	Nephite society disintegrates	3 Ne. 6:14–7:13
		34	Destruction; Christ appears	3 Ne. 8:2–28:12
		36	All converted; property held in common	4 Ne. 1:2–3
		201	Private ownership reinstituted	4 Ne. 1:24–25
		231	Tribalization reemerges	4 Ne. 1:35–38
		245	The wicked outnumber righteous	4 Ne. 1:40
		300	Nephites as wicked as Lamanites	4 Ne. 1:45
		326	Mormon leads army	Morm. 2:2
		350	Treaty with Lamanites and robbers	Morm. 2:28
		362	Mormon refuses to lead Nephites	Morm. 3:8–11
		385	Nephites destroyed; Mormon dies	Morm. 6:5–8:3
		421	Moroni seals up the record	Moro. 10:1–2

NOTE: Years in parentheses are calculated, with the year −600 beginning just over 600 Nephite years before the birth of Christ.

This may imply that Nephite months at that time were not lunar and that their civil calendar may have differed from their religious calendar.

John L. Sorenson (1990) has observed that during the reign of the judges warfare was mostly limited to four consecutive Nephite months. These months can be approximately correlated with our calendar because even today warfare in Mesoamerica (the probable area of BOOK OF MORMON GEOGRAPHY for most of Nephite history) is conducted mostly during the dry season after the fall harvest. This correlation implies that the Nephite year at that time began in December (*see* BOOK OF MORMON, HISTORY OF WARFARE IN). This would mean that because the crucifixion of Christ (presumably in early April) occurred in the first Nephite month, the Nephites probably shifted their calendar to begin the first month in April at the same time they began reckoning time from the birth of Christ. This conclusion is consistent with the Nephite record that Christ was born some time after the end of the Nephite year (3 Ne. 1:1–9).

EXTERNAL CHRONOLOGY.   Evidence supports two possible lengths for Nephite years: 365 days and 360 days. Each can be correlated to external history. The internal chronology is consistent, so that if the exact nature of the Nephite calendar were known, only one reference point in external history would be needed to fix the entire Nephite chronology. However, at least two such dates would be required to determine the length of the Nephite year. Three principal events are common to both Nephite and Old World sources: (1) the first year of the reign of Zedekiah, King of Judah; (2) the birth of Christ; and (3) the death of Christ. Because there are varying degrees of uncertainty about these three reference points, alternative correlation methods have been proposed, each using two of these dates.

First, Orson Pratt proposed that the Nephites used a 365-day year, as had the Egyptians previously and as did the Mesoamericans afterward (*Millennial Star* 28 [Dec. 22, 1866]:810). It has been noted (Lefgren) that such a year agrees, to the very day, with one choice for the birth and death dates of Christ—namely, Thursday, April 6, 1 B.C., and Friday, April 1, A.D. 33, respectively (Gregorian calendar). Both of these dates are supported by other arguments (J. Pratt, 1985 and 1990). This theory assumes that the third system of Nephite reckoning began on the very day of the birth of Christ, which is not explicitly stated in the Book of Mormon but is consistent with Sorenson's conclusions above.

Second, most historians believe that the first year of King Zedekiah began in 598–96 B.C. Lehi left Jerusalem shortly afterward (1 Ne. 1:4; 2:4). The date of the birth of Christ is not known directly from historical sources, but it is believed that King Herod died in 5–4 B.C., implying that Christ was born shortly before (Matt. 2:1). Using these two events as reference points, Huber has proposed a 360-day Nephite year because 600 such years fit the interval from Lehi to Christ (3 Ne. 1:1); such a system has historical precedent, and apparently underlies certain prophecies in which the word "time" may equal 360 days (e.g., Rev. 12:6, 14).

BIBLIOGRAPHY

Brown, S. Kent; C. Wilfred Griggs; and H. Kimball Hansen. "Review of *April Sixth* by John C. Lefgren." *BYU Studies* 22 (Summer 1982):375–83. See rebuttal and response in *BYU Studies* 23 (Spring 1983):252–55.

Huber, Jay H. "Lehi's 600 Year Prophecy and the Birth of Christ." *F.A.R.M.S. Paper.* Provo, Utah, 1982.

Lefgren, John C. *April Sixth.* Salt Lake City, 1980.

Pratt, John P. "The Restoration of Priesthood Keys on Easter 1836. Part 1: Dating the First Easter." *Ensign* 15 (June 1985):59–68.

———. "Yet Another Eclipse for Herod." *The Planetarian* 19 (Dec. 1990):8–14.

Sorenson, John L. "The Years of the Jaredites." *F.A.R.M.S. Paper.* Provo, Utah, 1969.

———. "Seasonality of Warfare in the Book of Mormon and in Mesoamerica." In *Warfare in the Book of Mormon,* ed. S. Ricks and W. Hamblin, pp. 445–77. Salt Lake City, 1990.

JOHN P. PRATT

BOOK OF MORMON COMMENTARIES

Because the Book of Mormon is the best known and most widely circulated LDS book, many commentaries on and reference books about it have been written to assist readers. Inasmuch as its historical timeline spans from c. 2200 B.C. to A.D. 421 and its doctrinal content is extensive, it is difficult for a one-volume work to meet the many needs and interests. The references cited herein contain bibliographies that will provide readers with additional sources.

George Reynolds and Janne M. Sjodahl coauthored a *Commentary on the Book of Mormon* (1955–1961), a seven-volume work (published posthumously to both authors) that has been widely circulated. Hugh Nibley's *Lehi in the Desert and the World of the Jaredites* (1952; rev. 1988) provides insightful historical material on the travels of Lehi's party from Jerusalem, which occurred about c. 600 B.C., through the Arabian Peninsula, to the Western Hemisphere, and also on the journey of the Jaredite colony at about c. 2200 B.C. from the Near East to the Western Hemisphere. Francis W. Kirkham wrote a two-volume work entitled *A New Witness for Christ in America* (rev. ed. 1959–1960) that discusses the coming forth and the translation and printing of the Book of Mormon and non-LDS explanations of the same topics. B. H. Roberts authored a three-volume work titled *New Witnesses for God* (1909). Volumes 2 and 3 addressed four topics: the Book of Mormon as a witness of the Bible; the discovery, translation, and people of the Book of Mormon; evidence of its truth; and Roberts's responses to various objections to the book. Sidney B. Sperry authored *Our Book of Mormon* (1947); *The Book of Mormon Testifies* (1952); and *Book of Mormon Compendium* (1968). Daniel H. Ludlow wrote a popular one-volume work, *A Companion to Your Study of the Book of Mormon* (1976).

The Religious Studies Center at Brigham Young University sponsors an annual symposium on the Book of Mormon. Beginning in 1985, it has published a volume of selected lectures for each symposium. Both doctrinal and historical materials are included. Other volumes are planned as additional symposia are held. A volume entitled *A Book of Mormon Treasury* (1959), taken from the pages of the *Improvement Era*, contains thirty-six articles by General Authorities and other respected students of the Book of Mormon on historical, geographical, and doctrinal matters, as well as biblical relationships. Following a similar format, Kent P. Jackson compiled a two-volume work, *Studies in Scripture, Volume Seven: 1st Nephi to Alma 29* (1987) and *Studies in Scripture, Volume Eight: Alma 30 to Moroni* (1988). Jackson also edited a special Book of Mormon issue of *BYU Studies* 30 (Summer 1990):1–140. Other scholarly materials related to Book of Mormon topics are available through F.A.R.M.S. (Foundation for Ancient Research and Mormon Studies).

Others who have contributed to the literature about the Book of Mormon are Paul R. Cheesman, whose works include *The World of the Book of Mormon* (1984), and Monte S. Nyman, whose publications include *An Ensign to All People: The Sacred Message and Mission of the Book of Mormon* (1987).

Church headquarters publishes materials for use in weekly priesthood quorum meetings, Relief Society meetings, Sunday School classes, and Institute and Seminary classes to assist members in better understanding the Book of Mormon.

Several authors have written on Book of Mormon archaeology and geology. Two popular books with an archaeological approach are Dewey and Edith Farnsworth, *The Americas Before Columbus* (1947), and Milton R. Hunter and Thomas Stuart Ferguson, *Ancient America and the Book of Mormon* (1950). More recent studies on Book of Mormon geography include John L. Sorenson, *An Ancient American Setting for the Book of Mormon* (1985); F. Richard Hauck, *Deciphering the Geography of the Book of Mormon* (1988); and Joseph L. Allen, *Exploring the Lands of the Book of Mormon* (1989). The Nephites, Lamanites, Mulekites, and Jaredites were historical cultures that occupied time and space; however, Church leaders have declared no official position as to where the Book of Mormon civilizations were situated other than that they were in the Western Hemisphere.

[*See also* other Book of Mormon entries.]

H. DONL PETERSON

BOOK OF MORMON ECONOMY AND TECHNOLOGY

The Book of Mormon reports information about three pre-Hispanic American peoples. Although its writers do not offer a detailed picture of the economic and material culture of their societies, numerous incidental details are preserved in the account. In many cases, though not in every instance, archaeology confirms the general details. The problems that remain in matching the Book of Mormon to its presumed ancient setting are no doubt due both to the scant information given in the book itself and to incompleteness in the archaeological record.

Testing what the Book of Mormon says about pre-Columbian

material culture is more difficult than it might at first appear to be. For instance, it is a historically well-established fact that craft techniques can be lost; thus one cannot confidently assume that technologies mentioned for limited Book of Mormon populations survived after the destruction of the Nephites. Nor can one assume what Old World technologies were successfully transferred to the New. Many crafts would not have been known to the small colonist parties, and even among the skills that were transported across the sea, many may not have proved useful or adaptable in the new environment. For that matter, items attested in early portions of the Book of Mormon may not safely be assumed to have survived into subsequent history within the record itself.

The economy of Book of Mormon peoples seems, on the whole, to have been relatively simple. Although many Nephites and Jaredites lived in cities of modest size (a point whose plausibility has been enhanced by recent research), their societies were agriculturally based. Trade was mentioned for some periods, but was constrained by frequent wars. In the infrequently mentioned times of free travel, trade barriers fell, and Lamanites and Nephites predictably prospered (e.g., Hel. 6:7–9).

Despite the economy's agrarian base, wealth was manifested in terms of movable flocks, herds, costly clothing, gold, silver, and "precious things" rather than land (Jacob 2:12–13; Enos 1:21; Jarom 1:8; Mosiah 9:12; Alma 1:6, 29; 17:25; 32:2; Ether 10:12). The ideology of the leading Book of Mormon peoples undoubtedly contributed to this phenomenon: They referred to themselves as a righteous remnant obliged to abandon their comfortable dwellings and depart into the wilderness because of their religious convictions. Since entire populations seem to have moved often, land may not have been a stable source of wealth (2 Ne. 5:5–11; Omni 12–13, 27–30; Mosiah 9; 18:34–35; 22; 24:16–25; Alma 27; 35:6–14; 63:4–10; Hel. 2:11; 3:3–12; 4:5–6, 19; 3 Ne. 3:21–4:1; 7:1–2). Ideally, wealth was to be shared with the poor and for the common good, but strong contrasts between rich and poor are evident more often than not.

Agriculture in the Book of Mormon involved livestock and sown crops. For example, in the fifth century B.C., the Nephites "did till the land, and raise all manner of grain, and of fruit, and flocks of herds, and flocks of all manner of cattle of every kind, and goats, and wild goats, and also many horses" (Enos 1:21). In the second century B.C., the people of Zeniff cultivated corn, wheat, barley, "neas," and "sheum" (Mosiah 9:9; cf. Alma 11:7). Early nineteenth-century American language usage suggests that Book of Mormon "corn" may denote maize or "Indian corn," which was and is a staple in diets in most parts of native America. Some of the other listed items remain less certain. Only in 1982 was evidence published demonstrating the presence of cultivated pre-Columbian barley in the New World (Sorenson, 1985, p. 184). "Neas" is not identifiable; but the word "sheum" appears to be cognate with early Akkadian *she-um,* a grain probably of the barley type (see F.A.R.M.S. Staff, "Weights and Measures").

Book of Mormon mention of horses in pre-Columbian America has drawn much criticism, and no definitive answer to this question is at present available. Linguistic data suggest that Book of Mormon "horse" need not refer to *equus,* but could indicate some other quadruped suitable for human riding, as Mesoamerican art suggests (Sorenson, 1985, p. 295). Moreover, some little-noticed archaeological evidence indicates that in certain areas the American Pleistocene horse could have survived into Book of Mormon times (*Update,* June 1984).

Most transportation was evidently on human backs; in the two contexts that the Book of Mormon mentions "chariots," it appears that their use was quite limited (Alma 18:9–12; 20:6; 3 Ne. 3:22). Chariots are never mentioned in military settings. Wheels are nowhere mentioned in the Book of Mormon (except in a quote from Isaiah). Thus, it is unknown what Nephite "chariots" may have been. "Highways" and "roads" are mentioned as used by the Nephites (3 Ne. 6:8). Some Latter-day Saints consider these to be reflected in the extensively documented road systems of ancient Mexico. "Ships" of unknown form were used during the middle of the first century B.C. for travel on the "west sea" coast (Alma 63:6) and for shipping timber to the north (Hel. 3:10), and at times maritime travel was evidently extensive (Hel. 3:14). Fine pearls are also mentioned as costly items (4 Ne. 1:24).

"Silk and fine-twined linen" are mentioned (e.g., Alma 1:29; Ether 10:24) along with common (cotton?) cloth. The "silk" is unlikely to have been produced from silkworms as in China, but similar fabrics were known, at least in Mesoamerica. For example, in Guatemala fiber from the wild pineapple plant, and among the Aztecs rabbit hair, served to make silklike fabrics. Although flax apparently was not known in America prior to the arrival of the Spaniards (linen was made from flax in the Old World), several vegetable-based fabrics with similar characteristics are well attested in ancient America (*Update*, Nov. 1988).

Care must be exercised when reading the Book of Mormon, or any other text originating in a foreign or ancient culture, to avoid misunderstanding unfamiliar things in light of what is familiar. For instance, the Nephites are said to have used "money," but since the Israelites in Lehi's day lacked minted coinage, Nephite "money" was probably noncoined.

A well-integrated system of dry measures and metal-weight units is outlined in Alma 11; some analysts have pointed out that the system sketched is strikingly simple, efficient, and rational (Smith). In its binary mathematical configuration and its use of barley and silver as basic media of exchange, the Nephite system recalls similar systems known in Egypt and in the Babylonian laws of Eshnunna (F.A.R.M.S. Staff, "Weights and Measures"; *Update*, March 1987).

Making weapons of "steel" and "iron" is mentioned by the Nephites only during their first few generations (2 Ne. 5:15; Jarom 1:8; iron is mentioned only as a "precious" ornamental metal during the time of Mosiah 11:8). Just what these terms originally meant may not be clear. Jaredite "steel" and "iron" and other metals are mentioned twice but are not described (Ether 7:9; 10:23). The weapons of the common soldier were distinctly simpler: stones, clubs, spears, and the bow and arrow (e.g., Alma 49:18–22).

The relative simplicity of Book of Mormon society does not imply lack of sophistication by ancient standards. For example, it would seem that literacy was not uncommon among either Nephites or Jaredites. The founding leaders of the migrations were definitely literate, and the Nephites in their middle era are said to have produced "many books and many records of every kind" (Hel. 3:15). The Lamanites and Mulekites, on the other hand, were less consistent record keepers (Omni 1:17–18; Mosiah 24:4–6; Hel. 3:15). The Jaredites and Nephites kept their most sacred records on almost imperishable metal PLATES, although some of their books were on flammable material (Alma 14:8). The plates that Joseph Smith had in his possession, and that he and other contemporary eyewitnesses described, seem well within the skill of pre-Hispanic metallurgists (Putnam; Sorenson, 1985, pp. 278–88), and the manner of their burial has rich precedent in the Eastern Hemisphere (Wright).

BIBLIOGRAPHY

Cheesman, Paul R. *Ancient Writing on Metal Plates.* Bountiful, Utah, 1985.

F.A.R.M.S. *Updates* (Provo, Utah), contain useful discussions, including bibliographies, of pre-Columbian horses (June 1984), metallurgy of golden plates (Oct. 1984), pre-Hispanic domesticated barley (Dec. 1984), the loss of technologies (July 1985), the legal implementation of the Nephite system of weights and measures (Mar. 1987), and possible silks and linens (Nov. 1988).

F.A.R.M.S. Staff. "Weights and Measures in the Time of Mosiah II." Provo, Utah, 1983.

Nibley, Hugh. *The Prophetic Book of Mormon,* in *CWHN* 8:245–46, 385–86, and *Since Cumorah,* in *CWHN* 7:220–27. Discusses metallic plates, steel, cement, money, and fauna.

Putnam, Reed. "Were the Golden Plates Made of Tumbaga?" *IE* (Sept. 1966):788–89, 828–31.

Smith, R. P. "The Nephite Monetary System." *IE* 57 (May 1954):316–17.

Sorenson, John L. "A Reconsideration of Early Metal in Mesoamerica." *Katunob* 9 (Mar. 1976):1–18.

———. *An Ancient American Setting for the Book of Mormon.* Salt Lake City, 1985.

Wright, H. Curtis. "Ancient Burials of Metallic Foundation Documents in Stone Boxes." In *Occasional Papers, University of Illinois Graduate School of Library and Information Science* 157 (1982):1–42.

DANIEL C. PETERSON

BOOK OF MORMON EDITIONS (1830–1981)

Two major goals of each published edition of the Book of Mormon have been (1) to faithfully reproduce the text; and (2) to make the text accessible to the reader. The goal of textual accuracy has led later editors to earlier editions and, when available, to the original and printer's manuscripts (*see* BOOK OF MORMON MANUSCRIPTS). The goal of accessibility has led to some modernization and standardization of the text itself and the addition of reader's helps (introductory material, versification, footnotes, chapter summaries, dates, pronunciation guides, and indexes).

Four editions were published during Joseph Smith's lifetime:

1. 1830: 5,000 copies; published by E. B. Grandin in Palmyra, New York. In general, the first edition is a faithful copy of the printer's

manuscript (although on one occasion the original manuscript rather than the printer's was used for typesetting). For the most part, this edition reproduces what the compositor, John H. Gilbert, considered grammatical "errors." Gilbert added punctuation and determined the paragraphing for the first edition. In the Preface, Joseph Smith explains the loss of the Book of Lehi—116 pages of manuscript (*see* MANUSCRIPT, LOST 116 PAGES). The testimonies of the Three and the Eight Witnesses were placed at the end of the book. In this and all other early editions, there is no versification.

2. 1837: Either 3,000 or 5,000 copies; published by Parley P. Pratt and John Goodson, Kirtland, Ohio. For this edition, hundreds of grammatical changes and a few emendations were made in the text. The 1830 edition and the printer's manuscript were used as the basis for this edition.

3. 1840: 2,000 copies; published for Ebenezer Robinson and Don Carlos Smith (by Shepard and Stearns, Cincinnati, Ohio), Nauvoo, Illinois. Joseph Smith compared the printed text with the original manuscript and discovered a number of errors made in copying the printer's manuscript from the original. Thus the 1840 edition restores some of the readings of the original manuscript.

4. 1841: 4,050 copies (5,000 contracted); published for Brigham Young, Heber C. Kimball, and Parley P. Pratt (by J. Tompkins, Liverpool, England). This first European edition was printed with the permission of Joseph Smith; it is essentially a reprinting of the 1837 edition with British spellings.

Two additional British editions, one in 1849 (edited by Orson Pratt) and the other in 1852 (edited by Franklin D. Richards), show minor editing of the text. In the 1852 edition, Richards added numbers to the paragraphs to aid in finding passages, thereby creating the first—although primitive—versification for the Book of Mormon.

Three other important LDS editions have involved major changes in format as well as minor editing:

1. 1879: Edited by Orson Pratt. Major changes in the format of the text included division of the long chapters in the original text, a true versification system (which has been followed in all subsequent LDS editions), and footnotes (mostly scriptural references).

2. 1920: Edited by James E. Talmage. Further changes in format included introductory material, double columns, chapter summaries, and new footnotes. Some of the minor editing found in this edition appeared earlier in the 1905 and 1911 editions, also under the editorship of Talmage.

3. 1981: Edited by a committee headed by members of the Quorum of the Twelve. This edition is a major reworking of the 1920 edition: The text appears again in double columns, but new introductory material, chapter summaries, and footnotes are provided. About twenty significant textual errors that had entered the printer's manuscript are corrected by reference to the original manuscript. Other corrections were made from comparison with the printer's manuscript and the 1840 Nauvoo edition.

The Reorganized Church of Jesus Christ of Latter Day Saints (RLDS) also has its own textual tradition. Prior to 1874, the RLDS used an edition of the Book of Mormon published by James O. Wright (1858, New York), basically a reprinting of the 1840 Nauvoo edition. The first and second RLDS editions (1874, Plano, Illinois; and 1892, Lamoni, Iowa) followed the 1840 text and had their own system of versification. Unlike the later LDS editions, all RLDS editions have retained the original longer chapters.

In 1903 the RLDS obtained the printer's manuscript and used it to produce their third edition (1908, Lamoni, Iowa). The text of the 1908 edition restored many of the readings found in that manuscript, but generally did not alter the grammatical changes made in the 1837 Kirtland edition. This edition also included a new versification, which has remained unchanged in all subsequent RLDS editions. In 1966 the RLDS published a thoroughly modernized Book of Mormon text. Both the 1908 (with minor editing) and the 1966 texts are available, but only the 1908 edition is authorized for use in the RLDS Church.

A critical text of the Book of Mormon was published in 1984–1987 by the Foundation for Ancient Research and Mormon Studies. This is the first published text of the Book of Mormon to show the precise history of many textual variants. Although this textual study of the editions and manuscripts of the Book of Mormon is incomplete and preliminary, it is helpful for a general overview of the textual history of the Book of Mormon.

BIBLIOGRAPHY

Anderson, Richard L. "Gold Plates and Printer's Ink." *Ensign*, 6 (Sept. 1976):71–76.

Heater, Shirley R. "Gold Plates, Foolscap, & Printer's Ink; Part II: Editions of the Book of Mormon." *Zarahemla Record* 37–38 (1987):2–15.

Larson, Stanley R. "A Study of Some Textual Variations in the Book of Mormon Comparing the Original and the Printer's Manuscripts and the 1830, the 1837, and the 1840 Editions." Master's thesis, Brigham Young University, 1974.

Matthews, Robert J. "The New Publication of the Standard Works 1979, 1981." *BYU Studies* 22 (1982):387–424.

Skousen, Royal. "Towards a Critical Edition of the Book of Mormon." *BYU Studies* 30 (1990):41–69.

Stocks, Hugh G. "The Book of Mormon, 1830–1879: A Publishing History." Master's thesis, UCLA, 1979.

———. "The Book of Mormon in English, 1870–1920: A Publishing History and Analytical Bibliography." Ph.D. diss., UCLA, 1986.

ROYAL SKOUSEN

BOOK OF MORMON GEOGRAPHY

Although the Book of Mormon is primarily a religious record of the NEPHITES, LAMANITES, and JAREDITES, enough geographic details are embedded in the narrative to allow reconstruction of at least a rudimentary geography of Book of Mormon lands. In the technical usage of the term "geography" (e.g., physical, economic, cultural, or political), no Book of Mormon geography has yet been written. Most Latter-day Saints who write geographies have in mind one or both of two activities: first, internal reconstruction of the relative size and configuration of Book of Mormon lands based upon textual statements and allusions; second, speculative attempts to match an internal geography to a location within North or South America. Three questions relating to Book of Mormon geography are discussed here: (1) How can one reconstruct a Book of Mormon geography? (2) What does a Book of Mormon geography look like? (3) What hypothetical locations have been suggested for Book of Mormon lands?

RECONSTRUCTING INTERNAL BOOK OF MORMON GEOGRAPHY. Although Church leadership officially and consistently distances itself from issues regarding Book of Mormon geography in order to focus attention on the spiritual message of the book, private speculation and scholarship in this area have been abundant. Using textual clues, laymen and scholars have formulated over sixty possible geographies. Dissimilarities among them stem from differences in (1) the interpretation of scriptural passages and statements of General Authorities; (2) procedures for reconciling scriptural information; (3) initial assumptions concerning the text and traditional LDS identification of certain features mentioned (especially the hill CUMORAH and the "narrow neck of land," which figure prominently in the text); and (4) personal penchants and disciplinary training.

Those who believe that reconstructing a Book of Mormon geography is possible must first deal with the usual problems of interpreting historical texts. Different weights must be given to various passages, depending upon the amount and precision of the information conveyed. Many Book of Mormon cities cannot be situated because of insufficient textual information; this is especially true for Lamanite and Jaredite cities. The Book of Mormon is essentially a Nephite record, and most geographic elements mentioned are in Nephite territory.

From textual evidence, one can approximate some spatial relationships of various natural features and cities. Distances in the Book of Mormon are recorded in terms of the time required to travel from place to place. The best information for reconstructing internal geography comes from the accounts of wars between Nephites and Lamanites during the first century B.C., with more limited information from Nephite missionary journeys. Travel distance can be standardized to a degree by controlling, where possible, for the nature of the terrain (e.g., mountains versus plains) and the relative velocity (e.g., an army's march versus travel with children or animals). The elementary internal geography presented below is based on an interpretation of distances thus standardized and directions based on the text.

AN INTERNAL BOOK OF MORMON GEOGRAPHY. Numerous attempts have been made to diagram physical and political geographies depicting features mentioned in the text, but this requires many additional assumptions and is difficult to accomplish without making approximate relationships appear precise (Sorenson, 1991). The description presented below of the size and configuration of Book of Mormon lands and the locations of settlements within it summarizes the least ambiguous evidence.

Book of Mormon lands were longer from north to south than from east to west. They consisted of two land masses connected by an isthmus ("a narrow neck of land") flanked by an "east sea" and a "west sea" (Alma 22:27, 32). The land north of the narrow neck was known as the "land northward" and that to the south as the "land southward" (Alma 22:32). The Jaredite narrative took place entirely in the land northward (Omni 1:22; Ether 10:21), but details are insufficient to place their cities relative to one another. Most of the Nephite narrative, on the other hand, took place in the land southward. Travel accounts for the land southward indicate that the Nephites and Lamanites occupied an area that could be traversed north to south by normal travel in perhaps thirty days.

The land southward was divided by a "narrow strip of wilderness" that ran from the "sea east" to the "sea west" (Alma 22:27). Nephites occupied the land to the north of this wilderness, and the Lamanites, that to the south. Sidon, the only river mentioned by name, ran northward between eastern and western wildernesses from headwaters in the narrow strip of wilderness (Alma 22:29). The Sidon probably emptied into the east sea—based on the description of the east wilderness as a rather wide, coastal zone—but its mouth is nowhere specified.

The relative locations of some important Nephite cities can be inferred from the text. Zarahemla was the Nephite capital in the first century B.C. That portion of the land southward occupied by the Nephites was known as the "land of Zarahemla" (Hel. 1:18). The city of Nephi, the original Nephite colony, by this time had been occupied by Lamanites and served at times as one of their capitals for the land south of the narrow wilderness divide (Alma 47:20). Based upon the migration account of Alma$_1$, the distance between the cities of Zarahemla and Nephi can be estimated to be about twenty-two days' travel by a company that includes children and flocks, mostly through mountainous terrain (cf. Mosiah 23:3; 24:20, 25).

The distance from Zarahemla to the narrow neck was probably less than that between Zarahemla and Nephi. The principal settlement near the narrow neck was the city of Bountiful, located near the east sea (Alma 52:17–23). This lowland city was of key military importance in controlling access to the land northward from the east-sea side.

The relative location of the hill Cumorah is most tenuous, since travel time from Bountiful, or the narrow neck, to Cumorah is nowhere specified. Cumorah was near the east sea in the land northward, and the limited evidence suggests that it was probably not many days' travel from the narrow neck of land (Mosiah 8:8; Ether 9:3). It is also probable that the portion of the land northward occupied by the Jaredites was smaller than the Nephite-Lamanite land southward.

Book of Mormon lands encompassed mountainous wildernesses, coastal plains, valleys, a large river, a highland lake, and lowland wetlands. The land also apparently experienced occasional volcanic eruptions and earthquakes (3 Ne. 8:5–18). Culturally, the Book of Mormon describes an urbanized, agrarian people having metallurgy (Hel. 6:11), writing (1 Ne. 1:1–3), lunar and solar calendars (2 Ne. 5:28; Omni 1:21), domestic animals (2 Ne. 5:11), various grains (1 Ne. 8:1), gold, silver, pearls, and "costly apparel" (Alma 1:29; 4 Ne. 1:24). Based upon these criteria, many scholars currently see northern Central America and southern Mexico (Mesoamerica) as the most likely location of Book of Mormon lands. However, such views are private and do not represent an official position of the Church.

HYPOTHESIZED LOCATIONS OF BOOK OF MORMON LANDS.   Two issues merit consideration in relation to possible external correlations of Book of Mormon geography. What is the official position of the Church, and what are the pervading opinions of its members?

In early Church history, the most common opinion among members and Church leaders was that Book of Mormon lands encompassed all of North and South America, although at least one more limited alternative view was also held for a time by some. The official position of the Church is that the events narrated in the Book of Mormon occurred somewhere in the Americas, but that the specific location has not been revealed. This position applies both to internal geographies and to external correlations. No internal geography has yet been proposed or approved by the Church, and none of the internal or external geographies proposed by individual members (including that proposed above) has received approval. Efforts in that direction by members are neither encouraged nor discouraged. In the words of John A. Widtsoe, an apostle, "All such studies are legitimate, but the conclusions drawn from them, though they may be correct, must at the best be held as intelligent conjectures" (Vol. 3, p. 93).

Three statements sometimes attributed to the Prophet Joseph Smith are often cited as evidence of an official Church position. An 1836 statement asserts that "Lehi and his company . . . landed on the continent of South America, in Chili [sic], thirty degrees, south latitude" (Richards, Little, p. 272). This view was accepted by Orson Pratt and printed in the footnotes to the 1879 edition of the Book of Mormon, but insufficient evidence exists to clearly attribute it to Joseph Smith ("Did Lehi Land in Chili [sic]?"; cf. Roberts, Vol. 3, pp. 501–503, and Widtsoe, Vol. 3, pp. 93–98).

In 1842 an editorial in the Church newspaper claimed that "Lehi . . . landed a little south of the Isthmus of Darien [Panama]" (*T&S* 3 [Sept. 15, 1842]:921–22). This would move the location of Lehi's landing some 3,000 miles north of the proposed site in Chile. Although Joseph Smith had assumed editorial responsibility for the paper by this time, it is not known whether this statement originated with him or even represented his views. Two weeks later, another editorial appeared in the *Times and Seasons* that, in effect, constituted a book review of *Incidents of Travel in Central America, Chiapas and Yucatan,* by John Lloyd Stephens. This was the first accessible book in English containing detailed descriptions and drawings of ancient Mayan ruins. Excerpts from it were included in the *Times and Seasons,* along with the comment that "it will not be a bad plan to compare Mr. Stephens' ruined cities with those in the Book of Mormon: light cleaves to light, and facts are supported by facts. The truth injures no one" (*T&S* 3 [Oct. 1, 1842]:927).

In statements since then, Church leaders have generally declined to give any opinion on issues of Book of Mormon geography. When asked to review a map showing the supposed landing place of Lehi's company, President Joseph F. Smith declared that the "Lord had not yet revealed it" (Cannon, p. 160 n.). In 1929, Anthony W. Ivins, counselor in the First Presidency, added, "There has never been anything yet set forth that definitely settles that question [of Book of Mormon geography]. . . . We are just waiting until we discover the truth" (*CR,* Apr. 1929, p. 16). While the Church has not taken an official position with regard to location of geographical places, the authorities do not discourage private efforts to deal with the subject (Cannon).

The unidentified *Times and Seasons* editorialist seems to have favored modern Central America as the setting for Book of Mormon events. As noted, recent geographies by some Church members promote this identification, but others consider upstate New York or South America the correct setting. Considerable diversity of opinion remains among Church members regarding Book of Mormon geography; however, most students of the problem agree that the hundreds of geographical references in the Book of Mormon are remarkably consistent—even if the students cannot always agree upon precise locations.

Of the numerous proposed external Book of Mormon geographies, none has been positively and unambiguously confirmed by archaeology. More fundamentally, there is no agreement on whether such positive identification could be made or, if so, what form a "proof" would take; nor is it clear what would constitute "falsification" or "disproof" of various proposed geographies. Until these methodological issues have been resolved, all internal and external geographies—including supposed archaeological tests of them—should, at best, be considered only intelligent conjectures.

BIBLIOGRAPHY

Allen, Joseph L. *Exploring the Lands of the Book of Mormon.* Orem, Utah, 1989.

Cannon, George Q. "Book of Mormon Geography." *Juvenile Instructor* 25 (Jan. 1, 1890):18–19; repr., *Instructor* 73 (Apr. 1938):159–60.

Clark, John E. "A Key for Evaluating Nephite Geographies." *Review of Books on the Book of Mormon* 1 (1989):20–70.

Hauck, F. Richard. *Deciphering the Geography of the Book of Mormon.* Salt Lake City, 1988.

Palmer, David A. *In Search of Cumorah: New Evidences for the Book of Mormon from Ancient Mexico.* Bountiful, Utah, 1981.

Richards, F., and J. Little, eds. *Compendium of the Doctrines of the Gospel,* rev. ed. Salt Lake City, 1925.

Roberts, B. H. *New Witnesses for God,* 3 vols. Salt Lake City, 1909.

Sorenson, John L. *An Ancient American Setting for the Book of Mormon.* Salt Lake City, 1985.

———. *A Hundred and Fifty Years of Book of Mormon Geographies: A History of the Ideas.* Salt Lake City, 1991.

Warren, Bruce W., and Thomas Stuart Ferguson. *The Messiah in Ancient America.* Provo, Utah, 1987.

Washburn, J. Nile. *Book of Mormon Lands and Times.* Salt Lake City, 1974.

Widtsoe, John A. *Evidences and Reconciliations,* 3 vols. Salt Lake City, 1951.

JOHN E. CLARK

BOOK OF MORMON LANGUAGE

The language of the Book of Mormon exhibits features typical of a translation from an ancient Near Eastern text as well as the stamp of nineteenth-century English and the style of the King James Version (KJV) of the Bible. That the language of the Book of Mormon should resemble that of the KJV seems only natural, since in the time of the Prophet Joseph Smith, the KJV was the most widely read book in America and formed the standard of religious language for most English-speaking people (see *CWHN* 8:212–18). Furthermore, the Book of Mormon shares certain affinities with the KJV: both include works of ancient PROPHETS of ISRAEL as well as accounts of part of the ministry of Jesus Christ, both are translations into English, and both are to become "one" in God's hand as collections of his word to his children (Ezek. 37:16–17; 1 Ne. 13:41; D&C 42:12).

LANGUAGES USED BY THE NEPHITES. Statements in the Book of Mormon have spawned differing views about the language in which the book was originally written. In approximately 600 B.C., NEPHI₁— the first Book of Mormon author and one who had spent his youth in JERUSALEM—wrote, "I make a record [the small plates of Nephi] in the language of my father, which consists of the learning of the Jews and the language of the Egyptians" (1 Ne. 1:2). One thousand years later, MORONI₂, the last Nephite prophet, noted concerning the PLATES of Mormon that "we have written this record . . . in the characters which are called among us the reformed Egyptian, being handed down and altered by us, according to our manner of speech. And if our plates [metal leaves] had been sufficiently large we should have written in Hebrew; but the Hebrew hath been altered by us also. . . . But the Lord knoweth . . . that none other people knoweth our language" (Morm. 9:32–34). In light of these two passages, it is evident that Nephite record keepers knew Hebrew and something of Egyptian. It is unknown whether Nephi, Mormon, or Moroni wrote Hebrew in modified Egyptian characters or inscribed their plates in both the Egyptian language and Egyptian characters or whether Nephi wrote in one language and Mormon and Moroni, who lived some nine hundred years later, in another. The mention of "characters" called "reformed Egyptian" tends to support the hypothesis of Hebrew in Egyptian script. Although Nephi's observation (1 Ne. 1:2) is troublesome for that view, the statement is ambiguous and inconclusive for both views.

Nephite authors seem to have patterned their writing after the plates of brass, a record containing biblical texts composed before 600 B.C. that was in the possession of descendants of JOSEPH OF EGYPT (1 Ne. 5:11–16). At least portions of this record were written in Egyptian, since knowledge of "the language of the Egyptians" enabled LEHI, father of Nephi, to "read these engravings" (Mosiah 1:2–4). But whether it was the Egyptian language or Hebrew written in Egyptian script is again not clear. Egyptian was widely used in Lehi's day, but because poetic writings are skewed in translation, because prophetic writings were generally esteemed as sacred, and because Hebrew was the language of the Israelites in the seventh century B.C., it would have been unusual for the writings of Isaiah and Jeremiah—substantially preserved on the brass plates (1 Ne. 5:13; 19:23)—to have been translated from Hebrew into a foreign tongue at this early date. Thus, Hebrew portions written in Hebrew script, Egyptian portions in Egyptian script, and Hebrew portions in Egyptian script are all possibilities. If the brass plates came into being while the Israelites were still in Egypt, then earlier portions (e.g., prophecies of Joseph in Egypt) were possibly written in Egyptian and later portions (e.g., words of Jeremiah) in Hebrew.

Concerning Book of Mormon composition, Mormon 9:33 indicates that limited space on the GOLD PLATES dictated using Egyptian characters rather than Hebrew. In Lehi's day, both Hebrew and Egyptian were written with consonants only. Unlike Hebrew, Egyptian had biconsonantal and even triconsonantal signs. Employing such characters—particularly in modified form—would save space.

Written characters were handed down and altered according to Nephite speech (Morm. 9:32). This observation suggests that at least later generations of Nephites used Egyptian characters to write their contemporary spoken language, an altered form of Hebrew. It is extremely unlikely that a people isolated from simultaneous contact with the two languages could have maintained a conversational distinction between, and fluency in the two languages over a thousand-year period. Thus, if Egyptian characters were altered as the living language changed, then the Nephites were probably using such characters to write their spoken language, which was largely Hebrew.

Though some of Lehi's group that left Jerusalem may have spoken Egyptian, a reading knowledge of the script on the brass plates would have allowed them to "read these engravings" (Mosiah 1:4). But the possibility that Lehi's colony could maintain spoken Egyptian as a second language through a thousand years without merging it with Hebrew or losing it is beyond probability. Therefore, the fact that the Nephites had "altered" the Egyptian characters according to their "manner of speech" underscores the probability that they were writing Hebrew with Egyptian characters. In addition, Moroni's language (c. A.D. 400) was probably different enough from that of Lehi (c. 600 B.C.) that reading Lehi's language may have required as much study in Moroni's day as Old English requires of modern English-speaking people.

LANGUAGE AMONG NATIVE AMERICANS.   Because Moroni's time represents a near midpoint between Lehi and the present, a consideration of the near end of the continuum could be helpful. The vague picture presented by statements in the text might be brought into focus by examining American Indian languages. The time depth from Latin to modern Romance languages is only slightly less than that from Lehi to the present. Similarities among Romance languages are plentiful and obvious, while language similarities between Native American languages and Hebrew or Egyptian are generally viewed as neither plentiful nor obvious. Though some professionals have alluded to similarities, no study has yet convinced scholars of Near Eastern links with any pre-Columbian American language.

One study, however, holds promise for demonstrating links to the Uto-Aztecan language family (Stubbs, 1988). Though other language groups offer suggestive leads, Uto-Aztecan yields more than seven hundred similarities to Hebrew, in phonological, morphological, and semantic patterns consistent with modern linguistic methods. While a handful of Egyptian words are identifiable, they are minimal compared to their Hebrew correspondents.

HEBRAISMS IN THE BOOK OF MORMON.   Many typical Hebrew language patterns have been identified in the Book of Mormon, though several are also characteristic of other Near Eastern languages. For example, the cognate accusative, literarily redundant in English, is used in Hebrew for emphasis: "They feared a fear" (Ps. 14:5, Hebrew text). Similar structures appear in the Book of Mormon: "to fear exceedingly, with fear" (Alma 18:5), another possible translation of the same cognate accusative (cf. 1 Ne. 3:2; 8:2; Enos 1:13).

Hebrew employs prepositional phrases as adverbs more often than individual adverbs, a feature typical of Book of Mormon language: "in haste" (3 Ne. 21:29) instead of "hastily" and "with gladness" (2 Ne. 28:28) instead of "gladly."

Tvedtnes has noted a possible example of Hebrew agreement: "This people *is* a free people" (Alma 30:24; emphasis added). In English, "people" is usually considered grammatically plural, but in Hebrew it is often singular. While this phrase in Alma may have been verbless, it may also have contained the third-person singular pronoun /hu/ placed between the two noun phrases or at the end as an anaphoric demonstrative functioning as a copula verb. Uto-Aztecan Indian languages also have the word /hu/, which is a third-person singular pronoun in some languages but a "be" verb in others.

Possession in English is shown in two constructs—"the man's house" and "the house of the man"—but only the latter construct is employed in Hebrew. The lack of apostrophe possession in the Book of Mormon is consistent with a translation from the Hebrew construct. Further, the "of" construct is common for adjectival relationships in Hebrew. Correspondingly, the Book of Mormon consistently employs phrases such as "plates of brass" (1 Ne. 3:12) instead of "brass plates" and "walls of stone" (Alma 48:8) rather than "stone walls."

Sentence structures and clause-combining mechanisms in Hebrew differ from those in English. Long strings of subordinate clauses and verbal expressions, such as those in Helaman 1:16–17 and Mosiah 2:20–21 and 7:21–22, are acceptable in Hebrew, though unorthodox and discouraged in English: "Ye all are witnesses . . . that Zeniff, who was made king, . . . he being over-zealous, . . . therefore being deceived by . . . king Laman, who having entered into a treaty, . . . and having yielded up [various cities], . . . and the land round about—and all this he did, for the sole purpose of bringing this people . . . into bondage" (Mosiah 7:21–22).

Frequent phrases such as "from before" and "by the hand of" represent rather literal translations from Hebrew. For example, "he fled from before them" (Mosiah 17:4), instead of the more typically English "he fled from them," portrays the common Hebrew compound preposition /millifne/.

While many words and names found in the Book of Mormon have exact equivalents in the Hebrew Bible, certain others exhibit Semitic characteristics, though their spelling does not always match known Hebrew forms. For example, "Rabbanah" as "great king" (Alma 18:13) may have affinities with the Hebrew root /rbb/, meaning "to be great or many." "Rameumptom" (Alma 31:21), meaning "holy stand," contains consonantal patterns suggesting the stems /rmm/ramah/, "to be high," and /tmm/tam/tom/, "to be complete, perfect, holy." The /p/ between the /m/ and /t/ is a linguistically natural outgrowth of a bilabial /m/ in cluster with a stop /t/, such as the /p/ in /assumption/ from /assume + tion/, and the /b/ in Spanish /hombre/ from Latin /homere/.

Claims that Joseph Smith composed the Book of Mormon by merely imitating King James English, using biblical names and inventing others, typically exhibit insensitivities about its linguistic character. Names such as "Alma" have been thought peculiar inventions. However, the discovery of the name "Alma" in a Jewish text (second century A.D.), the seven hundred observed similarities between Hebrew and Uto-Aztecan, literary patterns such as chiasmus, and numerous other features noted in studies since 1830 combine to make the fabrication of the book an overwhelming challenge for anyone in Joseph Smith's day.

[*See also* Book of Mormon Authorship; Book of Mormon as Literature; Book of Mormon Names; Book of Mormon, Near Eastern Background; Book of Mormon Translation by Joseph Smith.]

BIBLIOGRAPHY

Hoskisson, Paul Y. "Ancient Near Eastern Background of the Book of Mormon." *F.A.R.M.S. Reprint.* Provo, Utah, 1982.

Nibley, Hugh. *Lehi in the Desert and the World of the Jaredites. CWHN* 5.

———. *An Approach to the Book of Mormon. CWHN* 6.

Sperry, Sidney B. "The Book of Mormon as Translation English." *IE* 38 (Mar. 1935):141, 187–88.

———. "Hebrew Idioms in the Book of Mormon." *IE* 57 (Oct. 1954):703, 728–29.

———. *Book of Mormon Compendium.* Salt Lake City, 1968.

Stubbs, Brian D. "A Creolized Base in Uto-Aztecan." *F.A.R.M.S. Paper.* Provo, Utah, 1988.

Tvedtnes, John A. "Hebraisms in the Book of Mormon: A Preliminary Survey." *BYU Studies* 11 (Autumn 1970):50–60.

BRIAN D. STUBBS

BOOK OF MORMON MANUSCRIPTS

The printed versions of the Book of Mormon derive from two manuscripts. The first, called the original manuscript (O), was written by at least three scribes as Joseph Smith translated and dictated. The most important scribe was Oliver Cowdery. This manuscript was begun no later than April 1829 and finished in June 1829.

A copy of the original was then made by Oliver Cowdery and two other scribes. This copy is called the printer's manuscript (P), since it was the one normally used to set the type for the first (1830) edition of the Book of Mormon. It was begun in July 1829 and finished early in 1830.

The printer's manuscript is not an exact copy of the original manuscript. There are on the average three changes per original manuscript page. These changes appear to be natural scribal errors; there is little or no evidence of conscious editing. Most of the changes are minor, and about one in five produce a discernible difference in meaning. Because they were all relatively minor, most of the errors thus introduced into the text have remained in the printed editions of the Book of Mormon and have not been detected and corrected except by reference to the original manuscript. About twenty of these errors were corrected in the 1981 edition.

The compositor for the 1830 edition added punctuation, paragraphing, and other printing marks to about one-third of the pages of the printer's manuscript. These same marks appear on one fragment of the original, indicating that it was used at least once in typesetting the 1830 edition.

In preparation for the second (1837) edition, hundreds of grammatical changes and a few textual emendations were made in P. After the publication of this edition, P was retained by Oliver Cowdery. After his death in 1850, his brother-in-law, David Whitmer, kept P until his death in 1888. In 1903 Whitmer's grandson sold P to the Reorganized Church of Jesus Christ of Latter Day Saints, which owns it today. It is wholly extant except for two lines at the bottom of the first leaf.

The original manuscript was not consulted for the editing of the 1837 edition. However, in producing the 1840 edition, Joseph Smith used O to restore some of its original readings. In October 1841,

Joseph Smith placed O in the cornerstone of the Nauvoo House. Over forty years later, Lewis Bidamon, Emma Smith's second husband, opened the cornerstone and found that water seepage had destroyed most of O. The surviving pages were handed out to various individuals during the 1880s.

Today approximately 25 percent of the text of O survives: 1 Nephi 2 through 2 Nephi 1, with gaps; Alma 22 through Helaman 3, with gaps; and a few other fragments. All but one of the authentic pages and fragments of O are housed in the archives of the LDS Historical Department; one-half of a sheet (from 1 Nephi 14) is owned by the University of Utah.

BIBLIOGRAPHY

Heater, Shirley R. "Gold Plates, Foolscap, & Printer's Ink, Part I: Manuscripts of the Book of Mormon." *Zarahemla Record* 35–36 (1987):3–15.

Jessee, Dean C. "The Original Book of Mormon Manuscript." *BYU Studies* 10 (1970):259–78.

ROYAL SKOUSEN

BOOK OF MORMON NAMES

The Book of Mormon contains 337 proper names and 21 gentilics (or analogous forms) based on proper names. Included in this count are names that normally would not be called proper, such as kinds of animals, if they appear as transliterations in the English text and not as translations. Conversely, proper names that appear only in translation are not included, such as Bountiful and Desolation. Of these 337 proper names, 188 are unique to the Book of Mormon, while 149 are common to the Book of Mormon and the Bible. If the textual passages common to the Book of Mormon and the Bible are excluded, 53 names occur in both books.

It would seem convenient to divide the Book of Mormon collection or listing of names (onomasticon) into three groups because it mentions (1) JAREDITES, (2) the community founded by LEHI (which might be termed "Lehites"), and (3) the people referred to as the people of Zarahemla (who might be called "Mulekites"), each of which contributed to the history of the Book of Mormon and therefore to the list of proper names (*see* BOOK OF MORMON PEOPLES). While this grouping can be made with some degree of accuracy for Jaredite names, it is not easy to maintain the distinction between Lehite and Mulekite, because a portion of the Lehites united with the Mulekites sometime before 130 B.C.; practically nothing is known about Mulekite names before that time. For the present, Lehite and Mulekite names must be treated together. Given this grouping of the Book of Mormon onomasticon, 142 of the 188 unique Book of Mormon names are Lehite-Mulekite, 41 are Jaredite, and 5 are common to both groups.

Much preliminary work remains to be done on the Book of Mormon onomasticon. The transliteration system of the English text must be clarified: does the *j* of the text indicate only the Nephite phoneme /y/ or can it also represent /h/ in the name "Job," as it does once in the King James Version? A reliable critical analysis of the text is needed: what is the range of possible spellings of Cumorah that might indicate phonemic values? Linguistic phenomena beg explanation: there are no exclusively Book of Mormon names that begin with /b/; but several begin with /p/. *Q* and *x* do not occur in any Book of Mormon name. *V*, *w*, and *y* do not occur in any exclusively Book of Mormon name. *D*, *f*, and *u* do not begin any exclusively Book of Mormon name.

The Lehite-Mulekite names often show greatest affinity with Semitic languages (*CWHN* 6:281–94). For instance, *Abish* and *Abinadi* resemble *ab*, father, names in Hebrew; *Alma* appears in a Bar Kokhba letter (c. A.D. 130) found in the Judean desert; *Mulek* could be a diminutive of West Semitic *mlk*, king; *Omni* and *Limhi* appear to have the same morphology as Old Testament *Omri* and *Zimri*; *Jershon* is remarkably close to a noun form of the Hebrew root *yrš* (see below). Some Lehite-Mulekite names more closely resemble Egyptian: Ammon, Korihor, Pahoran, and Paanchi (*CWHN* 5:25–34). Jaredite names exhibit no consistently obvious linguistic affinity.

Like proper names in most languages, the proper names of the Book of Mormon probably had semantic meanings for Book of Mormon peoples. Such meanings are evident from several instances wherein the Book of Mormon provides a translation for a proper name. For example, *Irreantum* means "many waters" (1 Ne. 17:5), and *Rabbanah* is interpreted as "powerful or great king" (Alma 18:13). The single greatest impediment to understanding the semantic possibilities for the Book of Mormon proper names remains the lack of the original Nephite text. The transliterations of the English text allow only educated conjectures and approximations about the nature of the names and their possible semantic range. In addition, such postulations, if to be of any value, must be based on a knowledge of the possible linguistic origins of the names, such as Iron Age Hebrew and Egyptian for Lehite and Mulekite names.

The proper names of the Book of Mormon can provide information about the text and the language(s) used to compose it. When studied with apposite methodology, these names testify to the ancient origin of the Book of Mormon. For example, Jershon is the toponym for a land given by the Nephites to a group of Lamanites as an inheritance; based on the usual correspondence in the King James Version of *j* for the Hebrew phoneme /y/, Book of Mormon *Jershon* could correspond to the Hebrew root *yrš* meaning "to inherit," thus providing an appropriate play on words in Alma 27:22: "and this land Jershon is the land which we will give unto our brethren for an inheritance." Similarly, one Book of Mormon name used for a man that might have seemed awkward, *Alma,* now is known from two second-century A.D. Hebrew documents of the Bar Kokhba period (Yadin, p. 176) and thus speaks for a strong and continuing Hebrew presence among Book of Mormon peoples.

BIBLIOGRAPHY
Hoskisson, Paul Y. "An Introduction to the Relevance of and a Methodology for a Study of the Proper Names of the Book of Mormon." In *By Study and Also by Faith,* ed. J. Lundquist and S. Ricks, Vol. 2, pp. 126–35. Salt Lake City, 1990.
Tvedtnes, John A. "A Phonemic Analysis of Nephite and Jaredite Proper Names." *F.A.R.M.S. Paper.* Provo, Utah, 1977.
Yadin, Y. *Bar Kokhba,* p. 176. Jerusalem, 1971.

PAUL Y. HOSKISSON

BOOK OF MORMON NEAR EASTERN BACKGROUND

According to the Book of Mormon, the JAREDITES, the NEPHITES, and the "Mulekites" (*see* MULEK) migrated to the Western Hemisphere from the Near East in antiquity, a claim that has been challenged. While Book of Mormon students readily admit that no direct, concrete evidence currently exists substantiating the links with the ancient Near East that are noted in the book, evidence can be adduced—largely external and circumstantial—that commands respect for the claims of the Book of Mormon concerning its ancient Near Eastern background (*CWHN* 8:65–72). A few examples will indicate the nature and strength of these ties, particularly because such details were not available to Joseph Smith, the translator of the Book of Mormon, from any sources that existed in the early nineteenth century (*see* BOOK OF MORMON TRANSLATION BY JOSEPH SMITH).

1. LEHI (c. 600 B.C.) was a righteous, wellborn, and prosperous man of the tribe of Manasseh who lived in or near Jerusalem. He traveled much, has a rich estate in the country, and had an eye for fine metalwork. His family was strongly influenced by the contemporary Egyptian culture. At a time of mounting tensions in Jerusalem (the officials were holding secret meetings by night), he favored the religious reform party of Jeremiah, while members of his family were torn by divided loyalties. One of many prophets of doom in the land, "a visionary man," he was forced to flee with his family, fearing pursuit by the troops of one Laban, a high military official of the city. Important records that Lehi needed were kept in the house of Laban (1 Ne. 1–5; *CWHN* 6:46–131; 8:534–35). This closely parallels the situation in Lachish at the time, as described in contemporary records discovered in 1934–1935 (H. Torczyner, *The Lachish Letters,* 2 vols., Oxford, 1938; cf. *CWHN* 8:380–406). The Bar Kokhba letters, discovered in 1965–1966, recount the manner in which the wealthy escaped from Jerusalem under like circumstances in both earlier and later centuries (Y. Yadin, *Bar Kokhba,* Chaps. 10 and 16, Jerusalem, 1971; cf. *CWHN* 8:274–88).

2. Lehi's flight recalls the later retreat of the Desert Sectaries of the Dead Sea, both parties being bent on "keeping the commandments of the Lord" (cf. 1 Ne. 4:33–37; *Battle Scroll* [1QM] x.7–8). Among the Desert Sectaries, all volunteers were sworn in by covenant (*Battle Scroll* [1QM] vii.5–6). In the case of NEPHI$_1$, son of Lehi, he is charged with having "taken it upon him to be our ruler and our teacher. . . . He says that the Lord has talked with him. . . [to] lead us away into some strange wilderness" (1 Ne. 16:37–38). Later in the New World, Nephi, then MOSIAH$_1$, and then ALMA$_1$ (c. 150 B.C.)

led out more devotees, for example, the last-named, to a place of trees by "the waters of Mormon" (2 Ne. 5:10–11; Omni 1:12–13; Mosiah 18). The organization and practices instigated by Alma are like those in the Old World communities: swearing in, baptism, one priest to fifty members, traveling teachers or inspectors, a special day for assembly, all labor and share alike, called "the children of God," all defer to one preeminent Teacher, and so on (Mosiah 18; 25). Parallels with the Dead Sea Scroll communities are striking, even to the rival Dead Sea colonies led by the False Teacher (*CWHN* 6:135–44, 157–67, 183–93; 7:264–70; 8:289–327).

3. "And my father dwelt in a tent" (1 Ne. 2:15). Mentioned fourteen times in 1 Nephi, the sheikh's tent is the center of everything. When Lehi's sons returned from Jerusalem safely after fleeing Laban's men and hiding in caves, "they did rejoice . . . and did offer sacrifices . . . on an alter of stones . . . and gave thanks" (1 Ne. 2:7; 5:9). Taking "seeds of every kind" for a protracted settlement, "keeping to the more fertile parts of the wilderness," they hunt along the way, making "not much fire," living on raw meat, guided at times by a "Liahona"—a brass ball "of curious workmanship" with two divination arrows that show the way. One long camping was "at a place we call Shazer" (cf. Arabic *shajer,* trees or place of trees); and they buried Ishmael at Nahom, where his daughters mourned and chided Lehi (1 Ne. 16; cf. Arabic *Nahm,* a moaning or sighing together, a chiding). Lehi vividly describes a *sayl,* a flash flood of "filthy water" out of a wadi or stream bed that can sweep one's camp away (1 Ne. 8:13, 32; 12:16), a common event in the area where he was traveling. At their first "river of water" Lehi recited a formal "qasida," an old form of desert poetry, to his sons Laman and Lemuel, urging them to be like the stream and the valley in keeping God's commands (1 Ne. 2). He describes the terror of those who in "a mist of darkness . . . did lose their way, wandered off and were lost." He sees "a great and spacious building," appearing to stand high "in the air . . . filled with people, . . . and their manner of dress was exceeding fine" (1 Ne. 8; cf. the "skyscrapers" of southern Arabia, e.g., the town of Shibam). The building fell in all its pride like the fabled Castle of Ghumdan. Other desert imagery abounds (*CWHN* 5:43–92).

4. Among lengthier connected accounts, MORONI₁ (c. 75 B.C.), leading an uprising against an oppressor, "went forth among the people
waving the rent part of his garment" to show the writing on it
(Alma 46:19–20). The legendary Persian hero Kawe did the same
thing with his garment. The men of Moroni "came running. . . .
rending their garments . . . as a covenant [saying] . . . may [God]
cast us at the feet of our enemies . . . to be trodden underfoot"
(Alma 46:21–22). Both the rending of and the treading on the garments were ancient practices (*CWHN* 6:216–18; 7:198–202;
8:92–95). The inscription on the banner, "in memory of our God,
our religion, and our peace, our wives, and our children" (Alma
46:12), is similar to the banners and trumpets of the armies in the
Dead Sea *Battle Scroll* ([IQM] iii.1–iv.2). Before the battle Moroni
goes before the army and dedicates the land southward as
Desolation, and the rest he named "a chosen land, and the land of
liberty" (Alma 46:17). In the *Battle Scroll* ([1QM] vii.8ff.) the high
priest similarly goes before the army and dedicates the land of the
enemy to destruction and that of Israel to salvation (*CWHN*
6:213–16). Moroni compares his torn garment-banner to the coat
of Joseph, half of which was preserved and half decayed: "Let us
remember the words of Jacob, before his death. . . as this remnant
of [the coat] hath been preserved, so shall a remnant of [Joseph]
be preserved." So Jacob had both "sorrow . . . [and] joy" at the
same time (Alma 46:24–25). An almost identical story is told by
the tenth-century savant Tha'labi, the collector of traditions from
Jewish refugees in Persia (*CWHN* 6:209–21; 8:249, 280–81).

5. There is a detailed description of a coronation in the Book of
Mormon that is paralleled only in ancient nonbiblical sources,
notably Nathan ha-Bablil's description of the coronation of the
Prince of the Captivity. The Book of Mormon version in Mosiah 2–6
(c. 125 B.C.) is a classic account of the well-documented ancient
"Year Rite": (a) The people gather at the temple, (b) bringing first-
fruits and offerings (Mosiah 2:3–4); (c) they camp by families, all
tent doors facing the temple; (d) a special tower is erected, (e) from
which the king addresses the people, (f) unfolding unto them "the
mysteries" (the real ruler is God, etc.); (g) all accept the covenant
in a great acclamation; (h) it is the universal birthday, all are reborn;
(i) they receive a new name, are duly sealed, and registered in a

national census; (j) there is stirring choral music (cf. Mosiah 2:28; 5:2–5); (k) they feast by families (cf. Mosiah 2:5) and return to their homes (*CWHN* 6:295–310). This "patternism" has been recognized only since the 1930s.

6. The literary evidence of Old World ties with the Book of Mormon is centered on Egyptian influences, requiring special treatment. The opening colophon to Nephi's autobiography in the Book of Mormon is characteristic: "I, Nephi . . . I make it with mine own hand" (1 Ne. 1:1, 3). The characters of the original Book of Mormon writing most closely resemble Meroitic, a "reformed Egyptian" known from an Egyptian colony established on the upper Nile River in the same period (*see* ANTHON TRANSCRIPT; BOOK OF MORMON LANGUAGE). Proper names in the Book of Mormon include Ammon (the most common name in both 26th Dynasty Egypt [664–525 B.C.] and the Book of Mormon); Alma, which has long been derided for its usage as a man's name (now found in the Bar Kokhba letters as "Alma, son of Judah"); Aha, a Nephite general (cf. Egyptian *aha*, "warrior"); Paankhi (an important royal name of the Egyptian Late Period [525–332 B.C.]); Hermounts, a country of wild beasts (cf. Egyptian Hermonthis, God of wild places); Laman and Lemuel, "pendant names" commonly given to eldest sons (cf. Qabil and Habil, Harut and Marut); Lehi, a proper name (found on an ancient potsherd in Ebion Gezer about 1938); Manti, a form of the Egyptian God Month; Korihor (cf. Egyptian Herhor, Horihor); and Giddianhi (cf. Egyptian Djhwti-ankhi, "Thoth is my life"), etc. (*CWHN* 5:25–34; 6:281–94; 7:149–52, 168–72; 8:281–82; *see* BOOK OF MORMON NAMES).

7. The authenticity of the GOLD PLATES on which the Book of Mormon was inscribed has often been questioned until the finding of the Darius Plates in 1938. Many other examples of sacred and historical writing on metal plates have been found since (C. Wright in *By Study and Also by Faith*, 2:273–334, ed. J. Lundquist and S. Ricks, Salt Lake City, 1990). The brass (bronze) plates recall the Copper Scroll of the Dead Sea Scrolls, the metal being used to preserve particularly valuable information, namely the hiding places of treasures—scrolls, money, sacred utensils—concealed from the enemy. The Nephites were commanded, "They shall hide up their treasures . . . when they shall flee before their enemies;" but if

such treasures are used for private purposes thereafter, "because they will not hide them up unto [God], cursed be they and also their treasures" (Hel. 13:19–20; *CWHN* 5:105–107; 6:21–28; 7:56–57, 220–21, 272–74).

8. In sharp contrast to other cultures in the book, the Jaredites carried on the warring ways of the steppes of Asia "upon this north country" (Ether 1, 3–6). Issuing forth from the well-known dispersion center of the great migrations in western Asia, they accepted all volunteers in a mass migration (Ether 1:41–42). Moving across central Asia they crossed shallow seas in barges (Ether 2:5–6). Such great inland seas were left over from the last ice age (*CWHN* 5:183–85, 194–96). Reaching the "great sea" (possibly the Pacific), they built ships with covered decks and peaked ends, "after the manner of Noah's ark" (Ether 6:7), closely resembling the prehistoric "magur boats" of Mesopotamia. The eight ships were lit by shining stones, as was Noah's ark according to the Palestinian Talmud, the stones mentioned in the Talmud and elsewhere being produced by a peculiar process described in ancient legends. Such arrangements were necessary because of "the furious wind . . . [that] did never cease to blow" (Ether 6:5, 8). In this connection, there are many ancient accounts of the "windflood"—tremendous winds sustained over a period of time—that followed the Flood and destroyed the Tower (*CWHN* 5:359–79; 6:329–34; 7:208–10).

9. The society of the Book of Ether is that of the "Epic Milieu" or "Heroic Age," a product of world upheaval and forced migrations (cf. descriptions in H. M. Chadwick, *The Growth of Literature*, 3 vols., Cambridge, 1932–1940). On the boundless plains loyalty must be secured by oaths, which are broken as individuals seek ever more power and gain. Kings' sons or brothers rebel to form new armies and empires, sometimes putting the king and his family under lifelong house arrest, while "drawing off" followers by gifts and lands in feudal fashion. Regal splendor is built on prison labor; there are plots and counterplots, feuds, and vendettas. War is played like a chess game with times and places set for battle and challenges by trumpet and messenger, all culminating in the personal duel of the rulers, winner take all. This makes for wars of extermination and total social breakdown with "every man with his band fighting for that which he desired" (Ether 7–15; *CWHN* 5:231–37, 285–307).

10. Elements of the archaic matriarchy were brought from the Old World by Book of Mormon peoples (Ether 8:9–10). For instance, a Jaredite queen plots to put a young successor on the throne by teachery or a duel, and then supplants him with another, remaining in charge like the ancient perennial Great Mother in a royal court (cf. *CWHN* 5:210–13). The mother-goddess apparently turns up also among the Nephites in a cult-place (Siron), where the harlot Isabel and her associates were visited by crowds of devotees (Alma 39:3–4, 11); Isabel was the name of the great hierodule of the Phoenicians (*CWHN* 8:542).

BIBLIOGRAPHY
Nibley, Hugh. *CWHN*, Vols. 5–8. Salt Lake City, 1988–1989.

HUGH W. NIBLEY

BOOK OF MORMON PEOPLES

At least fifteen distinct groups of people are mentioned in the Book of Mormon. Four (NEPHITES, LAMANITES, JAREDITES, and the people of Zarahemla [Mulekites]) played a primary role; five were of secondary concern; and six more were tertiary elements.

NEPHITES.   The core of this group were direct descendants of NEPHI$_1$, the son of founding father LEHI. Political leadership within the Nephite wing of the colony was "conferred upon none but those who were descendants of Nephi" (Mosiah 25:13). Not only the early kings and judges but even the last military commander of the Nephites, MORMON, qualified in this regard (he explicitly notes that he was "a pure descendant of Lehi" [3 Ne. 5:20] and "a descendant of Nephi" [Morm. 1:5]).

In a broader sense, "Nephites" was a label given all those governed by a Nephite ruler, as in Jacob 1:13: "The people which were not Lamanites were Nephites; nevertheless, they were called [when specified according to descent] Nephites, Jacobites, Josephites, Zoramites, Lamanites, Lemuelites, and Ishmaelites." It is interesting to note that groups without direct ancestral connections could come under the Nephite sociopolitical umbrella. Thus, "all the people of Zarahemla were numbered with the Nephites" (Mosiah 25:13). This process of political amalgamation had kinship overtones in many instances, as when a body of converted Lamanites "took upon themselves the name of Nephi, that they might be called the children of Nephi and be numbered among those who were called Nephites" (Mosiah 25:12). The odd phrase "the people of the Nephites" in such places as Alma 54:14 and Helaman 1:1 suggests a social structure where possibly varied populations ("the people") were controlled by an elite ("the Nephites").

Being a Nephite could also entail a set of religious beliefs and practices (Alma 48:9–10; 4 Ne. 1:36–37) as well as participation in a cultural tradition (Enos 1:21; Hel. 3:16). Most Nephites seem to have been physically distinguishable from the Lamanites (Jacob 3:5; Alma 55:4, 8; 3 Ne. 2:15).

The sociocultural and political unity implied by the use of the general title "Nephites" is belied by the historical record, which documents a long series of "dissensions" within and from Nephite rule, with large numbers periodically leaving to join the Lamanites (Alma 31:8; 43:13; Hel. 1:15).

The Book of Mormon—a religiously oriented lineage history— is primarily a record of events kept by and centrally involving the Nephites. Since the account was written from the perspective of this people (actually, of its leaders), all other groups are understood and represented from the point of view of Nephite elites. There are only fragments in the Nephite record that indicate directly the perspectives of other groups, or even of Nephite commoners.

LAMANITES. This name, too, was applied in several ways. Direct descendants of Laman, Lehi's eldest son, constituted the backbone of the Lamanites, broadly speaking (Jacob 1:13–14; 4 Ne. 1:38–39). The "Lemuelites" and "Ishmaelites," who allied themselves with the descendants of Laman in belief and behavior, were also called Lamanites (Jacob 1:13–14). So were "all the dissenters of [from] the Nephites" (Alma 47:35). This terminology was used in the Nephite record, although one cannot be sure that all dissenters applied the term to themselves. However, at least one such dissenter, Ammoron, a Zoramite, bragged, "I am a bold Lamanite" (Alma 54:24).

Rulers in the Lamanite system appear to have had more difficulty than Nephite rulers in binding component social groups into a common polity (Alma 17:27–35; 20:4, 7, 9, 14–15; 47:1–3). They seem to have depended more on charisma or compulsion than on shared tradition, ideals, or an apparatus of officials. Whether a rule existed that Lamanite kings be descendants of Laman is unclear. Early in the second century B.C. two successive Lamanite kings were called Laman (Mosiah 7:21; 24:3); since this designation was being interpreted across a cultural boundary by a record keeper of Nephite culture, it is possible that "Laman" was really a title of office, in the same manner that Nephite kings bore the title "Nephi" (Jacob 1:9–11). Later, however, Lamoni, a local Lamanite ruler, is described as "a descendant of Ishmael," not of Laman (Alma 17:21), and his father, king over the entire land of Nephi (originally a homeland of the Nephites, but taken and occupied by the Lamanites throughout much of the remainder of Book of Mormon history), would have had the same ancestry. Evidently, if there was a rule that Laman's descendants inherit the throne, it was inconsistently applied. Moreover, Amalickiah and his brother, both Nephite dissenters, gained the Lamanite throne and claimed legitimacy (Alma 47:35; 52:3).

Repeatedly, the Lamanites are said to have been far more numerous than the Nephites (Jarom 1:6; Mosiah 25:3; Hel. 4:25), a fact that might appear to be inconsistent with the early Nephite characterization of them as savage hunters, which normally require much more land per person than farmers require (Enos 1:20; Jarom 1:6). The expression "people of the Lamanites" (Alma 23:9–12) may indicate that Lamanite elites dominated a disparate peasantry.

The few direct glimpses that Nephite history allows of the Lamanites indicate a level well beyond "savage" culture, though short of the "civilization" claimed for the Nephites. Perhaps their sophistication was due somewhat to the influence of Nephite dissenters among them (see Mosiah 24:3–7). Apparently some Lamanites proved apt learners from this source; moreover, those converted to the prophetic religion taught by Nephite missionaries are usually described as exemplary (Alma 23:5–7; 56; Hel. 6:1).

THE PEOPLE OF ZARAHEMLA (MULEKITES).   In the third century B.C., when the Nephite leader Mosiah₁ and his company moved from the land of Nephi down to the Sidon river, "they discovered a people, who were called the people of Zarahemla" (Omni 1:13–14) because their ruler bore that name. These people were descendants of a party that fled the Babylonian conquest of Jerusalem in 586 B.C., among whom was a son of the Jewish king Zedekiah, MULEK. Hence Latter-day Saints often refer to the descendants of this group of people as Mulekites, although the Book of Mormon never uses the term. When discovered by the Nephites around 200 B.C., this people was "exceedingly numerous," although culturally degenerate due to illiteracy and warfare (Omni 1:16–17). The Nephite account says the combined population welcomed Mosiah as king.

Mosiah found that the people of Zarahemla had discovered the last known survivor of the Jaredites shortly before his death. By that means, or through survivors not mentioned, elements of Jaredite culture seem to have been brought to the Nephites by the people of Zarahemla (*CWHN* 5:238–47). The fact that the people of Zarahemla spoke a language unintelligible to the Nephites further hints at an ethnic makeup more diverse than the brief text suggests, which assumes a solely Jewish origin.

The Mulekites are little referred to later, probably because they were amalgamated thoroughly into eclectic Nephite society (Mosiah 25:13). However, as late as 51 B.C., a Lamanite affiliate who was a descendant of king Zarahemla attacked and gained brief control over the Nephite capital (Hel. 1:15–34).

JAREDITES.   This earliest people referred to in the Book of Mormon originated in Mesopotamia at the "great tower" referred to in Genesis 11. From there a group of probably eight families journeyed to American under divine guidance.

The existing record is a summary by MORONI$_2$, last custodian of the Nephite records, of a history written on gold plates by Ether, the final Jaredite prophet, around the middle of the first millennium B.C. Shaped by the editorial hands of Ether, Moroni$_2$, and MOSIAH$_2$ (Mosiah 28:11–17), and by the demand for brevity, the account gives but a skeletal narrative covering more than two millennia of Jaredite history. Most of it concerns just one of the eight lineages, Jared's, the ruling line to which Ether belonged, hence the name Jaredites (*see* BOOK OF MORMON PLATES AND RECORDS).

Eventually a flourishing cultural tradition developed (Ether 10:21–27), although maintaining a viable population seems to have been a struggle at times (Ether 9:30–34; 11:6–7). By the end, millions were reported victims of wars of extermination witnessed by the prophet Ether (Ether 15:2). A single survivor, Coriantumr, the last king, was encountered by the people of Zarahemla sometime before 200 B.C., although it is plausible that several remote groups also could have survived to meld unnoticed by historians into the successor Mulekite and Lamanite populations.

SECONDARY GROUPS.   The same seven lineage groups are mentioned among Lehi's descendants near the beginning of the Nephite record and again 900 years later (Jacob 1:13; Morm. 1:8). Each was named after a first-generation ancestor and presumably consisted of his descendants. Among the Nephites there were four: Nephites proper, Jacobites, Josephites, and Zoramites. Within the Lamanite faction, Laman's own descendants were joined by the Lemuelites and Ishmaelites. These divisions disappeared after the appearance of Christ at Bountiful (there were neither "Lamanites, nor any manner of -ites" [4 Ne. 1:17]), but that descent was not forgotten, for the old lineages later reappeared (4 Ne. 1:20, 36–37). What might have happened was that some public functions that the groups had filled were taken over for several generations by the Christian church, which they all had joined. Based on analogy to social systems in related lands, it is possible that membership in these seven groups governed marriage selection and property inheritance, and perhaps residence (Alma 31:3). The Lemuelites evidently had their own city (Alma 23:12–13), and descent determined where the Nephites and the people of Zarahemla sat during Mosiah$_2$'s politico-religious assembly (Mosiah 25:4; cf. 25:21–23). Such functions may also have been filled by groups other than the seven lineages.

The seven lineage groups may be referred to as "tribes," as in 3 Nephi 7:2–4. Immediately before the natural disasters that signaled the crucifixion of Jesus Christ, Nephite social unity collapsed, and they "did separate one from another into tribes, every man according to his family and his kindred and friends; . . . therefore their tribes became exceedingly great" (3 Ne. 7:2–4).

The **Jacobites** are always listed first of the three secondary peoples among the Nephites. They were descendants of Nephi's younger brother, Jacob. Nothing is said of them as a group except that they were counted as Nephites politically and culturally. Since Jacob himself was chief priest under the kingship of his brother Nephi, and since he and his descendants maintained the religious records begun by Nephi, it is possible that the Jacobites as a lineage group bore some special priestly responsibilites.

The **Josephites** are implied to have been descendants of Joseph, Nephi's youngest brother. The text is silent on any distinctive characteristics.

The **Zoramites** descended from Zoram, Laban's servant who agreed under duress to join the party of Lehi following the slaying of Laban in Jerusalem (1 Ne. 4:31–37). Both early and late in the account (Jacob 1:13 and 4 Ne. 1:36), the Zoramites are listed in alignment with Nephi's descendants, although around 75 B.C. at least some of them dissented for a time and joined the Lamanite alliance (Alma 43:4). As they were then "appointed . . . chief captains" over the Lamanite armies (Alma 48:5), they may earlier have played a formal military role among the Nephites. A reason for their split with the Nephites was evidently recollection of what had happened to their founding ancestor: Ammoron, dissenter from the Nephites and king of the Lamanites in the first century B.C., recalled: "I am . . . a descendant of Zoram, whom your fathers pressed and brought out of Jerusalem" (Alma 54:23).

During their dissidence, their worship, characterized as idolatrous yet directed to a God of spirit, was conducted in "synagogues" from which the wealthy drove out the poor (Alma 31:1, 9–11; 32:5). Their practices departed from both Nephite ways and the LAW OF MOSES (Alma 31:9–12). Shortly after the signs marking the birth of Christ and almost eight years after the earliest mention of their separation from the Nephites, these Zoramites were still dissident and were luring naive Nephites to join the Gadianton robbers by means of "lyings" and "flattering words" (3 Ne. 1:29). Yet two centuries later they were back in the Nephite fold (4 Ne. 1:36).

The list of secondary peoples among the Lamanites starts with the **Lemuelites**. Presumably they were the posterity of Lehi's second eldest son, Lemuel. Nothing is said of the group as a separate entity other than routine listings among the Nephites' enemies (Jacob 1:13–14; Morm. 1:8–9), although a "city of Lemuel" is mentioned in Alma 23:12.

The **Ishmaelites** were descendants of the father-in-law of Nephi and his brothers (1 Ne. 7:2–5). Why Ishmael's sons (1 Ne. 7:6) did not found separate lineages of their own is nowhere indicated. As

with the other secondary groups, there is little to go on in character-
izing the Ishmaelites. At one time they occupied a particular land of
Ishmael within the greater land of Nephi, where one of their number,
Lamoni, ruled (Alma 17:21).

Somehow, by the days of Ammon and his fellow missionaries
(first century B.C.), the Ishmaelites had gained the throne over the
entire land of Nephi as well as kingship over some component kingdoms. (Alma 20:9 has the grand king implying that Lamoni's brothers, too, were rulers.) Yet the king recited the familiar Lamanite
litany of complaint about how in the first generation Nephi had
"robbed our fathers" of the right to rule (Alma 20:13). Evidently he
was a culturally loyal Lamanite even though of a minor lineage.

The final information known about both Ishmaelites and
Lemuelites is their presence in the combined armies fighting against
the Nephites in Mormon's day (Morm. 1:8). Presumably their contin-
gents were involved in the final slaughter of the Nephites at
CUMORAH.

TERTIARY GROUPS.   Six other groups qualify as peoples, even though
they did not exhibit the staying power of the seven lineages.

The earliest described are the **people of Zeniff** (Zeniffites).
Zeniff, a Nephite, about half a century after Mosiah had first discovered the people and land of Zarahemla, led a group out of Zarahemla
who were anxious to resettle "the land of Nephi, or . . . the land of
our fathers' first inheritance" (Mosiah 9:1). Welcomed at first by the
Lamanites there, in time they found themselves forced to pay a high
tax to their overlords. A long section on them in the book of Mosiah
(Mosiah 9–24) relates their dramatic temporal and spiritual experiences over three generations until they were able to escape back to
Zarahemla. There they became Nephites again, although perhaps
they retained some residential and religious autonomy as one of the
"seven churches" (Mosiah 25:23).

Two groups splintered off from the people of Zeniff. The **people
of Alma**$_1$ were religious refugees who believed in the words of the
prophet Abinadi and fled from oppression and wickedness under
King Noah, the second Zeniffite king (Mosiah 18, 23–24).
Numbering in the hundreds, they maintained independent social and
political status for less than twenty-five years before escaping from
Lamanite control and returning to Nephite territory, where they

established the "church of God" in Zarahemla (Mosiah 25:18) but soon disappeared from the record as an identifiable group.

The second Zeniffite fragment started when the priests of King Noah, headed by Amulon, fled into the wilderness to avoid execution by their rebellious subjects. In the course of their escape, they kidnapped Lamanite women and took them as wives, thus founding the **Amulonites** in a land where they established their own version of Nephite culture (Mosiah 24:1). In time, they adopted the religious "order of Nehor" (see below), usurped political and military leadership, and "stirred up" the Lamanites to attack the Nephites (Alma 21:4; 24:1–2; 25:1–5). They and the Amalekites (see below) helped the Lamanites construct a city named Jerusalem in the land of Nephi. Judging from brief statements by the Nephites (Mosiah 12–13; Alma 21:5–10), both Amulonites and Amalekites saw themselves as defenders of a belief system based on the Old Testament, which no doubt explains the naming of their city.

One of the earliest groups of Nephite dissenters was the **Amlicites**. Ambitious Amlici, a disciple of Nehor, likely claiming noble birth (Alma 51:8), gathered a large body of followers and challenged the innovative Nephite system of rule by judges instituted by Mosiah$_2$; Amlici wished to be king. When his aim was defeated by "the voice of the people," he plotted an attack coordinated with the Lamanites that nearly succeeded in capturing Zarahemla, the Nephite capital. Loyal forces under ALMA$_2$ finally succeeded in destroying or scattering the enemy (Alma 2:1–31). Amlici was slain, but the fate of his forces is unclear. Likely, elements of them went with the defeated Lamanite army to the land of Nephi. The name Amlicite is not used thereafter.

Another group of Nephite dissenters, the **Amalekites**, lived in the land of Nephi (Alma 21:2–3; 43:13). Their origin is never explained. However, based on the names and dates, it is possible that they constituted the Amlicite remnant previously mentioned, their new name possibly arising by "lamanitization" of the original. They were better armed than common Lamanites (Alma 43:20) and, like some Zoramites, were made military leaders within the Lamanite army because of their "more wicked and murderous disposition" (Alma 43:6). From the record of the Nephite missionaries, we learn that they believed in a God (Alma 22:7). Many of them, like the

Amlicites, belonged to the religious order of Nehor and built sanctuaries or synagogues where they worshipped (Alma 21:4, 6). Like the Amulonites, they adamantly resisted accepting Nephite orthodox religion (Alma 23:14). Instead, they believed that God would save all people. From their first mention to the last, only about fifteen years elapsed.

During a fourteen-year mission in the land of Nephi, the Nephite missionaries Ammon and his brothers gained many Lamanite converts (Alma 17–26). A Lamanite king, Lamoni, who was among these converts, gave the Lamanite converts the name **Anti-Nephi-Lehies.** These people were singularly distinguished by their firm commitment to the gospel of Jesus Christ, including, most prominently, the Savior's injunctions to love one's enemies and not to resist evil (3 Ne. 12:39, 44; Matt. 5:39, 44). Ammon maintained that in Christlike love this people exceeded the Nephites (Alma 26:33). After their conversion, the Book of Mormon says, they "had no more desire to do evil" (Alma 19:33) and "did not fight against God any more, neither against any of their brethren" (Alma 23:7). Having previously shed human blood, they covenanted as a people never again to take human life (Alma 24:6) and even buried all their weapons (Alma 24:17). They would not defend themselves when attacked by Lamanites, and 1,005 of them were killed (Alma 24:22). Ammon urged the vulnerable Anti-Nephi-Lehies to flee to Nephite territory. Among the Nephites they became known as the **people of Ammon** (or **Ammonites;** see Alma 56:57). They ended up in a separate locale within the Nephite domain, the land of Jershon (Alma 27:26). Later, they moved en masse to the land of Melek (Alma 35:13), where they were joined from time to time by other Lamanite refugees.

Some years later, desiring to assist the Nephite armies in defending the land but not wishing to break their covenant (Alma 53:13), the people of Ammon sent 2,000 of their willing sons to be soldiers, since their sons had not taken the covenant of nonviolence that they had. These "two thousand stripling soldiers" (Alma 53:22) became known as the sons of Helaman, their Nephite leader, and had much success in battle (Alma 56:56). Although they were all wounded, none were ever killed, a remarkable blessing ascribed "to the miraculous power of God, because of their exceeding faith" (Alma 57:26; cf. 56:47).

According to Helaman 3:11, a generation later some of the people of Ammon migrated into "the land northward." This is the last mention of them in the Book of Mormon.

OTHER GROUPS.   Among the other groups mentioned in the Book of Mormon are the widespread secret combinations or "robbers." Yet these groups do not qualify as "peoples" but as associations, which individuals could join or leave on their own volition.

Another group, the "order of Nehor," was a cult centered around the ideas that priests should be paid and that God would redeem all people. They were not really a "people" in the technical sense—the term implies a biological continuity that a cult lacks.

The inhabitants of separate cities were also sometimes called peoples. Local beliefs and customs no doubt distinguished them from each other, but insufficient detail prohibits describing units of this scale.

BIBLIOGRAPHY
Nibley, Hugh. *Lehi in the Desert; The World of the Jaredites; There Were Jaredites.* CWHN 5. Salt Lake City, 1988.
Sorenson, John L. *An Ancient American Setting for the Book of Mormon.* Salt Lake City, 1985.
Welch, John W. "Lehi's Last Will and Testament: A Legal Approach." In *The Book of Mormon: Second Nephi, The Doctrinal Structure*, ed. M. Nyman and C. Tate, pp. 61–82. Provo, Utah, 1989.

JOHN L. SORENSON

BOOK OF MORMON PERSONALITIES

[*The experiences, thoughts, feelings, and personalities of several individuals are brought to light in the Book of Mormon. Jesus Christ is
central in the book.*

*The founding prophet was Lehi. For articles concerning him and
members of his family, see* Lehi; Laman; Nephi$_1$; Jacob; *and* Ishmael.
*Concerning Lehi's wife, Sariah, and the other women of the Book of
Mormon, see* Women in the Book of Mormon.

The last Nephite king (153–90 B.C.) was Mosiah$_2$. *For articles on
his grandfather, father, and brother, see* Mosiah$_1$, Benjamin,
Helaman$_1$. *From 90 B.C. to A.D. 321 the Nephite records were kept by*

descendants of Alma$_1$; see Alma$_1$; Alma$_2$; Helaman$_2$; Helaman$_3$; Nephi$_2$; Nephi$_3$; Nephi$_4$. *The last Nephite prophets, military leaders, and historians were* Mormon *and his son,* Moroni$_2$, *named after an earlier chief captain* Moroni$_1$.

Four other prophets figure prominently in the Book of Mormon; see Abinadi; Amulek; Samuel the Lamanite; *and* Brother of Jared. *Prophets from the Old World quoted in the Book of Mormon include* Ezias; Isaiah; Joseph; Moses; Neum; Zenock; *and* Zenos. *Regarding the various groups of people in the Book of Mormon, see* Book of Mormon Peoples; Jaredites; Lamanites; Mulek; *and* Nephites. *See also* Book of Mormon Names.]

BOOK OF MORMON PLATES AND RECORDS

The Book of Mormon is a complex text with a complicated history. It is primarily an abridgment of several earlier records by its chief editor and namesake, MORMON. All these records are referred to as "plates" because they were engraved on thin sheets of metal. Various source documents were used by Mormon in his compilation, leading to abrupt transitions and chronological disjunctions that can confuse readers. However, when one is aware of the history of the text, these are consistent and make good sense. The various plates and records referred to in the Book of Mormon and used in making it are (1) the plates of brass; (2) the record of LEHI; (3) the large plates of NEPHI$_1$; (4) the small plates of Nephi; (5) the plates of Mormon; and (6) the twenty-four gold plates of Ether.

THE GOLD PLATES.   The GOLD PLATES that the Prophet Joseph Smith received and translated were the plates of Mormon on which Mormon and his son MORONI$_2$ made their abridgment. Mormon, a prophet and military leader who lived at the end of the NEPHITE era (c. A.D. 385), was the penultimate custodian of the records of earlier Nephite prophets and rulers. In particular, he had the large plates of Nephi, which were the official Nephite chronicle and which he was commanded to continue (Morm. 1:4). He later made his own plates of Mormon, on which he compiled an abridgment of the large plates of Nephi (W of M 1:3–5; 3 Ne. 5:9–10), which covered 985 years of Nephite history, from Lehi's day to his. The large plates drew on still earlier records and the writings of various prophets and frequently included various source materials such as letters, blessings, discourses, and memoirs.

After Mormon had completed his abridgment through the reign of King BENJAMIN (c. 130 B.C.), he discovered the small plates of Nephi, a separate history of the same time period focusing on the spiritual events of those years and quoting extensively from the plates of brass. Inspired to add the small plates of Nephi to his own record, Mormon inserted a brief explanation for the double account of early Nephite history (W of M 1:2–9).

Mormon continued his abridgment, selecting from the large plates, paraphrasing, and often adding his own comments, extending the account down to his time. Anticipating death, he passed the plates to his son Moroni. Over the next few decades, Moroni wandered alone, making additions to his father's record, including two chapters now included in a book previously abridged by his father (Morm. 7–8) and an account of the JAREDITES that he had abridged from the twenty-four gold plates of Ether. He also copied an extensive vision of the last days that had been recorded by an early Jaredite prophet, the BROTHER OF JARED, and which Moroni was commanded to seal (Ether 4:4–5). He also added brief notes on church rituals (Moro. 1–6), a sermon and two letters from his father (Moro. 7–9), and an exhortation to future readers (Moro. 10). Finally, Moroni took this somewhat heterogeneous collection of records—the plates of Mormon, the small plates of Nephi, his abridgment of the plates of Ether, and the sealed portion containing the vision of the brother of Jared—and buried them in the earth. About 1,400 years later, in 1823, Moroni, now resurrected, appeared to the Prophet Joseph Smith and revealed the location of these records. The plates of Mormon, which, except for the sealed portion, were subsequently translated by Joseph Smith, are known today as the gold plates.

The present English Book of Mormon, however, is not simply a translation of all those gold plates. Joseph Smith and Martin Harris began by translating the plates of Mormon, and when they had reached the reign of King Benjamin, they had 116 pages of translation. Harris borrowed these pages to show to his wife, then lost them, and they were never recovered (see MANUSCRIPT, LOST 116 PAGES). Joseph was commanded not to retranslate this material (D&C

10:30–46), but instead to substitute a translation of the parallel small plates of Nephi, which includes the books of 1 Nephi, 2 Nephi, Jacob, Enos, Jarom, and Omni. Thus, the present Book of Mormon contains only the second account of early Nephite history.

The translation continues from the rest of the plates of Mormon, which were abridged from the large plates of Nephi, and includes the books of Mosiah, Alma, Helaman, 3 Nephi, 4 Nephi, and Mormon (the last two chapters of which were written by Moroni). Next follow Moroni's abridgment of Jaredite history (the book of Ether) and his closing notes (the book of Moroni). Joseph Smith was commanded not to translate the sealed vision of the brother of Jared, which apparently made up a substantial portion of the gold plates (Ludlow, p. 320). Although Joseph Smith translated only from the gold plates, he and his associates saw many other records (*JD* 19:38; *Millennial Star* 40 [1878]:771–72).

THE PLATES OF BRASS. It is now known that many ancients of the Mediterranean area wrote on metal plates. "Where the record was one of real importance, plates of copper, bronze, or even more precious metal were used instead of the usual wooden, lead, or clay tablets" (*CWHN* 5:119; see also H. C. Wright, in *Journal of Library History* 16 [1981]:48–70). Such a metal record was in the possession of one Laban, a leader in Jerusalem in 600 B.C. How Laban obtained these plates and where they originally came from are not known. Several theories have been advanced, including the possibility that the plates of brass originated in the days of JOSEPH OF EGYPT (Ludlow, p. 56). The Book of Mormon indicates that Laban and his father had inherited and preserved the record because they were descendants of this Joseph (1 Ne. 5:16).

The Book of Mormon does tell how the prophet Lehi came to possess the plates of brass. After fleeing Jerusalem, Lehi was commanded by God to send his sons back to the city to obtain the plates from Laban. When he received them, Lehi found that they contained the five books of Moses, a record of the Jews from the beginning down to the reign of Zedekiah, the prophecies of the holy prophets for that same time period (including some of JEREMIAH's prophecies), and a genealogy of Lehi's fathers (1 Ne. 3–5).

Nephi and succeeding spiritual leaders highly valued the plates of brass. They were passed down by major prophets from Nephi to

Mormon, and since they were written in an adapted form of Egyptian (*see* BOOK OF MORMON LANGUAGE), their keepers were taught to read that language (Mosiah 1:2–4). The plates of brass were the basic scriptures of the Nephite nation, and for centuries their prophets read them, quoted them in sermons, and excerpted material from them to enrich their own writings. For example, when the prophet ABINADI cited the Ten Commandments in a disputation with the priests of Noah, his knowledge of the Ten Commandments was due, at least indirectly, to the plates of brass (Mosiah 12–13). As MOSIAH₂ stated, "For it were not possible that our father, Lehi, could have remembered all these things, to have taught them to his children, except it were for the help of these plates" (Mosiah 1:4).

Book of Mormon records, particularly the small plates of Nephi, occasionally quote at length from the plates of brass, and these quotations include twenty-one complete chapters from Isaiah. Although the translation of these quotations generally follows the wording of the King James Version of the Bible, there are many significant differences, which may indicate the existence of older textual sources (Tvedtnes, pp. 165–77). It is also evident from the scriptural quotations in the Book of Mormon that the plates of brass contained a more extensive record of the writings of Hebrew prophets than does the present Old Testament. For example, the Book of Mormon includes prophecies of Joseph of Egypt that are not found in the Bible, as well as writings of ZENOS, ZENOCK, NEUM, and EZIAS, prophets who are not specifically named in the Old Testament.

THE RECORD OF LEHI.   Unfortunately, Mormon's abridgment of the record of Lehi was the material translated in the 116 manuscript pages that were lost, and consequently it is not available in the present Book of Mormon. Lehi wrote an account of his life and spiritual experiences that was included in the large plates of Nephi (1 Ne. 19:1). Mormon abridged this record in his plates, and Joseph Smith translated it, but since it was lost by Martin Harris, very little is now known about it except what can be inferred from references in other texts (Brown, pp. 25–32; see also the preface to the first edition [1830] of the Book of Mormon). When Nephi and JACOB cite the words of Lehi, they seem to be quoting from this now-lost text, and at least the first eight chapters of 1 Nephi (part of the small plates) appear to be based on the record of Lehi. Other passages in the small plates may also have been derived from that record.

THE LARGE PLATES OF NEPHI.   Nephi began the large plates soon after his arrival in the New World. They were the official continuous chronicle of the Nephites from the time they left Jerusalem (c. 600 B.C.) until they were destroyed (A.D. 385). Apparently the large plates were divided into books, each named for its primary author. These plates "contained a 'full account of the history of [Nephi's] people' (1 Ne. 9:2, 4; 2 Ne. 4:14; Jacob 1:2–3), the genealogy of Lehi (1 Ne. 19:2) and the 'more part' of the teachings of the resurrected Jesus Christ to the Nephite nation (3 Ne. 26:7)" (Ludlow, p. 57). Begun as basically a secular history, they later became a combined record, mingling a thousand years of Nephite history and religious experiences.

The large plates emphasize the covenants made with the house of Israel and quote messianic prophecies of Old World prophets not found in the Old Testament. This information was excerpted from the plates of brass that Lehi's colony brought with it from Jerusalem. They also record wars and contentions, correspondence between military leaders, and information on various missionary journeys. The interventions and miraculous power of God permeate this history. The recorded sermons of King Benjamin, Abinadi, and ALMA₂ are indicative of these individuals' deep understanding of the gospel of Jesus Christ and of their faith in his prophesied coming. These plates feature an account of the post-Resurrection ministry and teachings of Christ to the people of the western world (3 Ne. 11–28).

The large plates of Nephi were passed down from king to king until they came into the possession of Mosiah₂. He added such records as those of Zeniff and ALMA₁ to the large plates and then gave them to Alma₂. The plates subsequently passed through a line of prophets until Ammaron's day in the early fourth century A.D. Ammaron chose Mormon, then only a child, to continue the record when he was mature. Mormon recorded the events of his day on the large plates and then used them as the source for his abridgment, which was later buried in the hill CUMORAH. Joseph Smith did not receive the large plates, but the Book of Mormon suggests that they may yet be published to the world (3 Ne. 26:6–10).

THE SMALL PLATES OF NEPHI.   Approximately twenty years after beginning the large plates, Nephi was commanded to make another set of plates. This second set was to be reserved for an account of the ministry of his people (1 Ne. 9; 2 Ne. 5:28–33). They were to contain the things considered most precious—"preaching which was sacred, or revelation which was great, or prophesying" (Jacob 1:2–4).

The small plates were kept for over four centuries, not quite half the time covered by the large plates, by nine writers: Nephi, Jacob, Enos, Jarom, Omni, Amaron, Chemish, Abinadom, and Amaleki. All of these authors were the sons or brothers of their predecessors. Though these plates include the writings of many over a long time period, 80 percent of the text was written by Nephi, the first writer, and an additional 12 percent by his brother Jacob.

Mormon included the small plates with his record when he delivered the plates of Mormon to his son Moroni because their witness of Christ pleased him and because he was impressed by the Spirit of the Lord to include them "for a wise purpose" (W of M 1:3–7). However, since the small plates covered the historical period already recorded in his abridgment of the record of Lehi (namely, from Lehi down to the reign of King Benjamin) and since the book of Mosiah began with the end of King Benjamin's reign, Mormon found it necessary to write a brief explanation to show how the small plates of Nephi connect with the book of Mosiah. He entitled this explanation "Words of Mormon."

While the writers of the small plates recognized the need to provide a historical narrative, their main purpose was to talk of Christ, to preach of Christ, and to prophesy of Christ (2 Ne. 25:26). Because Nephi was concerned with teaching his people the covenants and promises made to ancient Israel, he extracted these teachings from earlier prophets as recorded on the plates of brass. He quoted extensively from the prophet Isaiah (2 Ne. 12–24; cf. Isa. 2–14) and then wrote a commentary on it, predicting the future of Jews, Lamanites, and Gentiles and prophesying much that would happen in the latter days (2 Ne. 25–30).

Jacob continued his brother's approach by recording his own sermons and a long quotation from and explanation of a prophecy of Zenos. The writings of later authors in the small plates are much briefer and less concerned with spiritual matters.

Amaleki noted in his writings that the small plates were full and turned them over to King Benjamin (Omni 1:25, 30), who then possessed both the large and the small plates of Nephi, as well as the plates of brass. All these sets of plates were handed down from generation to generation until they were entrusted to Mormon.

THE PLATES OF MORMON.   After Mormon received the plates, he made a new set on which he engraved his abridgment of the large plates of Nephi (3 Ne. 5:10–11). It is this abridgment plus some additions by Mormon's son Moroni that constitute the gold plates given to Joseph Smith. He described them as follows:

> These records were engraven on plates which had the appearance of gold, each plate was six inches wide and eight inches long and not quite so thick as common tin. They were filled with engravings, in Egyptian characters and bound together in a volume, as the leaves of a book with three rings running through the whole. The volume was something near six inches in thickness, a part of which was sealed. The characters on the unsealed part were small, and beautifully engraved [Jessee, p. 214].

The descriptions reported by other witnesses add details which suggest that the plates were composed of a gold alloy (possibly tumbaga) and that they weighed about fifty pounds (Putnam, pp. 788–89, 829–31). Each plate was as thick as parchment or thick paper.

Most of the time, Mormon relied on the large plates of Nephi for his information. Much of the historical narrative in the Book of Mormon appears to be his paraphrase of earlier records, but occasionally first-person documents are worked into the text. For example, in Mosiah 9 and 10 the narrative suddenly includes a first-person account of Zeniff (apparently an earlier document that Mormon simply copied), and then in chapter 11 Mormon's paraphrase resumes. In addition, many sermons, blessings, and letters appear to be reproduced intact.

Nevertheless, some passages can definitely be ascribed to Mormon: the abridgment of his contributions to the large plates (Morm. 1–7), his sermon and letters recorded by Moroni (Moro. 7–9), and the explanatory comments that he inserted into his narrative. In some of these interpolations he identifies himself (W of M; 3 Ne. 5:8–26; 26:6–12; 28:24; 4 Ne. 1:23), but it seems likely that the frequent "thus we see" comments are also Mormon attempting to stress matters of particular spiritual importance to his readers (e.g., Alma 24:19, 27; 50:19–23; Hel. 3:27–30; 12:1–2).

THE TWENTY-FOUR GOLD PLATES OF ETHER.   These twenty-four gold plates were a record of ancient Jaredites, inhabitants of the Americas before the Nephites. This particular people left the Tower of Babel at the time of the confusion of tongues. Their prophet-leaders were led to the ocean, where they constructed eight peculiar barges. These were driven by the wind across the waters to America, where the Jaredites became a large and powerful nation. After many centuries, wickedness and wars led to a final war of annihilation. During that final war, Ether, a prophet of God, wrote their history and spiritual experiences on twenty-four gold plates, perhaps relying on earlier Jaredite records (see J. Welch, "Preliminary Comments on the Sources behind the Book of Ether," in *F.A.R.M.S. Manuscript Collection*, pp. 3–7. Provo, Utah, 1986).

After witnessing the destruction of his people, Ether hid the twenty-four gold plates. Many years later (c. 121 B.C.) they were discovered by a small Nephite exploring party and given to Mosiah$_2$, a prophet-king, who translated them into the Nephite language through the use of SEER STONES (Mosiah 8:8–9; 28:11–16). Much later (c. A.D. 400) Moroni abridged this history of the Jaredites as his father Mormon had intended, concentrating on spiritual matters and adding inspired commentaries. Moroni included this abridgment, now known as the book of Ether, with what he and his father had already written. (The twenty-four gold plates of Ether were not among the plates received by Joseph Smith.)

CHARACTERISTICS OF MORMON'S EDITING.   The Book of Mormon is quite complicated. The foregoing summary of the plates and other records from which the book was derived is drawn from a number of scattered but consistent comments included in the present text. The narrative itself is often complex. For instance, in Mosiah 1–25, Mormon narrates the stories of three separate groups and subgroups of people—principally the people of Mosiah, of Limhi, and of Alma—with their respective histories and interactions with each other and with the Lamanites (*see* BOOK OF MORMON PEOPLES). The story might have been quite confusing, as it jumps from one people to another, and back and forth in time, but Mormon has kept it remarkably clear. Alma 17–26 is a lengthy flashback recounting the histories of several missionaries on the occasion of their reunion with old friends, and Alma 43–63 narrates the history of a war with the Lamanites, keeping straight the events that happened on two fronts.

Mormon's account might have been much more complex. He emphasizes that he is presenting less than one hundredth of the material available to him (e.g., W of M 1:5; 3 Ne. 26:6–7). Furthermore, his source materials give a lineage history of one family, Lehi and his descendants, and do not encompass all events in the ancient western world (Sorenson, 1985, pp. 50–56). Mormon further simplifies his record by continuing Jacob's practice of lumping diverse peoples into two major groups:

> Now the people which were not Lamanites were Nephites; nevertheless, they were called Nephites, Jacobites, Josephites, Zoramites, Lamanites, Lemuelites, and Ishmaelites. But I, Jacob, shall not hereafter distinguish them by these names, but I shall call them Lamanites that seek to destroy the people of Nephi, and those who are friendly to Nephi I shall call Nephites, or the people of Nephi, according to the reigns of the kings [Jacob 1:13–14; see also Morm. 1:8–9].

The vast editing project that produced the Book of Mormon would require clear guidelines for selecting materials for inclusion. Mormon is quite explicit about the purpose of his abridgment. Like Nephi, he is writing a history to lead people to Christ, and he is writing specifically for the people of later times (2 Ne. 25:23; Morm. 7). The plates of Mormon were created to come forth in the latter days. Mormon is interested in pointing out the principles that will be of most use to such people, and his careful editing and his "thus" and "thus we see" passages are all directed at making the moral lessons easier to identify and understand.

Finally, Mormon took his job as record keeper and abridger very seriously. He was commanded by God to make his record (title page to the Book of Mormon; 3 Ne. 26:12). Also, Nephite society had a strong tradition of the importance of written records, and this was one of the criteria by which they distinguished themselves from the more numerous Mulekites (Omni 1:14–19). Furthermore, the various plates seem to have been handed down from one prophet or king to another as sacred relics and symbols of authority (Mosiah 28:20; 3 Ne. 1:2). In addition, the Nephites had a ceremonial record exchange when different branches of the family were reunited

(Mosiah 8:1–5; 22:14). Most important, the Nephites knew that they would be held responsible for and would be judged by what was written in the records, just as all people will be (2 Ne. 25:21–22; 33:10–15; Morm. 8:12).

BIBLIOGRAPHY

Brown, S. Kent. "Lehi's Personal Record: Quest for a Missing Source." *BYU Studies* 24 (Winter 1984):19–42.

Doxey, Roy W. "What is the Approximate Weight of the Gold Plates from Which the Book of Mormon Was Translated?" In *A Sure Foundation: Answers to Difficult Gospel Questions*, pp. 50–52. Salt Lake City, 1988.

Jessee, Dean C. *Personal Writings of Joseph Smith.* Salt Lake City, 1984.

Ludlow, Daniel H. *A Companion to Your Study of the Book of Mormon.* Salt Lake City, 1976.

Putnam, Read H. "Were the Golden Plates Made of Tumbaga?" *IE* 69 (Sept. 1966):788–89, 828.

Sorenson, John L. "The 'Brass Plates' and Biblical Scholarship." *Dialogue* 10 (Autumn 1977):31–39.

———. *An Ancient American Setting for the Book of Mormon.* Salt Lake City, 1985.

Sperry, Sidney B. *Our Book of Mormon.* Salt Lake City, 1950.

Tvedtnes, J. "Isaiah Variants in the Book of Mormon." In *Isaiah and the Prophets*, ed. M. Nyman, pp. 165–77. Provo, Utah, 1984.

GRANT R. HARDY
ROBERT E. PARSONS

BOOK OF MORMON RELIGIOUS TEACHINGS AND PRACTICES

Most of the Book of Mormon is about a group of Israelites who were guided by prophets, had the doctrines and ordinances of the gospel of Jesus Christ, but lived the law of Moses until the coming of Christ. After his resurrection, Jesus appeared to some of them, and organized his church, and for four generations they lived in peace and happiness. Many details about the religious teachings and practices of these people are found in the Book of Mormon. Latter-day Saints believe that these Christian teachings are applicable in the world today, both because the eternal doctrine of God is as binding on one generation as on the next and because the contents of the Book of Mormon were selected and preserved by prophets with the modern world in mind. These teachings are also found in the revelations that established contemporary LDS practices and ordinances.

In 3 Nephi and Moroni, documents recorded by firsthand witnesses preserve many words of the resurrected Jesus and give the basic doctrines, covenants, and ordinances of his church. Some of the main points follow:

1. Jesus defined his doctrine. Ye must "repent, and believe in me . . . and be baptized in my name, and become as a little child. . . . This is my doctrine" (3 Ne. 11:32, 38–39). The promise is given that God will visit such people "with fire and with the Holy Ghost" (3 Ne. 11:35).

2. Jesus instructed the people to be baptized by immersion, and gave the words of the baptismal prayer (3 Ne. 11:26–27). Only those who were "accountable and capable of committing sin" were baptized (Moro. 8:9–15; cf. 6:3).

3. Jesus ordained twelve disciples and gave them authority to baptize (3 Ne. 11:21–22). Moroni 2:2 preserves the words that Jesus spoke when he laid his hands on these disciples and gave them power to give the Holy Ghost (3 Ne. 18:36–37). The words the disciples used in subsequent ordinations of priests and teachers are found in Moroni 3:1–4.

4. The sacrament prayers are recorded in Moroni 4–5. The words of these prayers derive from the first-person expressions that Jesus spoke when he administered the sacrament in 3 Nephi 18:6–11.

5. The Nephite church met together often "to fast and to pray, and to speak one with another concerning the welfare of their souls, and . . . to partake of bread and wine, in remembrance of the Lord Jesus" (Moro. 6:5–6).

6. These Christians regularly renewed their covenant to keep the commandments Jesus had given them: for instance, to have no contention, anger, or derision; to offer a sacrifice of a broken heart and contrite spirit; to keep the law of chastity in thought and in deed; to love their enemies; to give sustenance to the poor; to do secret acts of charity; to pray alone and with others; to serve only God, not the things of the world; and to strive to become perfected like God and Jesus (3 Ne. 11–14; *see* SERMON ON THE MOUNT). They were promised that Jesus' spirit would continue with them and that they would be raised up at the last day.

7. This church was led by Nephi₃, one of the twelve disciples chosen by Jesus and sent out to preach the things they had heard him say and had seen him do (3 Ne. 27:1). The people were admonished to "give heed unto the words of these twelve" (3 Ne. 12:1).

8. At the Lord's instruction, the church was called by the name of Jesus Christ, and members called on the Father in the name of Christ in all things (3 Ne. 27:8–9).

9. The disciples healed the sick and worked miracles in the name of Jesus (4 Ne. 1:5).

10. They followed Jesus' examples in prayer, reverencing and praising God, asking for forgiveness, and praying that the will of God would be done (3 Ne. 13:9–13; 19:16–35). The people were commanded to "pray in [their] families" (3 Ne. 18:21).

11. They had "all things common among them, every man dealing justly, one with another. . . . Therefore there were not rich and poor" (3 Ne. 26:19; 4 Ne. 1:3).

12. As Jesus had instructed, his followers were strict in keeping iniquity out of their communities and synagogues, with "three witnesses of the church" being required to excommunicate offenders; nevertheless, all were helped, and those who sincerely repented were forgiven (3 Ne. 18:28–32; Moro. 6:7–8).

During the centuries before Christ, Nephite prophets had taught the fulness of the gospel and prepared the people for the coming of Jesus Christ. With respect to the points mentioned above, compare the following antecedents in Nephite history. Some can be traced back into ancient Israel; others were introduced at various times through inspiration or revelation:

1. The doctrine of Christ—faith in the Lord Jesus Christ, repentance, baptism, and the purging of sin by the fire of the Holy Ghost—was taught in the Book of Mormon as early as the time of Nephi₁ (2 Ne. 31). Nephite prophets frequently spoke about the "plan of redemption" or, as Alma called it, "the great plan of happiness" (Alma 42:8). They looked forward to the coming of God himself to earth to redeem mankind from their lost and fallen state. They knew that he would atone for the transgression of Adam and for all the sins of

those who would "not procrastinate the day of [their] repentance" (Alma 34:33), and that all mankind would be physically resurrected and then judged according to the justice and mercy of God (Alma 40–42).

2. Covenantal baptisms were performed from the beginning of the record, notably by Alma₁ at the waters of Mormon (Mosiah 18). His baptismal prayer sought sanctification of the heart as the covenantor promised to serve God "even until death" so that he or she might be granted eternal life through the redemption of Christ (Mosiah 18:12–13). Alma's group remained intact even after they took up residence among other Nephites, and those Nephites who submitted to baptism "after the manner he [had baptized] his brethren in the waters of Mormon" belonged to this church (Mosiah 25:18).

3. Centuries before the time of Christ, Nephite priests and teachers were consecrated (2 Ne. 5:26), appointed (Mosiah 6:3; Alma 45:22–23), or ordained by the laying on of hands (Alma 6:1; cf. Num. 27:23). They watched over the church, stirred the people to remember their covenants (Mosiah 6:3), preached the law and the coming of the Son of God (Alma 16:18–19), and offered their firstlings in "sacrifice and burnt offerings according to the law of Moses" (Mosiah 2:3; cf. Deut. 15:19–23), which they understood to be a type of Christ (2 Ne. 11:4). Nephites and Lamanites had temples, the first one being built "after the manner of the temple of Solomon" (2 Ne. 5:16). The altar was a place of worship where the people assembled, "watching and praying continually, that they might be delivered from Satan, and from death, and from destruction" (Alma 15:17). Nephite priests also taught in synagogues, or gathering places, and ideally no one was excluded (2 Ne. 26:26; Alma 32:2–12). Because they held the Melchizedek Priesthood (Alma 13:6–19), they could function in the ordinances of the Aaronic Priesthood even though they were not Levites. Nephite priests were ordained in a manner that looked "forward on the Son of God, [the ordination] being a type of his order" (Alma 13:16).

4. The covenantal language used by King BENJAMIN (c. 124 B.C.) was similar to the language of the Nephite sacrament prayers. Benjamin's people witnessed that they were willing to keep God's commandments, took upon them the name of Christ, and promised

to "remember to retain the name written always in [their] hearts" (Mosiah 5:5–12; cf. Num. 6:27).

5. The Nephites gathered to fast and pray for spiritual blessings (Mosiah 27:22; Hel. 3:35). In addition, like their Israelite ances-tors, they fasted in connection with mourning for the dead (Hel. 9:10; cf. 2 Sam. 3:35).

6. Covenant renewals were a long-standing part of the law of Moses, pursuant to which all men, women, and children were required to gather around the temple at appointed times to hear and recommit themselves to keep the law of God (Deut. 31:10–13; cf. Mosiah 2:5). Nephite religious law at the time of $Alma_2$ prohibited sorcery, idol worship, idleness, babbling, envy, strife, wearing costly apparel, pride, lying, deceit, malice, reviling, stealing, robbing, whoredom, adultery, murder, and all manner of wickedness (Alma 1:32; 16:18). In addition, $Nephi_2$ counseled against oppressing the poor, withholding food from the hungry, sacrilege, denying the spirit of prophecy, and deserting to the Lamanites (Hel. 4:12).

7. The righteous Nephites were accustomed to being led by prophets, inspired kings, high priests, and chief judges. These leaders kept the sacred records that were frequently cited in Nephite religious observances. The institutions of Nephite prophecy varied from time to time: some prophets were also kings; subsidiary prophets worked under King Benjamin (W of M 1:17–18); others, like ABINADI, were lone voices crying repentance. Their surviving mes-sages, however, were constant and accurate: they preached the gospel and the coming of Christ, and they knew that when he came he would ordain twelve authorized leaders both in the East (1 Ne. 1:10; 11:29) and in the West (1 Ne. 12:7–10).

8. The name of Jesus Christ was revealed to the early Nephite prophets (2 Ne. 10:3; 25:19), and thereafter the Nephites prayed and acted in the name of Jesus Christ (2 Ne. 32:9; Jacob 4:6). $Alma_1$ called his followers "the church of Christ" (Mosiah 18:17).

9. Like the Israelite prophets, the Nephite prophets performed miracles in the name of the Lord. As had Elijah (1 Kgs. 17), for example, $Nephi_2$ closed the heavens and caused a famine (Hel. 11:4), and $Nephi_3$ raised the dead and healed the sick (3 Ne. 7:19–22).

10. The Nephites watched and prayed continually (Alma 15:17). They were counseled to pray three times a day—morning, noon, and night—for mercy, for deliverance from the power of the devil, for prosperity, and for the welfare of their families (Alma 34:18–25; cf. Ps. 55:17). They taught that effective prayer had to be coupled with charitable actions (Alma 34:26–29), which are necessary to retain a remission of sin (Mosiah 4:26).

11. Regarding wealth and possessions, many early Book of Mormon prophets condemned the evils of seeking power and riches. The cycle leading from prosperity to pride, wickedness, and then catastrophe was often repeated, echoing formulas characteristic of DEUTERONOMY. The righteous Nephites covenanted to give liberally to the poor and to bear one another's burdens.

12. Typically, those who entered into the required covenant became "numbered" among the Nephites. If they transgressed, their names were "blotted out," presumably being removed from a roster (Mosiah 5:11; 6:1). Detailed procedures for excommunicating transgressors were established by Alma$_1$, who was given authority by King MOSIAH$_2$ to judge members of the church. Forgiveness was to be extended "as often as [the] people repent" (Mosiah 26:29–30).

Teachings and practices such as these specifically prepared the way for the personal coming of Jesus Christ after his resurrection. Despite years of preparation, the immediate reaction of some of the Nephite multitude to the initial words of the resurrected Christ was still to wonder "what he would concerning the law of Moses" (3 Ne. 15:2). Even though the prophets had long explained the limited function of the law, it remained a sacred and integral part of their lives until it was fulfilled by Jesus (e.g., 2 Ne. 25:24–25; Alma 30:3; 3 Ne. 1:24). When Jesus spoke, it became evident how old things "had become new" (3 Ne. 15:2).

The diversity of religious experience in the Book of Mormon is further seen in the great number of religious communities it mentions in varying situations. Outside of orthodox Nephite circles (whose own success varied from time to time), there were an extravagant royal cult of King Noah and his temple priests (Mosiah 11); a false, rivaling church in Zarahemla formed by Nehor (Alma 1); centers of worship among the Lamanites (Alma 23:2); the wicked and agnostic Korihor (Alma 30); an astounding aristocratic and apostate prayer stand (an elevated platform for a single worshipper) of the Zoramites (Alma 31:13–14); and secret combinations or societies with staunch oath-swearing adherents intent on murder and gain (3 Ne. 3:9). Frequent efforts were made by Nephite missionaries, such as Alma$_2$, Ammon, and Nephi$_2$, to convert people from these groups to the gospel of Jesus Christ and to organize them into righteous churches and communities. On occasion, the converts became more righteous than all their contemporaries. Even among the righteous, there were varying degrees of comprehension and knowledge, for the mysteries of God were imparted by God and his prophets according to the diligence of the hearers (Alma 12:9–11).

Many doctrinal points and practical insights fill the pages of the Book of Mormon. A few of them are the following: Alma$_2$ explains that by his suffering Jesus came to "know according to the flesh how to succor his people" (Alma 7:12). Alma$_2$ describes how faith may be nurtured into knowledge (Alma 32). Benjamin identifies sin as "rebellion against God" (Mosiah 2:36–37) and presents a hopeful outlook for all who will "yield to the enticings of the Holy Spirit and put off the natural man" (Mosiah 3:19). Alma$_2$ depicts the condition of spirits after death as they return to God, "who gave them life" (Alma 40:11). Jacob speaks poignantly of the nakedness of the unrepentant, who will stand filthy before the judgment of God (2 Ne. 9:14). Benjamin extols the "blessed and happy state" of the righteous who taste the love and goodness of God (Mosiah 2:41; 4:11). And Lehi states the purpose of existence: "Men are that they might have joy" (2 Ne. 2:25). The Book of Mormon teaches the one pathway to eternal happiness by numerous inspiring images, instructions, and examples.

Many Book of Mormon prophetic teachings have already been fulfilled (e.g., 1 Ne. 13; 2 Ne. 3; Hel. 14), but several still look to the future. One reason some people were puzzled when Jesus declared he had fulfilled the law and the prophets was that many prophecies of Isaiah, Nephi$_1$, and others remained open—in particular, the Nephites had not yet been reunited with a redeemed people of Israel. Jesus explained: "I do not destroy that which hath been spoken concerning things which are to come" (3 Ne. 15:7). Yet to be fulfilled in the prophetic view of the Book of Mormon are promises that the branches of scattered Israel will be gathered in Christ and will combine their records into one (2 Ne. 29:13–14), that the remnants of Lehi's descendants will be greatly strengthened in the Lord (2 Ne. 30:3–6; 3 Ne. 21:7–13), and that a great division will occur: a New Jerusalem will be built in the Western Hemisphere by the righteous (3 Ne. 21:23; Ether 13: 1–9), while the wicked will be destroyed (1 Ne. 30:10). "Then," Jesus said, "shall the power of heaven come down among them; and I also will be in the midst" (3 Ne. 21:25).

BIBLIOGRAPHY
Most Latter-day Saint doctrinal writings refer to the Book of Mormon on particular topics, but no comprehensive analysis of Nephite religious experience as such has been written.
In general, see Sidney B. Sperry, *Book of Mormon Compendium* (Salt Lake City, 1968); and Rodney Turner, "The Three Nephite Churches of Christ," in *The Keystone Scripture*, ed. P. Cheesman, pp. 100–126 (Provo, Utah, 1988).
For a cultural anthropologist's approach to Nephite religious institutions and practices, see John L. Sorenson, *An Ancient American Setting for the Book of Mormon* (Salt Lake City, 1985).

JOHN W. WELCH

BOOK OF MORMON STUDIES

Since the publication of the Book of Mormon in 1830, a substantial amount of material analyzing, defending, and attacking it has been published. Studies of this complex record have taken various approaches, for the book itself invites close scrutiny and rewards patient and reflective research.

For most Latter-day Saints the primary purpose of scripture study is not to prove to themselves the truth of scriptural records— which they already accept—but to gain wisdom and understanding about the teachings of these sacred writings and to apply in daily life gospel principles learned there. Because of the origins of the Book of Mormon, however, many people have also explored the secondary features of this document: its vocabulary, style, factual assertions, main themes, and subtle nuances.

Book of Mormon research has generally followed many of the same forms as biblical research. In both fields, writings range from expository texts to doctrinal, historical, geographical, textual, literary, and comparative commentaries. But there are also several salient differences. For example, unlike the authors of the Bible, the prophets, compilers, and abridgers of the Book of Mormon frequently state explicitly the dates when they worked, their purposes in writing, and the sources from which they drew, thus clarifying many compositional and interpretive issues; furthermore, academic and archaeological studies of the Book of Mormon are more limited than in biblical research because the earliest extant text is Joseph Smith's 1829 English translation and the precise locations of Book of Mormon settlements are unknown. Nevertheless, a significant number of internal and comparative analyses have been pursued. The works of the following individuals are most notable.

ALEXANDER CAMPBELL. The founder of the Disciples of Christ and a colleague of Sidney Rigdon before Rigdon converted to Mormonism, Alexander Campbell (1788–1866) composed a response to the Book of Mormon that he published on February 7, 1831, in his paper the *Millennial Harbinger* (reprinted as a pamphlet called *Delusions*). In it, Campbell challenged the idea that the Book of Mormon had been written by multiple ancient prophets and attacked the character of Joseph Smith. He said that the book was solely the product of Joseph Smith, written by him alone and "certainly conceived in one cranium" (p. 13). Campbell claimed that the book simply represents the reflections of Joseph Smith on the social, political, and religious controversies of his day: "infant baptism, ordination, the trinity, regeneration, repentance, justification, the fall of man, the atonement, transubstantiation, fasting, penance, church government, religious experience, the call to the ministry, the general resurrection, eternal punishment, who may baptize, and even the question of freemasonry, republican government, and the rights of man" (p. 13). He also asserted that the Book of Mormon misunderstands Israelite and Jewish history (portraying the Nephites as Christians hundreds of years before the birth of Christ) and is written in abysmal English grammar. Campbell characterized Joseph Smith as a "knave" who was "ignorant" and "impudent" (p. 11). *Delusions* is significant among Book of Mormon studies because in many ways it set the agenda for most subsequent critiques of the Book of Mormon (e.g., that the book derives from, or responds to, various trends in early-nineteenth-century upstate New York). Subsequently, however, Campbell changed his position, adopting the Spaulding-Rigdon theory, according to which Sidney Rigdon purloined a copy of a manuscript by Solomon Spaulding, developed from it what became the Book of Mormon, which he passed on to Joseph Smith in the late 1820s, and later pretended to have met Joseph for the first time in 1830 (*see* SPAULDING MANUSCRIPT).

ORSON PRATT.   In *Divine Authenticity of the Book of Mormon* (1850–1851), a series of six pamphlets, Orson Pratt (1811–1881), a member of the Quorum of the Twelve Apostles, drew together early Latter-day Saint thinking about the Book of Mormon. He argued on logical grounds for the divine authenticity of the Book of Mormon, confronted criticisms of it, and presented evidence in favor of its truth, relying heavily on biblical and historical evidences. He did not discuss the contents of the Book of Mormon directly, but addressed ideas of other churches that hindered their acceptance, or even serious consideration, of the Book of Mormon.

The first three pamphlets discussed the nature of revelation, giving evidence to support Pratt's claim that continued communication from God is both necessary and scriptural. The final three pamphlets reported on many witnesses who received heavenly visions substantiating Joseph Smith's claims (*see* BOOK OF MORMON WITNESSES), and asserted that the divinity of the Book of Mormon is confirmed by many miracles, similar to those recorded in the Bible, experienced by Latter-day Saints. Finally, he appealed to prophetic evidence for the Book of Mormon, taken from Daniel and Isaiah. In an 1872 discourse, Pratt proposed a geography for the Book of Mormon that has greatly influenced LDS thinking (*see* BOOK OF MORMON GEOGRAPHY).

GEORGE REYNOLDS AND JANNE M. SJODAHL.   During the nineteenth century, most defenses of, and attacks on, the Book of Mormon were based primarily on reason, on examinations of the environment contemporary with the book, or on the Bible. But George Reynolds (1842–1909) and Janne M. Sjodahl (1853–1939), in their seven-volume *Commentary on the Book of Mormon* (reissued 1955–1961), investigated the plausibility of the claims of the Book of Mormon by examining external evidences of a historical, cultural, linguistic, or religious nature from the Old World and the New. Although their examples and explanations are often not heavily documented and were sometimes mistaken, this work was the first major effort to study the cultural and historical contexts of the Book of Mormon (i.e., to place the book in a historical context by adducing relevant materials from the ancient world).

Whereas in *The Story of the Book of Mormon,* an earlier work, Reynolds had agreed with Orson Pratt on Book of Mormon geography, in their *Commentary* he and Sjodahl placed geography at a low level of priority and were interested primarily in establishing an internally consistent map of all Book of Mormon sites, without attempting to identify those sites with modern locations (Reynolds, pp. 19, 49, 301–330; Reynolds and Sjodahl, Vol. 1, pp. ix–xi). Reynolds eventually authored nearly three hundred articles and several Book of Mormon resource works. Sjodahl published *An Introduction to the Study of the Book of Mormon,* featuring a wide variety of cultural and linguistic theories.

B. H. ROBERTS. Among the most influential Latter-day Saint writers of his time, B. H. Roberts (1857–1933) wrote widely on a variety of Church-related topics, including the Book of Mormon. Like Reynolds and Sjodahl, he was interested not only in the theological implications of the Book of Mormon but also in its historical, geographical, and cultural setting (1909, Vol. 2, pp. 143–44, 162, 347–458; Vol. 3, pp. 3–92). Roberts was not afraid to ask difficult— and, for him, sometimes unanswerable—questions about the Book of Mormon, but affirmed his faith in the Book of Mormon to the end of his life (1985, pp. 61–148; J. Welch, *Ensign* 16 [Mar. 1986]:58–62).

FRANCIS KIRKHAM. In his two-volume study *A New Witness for Christ in America* (1942), Francis Kirkham (1877–1972) examined the 1820s historical evidence relating to the coming forth of the Book of Mormon. Kirkham showed that the testimonies of Joseph Smith and his friends are consistent and coherent, while those of his enemies are frequently inconsistent and contradictory. He carefully documented how alternative explanations for the origin of the Book of Mormon sometimes changed or were abandoned. While favoring the traditional view of Book of Mormon origins, Kirkham allowed all to speak for themselves with little commentary. He liberally presented the primary materials, published and unpublished, from libraries and archives across the United States. His use of the widest available range of primary sources set a new standard in the study of the origins of the Book of Mormon.

Kirkham's second volume of *A New Witness for Christ in America* (1951) examined the alternative explanations of Book of Mormon origins. Regarding the assertion that Joseph Smith wrote the book personally, Kirkham presented statements of some who knew Joseph well, with views representing both sides of the issue of whether he was capable of writing such a book. Kirkham also gave extensive evidence to show that the Spaulding hypothesis was fraught with difficulties. The theory provides only the most circumstantial and dubious evidence for Rigdon's theft of the manuscript and for his passing it on to Joseph Smith with no one else's knowledge. Even though the Spaulding hypothesis has fallen into disfavor as an explanation of the Book of Mormon during the past several decades, it is still occasionally revived.

HUGH W. NIBLEY.   In his considerable corpus of writings on the Book of Mormon, written over a period of some forty years, Hugh W. Nibley (b. 1910) has taken several approaches, mainly historical contextualization based on the internal claims of the Book of Mormon as a document of people who come from the ancient Near East, but also testing the book for authenticity on the basis of internal evidence alone, and seeing the fateful collapse of mighty civilizations as an ominous warning to people today.

In *Lehi in the Desert* (1949–1952), after reviewing the great American archaeologist William F. Albright's criteria for determining the historical plausibility of ancient accounts, Nibley asks these questions about the story of Lehi: "Does it correctly reflect 'the cultural horizon and religious and social ideas and practices of the time'? Does it have authentic historical and geographical background? Is the *mise-en-scène* mythical, highly imaginative, or extravagantly improbable? Is its local color correct, and are its proper names convincing?" (*CWHN* 5:4). The proper approach to the Book of Mormon, according to Nibley, is simply to give the book the benefit of the doubt, granting that it is what it claims to be (a historically authentic ancient document of a people who originated in ancient Israel) and then testing the internal evidence of the book itself (names, cultural and religious ideas) against what can be known about the ancient Near East. When this is done, a picture emerges that is strikingly consistent with what can be determined about the ancient Near East. Most of Nibley's examples come from the Arabs, Egyptians, and Israelites.

With wit and erudition, Nibley argues against alternative explanations of the Book of Mormon. For example, in discussing Thomas O'Dea's environmentalist assertion that the book is obviously an American work, Nibley calls for greater specificity and uniqueness of the American sentiments that allegedly permeate the work (*CWHN* 8:185–86). With skillful parry and thrust, Nibley proceeds in his studies on the Book of Mormon, sometimes defending points in the book, sometimes taking the offensive against those who attack it, always enriching the reader's understanding of its setting. As a teacher, lecturer, and writer, Nibley has been widely influential on subsequent studies of the Book of Mormon.

JOHN L. SORENSON.   Devoting his attention to Mesoamerica in an effort to understand better the geographical, anthropological, and cultural setting of BOOK OF MORMON PEOPLES, John L. Sorenson (b. 1924) examines the text of the Book of Mormon. He carefully analyzes the Mesoamerican evidence, particularly the geography, climatic conditions, modes of life and warfare, and archaeological remains in *An Ancient American Setting for the Book of Mormon,* in order to create a plausible, coherent matrix for understanding the book. With regard to Book of Mormon geography, Sorenson concludes that the events recorded in the Book of Mormon occurred in a fairly restricted area of southern Mexico and Guatemala:

> The narrow neck of land is the Isthmus of Tehuantepec. The east sea is the Gulf of Mexico or its component, the Gulf of Campeche. The west sea is the Pacific Ocean to the west of Mexico and Guatemala. The land southward comprises that portion of Mexico east and south of the Isthmus of Tehuantepec. . . . The land northward consists of part of Mexico west and north of the Isthmus of Tehuantepec. . . . The final battleground where both Jaredite and Nephite peoples met their end was around the Tuxtla Mountains of south-central Veracruz [pp. 46–47].

An Ancient American Setting for the Book of Mormon has placed the study of the ancient American background of the Book of Mormon on a scholarly footing as no previous work (*see* BOOK OF MORMON GEOGRAPHY).

CURRENT DIRECTIONS IN BOOK OF MORMON STUDIES. Much of the scholarly work on the Book of Mormon has been devoted to a fuller understanding of its theological riches or concerned with applying the Book of Mormon principle to "liken all scriptures unto us" (1 Ne. 19:23). Some of the recent publications of the Religious Studies Center at Brigham Young University have focused on various theological aspects of the Book of Mormon and on seeking life applications from the book (e.g., essays by various authors in Cheesman, in McConkie and Millet, and in Nyman and Tate).

Following the lead of Nibley, Sorenson, and others, several recent studies on the Book of Mormon have been concerned with enhancing an understanding of its Old World background and American setting. The research and publications of the Foundation for Ancient Research and Mormon Studies (F.A.R.M.S.), the Society for Early Historic Archaeology (SEHA), and the Archaeological Research Institute have been particularly concerned with the historical and geographic context of the Book of Mormon.

In certain circles, one of the major focuses in current Book of Mormon studies is concerned with its historicity. Whereas in the past, positions on the Book of Mormon divided themselves roughly between those who accepted it as an inspired and historically authentic ancient document and those who rejected it in both these regards, several different lines of approach have developed.

According to one view—a position that has existed since even before its first publication—the Book of Mormon is a conscious fabrication of Joseph Smith. Those holding to this view see the book as reflecting no inspiration and having no historical value, although they may see some religious value in it as a statement of Joseph Smith's religious feelings. The assumption underlying this view may be either a doctrinaire rejection of divine intervention in human affairs or a specific rejection of Joseph Smith's claims to experience with the divine. Those maintaining this position may accept either the Spaulding theory or, more commonly, various environmentalist explanations for the contents of the book (*see* VIEW OF THE HEBREWS). One environmentalist explanation that has attracted some interest in the recent past among both believers and nonbelievers is based on the purported "magic worldview" that suffused the environment in which Joseph Smith grew up. However, this position has been heavily criticized and has not been widely received.

Another view of the Book of Mormon accepts its inspiration but rejects its historical authenticity, seeing it as in some sense inspired but not the product of antiquity, coming rather from the pen of Joseph Smith.

A third position accepts parts of the Book of Mormon as ancient, but views other parts of the book as inspired expansions on the text. This view has suffered because a concession that any part of the book is authentically ancient (and beyond the powers of Joseph Smith to have established through research) seems an admission that the Book of Mormon is what it claims to be and what has traditionally been claimed for it: that it is ancient.

While these views have been articulated by some members in the LDS community, the majority of LDS students of the Book of Mormon accept the traditional view of its divine authenticity and study it as both an ancient document and a tract for modern days, thereby enhancing their appreciation of, and benefit from, the book.

BIBLIOGRAPHY

For bibliographies, see annual issues of the *Review of Books on the Book of Mormon* and John W. Welch, Gary P. Gillum, and DeeAnn Hofer, *Comprehensive Bibliography of the Book of Mormon*, F.A.R.M.S. Report, Provo, Utah, 1982. For essays on Pratt, Reynolds, Roberts, Kirkham, Sperry, and Nibley, see articles in the *Ensign*, 1984–1986.

Bush, Lester E., Jr. "The Spalding Theory Then and Now." *Dialogue* 10 (Autumn 1977):40–69.

Cheesman, Paul R., ed. *The Book of Mormon: The Keystone Scripture*. Provo, Utah, 1988.

Clark, John. "A Key for Evaluating Nephite Geographies" (review of F. Richard Hauck, *Deciphering the Geography of the Book of Mormon*). *Review of Books on the Book of Mormon*, 1 (1989):20–70.

Kirkham, Francis W. *A New Witness for Christ in America*, rev. ed., 2 vols. Salt Lake City, 1959–1960.

McConkie, Joseph Fielding, and Robert L. Millet. *Doctrinal Commentary on the Book of Mormon*, 2 vols. Salt Lake City, 1987–1988.

Nibley, Hugh. *Lehi in the Desert/The World of the Jaredites/There Were Jaredites; An Approach to the Book of Mormon; Since Cumorah;* and *The Prophetic Book of Mormon*. In *CWHN* 5–8.

Nyman, Monte S., and Charles D. Tate, eds. *The Book of Mormon: First Nephi, The Doctrinal Foundation; Second Nephi, The Doctrinal Structure; Jacob Through Words of Mormon, to Learn with Joy*. Provo, Utah, 1988–1990.

Reynolds, George. *The Story of the Book of Mormon*. Salt Lake City, 1888.

————, and Janne M. Sjodahl. *Commentary on the Book of Mormon,* 5th ed., 7 vols. Salt Lake City, 1972.

Reynolds, Noel B., ed. *Book of Mormon Authorship: New Light on Ancient Origins.* Provo, Utah, 1982.

Ricks, Stephen D., and William J. Hamblin, eds. *Warfare in the Book of Mormon.* Salt Lake City, 1990.

Roberts, B. H. *New Witnesses for God,* Vols. 2–3. Salt Lake City, 1909.

————. *Studies of the Book of Mormon,* ed. B. Madsen. Urbana, Ill., 1985.

Sjodahl, Janne M. *An Introduction to the Study of the Book of Mormon.* Salt Lake City, 1927.

Sorenson, John L. *An Ancient American Setting for the Book of Mormon.* Salt Lake City, 1985.

Sperry, Sidney B. *Book of Mormon Compendium.* Salt Lake City, 1968.

STEPHEN D. RICKS

BOOK OF MORMON TRANSLATION BY JOSEPH SMITH

By its own terms, the Book of Mormon is a translation of an ancient book; yet Joseph Smith knew no ancient languages at the time he dictated this text to his scribes. He and several of his close associates testified that the translation was accomplished "by the gift and power of God" (*HC* 1:315; see also D&C 1:29; 20:8).

Little is known about the translation process itself. Few details can be gleaned from comments made by Joseph's scribes and close associates. Only Joseph Smith knew the actual process, and he declined to describe it in public. At a Church conference in 1831, Hyrum Smith invited the Prophet to explain more fully how the Book of Mormon came forth. Joseph Smith responded that "it was not intended to tell the world all the particulars of the coming forth of the Book of Mormon; and . . . it was not expedient for him to relate these things" (*HC* 1:220).

Much is known, however, about when and where the work of translation occurred. The events are documented by several independent firsthand witnesses. Joseph Smith first obtained the GOLD PLATES at the hill CUMORAH in New York, in the early morning hours of September 22, 1827. To avoid local harassment and mobs, he moved to Harmony, Pennsylvania, in December 1827. There he copied and translated some of the characters from the plates, with his wife Emma and her brother Reuben Hale acting as scribes. In 1856,

Emma recalled that Joseph dictated the translation to her word for word, spelled out the proper names, and would correct her scribal errors even though he could not see what she had written. At one point while translating, Joseph was surprised to learn that Jerusalem had walls around it (E. C. Briggs, "Interview with David Whitmer," *Saints' Herald* 31 [June 21, 1884]:396–97). Emma was once asked in a later interview if Joseph had read from any books or notes while dictating. She answered, "He had neither," and when pressed, added: "If he had anything of the kind he could not have concealed it from me" (*Saints' Herald* 26 [Oct. 1, 1879]:290).

Martin Harris came to Harmony in February 1828, and shortly afterward took a transcript and translation of some of the characters to New York City, where he showed them to Professor Charles Anthon at Columbia College (*see* ANTHON TRANSCRIPT). He returned fully satisfied that Joseph was telling the truth, and from April 12 to June 14, 1828, Harris acted as scribe while Joseph Smith translated the book of Lehi.

On June 15, 1828, Joseph and Emma's first son was born but died a few hours later. About July 15, Joseph learned that Martin Harris had lost the 116 pages they had translated (*see* MANUSCRIPT, LOST 116 PAGES), and subsequently the angel MORONI took the plates and the interpreters temporarily from Joseph, who was chastened but reassured by the Lord that the work would go forth (D&C 3:15–16).

On September 22, 1828, the plates and translation tools were returned to Joseph Smith, and during that winter he translated "a few more pages" (D&C 5:30). The work progressed slowly until April 5, 1829, when Oliver Cowdery, a school teacher who had seen the Lord and the plates in a vision (*PWJS*, p. 8), arrived in Harmony and offered his scribal services to Joseph. Virtually all of the English text of the Book of Mormon was then translated between April 7 and the last week of June, less than sixty working days.

The dictation flowed smoothly. From the surviving portions of the Original Manuscript it appears that Joseph dictated about a dozen words at a time. Oliver would read those words back for verification, and then they would go on. Emma later added that after a meal or a night's rest, Joseph would begin, without prompting, where he had previously left off (*The Saints' Herald* 26 [Oct. 1, 1879]:290). No time was taken for research, internal cross-checking, or editorial rewriting. In

1834 Oliver wrote: "These were days never to be forgotten—to sit under the sound of a voice dictated by the inspiration of heaven, awakened the utmost gratitude of this bosom! Day after day I continued, uninterrupted, to write from his mouth as he translated" (*Messenger and Advocate* 1 [Oct. 1834]:14).

During April, May, and June 1829, many events occurred in concert with the translation of the Book of Mormon. By May 15, the account of Christ's ministry in 3 Nephi had been translated. That text explicitly mentions the necessity of being baptized by proper authority, and this injunction inspired Joseph Smith and Oliver Cowdery to pray, leading to the restoration of the Aaronic Priesthood on May 15 (JS—H 1:68–74) and of the Melchizedek Priesthood soon afterward. Time was also required for trips to Colesville, New York, for supplies (thirty miles away); to earn money to purchase paper; to obtain a federal copyright on June 11, 1829; to baptize Samuel and Hyrum Smith; to preach to several interested people; and, during the first week of June, to move by buckboard over 100 miles to the Peter Whitmer farm in Fayette, New York, where about 150 final pages were translated, with some of the Whitmers also acting as scribes. The work was completed before the end of June, at which time the Three and the Eight Witnesses were allowed to see the plates (*see* BOOK OF MORMON WITNESSES).

Most evidence supports the idea that Joseph and Oliver began their work in April 1829 with the speech of BENJAMIN (Mosiah 1–6), translated to the end of the book of Moroni in May, then translated the Title Page, and finally translated the small plates of Nephi (1 Nephi–Omni) and the Words of Mormon before the end of June (Welch and Rathbone). The text of the Title Page, "the last leaf" of the plates of Mormon (*HC* 1:71), was used as the book's description on the copyright form filed on June 11, 1829.

Many factors, including divine sources of knowledge and Joseph's own spiritual efforts and personal vocabulary, apparently played their roles in producing the English text of the Book of Mormon. Some accounts emphasize the divine factor. Years later, David Whitmer indicated that words would appear to Joseph on something resembling a piece of parchment and that he would read the words off to his scribe (*An Address to All Believers in Christ,* 1887, p. 12). Other accounts indicate that human effort was also involved.

When Oliver Cowdery attempted to translate in April 1829, he was told by the Lord: "You must study it out in your mind; then you must ask me if it be right" (D&C 9:8). According to David Whitmer, Joseph could only translate when he was humble and faithful. One morning something had gone wrong about the house; Joseph could not translate a single syllable until he went into an orchard, prayed, and then he and Emma made amends (*CHC* 1:131). Joseph's ability to translate apparently increased as the work progressed.

Most reports state that throughout the project Joseph used the "Nephite interpreters" or, for convenience, he would use a SEER STONE (see *CHC* 1:128–30). Both instruments were sometimes called by others the URIM AND THUMMIM. In 1830, Oliver Cowdery is reported to have testified in court that these tools enabled Joseph "to read in English, the reformed Egyptian characters, which were engraved on the plates" (Benton, *Evangelical Magazine and Gospel Advocate* 2 [Apr. 9, 1831]:15). In an 1891 interview, William Smith indicated that when his brother Joseph used the "interpreters" (which were like a silver bow twisted into the shape of a figure eight with two stones between the rims of the bow connected by a rod to a breastplate), his hands were left free to hold the plates. Other late reports mention a variety of further details, but they cannot be historically confirmed or denied.

Regarding the nature of the English translation, its language is unambiguous and straightforward. Joseph once commented that the book was "translated into our own language" (*TPJS*, p. 17; cf. D&C 1:24). In several chapters, for good and useful reasons, this meant that the language would follow the King James idiom of the day (see *CWHN* 8:212–16; Welch, 1990, pp. 134–63). It also assured that the manuscript would contain human misspellings and grammatical oddities, implying that if it had been translated in another decade its phraseology and vocabulary might have been slightly different.

At the same time, circumstantial evidence in the English text suggests that the translation was quite precise. For example, the independent and identical translations of 1 Nephi 1:8 and of Alma 36:22 (precisely quoting twenty-one of Lehi's words in 1 Nephi 1:8) typify the internal accuracy manifested in this long and complex record. Moreover, several formulaic terms, Hebraisms, stylistic indications of multiple authorship, varieties of parallelism and extended chiasmus (see BOOK OF MORMON AUTHORSHIP; BOOK OF MORMON AS LIT-ERATURE), as well as certain Semitic proper names and some textual variants, not at all evident from the King James Bible, corroborate the claim that the translation was faithful to a consistent underlying text.

Naturally, it is rarely possible to translate exactly the same range of meanings, word for word, from one language into another, and thus opinions have varied about the nature of the correspondence of the ancient text to the English translation. David Whitmer is quoted as saying that "frequently one character would make two lines of man-uscript while others made but a word or two words" (*Deseret News*, Nov. 10, 1881). Nevertheless, the linguistic relationship between the English translation and the characters on the plates cannot be deter-mined without consulting the Nephite original, which was returned to the angel Moroni in 1829 (see MORONI, ANGEL; MORONI₂).

BIBLIOGRAPHY

Roberts, B. H. "Translation of the Book of Mormon." *IE* 9 (Apr. 1906):706–136.

Ricks, Stephen D. "Joseph Smith's Means and Methods of Translating the Book of Mormon." *F.A.R.M.S. Paper.* Provo, Utah, 1984.

Welch, John W. "How Long Did It Take Joseph Smith to Translate the Book of Mormon?" *Ensign* 18 (Jan. 1988):46.

———. *The Sermon at the Temple and the Sermon on the Mount*, pp. 130–63. Salt Lake City, 1990.

Welch, John W., and Tim Rathbone. "The Translation of the Book of Mormon: Basic Historical Information." *F.A.R.M.S. Paper.* Provo, Utah, 1986.

JOHN W. WELCH
TIM RATHBONE

BOOK OF MORMON TRANSLATIONS

After the Prophet Joseph Smith's original translation of the Book of Mormon from the gold plates into English in 1829 and the return of those plates to the angel Moroni, no translations from English into other languages appeared until the 1850s. During the late nineteenth and early twentieth centuries, the Church produced translations of the Book of Mormon irregularly, often in groups of languages, and at widely separated intervals. However, in the 1970s and later, translations from the English text of the Book of Mormon became systematic and frequent.

Making the Book of Mormon and other STANDARD WORKS available in many languages is foreshadowed by the divine injunction "that every man shall hear the fulness of the gospel in his own tongue, and in his own language" (D&C 90:11). As missions were opened on the continent of Europe in 1850 and 1851, Church leaders in many of the newly opened missions mounted simultaneous translation efforts. The Danish edition (1851), produced by Erastus Snow for the Scandinavian Mission from a Danish translation by Peter Olsen Hansen, was the first printed. At the same time, John Taylor supervised translations into French by Curtis E. Bolton and German by George P. Dykes, while Lorenzo Snow was working on the Italian edition and John Davis on a Welsh one. All of these appeared in 1852, and culminated with George Q. Cannon's translation of the Book of Mormon into Hawaiian in 1855. No further translations were published for twenty years.

In 1875 Meliton G. Trejo and Daniel W. Jones produced the first translation of selections from the Book of Mormon into Spanish. This ninety-six-page document, comprising only the books of 1 and 2 Nephi, Omni, 3 Nephi, and Mormon, was the first partial translation and one of only two partial printings of the Book of Mormon in book form at the time. (The other was the publication of 1 Nephi–Words of Mormon in the Deseret Alphabet.) Trejo and James Z. Stewart completed a translation of the entire book into Spanish in 1886. The remainder of the nineteenth century produced three further translations: Swedish (1878), Maori (1889), and Dutch (1890). Sixteen more, including the first in Asian languages and several in South Pacific tongues, appeared between 1903 and 1977.

In 1971, in support of an expanding missionary program, the Church organized a Translation Services Department to direct a systematic program of scripture translation. They began with the production of a large number of translations of *Selections from the Book of Mormon,* designed to place selected chapters in the hands of missionaries, general readers, and members as quickly as possible and to train translators. The *Selections,* chosen and approved by the First Presidency and the Quorum of the Twelve Apostles, were the same in all languages, and consisted of the following:

Book	Chapters
1 Nephi	1–7, 16–18
2 Nephi	1–4; 5:1–20; 9, 29, 31–33
Enos	all
Mosiah	2–5, 17, 18
Alma	5, 11, 12, 32, 34, 39–42
Helaman	13–16
3 Nephi	1, 8, 11–30
4 Nephi	all
Mormon	1, 4, 6–9
Moroni	all

This *Selections* volume is being progressively replaced by full translations. As of 1990, the entire Book of Mormon was available in 36 languages (including English), while *Selections* was available in 44 additional languages.

Retranslations of early editions began in 1952 with the second translation into Spanish. Subsequently, the Japanese, Italian, and German editions were retranslated; other retranslations appeared as *Selections* from 1980 on. With the issuance of the 1981 English edition of the Book of Mormon (*see* BOOK OF MORMON EDITIONS), the Church Translation Department began systematically reviewing all existing translations, setting priorities for retranslation, and producing new editions more in conformity with the English format.

BIBLIOGRAPHY

"Book of Mormon Editions, Translated and Published." *Deseret News 1989–90 Church Almanac.* Salt Lake City, 1988.
The Millennial Star, Vols. 13–14 (1850–1851).

HUGH G. STOCKS

BOOK OF MORMON WITNESSES

Beginning with the first edition of 1830, the Book of Mormon has generally contained two sets of testimonies—the "Testimony of Three Witnesses" and the "Testimony of Eight Witnesses." When Joseph Smith first obtained the GOLD PLATES, he was told to show them to no one. As translation progressed, he and those assisting him learned, both in the pages of the book and by additional revelation, that three special witnesses would know, by the power of God, "that these things are true" and that several besides himself would see the plates and testify to their existence (Ether 5:2–4; 2 Ne. 27:12–13; D&C 5:11–13). The testimonies of the witnesses affirm that these things occurred.

The witnesses were men known for truthfulness and sobriety. Though each of the Three Witnesses was eventually excommunicated from the Church (two returned), none ever denied or retracted his published testimony. Each reaffirmed at every opportunity the veracity of his testimony and the reality of what he had seen and experienced.

A June 1829 revelation confirmed that Oliver Cowdery, David Whitmer, and Martin Harris would be the Three Witnesses (D&C 17). Soon thereafter, they, with Joseph Smith, retired to the woods near Fayette, New York, and prayed for the promised divine manifestation. The "Testimony of Three Witnesses" summarizes the supernatural event that followed, when an angel appeared and showed them the plates and engravings and they heard the Lord declare that the Book of Mormon was "translated by the gift and power of God." They said that the same divine voice "commanded us that we should bear record of it."

Joseph Smith's mother later recounted Joseph's great relief at no longer being the sole witness of the divine experiences of the restoration (see WITNESSES, LAW OF). That others had also seen an angel and "will have to testify to the truth of what I have said for now they know for themselves" relieved him of a great burden (Lucy Smith Preliminary Manuscript, Church Archives).

Soon afterward, at the Smith farm in New York, eight others were allowed to view and handle the plates: Christian Whitmer, Jacob Whitmer, Peter Whitmer, Jr., John Whitmer, Hiram Page, Joseph Smith, Sr., Hyrum Smith, and Samuel H. Smith. Their signed "Testimony of Eight Witnesses" reports that Joseph Smith showed these eight men the metal plates, which they "hefted" while turning the individual "leaves" and examining the engravings of "curious workmanship." In 1829 the word *curious* carried the meaning of the Latin word for "careful," suggesting that the plates were wrought "with care and art." Five of these Eight Witnesses remained solidly with the Church; John Whitmer was excommunicated in 1838, and his brother Jacob Whitmer and brother-in-law Hiram Page then became inactive.

Most of these eleven witnesses were members of the large Smith and Whitmer families—families who had assisted in guarding and in translating the ancient record. Not surprisingly, other family members reported indirect contact with the plates and the translation. Young William Smith once helped his brother Joseph carry the plates wrapped in a work frock. Joseph's wife Emma Smith felt the pliable plates as she dusted around the cloth-covered record on her husband's translating table. Burdened with daily chores and caring for her family and visitors working on the translation, Mother Whitmer (Peter Whitmer, Sr.'s, wife) was shown the plates by a heavenly messenger to assure her that the work was of God.

Martin Harris, a prosperous farmer of Palmyra, New York, who had long sought a religion fulfilling biblical prophecy, assisted with the translation previous to his experience as a witness. In 1828 he spent two months transcribing as Joseph Smith dictated the first major segment of Book of Mormon translation—116 handwritten pages. After Martin lost these pages, he wrote no more for the Prophet, but he later financed the publication of the book.

Oliver Cowdery was the main scribe for the Book of Mormon. A schoolteacher, he learned of the gold plates and the translation while boarding with Joseph Smith's parents near Palmyra, New York. In early April 1829, Oliver walked from the Smith home to Harmony, Pennsylvania, where Joseph Smith was translating. On the way Oliver visited his friend David Whitmer, who also developed an intense interest in the new scripture. When persecution increased in Harmony, David came as requested and moved Joseph and Oliver to his family farm near Fayette (more than 100 miles away), about June 1.

Joseph Smith later recalled the insistent pleading of Harris, Whitmer, and Cowdery after they learned that three would be permitted to see the plates. The June 1829 revelation confirmed that they would be the Three Witnesses—and that they would then testify both from firsthand knowledge and "by the power of God" to the end "that my servant Joseph Smith, Jr., may not be destroyed" (D&C 17:3–4). Of the perhaps 200 recorded interviews with the Three

Witnesses, a significant percentage stress the spiritual intensity of the witnesses as they described the angel and the plates. By themselves, the Prophet's reputation and claims were vulnerable, but the testimony of additional reputable, solemn witnesses who shared a divine experience added credibility.

Lucy Smith's autobiography records the overwhelming gratitude of the Three Witnesses as they returned to the Whitmer house after sharing this experience. Joseph Smith's own history gives the fullest details of the event: repeated prayers followed by a vision given simultaneously to the Prophet, Cowdery, and Whitmer, and soon after a nearly identical vision experienced by the Prophet with Harris. According to Joseph, the intense glory of God enveloped the natural surroundings, and in this divine light the angel appeared, carefully displayed the plates, specifically counseled David Whitmer—the only one of the three who did not eventually return to the Church—to endure to the end, and the voice of God declared the book divine (*HC* 1:54–56).

By early 1838, disagreements on Church policies brought disaffection and excommunication for each of the Three Witnesses, and they separated; Cowdery died in 1850, Harris in 1875, and Whitmer in 1888. Throughout their lives, each witness freely answered questions about his firsthand experience with the angel and the plates. Obviously not relying on Joseph Smith's account, which was not written until the months following their excommunication, each spoke spontaneously and independently; yet the details harmonized with each other and with Joseph Smith's history.

The alienation of the witnesses from the Church stemmed largely from conflicts regarding authority. After receiving revelation, the Three Witnesses felt they shared equally with Joseph Smith in foundational experiences, and their certainty about a past vision contributed to their inflexibility concerning future revelations. They sided with the Prophet's critics who reacted negatively to the failure of the Kirtland Safety Society, and they opposed Joseph Smith's vigorous doctrinal and administrative leadership. After their excommunication, each felt deep rejection, resulting, predictably, in their harsh criticisms of Church leadership. Even in these circumstances, each of the Three Witnesses continued to maintain vigorously the authenticity of their published testimony. None expressed any doubt as to what they had testified. Both Oliver Cowdery and Martin Harris returned to the Church at the end of their lives; David Whitmer retained religious independence but to the end aggressively defended the Book of Mormon.

Skeptics have discounted the "Testimony of Three Witnesses" on the ground of collusion or deception. Yet each of the three was a respected and independent member of non-Mormon society, active in his community. Their lives, fully documented, clearly demonstrate their honesty and intelligence. David Whitmer repeatedly reacted against charges of possible "delusion." To one skeptic, he responded: "Of course we were in the spirit when we had the view . . . but we were in the body also, and everything was as natural to us, as it is at any time" (Anderson, p. 87). Perhaps their later alienation makes them even more credible as witnesses, for no collusion could have withstood their years of separation from the Church and from each other.

The testimonies of the Three and Eight Witnesses balance the supernatural and the natural, the one stressing the angel and heavenly voice, the other the existence of a tangible record on gold plates. To the end of their lives, each of the Three said he had seen the plates, and each of the Eight insisted that he had handled them. Most of the Eight and all of the Three Witnesses reiterated their Book of Mormon testimonies just before death. Together with Joseph Smith they fulfill Nephi's prophecy: "They shall testify to the truth of the book and the things therein" (2 Ne. 27:12).

BIBLIOGRAPHY

Contributions of the Three Witnesses to the translation of the Book of Mormon are detailed in Lucy Mack Smith, *Biographical Sketches of Joseph Smith the Prophet and His Progenitors for Many Generations* (Liverpool, 1853 [reprinted Salt Lake City, 1902 under the title *History of the Prophet Joseph by His Mother Lucy Mack Smith*]). Joseph Smith's recollections of the events of June 1829 are found in Dean C. Jessee, ed., *The Papers of Joseph Smith*, Vol. 1 (Salt Lake City, 1989) (see transcriptions of the 1839 draft and 1839 manuscript history). See also Joseph Smith's published *History of the Church*.

For the Witnesses' testimonies, and their lives outside the Church, see Richard Lloyd Anderson, *Investigating the Book of Mormon Witnesses* (corr. ed.; Salt Lake City, 1989). Primary documents concerning their testimonies appear in Preston Nibley, *Witnesses of the Book of Mormon* (Salt Lake City, 1953). For life sketches, see Andrew Jenson, *Latter-day Saints Biographical Encyclopedia*, Vol. 1 (Salt Lake City, 1901). Profiles for most of the Witnesses are also in Lyndon Cook, *Revelations of the Prophet Joseph Smith* (Salt Lake City, 1985).

RICHARD LLOYD ANDERSON

BOOK OF MOSES

The book of Moses is an extract of several chapters from Genesis in the JOSEPH SMITH TRANSLATION OF THE BIBLE (JST) and constitutes one of the texts in the PEARL OF GREAT PRICE. The Prophet Joseph Smith began an inspired revision of the Old Testament in June 1830 to restore and clarify vital points of history and doctrine missing from the Bible.

As for other ancient books, the original title of the first chapter of Moses may have been its opening line, "The words of God" (Moses 1:1). The account deals with Moses' revelation, and beginning with chapter 2 largely parallels Genesis 1:1–6:13. The revelation came to Moses after his call to deliver the Israelites from bondage in Egypt (Moses 1:26). Much of it concerns God's dealings with Adam and Eve and their immediate posterity following their expulsion from the GARDEN OF EDEN, a topic on which the current text of Genesis is silent. Structurally, a series of orienting visions (chap. 1) is followed by a revelation of the Creation and its aftermath (2:1–8:1). Embedded within this revelation is an extended account of ENOCH (6:25–51; 7:1–8:1), which itself quotes from a record of Adam (6:51–68). A narrative concerning Enoch's descendants, chiefly Noah, appears next (8:2–30).

An outline of the book of Moses follows:

Chapter 1. God reveals himself and his creations to Moses; Satan tries to deceive Moses; God's work and glory are characterized.

Chapter 2. God reveals to Moses—and commands him to write— the creation of the heavens and the earth; man has dominion over other living things.

Chapter 3. All things were created in a spirit state before being created naturally on the earth; man and woman are created in God's image.

Chapter 4. Satan, who had rebelled in the pre-earthly council, tempts Eve; Adam and Eve transgress and are expelled from the Garden, becoming subject to death.

Chapter 5. Children are born to Adam and Eve; Adam offers animal sacrifice as a type and shadow of the anticipated Savior's atoning sacrifice; the gospel of the future Jesus Christ is preached; Cain rebels, and wickedness spreads.

Chapter 6. Adam and his faithful posterity have a "pure and undefiled" language, both written and spoken, and keep records (*see* ADAMIC LANGUAGE); Enoch preaches the word of God and proclaims that the plan of salvation was revealed to Adam; faith, repentance, baptism, and the gift of the Holy Ghost are taught.

Chapter 7. God reveals himself to Enoch, who preaches and establishes the city of ZION; Enoch foresees the coming of Christ, his Atonement and his resurrection; Enoch foresees the restoration of the gospel in the last days, the NEW JERUSALEM, and the second coming of the Savior.

Chapter 8. Great wickedness arises at the time of Noah; he and his sons preach the gospel, but it goes unheeded; all flesh is destroyed by the flood.

A comparison of the book of Moses with Old Testament pseudepigraphic texts shows parallels not found in the present text of Genesis. For example, Adam and Eve were to offer sacrifices to God after being driven from the Garden (Moses 5:5–7; cf. *Life of Adam and Eve*, 29.4), and Satan rebelled against God and was expelled from heaven (Moses 4:3–4; cf. *Life*, 12–16).

A major point of doctrine restored by the book of Moses is that the gospel of salvation was preached "from the beginning" (Moses 5:58), an idea echoed both by Paul's statement that the gospel was preached to Abraham (Gal. 3:8) and by the Book of Mormon (Jacob 4:4–5; 7:10–11; cf. D&C 29:41–42). Similarly, Eusebius (c. A.D. 263–339) maintained that the teaching of Christianity was neither new nor strange and that the religion of the patriarchs was identical with that of the Christians (*Ecclesiastical History* 1.2.1–22).

In this connection, the book of Moses clarifies the fact that Adam and Eve understood the coming mission of Jesus Christ (Moses 6:51–63). Sacrificial offerings, Adam learned, were "a similitude of the sacrifice of the Only Begotten" (5:6–8). Further, Adam was baptized in water, received the Holy Ghost (5:9; 6:64–68), and was taught the plan of salvation (6:62). Adam and Eve and their posterity were also taught the purpose of the Fall and rejoiced in the Lord's plan for redemption (5:10–12).

The book of Moses augments the biblical account of Enoch, who is briefly referred to in Genesis 5:22–24 as one who "walked with God." This restoration of Moses' account includes the fact that Enoch beheld in a vision the Savior's ministry (Moses 7:55–57), the spirit world (6:35–36; 7:56–57), the restoration of the gospel in the last days (7:62), and the second advent of the Savior (7:60, 65). Enoch's importance in the book of Moses parallels his significant role in other Enoch texts (Nibley, p. vii).

BIBLIOGRAPHY

Charlesworth, James H. *The Old Testament Pseudepigrapha*, Vol. 2, p. 285. Garden City, N.Y., 1983, 1985.

Nibley, Hugh. *Enoch The Prophet.* In *CWHN*, 2. Salt Lake City, 1986.

Reynolds, Noel B. "The Brass Plates Version of Genesis." In *By Study and Also by Faith*, ed. J. Lundquist and S. Ricks, Vol. 2, pp. 136–73. Salt Lake City, 1990.

BRUCE T. TAYLOR

BOOK OF REMEMBRANCE

From antiquity God has commanded his people to keep records. In the days of Adam the people wrote a book of remembrance "by the spirit of inspiration" (Moses 6:5) to identify the faithful, to "know" their fathers (Moses 6:45–46), to define "the right of priesthood" (Abr. 1:31), and to promote literacy (see Moses 6:6). Biblical records indicate similar practices (see Ezra 2:62; Neh. 7:5; Ezek. 13:9; Mal. 3:16). NEPHI₁, in the Book of Mormon, stressed the importance of family history. In 1 Nephi 3–5, the Lord commanded LEHI to obtain the brass plates containing a history of his ancestors before leaving Jerusalem, to "enlarge their memory" (Alma 37:8) so that his posterity might know whence and from whom they came and might not lose the language of their fathers. Later, the Savior admonished the Nephites to be accurate and complete in their record keeping (3 Ne. 23:7–13). He also quoted Malachi 3:16–18, which includes a statement about keeping a book of remembrance (3 Ne. 24:16–18).

Latter-day Saints are encouraged to prepare family records as a Book of Remembrance, containing patriarchal blessings, records of ordinations and other sacred information, as well as personal and family histories, spiritual experiences, and other evidences of God's goodness and love (D&C 85:9; 128:7–8, 24). As a latter-day prophet said, "Those who keep a book of remembrance are more likely to keep the Lord in remembrance in their daily lives. Journals are a way of counting our blessings and of leaving an inventory of these blessings for our posterity" (Kimball, p. 76).

BIBLIOGRAPHY

Kimball, Spencer W. "Listen to the Prophets." *Ensign* (May 1978):76.

CYNTHIA M. GARDNER

BROTHER OF JARED

The brother of Jared (c. 2200 B.C.) was the first JAREDITE prophet (*see* BOOK OF MORMON: BOOK OF ETHER). He led his people from "the great tower" in Mesopotamia to the Western Hemisphere. "A large and mighty man, and a man highly favored of the Lord" (Ether 1:34), he is remembered most for his very great faith that allowed him to see and converse face to face with the premortal Jesus Christ (Ether 3:13; 12:19–21) and to be shown in VISION all the inhabitants and events of the earth from beginning to end (Ether 3:25).

Only a few details are known about the life and revelations of this ancient PROPHET. In response to his prayer of faith, the Lord did not confound his language or that of his family and friends at the time of the Tower of Babel. Instead, the Lord instructed him to lead those people to a land "choice above all the lands of the earth" (Ether 1:42), and he was promised that his descendants would become a great and righteous nation. They were called the Jaredites. The Lord came in a cloud to tell the brother of Jared where they should travel, but he did not see him (Ether 2:4). They gathered flocks and seeds, and journeyed to a place on the sea that they called Moriancumer (Ether 2:13). Although the Book of Mormon does not give this prophet's name, Joseph Smith later identified it as Mahonri Moriancumer (*T&S* 2 [1841]:362; *Juvenile Instructor,* Vol. 27 [May 1, 1892]:282).

For four years the Jaredites dwelt in tents on the seashore. During those years, the brother of Jared apparently ceased praying for guidance, and when the Lord appeared again in a cloud, he talked with him for three hours and chastened him, which caused him to repent and return to favor with God. Latter-day Saints see this as evidence of God's concern for his children, of the importance of daily prayer, and of the fact that the Spirit of the Lord will not always strive with man, even with a great prophet, unless he continues to petition the Lord in righteousness (Ether 2:15).

The brother of Jared built eight unique barges (Ether 2:16–25) in which to cross the ocean. Then he prepared sixteen clear molten stones and asked the Lord to make them shine to illuminate the inside of the barges (Ether 3:1–5). As the Lord touched the stones, the brother of Jared saw the finger of the Lord and was "struck with fear" (Ether 3:6). Never before, the record states, had man come before God xwith such exceeding faith; as a result, he was brought into the presence of the Lord Jesus Christ and saw the premortal spirit body of Christ (Ether 3:9–13).

In this vision, the brother of Jared learned many things: he was told that he had been redeemed from the Fall; he saw that human beings were physically created in the image of God and that the spirit body of Jesus looked the same as would his future physical body; he beheld all the inhabitants of the earth from the beginning to the end; and he learned many other sacred things, which he was commanded to record in a cryptic language, sealed up to come forth in the "due time" of the Lord (Ether 3:24; 4:1–2). With that record he included two stones that had been prepared by the Lord to aid future prophets in interpreting the record. For all these reasons, Latter-day Saints esteem the brother of Jared as one of the mightiest prophets who ever lived.

The brother of Jared and his people crossed the sea to the promised land. His great faith, as noted by Moroni, once caused a mountain, Zerin, to be removed (Ether 12:30). He had twenty-two sons and daughters. He lived to see his people begin to prosper and his nephew, Orihah, anointed as their king.

BIBLIOGRAPHY

Eyring, Henry B. "The Brother of Jared." *Ensign* 8 (July 1978):62–65.

REX C. REEVE, JR.

C

CAIN

Although the Bible says little about Cain, latter-day scriptures give considerable information. These tell that Cain, son of Adam and Eve, came under the influence of Satan, whom "he loved . . . more than God" (Moses 5:18), and thereafter became the founder of secret societies whose purposes include to "murder and get gain" (Moses 5:31; cf. 5:49–51).

When Eve bore Cain, she rejoiced in the prospect of a child who would accept his parents' teaching concerning the true Son (Moses 5:7–8) saying, "I have gotten a man from the Lord; wherefore he may not reject his words. But behold, Cain hearkened not, saying: Who is the Lord that I should know him?" (Moses 5:16).

It was Satan who commanded Cain to make an offering to the Lord. When Cain followed Satan's instruction, his offering was rejected by the Lord. In the words of Moses, "Satan commanded him, saying: Make an offering unto the Lord. . . . But unto Cain, and to his offering, [the Lord] had not respect. Now Satan knew this, and it pleased him" (Moses 5:18, 21).

Earlier instructions from an angel to Adam and Eve had emphasized that animal sacrifice "is a similitude of the sacrifice of the Only Begotten of the Father. . . . Wherefore, thou shalt do all that thou doest in the name of the Son" (Moses 5:7–8). Thus, Cain already knew what was acceptable to God, but he refused to follow counsel (*TPJS*, pp. 58, 169).

In the aftermath of his offering, the Lord assured Cain that "if thou doest well, thou shalt be accepted." However, he warned, "if thou doest not well, sin lieth at the door, and Satan desireth to have thee; and except thou shalt hearken unto my commandments, I will deliver thee up" (Moses 5:23). Cain's course of action, the Lord continued, would have long-lasting, even eternal consequences, for "thou [Cain] shalt rule over him [Satan]; for from this time forth thou shalt be the father of his [Satan's] lies; thou shalt be called Perdition; for thou wast also before the world. And it shall be said in time to come—That these abominations were had from Cain; for he rejected the greater counsel which was had from God" (Moses 5:23–25; cf. *TPJS*, p. 190).

Cain grew up with a knowledge of God and even conversed with him person to person. Yet he rejected the counsel of God and also killed his own brother ABEL. Afterward, the Lord said to Cain, "The voice of thy brother's blood cries unto me from the ground. And now thou shalt be cursed from the earth which hath opened her mouth to receive thy brother's blood from thy hand. . . . And Cain said unto the Lord: Satan tempted me because of my brother's flocks. And I was wroth also; for his offering thou didst accept and not mine" (Moses 5:35–38).

In consequence of Cain's rebellion, the Lord cast him out of his presence (Moses 5:38–39) and "set a mark upon Cain, lest any finding him should kill him" (Moses 5:40), protecting him from death by the hand of any avenger (cf. also Moses 7:22). Moreover, Satan had convinced Cain that by committing murder he would acquire both power and wealth. "Cain said: Truly I am Mahan, the master of this great secret, that I may murder and get gain" (Moses 5:31). This latter point became the foundation of the SECRET COMBINATIONS instituted by Cain in collusion with Satan and perpetuated by Cain's descendant Lamech (Moses 5:47–52).

In the Book of Mormon, although the origin and even the operating procedures of such secret organizations are mentioned and condemned from time to time (e.g. Hel. 6:22–30), MORONI₂, like others, purposely limits himself to general remarks when discussing their evils.

And now I, Moroni, do not write the manner of their oaths and combinations, for it hath been made known unto me that they are had among all people. . . . Whoso buildeth it [a secret combination] up seeketh to overthrow the freedom of all lands, nations, and countries; and it bringeth to pass the destruction of all people, for it is built up by the devil, who is the father of all lies; even that same liar . . . who caused man to commit murder from the beginning [Ether 8:20, 25].

BIBLIOGRAPHY
McConkie, Bruce R. *A New Witness for the Articles of Faith*, pp. 167–68, 340, 658–59. Salt Lake City, 1985.
Smith, Joseph Fielding. *DS* 1:49, 61.

JAMES R. HARRIS, SR.

CANON

[*In one of its religious senses, the term "canon" refers to the literary works accepted by a religion as* Scripture. *The word derives from the Hebrew* qaneh *(reed), which came to mean "measuring rod" and then "rule." It thus indicates the norm or the standard by which all things are measured. Latter-day Saints accept a more extensive and more open canon of scripture than those accepted by other Christians and by Jews. Latter-day Saints accept, in addition to the* Bible, *the* Book of Mormon, *the* Doctrine and Covenants, *and the* Pearl of Great Price. *These four scriptural collections are called the* Standard Works. *Related topics include* Joseph Smith Translation of the Bible (JST); New Testament; Old Testament; *and* "Voice from the Dust."]

CIRCUMCISION

Circumcision (Gen. 17:9–14) was the sign of the covenant Abram made with God (Gen. 17:10), in token of which his name was changed to Abraham (Gen. 17:5; cf. Luke 1:59, 2:21). Joseph Smith's translation of the Bible indicates that the performance of circumcision on the eighth day after birth symbolized "that children are not accountable before me until they are eight years old" (JST Gen.

17:4–20; cf. D&C 68:25; 74:1–7). The rite is attested in the inter-testamental period (1 Macc. 1:15, 60–61; 2 Macc. 6:10) and is still observed in Judaism and Islam. Circumcision as a necessity for salvation became a major controversy in early Christianity (Acts 10:45; 11:2; 15:1–31), since it had become associated with the law of Moses.

The Book of Mormon seems to imply the continuing practice of circumcision among its peoples from about 600 B.C. They "were strict in observing the ordinances of God, according to the law of Moses" (e.g., Alma 30:3), apparently including the practice of circumcision. Near the end of Nephite history the Lord revealed to the prophet Mormon that "the law of circumcision is done away in me" (Moro. 8:8).

In modern times, Joseph Smith affirmed the perpetuity of the Abrahamic covenant and defended the integrity of Judaism. Today, however, if Latter-day Saint males are circumcised, it is for cleanliness and health, not religious, reasons. From the beginning of the modern Church, the emphasis has been on circumcision of heart (cf. Deut. 10:16; 30:6; Jer. 4:4; Ezek. 44:9). Such a heart is taken as a sign or token of one's covenants with Christ. This may be the understanding of "broken heart and contrite spirit" among Book of Mormon prophets (2 Ne. 2:7; 3 Ne. 12:19; Moro. 6:2) and in modern revelation (e.g., D&C 59:8).

GORDON C. THOMASSON

CIVIL WAR PROPHECY

Joseph Smith's Civil War prophecy is contained in sections 87 and 130 of the Doctrine and Covenants. He prophesied on December 25, 1832, that a war would begin in South Carolina; that the southern states would divide against the northern states; that the South would seek support from other nations, including Great Britain; and that the war would lead to the death and misery of many souls. These items in the prophecy were all fulfilled in the Civil War (1861–1865). In 1843 the Prophet noted (D&C 130:12–13) that he had also learned by revelation in 1832 that slavery would be the probable cause of the upcoming crisis. These matters are all history now, but certain verses in the Civil War prophecy have broader applications and it appears that portions of the revelation are yet to be fulfilled.

Section 87 was not published by the Church until 1851 and was not canonized until 1876. It was, however, copied and circulated by some Church leaders and missionaries in the 1830s. The Civil War prophecy became one of the most widely published revelations in the Doctrine and Covenants. Not surprisingly, it received greatest attention during the Civil War, as many viewed the conflict as a vindication of the prophetic powers of Joseph Smith.

BIBLIOGRAPHY
Cannon, Donald Q. "A Prophecy of War." In *Studies in Scripture,* ed. R. Millet and K. Jackson, Vol. 1, pp. 335–39. Salt Lake City, 1989.

PAUL H. PETERSON

COVENANTS IN BIBLICAL TIMES

The idea of making and keeping covenants is essential to Latter-day Saints, who would readily agree "that the central message of the Bible is God's covenant with men" (Bruce, p. 139). The "covenant theme pervades Old Testament teachings" and all scripture (Ludlow). A consistent and enduring pattern in God's dealings with mankind from the beginning of the earth's history down to present time is that sacred covenants are used to unite individuals to God and to each other.

Bringing extrabiblical revelations to bear on their understanding of biblical covenants, Latter-day Saints consider the history of God's dealings with mankind to be arranged according to dispensations of the gospel, in which the gospel (including the priesthood and all the necessary ordinances) is bestowed by God upon man, and received by covenant. Each dispensation is presided over by priesthood leaders who hold keys entitling them to put people under covenantal obligations that are bound in heaven as well as on earth. Thus, Moses (Deut. 29:10–15), Joshua (Josh. 24:14–28), and Peter (Matt. 16:19) were among those having authority to act on behalf of God in making and renewing binding covenants between God and his people.

God's covenant relationship with mankind began with Adam and

Eve. Texts in the PEARL OF GREAT PRICE show that Adam and Eve were the first after the Fall to enter into a covenant relationship with God—through sacrifice, baptism (Moses 6:64–66), and receiving the priesthood and ordinances associated with the temple: "Thus all things were confirmed unto Adam, by an holy ordinance" (Moses 5:59; see also 4:4–5, 8, 10–12). Adam and Eve were promised a savior and were instructed to be obedient, to be repentant, and to do all things in the name of the Son of God (Moses 5:6–8).

Whereas the Bible first uses the term "covenant" in conjunction with Noah (Gen. 6:18; 9:9–17), its first use in other LDS scriptures is with Enoch (Moses 7:51; 8:2). Non-LDS Bible scholars (e.g., Fensham) usually arrange the principal biblical covenants into a five-fold sequence (Noah, Abraham, Moses, David, and the New Testament covenant), but Latter-day Saints follow a sequence of seven main dispensations (Adam, Enoch, Noah, Abraham, Moses, Christ and his apostles, and Joseph Smith), and recognize those also of the brother of Jared, Lehi, and Alma in Book of Mormon history. Where non-LDS scholars explore both connections and distinctions between the covenants mentioned in the Bible (e.g., the patriarchal covenant of Abraham continued even when the covenant at Sinai was broken), Latter-day Saints see general uniformity of the principal covenant occurrences, all of them reflecting the same underlying principles of the gospel of Jesus Christ.

Central as they are to subsequent biblical references to covenants (e.g., Ex. 2:24; Luke 1:72–73; Acts 3:25; Gal. 3:13–14), the promises made explicit in the Abrahamic covenant receive particular emphasis in LDS teachings (Ricks, 1985; Nyman). The book of Abraham in the Pearl of Great Price adds to the understanding of the promises to Abraham and Sarah. To the promises of a land of inheritance (Gen. 15:18; 17:8; cf. Abr. 2:6) and of innumerable posterity (Gen. 15:5; 17:2–6; cf. Abr. 2:9; 3:14), the book of Abraham adds priesthood blessings (Abr. 1:3–4, 18) and the promise that Abraham's seed will be the means whereby the gospel will be ministered throughout the earth so that all people might receive the gospel and obtain salvation (Abr. 2:10–11). Latter-day Saints believe that the power to give these ancient promises by way of covenant was reinstated on April 3, 1836, when Elijah, Elias, Moses, and other ancient prophets restored to Joseph Smith and Oliver Cowdery the keys of "the dispensation of the gospel of Abraham, saying that in us and our seed all generations after us should be blessed" (D&C 110:12; 124:58; 132:30–31).

In biblical times, political and legal covenants were made in various ways. Religious covenants often drew upon these secular practices by way of analogy. For example, in the language of the Bible, one "cuts" a covenant, reminiscent of the legal procedure of cutting a small animal in a ceremony when solemnizing a contract or treaty (Gen. 15:10; Hillers, pp. 40–45).

The process of renewing covenants, individually and communally, was also an important part of religious life in biblical times. Just as individual Latter-day Saints "renew" their covenant of baptism by partaking of the sacrament of the Lord's Supper, so there are scriptural instances of communal rites of covenant renewal (e.g., Deut. 31:10–13; Josh. 1:16–18). Covenant renewals are also found in the Book of Mormon, where Near Eastern (especially Hittite) analogues are evident (Ricks, 1984, 1990).

Despite such renewals, it is clear that the old covenant, or Mosaic law, was to be replaced by a new one, as Jeremiah prophesied (Jer. 31:31). Latter-day Saints believe that this prophecy was fulfilled in the New Testament (or, more exactly, the New Covenant). Christ "is the mediator of a better covenant, which was established upon better promises" (Heb. 8:6). The recurring symbol of renewal in the new covenant is the sacrament, instituted at the Last Supper and centered in the commitment to remember Christ always, evoking the Passover imagery of the old covenant and the covenantal cry of the prophets to know God (Hosea 4:6).

BIBLIOGRAPHY

Bruce, F. F. "Bible." In *The New Bible Dictionary*, 2nd ed., ed. J. D. Douglas et al., pp. 137–40. Wheaton, Ill., 1982.

Fensham, F. C., "Covenant, Alliance." In *The New Bible Dictionary*, 2nd ed., ed. J. D. Douglas et al., pp. 137–40. Wheaton, Ill., 1982.

Hillers, Delbert R. *Covenant: The History of a Biblical Idea.* Baltimore, 1969.

Ludlow, Victor L. "Unlocking the Covenant Teachings in the Scriptures." *Religious Studies Center Newsletter, Brigham Young University* 4, no. 2 (1990):1, 4.

Nyman, Monte S. "The Covenant of Abraham." In *The Pearl of Great Price: Revelations from God*, pp. 155–70, ed. H. Donl Peterson and C. Tate. Provo, Utah, 1989.

Ricks, Stephen D. "The Treaty/Covenant Pattern in King Benjamin's Address (Mosiah 1–6)." *BYU Studies* 25 (Spring 1984):151–62.

————. "The Early Ministry of Abraham." In *Studies in Scripture*, ed. R. Millet and K. Jackson, Vol. 2, pp. 217–24. Salt Lake City, 1985.

————. "Deuteronomy: A Covenant of Love." *Ensign* 20 (Apr. 1990):55–59.

Whittaker, David J. "A Covenant People: Old Testament Light on Modern Covenants." *Ensign* 10 (Aug. 1980):36–40.

GEORGE S. TATE

CREATION, CREATION ACCOUNTS

Latter-day Saints have, in addition to the biblical Genesis, two modern restorations of ancient scriptural accounts of the Creation in the BOOK OF MOSES and the BOOK OF ABRAHAM. Related authoritative information also appears in the Book of Mormon, the Doctrine and Covenants, and the LDS temple ceremony. Drawing on this wealth of creation literature, Latter-day Saints understand that Jesus Christ, acting under the direction of God the Father, created this and other worlds to make possible the immortality and eternal life of human beings who already existed as spirit children of the Father. This understanding differs from both scientific and traditional Christian accounts in that it affirms God's purpose and role, while recognizing creation as organization of preexisting materials, and not as an ex nihilo event (creation from nothing). Furthermore, these accounts describe an active role for God's spirit children in the Creation and include a more detailed version of the origins of evil.

The frequent occurrence of creation accounts in LDS scriptures and sacred ceremonies reflects a pattern of the ancient world generally, and ancient Israel in particular, where the Creation was regularly recited or reenacted. The Creation—including its ritual recitation and reenactment—was viewed by the Israelites and other peoples of the ancient Near East as possessing a dynamic, not a static, quality. According to Raffaele Pettazzoni, a noted historian of religions, "What happened in the beginning has an exemplary and defining value for what is happening today and what will happen in the future" (p. 26).

Creation plays a central theological role in the Book of Mormon. The events surrounding creation are linked with the fall of that angel who became the devil (2 Ne. 2:17; 9:8). His fall, in turn, led to the fall of Adam; opposition as a feature of mortal existence; and, ultimately, the need for a divine redemption of mankind (2 Ne. 2:18–27). Book of Mormon prophets invoked the Creation as a symbol of God's goodness and a touchstone of human stewardship: "The Lord hath created the earth that it should be inhabited; and he hath created his children that they should possess it" (1 Ne. 17:36). Those who reject God's goodness, as symbolized by the Creation (and the Atonement), will inevitably be judged and punished (cf. 2 Ne. 1:10).

The creation account in the book of Moses (revealed in 1830 as the beginning of the JOSEPH SMITH TRANSLATION OF THE BIBLE) provides several insights in addition to those found in Genesis.

First, the book of Moses establishes Mosaic authorship of its creation account indicating explicitly that it resulted from a revelation given to Moses sometime between the time of the burning bush and the exodus (Moses 1:17, 25).

Second, it clarifies the role of Jesus Christ in the Creation: "By the word of my power have I created [these lands and their inhabitants], which is mine Only Begotten Son" (Moses 1:32–33); "I, God, said unto mine Only Begotten, which was with me from the beginning: Let us make man in our image" (Moses 2:26–27); "And I, the Lord God, said unto mine Only Begotten: Behold, the man is become as one of us to know good and evil" (Moses 4:28). This is consistent with the teachings of John and Paul in the New Testament (John 1:3, 10; Eph. 3:9; Col. 1:13–16; Heb. 1:2, 10).

Third, the Creation is placed in a much larger context of ongoing creations of innumerable inhabited earths with their respective heavens (in all of which Christ played a central role): "And worlds without number have I created . . . for mine own purpose; and by the Son I created them, which is mine Only Begotten. . . . And as one earth shall pass away, and the heavens thereof even so shall another come; and there is no end to my works" (Moses 1:33, 38). Moses is given details of the creation of "this heaven, and this earth" only (Moses 2:1; cf. 1:35).

Fourth, the origin of evil is traced back to the rebellion of Satan, who sought (1) to replace God's Beloved Son, who had been "chosen from the beginning," and (2) to receive and use God's own power to redeem all humans by destroying their agency (Moses 4:1–4). The importance of human agency is reaffirmed in the command to ADAM and EVE concerning the tree of knowledge of good and evil: "Thou shalt not eat of it, nevertheless, thou mayest choose for thyself, for it is given unto thee; but remember that I forbid it, for in the day thou eatest thereof thou shalt surely die" (Moses 3:17).

Fifth, the account in Moses makes clear that there was a spirit creation of all living things in heaven before they were created physically upon the earth: "I, the Lord God, created all things, of which I have spoken, spiritually, before they were naturally upon the face of the earth. . . . And I, the Lord God, had created all the children of men; and not yet a man to till the ground; for in heaven created I them; and there was not yet flesh upon the earth, neither in the water, neither in the air" (Moses 3:5).

Certain LDS commentators have explored the possibility that the Moses account could resolve the apparent conflict in the order of God's creative acts between Genesis 1 and Genesis 2 by treating the first as a spirit creation (O. Pratt, pp. 21–22; Roberts, pp. 264–68; cf. *DS* 1:74–76, which explains a different view). Later revelations make it clear that mankind's spirit creation had taken place long before the events described in any of the accounts of the earth's creation. God, our Heavenly Father, is literally the "Father of spirits" (Heb. 12:9). "Man as a spirit was begotten and born of heavenly parents, and reared to maturity in the eternal mansions of the Father, prior to coming upon the earth in a temporal body" (see First Presidency, "The Origin of Man," Nov. 1909 [Appendix, *Jesus Christ and His Gospel: Selections from the Encyclopedia of Mormonism*]).

The Abrahamic account is distinctive among creation accounts. It describes a structured cosmos, with many stars, one above another, with their different periods and orders of government (Abr. 3:1–10). Within this context Abraham also learns about eternally existing spirits, one above the other in intelligence, all the way up to "the Lord thy God," who is "more intelligent than they all" (Abr. 3:19; see speeches cited in bibliography). He is shown a group of organized intelligences (or spirits, or souls—the words are here used interchangeably), over whom God rules and among whom he dwells, and is taught that "in the beginning" God came down in the midst of them, and said of some who were "noble and great": "These I will make my rulers. . . . And he said unto me: Abraham, thou art one of them; thou wast chosen before thou wast born" (Abr. 3:18–23). A purpose of this premortal assembly in heaven is explained by "one among them that was like unto God," who says to those who are with him, "We will go down . . . and we will make an earth whereon these may dwell; and we will prove them herewith, to see if they will do all things whatsoever the Lord their God shall command them" (Abr. 3:24–25). This is followed by a pronouncement of the glory to come upon those who prove worthy, the choosing of one "like unto the Son of Man" (who is to be sent to bring this about), and the rejection of Satan—all done by "the Lord," who is identified elsewhere as Jehovah (Abr. 3:25–28; cf. Abr. 1:15–16; 2:7–8). Thereafter, "the Lord said: Let us go down," whereupon the Gods "organized and formed the heavens and the earth" (Abr. 4:1). A significant feature of this revealed account is that both the space and the materials for the earth explicitly existed before its creation.

Within this context of the divine assembly, or Council in Heaven, Abraham's account of the Creation proceeds, generally following the structural outline of Genesis. By the time Joseph Smith published this "translation" in 1842, he had gained a much deeper understanding both through additional revelation and some through study of Hebrew. In light of the doctrine of the Council in Heaven, Joseph Smith had pointed out that the Hebrew term *Elohim*, a plural form, should be rendered the "Gods" in the creation account, not as the traditional "God" (*WJS*, p. 379). It is so rendered throughout Abraham's account. In light of the doctrine of the eternal nature of matter, the word traditionally translated as "created" becomes "organized." The phrase "without form and void" (Hebrew *tohu wa-bohu*) is rendered, quite properly, "empty and desolate" and describes the condition of the earth after it was organized, not before (Abr. 4:2).

The term "day" (Hebrew *yom*) for the seven "days" of creation is given as "time," a permissible alternative in both Hebrew and English; and it is explicitly pointed out that the "time" in which Adam should die if he partook of the forbidden fruit "was after the Lord's time, which was after the time of Kolob [a great star that Abraham had seen nearest to the throne of God, whose revolution, one thousand years by our reckoning, is a day unto the Lord]; for as yet the Gods had not appointed unto Adam his reckoning" (Abr. 5:13; 3:2–4).

On the basis of the above passage, which clearly excludes the possibility of earthly twenty-four-hour days being the "days" or "times" of creation, some Latter-day Saint commentators have argued for one-thousand-year periods as the "times" of creation as well as the "time" of Adam's earthly life after the fall; others have argued for indefinite periods of time, as long as it would take to accomplish the work involved. Abraham's account does contain the interesting passage, in connection with the "organizing" of the lights in the "expanse" of heaven, "The Gods watched those things which they had ordered until they obeyed" (Abr. 4:14–18). Abraham's account actually includes twelve different "labors" of the Gods, divided up among the "days" in the manner of Genesis. The later temple account of creation gives an abbreviated version of those labors, divided up differently among the seven days while retaining the same order, suggesting that it may not be significant which labor is assigned to which day.

Abraham connects the seemingly differing accounts of Genesis 1 and 2 within the context of the Council in Heaven. Abraham's seven-day account proceeds through the work of the first five creative times and part of the sixth as the physical creation of the earth and its preparation to support life before life was actually placed upon it. Thus, during the third time, "the Gods organized the earth *to bring forth* grass . . . and the earth *to bring forth* the tree from its own seed" (Abr. 4:12; emphasis added). And during the fifth time, the Gods "prepared the waters that they might bring forth great whales, and every living creature, . . . and every winged fowl after their kind" (Abr. 4:21). Similarly, on the sixth time "the Gods prepared the earth *to bring forth* the living creature after his kind. . . . And the Gods saw they would obey" (Abr. 4:24–25). Then upon the sixth time, the Gods again took counsel among themselves and determined to form man, and to give them dominion over the plants and animals that should come upon the earth (Abr. 4:26–29). "And the Gods said among themselves: On the seventh time we will end our work, which we have counseled; and we will rest. . . . And thus were their decisions at the time that they counseled among themselves" (Abr. 5:2–3). The account paralleling Genesis 2 then follows smoothly as an account of the actual placing of life upon the earth: "And the Gods came down and formed these the generations of the heavens and of the earth, when they were formed in the day that the Gods formed the earth and the heavens, according to all that which they had said concerning every plant of the field before it was in the earth" (Abr. 5:4–5).

Several themes in other ancient creation accounts—premortal conflict in heaven, divine victory over the opposing powers of chaos, and the promulgation of law at the time of creation—are also familiar from creation accounts in LDS scripture and theology (2 Ne. 2:17; 9:8; Moses 4:3–4; Abr. 3:27–28; *see also* WAR IN HEAVEN). These ideas are alluded to in several places in the Bible (cf. Ex. 15; Job 38–41; Isa. 40–42; Ps. 18; 19; 24; 33; 68; 93; 104; Prov. 8:22–33; Hab. 3:8; Rev. 12:7–12). From the early Christian era until the end of the nineteenth century, traditional Christian interpretation has generally treated these biblical texts allegorically or has not considered them at all in discussions of the Creation. A profound transformation in the Christian interpretation of these passages took place during the latter part of the nineteenth century with the discovery and translation of creation accounts from ancient Mesopotamia and Egypt. While these accounts vary considerably in detail, they usually mention premortal combats, the establishment of the divine order before creation, and creation from chaos. The biblical passages mentioned above are now often understood in light of these descriptions of extrabiblical accounts.

The doctrine of ex nihilo creation has been the traditional Christian explanation. In recent discussion of the subject, many Jewish scholars agreed that the belief in an ex nihilo creation is not to be found before the Hellenistic period, while Christian scholars see no evidence of this doctrine in the Christian church until the end of the second century A.D. The rejection of ex nihilo creation in the teaching of the Latter-day Saints thus accords with the evidence of the earliest understanding of the Creation in ancient Israel and in early Christianity. Similarly, Latter-day Saints have understood such biblical passages as John 9:2 and Jeremiah 1:4–5 to refer to individual premortal existence, with implications for subsequent earthly existence. In support of this, it may be pointed out that various Christians and Christian groups in the early Christian centuries taught the same doctrine (cf. Origen, *De principiis* 1:7; 2:8; 4:1), and that it is also to be found in Jewish belief of the same period, including Philo (*De mutatione nominum* 39; *De opificio mundi* 51; *De cherubim* 32); in some apocryphal writings (Wisdom of Solomon

8:19–20; 15:3); and among the Essenes (Josephus, *Jewish War* 2.8.11, as well as in the Jewish Talmud and Midrash).

BIBLIOGRAPHY

Anderson, Bernhard W. "Creation." In *Interpreter's Dictionary of the Bible*, Vol. 1, pp. 725–32. New York, 1962.

Eliade, Mircea. "The Prestige of the Cosmogonic Myth." *Diogenes* 23 (Fall 1958):1–13.

Goldstein, Jonathan A. "The Origins of the Doctrine of Creation *Ex Nihilo*." *Journal of Jewish Studies* 35 (Autumn 1984):127–35.

McConkie, Bruce R. "Christ and the Creation." *Ensign* 12 (June 1982):9–15.

Pettazzoni, Raffaele. "Myths of Beginnings and Creation-Myths." In Pettazzoni, *Essays on the History of Religions*, H. J. Rose, trans., Vol. 1, pp. 24–36. Leiden, 1954.

Pratt, Orson. "The Pre-existence of Man." Serialized in *The Seer* (1853–1854). Photo repr., Salt Lake City, 1990.

Pratt, Parley P. "Origin of the Universe." In Pratt, *The Key to the Science of Theology*, pp. 26–32. Salt Lake City, 1978.

Roberts, B. H. *The Gospel and Man's Relationship to Deity*, pp. 256–73. Salt Lake City, 1966.

Salisbury, Frank B. *The Creation*. Salt Lake City, 1976.

Smith, Joseph. See speeches reported in *WJS*, pp. 9, 33, 60, 341, 346, 351–52, and 359 and their contexts.

Smith, Joseph Fielding. *Man, His Origin and Destiny*. Salt Lake City, 1954.

Winston, David. "Creation Ex Nihilo Revisited: A Reply to Jonathan Goldstein." *Journal of Jewish Studies* 37 (Spring 1986):88–91.

Young, Brigham. *Discourses of Brigham Young*, chaps. 2, 4, 9. Salt Lake City, 1954.

F. KENT NIELSEN
STEPHEN D. RICKS

CUMORAH

Cumorah in the Book of Mormon refers to a hill and surrounding area where the final battle between the NEPHITES and LAMANITES took place, resulting in the annihilation of the Nephite people (*see* BOOK OF MORMON PEOPLES). Sensing the impending destruction of his people, Mormon records that he concealed the plates of Nephi$_1$ and all the other records entrusted to him in a hill called Cumorah to prevent them from falling into the hands of the Lamanites (*see* BOOK OF MORMON PLATES AND RECORDS). He delivered his own abridgment of these records, called the plates of Mormon, and the small plates of Nephi, which he placed with them, to his son MORONI$_2$ (W of M 1:5;

Morm. 6:6), who continued writing on them before burying them in an unmentioned site more than thirty-six years later (Moro. 10:1–2).

The Book of Mormon mentions a number of separate records that would have been part of Mormon's final record respository in the hill Cumorah. Though the contents of these can be known to us only to the extent that they are summarized or mentioned in the Book of Mormon, Latter-day Saints expect them someday to become available. Alma₂ prophesied to his son Helaman that the brass plates of Laban (the Nephites' version of the Old Testament) would be "kept and preserved by the hand of the Lord until they should go forth unto every nation" (Alma 37:4; cf. 1 Ne. 5:17–19). He further explained that "all the plates" containing scripture are the "small and simple" means by which "great things are brought to pass" and by which the Lord will "show forth his power . . . unto future generations" (Alma 37:5–6, 19).

Cumorah had also been the site of the destruction of the JARED-ITES roughly 900 years earlier. Moroni states in the book of Ether that the Jaredites gathered for battle near "the hill Ramah," the same hill where his father, Mormon, hid up "the records unto the Lord, which were sacred" (Ether 15:11). It was near the first landing site of the people of Mulek (Alma 22:30), just north of the land Bountiful and a narrow neck of land (Alma 22:32).

The more common reference to Cumorah among Latter-day Saints is to the hill near present-day Palmyra and Manchester, New York, where the plates from which the Prophet Joseph Smith translated the Book of Mormon were found. During the night of September 21, 1823, Moroni₂ appeared to Joseph Smith as an angel sent from God to show him where these plates were deposited (JS—H 1:29–47).

In 1928 the Church purchased the western New York hill and in 1935 erected a monument recognizing the visit of the angel Moroni (see ANGEL MORONI STATUE). A visitors center was later built at the base of the hill. Each summer since 1937, the Church has staged the Hill Cumorah Pageant at this site. Entitled *America's Witness for Christ,* it depicts important events from Book of Mormon history. This annual pageant has reinforced the common assumption that Moroni buried the plates of Mormon in the same hill where his father had buried the other plates, thus equating this New York hill with the

Book of Mormon Cumorah. Because the New York site does not readily fit the Book of Mormon description of BOOK OF MORMON GEOGRAPHY, some Latter-day Saints have looked for other possible explanations and locations, including Mesoamerica. Although some have identified possible sites that may seem to fit better (Palmer), there are no conclusive connections between the Book of Mormon text and any specific site that has been suggested.

BIBLIOGRAPHY

Clark, John. "A Key for Evaluating Nephite Geographies." *Review of Books on the Book of Mormon* 1 (1989):20–70.

Palmer, David A. *In Search of Cumorah: New Evidences for the Book of Mormon from Ancient Mexico.* Bountiful, Utah, 1981.

Sorenson, John L. "Digging into the Book of Mormon: Part One." *Ensign* 14 (1984):26–37.

DAVID A. PALMER

D

DANIEL, PROPHECIES OF

The Church of Jesus Christ of Latter-day Saints regards the book of Daniel as the writings of Daniel, who was deported from Jerusalem to Babylon (c. 606 B.C.), and accepts the work as SCRIPTURE. It sees in the work significant PROPHECIES about the latter days, including the apostasy from and RESTORATION OF THE GOSPEL of Jesus Christ.

According to Wilford Woodruff, the angel Moroni quoted to the Prophet Joseph Smith from Daniel chapter two which features a prophecy of the latter-day restoration of the gospel in Nebuchadnezzar's dream concerning "what shall be in the latter days" (Dan. 2:28; Whittaker, p. 159). Daniel identified the "head of gold" in the dream as a symbol of Nebuchadnezzar's empire, and latter-day PROPHETS have specified that the stone "cut out without hands" (Dan. 2:34) represents the latter-day kingdom of God (D&C 65:2; *HC* 1:xxxiv–xl). The remaining symbols have been interpreted as follows: The "breast and arms of silver" represent the Persian realm that superseded Babylon. The "belly and thighs of brass" prefigure the succeeding Hellenistic states. The two "legs of iron" point to the Roman Empire, foreshadowing the division between Rome and Constantinople. The feet of the image, "part of iron and part of clay," symbolize the European kingdoms that grew out of the dissolving Roman Empire, beginning in the fifth century. Those kingdoms merged the culture of Rome with that of northern and eastern European tribes; hence, the symbolic mixing of iron and clay.

In the days of those kingdoms, Daniel predicted, "the God of heaven [will] set up a kingdom, which . . . shall stand for ever" (2:44). This final kingdom, represented by the stone "cut out without hands," is The Church of Jesus Christ of Latter-day Saints, restored to the earth in 1830, when European monarchs still ruled. That the Church would spread throughout the world is seen when "the stone that smote the image became a great mountain, and filled the whole earth" (2:34–35; Kimball, p. 8).

Daniel's vision in chapter seven is also interpreted in the context of the last days. The "four great beasts" (Dan. 7:3) seem to represent successive empires of Babylon, Persia, Macedonia, and Rome; and the "ten horns" (7:7) of the fourth beast appear to symbolize again the kingdoms that succeeded the Roman Empire. Latter-day prophets identify the "Ancient of Days" (7:22) as Adam, who will preside at a gathering to be held at Adam-ondi-Ahman in Missouri before Jesus' second coming (D&C 116). At that assembly, Jesus, "the Son of Man," will appear. Acting for priesthood leaders in all dispensations, Adam will return to the risen Jesus the priesthood keys which represent everlasting dominion.

The prophecy of the "seventy weeks" in chapter nine interests Latter-day Saints because it suggests that the New Testament church would fall into apostasy. The sixty-nine weeks (Dan. 9:24–26) may be symbolic of the period between the Jews' return to Jerusalem (537 B.C.) and the coming of Jesus the Messiah, who would atone ("be cut off") for his people. Verse 27 reports that the Lord would "confirm the covenant with many for one week." This seventieth week may typify the decades that Christ's true church endured, led then by living apostles and prophets, ending shortly after A.D. 100, following the ministry of John the Apostle. The prophecy also notes that Jerusalem and its temple would be destroyed "in the midst of the week" (A.D. 70), mentioning the abomination of desolation and the cessation of temple SACRIFICE (cf. Mark 13:14).

BIBLIOGRAPHY

Kimball, Spencer W. "A Stone Cut Without Hands." *Ensign* 6 (May 1976):4–9.

McConkie, Bruce R. *The Millennial Messiah*, chap. 11, 47. Salt Lake City, 1982.

Sperry, Sidney B. *The Voice of Israel's Prophets.* Salt Lake City, 1952.

Whittaker, David J. "The Book of Daniel in Early Mormon Thought." In *By Study and Also by Faith*, ed. J. Lundquist and S. Ricks, Vol. 1, pp. 155–201. Salt Lake City, 1990.

JEFFREY R. CHADWICK

DAVID, KING

David, king of ISRAEL, was the youngest of eight brothers, sons of Jesse (1 Sam. 16:6–12), a descendent of Boaz and RUTH (Ruth 4:21–22) and an ancestor to Jesus Christ (Matt. 1:6–17; Luke 3:23–31). He was born at Bethlehem and died in Jerusalem c. 1015 B.C., after reigning over Judah for seven years and the united kingdom of Israel for an additional thirty-three (1 Kgs. 2:11). He was buried in the ancestral home, in Bethlehem (1 Kgs. 2:10). He was perhaps the greatest king of Israel, once called "a man after [God's] own heart" (1 Sam. 13:14). Mormon interests in David have often dwelt on the issues of his plural marriages and his status in the afterlife.

While the scriptures relate different stories of his introduction at Saul's court (1 Sam. 16:14–23; 17:55–58), David's vault from obscurity to national awareness seems to have come as a result of his courageous defeat of the giant Goliath (1 Sam. 17:49).

David's strength and reliance on the Lord marked him as an exceptional leader and the epitome of Israelite heroism (2 Sam. 5:1–3; 22:2–51). Subsequent rulers were measured against his stature (cf. 1 Kgs. 15:3–5, 11), and his name was linked with that of the awaited Messiah (Mark 12:35; Luke 1:32; Rom. 1:3). Scripture indicates that David's blessings, including his wives, were given to him as a result of God's favor (2 Sam. 5:12–13; 12:8; D&C 132:39).

But when David also acquired wives and concubines, apparently under his own authority, he was condemned by God (Jacob 2:23–24). Certainly David lost divine approval as a result of his adulterous union with Bathsheba and the subsequent contrived murder of her husband, Uriah (2 Sam. 12:1–12; D&C 132:38–39).

Because of David's transgressions, his eternal blessings were taken from him (*TPJS*, pp. 188–89). The Lord granted David a continuation of life for another twenty-one years, perhaps because of his immediate and deep remorse (cf. Ps. 51), his acts of repentance, and his continued faithfulness to Jehovah (2 Sam. 12:13, 16; cf. *WJS*, p. 335). However, he must await in the spirit prison the redemption promised to him (Acts 2:34; *WJS*, p. 74). Even with the assurance of the Lord's ultimate mercy (Ps. 86:13), David lost much that God had given him on earth, he fell "from his exaltation" and his wives were given "unto another" (D&C 132:39). Yet his personal integrity appears in his insistence that he be punished in place of his people, whom he saw in vision being destroyed (2 Sam. 24:15–17).

BIBLIOGRAPHY
Bright, John. *A History of Israel.* 3rd ed., pp. 184–228. Philadelphia, 1981.
McCarter, P. Kyle. *Second Samuel. Anchor Bible.* New York, 1984.

NORMAN J. BARLOW

DAVID, PROPHETIC FIGURE OF LAST DAYS

King David (c. 1000 B.C.) remains today one of the most renowned Old Testament figures. His personality, spiritual sensitivity, creative abilities, military victories, and leadership carried him to the pinnacle of popularity. He had the potential to become an ideal king, but his kingship deteriorated after his adultery with Bathsheba and his involvement in Uriah's death. However, prophecy states that a model ruler in the last days will be "raised up" from David's lineage.

The Prophet Joseph Smith taught that "the throne and kingdom of David is to be taken from him and given to another by the name of David in the last days, raised up out of his lineage" (*TPJS*, p. 339). Elder Orson Hyde, in his dedicatory prayer on the Mount of Olives, October 24, 1841, prophesied that the Jews would return to Jerusalem and that in time a leader called David, "even a descendant from the loins of ancient David, [would] be their king" (*HC* 4:457).

This predicted figure corresponds to a promised messianic servant. Hosea, speaking shortly before the loss of northern Israel, foretold that Israelites would return in the latter days "and seek the LORD their God, and David their king" (Hosea 3:5). JEREMIAH prophesied of Israel and Judah's future righteousness, and of "David their king, whom I [the LORD] will raise up unto them" (Jer. 30:9; cf. 23:5; 33:15–22). And in Ezekiel it is written, "And I will set up one shepherd over them, and he shall feed them, even my servant David; he shall feed them, and he shall be their shepherd. And I the LORD will be their God, and my servant David a prince among them" (Ezek. 34:23–24; cf. also 44:1–3).

Speaking to Joseph Smith, the angel Moroni₂ cited Old Testament passages telling of significant figures who would be involved with Christ's millennial reign (JS—H 1:40). As prophesied in Isaiah, it appears that two persons are spoken of, a "rod" and a "root" (11:1, 10)—one a leader "on whom there is laid much power," the other a person with special priesthood keys (D&C 113:3–6). These leaders are believed by some to be among the "messianic figures" spoken of in the Dead Sea Scrolls and in rabbinic literature (*Encyclopedia Judaica*, 11:1411).

Although noble attributes and spiritual powers characterize such messianic servants, Jesus Christ exemplifies these qualities perfectly (D&C 113:1–2). Jesus is the exemplar PROPHET, priest, and king. He identified himself as the prophet "like unto Moses" (Deut. 18:15; Acts 3:22–23; 3 Ne. 20:23) and was a high priest after the order of Melchizedek (Heb. 5:9–10; 7:15–22). Jesus is King of Kings (Rev. 19:16), greater than all other leaders of all time. Some see in Jesus Christ the complete fulfillment of the prophecy of a future David. Others feel that, while the titles and functions of the future Davidic king apply to Jesus, there will also be another righteous king by the name of David in the last days, a leader from the loins of Jesse (and thus of Judah).

VICTOR L. LUDLOW

DEUTERONOMY

Deuteronomy (Greek for "duplication of the law") is the fifth book of the Old Testament. Latter-day Saints have specific interests in this work. It distinctively teaches that those who inherit a PROMISED LAND do so on condition that they remain faithful to the Lord, pure in heart, generous to the poor, and devoted to God's Law. In a formula that appears several times, the people are promised that they will receive blessings for obedience to God and punishment for disobedience (Deut. 27–30). Book of Mormon prophets taught similar doctrines, and they also indicated that such principles were divinely given long before Moses. Latter-day scriptures are replete with deuteronomic teachings. Significantly, Jesus Christ quoted Deuteronomy regularly.

JESUS' USE OF DEUTERONOMY.   When Satan tempted Jesus, saying that if he were the Son of God he would turn stones to bread, leap from the temple's pinnacle to test God's care, and gain worldly king-doms and glory by worshiping Satan, the Savior responded with quo-tations from Deuteronomy (Matt. 4:1–10; cf. Deut. 8:3; 6:16, 13). He cited Deuteronomy regarding the law of witnesses and levirate mar-riage (John 8:17; Luke 20:28; cf. Deut. 19:15; 25:5). Twice he quoted the law on loving God (Deut. 6:4–5), calling it "the first and great commandment" (Matt. 22:35–38; cf. Luke 10:25–27). Many of Jesus' teachings admonishing good and warning against evil reiterate the deuteronomic principle of human action and divine response. Indeed, the Book of Mormon teaches that the premortal Jesus gave the law of Moses (3 Ne. 11:14; 12:17–18; 15:4–6).

DEUTERONOMIC TEACHINGS IN THE BOOK OF MORMON.   The Jerusalem emigrants who became a BOOK OF MORMON PEOPLE retained a copy of the five books of Moses on plates of brass (1 Ne. 4:38; 5:11–16). They were taught the law of Moses and were promised security and hap-piness if they obeyed it (e.g., 2 Ne. 1:16–20). Retention of their promised land depended upon continued obedience (e.g., 1 Ne. 2:20–23; 4:14; 7:13; 14:1–2; cf. Deut. 18:9–13). Just as deutero-nomic teachings were a stimulus for righteous commitment in King Josiah's Jerusalem (2 Kgs. 23:2–8), so were they in the Book of Mormon (e.g., 1 Ne. 17:33–38; 2 Ne. 5:10; Omni 1:2; Mosiah 1:1–7; Alma 8:17). Certain summary statements in the Book of Mormon may also reflect deuteronomic law (e.g., Alma 58:40; Hel. 3:20; 6:34; 15:5; 3 Ne. 25:4). Further, the prophecy of God's raising up a prophet in Deuteronomy 18:15–19 is declared by the Book of Mormon to be fulfilled in Jesus Christ (1 Ne. 22:20; 3 Ne. 20:23; cf. John 6:14; Acts 3:22; 7:37).

Book of Mormon writers observed that the prophet Alma$_2$ may have been taken up by God as Moses was, reflecting a possible vari-ant in their copy of Deuteronomy 34:5–6: "The scriptures saith the Lord took Moses unto himself" (Alma 45:19).

The book of Ether describes a people from the time of "the great tower" of Babel (Ether 1:3), with whom God covenanted that they could escape the fate of the wicked and be blessed in their land of promise if they would serve him in righteousness. This account from an epoch long before Moses is nevertheless in harmony with deuteronomic principles (Ether 2:6–10; 7:23; 9:20; 10:28; 11:6). When their descendants became wicked, they destroyed each other in successive wars (Ether 11:13, 20–21; 15:19).

DEUTERONOMIC IDEAS IN OTHER LDS SCRIPTURES.   As recorded in the PEARL OF GREAT PRICE, Adam and Eve were taught about choices and consequences in the beginning (Moses 3:15–17; 4:8–9, 22–25, 28). Generations of their descendants taught others righteousness and warned them about wickedness (Moses 6:22–23; 7:10, 15, 17–18). Noah taught the same doctrines; and the deluge followed rejection of his divine counsel (Moses 8:16–20).

The Doctrine and Covenants contains scores of passages about keeping the commandments of God (e.g., D&C 5:22; 6:6, 9, 37; 8:5; 11:6, 9, 18, 20). Those who keep them are promised blessings (e.g., D&C 14:7; 63:23; 76:52–55; 89:18–21; 93:19–20). Violators, of course, will suffer negative consequences (e.g., D&C 10:56; 18:46; 56:2–3). Thus, so-called deuteronomic precepts persist as divinely ordained principles.

[*See also* Covenants in Biblical Times; Law of Moses; Old Testament.]

BIBLIOGRAPHY

Nibley, Hugh. "How to Get Rich." *CWHN*, Vol. 9, pp. 178–201.

Rasmussen, Ellis T. "The Unchanging Gospel of Two Testaments." *Ensign* 3 (Oct. 1973):34–35.

Sperry, Sidney B. *The Spirit of the Old Testament.* 2nd ed., chaps. 5, 12, 13. Salt Lake City, 1970.

ELLIS T. RASMUSSEN

DOCTRINE AND COVENANTS

[*This entry consists of twenty articles:*

Overview
Contents
Section 1
Sections 20–22
Section 25
Section 42

Section 45
Section 76
Section 84
Section 88
Section 89
Section 93
Section 107
Sections 109–110
Sections 121–123
Section 124
Sections 127–128
Sections 131–132
Sections 137–138
Official Declaration—2

The first article is an introduction to the Latter-day Saint scripture known as the Doctrine and Covenants, its meaning, significance, and use in The Church of Jesus Christ of Latter-day Saints. The second article summarizes the main contents of this collection of revelations and official statements of the Church. A series of individual articles follows on selected sections of the Doctrine and Covenants, summarizing their contents and importance. Commentaries on, editions of, and literary features of the Doctrine and Covenants are also discussed in the separate articles.]

OVERVIEW

The Doctrine and Covenants is a compilation of revelations, most of which were received by the Prophet Joseph Smith for the establishment and governance of the kingdom of God in the latter days. It is a STANDARD WORK of the Church and functions as its open, ever-expanding, ecclesiastical constitution. Its main focus is to build up the Church of Jesus Christ and to bring people into harmony with Christ's kingdom. It is viewed as the capstone of the Church; its companion volume, the Book of Mormon, is seen as the keystone (Benson, pp. 83–85). The Book of Mormon was written to convince all individuals that Jesus is the Christ (*see* BOOK OF MORMON: OVERVIEW); the Doctrine and Covenants was given to organize and orient them according to God's mind and kingdom.

Of the 138 sections and two declarations presently in this

collection, 133 were received principally through Joseph Smith, the
first prophet and President of the Church. The seven remaining sec-
tions were received or written by or under the direction of Oliver
Cowdery (sections 102 and 134), John Taylor (section 135), Brigham
Young (section 136), Joseph F. Smith (section 138), Wilford Woodruff
(Official Declaration—1), and Spencer W. Kimball (Official
Declaration—2).

While most passages in the Doctrine and Covenants have a specific historical setting, virtually every verse is one of wisdom, general
instruction, religious principle, or doctrine. Most of the revelations
were received in answer to specific prayerful requests. Although
many were given for the benefit of particular individuals, by and
large their guidance has universal application, making these revelations as relevant today as when first received. They were given to the
servants of the Lord "in their weakness, after the manner of their language, that they might come to understanding" (1:24). They are recognized by Latter-day Saints as "the will of the Lord, . . . the mind of
the Lord, . . . the word of the Lord, . . . the voice of the Lord, and the
power of God unto salvation" (68:4).

The revelations in the Doctrine and Covenants were received
by various methods. Some were received by INSPIRATION, the mind
being enlightened by the Holy Spirit (e.g., sections 20–22); others
came from an angel (sections 2, 13, 27, 110); in VISIONS, or sight-
knowledge, usually through the spiritual eyes of the prophet (sections
76, 137–38); by the still small voice, a voice that comes into the
mind (section 85); or by an audible voice (section 130:12–13). At
times, other people were present and shared the spiritual manifestations.

The sections are of many types, containing various kinds of
materials and historical documents. For example, section 102 contains the minutes of a high council meeting; section 113 answers
questions on the writings of Isaiah; sections 121–23 are part of a letter written by Joseph Smith in relation to persecution; sections
127–28 are epistles on baptisms for the dead; section 134 is an
article on government and laws; and section 135 reports the martyrdom of Joseph and Hyrum Smith. Section 7 is a translation of a
record written and hidden up by the Apostle John; sections 65 and
109 are prayers; other sections are items of instruction (sections

130–31) and prophecies (sections 87 and 121). Section 1 is the Lord's Preface to the other revelations. Section 133 is known as the Appendix; it was given two days after the Preface and contains eschatological information. Both sections 1 and 133 were provided in preparation for the publication of the revelations.

The first compilation of the revelations given to Joseph Smith was printed in 1833 and was known as *A Book of Commandments, for the Government of the Church of Christ* (*see* BOOK OF COMMANDMENTS). It contained sixty-five chapters. This collection was submitted to a priesthood conference of the Church on November 1, 1831, for approval prior to publication. Because of the unpolished language of the revelations, one member doubted their authenticity. A revelation, section 67 in modern editions, challenged any person to write a revelation; when the doubter confessed that he was unable to do so, the compilation was approved by those assembled. Because the printing office of the Church in Independence, Missouri, was destroyed by a mob in July 1833 while the book was in production, only a few copies of this first compilation have survived.

Over the years after the first printing, other revelations were received and some earlier materials were deleted. An 1835 edition, published in Kirtland, Ohio, was entitled *Doctrine and Covenants of the Church of the Latter Day Saints* and contained 103 sections. In subsequent editions, more sections were added (*see* DOCTRINE AND COVENANTS EDITIONS). The most recent additions were sections 137 (1836) and 138 (1918) on salvation of the dead, and the Official Declaration—2 announcing the priesthood available to every worthy male member of the Church (1978). An article on marriage written by Oliver Cowdery in 1835 was deleted from the 1876 edition. Beginning with the 1921 edition, a set of lessons called the LECTURES ON FAITH have not been included.

One hundred of the revelations were received before 1834, during the early, formative years of the Church. Many of them were addressed to specific individuals who sought wisdom from the Prophet. Gospel doctrines were often not revealed in their fulness at first, but were received progressively from time to time. As the Church grew and relocated, questions regarding Church administration, duties of officers, guidance for the members of the Church, and events of the future became the subjects of further revelations.

Not all the revelations received by Joseph Smith are included in the Doctrine and Covenants (*see* REVELATIONS, UNPUBLISHED). Some are contained in the *History of the Church,* giving counsel and instruction to individuals (*HC* 1:229), concerning the Saints being driven to the Rocky Mountains (*HC* 5:85), and a prophecy about Stephen A. Douglas (*HC* 5:393–94).

Deciding which revelations to include in the Doctrine and Covenants is a prerogative of the First Presidency and the Quorum of the Twelve Apostles. The selection is then affirmed by the common consent of Church members.

The Doctrine and Covenants is directed to the people of this generation. To the Latter-day Saints it is the voice of the Lord Jesus Christ confirming and revealing the way of salvation and instruction for the government of his Church. It warns individuals and nations of impending destruction if they do not repent. It witnesses to the reality of life beyond the grave.

Prominent among its teachings are the specific principles, covenants, and ordinances that lead to eternal life. It prescribes priesthood ordinances from baptism to marriage sealed for eternity. Salvation for the dead also is made known by revelations concerning baptism for the dead and visions of preaching to the spirits who are awaiting resurrection.

Its emphasis upon the spiritual nature of temporal matters heightens one's appreciation of and respect for this life. For example, its code of health, known as the Word of Wisdom, promises both spiritual and physical health to those who obey it (section 89).

The Doctrine and Covenants contains numerous teachings and pithy sayings that powerfully influence the daily lives and feelings of Latter-day Saints, which set the tone of Church service and instill vitality into the work. Among its frequently quoted lines are the following maxims and words of counsel and divine assurance: "If ye are prepared ye shall not fear" (D&C 38:30); "Seek not for riches but for wisdom" (11:7); "He who doeth the works of righteousness shall receive his reward, even peace in this world, and eternal life in the world to come" (59:23); "Seek ye out of the best books words of wisdom; seek learning, even by study and also by faith" (88:118); "Without faith you can do nothing" (8:10); "Of you it is required to forgive all men" (64:10); "Men should be anxiously engaged in a good cause, and do many things of their own free will" (58:27); "All these things shall give thee experience, and shall be for thy good" (122:7); "For I will raise up unto myself a pure people, that will serve me in righteousness" (100:16); "Be not weary in well-doing" (64:33); "Search diligently, pray always, and be believing, and all things shall work together for your good" (90:24); and "Now what do we hear in the gospel which we have received? A voice of gladness! A voice of mercy from heaven; and a voice of truth out of the earth; glad tidings for the dead; a voice of gladness for the living and the dead; glad tidings of great joy" (128:19).

BIBLIOGRAPHY

Benson, Ezra Taft. "The Book of Mormon and Doctrine and Covenants." *Ensign* 17 (May 1987):83–85.

Doxey, Roy W. *The Latter-day Prophets and the Doctrine and Covenants,* 4 vols. Salt Lake City, 1963–1970.

———. *The Doctrine and Covenants Speaks,* 2 vols. Salt Lake City, 1969–1970.

Ludlow, Daniel H. *A Companion to Your Study of the Doctrine and Covenants,* 2 vols. Salt Lake City, 1978.

Millet, Robert L., and Larry E. Dahl, eds. *The Capstone of Our Religion.* Salt Lake City, 1989.

ROY W. DOXEY

CONTENTS

The revelations compiled in the Doctrine and Covenants contain directions and doctrine needed to inspire, organize, and administer the affairs of the Church. They were not received or written as a textbook, treatise, or organized curriculum of lesson plans, but were received intermittently when the Prophet Joseph Smith and others sought divine guidance in various circumstances.

Despite the fact that many of these revelations are personally directed to certain individuals or groups in nineteenth-century times and places, they contain principles that have eternal application and thus current value. The revelations include warnings of divine judgments upon the wicked; teachings about the progression of human souls toward exaltation and eternal life through the gospel of Jesus Christ; information about scripture, including the coming forth of the Book of Mormon and the translation of the Bible by Joseph Smith; instructions about the priesthood, its restoration, functions, offices, and ordinances; commandments and instructions to people of the Church regarding personal behavior, education, lands and property, buildings, and caring for the poor; and callings and counsel to preach and live the gospel.

Section 1 is the Preface, given at a conference of the Church on November 1, 1831. It came in response to Joseph Smith's request for authority from the Lord to publish some of the revelations that he had previously received. In it, the Lord authorized the request and issued the following challenge and declaration to all who would read it: "Search these commandments, for they are true and faithful, and the prophecies and promises which are in them shall all be fulfilled" (D&C 1:37).

Sections 2–19 are revelations received prior to the organization of the Church in 1830. In them, the Lord instructed Joseph Smith and his companions on many subjects, especially the translation, publication, and value of the Book of Mormon, and the need to trust completely in the Lord and to safeguard sacred things (sections 3, 5, 10, 17, 20). Joseph Smith, Sr.; Hyrum Smith; Joseph Knight, Sr.; John, Peter, and David Whitmer; Oliver Cowdery; and Martin Harris were taught how they might be a part of the work that was about to come forth and were instructed about its sacredness (sections 4, 6, 8–9, 11–12, 14–19). They were also counseled to become worthy to receive the Lord's Spirit so that they might recognize God's revelations and carry out his will (sections 6, 8–9, 11).

Also during this time, the authority to act in the name of the Lord was restored, and the purpose and scope of that authority were explained (sections 13, 18, 20; cf. 27). The Lord gave counsel concerning the value of individual souls and encouraged his servants to labor for one another's salvation by teaching the restored gospel and bringing people to repentance (section 18). The value of and need for the atonement of Jesus Christ were revealed, and people were directed to come to him for forgiveness and spiritual strength (section 19).

Sections 20–40 gave instructions in 1830 to the newly organized Church in New York. The basic doctrines of the Church as contained in the Bible and the Book of Mormon and the criteria for establishing covenants with the Lord were summarized, and the responsibilities of members and priesthood holders in the Church were established (section 20).

The Lord gave a revelation concerning the relationship of the

Prophet to the Lord and of Church members to the word of the Lord through his Prophet (section 21). This is a major topic in the Doctrine and Covenants and provides the basis for understanding the process of continuing revelation through the President of the Church (section 28; cf. 43, 68, 81, 90, 124).

Further revelations were received for the benefit of various individuals and for the Church in general, in which many doctrinal insights were provided on such subjects as baptism (section 22); following counsel (sections 23–24, 31); music, and counsel to the Prophet's wife, Emma Smith (section 25); common consent (section 26); the SACRAMENT (section 27); the Holy Spirit (sections 29–30, 34, cf. 46, 50, 75, 79); preaching to the American Indians, or Lamanites (section 30, 32); proclaiming the gospel to all the world in the last days (sections 29, 33, 35, 38; cf. 43, 45, 86–87, 90, 101, 116, 133); and Joseph Smith's work on translating the Bible and other records (sections 35, 37; cf. 41–42, 45, 73–74, 76–77, 86, 91, 93–94, 124:89). It was through this translation activity that many of the doctrines of the Church were revealed to Joseph Smith.

The Lord directed members of the Church to gather to Ohio, where he promised that he would give them his law, establish Zion, and endow them with power from on high (sections 37–38, 42). The making and keeping of covenants are identified as the basis for individuals becoming God's people or his disciples (sections 39–41).

Sections 41–123 were given during the Ohio and Missouri periods of the Church (1831–1839) and contain various instructions concerning the affairs of the Church. During these years many doctrines and principles of the gospel were revealed that helped to build a vital doctrinal framework for the Church. The first revelation recorded by Joseph Smith in Ohio called Edward Partridge to serve as the first bishop of the Church (section 41). As promised, the Saints were given the Lord's laws by which members of the Church are governed, including the law of teaching (sections 42, 68, 88, 93, 100); moral laws (sections 42, 58–59); the law of consecration (sections 42, 51, 54, 70, 78, 82–83, 104); the law of labor (sections 42, 60, 68, 75); instructions concerning administration to the sick (sections 42, 46, 63); laws of remuneration for goods and services (sections 42, 43, 70, 106); and laws pertaining to transgressors (sections 42, 58, 102, 107). Joseph Smith also received instruction concerning the importance of marriage and the family (section 49; cf. 131–32), and the Lord revealed information by which counterfeit and evil practices might be detected and avoided (sections 43, 46, 50, 52; cf. 129).

A major theme of the Doctrine and Covenants is the establishment and building of ZION, both as a place (*see* NEW JERUSALEM) and as a condition of the people (the pure in heart; D&C 97:21). Joseph Smith was instructed to go to Missouri, where the site for the city of Zion would be made known (section 52). While there, he received guidance from the Lord concerning the establishment of Zion and its people (sections 57–59). The Saints began to gather in Missouri to fulfill the Lord's requirements, and additional revelations were received pertaining to their various responsibilities (sections 63–64). They were taught the necessity of building and having a temple, or house of the Lord, in connection with becoming a people of Zion (sections 57, 84, 88, 97, 101, 109–110; cf. 124). Since some members did not reach levels of consecrated faith and obedience reflective of a Zion society, they failed to establish Zion at that time. They were expelled from Missouri, and the building of Zion in that place was temporarily suspended (sections 101, 103, 105).

During this same time and later, other insightful revelations were provided concerning health rules (sections 49, 89); the life, light, spirit, and power of Christ (sections 50, 84, 88, 93); missionary work (sections 75, 79–80, 84, 99); the SABBATH (section 59); obedience and sacrifice (sections 58–59, 82, 97, 117–18); obtaining and extending forgiveness (sections 58, 64, 82, 98); the plan of salvation for all humankind (sections 76, 93; cf. 131, 137–38); priesthood functions and quorums (sections 81, 84, 90, 107, 112, 121; cf. 124; and Official Declaration—2 of 1978); impending wars (section 87); biblical texts (sections 74, 77, 113); and tithing (sections 119–20).

Sections 124–135 were recorded in Nauvoo during the last years of Joseph Smith's life (1839–1844). They include directions to the Church regarding the Nauvoo Temple, the first full-ordinance temple (section 124); ordinances and salvation for the dead (sections 124, 127–128); the nature of the Godhead and exalted beings (sections 130, 132); eternal and plural marriage (sections 131–32; see also Official Declaration—1); political laws and governments (section 134); and a statement of the contributions of Joseph Smith and of his testimony at the time of his martyrdom (sections 135–36).

BIBLIOGRAPHY

Berrett, William E. *Teachings of the Doctrine and Covenants.* Salt Lake City, 1956.

Cook, Lyndon W. *The Revelations of Joseph Smith.* Provo, Utah, 1981.

Matthews, Robert J. "The Joseph Smith Translation and The Doctrine and Covenants: Historical and Doctrinal Companions." In *The Capstone of Our Religion: Insights into the Doctrine and Covenants,* ed. Robert L. Millet and Larry E. Dahl. Salt Lake City, 1989.

Otten, Leaun G., and C. Max Caldwell. *Sacred Truths of the Doctrine and Covenants,* 2 vols. Springville, Utah, 1983.

Smith, Hyrum M., and Janne M. Sjodahl. *Doctrine and Covenants Commentary.* Salt Lake City, 1954.

Smith, Joseph Fielding. *Church History and Modern Revelation,* 2 vols. Salt Lake City, 1946.

Welch, John W., and Jeannie Welch. *The Doctrine and Covenants by Themes.* Salt Lake City, 1986.

Widtsoe, John A. *The Message of the Doctrine and Covenants,* ed. G. Homer Durham. Salt Lake City, 1969.

Woodford, Robert J. "The Historical Development of the Doctrine and Covenants," 3 vols. Ph.D. diss., Brigham Young University, 1974.

C. MAX CALDWELL

SECTION 1

Section 1 of the Doctrine and Covenants is called the "Preface." It was a revelation received by Joseph Smith between sessions of a conference in Hiram, Ohio, on November 1, 1831. The conference had been convened to consider publishing sixty-three of the revelations Joseph Smith had received (*see* BOOK OF COMMANDMENTS). The conference voted unanimously to publish them as the word of the Lord. In accordance with the Lord's declaration, this section was published as "my preface unto the book of my commandments" (D&C 1:6). It sets an urgent tone for the entire Doctrine and Covenants.

Like the revelations it introduces, section 1 is written predominantly in the first person as the word of the Lord: "What I the Lord have spoken, I have spoken" (verse 38). It proclaims to the world that through the RESTORATION of his Church, God has set his hand the last time to redeem his children and prepare the earth for the Savior's return.

Section 1 is a bold declaration that God sees all things and speaks to all people, that his words will go to all nations through his chosen disciples, that every person eventually will hear the gospel in his or her own language so that each may understand, and that weak things of the world will break down the mighty and strong and the

Church will be brought out of obscurity by the power of God (see also the revelation given two days later, D&C 133).

Section 1 balances judgment and relief. It is a voice of warning of impending judgments: "Prepare ye, prepare ye" (verse 12). It warns that those who do not repent will suffer much sorrow, for world-wide sin has kindled the "anger of the Lord" and people "have strayed from [his] ordinances and have broken [his] everlasting covenant" (verses 13–15). Those who hearken, however, are promised instruction, chastening, correction, knowledge, and blessings from God.

The section ends with the certification of the Lord that all his prophecies and promises, though given to men in their weakness, are true and will be fulfilled.

GEORGE W. PACE

SECTIONS 20–22

Sections 20–22 of the Doctrine and Covenants are fundamental, formative documents in early Church history. They continue to serve as a definitive statement of beliefs and priesthood functions. Originally sections 20 and 22 were published together as "Articles and Covenants of the Church of Christ." They were first published in the *Painesville* (Ohio) *Telegraph* in April 1831 and later on the first page of the first issue of *The Evening and the Morning Star* in June 1832. The earliest known version of section 20 is dated June 1829. Many early copies were made of a draft in Oliver Cowdery's hand.

Sections 20–22 were officially adopted as doctrinal revelations by the Church at its first conference on June 9, 1830, and were the first sections of the Doctrine and Covenants to be thus approved. Later, missionaries often would read manuscript copies of these "Articles" at public meetings and conferences because they had been instructed to include the "Church Articles" in their teachings (D&C 42:13). Section 20 was Chapter II in the 1835 edition of the Doctrine and Covenants, right after the revealed Preface. The present order was established in the 1876 edition.

Section 20 is a composite text that divides into a historical prologue (verses 1–16), a statement of beliefs (verses 17–36), and a collection of policies and procedures (verses 37–84). While its principles continue to guide Latter-day Saints today, its provisions also provide glimpses of Church life in its initial years. The prologue contains the earliest published references to the ordination of Joseph Smith and Oliver Cowdery as apostles (verses 2–3) and to Joseph Smith's first vision: "It was truly manifested unto this first elder that he had received a remission of his sins" (verse 5). The personal dimension of this account is consistent with Joseph's 1832 and 1835 accounts of his first vision.

Section 20 also contains the Church's earliest known declaration of faith. It affirms basic Christian doctrines, following the sequence common to most Protestant confessions, beginning with the nature of God (verse 17), the Creation (verses 18–19), the Fall (verse 20), Jesus Christ, the Atonement, and the plan of salvation (verses 21–28). Additional comments discuss the possibility of "falling from grace" and the nature of sanctification, which were lively issues in the 1820s. Sensitivity to the surrounding Christian world is shown in verse 35, which assures that these articles are "neither adding to, nor diminishing from the prophecy of [John's] book, the holy scriptures, or the revelations of God that will come hereafter."

Most of section 20 gives guidelines for Church government. Drawing partly upon texts from the Book of Mormon, it explains the ordinances of baptism and the SACRAMENT, and the duties of baptized members. Originally, priests, teachers, and deacons were local adult priesthood leaders, which explains the significant pastoral charge given them (verses 46–59) and their role in signing certificates of worthiness for members moving from one branch of the Church to another (verse 84). The Aaronic Priesthood had a public ministry to "preach, teach, expound, exhort" (verse 46) and needed to be properly "licensed" (verse 64).

Received on the day the Church was incorporated, section 21 defines Joseph Smith's leadership of the new Church as "a seer, a translator, a prophet, an apostle of Jesus Christ" (verse 1), with Oliver Cowdery as an elder "under his hand" (verse 11). Church members are counseled to keep records and to receive Joseph's words "as if from mine own mouth" (verses 1, 5).

Section 22, received the same month, requires all people, even

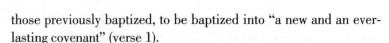

those previously baptized, to be baptized into "a new and an everlasting covenant" (verse 1).

Together, these three sections provide a firm organizational foundation for the restored Church of Christ.

BIBLIOGRAPHY

Anderson, Richard L. "The Organization Revelations: D&C 20, 21, and 22." In *Studies in Scripture*, Vol. 1, pp. 109–23, ed. R. Millet and K. Jackson. Sandy, Utah, 1984.

Woodford, Robert J. "The Articles and Covenants of the Church of Christ and the Book of Mormon." In *Doctrines for Exaltation*, pp. 262–73. Salt Lake City, 1989.

GRANT UNDERWOOD

SECTION 25

This revelation was given in Harmony, Pennsylvania, in July 1830, three months after the organization of the Church. It was first printed in the BOOK OF COMMANDMENTS in 1833 as Chapter XXVI. It is addressed to Emma Smith, wife of the Prophet Joseph Smith. In the earliest version, Emma Smith is addressed as "my daughter in Zion." Joseph Smith later expanded this verse to add, "All those who receive my Gospel are sons and daughters in my kingdom."

The section has five main components:

1. Emma is designated as an "elect lady" (verse 3). Later, on March 17, 1842, when Emma Smith became the first president of the Relief Society and the women were organized in the order of the priesthood, Joseph explained that this was the office of her "elect" calling. The benevolent organization that she led had grown to more than 3 million women by 1990.

2. Emma is admonished to unity with her husband to "be unto him for a scribe" and to "go with him at the time of his going" (verse 6). She accepted these callings, though she was later required to abandon home and security.

3. Emma is called to "be ordained under [Joseph's] hand to expound scriptures, and exhort the church," as "given thee by my Spirit" (verse 7). She is also commanded to study and devote her time "to writing, and to learning much" (verse 8). In the course of her life, she taught, expounded, exhorted, presided, and served in many Church organizations. The mandate has remained with LDS

women: to master the scriptures, thus the more powerfully to lead, teach, minister, and serve.

4. Emma is charged to select sacred hymns, and a manifesto is given of the spiritual power of music: "The song of the righteous is a prayer unto me" (verse 12). Her hymnal was first published in 1836 (although 1835 appears on the title page). This collection utilizes many classical Christian words and melodies but also embodies songs related to most of the unique events and teachings of the RESTORATION.

5. Emma is counseled against murmuring, putting her public ministry before her role as companion of her husband, seeking "the things of this world" (verse 10), and pride. "Let thy soul delight in thy husband" (verse 14). She is to glorify her husband while involved in a public ministry. Emma fulfilled each of these callings, endured the loss of five children, and stood by Joseph until his martyrdom.

This inclusion of women in leading roles of the Church, presiding in some organizations and over certain sacral functions, was a marked departure from nineteenth-century patterns. Church leaders, both men and women, continue to cite passages from this inspired calling of Emma to exemplify some of the potentials of women and facilitate their full participation in all spiritual callings and blessings of the Gospel.

BIBLIOGRAPHY
Hinckley, Gordon B. "If Thou Art Faithful." *Ensign* 14 (Nov. 84):89–92.

KLIS HALE VOLKENING

SECTION 42

This section is called the "law of Christ" and the "law of the Church," and receiving it fulfilled a promise made on January 2, 1831, in Doctrine and Covenants 38:32, that the law would be given to the Church in Ohio. As a precondition (see D&C 41:2–3), the elders were to unite in the prayer of faith. The first seventy verses of section 42 were given February 9, 1831, while twelve elders were, as the record states, "united in mighty prayer." Verses 71–93 were received two weeks later in similar circumstances. The revelation was first published in *The Evening and the Morning Star*, in July and

October 1832, and was included as chapters 44 and 47 of the BOOK OF COMMANDMENTS in 1833.

High requirements were here imposed on the infant Church, with a small and scattered membership and little instruction and experience. They can be divided into six main segments:

1. A missionary commission to travel to the West (verses 1–17). Its members were to go two by two, under proper ordination and authority, to teach the principles of the gospel from the Bible and Book of Mormon and to teach only "by the Spirit."

2. A reaffirmation of the TEN COMMANDMENTS (verses 18–29). The ancient decalogue of Moses stressed the laws of behavior. The New Testament, especially the SERMON ON THE MOUNT, and a similar sermon in 3 Nephi emphasize both the act and the inner condition, letter and spirit. Section 42 also affirms the more inclusive expectations and aspirations of the new and everlasting covenant. Additions include "Thou shalt not lie . . . [nor] speak evil of thy neighbor, nor do him any harm" and "Thou shalt love thy wife with all thy heart, and shalt cleave unto her and none else." Violators, it is said, "shall not have the Spirit" and shall fear.

3. A statement on the laws of stewardship and consecration (verses 30–39). Properties were to be consecrated by a covenant "which cannot be broken," for support of the poor, each person acting as a steward over his own property, and a high council and bishop as stewards over the Church storehouse. The storehouse, replenished by "residues," would administer to the poor and needy. "Inasmuch as ye do it unto the least of these, ye do it unto me." Through these principles, the Church was to procure land, build houses of worship, and eventually establish the NEW JERUSALEM.

4. Warnings against pride of heart, ostentation, idleness, and uncleanness (verses 40–42).

5. Admonitions to compassionate care for the sick who are without the gift of faith unto healing (verses 43–52). Signs, including healing, will follow specific gifts of faith, but the highest form of faith is to "have power to become my sons." Reassurance is given those who die unto the Lord, for their death "shall be sweet unto them" (verse 46).

6. Instructions on Church procedures regarding transgressors, trials, witnesses, Church discipline in relation to the laws of the land, and patterns of confession and reconciliation (verses 53–93).

BIBLIOGRAPHY

Otten, L. G., and C. M. Caldwell. *Sacred Truths of the Doctrine and Covenants*, Vol. 1, pp. 195–206. Springville, Utah, 1982.

VICTOR L. BROWN, SR.

SECTION 45

This revelation of the Doctrine and Covenants was received in early March 1831, a time when "many false reports, lies, and foolish stories, were published in the newspapers, and circulated in every direction, to prevent people from investigating the work, or embracing the faith" (*HC* 1:158). In it the Lord called the Saints to hearken to his voice, and noted that he was pleading unto the Father for them (D&C 45:1–7). He then told them he would "prophesy, as unto men in days of old," and gave them what he had given his disciples in Jerusalem concerning events that would take place in that day, in the last days, and at his second coming.

Three events would take place during the time of the Savior's own generation: (1) the temple in Jerusalem would be destroyed (verses 18–20); (2) the Jewish nation would be desolated and destroyed (verse 21); and (3) the Jews would be scattered among all nations (verse 24). History shows that these prophecies were fulfilled. Before the end of first century, Roman conquests brought about a literal and exact fulfillment of all that Jesus had described. Some who heard him prophesy lived to witness those events.

Many events would happen in the last days preceding the Lord's second coming:

1. The Jews shall be gathered to Jerusalem (verse 25).

2. There shall be wars and rumors of wars (verse 26).

3. Men's hearts shall fail them (verse 26).

4. There shall be claims of a delay in Christ's coming (verse 26).

5. The love of men shall wax cold (verse 27).

6. Iniquity shall abound (verse 27).

7. The fulness of the gospel shall be restored (verse 28).

8. Times of the Gentiles shall be fulfilled (verse 30).

9. There shall be an overflowing scourge and desolating sickness (verse 31).

10. The wicked shall curse God (verse 32).

11. There shall be earthquakes and many desolations (verse 33).

12. There shall be displays of heavenly phenomena—sun, moon, stars (verses 40–44).

The Times of the Gentiles referred to in item 8 began with the taking of the gospel to the Gentiles by the apostles after the death of Christ. The second opportunity for the Gentiles came with the restoration of the gospel through Joseph Smith, to be preached first to the Gentiles and then to the Jews.

When the Savior comes a second time, he will make at least three general appearances:

1. He will appear to the Saints or covenant members of his church (verses 45–46, 56–57). The Savior likened those faithful members to the five wise virgins who had taken the Holy Spirit to be their guide (cf. Matt. 25:1–13).

2. He will appear to the Jews at Jerusalem (verses 47–53). When the Jews are engaged in a battle for survival, the Savior will appear and intervene in their behalf and they will recognize him as their Messiah.

3. He will appear to the world (verses 74–75). This appearance will not be to a select group, but rather will be of such magnitude that the wicked will be destroyed, leaving only the righteous to enjoy the millennial reign of the Savior. The second coming of the Savior will coincide with the resurrection of faithful covenant members of his Church who shall be caught up to meet him when he comes in his glory (verse 45). And the heathen who lived without the law will be resurrected, and also "they that knew no law" (verse 54).

The revelation known as section 45 then focuses on Joseph Smith's work on the Bible translation (verses 60–62), and also mentions wars abroad and at home (verse 63). The last verses call the Saints to gather "with one heart and with one mind . . . [to build] the New Jerusalem, a land of peace, a city of refuge, a place of safety" (verses 65–66).

BIBLIOGRAPHY
Church Educational System. *The Doctrine and Covenants Student Manual.* Salt Lake City, 1981.
Cook, Lyndon W. *The Revelations of the Prophet Joseph Smith.* Provo, 1981.
Otten, Leaun G., and C. Max Caldwell. *Sacred Truths of the Doctrine and Covenants,* Vol. 1. Springville, Utah, 1982.

C. MAX CALDWELL

SECTION 76

Section 76 presents a vision about the plan of salvation, particularly the nature of the three kingdoms or heavens of glory that mankind may inherit following the Resurrection, depending on their personal faithfulness.

As Joseph Smith and Sidney Rigdon were working on the JOSEPH SMITH TRANSLATION OF THE BIBLE (JST) on February 16, 1832, they came to John 5:29, concerning the resurrection of the just and the unjust. Of that experience, Joseph explained, "It appeared self-evident that . . . if God rewarded every one according to the deeds done in the body, the term 'Heaven,' as intended for the Saints' eternal home must include more kingdoms than one. . . . While translating St. John's Gospel, myself and Elder Rigdon saw the following vision" (*HC* 1:245). At least ten people were in the room when this revelation was received. One of them, Philo Dibble, sixty years later recalled how Joseph and Sidney, almost motionless for about one hour, would alternately relate and confirm to each other what they were concurrently seeing in the vision (Cannon, pp. 303–304).

The revelation contains a series of six visions: They see the Son of God on the right hand of God (verses 1–24); they see how the devil and his followers rebelled and were cast down (25–49); they see the celestial kingdom (50–70), terrestrial kingdom (71–80), and telestial kingdom (81–90), and those who will inherit each of these degrees of glory; and they see the three kingdoms of glory compared (91–119). The text was first published in *The Evening and the Morning Star* in July 1832 and was included as section 91 in the 1835 edition of the Doctrine and Covenants.

Because this section, called "The Vision," departed significantly from the mainstream Christian view of one heaven and one hell, it was not easily received by some at first. Brigham Young said, "My traditions were such, that when the Vision came first to me, it was so directly contrary and opposed to my former education, I said, wait a little; I did not reject it, but I could not understand it" (*Deseret News, Extra,* September 14, 1852, p. 24). Entire branches of the Church had the same problem. John Murdock and Orson Pratt, serving missions in Ohio at the time, struggled to help Church members there accept these new outlooks on eternity. Soon, however, most members believed and understood the concepts, and came to revere this vision as one of the most beautiful and awe-inspiring ever given.

Joseph Smith himself rejoiced in "the light which burst upon the world through the foregoing vision" (*PJS* 1:372), which he said was "a transcript from the records of the eternal world. The sublimity of the ideas; the purity of the language; the scope for action; the continued duration for completion, in order that the heirs of salvation may confess the Lord and bow the knee; the rewards for faithfulness, and the punishments for sins; are so much beyond the narrow-mindedness of men, that every man is constrained to exclaim: "It came from God'" (*TPJS*, p. 11).

BIBLIOGRAPHY

Cannon, George Q., ed. "Recollections of the Prophet Joseph Smith." *Juvenile Instructor,* 27 (May 15, 1892):302–4.

Cook, Lyndon W. *The Revelations of the Prophet Joseph Smith,* pp. 157–66, 311–12. Provo, Utah, 1981.

Dahl, Larry E. "The Vision of the Glories." In *Studies in Scripture,* Vol. 1, pp. 279–308. Sandy, Utah, 1984.

DONALD Q. CANNON

SECTION 84

Given on September 22–23, 1832, at Kirtland, Ohio, section 84 was first published as Chapter IV in the 1835 edition of the Doctrine and Covenants. It is called a revelation on priesthood and was given in the presence of six elders who had just returned from their missions to the eastern states. The revelation has four main themes.

ZION. Earlier, the establishment of ZION and the need for a temple as its center had been revealed (D&C 57:1–3). Section 84 makes the Church responsible for assembling the Saints and building the NEW JERUSALEM (Zion), beginning with the temple. Both undertakings are to be completed in a "generation." Zion is to be established through the power and authority of the Melchizedek Priesthood (verses 1–5).

PRIESTHOOD.   Priesthood is the power and authority delegated to man to act for God in saving souls, and it cannot be assumed, but must be passed on from one who already has it. Section 84 clearly distinguishes two priesthoods, namely, the Melchizedek and Aaronic. Moses, for example, received the Melchizedek Priesthood from Jethro, who received it through rightful heirs back to "Adam, who was the first man" (verses 6–17). The Melchizedek Priesthood administers the gospel and holds the keys of the mysteries of the kingdom and knowledge of God. Through the ordinances administered by this priesthood, men and women partake of the powers of godliness. Only thus may they behold his face and endure his presence (verses 19–22).

The Aaronic Priesthood holds the keys of the ministering of angels and the preparatory gospel. It continued in an unbroken line from Aaron and was the priesthood of the law of Moses. It was also the priesthood held by John the Baptist. This preparatory gospel includes faith, repentance, and baptism, and leads to the Melchizedek Priesthood and its ordinances (verses 26–27).

OATH AND COVENANT OF THE PRIESTHOOD.   When worthy men receive the Melchizedek Priesthood, they enter into a covenant relationship with the Lord. They covenant that in faithfulness and obedience they will magnify their priesthood callings—that is, wholeheartedly honor and fulfill their stewardships. By keeping this covenant, the priesthood holder receives the oath of the Father, which leads to receiving the Father's kingdom and "all that [the] Father hath" (verse 38). Those who violate or break this covenant and altogether turn from it "shall not have forgiveness of sins in this world nor in the world to come" (verse 41).

The elders of the Church are told that because of "vanity and unbelief" they and all the children of Zion have been spiritually darkened and are under condemnation before the Lord. They are to repent and remember the "new covenant," even the Book of Mormon. Through obeying this counsel, they will be forgiven their sins and bring forth fruit worthy for the kingdom (verses 54–61).

MISSIONARY COUNSEL.   Section 84 gives instruction and promises to those who are emissaries of Jesus Christ. Under their direction, the gospel is to be taken to all the world. Those who desire to enter into the kingdom of Christ are to be baptized and receive the gift of the Holy Ghost. Signs will follow those who believe. The missionaries are promised protection as well as necessities of life (verses 62–119; cf. Matt. 10).

In summary, priesthood bearers are counseled to learn their duties and faithfully function in their offices and callings. Each calling is essential within the kingdom of Christ (verses 109–110).

BIBLIOGRAPHY

Otten, Leaun G., and C. Max Caldwell. *Sacred Truths of the Doctrine and Covenants,* 2 vols. Springville, Utah, 1983.

Smith, Hyrum M., and Janne M. Sjodahl. *Doctrine and Covenants Commentary,* rev. ed. Salt Lake City, 1978.

LEAUN G. OTTEN

SECTION 88

Section 88 was given through Joseph Smith in the "translating room" of the Whitney store in Kirtland, Ohio. Verses 1–126 were given on December 27 and 28, 1832, and verses 127–141 on January 3, 1833. The revelation was recorded in the Kirtland Council Minute Book, and portions of it were published in *The Evening and the Morning Star* in February and March 1833. It was printed as section 7 in the 1835 edition of the Doctrine and Covenants.

On Christmas Day 1832, Joseph Smith received what has become known as the prophecy on war (D&C 87), which predicted "the death and misery of many souls." His brethren were troubled at this. They united in fasting and prayer before the Lord, seeking his will concerning the upbuilding of Zion. The Prophet designated the subsequent revelation (D&C 88) the "olive leaf" and "the Lord's message of peace to us" (*HC* 1:316).

The section opens with an intimate promise "even upon you my friends," which is given of God through Jesus Christ, his Son (D&C 88:3–5) and is comparable with the promise of John 14 of the Comforter and the Holy Spirit of promise.

Passages follow on the pervasive immanence of divine light: The Light of Christ enlightens the eyes and quickens the understanding. It is in and through all things, the very light of the sun, moon, and stars. It "proceedeth forth from the presence of God to fill the immensity of space" (verse 12). It is equated with the life, the law, and the power of God.

In this context the following doctrines are clarified:

The spirit and body are the soul of man. There are three degrees of glory and three orders of glorified bodies. One receives a resurrected body according to the law by which one abides while in this world: "Your glory shall be that glory by which your bodies are quickened" (verse 28). In the resurrection one receives in full what in this world one has had only in part. A fourth order of resurrected bodies pertains to the Sons of Perdition, who, though resurrected, receive no glory (verses 32–33).

The earth itself is alive. It will die and be glorified, and the bodies who are quickened by a celestial spirit will inherit; "for this intent was it made and created, and for this intent are they sanctified" (verse 20).

There are multiple worlds, multiple creations, all governed by law. "Unto every kingdom is given a law; and unto every law there are certain bounds also and conditions" (verse 38). Law includes appointed cosmic times, seasons, and orders, as well as the divine attributes and powers of mercy, justice, and judgment. "All beings who abide not in those conditions are not justified" (verse 39). Those who seek to become a law unto themselves will not, and cannot, be sanctified.

A parable of laborers in a field teaches the magnitude of the Lord's creations (verses 46–61), that glorification comes only in appointed time and sequence, "every man in his own order" (verse 60).

The call is given to build a temple and hold a solemn assembly. The temple is to become a house of God: of prayer, fasting, faith, learning, glory, and order. All incomings, outgoings, and salutations will be in the name of the Lord. The Saints are commanded to "organize yourselves, and prepare yourselves, and sanctify yourselves" (verse 74) through solemnity and sober study, to be ready for the temple experience.

A comprehensive curriculum for the School of the Prophets is introduced. It includes languages, history, and a study of "the wars and the perplexities of the nations, . . . and a knowledge also of countries and of kingdoms" (verse 79).

Prophecies are reiterated concerning the changes, earthquakes, tempests, and commotion in the earth and the heavens that will precede the second coming of Christ. Six periods or epochs of one thousand years each are designated. These are to culminate in the seventh or millennial era. An angel and an angelic trump symbolize each period.

The revelation concludes with specific instructions on the conduct of meetings, the duties of the presidency, admission into the School of the Prophets, and WASHING OF FEET, in the pattern of John 13, as an initiatory and purifying ordinance for members of the school.

BIBLIOGRAPHY
Cook, Lyndon W. *The Revelations of the Prophet Joseph Smith.* Provo, Utah, 1981.

BARBARA R. CARTER

SECTION 89
This section, known as the Word of Wisdom from its first words, was received at a meeting of the School of the Prophets in the upper level of the Whitney store on February 27, 1833, in Kirtland, Ohio. According to Zebedee Coltrin, one of twenty-two Church leaders in attendance, Joseph Smith received the revelation in an adjoining room in the presence of two or three brethren, walked in with the document in hand, and read the contents to the assembled school members. The revelation was first printed in December 1833 or January 1834 on a broadsheet and was included in the 1835 edition of the Doctrine and Covenants.

The Word of Wisdom was given "in consequence of evils and designs which do and will exist in the hearts of conspiring men in the last days" (verse 4). As some of these designs pertain to what people eat and drink, the Word of Wisdom gives basic directions on what is good and not good, and posits a strong relationship between what individuals take into their bodies and their physical and spiritual well-being. The revelation prohibits three things: tobacco, strong drinks, and hot drinks (verses 5–9). "Strong drinks" were understood as alcoholic beverages; "hot drinks" were defined by early Church leaders as tea and coffee. Church leaders have traditionally confined relevant worthiness requirements to the prohibited items. The revelation also recommends the prudent use of herbs and fruits, the sparing consumption of meat, and the use of "all grain," but especially "wheat for man" (verses 10–17). Saints who obey the admonitions are promised health and strength, wisdom and knowledge, and protection from the destroying angel (verses 18–21).

The Word of Wisdom was an inspired response to specific problems or paradoxes within the Church and to pressing social issues in contemporary American society. Brigham Young recalled in 1868 that Joseph Smith was bothered by the seeming incongruity of discussing spiritual matters in a cloud of tobacco smoke and that Joseph's wife, Emma Smith, was bothered at having to clean the quid-littered floor. It is also probable that the Prophet was sensitive to, and supportive of, the widespread temperance sentiment of the 1830s. As was his custom, the Prophet went to the Lord for instructions, and section 89 is distinctive in the sense that it is a divinely approved code of health.

Interpretations and applications of the Word of Wisdom have gradually changed through the years. In part, this change is consistent with the Church's belief in continuing revelation through living prophets. With regard to this particular section, the varied interpretations also reflect some ambiguity in verse 2, which states that the revelation was given "not by commandment or constraint." Since verses 1–4 were part of the introduction to this section in the 1835 edition of the Doctrine and Covenants, through the years there have been differences of opinion as to whether the Word of Wisdom is a commandment in the sense that observance is obligatory to enjoy full Church fellowship as well as whether observance implies abstinence or merely moderation.

In the mid-1830s, many Church members felt that abstinence from alcohol, tobacco, tea, and coffee was a criterion for fellowship. The one possible exception to this otherwise strict interpretation was wine, which some early Church leaders may not have considered "strong drink." This early emphasis on abstinence or near abstinence failed to gain Church-wide or official acceptance, although Joseph Smith said no member "is worthy to hold an office" who has been taught the Word of Wisdom and fails "to comply with and obey it" (TPJS, p.117, fn.). Even so, the early statement gradually gave way to an emphasis on moderation. President Joseph F. Smith later taught that the Lord did not insist on strict compliance in these early years in order to allow a generation addicted to noxious substances some years to discard bad habits. This early pattern of moderation, observable by the 1840s, continued throughout the nineteenth century. President John Taylor initiated a reform in the early 1880s in which he stressed that all Church officers should abstain from the prohibited items, but his efforts were cut short by the social disruption caused by federal antipolygamy raids. While Church leaders did not require abstinence in the nineteenth century, they stressed moderation, counseled strongly against drunkenness, and opposed or carefully regulated the establishment of distilleries and grog shops. The numerous observations by visitors in Utah Territory attest to the prevailing orderliness and sobriety of Mormon communities and evidence the effectiveness of such preaching.

The path leading to the present position on the Word of Wisdom began with the presidency of Joseph F. Smith (1901–1918) and culminated in the administration of Heber J. Grant (1918–1945), who, more than any other Church leader, preached strict compliance with frequency and fervor. By the early 1930s, abstinence from alcohol, tobacco, tea, and coffee had become an established test of Church fellowship. There was no known specific revelation that brought this about. It resulted from Church leaders' long-term concern over the deleterious physical and spiritual effects of alcohol, tobacco, tea, and coffee on both individuals and communities. National and local agitation over prohibition and the mounting scientific evidence attesting to the harmful effects of certain substances intensified that concern.

The Word of Wisdom has resulted in, among other things, better physical health among LDS people and physical affirmations of truths received through revelation. It has also brought about a distinguishing separateness that reminds Latter-day Saints of their religious commitments and responsibilities.

BIBLIOGRAPHY
Alexander, Thomas G. *Mormonism in Transition,* pp. 258–71. Urbana, Ill., 1986.
Bush, Lester E., Jr. "The Word of Wisdom in Early Nineteenth-Century Perspective." *Dialogue* 14 (Fall 1981):47–65.

PAUL H. PETERSON

SECTION 93

Section 93 is a revelation received through the Prophet Joseph Smith on May 6, 1833, during a conference of high priests at Kirtland,

Ohio. It was first printed as chapter 82 of the 1835 edition of the Doctrine and Covenants. The insights of this revelation pervade LDS understanding of the nature and relationship of God and man.

It begins with the divine promise that every soul who forsakes sin, comes unto Christ, calls upon his name, obeys his voice, and keeps his commandments shall see his face "and know that I am, and that I am the true light that lighteth every man that cometh into the world" (verses 1–2).

The next verses refer to sayings from a record of John yet to be revealed in full. They are reminiscent of the prologue to John's Gospel, but they also witness to Jesus' baptism by John the Baptist.

Christ is called the Father and is one with the Father because "he gave me of his fulness" (verse 4). He is called the Word because he is the "messenger of salvation" (verse 8). In him is "the life of men and the light of men" (verse 9). "The worlds were made by him; men were made by him; all things were made by him, and through him, and of him" (verse 10).

In contrast with theologies of static being, several verses affirm Christ's becoming. Three times they reiterate that Christ did not receive a fulness at the beginning but continued "from grace to grace" until he received a fulness of the glory of the Father (verses 12, 13, 14; cf. Luke 2:40; Heb. 5:8–9). Christ became like the Father in the exalted sense only after his resurrection and glorification (cf. Rev. 5:12–13). An understanding of this process is the foundation of authentic worship.

The revelation denies the notion of *ex nihilo* creation. The intelligence of man, "the light of truth," (verse 29), is not created but is self-existent. Man, like Christ himself, "was . . . in the beginning with God" (verse 29). Furthermore, "The elements are eternal" (verse 33).

Truth is "knowledge of things as they are, and as they were, and as they are to come" (verse 24). Truth and intelligence are independent in the spheres in which God has placed them (verse 30). The spirit of man is native to the spirit of truth, which is "plainly manifest" from the beginning (verse 31). This is the basis of agency and accountability. "Every man whose spirit receiveth not the light is under condemnation" (verse 32).

Christ is the exemplar in all things. All may "come unto the Father in my name" (verse 19) and, in due time, "be glorified in me as I am in the Father" (verse 20). Man is a temple and a defiled temple will be destroyed. "Spirit and element" inseparably connected (resurrected) can receive a fulness of joy. "The glory of God is intelligence" defined as "light and truth." One who receives light and truth forsakes the evil one (verse 37).

"Every spirit of man was innocent in the beginning; and God having redeemed man from the fall, men became again, in their infant state, innocent before God" (verse 38). Through disobedience men become sinful, "light and truth" taken as they embrace the "traditions of their fathers" (verse 39).

The revelation closes with admonitions to the assembled high priests to set their houses in order by teaching the gospel more fully to their families (verses 42–50). Sidney Rigdon is to proclaim "the gospel of salvation" (verse 51) and the brethren are to "hasten to translate my scriptures" (Bible) and "to obtain a knowledge of history, and of countries, and of kingdoms, of laws of God and man," all "for the salvation of Zion" (verse 53).

DAN J. WORKMAN

SECTION 107

Section 107 is one of the most important statements in latter-day scripture on the divisions, offices, quorums, and councils of the priesthood. Section 107 establishes an orderly arrangement of lay priesthood responsibilities at several levels. It was first published as Chapter III in the 1835 edition of the Doctrine and Covenants and was entitled "On Priesthood." Over the years it has been accepted as a major document and has been viewed as a wise and effective charter on priesthood keys and offices. It is the foundation of the priesthood administration of the Church.

On March 28, 1835, in Kirtland, Ohio, the recently organized Quorum of the Twelve Apostles met in preparation for their mission to the eastern United States. Feeling a sense of inadequacy in their new callings as special witnesses for Christ, the quorum drafted a letter to the Prophet Joseph Smith requesting a revelation on their behalf: "The time when we are about to separate is near; and when we shall meet again, God only knows; we therefore feel to ask of him whom we have acknowledged to be our Prophet and Seer, that he inquire of God for us, and obtain a revelation, (if consistent) that we may look upon it when we are separated, that our hearts may be comforted" (*HC* 2:209–210).

Joseph "inquired of the Lord" and received section 107:1–57. The document distinguishes the Melchizedek Priesthood from the Aaronic Priesthood and defines which offices fall under each: the First Presidency, and under it the twelve apostles, high priests, and elders, officiate in the Melchizedek Priesthood and function in all "spiritual things" (verses 1–12, 18–19, 21–26); the bishop, with his counselors, serves in the Aaronic Priesthood, which administers the "outward ordinances" of the Church, including baptism (verses 13–17, 20). The First Presidency presides over the Church; the Twelve are "special witnesses of the name of Christ in all the world" (verse 23); and the Seventy are called to preach the gospel abroad (verse 25).

The principles of priesthood organization established by this revelation combine democratic and hierarchic elements. "Of necessity there are presidents" over the several offices (verse 21), but every decision of one of the three governing quorums of the Church "must be by the unanimous voice of the same" (verse 27), made "in all righteousness, in holiness, and lowliness of heart" (verse 30). These quorums—the First Presidency, the Quorum of the Twelve, and the quorums of the Seventy—are "equal in authority" but function under the priesthood keys of the First Presidency, or of the Quorum of the Twelve when the presidency is dissolved on the death of the President (verses 22–26). The revelation also traces the lineage of the patriarchal priesthood in ancient times from Adam to Noah (verses 39–57).

With few exceptions, verses 58–100 were excerpted from an earlier revelation and vision that Joseph Smith had received. It declared that the President of the High Priesthood is "to preside over the whole Church, . . . like unto Moses" (verse 91), and defined the duties, presidencies, and membership limits for quorums of elders, priests, teachers, and deacons. It also specified the duties of the bishop as a judge in Zion and gave the procedures for trying the conduct of a general officer of the Church.

BIBLIOGRAPHY

Cook, Lyndon W. *The Revelations of the Prophet Joseph Smith*, pp. 215–16, 326–29. Provo, Utah, 1981.

WALTER D. BOWEN

SECTIONS 109–110

Section 109 is the dedicatory prayer for the Kirtland Temple. Joseph Smith records that he received this prayer under the spirit of revelation (*HC* 2:420). The prayer contains some temple language repeated from Doctrine and Covenants section 88 (see verses 119–21), and some passages in it pertaining to the redemption of Jerusalem are paralleled in the Orson Hyde prayer given on the Mount of Olives five years later.

Section 109 is Hebraic in tone and reminiscent of the Solomonic dedication of the first temple and the temple-related benedictions of Jewish tradition (cf. 1 Kgs. 8).

It begins with thanksgiving, "Thanks be to thy name, O Lord God of Israel, who keepest covenant and showest mercy"; seeks divine acceptance and visible manifestation of divine glory upon the temple and the faithful; petitions that God accept what has been done in the spirit of sacrifice; designates the building as a house of God, of prayer, fasting, faith, learning, glory, and order (verse 8; cf. verse 16), where the divine name may be put upon his servants; asks forgiveness and the blotting out of sin; pleads for emissaries of truth to go forth in power and seal their witness with power; pleads for protection from enemies and deliverance from the calamities in Missouri; and prays for mercy on the nations of the earth, for expansion of stakes, for the gathering of scattered Jacob and Judah, for the redemption of Jerusalem "from this hour" (verse 62), and finally for blessings on the homes and families of the leaders of the Church. It ends with "O hear, O hear, O hear us, O Lord . . . that we may mingle our voices with those bright, shining seraphs around thy throne" and an "Amen, and Amen" (verses 78, 80).

Section 110 is the record of events following the temple dedication on April 3, 1836. The account (not canonical in the RLDS church) was recorded by Joseph's scribe Warren Cowdery, and first published one week after the events it describes in the *Messenger and Advocate*, and later was included in the 1876 edition of the Doctrine and Covenants (see headnote). After partaking of the sacrament and bowing in "solemn and silent prayer," Joseph Smith and Oliver Cowdery received a shared vision. The Savior appeared and accepted the temple, saying, "My name shall be here; and I will manifest myself to my people in mercy in this house" (verse 7). Moses next appeared to restore the "keys of the gathering of Israel from the four parts of the earth" (verse 11) preparatory to the renewal of temples and temple worship (*see* ISRAEL: GATHERING OF ISRAEL). Elias "committed the dispensation of the Gospel of Abraham" (verse 12) to restore the covenant promise made to Abraham that through him and his seed all generations would be blessed. Finally Elijah appeared and bestowed the keys of sealing for all priesthood ordinances, including the sealing of families, and announced the imminence of the second coming of the Messiah (verses 13–16). This was in keeping with the final prophecy of Malachi that Elijah would come to turn the hearts of the children to the fathers before the great and dreadful day of the Lord (Mal. 4:5–6; *see* ELIJAH).

BIBLIOGRAPHY
Sperry, Sidney B. *Doctrine and Covenants Compendium.* Salt Lake City, 1960.

S. MICHAEL WILCOX

SECTIONS 121–123

These sections are selections from a long letter written by Joseph Smith in Liberty Jail, Missouri, on March 20, 1839, addressed "To the Church of Latter-day Saints at Quincy, Illinois and scattered abroad and to Bishop Partridge in particular" (*HC* 3:289). The power and richness of the letter, both its doctrinal content and its literary images, may have resulted from the Prophet's personal suffering.

Section 121 begins with a prayer, a cry of "O God, where art thou?" a plea that God will recognize the sufferings of the Saints, punish their enemies, and avenge their wrongs (verses 1–6). In the next verse, the Prophet hears the consoling voice of inspiration saying, "My son, peace be unto thy soul; thine adversity and thine afflictions shall be but a small moment" (verse 7). He is reminded "Thy friends do stand by thee," and promised "They shall hail thee again with warm hearts and friendly hands" (verse 9). "Thou art not yet as Job" (verse 10). The righteousness of the Saints' actions is confirmed; in the Lord's time those who have afflicted the Saints will be punished (verses 11–25).

Verses 26–33 promise blessings of knowledge that will soon be poured out upon the Latter-day Saints by the Holy Spirit, including a knowledge of all God's dominions and the laws by which they operate. The last part of section 121 includes some of the most sensitive and powerful verses in LDS scripture. Here the Prophet teaches against all forms of unrighteous dominion. True authority, he writes, is always linked to love. "No power or influence can or ought to be maintained by virtue of the priesthood, only by persuasion, by long-suffering, by gentleness and meekness, and by love unfeigned" (verse 41).

Section 122 is a revelation directed specifically to Joseph Smith, to help him understand the trials he is suffering. It assures him that he will be known for good among the noble and virtuous of the earth, and that his own people will never be turned against him by "the testimony of traitors" (verse 3). The verses graphically name perils and betrayals he has suffered or has yet to suffer, and then continues "Know thou, my son, that all these things shall give thee experience, and shall be for thy good" (verse 7). The section ends by reminding the young prophet that "the Son of Man hath descended below them all" (verse 8).

Section 123 instructs the Saints in the steps they should take to seek redress for their persecution and losses in Missouri. They are admonished to compile lists of property damages and character and personal injuries, to take affidavits, and to gather libelous publications so that they may present their case before government officials. This course of action is explained as the last duty they owe to God, to their families, and to the rising generation. The section ends by assuring the Saints that these efforts, although they may not understand their value, will be important to the Church in the future (verse 15).

BIBLIOGRAPHY
Christianson, James R. "A Ray of Light in an Hour of Darkness." In *Studies in Scripture*, ed. R. Millett and K. Jackson 1:463–75. Salt Lake City, 1984.
Maxwell, Neal A. *But for a Small Moment.* Salt Lake City, 1986.

SUSAN HOWE

SECTION 124

Section 124, given January 19, 1841, to the Prophet Joseph Smith, is the longest revelation in the Doctrine and Covenants. It was the first section received at Nauvoo, Illinois, and was first printed in the 1844 edition of the Doctrine and Covenants as number 103.

Church members had fled from Missouri to Illinois in 1839 to escape the Extermination Order of Governor Lilburn W. Boggs. The eastern banks of the Mississippi River became a place of refuge and the Church headquarters. By 1841, Nauvoo had been established there and the village had grown to approximately 3,000 inhabitants. In that setting, section 124 served as an important inaugural, a kind of constitution for further development of Nauvoo and the Church. It provided instruction on temporal, doctrinal, and organizational matters, and gave assignments and counsel to fifty-five individuals.

Section 124 includes the following:

- A charge to Joseph Smith to "make a solemn proclamation" of the gospel to rulers of all nations (verses 2–14, 16–17, 107).

- Directions to build the Nauvoo House, a hotel where "the weary traveler may find health and safety" while contemplating the word of the Lord (verses 22–24, 56–82).

- A commandment to members to assist in building the Nauvoo Temple, begun three months earlier. It was to be a place for the Lord to restore the fulness of the priesthood and reveal "things which have been kept hid from before the foundation of the world" pertaining to the Dispensation of the Fulness of Times (verses 25–28, 40–44).

- A promise that if members would hearken unto the voice of God and his servants, "they shall not be moved out of their place" (verses 45–46).

- A clarification on baptism for the dead, defined as a temple ordinance. The revelation said Moses had received a similar charge to build a tabernacle for ordinance work (verses 25–48).

- A declaration that efforts of the Saints to establish a city and temple in Missouri were accepted by the Lord, even though persecutions prevented their establishment at that time (verses 49–54).

- Callings and confirmations of various positions in the Church, including a listing of some new officers and a reiteration of some previous callings. For example, Hyrum Smith was named as patriarch, replacing his father, who had died September 14, 1840. Joseph Smith, Sidney Rigdon, and William Law were appointed to the First Presidency. Brigham Young was renamed President of the Quorum of the Twelve Apostles (he had been sustained in this position on

April 14, 1840), and assignments were made to that quorum. Twelve members were named for a stake high council, and others were called to serve in the presidencies of the high priests, elders, seventies, two bishoprics, and priests. Teachers, deacons, and stake organizations were mentioned, but no leadership assignments in these were made (verses 20–21, 123–42).

PAUL C. RICHARDS

SECTIONS 127–128

Sections 127 and 128 constitute two doctrinal letters dictated by the Prophet Joseph Smith while "in exile" near Nauvoo, Illinois, during the first week of September 1842. His scribe was William Clayton. The sections were first published in the *Times and Seasons* on September 14 and October 1, 1842, and first appeared in the Doctrine and Covenants in 1844 as numbers 105 and 106.

These documents clarified and formalized the LDS doctrine and practice of baptism for the dead, a practice attested to in the first century at Corinth (1 Cor. 15:29). Two years earlier, while speaking at a funeral on August 15, 1840, Joseph Smith first publicly announced the privilege and the responsibility of Church members to perform baptisms for the dead (*TPJS*, p. 179). "It presents the Gospel of Christ in probably a more enlarged scale than some have imagined it" (*TPJS*, p. 180). Immediately thereafter, Church members began performing proxy baptisms in the Mississippi River. A year later, Joseph Smith declared, "There shall be no more baptism for the dead, until the ordinance can be attended to in the Lord's House" (*HC* 4:426). When the baptismal font in the Nauvoo Temple was completed November 21, 1841, baptisms for the dead were performed there (*HC* 4:454).

Sections 127 and 128 stress the requirement for eyewitnesses and a recorder at all such baptismal services. Without authenticated records on earth and in heaven, a baptism is not deemed valid (D&C 127:6–9; 128:3–10).

In Section 128, the Prophet expounded on Malachi 4:5–6 and explained that baptism for the dead is "a welding link" between parents and children (D&C 128:18). He further explained that unless children are sealed by temple ordinances to their deceased forebears, who are in turn sealed to each other in God's family, neither can be fully saved and exalted (verses 14, 15, 18). "They without us cannot be made perfect—neither can we without our dead be made perfect" (verse 15; cf. Hebrews 11:40).

Baptisms and other temple ordinances for the dead continue as a vital part of Church doctrine and practice.

GEORGE D. DURRANT

SECTIONS 131–132

These sections discuss the principle of eternal marriage as a requirement for obtaining the highest degree of glory in the celestial kingdom (D&C 131:1–4; cf. 76:50–70). In that exalted state, men and women become gods, continue to have children, and come to know God fully (D&C 132:23–24).

Section 131 contains selected statements made by Joseph Smith on May 16–17, 1843, during a visit to members of the Church in Ramus, Illinois, 22 miles east of Nauvoo (*HC* 5:391–93). They were recorded by William Clayton in his diary. In addition to its teachings on eternal marriage, section 131 also defines the phrase "more sure word of prophecy," declares that no one can be saved in ignorance (cf. *TPJS*, p. 217), and explains that spirit is purified matter.

Section 132 contains the doctrinal basis of the practice of plural marriage. Although some were distressed by it, others found plural marriage "the most holy and important doctrine ever revealed" (W. Clayton, in A. Jenson, *Historical Record* 6:226). This revelation was recorded on July 12, 1843, in the brick store in Nauvoo. At the urging of Hyrum Smith so that Emma Smith might be convinced of its truth, the Prophet Joseph Smith dictated it sentence by sentence. Clayton reported that "after the whole was written Joseph asked me to read it through, slowly and carefully, which I did, and he pronounced it correct" (*CHC* 2:106–7). That evening, Bishop Newel K. Whitney received permission to copy the revelation. The next day, his clerk, Joseph C. Kingsbury, copied the document, which Whitney and Kingsbury proofread against the original. This copy was given to Brigham Young in March 1847; it was officially adopted as revelation at a general conference in Salt Lake City in August 1852, and was first published for public review in a *Deseret News* extra of September 14, 1852.

The doctrines in this revelation were probably received

sometime in 1831 while the Prophet was translating the Bible. In response to questions about the legitimacy of the ancient prophets' plural marriages, the Lord revealed to Joseph Smith the conditions and requirements under which plural marriage was to be observed. Lyman Johnson told Orson Pratt that "Joseph had made known to him [Johnson] as early as 1831, that plural marriage was a correct principle," but had said it was not yet time to teach and practice it (*MS* 40 [1878]:788). That date was later confirmed in various statements and affidavits collected by Joseph F. Smith and others from those who had been close to Joseph Smith in Nauvoo.

Section 132 states that all covenants must be made in the proper manner, by proper authority, and be sealed by the Holy Spirit of Promise in order to be valid eternally (verses 7–19), and that through faithfulness eternal blessings are guaranteed to those who marry by this new and everlasting covenant: "Then shall they be gods, because they have no end; therefore shall they be from everlasting to everlasting, because they continue" (verse 20). This law was ordained before the world was, and through it Abraham received the promise of eternal lives through his seed (verses 28–37). Strict prohibitions against adultery accompany the law of eternal marriage (verses 38–44, 61–63). In concluding verses, Joseph Smith received divine affirmation of his eternal standing with God and acceptance of his labors (verses 45–50); and admonitions were given to Emma and others to observe this law and to multiply and replenish the earth so that God may be glorified (verses 51–66).

BIBLIOGRAPHY

Danel W. Bachman. "New Light on an Old Hypothesis: The Ohio Origins of the Revelation on Eternal Marriage." *Journal of Mormon History* 5 (1978):19–32.

PAUL G. GRANT

SECTIONS 137–138

Section 137 reports a vision of the celestial kingdom recorded in the diary of Joseph Smith. On January 21, 1836, he and several other Church leaders gathered in the Kirtland Temple for the ordinances of washing and anointing. Joseph blessed and anointed his aged father, Joseph Smith, Sr., who in turn anointed the members of the Church presidency and sealed blessings upon the Prophet. Joseph recorded that as the presidency laid their hands on his head and prophesied, "the heavens were opened upon us and I beheld the celestial kingdom of God, and the glory thereof" (verse 1). He saw its streets as if paved with gold. The Father and the Son sat on a blazing throne. ADAM and ABRAHAM were there; so were Joseph's parents, who were still alive at the time of the vision, and his brother Alvin, who had died before the priesthood was restored and hence had not been baptized for the remission of sins. The vision continued beyond that which is included in section 137 (*HC* 2:380–81; *PWJS*, pp. 145–46). Many present received visions and witnessed the glory of God fill the room.

Joseph's vision was the first doctrinal revelation to the Church disclosing that the Lord will provide all who die without hearing the gospel an opportunity to hear and accept it in the spirit world so they can enter the celestial kingdom (D&C 137:8–9; clarifying 76:72) and that children who die before the age of accountability (eight years) will be heirs of the celestial kingdom (D&C 137:10).

Section 138 is the record of a vision received by President Joseph F. Smith on October 3, 1918, as he was pondering the universal nature of the atonement of Jesus Christ and wondering how the Savior taught the spirits in prison in the brief time between his death and resurrection (D&C 138:1–11; cf. 1 Pet. 3:19; 4:6). He saw the visit of the Savior to the righteous spirits in paradise. He also observed that Jesus did not go in person among the wicked and disobedient but organized representatives from among the righteous spirits to carry the gospel to "all the spirits of men" (D&C 138:30). Those who were not taught the gospel on earth will be given the opportunity to hear it and accept its exalting fulness when taught by Christ's authorized representatives in the spirit world; those spirits who are "in darkness and under the bondage of sin . . . who repent will be redeemed" (verses 138:57–58; cf. 76:74).

The accounts of these two visions were canonized in the general conference of April 1976 as additions to the Pearl of Great Price. They became sections in the Doctrine and Covenants in 1981.

BIBLIOGRAPHY

Millet, Robert L. "Salvation Beyond the Grave (D&C 137 and 138)." In *Studies in Scripture*, Vol. 1, pp. 549–63, ed. R. Millet and K. Jackson. Sandy, Utah, 1984.

LEON R. HARTSHORN

OFFICIAL DECLARATION—2

Official Declaration—2 revealed that the "long-promised day has come when every faithful, worthy man in the Church may receive the holy priesthood." This "priesthood revelation" made it possible for all worthy males to be ordained to all levels of the priesthood. Previously black members of the Church had been denied the priesthood, which precluded their holding priesthood callings and participation in most temple ordinances.

The revelation was received by President Spencer W. Kimball "after extended meditation and prayer" in the Salt Lake Temple. That same revelation came to his counselors and to the Quorum of the Twelve Apostles in the temple, and then it was presented to all of the other General Authorities, who approved it unanimously. It was announced by letter to all priesthood officers of the Church and to the press on June 8, 1978. Official Declaration—2 contains the text of that letter and records its presentation and acceptance on September 30, 1978, in general conference by the common consent of the members of the Church. The revelation resolved problems for many members who had agonized over the prior practice (Bush and Mauss), the historical origins and ramifications of which had become the subject of considerable debate and reflection.

Since the announcement, missionaries have actively proselytized in many nations with large black populations, where thousands have become members of the Church. Dallin H. Oaks, an apostle, noted this growth in the LDS Afro-American Symposium held at Brigham Young University on the occasion of the tenth anniversary of the revelation (Oaks). In particular, he pointed to the rapid growth in black converts in the Caribbean islands, West Africa, and Brazil.

BIBLIOGRAPHY

Bush, Lester E., and Armand L. Mauss, eds. *Neither White nor Black: Mormon Scholars Confront the Race Issue in a Universal Church.* Midvale, Utah, 1984.

Grover, Mark L. "The Mormon Priesthood Revelation and the São Paulo Brazil Temple." *Dialogue* 23 (Spring 1990):39–53.

McConkie, Bruce R. "All Are Alike unto God." In *Second Annual CES Symposium*, pp. 3–5. Salt Lake City, 1978.

Oaks, Dallin H. "For the Blessing of All His Children." Address, LDS Afro-American Symposium. Provo, June 8, 1988.

CARDELL K. JACOBSON

DOCTRINE AND COVENANTS AS LITERATURE

The literary quality of the Doctrine and Covenants can best be seen in its similarities to a near literary relation—that "noblest monument of English prose," the King James Version of the BIBLE. Although a truly unique religious text, the Doctrine and Covenants contains more than 2,000 close parallels to biblical passages, and the literary manner of the book is similar to the Bible in subject matter. Like earlier scripture, the Doctrine and Covenants offers a rainbow of literary genres. The collection of revelations ranges from forms as transcendent as VISIONS (sections 3, 76, 110), angelic annunciations (sections 2, 13, 27), and PROPHECIES (sections 87, 121); through such ecclesiastical proclamations as prayers (sections 109, 121), epistles (sections 127, 128), scriptural explanations (sections 74, 77, 86), commandments (section 19), and official declarations; to down-to-earth instructions (sections 130, 131) and minutes of meetings (section 102).

The literary kinship of the Doctrine and Covenants with the Bible is more apparent in tone than in style. The Doctrine and Covenants, for instance, is impressive for a simple, condensed straightforwardness that lends itself to statements remarkably rich in implication. The following two examples are from a single section: "Truth is knowledge of things as they are, and as they were, and as they are to come" (D&C 93:24). "The glory of God is intelligence, or in other words, light and truth" (93:36). These lines are not set in contexts that illuminate them so much as they are parts of a sorites—conclusions without the use of thesis and antithesis.

Tonal richness sometimes expresses itself in vivid metaphor. A single section of the Doctrine and Covenants, for example, displays a sensitive sequence of images of water—progress like "rolling waters" that cannot "remain impure" (D&C 121:33), evil prospects that shall "melt away as the hoar frost melteth before the burning rays of the rising sun" (121:11), and doctrine that will "distil upon thy soul as the dews from heaven" (121:45).

As the most recent compilation of divine prophecy of The Church of Jesus Christ of Latter-day Saints, the Doctrine and Covenants provides the invaluable literary benefit of immediacy; divinity can be approached by modern readers through this book naturally and directly. It locates the reader not in the distant past of Ophir or Tarsus but in the recent history of such familiar landscapes as New York and Boston, where God reveals himself in close proximity. That closeness is apparent in his manner of address; he refers to recipients of his revelations a half dozen times in the book as "friends" (D&C 84:63; 84:77; 94:1; 98:1; 100:1; 104:1).

That is how the voice of the God of ABRAHAM and Isaac and of PETER and PAUL addresses readers in the Doctrine and Covenants— as friends. The most striking literary characteristic of the book is the directness of its access to God. When Joseph Smith cries out in a long and painful prayer of reproach, "O God, where art thou?" the Father's response is as immediately comforting to present readers as it was to the Prophet: "My son, peace be unto thy soul" (D&C 121:1, 7). The Doctrine and Covenants speaks with biblical power to the immediate conditions of modern life. In the most difficult moments of current circumstance, the Doctrine and Covenants lifts readers' eyes above mortal disappointments toward eternal hopes: "All these things shall give thee experience, and shall be for thy good" (122:7).

BIBLIOGRAPHY
Sperry, Sidney B. *Doctrine and Covenants Compendium.* Salt Lake City, 1960.
Walker, Steven C. "The Voice of the Prophet." *BYU Studies* 10 (Autumn 1969):95–106.

STEVEN C. WALKER

DOCTRINE AND COVENANTS COMMENTARIES

Commentaries on the Doctrine and Covenants follow the pattern of many biblical commentaries, supplying the historical context, that is, the time, circumstances, and situation of the revelations. In the most recent (1981) edition of the Doctrine and Covenants, headnotes for each section have been added or enlarged, with a brief synopsis of the historical setting. Additional notes and explanations are provided by the various separately published commentaries discussed here. Commentaries written by members of the Quorum of the Twelve Apostles are given special consideration. Others are recommended as helps to the membership of the Church to provide historical insight to their study of the scriptures.

An early (1916) and still useful one-volume commentary was written by Hyrum M. Smith, a member of the Quorum of the Twelve Apostles, and Janne M. Sjodahl. *Doctrine and Covenants Commentary* contains the text of the Doctrine and Covenants and gives historical background and commentary for each section. It is extensively footnoted with exegetical notes. The volume was later supplemented and expanded under the direction of Joseph Fielding Smith, Harold B. Lee, and Marion G. Romney of the Quorum of the Twelve.

The Message of the Doctrine and Covenants (1969, edited by G. Homer Durham) is a published version of a series of lectures delivered at the University of Southern California by John A. Widtsoe, also of the Quorum of the Twelve. The author's scientific background is apparent in his references to nineteenth- and twentieth-century scientific theory.

T. Edgar Lyon, former director of the institute of religion adjacent to the University of Utah in Salt Lake City, published his *Introduction to the Doctrine and Covenants and Pearl of Great Price* in 1948. He treats the work as a "connected message" and emphasizes the functional aspects of many topics, including priesthood, missionary work, Zion, gathering, ordinances, Christian teachings, economics, millennium, unique revelations, and literary value.

From 1947 through 1949 the Church published a series of manuals titled *Church History and Modern Revelation,* written by Joseph Fielding Smith of the Quorum of the Twelve. It was a study course for the Melchizedek Priesthood quorums of the Church. These volumes integrated each section of the Doctrine and Covenants with the life and times of the Prophet Joseph Smith. A more concise attempt at this approach was that of E. Cecil McGavin in a volume titled *The Historical Background of the Doctrine and Covenants,* published in 1949.

Sidney B. Sperry, longtime professor of Hebrew and ancient scripture at Brigham Young University, published *A Doctrine and Covenants Compendium* in 1960, which considered linguistic and doctrinal issues in detail.

A four-volume work titled *The Latter-day Prophets and the Doctrine and Covenants* (1963), by Roy W. Doxey, former dean of the College of Religious Instruction at Brigham Young University, includes statements of General Authorities on each section of the

Doctrine and Covenants. It demonstrates applications of Doctrine and Covenants texts in homiletic settings.

A historical account is *The Revelations of the Prophet Joseph Smith* by Lyndon W. Cook (1981), providing a compilation of background facts relevant to each section. Documented biographical profiles of the personalities mentioned in the text are included.

A commentary titled *The Edwards Commentary on the Doctrine and Covenants* was written by F. Henry Edwards of the Reorganized Church of Jesus Christ of Latter Day Saints and published in 1946. This book provides a brief historical overview for each section and commentary on the major themes of the sections, as these relate and apply to the problems of that church.

A critical analysis of the earliest texts and publication of the Doctrine and Covenants is Robert J. Woodford's *The Historical Development of the Doctrine and Covenants,* a Ph.D. dissertation, Brigham Young University, 1974. Other studies are those by William E. Berrett, *Teachings of the Doctrine and Covenants,* 1961; Roy W. Doxey, *Doctrine and Covenants Speaks,* 2 vols., 1970; Richard O. Cowan, *The Doctrine and Covenants, Our Modern Scripture,* 1978; Daniel H. Ludlow, *A Companion to Your Study of the Doctrine and Covenants,* 1978; Leaun G. Otten and C. Max Caldwell, *Sacred Truths of the Doctrine and Covenants,* 2 vols., 1982; and Robert L. Millet and Kent P. Jackson, eds., *Studies in Scripture, the Doctrine and Covenants,* 1985.

H. DEAN GARRETT

DOCTRINE AND COVENANTS EDITIONS

The Doctrine and Covenants contains revelations from God as given to the Prophet Joseph Smith and later Presidents of The Church of Jesus Christ of Latter-day Saints and includes other inspired writings and doctrinal declarations accepted as scripture by the Latter-day Saints. The first edition appeared in 1835. Later editions incorporated additional revelations and reference aids. The Doctrine and Covenants has been translated into many languages, though the English edition is the official version.

By the fall of 1831, Joseph Smith had recorded seventy or more revelations, most of which contained instructions to Church members. In a special conference held November 1, 1831, in Hiram, Ohio, the Church decided to publish a selection of these revelations, or "commandments." A new revelation was received on that occasion as "my preface unto the book of my commandments," from which the title of the 1833 compilation, the Book of Commandments, may have been taken (D&C 1:6). This publication was never completed; a mob destroyed the Independence, Missouri, press and all but about a hundred unfinished copies in July 1833. These few copies of the Book of Commandments were circulated within the Church and were often called the "Book of Covenants," in reference to the lead section, which had circulated widely in handwritten versions as "The Articles and Covenants of the Church." Received the day the Church was organized, this revelation is now section 20 of the Doctrine and Covenants.

THE 1835 EDITION.   Shortly after the unsuccessful 1833 effort to print the Book of Commandments was stopped, plans were made to publish the revelations in Kirtland, Ohio. Renamed the *Doctrine and Covenants of the Church of the Latter Day Saints,* the book was presented to, and accepted by, the members of the Church in an August 1835 conference as the word of God. The change in name to Doctrine and Covenants reflected a change in content. Unlike the Book of Commandments, which contained revelations only, the Doctrine and Covenants was divided into two parts. The new first part consisted of seven theological presentations now known as the Lectures on Faith but then titled "On the Doctrine of the Church of the Latter Day Saints." The part including the revelations published previously, the original preface, and a number of new revelations not in the 1833 compilation, were titled "Part Second, Covenants and Commandments." The title of the Doctrine and Covenants reflects the subtitles of these two parts.

In preparing the 1835 edition, Joseph Smith and a committee appointed to the task on September 24, 1834 (*HC* 2:165, 243–44) edited the revelations that had formerly appeared in the Book of Commandments. They corrected scribal and printing errors and occasionally clarified the text. They added explanations of the duties of officers that were new in the Church organization since the earlier revelations were received. They also combined some of the revelations to simplify publication and corrected grammatical problems.

The 1835 edition of the Doctrine and Covenants contained 103 sections, though two sections were inadvertently numbered 66, so that the last one's number was printed 102. Sections 1–100 were revelations to Joseph Smith. Section 101 prescribed practices for marriage. Section 102 stated the appropriate relationship of the Church to governments. These two sections were not revelations but were included as expressions of belief of the Church at that time. Oliver Cowdery (and possibly W. W. Phelps) wrote them, probably in response to critics of the doctrines and activities of the Church. Although Joseph Smith subsequently endorsed the statement on government, there is evidence that he opposed including the statement on marriage from the beginning, and it was eventually removed (see Cook, pp. 348–49, n. 11).

THE 1844 NAUVOO EDITION. By 1840 the Church needed a new edition of the Doctrine and Covenants. The 1835 edition had sold out, and Joseph Smith had received additional revelations. The new edition appeared in Nauvoo shortly after the death of Joseph Smith in 1844. The eight newly added revelations are numbered sections 103, 105, 112, 119, 124, 127, 128, and 135 in the 1981 edition. The metal printing plates from the 1844 edition were used in the 1845 and 1846 reprintings.

THE 1845 LIVERPOOL, ENGLAND, EDITION. In 1847, Brigham Young led the members of the Church to the Salt Lake Valley, where they had no facilities to print books. In 1845 Wilford Woodruff printed 3,000 copies of the Doctrine and Covenants in England for the growing LDS population in the British Isles. This edition included the new revelations published in the 1844 Nauvoo edition. Other Church representatives arranged reprintings in England in 1849, 1852, 1854, 1866, and 1869 and shipped most of the 1854 printing to Salt Lake City because of very limited facilities for printing there.

THE 1876 EDITION. In 1876 Orson Pratt, a member of the Quorum of the Twelve Apostles and Church historian, acting under the direction of President Brigham Young, prepared a new edition of the Doctrine and Covenants in Salt Lake City. He divided each revelation into verses and added twenty-six revelations not previously included. They are now sections 2, 13, 77, 85, 87, 108–11, 113–18, 120–23, 125, 126, 129–32, and 136. Since section 132 contained information about plural marriage inconsistent with the 1835 article on marriage, the latter was eliminated.

THE 1879 EDITION.   Three years later, Pratt published another edition in England in which he added footnotes to the text. He also requested permission from President John Taylor to drop the "Lectures on Faith," but was instructed that, though the time might come to do this, it was not yet. This edition was published in 1879 in England and in 1880 in Salt Lake City from duplicate plates. President George Q. Cannon, a counselor in the First Presidency, presented this edition to the members of the Church in a fiftieth jubilee conference held in October 1880; they accepted the book as scripture.

From 1880 to 1920 the Church published at least twenty-eight printings from this edition. Beginning in 1908, each printing included a concordance and excerpts from President of the Church Wilford Woodruff's "Manifesto," an official declaration ending plural marriage.

THE 1921 EDITION.   In 1920, President Heber J. Grant assigned a committee of six members of the Council of the Twelve to prepare a new edition of the Doctrine and Covenants. The major change in the 1921 edition was the removal of the "Lectures on Faith," which were not considered to be revelations. The committee also revised the footnotes and divided the pages into double columns. Even though the name of the collection had been changed in the 1835 edition to signal the addition of the "Lectures on Faith," it was not changed back when the lectures were deleted. The 1921 edition was the standard until 1981.

THE 1981 EDITION.   A committee appointed by the First Presidency of the Church directed the publication of a new edition of the Doctrine and Covenants in 1981. New features included completely revised footnotes and rewritten introductory headings for each section. Two additional sections and a second official declaration were also incorporated. Section 137 is a portion of a vision of the celestial kingdom given to Joseph Smith in the Kirtland Temple on January 21, 1836. Section 138 is a vision about the redemption of the dead given to Joseph F. Smith, sixth President of the Church, in 1918. Official Declaration—2 is the 1978 announcement by the First Presidency that all worthy male members of the Church can be ordained to the priesthood.

FOREIGN-LANGUAGE EDITIONS. The Church has also published the Doctrine and Covenants in many languages other than English. Beginning in 1851 with the Welsh edition, the Doctrine and Covenants has been translated and published in its entirety in a score or more languages and selections from it in many others.

BIBLIOGRAPHY
Cook, Lyndon W. *The Revelations of the Prophet Joseph Smith: A Historical and Bibliographical Commentary of the Doctrine and Covenants.* Salt Lake City, 1985.
Gentry, Leland H. "What of the Lectures on Faith?" *BYU Studies* 19 (Fall 1978):5–19.
Lambert, A. C. *The Published Editions of the Book of Doctrine and Covenants of the Church of Jesus Christ of Latter-day Saints in All Languages, 1833–1950.* Provo, Utah, 1950.
Woodford, Robert J. "The Historical Development of the Doctrine and Covenants." 3 vols. Ph.D. diss., Brigham Young University, 1974.
———. "The Doctrine and Covenants: A Historical Overview." In *Studies in Scripture*, ed. R. Millet and K. Jackson, Vol. 1, pp. 3–22. Sandy, Utah, 1984.

ROBERT J. WOODFORD

DOVE, SIGN OF THE

All four Gospel writers indicate that at the baptism of Jesus, JOHN THE BAPTIST saw the Spirit descend upon Jesus like a dove (Matt. 3:16; Mark 1:10; Luke 3:22; John 1:32). The JOSEPH SMITH TRANSLATION OF THE BIBLE, John 1:31–33, reads: "And John bare record, saying: When he was baptized of me, I saw the Spirit descending from heaven like a dove, and it abode upon him. And I knew him; for he who sent me to baptize with water, the same said unto me: Upon whom thou shalt see the Spirit descending, and remaining on him, the same is he who baptizeth with the Holy Ghost. And I saw, and bare record that this is the Son of God" (see also JST Matt. 3:45–46).

The Holy Ghost is a spirit person in the form of man (D&C 130:22) and does not transform himself into a dove or any other form. The Prophet Joseph Smith explained: "The sign of the dove was instituted before the creation of the world, a witness for the Holy Ghost, and the devil cannot come in the sign of a dove. The Holy Ghost is a personage [a man], and is in the form of a personage [a man]. It does not confine itself to the *form* of the dove, but in *sign* [symbol or representation] of the dove. The Holy Ghost cannot be transformed into a dove; but the sign of a dove was given to John to signify the truth of the deed, as the dove is an emblem or token of truth and innocence" (*TPJS,* p. 276). The dove was a supernatural sign given to John to witness the identity of the Messiah. Some non-LDS scholars have entertained differing opinions as to whether or not a real dove was present. Joseph Smith's explanation leads toward a conclusion that the dove was not literally present.

Other references to the sign of the dove are 1 Nephi 11:27; 2 Nephi 31:8 and Doctrine and Covenants 93:15. The BOOK OF ABRAHAM states that to Abraham also was revealed "the sign of the Holy Ghost in the form of a dove" (Facsimile 2, Fig. 7).

ROBERT L. MARROTT

E

ELIAS

Elias is both a name and a title and has four meanings: (1) Elias was a man, presumably of Abraham's time, who "committed the dispensation of Abraham"—which included the blessings of God's covenant with Abraham—to the Prophet Joseph Smith and Oliver Cowdery on April 3, 1836, in the Kirtland Temple (D&C 110:12); nothing more is known about this man. (2) "Elias" appears in the New Testament as the Greek transliteration of the Hebrew name ELIJAH (e.g., Matt. 17:3; James 5:17–18). (3) A forerunner in building God's kingdom is called "an Elias" (*TPJS*, pp. 335–36). (4) A prophet who helps restore something of particular importance is also referred to as an "Elias" (cf. JST Matt. 17:13–14). In scripture, therefore, the name Elias may refer to a preparer, a forerunner, a restorer, to Elias himself, or to Elijah.

Individuals who have acted as forerunners or restorers include Jesus Christ (JST John 1:21–28); Noah as Gabriel (D&C 27:6–7; *TPJS*, p. 157); John the Baptist (Luke 1:17); John the Revelator (D&C 77:9, 14); Adam as Michael, Moroni$_2$, and Peter, James, and John (D&C 27:5–13; 128:20–21); and Joseph Smith (D&C 1:17–18; *TPJS*, p. 335). Each of these may be considered an Elias.

Preparatory work in the Church is primarily associated with the Aaronic Priesthood; but when performed by the Melchizedek Priesthood, it is done under the spirit and power of Elijah (*TPJS*, pp.

336–37). In this connection, the keys given by Elias in the Kirtland Temple (D&C 110:12) were specifically for the Abrahamic covenant.

GEORGE A. HORTON, JR.

ELIJAH

[*Because of Elijah's prophesied role (Mal. 4:5–6), he has become the subject of tradition and legend, as the article* Ancient Sources *explains. Moreover, as expressed in the companion essay,* LDS Sources, *Latter-day Saint teaching illuminates Elijah's latter-day roles as well as the fulfillment of prophetic expectations associated with him.*]

LDS SOURCES

During a divine manifestation to the youthful Joseph Smith on the evening of September 21, 1823, the angel MORONI quoted Malachi 4:5–6, a prophecy that concerns Elijah's activities in the latter days. Moroni's rendering, which differs from the current biblical text, outlines and clarifies Elijah's prophesied role:

> Behold, I will reveal unto you the Priesthood, by the hand of Elijah the prophet, before the coming of the great and dreadful day of the Lord. And he shall plant in the hearts of the children the promises made to the fathers, and the hearts of the children shall turn to their fathers. If it were not so, the whole earth would be utterly wasted at his coming [JS—H 1:38–39; D&C 2].

Malachi's prophecy anticipates that Elijah would play an important role "before the coming of the great and dreadful day of the Lord" (Mal. 4:5). Elijah was endowed with the priesthood power of God. With this power, he declared to King Ahab that no rain would fall upon the land (1 Kgs. 17:1). Accordingly, the heavens were sealed and ancient Israel experienced a disastrous drought for three and a half years. When Elijah was carried up into heaven in a fiery chariot, his earthly mission appeared to have ended. But the sealing power that he exercised marked only the beginning of his responsibility regarding this eternal priesthood power.

At the conclusion of his mortal life, Elijah was translated; that is, he experienced some type of change from mortality without experiencing mortal death (*see* TRANSLATED BEINGS). Latter-day Saints conclude that a major reason for Elijah's translation was to enable him to return to the earth to confer keys of authority on the three chief apostles before Jesus' crucifixion and resurrection (see MOUNT OF TRANSFIGURATION). Since spirits cannot lay hands on mortal beings (D&C 129), and since Moses and Elijah could not return as resurrected beings because Jesus was the first to be resurrected (Packer, p. 109; cf. *TPJS*, p. 191), the need for the translation of Elijah and Moses is evident. On the Mount of Transfiguration (Matt. 17:1–9), Elijah specifically restored the priesthood keys of sealing, the power that binds and validates in the heavens all ordinances performed on the earth (cf. *TPJS*, p. 338).

On April 3, 1836, in a vision to Joseph Smith and Oliver Cowdery in the newly completed Kirtland Temple, Elijah appeared and announced that the time had come when Malachi's prophecy was to be fulfilled. He committed the sealing keys of the priesthood to Joseph Smith and Oliver Cowdery (D&C 110:13–16). This restoration was necessary so that the sealing ordinances and covenants of God could be administered in righteousness upon the earth (*DS* 2:117). Joseph Smith explained:

> The spirit, power, and calling of Elijah is, that ye have power to hold the key of the revelations, ordinances, oracles, powers and endowments of the fulness of the Melchizedek Priesthood and of the kingdom of God on the earth; and to receive, obtain, and perform all the ordinances belonging to the kingdom of God. . . . What you seal on earth, by the keys of Elijah, is sealed in heaven; and this is the power of Elijah [*TPJS*, pp. 337–38].

Through the sealing power of the priesthood, men and women may be sealed to each other in marriage for all eternity in one of the temples of God. In addition, children may be sealed to their parents forever. Thus the family organization continues eternally (Sperry, p. 139).

Because many have died without either a knowledge of saving gospel principles or the opportunity to receive priesthood ordinances, the latter-day mission of Elijah made it possible to have these sealing ordinances performed vicariously on the earth for those who have died, thus giving all an opportunity for salvation (cf. *DS* 2:118–19). The Prophet Joseph Smith offered the following explanation:

> The spirit of Elijah is to come, the Gospel to be established, . . . and the Saints to come up as saviors on Mount Zion. But how are they to become saviors on Mount Zion? By building their temples, erecting their baptismal fonts, and going forth and receiving all the ordinances, baptisms, confirmations, washings, anointings, ordinations and sealing powers upon their heads, in behalf of all their progenitors who are dead, and redeem them; . . . and herein is the chain that binds the hearts of the fathers to the children and the children to the fathers, which fulfills the mission of Elijah [*TPJS*, p. 330].

When Latter-day Saints speak of the spirit of Elijah, they mean at least two things. First, the promise of salvation made to the fathers has been renewed to the modern Church (JS—H 1:38–39; D&C 27:9–10). Second, the hearts of men and women have extensively turned to their fathers, as is evident in the dramatic growth in the number of genealogical societies, libraries, and individual genealogical or family history research organizations throughout much of the world. The spirit of Elijah has motivated thousands to make considerable investment in both money and time to search out the records of family ancestors and bring these records together to form a family history (*DS* 2:123–27). In addition to numerous family history centers, the Church has built many temples where sacred priesthood saving ordinances may be performed for both the living and the dead.

BIBLIOGRAPHY

Packer, Boyd K. *The Holy Temple.* Salt Lake City, 1980.
Smith, Joseph Fielding. *DS* 2:100–128. Salt Lake City, 1955.
Sperry, Sidney B. *The Spirit of the Old Testament.* Salt Lake City, 1970.
Widtsoe, John A. "Elijah, The Tishbite." *Utah Genealogical and Historical Magazine* 27 (Apr. 1936):53–60.

FRANKLIN D. DAY

ANCIENT SOURCES

Elijah in Jewish tradition was an Israelite prophet who was active in the northern kingdom during the reigns of King Ahab (and his consort Jezebel) and King Ahaziah (9th cent. B.C.). His name may be a cognomen: Eli-yahu (YHWH, or Jehovah, is God), expressing the main emphasis of his prophetic ministry: the exclusive and pure worship of YHWH, and uncompromising opposition to the Canaanite pagan cult of Baal. His activities are described in 1 Kings 17–2 Kings 2, and account for his becoming in Jewish tradition the symbol of uncompromising religious zeal. The latter came to a dramatic climax in his confrontation with the priests of Baal, after a long period of drought which Elijah had prophesied would come as punishment for the idolatrous Baal-worship, on Mount Carmel. (The Catholic monastic order of Carmelites, taking Elijah's ascetic life in the desert as a model, considers him as its spiritual father.) Unlike the later "literary" prophets, Elijah is also described as a worker of miracles, but he shares with them the strong emphasis on social justice, as evidenced by his other great clash with the king and queen in the matter of Naboth's vineyard (1 Kgs. 21), which the royal couple desired for themselves.

According to the biblical account, Elijah did not die an ordinary death but was taken up into heaven in a whirlwind by a chariot of fire drawn by horses of fire. Hence, unlike other prophets, a large number of legends and beliefs concerning him developed. He is said to return frequently to earth, usually in the guise of a poor peasant, beggar, or even Gentile and—unrecognized—to help those in distress or danger, disappearing as suddenly as he appeared. A chair is set and a cup of wine poured for Elijah at every Passover celebration. He is also believed to be present at every circumcision ceremony, and a special chair ("Elijah's chair") for his invisible presence is placed next to that of the godfather holding the male baby. This particular belief may be due to two factors: Elijah's angelic status (having ascended to heaven) and the prophet Malachi's reference to him (Mal. 3:1) as the "angel of the covenant." In Jewish usage the term *berith* ("covenant") signifies more specifically the "covenant of circumcision" (cf. Gen. 17:9–10). Elijah also plays an important role in Jewish mysticism, where he appears as a celestial messenger revealing divine mysteries.

More important, however, than all the other aspects is Elijah's eschatological role in Jewish tradition. How and why this role developed is difficult to reconstruct, but by the time of Malachi, one of the last Old Testament prophets, some such beliefs seem to have already been in existence: "Behold, I will send you Elijah the prophet before the coming of the great and dreadful day of the Lord" (Mal. 4:5). Elijah gradually assumed the role of precursor of the Messiah and the messenger announcing his advent. Some of the contemporaries of Jesus (cf. Matt. 16:13–14) seem to have thought that he might be Elijah (Matt. 11:14; 17:10–13) in a manner that suggests that John the Baptist, as the forerunner and announcer of the Messiah, was Elijah (namely, fulfilled his eschatological function). Later apocryphal writings (e.g., *The Apocalypse of Elijah*) connect the "revelations" concerning the last things they report with Elijah. Elements from the Jewish Elijah traditions and legends were also adopted and developed in different ways by Islam.

BIBLIOGRAPHY
"Elijah." *Encyclopaedia Judaica*, Vol. 6. Jerusalem, 1972.
Postbiblical Jewish sources are conveniently collected in Louis Ginzberg, *Legends of the Jews*, Vol. 6, 3rd reprint. Philadelphia, Pennsylvania, 1967, pp. 133–35 (under "Elijah"). A very good summary can be found in M. J. Stiassny, "Le Prophète Élie dans le Judaïsme," in *Élie le Prophète*, Études Carmélitaines, Vol. 2 (1956): 199–255.
For Islamic traditions, see "Ilyas" and "al-Khadir" in *Encyclopaedia of Islam*.

R. J. ZVI WERBLOWSKY

ELOHIM

Elohim (God; gods; Heavenly Father) is the plural form of the singular noun *'eloah* (compare Arabic *Allah*) in the Hebrew Bible, where it is used 2,570 times as compared to 57 times for its singular. But as one commentator has noted, why this "plural form for 'God' is used has not yet been explained satisfactorily" (Botterweck, Vol. 1, p. 272).

SINGULAR USAGE. Elohim appears in the Hebrew Bible as a common noun identifying Israel's God: "In the beginning God [*'elohim*] created [singular verb] the heaven and the earth" (Gen. 1:1). It was also frequently used interchangeably with Jehovah, the proper name for Israel's God: "And Jacob said, O God [*'elohim*] of my father Abraham, . . . the LORD [Jehovah] which saidst unto me, Return unto thy country" (Gen. 32:9).

Latter-day Saints use the name Elohim in a more restrictive

sense as a proper name-title identifying the Father in Heaven. The First Presidency of the Church has written, "God the Eternal Father, whom we designate by the exalted name-title 'Elohim,' is the literal Parent of our Lord and Savior Jesus Christ, and of the spirits of the human race" (*MFP* 5:26; *see also* Doctrinal Expositions of the First Presidency, "The Father and the Son," Appendix, *Jesus Christ and His Gospel: Selections from the Encyclopedia of Mormonism*).

PLURAL USAGE.   Ancient Israelites used *'elohim* also as a proper plural form to refer to gods of nations other than Israel. At such times, the accompanying verbs and adjectives used were also plural. "Thou shalt have no other gods before me" (Ex. 20:3; here "other" is a plural adjective).

Occasionally, Latter-day Saints use Elohim in its plural sense as a common noun to refer to the plurality of gods known to exist (*TPJS*, pp. 371–74). However, despite their belief that many lords and gods exist in addition to Elohim, Jehovah, and the Holy Ghost (D&C 121:28–32), they follow the example of Jesus and Paul, who worshiped the Father in Heaven (Matt. 19:17; 1 Cor. 8:4–6).

BIBLIOGRAPHY

Botterweck, G. Johannes, and Helmer Ringgren, eds. "Elohim." In *Theological Dictionary of the Old Testament*, rev. ed., Vol. 1, pp. 267–84. Grand Rapids, Mich., 1977.

KEITH H. MESERVY

ENOCH

[In three parts, this entry discusses Enoch, his visions, prophetic leadership, and significance.]

LDS SOURCES

Enoch holds a prominent place in Latter-day Saint scripture and tradition as a PROPHET, seer, and builder of ZION. The Bible states that "Enoch walked with God: and he was not; for God took him" (Gen. 5:21–24). In revelations to Joseph Smith much additional information is given about Enoch, his knowledge of the sanctifying atonement of Christ, the visions he saw of the future of the world, the messages he proclaimed, the wickedness he opposed, the miracles he worked, the priesthood ordinances he performed, and the promises he received from the premortal Lord Jesus Christ (*see* BOOK OF MOSES). Enoch and his city of Zion are powerful symbols among the Latter-day Saints, affirming that supreme righteousness can be attained on earth as it is in heaven.

MOSES 6–7 IN THE PEARL OF GREAT PRICE.   Enoch was the seventh in a chain of patriarchs extending back to ADAM (Moses 6:10–22). Adam's grandson Enos had fled with "the residue of the people of God" from a wicked land called Shulon into "a land of promise," which Enos named after his son, Cainan (6:17). The text implies that Enoch was born in this "land of righteousness" (6:41). Following the example of Adam and Eve, Enoch's father taught him "in all the ways of God" (6:21, 41; cf. 5:12).

When Enoch was said to be "but a lad" (although he was possibly over 65—Moses 6:25, 31), he was called to preach repentance to the wicked: "The Spirit of God descended out of heaven, and abode upon him" (6:26–30). Like other prophets, Enoch felt profoundly inadequate to the task: "All the people hate me; for I am slow of speech" (6:31–34; cf. 1:25–26; Ex. 4:10–12; Jer. 1:4–10; Isa. 6:1–10). The Lord instructed Enoch to anoint his eyes with clay and wash them, whereupon he saw a vision of "the spirits that God had created; and . . . things which were not visible to the natural eye" (Moses 6:35–36). The word "seer" thus applies to him.

Enoch then went forth preaching in the hills and high places, but the people took offense and considered him "a wild man" (6:37–38). One man named Mahijah was bold enough to ask Enoch who he was and whence he had come. Enoch then explained his vision of heaven and his understanding of the fall of Adam; he taught how humans after the Fall had become carnal and devilish by worshiping Satan, but how according to the plan of salvation they may repent and become "sons of God" through the blood of Jesus Christ, the Only Begotten Son of the Man of Holiness (6:42–7:1).

As Enoch continued his ministry, he told of another vision he had received in which he stood upon a mountain and saw the Lord face to face. The Lord showed Enoch the judgments of war and the barrenness that would come upon the wicked and commanded Enoch again to preach repentance and baptism in the name of the Father, Son, and Holy Ghost (7:2–11).

Enoch brought a large body of converts to the gospel of Jesus Christ, but his success did not come without fierce opposition (7:12–13). The enemies of the righteous mobilized against them. The scriptural account describes miracles of extraordinary power. By Enoch's words, "the earth trembled, and the mountains fled, . . . and rivers of water were turned out of their course" (7:13). Stricken by fear, Enoch's enemies and the giants of the land stood far off, and "the Lord came and dwelt with his people, and they dwelt in righteousness" (7:17).

Under Enoch's inspired leadership, the faithful achieved an extraordinary unity of heart and mind. Loving obedience to the laws of Christ was maintained; a state of economic equality was realized, and "there was no poor among them" (7:18). The spiritual unity of Enoch's people took on physical dimensions through the construction of a city "that was called the City of Holiness, even Zion" (7:19). Their lives were based on "the order of him who was without beginning of days or end of years [Jesus Christ]" (6:67), and "after the order of the covenant which God made with Enoch" (JST Gen. 14:27). This unique community matured over a period of 365 years, after which it was received up into heaven. Fulfilling his covenant to preserve the lineage of Enoch upon the earth, the Lord left behind Enoch's son, Methuselah, and grandson, Lamech (Moses 8:2, 5). Lamech's son NOAH was born four years after the city of Enoch was taken into heaven.

In a third vision, Enoch beheld "all the inhabitants of the earth" (7:21). In this panoramic revelation, he witnessed the wickedness and violence in the days of Noah; he saw Satan laughing, with a great chain in his hand, and the Lord weeping over his creations, for mankind had rejected God and had become "without affection" (7:33). Enoch saw the atoning sacrifice of Jesus Christ (7:47–48) and received a promise that "a remnant of his seed should always be found among all nations" (7:52). Finally, he saw the joyous reunion of his city with a latter-day Zion built in anticipation of Jesus' second coming (7:63–67).

According to the biblical account, Enoch lived 365 years (Gen. 5:23); according to the book of Moses, 430 years (8:1; i.e., 365 plus 65, which was Enoch's age when he begat Methuselah and was ordained).

DOCTRINE AND COVENANTS 76, 84, 107. Enoch's rapid rise to spiritual maturity is indicated by the fact that he received the priesthood before his father and grandfather. The priesthood held by Enoch is described in several passages in the Doctrine and Covenants. He was ordained at age twenty-five under the hand of Adam. His priesthood was "after the holiest order of God," holding "the key of the mysteries of the kingdom, even the key of the knowledge of God" (D&C 84:15–19). The scriptures confirm that Enoch "saw the Lord, and he walked with him, and was before his face continually" (D&C 107:48–49). Indicative of Enoch's eternal priesthood station, heirs of the celestial kingdom are described as "priests of the Most High, after the order of Melchizedek, which was after the order of Enoch, which was after the order of the Only Begotten Son" (D&C 76:57).

Enoch received two blessings from Adam: one when he was ordained to the priesthood, the other 240 years later at the council of Adam-ondi-Ahman, which seems to be more of a public blessing (D&C 107:48, 53). All the patriarchs in Enoch's ancestral line were present at this final reunion of Adam's righteous posterity, and Adam prophesied the future of his descendants "unto the latest generation" (107:56). These prophecies were written in the book of Enoch.

ENOCH AND THE LATTER-DAY SAINTS. Latter-day Saints believe that Enoch's righteousness was grounded on the same gospel principles that apply in all dispensations and eternally. For this reason, Latter-day Saints feel a spiritual kinship with Enoch and his people: Enoch's Zion represents every spiritual ideal for which Latter-day Saints strive. Called to build a modern Zion, the prophet and seer Joseph Smith used the name Enoch as one of the code names for himself in early editions of the Doctrine and Covenants. An economic system designed to promote material and spiritual equality within the Church, the Order of Enoch, has been implemented at various times in Church history. Church members look toward the day when the righteous will build the counterpart of Enoch's City of Holiness, the New Jerusalem, in Jackson County, Missouri. Missionaries around the world preach repentance, for the earth is to be cleansed by fire, as it was with the flood that followed Enoch's ministry. Church members anticipate the return of Enoch's city from above to be reunited with the Zion beneath (Moses 7:58), when the earth will rest under the millennial reign of Jesus Christ.

BIBLIOGRAPHY

Maxwell, Neal A. *Of One Heart: The Glory of the City of Enoch.* Salt Lake City, 1975.

Millet, Robert L. "Enoch and His City (Moses 6, 7)." In *Studies in Scripture*, Vol. 2, pp. 131–44. Salt Lake City, 1985.

Nibley, Hugh. *Enoch the Prophet.* In *CWHN* 2.

Ricks, Stephen D. "The Narrative Call Pattern in the Prophetic Commission of Enoch (Moses 6)." *BYU Studies* 26 (Fall 1986):97–105.

RULON D. EAMES

ANCIENT SOURCES

According to Genesis 5:22–25, "Enoch walked with God after the birth of Methuselah three hundred years, and had other sons and daughters. Thus all the days of Enoch were three hundred and sixty-five years. Enoch walked with God; and he was not, for God took him" (RSV).

Enoch, the father of Methuselah and great-grandfather of Noah, was honored by Jews and Christians because of the following reasons: (1) Genesis 5 says that he lived 365 years, a number attractive to Jews who were arguing for cultic alignment with the solar calendar (*1 Enoch*). (2) He "walked with God" and therefore pleased God and was perfect (*Wisdom of Solomon* 4:13). (3) He did not die—"God took him"—and hence would return from heaven (*1 Enoch* 14:21–24) to bring to fruition God's promises for his people. (4) He was "seventh" (seven is a perfect number) after Adam (Gen. 5; *1 Enoch* 93:3; Jude 1:14). Enoch is declared by "an angel" to be "the Son of man" (*1 Enoch* 71:14). He alone has seen everything (*1 Enoch* 19). He will reprimand the fallen angels (*1 Enoch* 14), reveal everything (*1 Enoch* 91), intercede for humans (*1 Enoch* 15:2), and bring eternal peace into the world that is to come, as indicated at creation, since righteousness never forsakes him (*1 Enoch* 71:14–17).

BOOKS OF ENOCH.   It is clear that early Jews and Christians honored the books of Enoch. The most ancient of these are excerpted in what is now called 1 (Ethiopic) Enoch. In the estimation of most experts today, all the documents preserved in 1 Enoch are Jewish and antedate the destruction of Jerusalem in A.D. 70. In probable chronological order these books of Enoch are as follows: *The Book of Astronomy* (*1 Enoch* 72–82) describes the movement of the sun, the reception of its light by the moon (73:7; 78:10), and the divinely ordained solar calendar. *The Book of the Watchers* (*1 Enoch* 1–36) is a composite work consisting of the Parables of Enoch (1–5), the Watchers (6–16), and Enoch's journeys (17–19 and 20–36); the main purpose of this compilation is to explain that evil entered into this world because of the fall of angels (cf. Gen. 6). *The Book of Dream Visions* (*1 Enoch* 83–90) contains a Vision of the Deluge (83–84) and an Animal Apocalypse (85–90), which describes the history of the world from before the Flood until the appearance of "one great horn," who is probably Judas Maccabeus. *The Epistle of Enoch* (*1 Enoch* 91–105; 106–107 is probably from the lost book of Noah, and 108 is a later addition) is addressed against the affluent sinners (94:8–9; 95:3; 96:4–8; 97:8–10), contains an older review of history (the Apocalypse of Weeks, *1 Enoch* 93:1–10, and 91:11–17, which is misplaced), and exhorts the righteous to continue in their hope (104) and to walk in the way of righteousness and avoid the way of wickedness. *The Similitudes of Enoch* (*1 Enoch* 36–71) is one of the most brilliant theological documents of Judaism before Jerusalem's destruction in 70 A.D; it describes the future appearance of the Messiah, the Righteous One, the Elect One, and the Son of Man, and tends to equate them as one figure, who is eventually revealed to be Enoch. Related to the books of Enoch is the *Book of the Giants*, which is preserved in Qumranic fragments that date from the first century B.C.

    2 Enoch is one of the most difficult Jewish writings to date and to understand because it is preserved only in medieval Slavonic manuscripts. It was beloved by the Bogomils, who were shaped by ancient Jewish sources but who also created or reshaped ancient documents. Many scholars trace *2 Enoch* back to a Jew who lived before A.D. 100. After an introduction in which he informs his sons of his impending assumption, Enoch describes his ascent through the seven heavens (3–21). Then the Lord reveals secrets to Enoch (22–38), who admonishes his sons (39–66) and is translated into the highest heaven (67; chap. 68 is extant only in the long recension). The apocalypse concludes with a description of Melchizedek's miraculous birth from Sophanima, who has died. He is then taken into paradise by the archangel Michael and will return at the end of time to be the head of the priests (69–73).

    3 Enoch in its present form is a medieval Jewish work; but it may go back to an earlier document and certainly preserves very ancient traditions. The forty-eight chapters of *3 Enoch* contain cosmological information, especially regarding the heavenly world of God's throne and chariot. The archangel Metatron informs the seer Ishmael that he is Enoch, who has been transformed into an angel.

THE EXIT OF ENOCH. Despite the fact that the author of Jude (verse 9) quoted from *1 Enoch* as prophecy and that the Ethiopian church has canonized the book and celebrated numerous other works that interpret it, the books of Enoch fell out of favor in mainstream Judaism and Christianity. With the compilation of the Mishnah by Rabbi Judah around A.D. 200 and the tendency to denigrate apocalypticism, Enoch fell out of favor. Hillel and his school were the norm for rabbinics. With the closing of the Christian canon, as a result of the emergence of the Holy Roman Empire in the fourth century, the books of Enoch were branded as extracanonical, and the veneration once given to the wise scribe Enoch was transferred to, or reserved for, Jesus Christ.

BIBLIOGRAPHY

Black, M., with J. C. VanderKam. *The Book of Enoch or I Enoch: A New English Edition.* Leiden, 1985.

Charles, R. H. *The Book of Enoch or 1 Enoch.* Oxford, 1912.

Charlesworth, J. H. *The Old Testament Pseudepigrapha*, 2 vols. Garden City, N.Y., 1983, 1985. (Contains introductions, translations, and notes to 1 Enoch, 2 Enoch, and 3 Enoch.)

Knibb, M., with E. Ullendorff. *The Ethiopic Book of Enoch: A New Edition in the Light of the Aramaic Dead Sea Fragments*, 2 vols. Oxford, 1978.

Milik, J. T., with M. Black. *The Books of Enoch: Aramaic Fragments of Qumrân Cave 4.* Oxford, 1976.

VanderKam, J. C. *Enoch and the Growth of an Apocalyptic Tradition.* Washington, D.C., 1984.

JAMES H. CHARLESWORTH

BOOK OF ENOCH

The book of Enoch is one of the ancient writings that Latter-day Saints anticipate receiving sometime in the future (*see* SCRIPTURE: FORTHCOMING SCRIPTURE). This is not to be confused with the pseudepigraphic books of Enoch, which nevertheless have garnered the interest of some Latter-day Saints since at least 1840 (Pratt, p. 61). In Doctrine & Covenants 107:53–57, reference is made to a meeting of Adam's righteous posterity held at Adam-ondi-Ahman three years before Adam's death. The influence of the Holy Spirit was manifested powerfully in prophecy as Adam blessed his posterity. While these verses give a précis of what happened, many more things were "written in the book of Enoch, and are to be testified of in due time" (D&C 107:57). Speaking of this book in December 1877, Elder Orson Pratt said, "When we get that, I think we shall know a great deal about the ante-diluvians of whom at present we know so little" (*JD* 19:218). An extract from the prophecy of Enoch was revealed and published in the BOOK OF MOSES (chaps. 6–7), the latter chapter being published in the *The Evening and The Morning Star* of August 1832 (*HC* 1:130–31).

BIBLIOGRAPHY

Pratt, Parley P. "The Apocryphal Book of Enoch." *MS* 1 (July 1840):61.

LEWIS R. CHURCH

EPHRAIM

Ephraim was the son of Joseph and Asenath and the younger brother of Manasseh (Gen. 41:50–52). According to the Bible, when Joseph brought his two sons to his father, Jacob, for a blessing, Ephraim received the birthright blessing in place of Manasseh (Gen. 48:13–20), one of the departures noted in the Bible from the custom of bestowing on the firstborn son the special privileges that belonged to him by right of primogeniture. The Lord continued to acknowledge Ephraim's blessing centuries later when he said, "I am a father to Israel, and Ephraim is my firstborn" (Jer. 31:9; cf. 1 Chr. 5:1–2). Ephraim's descendants will continue in significant roles. The Book of Mormon records that Joseph of old "obtained a promise of the Lord, that out of the fruit of his loins the Lord God would raise up a righteous branch unto the house of Israel . . . to be remembered in the covenants of the Lord" (2 Ne. 3:5). Further, a "choice seer" would arise from Joseph's descendants who would "do a work for the fruit of [Joseph's] loins, his brethren, which shall be of great worth unto them, even to the bringing of them to the knowledge of the covenants which I [the Lord] have made with thy fathers" (2 Ne. 3:7). Many Latter-day Saints believe that they are of the branch of Ephraim, of whom Joseph prophesied (2 Ne. 3:5–16; D&C 133:30–34) and that the Prophet Joseph Smith is the "choice seer" (3 Ne. 3:6).

Because of their rebellion against the Lord many centuries ago, Ephraim's descendants were scattered among the Gentile nations, along with members of the other tribes, beginning with the fall of the northern kingdom of Israel c. 722 B.C. (2 Kgs. 17:5–6; see also ISRAEL: SCATTERING OF ISRAEL and ISRAEL: LOST TRIBES OF ISRAEL).

In the last days, Ephraim's descendants have the privilege and responsibility to bear the message of the RESTORATION of the gospel to the world and to gather scattered Israel (D&C 113:3–6). "We believe in the literal gathering of Israel and in the restoration of the Ten Tribes; that Zion (the New Jerusalem) will be built upon the American continent" (A of F 10; cf. Deut. 4:27–31; 28; 29; 30; 3 Ne. 20–21). The keys of gathering Israel were committed to the Prophet Joseph Smith by MOSES on April 3, 1836, in the Kirtland Temple (D&C 110:11). Many of Ephraim's descendants are being gathered first, for they have the responsibility of preparing the way for the gathering of the other tribes (D&C 113). "And they [others of the tribes of Israel] shall bring forth their rich treasures unto the children of Ephraim, my servants . . . and there shall they fall down and be crowned with glory, even in Zion, by the hands of the servants of the Lord, even the children of Ephraim, and they shall be filled with songs of everlasting joy" (D&C 133:30–33; see also ISRAEL: GATHERING OF ISRAEL).

One of the tools to be used in the gathering is the Book of Mormon, also known among Latter-day Saints as the stick of Joseph or the stick of Ephraim (Ezek. 37:15–19; 2 Ne. 3:12; D&C 27:5). It is to play an important part in convincing Lamanites, Jews, and Gentiles that Jesus is the Messiah and that God does remember his covenant people (see BOOK OF MORMON: TITLE PAGE).

For Latter-day Saints, identification of a person's lineage in latter-day covenant Israel is made under the hands of inspired patriarchs through patriarchal blessings that declare lineage. Elder John A. Widtsoe, an apostle, declared, "In giving a blessing the patriarch may declare our lineage—that is, that we are of Israel, therefore of the family of Abraham, and of a specific tribe of Jacob. In the great majority of cases, Latter-day Saints are of the tribe of Ephraim, the tribe to which has been committed the leadership of the Latter-day work. Whether this lineage is of blood or adoption it does not matter" (p. 73; cf. Abr. 2:10).

The patriarchal blessings of most Latter-day Saints indicate that they are literal, blood descendants of ABRAHAM and of Israel. Those who are not literal descendants are adopted into the family of Abraham when they receive baptism and confirmation. They are then entitled to all the rights and privileges of heirs (*TPJS*, pp. 149–50). This doctrine of adoption was understood by ancient prophets and apostles (e.g., Rom. 11; 1 Ne. 10:14; Jacob 5; cf. D&C 84:33–34).

BIBLIOGRAPHY

McConkie, Bruce R. *A New Witness for the Articles of Faith*, pp. 541–75. Salt Lake City, 1985.

Smith, Joseph Fielding. *DS* 3:244–64.

Widtsoe, John A. *Evidences and Reconciliations*, pp. 72–77. Salt Lake City, 1943.

BRIAN L. SMITH

EVE

Eve, first woman of earthly creation, companion of ADAM, and mother and matriarch of the human race, is honored by Latter-day Saints as one of the most important, righteous, and heroic of all the human family. Eve's supreme gift to mankind, the opportunity of life on this earth, resulted from her choice to become mortal.

Eve, Adam, Abraham, and others were among the noble and great ones involved with the creation of the earth (Abr. 3:22–24; cf. McConkie, p. 59). God foreordained her and named her Eve, "the Mother of All Living"; in the GARDEN OF EDEN Adam called her Eve, reflecting that calling (Moses 4:26). She was created spiritually and physically in the same manner as was Adam (*MD*, p. 242). God called *their* name Adam, and "in the image of his own body, male and female, created he them" (Moses 6:9).

Eve and Adam faced a dilemma as they sought to obey God's commandments. They could not keep the primary commandment to have children as long as they remained nonmortals in the Garden (2 Ne. 2:22–23). The instruction not to eat of the tree of knowledge of good and evil, however, was uniquely modified with the words "nevertheless, thou mayest choose for thyself" (Moses 3:16–17), and becoming mortal was expressly stated as the consequence.

Satan was present to tempt Adam and Eve, much as he would try to thwart others in their divine missions: "And he sought also to beguile Eve, for he knew not the mind of God, wherefore he sought to destroy the world" (Moses 4:6; cf. Matt. 4:3–11; Moses 1:12–22; JS—H 1:15–16). Eve faced the choice between selfish ease and unselfishly facing tribulation and death (Widtsoe, p. 193). As befit her calling, she realized that there was no other way and deliberately chose mortal life so as to further the purpose of God and bring children into the world.

The Church of Jesus Christ of Latter-day Saints strongly affirms that in partaking of the fruit of the tree of knowledge of good and evil, Eve along with Adam acted in a manner pleasing to God and in accord with his ordained plan. Brigham Young explained: "The Lord knew they would do this and he had designed that they should" (*JD* 10:103). "We should never blame Mother Eve, not the least" (*JD* 13:145). Adam and Eve "accepted a great challenge. . . . They chose wisely in accordance with the heavenly law of love for others" (Widtsoe, p. 194). Afterward, in one of the earliest recorded statements in scripture, Eve recounted the plan of salvation as she expounded on the joy prepared for humankind in eternity: "Were it not for our transgression we never should have had seed, and never should have known good and evil, and the joy of our redemption, and the eternal life which God giveth unto all the obedient" (Moses 5:10–11).

Loving parents in heaven prepared Eve and Adam for their roles in mortality. After the Fall, God gave Adam and Eve the law of SAC-RIFICE so that they could obtain forgiveness of sins committed in mortality (Moses 5:5). He placed enmity (an abhorrence of evil) between Eve's seed and Satan and his followers (Moses 4:21). God granted to Eve the powers of motherhood, disclosing the difficult labor of childbirth. The Hebrew word rendered "sorrow" (Gen. 3:16–17) does not connote "sadness," but "labor," or "sweat," or "pain."

Adam and Eve were husband and wife. While in the Garden, God sealed them in eternal marriage (Gen. 2:22–24). God instructed

Eve, "Thy desire shall be to thy husband, and he shall rule over thee" (Gen. 3:16). President Spencer W. Kimball explained that the Hebrew word translated as "rule" would better be understood as " 'preside' because that's what he does" (*Ensign* [Mar. 1976]:72), and the husband presides only in righteousness. Correlatively, God introduced Eve to Adam in terms that are rendered into English by the phrase "an help meet for him"; these words mean "to be strong, to help, rescue, or save" and "to meet, to correspond to, to be equal," thus indicating that Eve was to be a strong, saving partner in righteousness (Gen. 2:18).

The Lord himself made coats of skins and clothed Adam and Eve (Moses 4:27). Eve bore unto Adam sons and daughters. She worked with Adam. They prayed to the Lord and heard his voice (Moses 5:4–5). They made "all things known" to their children and taught them to read, write, and to keep records of family remembrance (Moses 5:12; 6:5–6).

Eve is a "joint-participant with Adam in all his ministry, [and] will inherit jointly with him all the blessings appertaining to his high state of exaltation" (*MD*, p. 242). President Joseph F. Smith saw her in vision in 1918: among the great and mighty ones in the celestial congregation of the righteous, he beheld "our glorious Mother Eve, with many of her faithful daughters who had lived through the ages and worshipped the true and living God" (D&C 138:39).

The fall of Eve and Adam is profoundly significant: they opened the way of mortality for all humankind, and they subjected themselves to death in order to make continued progression toward eternal life possible. Mother Eve bestowed upon her daughters and sons a heritage of honor, for she acted with wisdom, love, and unselfish sacrifice.

BIBLIOGRAPHY

McConkie, Bruce R. "Eve and the Fall." In *Woman*, pp. 57–68. Salt Lake City, 1979.

Nibley, Hugh. "Patriarchy and Matriarchy." *CWHN* 1:87–114.

Smith, Joseph Fielding. "Was the Fall of Adam Necessary?" *Answers to Gospel Questions*, Vol. 4, pp. 79–83. Salt Lake City, 1963.

Widtsoe, John A. "Was the 'Fall' Inevitable?" *Evidences and Reconciliations*, pp. 192–95. Salt Lake City, 1987.

BEVERLY CAMPBELL

EZEKIEL, PROPHECIES OF

The prophecies of Ezekiel (593–c. 570 B.C.) interest Latter-day Saints because they contain unique insights into aspects of God's saving work with his children, such as the responsibilities of a watchman or leader (chaps. 3, 33), the nature of personal agency and accountability (chap. 18), divine mercy and forgiveness (chap. 18), and God's covenant relationships with Israel and Judah (chaps. 34–39). The principal attention of most Latter-day Saints to the book of Ezekiel focuses on chapters 34–48 because they shed light on God's latter-day work, including Israel's return to its land, the restoration of the land to full productivity, the rebuilding of the temple as a residence for God, and the appearance of important records that they identify with the Bible and Book of Mormon.

In chapter 34, Ezekiel described the scattering of Israelites among the nations of the earth as a leadership failure—Israel's "shepherds" had exploited rather than cared for the "sheep" (*see* ISRAEL: SCATTERING OF ISRAEL). Consequently, the Lord will become the Shepherd to seek out lost sheep and gather "them from the countries . . . to their own land" (34:11, 13). Finally a latter-day David will become their leader (34:24), the sterility of the land will be overcome (36:8–11), the Dead Sea will support fishing (47:1, 7–10), and Israel, as well as the nations, will know that the Lord is with them and "They shall know that I am the Lord" (34:23–28, 30).

Chapters 35–36 reflect the tensions that will develop when returning Israelites find their land inhabited by others who claim it as their own (35:10, 12, 15; 36:2–5). The Lord, however, promised that he would divide the land "by lot" among the returning Israelites for their inheritance, at the same time assuring any non-Israelites living in their midst that they, too, would be granted an "inheritance . . . among the tribes of Israel" (47:22 [13–23]).

The Lord emphasized how real this gathering would be (37:1–14). As in the Resurrection, scattered Israelites, like individual dry bones, might still hope to be formed into one body—with sinews and flesh, breath, and spirit—once more in their own land. The Resurrection thus serves as a metaphor of the gathering as well as a means whereby it will be accomplished, as promised by the Lord: "I will open your graves, and cause you to come up out of your graves, and bring you into the land of Israel" (37:12).

After Israelites gather and prosper, they will live peacefully in "unwalled villages," "at rest," dwelling "safely," "without walls" (38:11). At this point, they will be attacked by Gog, whose goal is to plunder their prosperous land. In the battles that follow, the Lord will refine Israel while bringing judgment against the nations—both those who attack Israel and those who live in distant lands (cf. Isa. 4:4; Zech. 12:2–3; 14:2–3; Zeph. 3:8; Ezek. 39:2–4, 6, 11, 21–24). Jerusalem will be rebuilt as a divine center, God's temple will be erected in their midst (chaps. 40–47), and he will reside there, so that Jerusalem will be "called Holy, for the Lord shall be there" (JST Ezek. 48:35).

In this gathering context, Ezekiel spoke of the unification of the so-called "sticks" of Judah and Ephraim (i.e., Israel), a joining that signals not only the beginning of the gathering of Israel (Ezek. 37:15–22; cf. 3 Ne. 20:46; 21:1–3, 7–13) but also the means by which the ultimate gathering—of peoples back to God—will be accomplished (cf. 1 Ne. 22:12; 2 Ne. 6:11).

Latter-day Saints identify Judah's record as the Bible and Ephraim's record as the Book of Mormon (D&C 27:5). They understand that when the Book of Mormon was translated and published, it became possible to join the two records. And since the stated purpose of the Book of Mormon is to convince "Jew and Gentile that Jesus is the Christ, the Eternal God, manifesting himself unto all nations" (title page of the Book of Mormon), they see this joining of testimonies as being a principal means whereby Israel will be brought back to God (*see* BOOK OF MORMON, BIBLICAL PROPHECIES ABOUT).

BIBLIOGRAPHY

Meservy, Keith H. "Ezekiel's Sticks and the Gathering of Israel." *Ensign* 17 (Feb. 1987):4–13.

Sperry, Sidney B. *The Voice of Israel's Prophets*, pp. 218–37. Salt Lake City, 1952.

KEITH H. MESERVY

EZIAS

Ezias was a prophet of Old Testament times whose prophecies were apparently recorded on the PLATES of brass, a record brought to the Western Hemisphere by the Book of Mormon prophet LEHI. Ezias was mentioned by NEPHI$_2$ (c. 22 B.C.) in a list of prophets who testified of the coming ministry and redemption of Christ (Hel. 8:13–20).

MELVIN J. THORNE

F

FATE

Fate, as usually interpreted, is the antithesis of self-determination and responsibility. Latter-day Saints reject on scriptural grounds all appeals to precausation whether as "fate," "the stars," "blind chance," or even the PREDESTINATION of man by God. Fate in these forms implies a precaused outcome of one's life. Instead, man is seen as having innate autonomies and capacities—the gift of agency—that the divine will guarantees all men: "I the Lord God make you free, therefore ye are free indeed: and the law also maketh you free" (D&C 98:8; cf. 2 Ne. 2:25–27; Alma 12:31; Moses 4:3). People are free to choose obedience or disobedience, good or evil, and most other aspects of their lives, and they are accountable for their choices. The belief that all is fated, stifles, discourages, and hinders the progress and growth possible for the children of God. Fate is considered a negative term in the gospel. Even one's own momentous decisions influence one's so-called fate or destiny only as long as the decisions are maintained. The gospel of Jesus Christ opens to all mankind the opportunity to rise above chance fate in this life and choose eternal life with God.

BIBLIOGRAPHY

The Church of Jesus Christ of Latter-day Saints. *Gospel Principles.* Salt Lake City, 1978, pp. 18–21.

GERALD E. JONES

G

GARDEN OF EDEN

The significance of the Garden of Eden is fundamental among the beliefs of The Church of Jesus Christ of Latter-day Saints and is referred to in each of the STANDARD WORKS. As one of the final steps in the Creation, God planted a garden eastward in Eden and placed in it varieties of animals and plants (Gen. 2:8–9). It was an idyllic environment, without enmity among living things and without death. ADAM and EVE were given dominion over all things and directed to cultivate and beautify the garden (Gen. 2:15). However, in this pristine condition, Adam and Eve would have had no children (2 Ne. 2:22–25; Moses 5:11).

God placed the tree of knowledge of good and evil in the midst of the garden and gave Adam and Eve their agency whether to partake of its fruit (Moses 7:32). Unless they ate, they would remain forever in the garden, limited in their ability to progress and without posterity. However, while partaking would bring opportunity to bear children and to learn good from evil by experience, including sorrow, pain, and death, they would be exiled temporarily from the presence of God. The decision of Eve and Adam to transgress a commandment of God and partake of the fruit of the tree brought mortality and death to them and to their posterity; for it made possible the human family upon the earth (2 Ne. 2:25). The fall of Adam also made the atonement of Jesus Christ necessary.

Neither biblical records nor secular history and archaeological research identify the dimensions or the location of the garden in terms of the present-day surface of the earth. Latter-day revelation specifies that as a mortal, Adam lived at Adam-ondi-Ahman in what is now Daviess County, Missouri (D&C 107:53–56; 116:1; 117:8). Several early LDS leaders, among them Brigham Young and Heber C. Kimball, stated that the Prophet Joseph Smith taught them that the Garden of Eden was located in what is now Jackson County, Missouri (*JD* 10:235; cf. 11:336–37; *DS* 3:74).

BIBLIOGRAPHY
Cowley, Matthias F. *Wilford Woodruff*, p. 481. Salt Lake City, 1964.

GRAHAM W. DOXEY

GATHERING

For Latter-day Saints, the gathering of ISRAEL involves bringing together the heirs of the covenant to designated places where they can enjoy the blessings of temples (*see* ISRAEL; PROMISED LAND, CONCEPT OF A). Latter-day Saints believe in "the literal gathering of Israel" and hold that, along with a vital future role for the Old World Jerusalem, "Zion (the New Jerusalem) will be built upon the American continent" (A of F 10). Church members still look for an eventual temple and permanent headquarters to be built in ZION, a NEW JERUSALEM in Missouri.

Early Latter-day Saints first encountered the concept of a New Jerusalem separate from the Old World Jerusalem in Book of Mormon prophecies that the land of America was to be "the place of the New Jerusalem" (3 Ne. 20:22; Ether 13:3). More information came in September 1830, soon after the Church was organized, when a revelation mentioned building a New Jerusalem near the Missouri River at a location soon to be revealed (D&C 28:9). Another revelation that same month enjoined the Saints to "bring to pass the gathering of [the Lord's] elect," suggesting both the work of missionaries and the physical gathering of the faithful to a designated location. It also stressed that the Saints should be "gathered in unto one place" (D&C 29:7–8).

In Nauvoo, Joseph Smith taught that "in any age of the world" the object of gathering the people of God was the same—"to build unto the Lord an house whereby he could reveal unto his people the ordinances" of his temple (*WJS*, p. 212). The gathering was necessary to build a temple, and a temple was a prerequisite for the establishment of Zion. Consequently, at each of the Saints' headquarters gathering places, a temple site was designated, and in Kirtland, Nauvoo, and Salt Lake City, temples were constructed. Gathering also provided a refuge, a place for mutual protection and spiritual reinforcement and instruction. It strengthened LDS communities and brought economic and political benefits as well.

The Kirtland area in northeastern Ohio was the first gathering place. But when converts from New York arrived there in May 1831, they learned that Ohio would be a gathering place only "for a little season" (D&C 51:16). Some left that same year for Missouri once it was revealed that Zion was to be built in Jackson County, Missouri, a land "appointed and consecrated for the gathering of the saints" (D&C 57:1–3).

For the following seven years the Church had two gathering places—Ohio, the site of the Saints' first temple, and Missouri, the site of the City of Zion. However, in 1838, less than two years after the dedication of the Kirtland Temple, opposition drove the Ohio faithful from that temple-city. The persecution in Missouri that earlier had forced the Saints from Jackson County now forced them from their new headquarters in Far West, Missouri, before temples could be built. Between 1839 and 1846, Latter-day Saints gathered by the thousands at Nauvoo, Illinois, where they again completed a temple before leaving, in the face of violence, for a gathering place in the Rocky Mountains.

Although the major current purposes for gathering the faithful into a single place have been accomplished, belief in the necessity of gathering the elect continues. Members in all parts of the world are now encouraged to remain in their own communities and "build Zion" in their own wards and stakes. Temples have now been built in many countries, and missionaries further the establishment of Zion by gathering "the pure in heart" (D&C 97:21) to the stakes of Zion throughout the world.

BIBLIOGRAPHY

Cook, Lyndon, and Andrew Ehat, eds. *Words of Joseph Smith*, pp. 209–216. Provo, Utah, 1980.

RONALD D. DENNIS

GENTILES

[*In the Bible, the Hebrew and Greek words translated into English as "Gentile" signified other peoples; i.e., "not Israelite" and later "not Jewish." For Latter-day Saints, "Gentile" generally means "not Latter-day Saint," although the meaning also extends to include "not Jewish" and "not Lamanite." These latter senses are rooted partly in scripture, where the distinction between Gentiles and Israelites or Jews is firmly maintained, and partly in the language adopted by early leaders of The Church of Jesus Christ of Latter-day Saints. In the LDS scriptural view, Gentiles play an important role in the restoration of the gospel in the latter days (1 Ne. 13:38–39; 22:6–11; 3 Ne. 21:1–6) and in the latter-day work of gathering Israel (1 Ne. 22:12; 3 Ne. 21:6, 22–29). For discussions related to this topic, see* Gentiles, Fulness of *and* Israel: Gathering of Israel.]

GENTILES, FULNESS OF

The "fulness of the Gentiles" is a term for a doctrine taught in the New Testament, the Book of Mormon, and the Doctrine and Covenants. It refers to a process whereby, after Jesus' ministry among his Jewish countrymen, the gospel was preached to Gentiles in the MERIDIAN OF TIME. Jesus told his Jewish listeners that the kingdom of God would be taken from them "and given to a nation bringing forth the fruits thereof" (Matt. 21:43). He also said that many Gentiles would sit down in the kingdom of heaven with Abraham, Isaac, and Jacob (Matt. 8:5–12). Paul taught that in his day the Gentiles would be given an opportunity to receive the gospel, be adopted into the house of Israel, and receive the blessings of the covenant people (Rom. 9–11), concluding that "blindness in part is happened to Israel, until the fulness of the Gentiles be come in" (Rom. 11:25).

Jesus prophesied the destruction of Jerusalem and the dispersion of the people of Judah among all nations "until the times of the Gentiles be fulfilled" (Luke 21:24; JST Luke 21:24, 32). As latter-day revelation makes clear, "the times" of the Gentiles refers to the time when the fulness of the gospel will come among them (D&C 45:24–28). Latter-day revelation further teaches that in the last days the restored gospel will "go forth unto the ends of the earth, unto the Gentiles first, and then, behold, and lo, they shall turn unto the Jews" (D&C 90:9–11), so "that all who will hear may hear" (D&C 1:11) and "all the families of the earth be blessed" (Abr. 2:11). When the Gentiles reject the gospel, "the times of the Gentiles [will] be fulfilled" (D&C 45:29–30).

In 1823 the angel Moroni told Joseph Smith "that the fulness of the Gentiles was soon to come in" (JS—H 1:41). During the ministry of the resurrected Jesus among Book of Mormon peoples, he foretold the coming forth of the restored gospel among the Gentiles and warned that when they reject the fulness of his gospel and are lifted up in pride and all manner of wickedness, he will take his gospel from among them (3 Ne. 16:7–10). After they reject the gospel, it will be offered to the house of Israel (3 Ne. 16:11–12). Thus, Gentiles who have accepted the gospel will be numbered with Israel and escape the judgments that are to come upon the wicked (3 Ne. 16:13–14). In the Dispensation of the Fulness of Times, the Gentiles will have been first to receive the gospel, and the first (Israel) will be the last (cf. 1 Ne. 13:42; *MD*, pp. 721–22).

BIBLIOGRAPHY

Nyman, Monte S. *An Ensign to All People*, pp. 49–56. Salt Lake City, 1987.

MONTE S. NYMAN

GOLD PLATES

On September 21, 1823, the angel Moroni appeared to Joseph Smith and instructed him about a record engraved on thin goldlike sheets. The record, written by MORONI$_2$, his father MORMON, and other ancient inhabitants of the Americas, was buried in a stone box in a hill not far from the Smith residence. Moroni eventually delivered these plates to Joseph, who translated and published them as the Book of Mormon and returned them to Moroni. While the plates were in Joseph's keeping, others saw them, including eleven witnesses whose testimonies appear in all editions of the book. Various descriptions provided by eyewitnesses suggest that the plates may have been made of a gold alloy, measured about 6 inches by 8 inches (15.2 cm by 20.3 cm), were 6 inches (15.2 cm) thick, and weighed about 50 pounds (22.7 kg).

[See also Book of Mormon Plates and Records; Book of Mormon Translation by Joseph Smith; Book of Mormon Witnesses; Plates, Metal.]

GRANT R. HARDY

GREAT AND ABOMINABLE CHURCH

The phrase "great and abominable church," which appears in an apocalyptic vision received by the Book of Mormon prophet NEPHI₁ in the sixth century B.C. (1 Ne. 13:6), refers to the church of the devil and is understood by Latter-day Saints to be equivalent to the "great whore that sitteth upon many waters" described in Revelation 17:1. This "whore of all the earth" is identified by Nephi's brother JACOB as all those who are against God and who fight against ZION, in all periods of time (2 Ne. 10:16). Nephi did not write a detailed account of everything he saw in the VISION, as this responsibility was reserved for JOHN the apostle, who was to receive the same vision; however, Nephi repeatedly refers to its content and teachings, using various images and phrases (1 Ne. 13:4–9, 26–27, 34; 14:1–4, 9–17).

Like John, Nephi and Jacob describe persecutions that evil people will inflict on God's people, particularly in the last days. The angel who explained the vision to Nephi emphasized that this great and abominable church would take away from the Bible and "the gospel of the Lamb many parts which are plain and most precious; and also many covenants of the Lord" (1 Ne. 13:26), causing men to "stumble" and giving Satan "great power" over them (1 Ne. 13:29; D&C 86:3; Robinson, "Early Christianity," p. 188). Though many Protestants, following the lead of Martin Luther, have linked this evil force described in Revelation 17 with the Roman Catholic church, the particular focus of these LDS and New Testament scriptures seems rather to be on earlier agents of apostasy in the Jewish and Christian traditions (see A. Clarke, *Clarke's Commentary*, Vol. 6, pp. 1036–38, Nashville, Tenn., 1977).

When Nephi speaks typologically rather than historically, he identifies all the enemies of the Saints with the church of the devil (1 Ne. 14:9–10; 2 Ne. 10:16). They are those from all nations and all time periods who desire "to get gain, and . . . power over the flesh, and . . . to become popular in the eyes of the world, . . . who seek the lusts of the flesh and the things of the world, and to do all manner of iniquity" (1 Ne. 22:23). Other scriptural terms related to the great and abominable church include "Babylon" and the "great harlot" (Rev. 17:5; 1 Ne. 22:13; D&C 1:16). Images of pride, greed, and covenant abandonment are associated with these terms, in sharp contrast to the church of God. The scriptures are consistent in warning people to flee from the church of evil and find refuge in the church of God (Jer. 51:6; Rev. 18:4; 1 Ne. 20:20; D&C 133:14; see also P. Minear, "Babylon," in *Interpreter's Dictionary of the Bible*, 1:338, Nashville, Tenn., 1962). The Book of Mormon image of a great and abominable church complements the biblical images of Babylon and the harlot.

The fate of the great and abominable church is described in both ancient and modern scriptures (Jer. 51:37; Rev. 18:21; 1 Ne. 14:15–16; 22:14; D&C 1:16): Though the nations of the earth will gather together against them, "the covenant people of the Lord, who were scattered upon all the face of the earth" are promised redemption even if it requires power sent down from heaven, as if by fire (1 Ne. 14:14; 22:17). When Jesus Christ returns, he will claim his own and reject those who have opposed him (Mal. 4:1–3; 2 Thes. 2:6–10; 1 Ne. 22:23–26). As the Savior institutes his millennial reign, great will be the fall of Babylon, the harlot, and the great and abominable church (Rev. 18; 2 Ne. 28:18), for every knee will bow and every tongue confess, with thankfulness, that Jesus is the Christ (Isa. 45:23; Mosiah 27:31).

BIBLIOGRAPHY

Nibley, Hugh. "The Passing of the Primitive Church: Forty Variations on an Unpopular Theme." In *CWHN* 4:168–208.

———. "Prophecy in the Book of Mormon: The Three Periods." In *CWHN* 7:410–35.

Robinson, Stephen E. "Warring Against the Saints of God." *Ensign* 18 (Jan. 1988):34–39.

———. "Early Christianity and 1 Nephi 13–14." In *The Book of Mormon: First Nephi, The Doctrinal Foundation,* ed. M. Nyman and C. Tate, pp. 177–91. Provo, Utah, 1988.

DENNIS A. WRIGHT

H

HEBREWS, EPISTLE TO THE

Many passages in this New Testament letter have particular significance for Latter-day Saints. In general conferences of the Church, the most frequently cited scriptures from the book of Hebrews are those concerning the Godhead (Heb. 1:1–3; 12:9; 13:8); the obedient suffering of Jesus (Heb. 2:14–18; 4:15–16; 5:8–9); the eternal priesthood of Jesus Christ (Heb. 7–8); how one must be called by God in order to hold the priesthood (Heb. 5:1–4); the nature of true faith, which motivates people to righteous action (Heb. 11); going on "unto perfection" (Heb. 6:1); and enduring to the end (Heb. 12:4–11). These themes are essential pillars of the gospel of Jesus Christ.

The main point at the center of the epistle is that Jesus Christ is the eternal "high priest, who is set on the right hand of the throne of the Majesty in the heavens; a minister of the sanctuary, and of the true tabernacle" of God (Heb. 8:1–2). This theme is developed throughout the epistle, showing how eternal salvation comes through the greatness, sufficiency, and supremacy of Jesus Christ. The letter was written to devoted converts from Judaism to the early Christian church, who already understood the first principles of the gospel and had received its basic ordinances (Heb. 6:1–4). Step by step, it systematically strives to persuade them "to hold fast to their faith" (Buchanan, p. 266), to keep the covenant, and to realize the incomparable hope and irrevocable promises given to them by God through the sacrifice of Jesus Christ. With its explication of the Atonement in terms of priesthood, oaths, covenants, and temple imagery, this entire epistle resonates and harmonizes with LDS concepts and practices.

Chapter 1 begins by boldly declaring that Jesus is the sole mediator between God and all human beings; he is superior to, and supersedes, both prophets and angels. As a separate and distinct personage in the Godhead, he is the God of creation and the perfect revelation of godhood for all time. He is the express image of his Father, both spiritually and physically; he alone purged the sins of mankind and sits on the right hand of God the Father (Heb. 1:1–3). The Father brought the Savior (who was his "firstbegotten" in the premortal existence) "into the world" (Heb. 1:6; cf. D&C 93:21; 1 Ne. 11:18). As the firstborn, Jesus is the heir of all things (Heb. 1:2), and those who are faithful become joint-heirs with him.

Chapter 2 holds a strong warning to heed the word of God given through Jesus Christ (Heb. 2:1–4). The next world is in subjugation to Christ alone (Heb 2:5–10). God made him a little lower than "the gods" (taking the marginal reading of Ps. 8:4–6). Because God is the Father of all, even Christ is subject to him. Christ is second only to the Father, yet he is the spirit brother of mankind (Heb. 2:17). Like his brothers and sisters in mortality, he suffered temptation, but unlike them, he never sinned (Heb. 2:18; 4:15–16). Through this suffering, he learned obedience and gained compassion for all God's children.

The admonition of chapter 3 counsels people to contemplate the greatness of the Lord and to commit themselves to him. The total obedience shown by the Savior to his Father marks the way. The time for commitment is "today." The gospel is not always available to mankind, and so it is necessary to respond covenantally "this day," lest individuals be left like the rebellious Israelites to die in the deserts of their own lives (Heb. 3:7–17; cf. Josh. 24:14–25; Jacob 6:5–7; D&C 64:23–25).

Chapter 4, drawing in part upon Israelite temple symbolism, admonishes the Saints to enter into the rest of the Lord (Heb. 4:1, 11). This comes by believing, softening the heart, laboring, standing openly before God, relying on the compassion of Jesus the High

Priest, and coming boldly to the mercy seat of God to find grace in time of need (Heb. 4:7, 11, 13, 15, 16).

Chapter 5 explains how Jesus obtained his authority to act as Israel's great High Priest. He did not presume to take this honor upon himself. As with Aaron, God chose him and bestowed authority upon him as "a priest for ever after the order of Melchisedec" (Heb. 5:6; Ps. 110:4).

Chapter 6 calls upon all members of the church to "lay hold upon the hope" of perfection and eternal life, which has been extended to them by an immutable oath and covenant (Heb. 6:1, 13–20). Diligence in serving Christ will bring a full assurance of extraordinary promises, as God covenanted with ABRAHAM and promised him eternal increase (Heb. 6:13–14; cf. D&C 132:30). This hope, made possible in Christ, is an anchor for the soul, since God cannot lie. However, those who once have tasted the good word of God and have partaken of the Holy Ghost and then fall away and "crucify to themselves the Son of God afresh," the sin is so grievous that they cannot be renewed again unto repentance (Heb. 6:6–10).

God's promises to Abraham are extended to all who come unto Christ: Jesus was a priest after the order of Melchizedek, who was the priest who blessed Abraham, in whose loins was Levi. The superiority of Christ's Melchizedek Priesthood over the Levitical priesthood and the LAW OF MOSES is developed in chapter 7. Melchizedek was a type of Christ. His priesthood was more enduring than the Levitical priesthood, which was limited to blood lines and was not given with an oath and whose priests did not continue because of death and needed daily renewal (Heb. 7:3, 21, 23, 27). The Melchizedek order of priesthood, however, was directed by Jesus Christ, who, unlike the high priest under the law of Moses on the annual Day of Atonement (Lev. 16:4), did not need to "offer sacrifice for his own sins, for he knew no sins" (JST Heb. 7:26). His priesthood was *aparabatos*, meaning "permanent, unchangeable, and incomparable" (Heb. 7:24). No other priesthood will succeed it. It will be the permanent power of salvation and eternal lives within Christ's church forever more (*TPJS*, pp. 166, 322).

As the great High Priest, Jesus offered himself as the eternal atoning sacrifice and became the mediator of this new and better covenant (Heb. 8:6), putting the law of God into the hearts of his people (Heb. 8:10; 10:16). The old law (of Moses), with its performances and sacrifices, had been fulfilled. Through the new covenant, God promised to remember the sins of the repentant no more (Heb. 10:17), and each Saint was challenged to enter into "a new and living way" through the blood of Christ (Heb. 10:15–20). Those who were willing to do so in patience and faith would be justified and receive the promise (Heb. 10:35–38).

Chapter 11 then concentrates on faith and its outward effects in the lives of Israel's spiritual heroes. Faith is the actual substance or substantiation or assurance (*hypostasis*) and the evidence or evincing (*elenchos*) of things not seen that are true (Heb. 11:1; Alma 32:21). True faith necessarily manifests itself in works of righteousness. Chapter 12 thus exhorts the faithful to endure the chastening and correction of God, who is the Father of their spirits. By inheriting the blessings of eternity as sons of the living God, his Saints are able to come to the new Mount Zion, the heavenly Jerusalem, being made perfect, an assembly of "firstborns" (*prototokōn*), having inherited all with the Firstborn.

Chapter 13 concludes by noting that "marriage is honourable in all," and by counseling all to "let brotherly love continue," to "be without covetousness," and to be loyal to Jesus alone, "bearing his reproach, for here [on earth] have we no continuing city, but we seek one to come" (Heb. 13:1, 4–5, 13–14). Those who enter into this holy order and keep its covenants prepare themselves for eternal life, and fulfillment of the invocation that "the God of peace, that brought again from the dead our Lord Jesus, that great shepherd of the sheep, through the blood of the everlasting covenant, make you perfect in every good work to do his will" (Heb. 13:20–21).

BIBLIOGRAPHY

Anderson, Richard L. *Understanding Paul.* Salt Lake City, 1983.

Buchanan, George W. *To the Hebrews.* Garden City, N.Y., 1972.

Gentry, Leland H. "Let Us Go On unto Perfection: Paul's Message in the Book of Hebrews." In *Sidney B. Sperry Symposium,* pp. 135–44. Provo, Utah, 1983.

RICHARD D. DRAPER

HELAMAN₁

The first Helaman noted in the Book of Mormon (c. 130 B.C.) was one of the three sons of BENJAMIN, king of the NEPHITES and the people of Zarahemla. He is mentioned only once in connection with his father's efforts to educate him and his brothers, MOSIAH₂ and Helorum. Benjamin taught them both the language of their fathers and the prophecies spoken by their fathers, "that thereby they might become men of understanding" (Mosiah 1:2).

MELVIN J. THORNE

HELAMAN₂

Helaman₂ (c. 100–57 B.C.) was a noted BOOK OF MORMON military commander and PROPHET. The eldest son of ALMA₂, he was brother to Shiblon and Corianton (Alma 31:7) and father to HELAMAN₃. He became a high priest (Alma 46:38) and was known for teaching repentance to his people.

While a young man, he remained behind during the mission of his father and brothers to the Zoramites (Alma 31:7), apparently to manage domestic and ecclesiastic affairs in Alma's absence. Later, his father gave him a special blessing, which is often quoted among Latter-day Saints, admonishing him to keep the commandments of God and promising that, if he did so, he would prosper in the land (Alma 36:30; 37:13). Helaman's father also instructed him to continue the record of his people and charged him with the sacred custody of the NEPHITE records, the plates of brass, the twenty-four plates of the JAREDITES, the interpreters, and the LIAHONA, that is, the divine compass that led Lehi's family to the new promised land in the Western Hemisphere (Alma 37:1–47). Before his father's death, Helaman recorded his father's prophecy concerning the final destruction of the Nephite people (45:9–14).

Although Helaman was known simply as one of "the high priests over the church" (Alma 46:6), apparently he was the chief priest because "Helaman and his brethren" (45:22–23; 46:1, 6; 62:45) or "Helaman and the high priests" (46:38) always performed the ecclesiastical functions; no other presiding high priest is named. When

Helaman and his brothers attempted "to establish the church again in all the land" (45:22) after a protracted war with the LAMANITES (43–44), their action triggered civil unrest led by Amalickiah, which in turn embroiled the Nephites in one of their most devastating wars.

During Helaman's youth, a large number of Lamanite converts, called Ammonites (*see* BOOK OF MORMON PEOPLES), moved to the Nephite territory of Jershon (Alma 27). They swore an oath that they would never again take anyone's life (Alma 24:17–18). Later, when other Lamanites attacked their Nephite protectors, the Ammonites offered to break their oath in order to help the Nephite army defend their families and land. It was "Helaman and his brethren" who persuaded them not to break their covenant. They did welcome 2,060 Ammonite young men, who were not under their parents' oath, who volunteered to fight in the Nephite cause and chose Helaman to lead them (53:10–22). Accepting their invitation, he became both military leader and spiritual father, an observation found in Helaman's long letter to his commander MORONI₁ (Alma 56–58). While Helaman led these "stripling soldiers" (53:22) into many battles, none was killed, although all received wounds (56:56; 57:25; 58:39). These young men credited God with their protection and paid solemn tribute to their mothers who had trained them in faith (56:47). During Helaman's military campaign as leader of these young men, he won victory after victory, often capturing enemies without shedding blood. Exhibiting extraordinary ingenuity and character, he always acknowledged God's blessings in his successes (56:19; 57:35; 58:33).

After the war, Helaman returned home and spent his remaining years regulating the affairs of the Church, convincing "many people of their wickedness, which did cause them to repent of their sins and to be baptized unto the Lord their God" (Alma 62:45). An era of peace resulted from his final efforts. He died in 57 B.C.

PAUL R. CHEESMAN

HELAMAN₃

Helaman₃, son of HELAMAN₂, was the record keeper and chief judge in the land of Zarahemla for the fourteen years prior to his death in 39 B.C. Little is known of his personal affairs. He was given charge of

NEPHITE historical records by his uncle, Shiblon, in 53 B.C. (Alma 63:11–13), and the book of Helaman in the BOOK OF MORMON takes its name from him.

After the assassination of the chief judge Pacumeni in 50 B.C., Helaman was elected by the people to this highest national office. A murder plot against him was subsequently uncovered, and the would-be assassin, Kishkumen, was mortally wounded. The murderous band, led by Gadianton, escaped into the wilderness. Of Gadianton, MORMON wrote "In the end of this book [Book of Mormon] ye shall see that this Gadianton did prove the overthrow . . . of the people of Nephi" (Hel. 2:13; *see also* SECRET COMBINATIONS).

During the three-year period 48–46 B.C., a substantial number of people left Zarahemla—because of unspecified dissensions—and "went forth unto the land northward" (Hel. 3:3). So extensive was the migration that only a fraction of its impact could be discussed in Mormon's record (Hel. 3:14). Despite dissension, emigration, and war, "Helaman did fill the judgment-seat with justice and equity; yea, he did observe to keep the statutes, and the judgments, and the commandments of God; and he did do that which was right in the sight of God continually; and he did walk after the ways of his father, insomuch that he did prosper in the land" (3:20). During his tenure, tens of thousands of people were baptized into the church, even to the astonishment of the high priests and teachers (3:24–25). Through the force of his personality, Helaman maintained peace throughout two-thirds of his political career.

When Helaman died, he left the spiritual responsibilities and the sacred records in the hands of his son, NEPHI$_2$ (Hel. 3:37; 5:5–14; 16:25).

BIBLIOGRAPHY
Moss, James R. "Six Nephite Judges." *Ensign* 7 (Sept. 1977): 61–65.

CHRISTINE PURVES BAKER

HOPE OF ISRAEL

The phrase "hope of Israel" appears three times in scripture: Jeremiah 14:8; 17:13; and Acts 28:20. These passages refer to

Israel's Lord and Savior as the "hope of Israel." Latter-day Saints believe that all blessings or promises associated with this hope are dependent upon acceptance of, and obedience to, Israel's God, Jesus Christ.

The phrase "hope of Israel" also calls to mind the expected fulfillment of divine promises made to Abraham, Isaac, Jacob, and their posterity. The promises included an inheritance in the PROMISED LAND, combined with prosperity and peace—conditioned on their obedience—and an endless posterity that will continue "in the world and out of the world" (D&C 132:29–33; cf. Gen. 15:5). Only through Jesus Christ and the latter-day restoration of his Church will the fulfillment come of these promises made to the fathers (cf. 3 Ne. 20:10–46; Isa. 11:10–12; Jer. 14:8, 13; 1 Tim. 1:1; Titus 2:11–13).

In his defense before King Agrippa, Paul referred to this hope (Acts 26:6–8). Apparently Paul, as well as other prophets, believed that the full redemption of Israel can be realized only after the Resurrection, when Jesus Christ comes to rule in his millennial kingdom (cf. Acts 24:15; 28:20; Ps. 16:9–11; 37:1–11; Isa. 26:19; Ezek. 37:1–14).

For Latter-day Saints, the phrase "hope of Israel" is well known through the words of a familiar hymn (*Hymns*, 259) which characterize the youth of ZION as the "Hope of Israel." They are to "rise in might" and wield "the sword of truth and right" above hosts marshaled in "ranks of sin." If the youth willingly heed the call to battle against sin and error, remaining watchful and prayerful, they will see victory.

[*See also* Israel.]

JOHN M. MADSEN

I

INFANT BAPTISM

[*This entry has two parts: the* LDS Perspective *concerning this practice, and the* Early Christian Origins.]

LDS PERSPECTIVE

Children are baptized as members of The Church of Jesus Christ of Latter-day Saints when they reach age eight and receive a bishop's interview to assess their understanding and commitment. This age for baptism was identified by revelation (D&C 68:25, 28). The Church does not baptize infants.

The practice of baptizing infants emerged among Christians in the third century A.D. and was controversial for some time. According to the Book of Mormon, it similarly became an issue and was denounced among the Nephites in the fourth century A.D. When MORMON, a Nephite prophet, inquired of the Lord concerning baptism of little children, he was told that they are incapable of committing sin and that the curse of Adam is removed from them through the atonement of Christ. Hence little children need neither repentance nor baptism (Moro. 8:8–22). They are to be taught "to pray and walk uprightly" so that by the age of accountability their baptism will be meaningful and effective for their lives.

BIBLIOGRAPHY
McConkie, Bruce R. "The Salvation of Little Children." *Ensign* 7 (Apr. 1977):3–7.

ROBERT E. PARSONS

EARLY CHRISTIAN ORIGINS

Although the New Testament never mentions infant baptism either to approve or to condemn the practice, many passages therein associate baptism with faith in Jesus Christ, repentance, and forgiveness of sins, none of which are appropriate requirements for infants (Mark 1:4–5; 16:15–16; Acts 2:37–38; 19:4; 22:16; Rom. 6:1–6; 1 Cor. 6:9–11; Gal. 3:26–27; Col. 2:12–13; Heb. 6:1–6; 10:22; 1 Pet. 3:21).

The assumption that those baptized are committed disciples continues through the second century in Christian literature (*Didache* 7.1; *Shepherd of Hermas*: "Vision" 3.7 and "Mandates" 4.3; *Epistle of Barnabas* 11; Justin, *First Apology* 1.11, 15). The earliest explicit reference to the practice of baptizing infants dates to shortly after A.D. 200 in the writings of Tertullian, a North African theologian who opposed it on the grounds that baptism carries an awesome responsibility and should be delayed until a person is fully committed to living righteously (*De baptismo* 18). A decade later Hippolytus, who would become a schismatic bishop in Rome, wrote a handbook of rules for church organization and practice. Some versions of his *Apostolic Tradition* (21.3–4) refer to baptizing "little ones," who should have an adult relative speak for them if they are unable to do so themselves. However, since Hippolytus prescribed a normative three-year preparatory period of teaching, reading, fasting, and prayer prior to baptism (*Apostolic Tradition* 17), the infant baptism passage has been questioned as a later interpolation.

The first Christian writer to defend infant baptism as an apostolic practice was apparently Origen, the preeminent theologian of the Greek-speaking church, who wrote on the subject around A.D. 240 in Alexandria, Egypt. Origen referred to the frequently asked question of why the church should baptize sinless infants (*Homily on Luke* 14). In response, he argued that baptism takes away the pollution of birth. Origen's *Commentary on Romans* further elaborates this theme, asserting that because of hereditary sin, "the church has a tradition from the apostles to give baptism even to infants" (5.9). However, this passage is suspect because it is found only in a Latin translation by Rufinus, who tended on several occasions to "correct" Origen according to later doctrine. A few years later, Cyprian, bishop of Carthage, addressing the question of the timing of infant baptism, wrote that a child's soul should not be placed in jeopardy of perdition even one day by delaying the grace of baptism (*De peccatorum meritis* 1.34).

Historically, then, infant baptism cannot be demonstrated as beginning before the third century, when it emerged as a topic of extended controversy. Not until Augustine wrote against the Donatists two centuries later was infant baptism established as a universal custom (Jeremias, pp. 94–97; Jewett, p. 16). Thereafter, the practice went largely unquestioned until the Protestant Reformation, when a radical group in Zurich broke with the reformer Zwingli over this and other issues in 1525. These so-called Anabaptists (those who denied the validity of their baptism as infants and were rebaptized as adults) were precursors of the Baptist movement.

BIBLIOGRAPHY

Beasley-Murray, G. R. *Baptism in the New Testament*. London, 1962.

Cullmann, Oscar. *Baptism in the New Testament*, trans. J. Reid. Chicago, 1950.

Jeremias, Joachim. *Infant Baptism in the First Four Centuries*, translated by D. Cairns. Philadelphia, Pa., 1962.

Jewett, Paul K. *Infant Baptism and the Covenant of Grace*. Grand Rapids, Mich., 1978.

KEITH E. NORMAN

INSPIRATION

All humans are entitled to inspiration, which is the influence of the Spirit of the Lord upon their minds and souls (Benson, p. 142). The Lord inspires men and women and calls them "to his holy work in this age and generation, as well as in generations of old" (D&C 20:11). Inspiration from God is essential to understanding spiritual matters. The Prophet Joseph Smith explained, "If a man learns nothing more than to eat, drink and sleep, and does not comprehend any of the designs of God, the beast comprehends the same things . . . it knows as much as we, unless we are able to comprehend by the inspiration of Almighty God" (*TPJS*, p. 343).

"Inspiration" and "revelation" are sometimes used interchangeably by LDS leaders in explaining the source of prophetic authority. The First Presidency of the Church said, "Moses wrote the history of the creation, and we believe that he had the inspiration of the

Almighty resting upon him. The Prophets who wrote after him were likewise endowed with the Spirit of revelation" (*MFP* 2:232). President Wilford Woodruff later noted, "This Church has never been led a day except by revelation. And He will never leave it. It matters not who lives or who dies, or who is called to lead this Church, they have got to lead it by inspiration of Almighty God" (*MFP* 3:225).

Latter-day Saints believe that their efforts can be enhanced and their personal capabilities expanded when they do their best work and at the same time depend upon the Lord "for light and inspiration beyond [their] own natural talents" (Benson, p. 173). Inspiration must be sought and then acted upon when it is received. This quest for inspiration is important in all the affairs of life. President Ezra Taft Benson's explanation of the necessity of inspiration is as valid in temporal, family, and all other matters as it is in Church concerns: "Inspiration is essential to properly lead (D&C 50:13–14). We must have the spirit of inspiration whether we are teaching (D&C 50:13–14) or administering the affairs of the kingdom (D&C 46:2). If we do our part in preparation and work and have the Spirit of the Lord, we can be led, though we do not know beforehand what needs to be done (1 Ne. 4:6; Alma 17:3). Therefore, we should always pray, especially prior to commencing the work of the Lord (2 Ne. 32:9)" (Benson, p. 433).

Inspiration comes from the Lord and may be received in various ways. It comes from prayer (D&C 63:64), from a personal manifestation of the spirit of the Lord (D&C 20:11), from reading and following the commandments, and from studying and pondering the scriptures. Women and men may also be inspired by good causes, such as protection of home, family, and personal freedoms (Alma 43:45). President Spencer W. Kimball explained, "We pray for enlightenment, then go to with all our might and our books and our thoughts and righteousness to get the inspiration" (Kimball, p. 122). Much of the world's fine music, art, and literature can inspire, as can the role models provided by noble people living in the past or present, because "every thing which inviteth and enticeth to do good, and to love God, and to serve him, is inspired of God" (Moro. 7:13).

The fruits of inspiration are many: inspiration from the Lord gives understanding (Job 32:8); those who call upon God may write by the spirit of inspiration (Moses 6:5); and those who believe in the words of the PROPHETS may speak as they are inspired by the gift of the Holy Ghost (D&C 20:26). Individuals may be inspired to take specific action, as the Prophet Joseph Smith was inspired to lay the foundation of The Church of Jesus Christ of Latter-day Saints (D&C 21:2,7). The Constitution of the United States "was given by inspiration of God" (*MFP* 3:12).

When called to specific Church duties, members have the right to receive inspiration from God in fulfilling them. They can also expect their leaders to serve with inspiration. "When you read the Book of Mormon, you know you are reading the truth. Why? Because God directed men to write events as they occurred, and he gave them the wisdom and inspiration to do this" (*DS* 2:202).

BIBLIOGRAPHY

Benson, Ezra Taft. *The Teachings of Ezra Taft Benson.* Salt Lake City, 1988.
Kimball, Spencer W. *The Teachings of Spencer W. Kimball,* ed. Edward L. Kimball. Salt Lake City, 1982.

CAROL L. CLARK

ISAIAH

[It is the emphasis on Isaiah's words in LDS scripture that necessitates a treatment of his writings under four titles:

Authorship
Texts in the Book of Mormon
Interpretations in Modern Scripture
Commentaries on Isaiah

The article Authorship *deals with the issue of the single authorship of the book of Isaiah in light of the existence of an Isaiah text possessed by Book of Mormon peoples as early as 600 B.C. The article* Texts in the Book of Mormon *focuses on the question of what can be learned about the history of the text of Isaiah's book from the portions preserved in the Book of Mormon. Many of Isaiah's words that are preserved and commented on in LDS scripture have to do with the latter days, a matter that is taken up in the article* Interpretations in Modern Scripture. *The resulting LDS interest in Isaiah has led to a number of studies that are treated in the article* Commentaries on Isaiah.]

AUTHORSHIP

Of the writings in the Old Testament, the message of Isaiah enjoys high priority among Latter-day Saints. The attraction derives primarily from the extensive use of Isaiah in the Book of Mormon. Secondarily, chapter 11 of Isaiah was quoted to Joseph Smith in a vision in his earliest days as a prophet (JS—H 1:40) and became the subject of a section in the Doctrine and Covenants (D&C 113). In addition, Jesus Christ has given revelations about, and prophets and apostles of the latter days have frequently quoted from and commented upon Isaiah's words when instructing the Saints.

Traditionally, the book of Isaiah has been ascribed to a prophet living in the kingdom of Judah between 740 and 690 B.C. In Germany during the late 1700s, several scholars challenged this view, claiming that chapters 40–66 were written by one or more other individuals as late as 400 B.C. because of the specific references to events that occurred after Isaiah's death. This outlook now permeates many Bible commentaries and has led to the postulation of a second prophetic writer who is commonly called in scholarly literature "Deutero-Isaiah." Indeed, a wide variety of theories regarding the date and authorship of Isaiah now exist. However, LDS belief in revelation and the seership of prophets, along with the quotations from Isaiah in the Book of Mormon and its admonitions to study his writings, have reinforced Latter-day Saints in the traditional view concerning the date and authorship of Isaiah, in the following ways.

First, while some scholars argue that prophets could not see the future and that, therefore, the later chapters of Isaiah must have been written after Isaiah's time (e.g., Isa. 45 concerning Cyrus), Latter-day Saints recognize that prophets can see and prophesy about the future. In chapters 40–66, Isaiah prophesies of the future, just as the apostle John does in Revelation 4–22, and the prophet Nephi$_1$ in 2 Nephi 25–30.

Second, the Book of Mormon prophet Lehi and his family left Jerusalem about 600 B.C. and took with them scriptural writings on plates of brass that contained much of the Old Testament, including Isaiah (1 Ne. 5:13; 19:22–23). Book of Mormon prophets taught from the brass plate records, not only from chapters 1–39, which are usually assigned by scholars to the prophet Isaiah of the eighth century B.C., but also from the later chapters, the so-called

Deutero-Isaiah. For example, Isaiah chapters 48–54 are all quoted in the Book of Mormon, with some passages mentioned a number of times (1 Ne. 20–21; 2 Ne. 6:16–8:25; Mosiah 12:21–24; 14; 15:29–31; 3 Ne. 16:18–20; 20:32–45; 22). Hence, the existence of a virtually complete Isaiah text in the late seventh century B.C., as witnessed by the Book of Mormon, negates arguments for later multiple authorship, whether those arguments be historical, theological, or literary.

Finally, other significant witnesses exist for the single authorship of Isaiah, including Jesus Christ in particular (cf. Matt. 13:14–15; 15:7–9; Luke 4:17–19; 3 Ne. 16, 20–22). Indeed, after quoting much from Isaiah 52 (3 Ne. 16:18–20; 20:32–45) and repeating Isaiah 54 in its entirety (3 Ne. 22), the resurrected Jesus Christ admonished his Book of Mormon disciples to study Isaiah's words and then said, "A commandment I give unto you that ye search these things diligently; for great are the words of Isaiah. For surely he spake as touching all things concerning my people which are of the house of Israel" (3 Ne. 23:1–2).

Jewish and Christian traditions from the earliest times have supported the single authorship of Isaiah. The Septuagint, the Dead Sea Scrolls, and other ancient texts also give no hint of multiple authorship. Latter-day Saints accept the words of the risen Jesus that Isaiah was a seer and revelator whose prophecies, as recorded throughout his book, will eventually all be fulfilled (3 Ne. 23:1–3). Particularly from Jesus' attribution of Isaiah 52 and 54 to the ancient prophet have Latter-day Saints concluded that the book of Isaiah is the inspired work of the eighth-century prophet Isaiah, son of Amoz.

BIBLIOGRAPHY

Adams, Larry L., and Alvin C. Rencher. "A Computer Analysis of the Isaiah Authorship Problem." *BYU Studies* 15 (Autumn 1974):95–102.

Anderson, Francis I. "Style and Authorship." *The Tyndale Paper* 21 (June 1976):2.

Gileadi, Avraham. *A Holistic Structure of the Book of Isaiah.* Ph.D. diss., Brigham Young University, 1981.

Kissane, E. J. *The Book of Isaiah,* 2 vols. Dublin, Ireland, 1941, 1943.

Ludlow, Victor L. *Isaiah: Prophet, Seer, and Poet.* Salt Lake City, 1981.

Tvedtnes, John A. "Isaiah Variants in the Book of Mormon." In *Isaiah and the Prophets,* ed. M. Nyman. Provo, Utah, 1984.

Young, Edward J. *Introduction to the Old Testament.* Grand Rapids, Mich., 1949.

VICTOR L. LUDLOW

TEXTS IN THE BOOK OF MORMON

The Isaiah texts quoted in the Book of Mormon are unique. They are the only extant Isaiah texts that have no "original" language source with which the translation can be textually compared. These English texts date to the translation and initial publication of the Book of Mormon (1829).

CHART OF ISAIAH CITATIONS IN THE BOOK OF MORMON

Book of Mormon	*Isaiah*
1 Ne. 20–21	48–49
1 Ne. 22:6	49:22
1 Ne. 22:8	49:22–23; 29:14
1 Ne. 22:10–11	52:10
2 Ne. 6:6b–7	49:22–23
2 Ne. 6:15	29:6
2 Ne. 6:16–8:25	49:24–52:2
2 Ne. 9:50–51	55:1–2
2 Ne. 12–24	2–14
2 Ne. 25:17 (mixed)	11:11 and 29:14
2 Ne. 26:15–16, 18	29:3–5
2 Ne. 26:25	55:1
2 Ne. 27:2–5	29:6–10
2 Ne. 26:6–9	29:4, 11
2 Ne. 27:15–19	29:11–12
2 Ne. 27:25–35	29:13–24
2 Ne. 28:9b	29:15
2 Ne. 28:14b	29:13b
2 Ne. 28:16a	29:21
2 Ne. 28:30a	28:10, 13
2 Ne. 28:32	9:12–13
2 Ne. 29:1	29:14, 11:11
2 Ne. 30:9, 12–15	11:4–9
Mosiah 12:21–24	52:7–10
Mosiah 14:1–12	53
Mosiah 15:10	53:10
Mosiah 15:14–18	52:7
Mosiah 15:29–31	52:8–10
3 Ne. 16:18–20	52:8–10
3 Ne. 20:32–35	52:8–10
3 Ne. 20:36–46	52:1–3, 6–7, 11–15
3 Ne. 21:8b	52:15b
3 Ne. 21:29	52:12
3 Ne. 22:1b–17	54
Moro. 10:31	52:17; 54:2

These Isaiah texts were quoted and paraphrased by many Book of Mormon prophets who had a copy of Isaiah on the PLATES of brass. Attempts to determine the authenticity of those Book of Mormon Isaiah texts by comparing them with Hebrew, Greek, and Latin texts of Isaiah hold interest, but such efforts are moot because the ancient texts behind the Book of Mormon Isaiah translation are not available for study. However, much can be learned by comparing the numerous ancient versions and translations of Isaiah with the Book of Mormon Isaiah texts. Such comparisons result in granting the Book of Mormon Isaiah full recensional status.

The Isaiah materials in the Book of Mormon exhibit many similarities to those in the King James translation of the Bible, which would seem to indicate that both share a Hebrew Masoretic origin. However, many other peculiarities in the Book of Mormon texts point to an origin related to texts similar to those from which the Greek Septuagint and the Latin Vulgate were derived. These peculiar readings are significant enough that they preclude relegating the Book of Mormon Isaiah texts to being a mere copy of the King James Version. The Isaiah texts found in English translation in the Book of Mormon possess a distinctive character that indicates a unique textual origin. The important question is not, "Are the Book of Mormon Isaiah texts authentic?" Rather, the issue is, "Do the Book of Mormon Isaiah texts provide clear evidence of variant texts besides those normally acknowledged?" Should they not be considered as valid as, say, the Dead Sea Isaiah texts?

One of the major criticisms of the Book of Mormon Isaiah texts is that they contain parts of what have come to be termed "First Isaiah" and "Deutero-Isaiah" by Bible scholars. It is evident that the Book of Mormon Isaiah texts provide evidence contravening modern theories of multiple authorship of Isaiah's book (see ISAIAH: AUTHORSHIP); for if the origins of the Isaiah material in the Book of Mormon are accepted as stated by its authors, then by 600 B.C. the book of Isaiah was essentially as it is today. The chief value of textual criticism, in this case, is to help identify special themes and language patterns, that is, to provide a better understanding of the message, not a determination of authorship. The most viable and certainly the most productive option for determining the origin of the Book of Mormon Isaiah texts is therefore an internal examination.

The Book of Mormon indicates that in "the first year of the reign of Zedekiah, king of Judah" (1 Ne. 1:4) the prophet NEPHI₁ and his brothers retrieved from Jerusalem a "record" written by their ancestors on plates of brass (1 Ne. 3–4), which they carried with them to the Western Hemisphere. Included in the record were prophecies of Isaiah (1 Ne. 19:22–23; cf. 5:13). All of the Isaiah texts in the Book of Mormon are quotations from that record, except perhaps those cited by the risen Jesus (cf. 1 Ne. 16, 21–22). Whether quoting directly or paraphrasing, Book of Mormon prophets were trying to do two things: "persuade [people] to believe in the Lord their Redeemer" (1 Ne. 19:23) and reveal the plans of God for his people, as noted by the prophet Isaiah (e.g., 2 Ne. 25:7; Hel. 8:18–20; 3 Ne. 23:1–2). These features give a singular quality to the Isaiah texts of the Book of Mormon, because it preserves almost exclusively the texts pertaining to salvation and saving principles and ignores Isaiah's historical material. The concerns of Book of Mormon prophets were doctrinal, and passages were utilized to expound their testimonies. Moreover, the passages that concern salvation from the later chapters of Isaiah are presented to show that Jesus was the promised Messiah (cf. Mosiah 13:33–15:31, which cites Isa. 53; 52:7, 8–10). While nineteenth-century biblical scholarship held that the concept of a "saving Messiah" arose after the Babylonian exile (587–538 B.C.) and therefore the later chapters of Isaiah are to be dated to the end of the sixth century or later, the Book of Mormon texts obviously undermine that theory.

Minor changes in the Book of Mormon Isaiah texts have been made since the publication of the work in 1830. These changes in recent editions have attempted to correct early errors in printing and to bring the Isaiah texts of the present edition into "conformity with prepublication manuscripts and early editions edited by the Prophet Joseph Smith" ("A Brief Explanation About the Book of Mormon," 1981 edition of the Book of Mormon). None of these changes has been substantive.

BIBLIOGRAPHY

Eissfeldt, Otto. *The Old Testament: An Introduction*, pp. 303–346. New York, 1965.

Nibley, Hugh. *Since Cumorah*, pp. 111–34. In *CWHN* 7.

Sperry, Sidney B. *Answers to Book of Mormon Questions*. Salt Lake City, 1967.

Tvedtnes, John A. "The Isaiah Variants in the Book of Mormon." *F.A.R.M.S.* Paper. Provo, Utah, 1981.

LEGRANDE DAVIES

INTERPRETATIONS IN MODERN SCRIPTURE

Isaiah was one of the most important prophetic writers in the Old Testament. The Book of Mormon and the Doctrine and Covenants, modern LDS scriptures, confirm this assessment and contain extensive commentaries on his writings. The Book of Mormon quotes 425 verses and paraphrases many others from the book of Isaiah, taken from the PLATES of brass, a record brought to the Western Hemisphere by the prophet LEHI and his family (c. 600 B.C.). The Book of Mormon quotations from Isaiah are accompanied by the interpretations of Nephite prophets and the resurrected Jesus Christ. The Doctrine and Covenants likewise contains quotations and paraphrases of Isaiah, many illuminating the setting for and relevance of the fulfillment of his prophecies.

THE BOOK OF MORMON. The prophets in the Book of Mormon explicitly praise the writings of Isaiah and provide a thorough commentary thereon. Besides three early NEPHITE prophets, NEPHI₁, JACOB, and ABINADI, who quoted extensively from and explained the meanings of Isaiah, the resurrected Jesus Christ, when he visited the Nephites (A.D. 34), commanded his hearers to "search these things diligently; for great are the words of Isaiah" (3 Ne. 23:1). Most Book of Mormon citations of Isaiah concern two themes: (1) the testimony that Jesus Christ would come into the world to save it (1 Ne. 19:23; cf. 2 Ne. 9:5–12), and (2) pronouncements that even though the Lord would scatter Israel, he would gather and restore them, fulfilling the covenants that he made with Abraham and Israel (2 Ne. 6:5; cf. 9:1–2).

Concerning the house of Israel, Nephi's earliest citation of Isaiah (chaps. 48–49) emphasized two types of scattering: that of large segments of the tribes of Israel, and that of small groups among the nations of the earth (1 Ne. 22:3–5; cf. Isa. 49:1–13). Scattered Israelites of both types would be nursed temporally and spiritually among the GENTILES. The temporal assistance to Israelites would lead to a dependency on Gentiles for survival. The spiritual nursing would come through a "marvelous work" that would gather Israel out of obscurity and darkness and bring them to the knowledge of their Redeemer (1 Ne. 22:6–12).

Nephi presented his longest quotation of Isaiah 2–14 (2 Ne. 12–24) as a third witness of Israel's Redeemer. Nephi, his brother

Jacob, and Isaiah had each seen the Redeemer (as the premortal Jesus Christ) face to face (2 Ne. 11:2–3; cf. 2 Ne. 16:1–7). Nephi's own vision (1 Ne. 11:13–20) clarified Isaiah's words pointing to the coming of Christ (cf. 2 Ne. 17:14; 19:6–7 [i.e., Isa. 7:14; 9:6–7]).

Nephi's commentary on Isaiah 2–14 describes what was to happen to the Jews (2 Ne. 25:9–21; cf. Isa. 3:1–15; 5:1–7), to Nephi's own people (2 Ne. 25:22–26:11; cf. Isa. 29:1–4), and among the Gentiles (2 Ne. 26:12–28:32; cf. Isa. 3:16–4:1). Nephi knew by revelation that when the Book of Mormon would come forth among Gentiles, churches would be lifted up in pride and learning, SECRET COMBINATIONS would prevail, and priestcraft would flourish (2 Ne. 26:14–33; cf. Isa. 3:16–4:1; 2 Ne. 13:16–14:1). By contrast, he foresaw that beautiful branches of Israel would be cleansed and grow in both ZION and JERUSALEM and that they would be protected by the Lord (Isa. 4:2–6; 2 Ne. 14:2–6). Expanding Isaiah's prophecy, Nephi prophesied that Gentiles who repented would be numbered with the house of Israel and become heirs of the promised blessings (2 Ne. 30:1–3). He affirmed that his own people would again receive the gospel of Jesus Christ and become a pure and delightsome people (2 Ne. 30:4–6). He foretold the gathering of Jews to Jerusalem, as they would begin to believe in Christ, and also as a delightsome people (2 Ne. 30:7).

The prophet Abinadi (c. 150 B.C.) said that all the prophets had spoken concerning Christ's coming (Mosiah 13:33–35), and he quoted Isaiah 53 as an example (cf. Mosiah 14). In one of the most lucid explanations of the ministry and atonement of Christ, Abinadi explained that chapter 53 of Isaiah underscored that "God himself shall come down among the children of men, and shall redeem his people," and that, because of his redemption, he would stand "betwixt them and justice; having broken the bands of death, taken upon himself their iniquity and their transgressions, . . . and satisfied the demands of [God's] justice" (Mosiah 15:1–9).

During his first visit among Book of Mormon peoples, the resurrected Jesus cited Isaiah 52 and 54 among his principal texts. He declared that when the words of Isaiah were fulfilled, the covenants made to the house of Israel would be fulfilled (3 Ne. 20:11–12). The gospel will be taught to Jews in their scattered locations and, after they accept it, they will return to Jerusalem and teach their own people (3 Ne. 20:29–35; cf. Isa. 52:8–10). Jesus gave his hearers a sign that the restoration of Jews to Jerusalem would indicate that the restoration had already begun among other Israelites in Zion, the Americas (3 Ne. 21:1–7; Isa. 52:1–3, 6–7, 11–12). In a reference to the "marred" servant of Isaiah 52:13–15, he spoke of the servant's "marvelous work." While the marred servant was clearly the mortal Jesus (Mosiah 15:1–9), Isaiah's words form a dual prophecy because the resurrected Jesus said that it also referred to a latter-day servant. Latter-day Saints believe that this servant was the Prophet Joseph Smith, and the marvelous work referred to was the coming forth of the Book of Mormon and the restoration of the gospel (3 Ne. 21:8–11).

While expanding on Isaiah's words, Jesus foretold the building of the NEW JERUSALEM in the Western Hemisphere by a remnant of the house of Israel, assisted by converted Gentiles (3 Ne. 21:22–25; cf. 20:22). The gospel is to be preached among the various groups of the house of Israel, including the Lamanites and the lost tribes (3 Ne. 21:26).

THE DOCTRINE AND COVENANTS. Also a rich source for interpreting and applying the prophecies of Isaiah, the Doctrine and Covenants has over seventy quotations from or paraphrases of Isaiah. Two themes are prevalent: the gospel will be restored, and Israel will be gathered. For example, the "marvelous work and a wonder" (Isa. 29:14) is the coming forth of the Book of Mormon (D&C 6:1); God's "strange act" (Isa. 28:21) refers to the RESTORATION of the Church and its temple ordinances (D&C 95:4); the "good tidings" published "upon the mountains" (Isa. 52:7) consist of the preaching of the gospel to all nations (D&C 19:29); and the restoration of the tribes of Jacob from among the nations (Isa. 49:6) means the return of scattered Israel to their lands of promise (D&C 133:26–33).

Other themes include the building of the latter-day Zion and her stakes (Isa. 54:1–2; D&C 82:14) as well as the old Jerusalem (Isa. 52:1–2; D&C 113:7–10); verification that Jesus is the only Savior of the world (Isa. 43:11; D&C 76:1); and details of his SECOND COMING (Isa. 63:3–6; 64:1–5; D&C 133:37–52). Finally, many anticipated events are interpreted to be millennial occurrences (Isa. 65; D&C 101:30–31).

CHART OF ISAIAH CITATIONS IN THE DOCTRINE AND COVENANTS

The following lists offer a sampling of Isaiah passages that are either quoted, paraphrased, or interpreted in the Doctrine and Covenants.

Isaiah	Doctrine and Covenants
1:2	76:1
1:18	45:10; 50:10–12
1:19	64:34
2:2–3	133:12–13
4:5	45:63–75; 84:5
4:6	115:6
5:1–7	101:43–62
8:16	88:84; 133:72
11:1–5	113:1–4
11:4	19:15
11:10	113:5–6
11:16	133:26–29
13:1	133:14
13:10	29:14; 34:9; 45:42; 88:87; 133:49
13:13	21:6; 35:24
14:12	76:26
24:5	1:15
24:20	49:23; 88:87
25:6	58:8
28:10	98:12; 128:21
28:15, 18	45:31; 5:19; 97:23
28:21	95:4; 101:95
29:14	4:1; 6:1; 11:1; 12:1; 14:1; 18:44; 76:9
33:22	1:13
34:5	38:22
35:1–2	49:24–25; 117:7
35:3	81:5
35:7–10	133:27–33
35:10	45:71; 66:11
40:3	33:10; 45:9; 65:1; 84:28
40:4	88:66
40:5	49:23; 133:22
40:6	101:23; 124:7–8
40:31	89:20; 124:99
42:7	128:22
43:11	76:1
45:17	35:25; 38:33
45:23	76:110; 88:104
49:1	1:1
49:2	6:2; 11:2; 12:2; 14:2; 15:2; 16:2; 33:1; 86:9
49:6	86:11
49:22	45:9; 115:5

Isaiah	Doctrine and Covenants
50:2–3	35:8; 133:66–69
50:11	133:70
51:9–11	101:18
52:1	82:14; 113:7–8
52:2	113:9–10
52:7	19:29; 31:3; 113:10
52:8	39:13; 84:98–99; 133:10
52:10	113:10; 133:3
52:11	38:42; 133:5
52:12	49:27; 58:56; 101:68, 72; 133:15
52:15	101:94
54:2	82:14; 133:9
54:17	71:9; 109:25
55:6	88:62–63
59:17	27:15–18
60:1–4	64:41–42
60:2	112:23
60:22	133:58
61:1	128:22
62:4	133:23–24
62:10	45:9; 115:5
63:1–2	133:46–48
63:3–6	76:107; 88:106; 133:50–52
63:7–9	133:52–53
64:1–2	34:8; 133:40–42
64:3–5	76:10; 133:43–45
65:17	29:23
65:20	63:51; 101:30
65:21–22	101:101
66:1	38:17
66:24	76:44

BIBLIOGRAPHY

Ludlow, Victor L. *Isaiah: Prophet, Seer, and Poet.* Salt Lake City, 1982.
Nyman, Monte S. *Great Are the Words of Isaiah.* Salt Lake City, 1980.

MONTE S. NYMAN

COMMENTARIES ON ISAIAH

The book of Isaiah is one of the most frequently cited prophetic works within LDS scripture. When the Book of Mormon people left Jerusalem, they carried records on PLATES of brass that contained many Old Testament books predating 600 B.C., including Isaiah. Early in their narratives, NEPHI₁ and his brother JACOB quoted extensively from Isaiah. Later, the resurrected Jesus admonished his hearers in the Americas to search the words of Isaiah diligently, for "great are the words of Isaiah" (3 Ne. 23:1).

Latter-day Saints see many of Isaiah's prophecies fulfilled in contemporary events. When the angel Moroni appeared to the Prophet Joseph Smith on September 21–22, 1823, he quoted Isaiah 11 and said it was "about to be fulfilled" (JS—H 1:40). Isaiah 29 is also seen as a prophecy anticipating the coming forth of the Book of Mormon. Joseph Smith's teachings contain many references to Isaiah, especially about the last days before the second coming of Christ. Additionally, Isaiah is often quoted in the Doctrine and Covenants (e.g., 45:10; 50:10–12; 64:34–35; 133), and in some cases interpretations are added (e.g., D&C 113).

Several books written by LDS authors since 1950 have sought to assist Church members and others to understand Isaiah's words. Some of these commentaries addressed a scholarly audience and others were written for general readers.

In 1952 Sidney B. Sperry commented on Isaiah in the first ten chapters of his book *The Voice of Israel's Prophets* (Salt Lake City). Its chief purpose was to offer commentary from an LDS perspective, including Joseph Smith's views, and to analyze the entire book of Isaiah historically and philologically. Sperry included Book of Mormon interpretations of various passages and a discussion of a unified authorship. He also utilized the Septuagint and his mastery of Hebrew to explain and sometimes retranslate passages. Although the earliest such study, it remains a classic of its kind.

In 1982 Avraham Gileadi published *The Apocalyptic Book of Isaiah* (Provo, Utah), a fresh translation of the Hebrew text with interpretive keys for general readers. The book's contributions include his translation and his Jewish-Mormon perspective. In 1988 he published a second volume, *The Book of Isaiah* (Salt Lake City), which included his earlier translation and an enlarged introduction containing four interpretive keys that he derived from the Book of Mormon. This work notes alternate readings in the Dead Sea scroll Isaiah text and the Septuagint.

Two volumes have served as textbooks. In 1980 Monte S. Nyman published *Great Are the Words of Isaiah* (Salt Lake City) as a commentary and study guide. The book's most distinctive contribution is a collection of references to Isaiah from Joseph Smith's writings, the New Testament, the Book of Mormon, the Doctrine and Covenants, and LDS General Authorities. In 1982 Victor L. Ludlow authored *Isaiah: Prophet, Seer, and Poet* (Salt Lake City). Important features are his chapter-by-chapter commentary, suggested multiple inter-pretations of some passages in the text, helpful maps and historical notes, and LDS doctrinal discussions using various translations of the text.

Other books were written for nonscholarly LDS audiences. L. LaMar Adams's *The Living Message of Isaiah* (Salt Lake City, 1981) aimed at helping his readers appreciate Isaiah's prophecies. Its distinctive contribution is its appendix on the apocryphal *Ascension of Isaiah.*

In 1984 W. Cleon Skousen published *Isaiah Speaks to Modern Times* (Salt Lake City) with the intent of assisting an LDS audience to understand Isaiah as one who saw and spoke of the modern era.

Elder Mark E. Petersen is the only General Authority who has written a book on Isaiah, *Isaiah for Today* (Salt Lake City, 1981). His purpose was to help a nonscholarly LDS audience relate Isaiah's prophecies to present-day events.

ANN N. MADSEN

ISHMAEL

Little is known of the Book of Mormon Ishmael. An Ephraimite from Jerusalem (cf. *JD* 23:184), he cooperated in fulfilling God's command (brought to him from the wilderness by Lehi's sons) that he, his wife, five daughters, two sons, and their households travel into the wilder-ness to join the exodus of the prophet LEHI from Jerusalem about 600 B.C. (1 Ne. 7:2–5).

While en route to Lehi's camp, a division arose in which four of Ishmael's children collaborated with LAMAN and Lemuel, the older sons of Lehi, against the others of their party. A reprimand by NEPHI$_1$, the fourth son of Lehi, provoked them to bind him and threaten to leave him to die. Their hearts were softened toward him only when other members of Ishmael's family pleaded for Nephi's safety (1 Ne. 7:6–21).

After joining with Lehi in the valley of Lemuel, Nephi, his

brothers, and ZORAM married the daughters of Ishmael (1 Ne. 16:7). As the journey continued Ishmael died and "was buried in the place which was called Nahom" (16:34). Ishmael's death and the combination of other adversities caused such grieving among his children that they again complained against Lehi and Nephi, repenting only after the voice of the Lord chastened them (16:34–39).

CHRISTINE PURVES BAKER

ISRAEL

[*Four articles are clustered under this entry:*

Overview
Scattering of Israel
Lost Tribes of Israel
Gathering of Israel

The first article is a general introduction of the distinctive LDS concept of Israel. The second article is a review of the scriptural scattering of Israel. The third article treats the scriptural promises of the restoration of the tribes to their homelands. The fourth article constitutes a review of the scriptural promises concerning the latter-day gathering of Israel. They reflect the breadth of interest in the topic among Latter-day Saints and the doctrinal and historical foundations of this interest. Other articles with a related historical component are Ephraim; Jerusalem; Moses; Promised Land; *and* Zionism. *Articles that incorporate doctrinal aspects of LDS interest are* Allegory of Zenos *and* New Jerusalem.]

OVERVIEW

The name Israel (Hebrew for "God rules" or "God shines") has two particularly distinctive modern applications to Latter-day Saints. First, it refers to members of the Church. Second, it points to modern descendants of ancient Israelite stock, who, because of God's fidelity to ancient covenants made with their forebears, are to become recipients of his blessings in the latter days.

HISTORY OF THE NAME.   The name Israel first appears in the Bible as the divinely bestowed second name of Jacob (Gen. 32:28; 35:10).

"Sons of Israel" or "children of Israel" initially meant Jacob's sons and their families (Gen. 50:25; Ex. 1:1) and, more distantly, all of Jacob's descendants (e.g., Ex. 1:7, 9). After Jacob's posterity settled in the land of Canaan, the name Israel referred to the league of tribes bound together by a covenant with the Lord (Josh. 24). Later, the united monarchy of Saul, David, and Solomon was known as Israel (e.g., 1 Sam. 9:16; 13:13; 2 Sam. 5:3). After the breach following Solomon's death, the name Israel denoted the northern kingdom (1 Kgs. 11:34–39; 12:3, 16), while the name Judah designated the southern realm (1 Kgs. 12:23, 27). After the northern kingdom fell to the Assyrians in 722 B.C., the name Israel became a spiritual designation for the southern kingdom (e.g., Isa. 5:7; Micah 3:1; Zech. 12:1; 1 Macc. 1:11, 62). The term "Jew" was first applied by outsiders to those living in the kingdom of Judah and first appears in 2 Kings 16:6.

In the New Testament, the name Israel refers to the people of God, not usually in a nationalistic sense but designating those who are, or will be, gathered to Jesus Christ by obeying the word of God (e.g., Matt. 10:6–7; Luke 24:21; John 1:31, 49; Acts 2:22, 36). It also refers to Christ's kingdom (Matt. 27:42; Mark 15:32), into which Gentiles will be grafted as if into an olive tree (Rom. 11:17–21). Two passages in Galatians clearly equate Israel with the early Christian church (Gal. 3:27–29; 6:15–16), and the connection is also affirmed by Jesus' statement that his apostles will judge the tribes of Israel (Matt. 19:28; cf. 1 Ne. 12:9; D&C 29:12).

In the Book of Mormon, several phrases appear with distinctive applications. The phrase "children of Israel" regularly refers back to Jacob's descendants in the Mosaic era, echoing the language of the Exodus account (e.g., Ex. 19:1; 1 Ne. 17:23; Jacob 1:7; Mosiah 7:19; cf. 3 Ne. 29:1–2). God's title Holy One of Israel, drawn from Isaiah (e.g., 48:17; 1 Ne. 20:17), appears in discussions of God's covenants, affirming him to be the faithful God who made covenants with ancient Israel (e.g., 1 Ne. 19:14–17). This title also appears in prophecies concerning God's future "reign in dominion, and might, and power, and great glory" (1 Ne. 22:24–25). The Holy One of Israel is identified as Jesus Christ (2 Ne. 25:29). "House of Israel" refers to the lineal posterity of Jacob and is frequently used in prophetic utterances that have to do with their scattering or latter-day gathering. Moreover,

Book of Mormon people saw themselves as a "remnant" or "branch" of the house of Israel whose descendants would receive the blessings promised to Israel in the latter days (1 Ne. 19:24; 3 Ne. 20:16).

For two major reasons, Latter-day Saints today apply the name Israel to themselves. First, Moses appeared to Joseph Smith and Oliver Cowdery in the Kirtland Temple on April 3, 1836, and conferred on them the keys, or authorization, for "the gathering of Israel" (D&C 110:11; cf. *PWJS*, pp. 145–46). This gathering consists not only in restoring people of Israelite ancestry "to the lands of their inheritance" but also in bringing them "out of obscurity and out of darkness; and they shall know that the Lord is . . . the Mighty One of Israel" (1 Ne. 22:12). This action means bringing them into the Church. Second, Latter-day Saints have often learned from their patriarchal blessings that they are literally of the lineage of Israel (D&C 86:8–9), primarily the tribes of EPHRAIM and Manasseh. The Lord has revealed that it is the particular responsibility of Israel to carry the message of the restored gospel to the world, and Ephraim has the responsibility of directing this work (D&C 133:26–34; cf. *TPJS*, p. 163). Those who are not of Israel's lineage become such through adoption at the time of their baptism and reception of the Holy Ghost (*TPJS*, pp. 149–50; Rom. 8:15–17; Gal. 4:5–7; Abr. 2:10).

LINEAL ISRAEL.   Israel's consciousness of lineal distinction was related at least in part to God's formal adoption of it by covenant at the holy mount. "Now therefore, if ye will obey my voice indeed, and keep my covenant, then ye shall be a peculiar treasure unto me above all people . . . and ye shall be unto me a kingdom of priests, and an holy nation" (Ex. 19:5–6). As the chosen people of God, Israel was under a divine obligation to bear the covenant and its promises to others, an obligation established earlier with Abraham and his seed (Abr. 2:9–11).

The Book of Mormon peoples were literally of Israel. Those who journeyed to the Western Hemisphere from Jerusalem with LEHI around 600 B.C. were descended from JOSEPH OF EGYPT through his sons Manasseh and Ephraim (Alma 10:3; cf. 1 Ne. 5:14–16; *JD* 23:184–85). A second group had links to the royal house of Judah through MULEK, son of Zedekiah (Hel. 6:10; Omni 1:14–16). Several prophecies deal with the eventual restoration of God's covenant among the descendants of these peoples (e.g., 1 Ne. 22:3–12; 3 Ne. 20:22–27; 21:1–7). As a natural corollary, several prophecies focus on the scattering and eventual return of many of the Jews to Jerusalem and the blessings that await them there (e.g., 2 Ne. 6:10–14; 3 Ne. 20:29–46; Ether 13:5). As with other covenants, promises are fulfilled only when people—whether Gentiles or Israelites—obey the commandments of God (e.g., 1 Ne. 14:5–6; 22:17–22).

Today, members of the Church—latter-day Israel, largely Joseph's descendants either by blood or adoption—are to seek out the other descendants of Israel and those who would become Israelites through adoption by baptism. The Prophet Joseph Smith observed that "as the Holy Ghost falls upon one of the literal seed of Abraham, it is calm and serene; . . . while the effect of the Holy Ghost upon a Gentile, is to purge out the old blood, and make him actually of the seed of Abraham. That man that has none of the blood of Abraham (naturally) must have a new creation by the Holy Ghost" (*TPJS*, pp. 149–50; cf. Rom. 6:4; 12:2).

SPIRITUAL ISRAEL.   In both ancient and modern times, keeping God's covenants has been the heart of becoming and remaining the people of God (e.g., Ex. 19:5–6; Deut. 4:32–40; D&C 100:15–16). At the physical center of Israel, so to speak, stood the house of God's spiritual blessings, where covenants were made and remade, first the tabernacle in the camp and later the temple in Jerusalem. Almost immediately after giving the Ten Commandments and other terms of the covenant (Ex. 20–23), God gave directions for fashioning the tabernacle (Ex. 24–27), the most sacred structure of Moses' Israel, "that I [God] may dwell among them" (Ex. 25:8). Latter-day Saints have also been commanded by the God of Israel to build temples for worship and for making covenants, so that the lives of men and women will be enriched through eternal family sealings (D&C 110:6–10; cf. *TPJS*, p. 186; *WJS*, p. 212).

In the New Testament era Gentiles were offered a broad opportunity to become full partakers of Israel's blessings. While Jesus limited his personal ministry to Israelites (Matt. 15:24; cf. 3 Ne. 15:23) and told the Twelve to proselytize only among Israel (Matt. 10:5), he visited Gentiles in the Decapolis, near Galilee (Matt. 8:28–34), and sent his seventy disciples into areas where there were many Gentiles

(Luke 10:1–17). He prophesied that many "shall come from the east and west, and shall sit down with Abraham, and Isaac, and Jacob, in the kingdom of heaven" (Matt. 8:11). John the Baptist proclaimed that "God is able of these stones to raise up children unto Abraham" (Matt. 3:9), evidently referring to the adoption of Gentiles into the house of Israel (*TPJS,* p. 319). Peter learned that the righteous in "every nation" who hearken to God are "accepted with him" (Acts 10:35). Even so, Paul reminded readers to "boast not against the branches" of the tree of Israel when they falter because "all Israel shall be saved" (Rom. 11:18, 26).

The Book of Mormon preserves a prophecy of Joseph of Egypt (2 Ne. 3:5–21) wherein the Lord promised Joseph that "a choice seer will I raise up out of the fruit of thy loins . . . [to bring] them to the knowledge of the covenants which I have made with thy fathers" (2 Ne. 3:7). The "work" of this seer includes bringing forth a record written by Joseph's descendants that will be joined to a record from the tribe of Judah, to bring Israelites "to the knowledge of their fathers in the latter days, and also to the knowledge of my covenants, saith the Lord" (2 Ne. 3:11–12). The record from Joseph's lineage is the Book of Mormon and that from Judah's is the Bible (cf. Ezek. 37:15–23; *see also* BOOK OF MORMON, BIBLICAL PROPHECIES ABOUT). The prophecy states that the seer "shall be called after me [Joseph]; and it shall be after the name of his father. And he shall be like unto me" (2 Ne. 3:15). For Latter-day Saints, this seer is Joseph Smith. Moreover, the Book of Mormon is an instrument for bringing about the restoration of gospel covenants and Israel's gathering. About 600 B.C. the Lord spoke to NEPHI₁ concerning both the Gentiles and Nephi's posterity: "I will manifest myself unto thy seed, that they shall write many things which I shall minister unto them, which shall be plain and precious; . . . behold, these things shall be hid up, to come forth unto the Gentiles, by the gift and power of the Lamb. And in them shall be written my gospel, saith the Lamb" (1 Ne. 13:35–36). On the title page of the Book of Mormon, one finds these words written about A.D. 400 stating the purpose of the work: "Which is to show unto the remnant of the House of Israel what great things the Lord hath done for their fathers; and that they may know the covenants of the Lord, that they are not cast off forever" (*see* BOOK OF MORMON: TITLE PAGE).

The gathering of Israel could not proceed until the restoration of the keys or authorization for this effort. On April 3, 1836 (Passover time), both Moses and Elijah appeared to Joseph Smith and Oliver Cowdery in the Kirtland Temple, Elijah restoring the sealing powers for turning the hearts of the children to the promises made to their ancestors (cf. Mal. 4:5–6; D&C 2:1–3; JS—H 1:38–39) and Moses the keys for gathering Israel (D&C 110:11, 13–16; cf. *TPJS*, pp. 337–38; *PWJS*, pp. 186–87).

LAND OF ISRAEL.   While the phrase "land of Israel" is used relatively infrequently in the earlier parts of the Old Testament and is likely the work of a later hand (e.g., 1 Sam. 13:19; 2 Kgs. 5:2), the concept of a definable land given to Israel as an inheritance is at least as old as Abraham (e.g., Gen. 12:7; Abr. 2:6; *see also* PROMISED LAND, CONCEPT OF A). Furthermore, it is clear that continued obedience was required for retaining possession of it. For the Lord promised Abraham—with a caution—that his descendants would receive a "land which I will give unto thy seed after thee for an everlasting possession, when they hearken to my voice" (Abr. 2:6; cf. also Lev. 18:25–28; Jer. 16:12–13).

The concept of multiple lands of inheritance is taught in the Book of Mormon. This plurality of territories is joined to the notion of inheritance, as expressed by Isaiah. In most cases, the Book of Mormon writer cites Isaiah about the gathering of Israel to its lands. For instance, Jacob predicted that the house of Israel "shall be gathered home to the lands of their inheritance, and shall be established in all their lands of promise" (2 Ne. 9:2, after quoting Isa. 49:24–52:2; cf. 2 Ne. 6:11; 10:7–8). Significantly, in each instance a spiritual transformation of Israel is to accompany the gathering to lands: "And they shall be brought out of obscurity and out of darkness; and they shall know that the Lord is their Savior and their Redeemer, the Mighty One of Israel" (1 Ne. 22:12). Again, God "has spoken unto the Jews, by the mouth of his holy prophets, even from the beginning [and will continue] . . . until the time comes that they shall be restored to the true church and fold of God" (2 Ne. 9:2; cf. 30:2; 3 Ne. 16:4; 20:13, 31).

The resurrected Jesus stated that there are at least two lands to which descendants of the house of Israel are to be gathered. To hearers of the lineage of Joseph in the Western Hemisphere, he declared that "the Father hath commanded me that I should give unto you this land, for your inheritance" (3 Ne. 20:14; cf. 20:22; Ether 13:6–10). Concerning the Jews, the risen Jesus said, "I will remember the covenant which I have made with my people . . . [that] I would give unto them again the land of their fathers for their inheritance, which is the land of Jerusalem, which is the promised land unto them forever, saith the Father" (3 Ne. 20:29; cf. Ether 13:5, 11). Latter-day scripture indicates that the ten tribes will come first to the Americas, where they will "be crowned with glory, even in Zion" (D&C 133:26–34) and then will inherit the land of their ancestors (3 Ne. 20–21).

STATE OF ISRAEL.   LDS leaders have viewed the creation of the modern state of Israel in the Middle East as a consequential world event but not as the complete fulfillment of prophecy. After noting the glory of God's work yet to be done among all branches of Israel and after discussing the redemption promised to Judah, Bruce R. McConkie, an apostle, wrote of the present immigration of a few million Jewish people to the Holy Land, "Is this the latter-day gathering of which the scriptures speak? No! It is not. . . . [It] is nonetheless part of divine plan" of a more complete gathering yet to occur (p. 229).

BIBLIOGRAPHY
Hunter, Howard W. "All Are Alike unto God." *Ensign* 9 (June 1979):72–74.
McConkie, Bruce R. *The Millennial Messiah,* pp. 182–329. Salt Lake City, 1982.
Nelson, Russell M. "Thanks for the Covenant." *Devotional and Fireside Speeches [BYU], 1988–89,* pp. 53–61. Provo, Utah, 1989.

S. KENT BROWN

SCATTERING OF ISRAEL

The scattering of Israel, as foretold throughout the Bible and the Book of Mormon, is evidence of fulfilled prophecy. On the one hand, Abraham received promises that his children would possess a dwelling place as long as they remained faithful to God's commands (Abr. 2:6); on the other, prophets from Moses on warned that spiritual rebellion would lead to their removal from the promised land (Lev. 18:26–28; 26:21–33). During the divided monarchy, Israelite prophets pled for a return to neglected covenants to assure the Lord's promised protection (e.g., Hosea 6:1–3; Amos 5:4–9; Isa. 49; 50:1–3;

51–52; Jer. 3:12–19; 18:11). After they rejected prophetic warnings, both Israel and Judah were scattered.

The scattering occurred in three primary phases: (1) the Assyrian captivity of the northern kingdom of ten of the tribes of Israel (c. 722 B.C.); (2) the Babylonian captivity of the kingdom of Judah (c. 587 B.C.); and (3) the destruction of the Judean state and second temple by Rome (A.D. 66–70). While other cases of scattering occurred, these phases accomplished the Lord's purposes of punishing his covenant people by scattering them; but he mercifully made preparation for gathering their descendants in the latter years when they "come to the knowledge of their Redeemer" (2 Ne. 6:8–14).

Numerous references to Israel's scattering appear in scripture. Isaiah, Jeremiah, Ezekiel, NEPHI₁, and others wrote much concerning it (e.g., Isa. 50–53; Jer. 3; 18; Ezek. 6:8–10; 11–12; 36; 2 Ne. 10). Perhaps the most notable of these is the prophecy of ZENOS given "unto the house of Israel" and cited in the Book of Mormon by JACOB, son of LEHI (Jacob 5). In language similar to Isaiah 5:1–7 and echoed in Romans 11:17–24, Zenos compared the history of the house of Israel to an olive tree planted in a vineyard, likening it to a "tame olive tree" that begins to decay. GENTILES, represented in Zenos' allegory as branches from a wild olive tree, were grafted onto the tame tree to preserve its natural fruit. Servants assisted the lord of the vineyard in providing the best conditions for growth—digging, pruning, fertilizing, and finally transplanting, grafting, and pruning. Meanwhile, they planted branches of the mother tree in remote parts of the orchard. In three "visits" to the vineyard (Jacob 5:4, 16, 30), the lord and his servants labored to produce desirable olives that could be stored for "the season, which speedily cometh" (5:76). Finally, the desired fruit appeared, which greatly pleased the lord of the vineyard (5:38–75).

Joseph Fielding Smith, a modern apostle, summed up this allegory thus: "It records the history of Israel down through the ages, the scattering of the tribes to all parts of the earth; . . . or in other words the mixing of the blood of Israel among the Gentiles by which the great blessings and promises of the Lord to Abraham are fulfilled" (*Answers to Gospel Questions*, Salt Lake City, 1963, Vol. 4, pp. 141–42).

Book of Mormon prophets and the resurrected Savior also spoke of the scattering. Reflecting on his people's situation in a new land, Nephi₁ noted that they were part of scattered Israel that would one day be gathered (1 Ne. 22:3–5, 7–12). Jacob observed, "We have been driven out of the land of our inheritance; but we have been led to a better land" (2 Ne. 10:20–22). The resurrected Jesus told hearers in the Americas that though the prophesied scattering was not yet complete, the promised gathering was certainly forthcoming (3 Ne. 20:11–18, 29–46; 21:1–9, 26–29).

The scattering of Israel interests Latter-day Saints because of the promise of the latter-day gathering, which began in 1829 when the Lord restored the priesthood through the Prophet Joseph Smith. Then, on April 3, 1836, Moses appeared and gave the keys, or authorization, of gathering to Joseph Smith and Oliver Cowdery in the Kirtland Temple. Today, commissioned by those with priesthood authority, missionaries gather latter-day Israel back to the covenant, to acceptance of their Redeemer, teaching them in the nations to which their ancestors were long ago dispersed.

BIBLIOGRAPHY

Jackson, Kent P. "Nourished by the Good Word of God." In *Studies in Scripture*, ed. K. Jackson, Vol. 7, pp. 185–95. Salt Lake City, 1987.

Richards, LeGrand. *Israel, Do You Know?* Salt Lake City, 1982.

DOUGLAS A. STEWART

LOST TRIBES OF ISRAEL

Events leading to the separation of the ten tribes of Israel—later known as the ten lost tribes—are linked to the division of the Israelite monarchy (c. 930 B.C.). Following their upstart king, Jeroboam, the northern kingdom of Israel apostatized from covenants they had made with the Lord (1 Kgs. 12:26–30). ISAIAH warned that the Assyrian army would become "the rod of [God's] anger" (Isa. 10:5); the PROPHECY was fulfilled when the Assyrians took most of the people in the northern tribes into captivity (2 Kgs. 17:23). For Latter-day Saints, the lost tribes are Israelites other than either the Jewish people or the LAMANITES of the Book of Mormon (2 Ne. 29:13). LDS sources provide some information about their situation and announce that descendants of these lost tribes will be vitally involved in events of the last days.

The Lord revealed through Old Testament PROPHETS that the ten tribes would return and receive promised blessings. Isaiah prophesied "that the Lord shall set his hand again . . . to recover the remnant of his people" (Isa. 11:11). JEREMIAH declared that "remnants" would come from "the land of the north" (Jer. 3:18; 16:14–15; cf. 23:7–8; 31:8) and that the Lord would "make a new covenant" with them (Jer. 31:31).

Book of Mormon prophets affirmed that the Lord had not forgotten the ten tribes, and that they are keeping records that will yet be revealed (2 Ne. 29:12–14). When the resurrected Jesus Christ appeared in the Americas, he spoke of being commanded of the Father to minister unto the lost tribes, "for they are not lost unto the Father" (3 Ne. 17:4). Jesus also promised that the Lord's redemptive work in the last days would include "the tribes which have been lost" (3 Ne. 21:26).

For the lost tribes to receive their promised blessings in the last days, priesthood keys or authorization had to be restored. On April 3, 1836, MOSES appeared to the Prophet Joseph Smith and Oliver Cowdery in the Kirtland Temple and committed to them the "keys of the gathering of Israel . . . and the leading of the ten tribes from the land of the north" (D&C 110:11). These keys still rest with the President of the Church. In time, the ten tribes are to be "crowned with glory . . . by the hands of the servants of the Lord, even the children of Ephraim" (D&C 133:26–34). Elder James E. Talmage also affirmed that "the tribes shall come; they are not lost unto the Lord; they shall be brought forth as hath been predicted" (*CR* [Oct. 1916]:76). Plainly, according to scripture and teachings of LDS leaders, descendants of the lost tribes—wherever they may be—have continued to receive divine attention and will receive future blessings.

BIBLIOGRAPHY

Smith, Joseph Fielding. *The Way to Perfection*, chap. 20. Salt Lake City, 1968.
Talmage, James E. "The Dispersion of Israel." In *AF*, pp. 314–29.

DAVID L. BOLLIGER

GATHERING OF ISRAEL

Latter-day Saints "believe in the literal gathering of Israel and in the restoration of the Ten Tribes; [and] that Zion (the New Jerusalem) will be built upon the American continent" (A of F 10). In the LDS perspective, gathering Israel in the latter days consists of the following: (1) the spiritual gathering, which includes coming to know that Jesus is the Christ and joining The Church of Jesus Christ of Latter-day Saints; (2) the assembling of Church members to organized stakes; and (3) the gathering of the descendants of Jacob's twelve sons— including the lost ten tribes (D&C 110:11)—to the lands of their inheritance. These gatherings are necessary because of ancient apostasies that resulted in the dispersion of Israel into all nations (Deut. 4:27; 28:64; Jer. 16:13; Hosea 9:17).

Israelite PROPHETS, foreseeing Israel's scattering, also foretold her gathering in the last days (1 Kgs. 22:17; Jer. 31:7–12; 32:37–40; Ezek. 36:24; etc.). According to ISAIAH, Israel will come to know that the Lord is Savior, be gathered again, direct her own affairs, and rebuild JERUSALEM (Isa. 52:1–2; D&C 113:7–10). Anciently, the Lord brought Israel out of Egypt, and Isaiah prophesied a future recovery of Israel from many lands (Isa. 11:11–13; cf. 2 Ne. 6:14; *TPJS*, pp. 14–15; Benson, 1977, pp. 137–38).

The spiritual gathering of Israel through conversion to the restored gospel of Jesus Christ is to be accomplished by the elders of the Church (D&C 133:8) who are set apart and sent out as "fishers" and "hunters" to "hunt them from every mountain, and from every hill, and out of the holes of the rocks" (Jer. 16:16) and to call them to ZION and her stakes (D&C 133:4–9; Isa. 54).

The Book of Mormon and Doctrine and Covenants are seen as tools "to gather out mine elect" from all the earth (Moses 7:62; Benson, *Ensign* 16 [Nov. 1986]:78–80). The risen Jesus declared "that when the words of Isaiah should be fulfilled . . . then is the fulfilling of the covenant" that the Father made to gather Israel (3 Ne. 20:11–13). Further, he proclaimed that the Book of Mormon would come forth as a sign that scattered Israel was about to be gathered (3 Ne. 20–21). NEPHI₁ quoted Isaiah 48 and 49, which he regarded as a herald of Israel's future gathering and glory (1 Ne. 20–22).

The priesthood keys, or authorization, to gather Israel were restored to the Prophet Joseph Smith and Oliver Cowdery on April 3, 1836, in the Kirtland Temple. "Moses appeared before us, and committed unto us the keys of the gathering of Israel from the four parts of the earth, and the leading of the ten tribes from the land of the north" (D&C 110:11). This authority is now held by the President of the Church. That portion of Israel known as the Ten Tribes will yet be led from the north. Their gathering will be accomplished in part as they are converted to the Lord, receive the blessings of the gospel, and return to "the land of their ancient inheritance" (McConkie, 1982, pp. 321, 324–26).

Both the spiritual and the literal characteristics of gathering were emphasized by the Lord in the following interpretation of the parable of the wheat and tares: "I must gather together my people, according to the parable of the wheat and the tares, that the wheat may be secured in the garners to possess eternal life, and be crowned with celestial glory" (D&C 101:65; also 86:7–10). Joseph Smith declared that in all ages the divine purpose of gathering is to build temples so that the Lord's children can receive the highest ordinances and thereby gain eternal life (*TPJS*, pp. 307–308, 314).

The gathering of Israel continues in the post-earthly spirit world where Christ "organized his forces and appointed messengers . . . and commissioned them to go forth and carry the light of the gospel to them that were in darkness, even to all the spirits of men" so that they too may be gathered (D&C 138:30, 34; cf. 1 Pet. 3:18–19). In the implementation of this gathering, ordinances such as baptism and confirmation are performed in latter-day temples by Church members on behalf of the dead (cf. 1 Cor. 15:29).

The physical gathering of Israel is a concomitant of the spiritual gathering. The Lord's servants are to unite and "come forth to Zion, or to her stakes, the places of thine appointment" (D&C 109:39). In 1830 the Lord commanded the Saints to gather into "one place" (D&C 29:8), the first place being in Ohio. In July of 1831 he revealed that "the land of Missouri" was "appointed and consecrated for the gathering of the saints" and Independence, Missouri, was established as the "center place" (D&C 57:1–3). In 1838, after the Church had expanded, the Lord spoke of "gathering together upon the land of Zion, and upon her stakes" (D&C 115:6; cf. Isa. 54:2–3; D&C 101:21–22).

Missionaries were sent out after the Church was organized (1830) to gather both spiritual and bloodline Israel. In the spirit of gathering, many converts immigrated from the eastern states, Canada, Britain, and Western Europe, first to Ohio, then Missouri, Illinois, and eventually the Great Basin. Between 1840 and 1890, more than eighty thousand converts came from continental Europe and fifty-five thousand from Great Britain (P. A. M. Taylor, *Expectations Westward* [Edinburgh, 1965], p. 144).

At the turn of the century and thereafter, converts were no longer asked to immigrate to America and the West. As Spencer W. Kimball reemphasized, converts were to remain in their own lands, where stakes of Zion would be established and temples built, allowing members all the privileges of the gospel in their native countries. He urged the Saints to establish "multiple Zions" and to gather together in their own "culture and nation" (Kimball, pp. 438–40; cf. Palmer, pp. 33–42).

The gathering of Israel includes the LAMANITES. To their ancestors in the Americas, the resurrected Jesus promised: "This people will I establish in this land, unto the fulfilling of the covenant which I made with your father Jacob" (3 Ne. 20:22, 25; 21:1–7).

The gathering of Jews to the state of Israel will continue. Joseph Smith's associates and successors predicted that their initial gathering would be in unbelief (*JD* 4:232; 11:245; 18:64–66; cf. 16:352; 18:225). Elder Bruce R. McConkie calls this a "gathering of the unconverted to Palestine . . . a political gathering" (1982, pp. 229–30). This "preliminary gathering" is to precede Christ's coming to the Jews on the Mount of Olives, when he will personally manifest himself to them (2 Ne. 6:14; cf. Zech. 13:6; D&C 45:48–53; JS—M 1:37).

The land of Canaan was promised to ABRAHAM and his posterity on condition of their righteousness (Abr. 2:6), a promise later reiterated to Isaac and Jacob (Gen. 12:7; 26:3; 35:12). Of the descendants of Jacob, the Jews have maintained their identity throughout the ages. As descendants of Abraham, Isaac, and Jacob, the people of Judah are to return to their ancestral lands (D&C 109:64). At the dedication of the Kirtland Temple, Joseph Smith pled with the Lord that "the children of Judah may begin to return to the lands which thou didst give to Abraham, their father" (D&C 109:62–64). Orson Hyde, an early apostle, was called and ordained by Joseph Smith to dedicate Palestine for the return of the Jews. On October 24, 1841, Hyde climbed the Mount of Olives, prayed to "dedicate and consecrate this land . . . for the gathering together of Judah's scattered remnants," and erected a mound of stones to commemorate the event (*HC* 4:456–59).

The Book of Mormon states that the Jews "shall be gathered in from their long dispersion, from the isles of the sea, and from the four parts of the earth" (2 Ne. 10:8; cf. 25:15–17). Moreover, MORMON, editor and compiler of the Book of Mormon, declared that "ye need not any longer hiss, nor spurn, nor make game of the Jews, nor any of the remnant of the house of Israel; for behold, the Lord remembereth his covenant unto them, and he will do unto them according to that which he hath sworn" (3 Ne. 29:8).

[*See also* Zionism.]

BIBLIOGRAPHY

Benson, Ezra Taft. "A Message to Judah from Joseph." *Ensign* 6 (Dec. 1976):67–72.

———. *This Nation Shall Endure.* Salt Lake City, 1977.

Kimball, Spencer W. *The Teachings of Spencer W. Kimball,* ed. Edward L. Kimball. Salt Lake City, 1982.

McConkie, Bruce R. "Come: Let Israel Build Zion." *Ensign* 7 (May 1977):115–18.

———. *The Millennial Messiah: The Second Coming of the Son of Man.* Salt Lake City, 1982.

Palmer, Spencer J. *The Expanding Church.* Salt Lake City, 1978.

Talmage, James E. "The Gathering of Israel." In *AF,* pp. 328–44.

TERRY L. NIEDERHAUSER

J

JACOB, SON OF LEHI

Jacob was the fifth son of LEHI and Sariah and the elder of the two sons born during the days of his parents' wilderness tribulation. His birth apparently occurred soon after the family left JERUSALEM (c. 599 B.C.). Jacob's life demonstrated him to be a spiritual leader: He was a defender of the faith, keeper of the sacred records, visionary, doctrinal teacher, expressive writer, and plainspoken servant of Christ.

From birth, Jacob was a child of affliction. As Lehi's firstborn in the wilderness, he never knew the family's earlier life in Jerusalem or indeed any period of sustained family harmony. Rather, he grew up knowing only the hardships of a nomadic life, coupled with deepening dissensions between his two oldest brothers and the rest of the family—conflicts that would erupt into open violence before Jacob was forty years old (2 Ne. 5:34). This bitter family strife, which nearly killed his parents from grief on the sea voyage from the Near East to the Western Hemisphere, deeply distressed young Jacob as well. Nephi records that Jacob and his younger brother, Joseph, "grieved because of the afflictions of their mother" while on the ship (1 Ne. 18:19). Lehi told young Jacob in a farewell blessing, "Thou hast suffered afflictions and much sorrow, because of the rudeness of thy brethren" (2 Ne. 2:1). Nevertheless, Lehi assured him that God "shall consecrate thine afflictions for thy gain" (2 Ne. 2:2).

Long affliction seems to have rendered Jacob all the more

spiritually sensitive, and he became one of the most profound doctrinal teachers in the Book of Mormon. Near the time of his death, he summarized the harsh, melancholic conditions of his life in words of haunting beauty and deep humanity: "Our lives passed away like as it were unto us a dream, we being a lonesome and a solemn people, wanderers, cast out from Jerusalem, born in tribulation, in a wilderness, and hated of our brethren, which caused wars and contentions; wherefore, we did mourn out our days" (Jacob 7:26).

Lehi blessed Jacob to spend his days in the service of God and to live safely with NEPHI₁ (2 Ne. 2:3). From his youth to his death, Jacob indeed labored in the Lord's service (2 Ne. 5:26; Jacob 1:18), working closely with Nephi for many years. Nephi consecrated him a priest and a teacher (Jacob 1:18; 2 Ne. 5:26; 6:2), recorded one of his sermons (2 Ne. 6–10), and gave him a stewardship over the records on the small PLATES and other sacred objects (Jacob 1:2). This latter fact had notable consequences for the Book of Mormon, for all subsequent authors of the small plates were direct descendants of Jacob (*see* BOOK OF MORMON: BOOK OF ENOS; BOOK OF JAROM; BOOK OF OMNI).

Jacob was a powerful personal witness of the anticipated Redeemer, which was his most prominent theme. Nephi noted that "Jacob also has seen him [the premortal Christ] as I have seen him" (2 Ne. 11:3), and Lehi indicated that it was in his youth that Jacob had beheld the glory of the Lord (2 Ne. 2:4). So firm was Jacob's faith in Christ that Sherem, an anti-Christ, could not shake him by subtle argument, for, declared Jacob, "I truly had seen angels, and they had ministered unto me. And also, I had heard the voice of the Lord speaking unto me in very word, from time to time" (Jacob 7:5; cf. 7:12). Jacob was the first Nephite prophet to reveal that the Savior would be called Christ, having received that information from an angel (2 Ne. 10:3). He characterized his ministry as persuading his people to come unto Christ (Jacob 1:7). Likewise, he explained that he wrote on the plates so that future generations "may know that we knew of Christ, and we had a hope of his glory many hundred years before his coming" (Jacob 4:1–4). (Note: "Christ" is a Greek-English title, equivalent to Hebrew "Messiah," and it means "anointed," that is, divinely appointed as the Savior of mankind.)

A second prominent theme in the book of Jacob is the scattering and subsequent gathering of ISRAEL. Jacob spoke often and longingly of the Lord's promises to scattered Israel. In his first sermon in the Book of Mormon, Jacob quoted and commented extensively on Isaiah 50 about Israel's restoration (2 Ne. 6–8), assuring his people that "the Lord remembereth all them who have been broken off, wherefore he remembereth us also" (2 Ne. 10:22). Likewise, Jacob quoted the words of a prophet named ZENOS, in which God's love for the scattered branches of Israel was depicted through an allegory of the olive trees. "How merciful is our God unto us," exclaimed Jacob as he explained the allegory to his people, "for he remembereth the house of Israel, both roots and branches" (Jacob 6:4).

Jacob employed a unique style, the distinctive features of which are conspicuous in an exhortation in which he condemned the pride, materialism, and unchastity of his people. He began his sermon by confessing his "anxiety" over his people and over his painful duty to rebuke them for their sins (Jacob 2:3). In like fashion, Jacob prefaced his two other discourses by alluding to his "anxiety" (2 Ne. 6:3; Jacob 4:18). No other Book of Mormon prophet so begins a sermon; indeed, half the references to "anxiety" in the Book of Mormon occur in his writing.

Jacob's stylistic stamp is also evident in other features throughout his writings, which are replete with a vivid, intimate vocabulary either unique to him or disproportionally present. Two-thirds of the uses of "grieve" and "tender" (or their derivatives) are attributable to Jacob. Likewise, he is the only Book of Mormon author to use "delicate," "contempt," "lonesome," "sobbings," "dread," and "daggers." He deploys this last term in a metaphor about spiritual anguish: "daggers placed to pierce their souls and wound their delicate minds" (Jacob 2:9). Similarly, Jacob alone uses "wound" in reference to emotions, and never uses it (as do many others) to describe a physical injury. Jacob uses "pierce" or its variants four of nine instances in the Book of Mormon, and he alone uses it in a spiritual sense.

Such stylistic evidence suggests that Jacob lived close to his feelings and was gifted in expressing them. Moreover, the complex consistency of his style, linking as it does widely separated passages from two different books (2 Nephi and Jacob), bears out the portrait of the man that emerges from the narrative. Story, style, and subject matter all reveal Jacob, Lehi's child of tribulation, to have become a sensitive and effective poet-prophet, preacher, writer, and powerful witness of Jesus Christ.

BIBLIOGRAPHY

Matthews, Robert J. "Jacob: Prophet, Theologian, Historian." In *The Book of Mormon: Jacob through Words of Mormon, To Learn With Joy,* ed. M. Nyman and C. Tate, pp. 33–53. Provo, Utah, 1990.

Tanner, John S. "Literary Reflections on Jacob and His Descendants." In *The Book of Mormon: Jacob through Words of Mormon, To Learn With Joy,* ed. M. Nyman and C. Tate, pp. 251–69.

Warner, C. Terry. "Jacob." *Ensign* 6 (Oct. 1976):24–30.

JOHN S. TANNER

JAMES, EPISTLE OF

The Epistle of James has great prominence for Latter-day Saints. They believe that it was composed by James, the brother of the Lord (Gal. 1:19); that it was written to all the house of Israel, but particularly to those in this dispensation or era; and that it directly inspired Joseph Smith to begin to seek answers from God in prayer. Several teachings from James, including those concerning "pure religion and undefiled," bridling the tongue and controlling anger, the interdependence of faith and works, and blessing the sick, are frequently cited in general conferences and in other Church talks.

That James addresses the lost tribes of Israel (James 1:1) is significant, since Latter-day Saints believe that the ten tribes will be literally gathered in the latter days (A of F 10) and that the tribe of Ephraim, strongly represented in the Church, has the responsibility of carrying the priesthood blessings of Abraham, Isaac, Jacob, and Joseph to the ten tribes (cf. D&C 133:20–35). The President of the Church holds the keys of the gathering of ISRAEL (cf. D&C 110:11). Since the RESTORATION OF THE GOSPEL through Joseph Smith will effect the gathering, it is notable that Joseph Smith, while reading James 1:5, was deeply moved to prayer, which led to his first vision in 1820, an event that opened the way for the latter-day gathering of Israel (*see* ISRAEL: GATHERING OF ISRAEL). James's statement about not doubting also characterized Joseph Smith. Quoting James 1:5–6 and Hebrews 11:6, President David O. McKay stated, "In this scripture lies the secret of Joseph Smith's emergence from obscurity to world-wide renown. His belief in God was absolute, his faith in divine guidance unwavering" (*IE* 65 [Mar. 1962]:149). Many conference talks and presentations apply James 1:5 and Joseph Smith's First Vision to the potentials of prayer in solving life's problems.

Another passage often quoted is James 1:22–24, together with 2:14–18 and 24–26, on the relation between faith and works. Latter-day Saints believe in the "infinite and eternal" power of the Atonement, that it will bring to all mankind an end to the basic effects of the fall of Adam: it automatically forgives the sins of those who are without the law (e.g., children under the age of eight, mentally handicapped, and those who have not known the gospel), provides a universal resurrection (cf. Mosiah 15), and restores mankind back to the presence of God for judgment. However, when individuals willfully rebel against the law that they know, they must repent, be obedient, and prove by their good works that they accept the grace of the Atonement for their personal sins. For such, forgiveness of personal sins through the Atonement is conditional upon their "works," as Latter-day Saints understand the word—faith, repentance, obedience, and serving others in many ways, including performing vicarious temple ordinances.

To underscore the need to serve others, Church leaders often cite James 1:27 on "pure religion and undefiled," relating it to Mosiah 2 in the Book of Mormon, wherein King BENJAMIN exhorts his people to serve selflessly and without concern for the recipient's social or economic status. By so living, people show the pure religion or charity of heart that is manifested in helping others without seeking personal credit. Much of this service is directed toward the young and the elderly, particularly when the traditional support of a nuclear family is not available. Thus, compassionate service becomes a major component of "pure religion and undefiled."

A fourth principle from the Epistle of James appreciated by Latter-day Saints is the admonition to control one's temper and tongue (James 1:26; 3:3–10) and be patient in affliction (James 5). These extensions of the SERMON ON THE MOUNT are principles enunciated frequently by Church leaders.

Of special prominence in Church sermons is James 4:17, regarding sins of omission. Latter-day Saints are encouraged to perform service and good works, and they are reminded that while God judges the intent of the heart, he also requires his people to do every good thing, "for of him unto whom much is given much is required" (D&C 82:3). Further, this scripture is linked with D&C 58:26–29, in which

members are encouraged to "be anxiously engaged in a good cause
. . . of their own free will."

Latter-day Saints hold a deep and firm belief in healing by faith
through blessings by priesthood holders. Concerning this ordinance,
D&C 42:43–44 corresponds to James 5:14–16. Olive oil is consecrated for the purpose of anointing the sick. Then in the healing ordinance one Melchizedek Priesthood bearer anoints, and another
"seals" the anointing through prayer and blesses the sick person as
inspired. Many can attest to miracles of healing through faith and the
power of the priesthood; they consider them private and sacred. Far
from being an "epistle of straw," as Luther called it, the Epistle of
James is profound and very relevant for LDS theology.

BIBLIOGRAPHY
Dahl, Larry E. "A String of Gospel Pearls (James)." In *Studies in Scripture*, ed. R.
  Millett, Vol. 6, pp. 207–24. Salt Lake City, 1987.
McConkie, Bruce R. *Doctrinal New Testament Commentary*, Vol. 3, pp. 243–79. Salt
  Lake City, 1973.
Swensen, Russel B. *The New Testament: The Acts and the Epistles*, pp. 270–76. Salt
  Lake City, 1955.

THOMAS W. MACKAY

JAMES THE APOSTLE

James, the son of Zebedee and one of the original apostles of Jesus
Christ, played an important part in the restoration of the gospel of
Jesus Christ when he and his brother John appeared with Peter as
heavenly messengers to the Prophet Joseph Smith and Oliver Cowdery
and conferred on them the Melchizedek Priesthood and the apostolic
office, including the keys, or authority, of presidency. This ordination
had been promised as forthcoming by John the Baptist on May 15,
1829, when he bestowed the Aaronic Priesthood on Joseph Smith and
Oliver Cowdery (D&C 13; JS—H 1:68–73). In a revelation dated
August 1830, the Lord refers to the restoration of the Melchizedek
Priesthood and notes the participation of James: "Peter, and James,
and John, whom I have sent unto you, by whom I have ordained you
and confirmed you to be apostles, and especial witnesses of my name"
(D&C 27:12). In a later epistle to the Church (D&C 128:20), Joseph

Smith, reviewing the major events of the restoration, mentions this event and locates its happening near the Susquehanna River between Harmony, Pennsylvania, and Colesville, New York.

In the twenty-two references to him in the New Testament, James is never mentioned apart from either his brother John or Peter. In the lists of the apostles, he is always given precedence after Peter except on two occasions when Andrew's name follows Peter's, where it is clear that this order is due to his family connection (Matt. 10:2; Luke 6:14). James's importance is due to his membership in what may be called a presiding council. This idea is borne out by the fact that Peter, James, and John were members of a select circle and were privileged to be present with Jesus on special occasions from which other apostles were excluded, including the raising of the daughter of Jairus (Mark 5:22–23, 35–43), the TRANSFIGURATION on the mountain (Mark 9:2–9), and the agony in Gethsemane (Mark 14:32–42).

According to Joseph Smith and later Presidents of the Church, James, with Peter and John, received special authority and keys from Jesus, Moses, and Elijah on the MOUNT OF TRANSFIGURATION. This was in addition to other keys received during their ordination as apostles that endowed them with power for their ministry as the Presidency of the Twelve and the Church (*HC* 3:386–87; *DS* 2:165).

If their mother, Salome, was a sister of Mary, the mother of Jesus, as is generally believed, then James and John were cousins of Jesus. This may account for Salome's presuming to importune Jesus to grant her sons a special position in his kingdom (Matt. 20:20–23). It may also explain their impetuous zeal against the Samaritan village that denied Jesus' party entry, for which they were called Boanerges ("Sons of Thunder") (Luke 9:52–56; Mark 3:17). James was present with the other apostles in Jerusalem and was a witness of the resurrection of Christ. He was the first of the apostles to be slain, being beheaded by Herod Agrippa I in A.D. 44 (Acts 12:2).

R. DOUGLAS PHILLIPS

JAREDITES

The Jaredites are a people described in the book of Ether (*see* BOOK OF MORMON: BOOK OF ETHER) whose name derives from their first leader, Jared. The Jaredites date to the time of the "great tower" mentioned in the Old Testament (Gen. 11:1–9), which was built in or around Mesopotamia. Led by God, the Jaredites left their homeland for a new land somewhere in the Americas, and there they established a kingdom. They grew to be a numerous population with kings and prophets, and, like the Nephites after them, were eventually annihilated by internecine war evidently sometime between 600 and 300 B.C. Their story was recorded by their last prophet, Ether. Around A.D. 400, the last Nephite survivor, MORONI$_2$, abridged the record of Ether and appended his summary to the account of the Nephites that had been prepared by his father, MORMON. Although the record is brief, it hints at an epic genre rooted in the ancient Near East.

The Jaredite origin in the Old World probably dates to the third millennium B.C., which due to the scarcity of historical material presents obstacles to the use of comparative literature or archaeology. Parallels with the ancient Near East can only be described in general forms, and no artifacts or writings identifiable as Jaredite have ever been found outside the Book of Mormon. But while parallels may be nebulous, certain Jaredite terms and names refer to practices, objects, or places in the ancient Near East. Several types, and a few specifics, may be analyzed in order to better understand the Jaredites and their civilization.

The principal theme of the Jaredite story is familiar in the genre of the ancient Near East. God calls a man to lead his people to a new and a promised land. Once settled in the land, the people alternate between stages of good and evil, relying on their king for guidance. When the king is good, the people tend to be good and follow God; when the king is evil, so too are the people. While parallels to the literature of the ancient Near East, especially the Old Testament, are apparent, the Jaredite narrative is unique in that the first leader, Jared, was not the one who received the call from God, but his brother (*see* BROTHER OF JARED). The roles of the two men differ, as do the roles of king and prophet in the Old Testament. From the earliest days after arriving in America, the Jaredites had a monarchical government apparently patterned after Bronze Age Mesopotamian society.

The story of the Jaredites has an epic flavor. Stories of heroes, kings, and princes who perform great deeds dominate the book of

Ether. The heroes are great warriors who win decisive battles. Accounts dealing with cycles of life and death, good and evil, prosperity and hardship are the types of things that were done and written about in the epics in the book of Ether and the epics of the ancient Near East (*CWHN* 5:283–443).

The book of Ether begins with a genealogy spanning at least thirty generations, from the final prophet and historian Ether back to Jared. The list is reminiscent of genealogies in Old Testament or king lists common to antiquity. The thirty listed by name are:

Name	*Number*
Jared	1
Orihah	2
Kib	3
Shule	4
Omer	5
Emer	6
Coriantum	7
Com	8
Heth	9
Shez	10
Riplakish	11
Morianton	12
Kim	13
Levi	14
Corom	15
Kish	16
Lib	17
Hearthom	18
Heth	19
Aaron	20
Amnigaddah	21
Coriantum	22
Com	23
Shiblon(m)	24
Seth	25
Ahah	26
Ethem	27
Moron	28
Coriantor	29
Ether	30

Except for the lengthy accounts concerning the first and the last of these figures, all information about the people in this lineage is found in Ether, chapters 7–11. This dynasty endured for many centuries, always passing directly from father to son, except possibly in the case of Morianton, who was "a descendant of Riplakish," following him by an interval of "many years" (Ether 10:9).

The Jaredites crossed the sea to the New World in eight "barges" in 344 days, driven by currents and winds. Their route is unknown. Perhaps coincidentally, the North Pacific current takes about the same time to cross from Japan to Mexico (Sorenson, p. 111). The question of ancient long-distance sea travel has been much debated, but extensive indications have been found of pre-Columbian transoceanic voyaging (Sorenson and Raish). The Bering land bridge "is no longer recognized as the only scientifically acceptable theory to explain the means and timing of human entry into the New World" (Dixon, p. 27).

The design of the Jaredite barges is unclear. They were built according to instructions given by God. Ether described them as being "light upon the water" like a fowl (Ether 2:16). They were "tight like unto a dish; and the ends thereof were peaked." To allow light and air inside they had some sort of a "hole in the top, and also in the bottom" (Ether 2:17, 20). Ether also compared the barges with Noah's ark (Ether 6:7). Thus it may be relevant that Utnapishtim, the Sumerian Noah in the *Epic of Gilgamesh,* similarly is said to have built his boat with a ceiling and water plugs, and to have waterproofed the entire inside with bitumen. Utnapishtim's story also recounts the raging winds that slammed water into the mountains and people, vividly paralleling the Jaredites' experience of being driven by a furious wind (Ether 6:6).

Stones were made to shine by the touch of God's finger to light these barges. Shining stones are not unique to the book of Ether. One reference to a shining stone in Noah's ark appears in the Jerusalem Talmud, stating that a stone in the ark shone brighter in the night than in the day so that Noah could distinguish the times of day (*Pesachim* I, 1; discussed in *CWHN* 6:337–38, 349). Shining stones were also said to be present in the Syrian temple of the goddess Aphek (see *CWHN* 5:373) and are mentioned several times in the pseudepigraphic *Pseudo-Philo* (e.g., 25:12).

Little original detail remains about the culture of the Jaredite people. Some of them were obviously literate. While their royalty was strictly hereditary, sons sometimes deposed their fathers or were rivals to their brothers. Kings held their opponents in captivity for long periods, entered into SECRET COMBINATIONS, and waged battles. The record indicates that some of these kings were "anointed" (e.g., Ether 6:27; 9:4; 10:10), sat upon beautiful thrones (Ether 10:6), and had concubines (Ether 10:5–6). Their economy was basically agrarian. They were settled people, the ruling lines living most of their long history in a single land called Moron, somewhere near and north of what would later be called the Nephite "narrow neck of land." In some eras, the Jaredites built many cities and buildings (Ether 9:23; 10:5–12). One of their kings "saw the Son of Righteousness" (Ether 9:22). They once fought off a plague of poisonous snakes that came upon the land as a curse (Ether 10:19). At times they mined several ores (e.g. gold, silver, iron, copper) and made metal weapons and tools (Ether 7:9; 10:23–25; *see* BOOK OF MORMON ECONOMY AND TECHNOLOGY). "Elephants" were useful to them (Ether 9:19). This may refer to the mastodon or mammoth, but it is not possible to date the final disappearance of these animals in the New World. A section in the book of Ether talks of the hunt (10:19–21), a common pattern known in the Near East of the king who is also hunter. In this passage, the Jaredite king Lib designated the land to the south as a hunting preserve. An early Mesopotamian example of a royal hunter is Nimrod, who comes from about the same period as Jared. Other Jaredite parallels are of interest. The dance of Jared's daughter for the life of Omer (Ether 8:10) has been compared with similar incidents from ancient lore (*CWHN* 5:213).

The theophany of the brother of Jared, in which he sees the finger of the Lord, parallels the story of MOSES. The brother of Jared goes up a mountain to pray (Ether 3:1; cf. Ex. 3:1–3); sees the finger of the Lord (Ether 3:6; cf. Ex. 31:18); fears the Lord (also meaning "held in awe"; Ether 3:6; cf. Ex. 3:6); sees the whole spirit body of the Lord (Ether 3:13, 16–18; cf. Ex. 33:11); learns the name of the Lord (Ether 3:14; cf. Ex. 3:14); and, finally, receives a symbol of power and authority (Ether 3:23; cf. Ex. 4:1–5). The unique aspect of the story of the brother of Jared is his extended revelation concerning the nature of God, who appeared to him in a spirit body "like unto flesh and blood" (Ether 3:6).

Some Jaredite prophets were apparently similar to the prophets in biblical Israel. They condemned idolatry and wickedness, and foretold the annihilation of the society and destruction of the people unless they repented. Although some prophets received the protection of the government, most were rejected by the people, and, like Ether, were forced to hide for fear of their lives. Ether's prophecies looked beyond the despair of the final destruction of his people toward the future destiny of the Jaredite land. He foresaw it as the place of "the New Jerusalem, which should come down out of heaven, and the holy sanctuary of the Lord" (Ether 13:3).

The final battle reported by Ether took place at the hill Ramah, the same place where Mormon later buried the sacred Nephite records (Ether 15:11). The war involved two vast armies, and hostilities continued several days until all the soldiers and one of the kings were slain. An exhausted Coriantumr culminated his victory over Shiz by decapitating him. Near Eastern examples of decapitation of enemies are evident in early art and literature, as on the Narmer palette; and decapitation of captured kings is represented in ancient Mesoamerica (Warren, pp. 230–33). Coriantumr was later discovered by the people of Zarahemla (Mulekites), with whom he lived for "nine moons" (Omni 1:21). Ether's plates (historical records), together with the decayed remains from the final Jaredite battle were later found by a group of lost Nephites who were searching for the city of Zarahemla (Mosiah 8:8–11).

Ether writes of the annihilation of his people, but this was not necessarily an extermination of the entire population. One may assume that many of the commoners were not in the two armies and thus survived after these wars. The Jaredite people were crushed and dispersed, but probably not exterminated, since explicit features of Jaredite culture (especially personal names) were later evident in the Nephite culture (*CWHN* 5:237–41; Sorenson, p. 119).

The similarity between the Jaredite and Nephite histories is striking. But the similarity may be chiefly one of literary convention, which Moroni used to compare the two peoples. Other than possessing similar epic tales of people who were led across the sea to build kingdoms that eventually fell, the underlying cultures were probably quite different; for example, the Jaredite laws and government pre-date the LAW OF MOSES, and thus their system of justice was different from that of the Israelites and Nephites.

The message drawn by Moroni from the histories of the Jaredites and the Nephites is, however, the same: God revealed himself to both peoples. He gave both a land of promise, where their prosperity was conditioned on righteousness. Both met their demise because of wickedness and secret combinations, and both endings are included in the Book of Mormon to teach this hard-learned lesson. Concerning this, Moroni states: "The Lord worketh not in secret combinations, neither doth he will that man should shed blood, but in all things hath forbidden it, from the beginning of man" (Ether 8:19).

BIBLIOGRAPHY

Hugh Nibley provides material on the Jaredites in *The World of the Jaredites* and *There Were Jaredites*, in Vol. 5 of *CWHN*; see also *CWHN* 6:329–58; reviewed and updated by D. Honey, "Ecological Nomadism Versus Epic Heroism in Ether," *Review of Books on the Book of Mormon* 2 (1990):143–63.

On the epic genre, see H. Munro Chadwick, *The Growth of Literature,* 3 vols. (Cambridge, England, 1932–1940), especially Vol. 1; Samuel Noah Kramer, "New Light on the Early History of the Ancient Near East," *American Journal of Archaeology* 52 (1948):156–64; David M. Knipe, "Epics," in *Encyclopedia of Religion,* Vol. 5, pp. 127–32; and T. G. Panches, "Heroes and Hero-Gods (Babylonian)," in James Hastings, ed., *Encyclopedia of Religion and Ethics,* Vol. 6, pp. 642–46 (New York, 1951).

Concerning kingship in the ancient Near East, see Henri Frankfort, *Kingship and the Gods* (Chicago, 1948). An English translation of the story of Noah's lighted stones may be found in Louis Ginzberg, ed., *The Legends of the Jews,* Vol. 1, pp. 162–63 (Philadelphia, 1937).

On possible ancient connections between the Old World and the New, see John L. Sorenson and Martin H. Raish, *Pre-Columbian Contact with the Americas Across the Oceans: An Annotated Bibliography* (Provo, Utah, 1990). See also Cyrus H. Gordon, *Before Columbus: Links Between the Old World and Ancient America* (New York, 1971); Carroll L. Riley, et al., eds., *Man Across the Sea: Problems of Pre-Columbian Contacts* (Austin, 1971), especially the chapter by Sorenson. See also E. James Dixon, "The Origins of the First Americans," *Archaeology* 38, no. 2 (1985):22–27; Thor Heyerdahl, *Early Man and the Ocean* (Garden City, N.Y., 1979); and Bruce W. Warren, "Secret Combinations, Warfare, and Captive Sacrifice in Mesoamerica and the Book of Mormon," in S. Ricks and W. Hamblin, eds., *Warfare in the Book of Mormon,* pp. 225–36 (Salt Lake City, 1990).

John L. Sorenson, *An Ancient American Setting for the Book of Mormon* (Salt Lake City, 1985), guides the reader through the archaeology of Mesoamerica and proposes possible Jaredite locations in areas occupied at comparable times, during the early and middle preclassic periods in Mexico, which include the Olmec civilization.

MORGAN W. TANNER

JEREMIAH, PROPHECIES OF

The book of Jeremiah presents a number of elements that are significant for Latter-day Saints. Such features range from important doctrinal teachings connected with Jeremiah's call to his prophecies of the latter days. Notably, his work reveals more about him as a person than most other prophetic works do about their authors. Moreover, his definition of a testimony, hard won through years of persecution, is a classic: The word of God "was in mine heart as a burning fire" (Jer. 20:9).

In calling Jeremiah to be a PROPHET, the Lord explained that he had known Jeremiah and ordained him to be a prophet before his conception and birth (Jer. 1:4–10). Latter-day Saints believe this refers to Jeremiah's premortal life, during which the Lord ordained him and others to special assignments. Though foreordained to be a prophet, Jeremiah was not compelled to serve, and his first reaction was to object (1:6). However, it is apparent that, as Jeremiah exercised his agency, he chose to accept the responsibilities conveyed by his foreordination and subsequent earthly calling to be a prophet.

A choice feature of Jeremiah's work is his portrait of the Lord's tender responses to people. Although through Jeremiah he denounced the behavior of his people and allowed them to be taken captive, the Lord still affirmed his affection for them. This attribute is seen in the divine laments recorded in Jeremiah 4:19–22, 8:18–9:3, and possibly 10:19–22. In Jeremiah 8:19, for example, the Lord says: "Behold the voice of the cry of the daughter of my people because of them that dwell in a far country: Is not the LORD in Zion? is not her king in her?" The Lord then responds to his own question: "For the hurt of the daughter of my people am I hurt" (8:21).

Another doctrinal contribution is Jeremiah's revelation of the Lord's foreknowledge of future events. Latter-day Saints see in Jeremiah's work evidence that the Lord knows the future and can reveal its relevant dimensions to his prophets. When Jeremiah was first called (627/6 B.C.), the ruling power in the Near East was Assyria. But he accurately predicted that Babylon would become dominant (Jer. 27:2–11), and warned his people that the Babylonian kings would conquer Jerusalem (32:28), take many captive (32:31–32), and then fall to another power (25:12) that would subsequently allow the Jews to return and rebuild Jerusalem (29:10).

Under inspiration, Jeremiah also saw the latter days, referring to them as "the days [to] come" (Jer. 30:3). In those days, he declared, the Lord would establish a "new" and "everlasting covenant" (31:31; 32:40). A significant feature of this new covenant would be the divinely authorized gathering of ISRAEL to former inheritances (23:5–8).

An element of interest in Jeremiah's prophetic work is the manner in which he taught object lessons. For instance, Jeremiah called attention to the impending fall of Jerusalem and captivity of her inhabitants by wearing the yoke of an ox (Jer. 27:2). He showed his faith in the eventual restoration of Israel to her homeland by buying a piece of land (32:1–15). He conveyed some of his messages with parables. In Jeremiah 18:1–10, the Lord inspired him to ask his listeners to observe a potter who had to rework some "marred" clay. He noted that the potter represented the Lord and the marred clay the inhabitants of Jerusalem. So poignantly disturbing was this parable that some of Jeremiah's listeners began to plot against his life (18:18–23). In Jeremiah 24:1–10 he declared that the Lord showed him two baskets of figs, one good and one inedible. The good figs represented those taken captive whom the Lord would "acknowledge." The inedible figs, which the Lord would discard, or have "removed," represented king Zedekiah, his princes, and those Judeans who had fled to Egypt.

Jeremiah and his writings were well respected by his contemporary, LEHI, and later Book of Mormon prophets who possessed a copy of some of Jeremiah's prophecies on the PLATES of brass (cf. 1 Ne. 5:13; 7:14). A later Book of Mormon prophet, NEPHI$_2$, indicates that Jeremiah had prophesied of the Messiah's first coming (Hel. 8:13–20). However, current texts of Jeremiah do not have clear references to this event, underscoring the observation that in the transmission of the biblical text parts may have been lost, or that Lehi may have possessed a fuller version. This is not surprising since ancient evidence both from Dead Sea fragments and from the Septuagint version of Jeremiah suggests that the text of his book has not been well preserved.

The book of Jeremiah presents rich insights into the attributes of God, the nature of prophets and prophecy, and varied teaching techniques. The available text of Jeremiah, however, suggests that scribes or others have allowed some parts that were "plain and precious" (cf. 1 Ne. 13:20–42) to be omitted.

BIBLIOGRAPHY

For Mormon thought on Jeremiah, see Sidney B. Sperry, *The Spirit of the Old Testament* (Salt Lake City, 1970), and S. Kent Brown, "History and Jeremiah's Crisis of Faith," in *Isaiah and the Prophets*, M. Nyman, ed. (Provo, Utah, 1984). For textual transmission, see William J. Adams, Jr., "Some Ways in which the 'Plain and Precious Parts' Became Lost (1 Ne. 13:20–42)," *Newsletter and Proceedings of the Society for Early Historic Archaeology* (No. 159 [July 1985]:1–6), and Ernst Würthwein, *The Text of the Old Testament* (Grand Rapids, Mich., 1979). For current views of Jeremiah, see Alexander Rofé, "Jeremiah, the book of," in *Harper's Bible Dictionary*, ed. P. J. Achtemeier (San Francisco, 1985), and John Bright, *Jeremiah*, The Anchor Bible (Garden City, N.Y., 1965).

WILLIAM J. ADAMS, JR.

JERUSALEM

Latter-day Saints view Jerusalem as a holy city, as do other Christians, Jews, and Muslims. The existence of Jerusalem as a unique holy place stems from at least the time that DAVID captured the city and made it his capital. With Solomon's efforts, the temple stood in Jerusalem as God's dwelling place (1 Kgs. 6). For a millennium, Jehovah was worshiped there, and his people looked for redemption in Jerusalem (Luke 2:38). Tradition holds that its former name was Salem (Gen. 14:18; Ps. 76:2), where Melchizedek reigned and ABRAHAM went to sacrifice Isaac. Later, Jesus Christ died there to atone for the sins of mankind. Concerning Jerusalem's future importance, latter-day scripture affirms biblical prophecies that Jerusalem is to be the scene of important events in the last days.

Old Testament prophets spoke of the rise and demise of Jerusalem (e.g., 1 Kgs. 9:3; Micah 3:12). About 600 B.C., the future Book of Mormon prophet LEHI lived in the land of Jerusalem and encountered opposition when he called its inhabitants to repentance and prophesied the coming of the Messiah. He and his family were subsequently commanded by the Lord to flee the city, eventually journeying to the Western Hemisphere, where his descendants became two rival Book of Mormon peoples, the NEPHITES and the LAMANITES. Thus, from Jerusalem sprang the Book of Mormon saga.

Jerusalem was the scene of important events in Jesus' ministry. He taught and performed miracles there. No place was more holy to his followers than the temple, which Jesus considered the legitimate sanctuary of God, calling it "my Father's house" (John 2:16) and "my house" (Matt. 21:13). In an upper room of a house in Jerusalem, Jesus celebrated the Passover with his apostles, instituted the SACRAMENT, gave special meaning to the washing of feet, and revealed who would betray him. In Gethsemane and on Golgotha, Jesus accomplished the most selfless suffering in history, leading to his atoning sacrifice and resurrection.

Jesus mourned over the city as he recalled its past and envisioned its future (Matt. 23:37–39; Luke 19:41–44; 13:34–35). Like Jesus, Jerusalem would suffer indignities, anguish, and death (JS—M 1:18–22). But as Jesus lives again, so will Jerusalem (Isa. 52:1–2, 9; D&C 109:62). As part of the RESTORATION of all things, the holy city must be restored. The Prophet Joseph Smith said, "Judah must return, Jerusalem must be rebuilt, and the temple, . . . and all this must be done before the Son of Man will make His appearance" (HC 5:337).

Jerusalem will be restored in its former place, be sanctified, and become a city of holiness, graced with a new temple (Zech. 2:12; 12:6; Ether 13:5, 11; 3 Ne. 20:29–36; D&C 77:15). Elder Orson Hyde, an apostle, journeyed to Jerusalem in 1841 to dedicate the land "for the building up of Jerusalem again . . . and for rearing a Temple in honor of [the Lord's] name" (HC 4:456).

Other events are yet to occur in Jerusalem: a major struggle will yet rage in Jerusalem's streets, that of Armageddon (Zech. 14); an earthquake will divide the Mount of Olives; and the Savior will appear to the Jews (D&C 45:48–53).

Two separate Jerusalems, the old and the new, will serve as headquarters of the millennial kingdom of God from which Jesus will rule. Old Jerusalem will be built up by Judah. The NEW JERUSALEM, also to be known as ZION (D&C 45:66–67), will be built up in Jackson County, Missouri, by EPHRAIM, whose descendants largely make up The Church of Jesus Christ of Latter-day Saints. Isaiah foresaw the day when this second Jerusalem or Zion would be established: "For out of Zion shall go forth the law, and the word of the Lord from Jerusalem" (Isa. 2:3; cf. 64:10). MORONI$_2$, the last Book of Mormon prophet, first described the Jerusalem of old, then quoted the prophecy of Ether that "a New Jerusalem should be built up upon the land, unto the remnant of the seed of Joseph," and finally mentioned the "New Jerusalem, which should come down out of heaven" (Ether 13:3–12). John the Revelator also envisioned this final "Jerusalem, coming down from God out of heaven" (Rev. 21:2, 10). From this New Jerusalem, the city of Zion, God and the Lamb will reign over a celestialized earth (Moses 7:62–63; cf. *DS* 3:55–79).

BIBLIOGRAPHY

Burton, Alma P. *Toward the New Jerusalem.* Salt Lake City, 1985.

Nibley, Hugh. "Jerusalem: In Early Christianity." In *CWHN,* Vol. 4, pp. 323–54.

D. KELLY OGDEN

JEWS

[Articles in this volume focus only indirectly on Jewish matters but indicate the place that Jews and elements of Judaica hold in LDS doctrine and prophecy: Abraham; Circumcision; Ephraim; Ezekiel, Prophecies of; Gentiles, Fulness of; Isaiah: Interpretations in Modern Scripture; Israel; Jerusalem; Law of Moses; Moses; New Jerusalem; Old Testament; Restoration of All Things; Sacrifice in Biblical Times; Ten Commandments; Zion; Zionism.]

JOHN, REVELATIONS OF

The apostle John, sometimes referred to as John the Beloved and John the Revelator, and scriptural texts linked to his name are esteemed highly by Latter-day Saints. Modern scripture adds to an understanding of the man and his writings in three important areas: John as a TRANSLATED BEING, an additional record of John, and clarification of the book of Revelation.

JOHN AS TRANSLATED BEING.   In April 1829 the Prophet Joseph Smith received a revelation (D&C 7) that clarified the Savior's statement about John's tarrying on earth until Jesus returned (John 21:22). This revelation teaches that John requested that he receive power over death so that he could bring more souls to Christ (3 Ne. 28:6–11); that the Lord promised him that he could tarry "until I come in my glory"; and that John is a translated being whose state is "as flaming fire and a ministering angel" (D&C 7:1–3, 6).

ADDITIONAL RECORD OF JOHN.   In another revelation to Joseph Smith on May 6, 1833, an excerpt of eleven verses appears from what is called the "fulness of the record of John" (D&C 93:7–18). Important similarities exist between these verses and the opening verses of John's gospel (John 1:1–34), but links to the experiences of JOHN THE BAPTIST are also apparent (cf. D&C 93:15; John 1:32–34). Since Doctrine and Covenants 93 mentions only the name John, without annotation, it is unclear whether John the Beloved or John the Baptist is meant (cf. McConkie, 1979, Vol. 1, pp. 426–27).

Whatever the source, these few lines from the "record of John" bear important witness of the Savior, reaffirming that Jesus is the Word, "even the messenger of salvation" (D&C 93:7–8); that he is the light and the redeemer of the world and the spirit of truth (93:9–10); and that he did not receive the fulness at first, but continued "from grace to grace" until he received "all power, both in heaven and on earth" (93:11–17).

BOOK OF REVELATION.   Two Book of Mormon passages underscore the importance of the Revelation of John for the latter days. The prophet NEPHI$_1$ (c. 600 B.C.) saw in vision many future events, but he was forbidden to write them, "for the Lord God hath ordained the apostle of the Lamb of God that he should write them. . . . [And] the name of the apostle of the Lamb was John" (1 Ne. 14:25, 27). Further, speaking of the last days, the Lord said, "Then shall my revelations which I have caused to be written by my servant John be unfolded in the eyes of all the people" (Ether 4:16).

In this connection, three important sources aid the interpretation of the Apocalypse.

1. Doctrine and Covenants section 77. Received by Joseph Smith while working on the JOSEPH SMITH TRANSLATION OF THE BIBLE (JST), this revelation contains fifteen questions and answers about the book of Revelation. "This Revelation [D&C 77] is not a complete interpretation of the book. It is a *key*. . . . It unlocks the door through which an entrance may be gained, but after the key has been turned, the searcher for treasure must find it for himself" (Smith, p. 478).

2. The Joseph Smith Translation. In addition to the questions and answers in section 77, Joseph Smith made significant revisions to the text of Revelation in the JST.

3. Other scriptural and prophetic writings. Much of the Apocalypse is couched in imagery. Both latter-day scripture and the writings of General Authorities provide interpretations that help unlock this imagery. Examples include the "rod of iron" as the word of God (Rev. 2:27; cf. 1 Ne. 15:23–24), the "beasts" of chapter 13 as the degenerate kingdoms of the world (*TPJS*, p. 289), and Babylon as the symbol of spiritual wickedness (Rev. 17:5; cf. D&C 133:14).

In brief, the book of Revelation is divided into two major segments—the letters to the seven churches of Asia (chaps. 2–3) and the vision of "things which must be hereafter" (4:1; see chaps. 4–22).

The seven letters written to churches in Asia are important to Christians of all ages. They outline beliefs and practices that the Lord found commendable, as well as those which displeased him. In capsule form, these chapters summarize blessings that await the faithful.

The vision of the future (Rev. 4–22) revolves around a "book," sealed with seven seals, which was in God's hand (5:1–8). According to Doctrine and Covenants section 77, that book represented God's plan for this earth during the seven thousand years of its "temporal existence," each seal representing a thousand years (D&C 77:6–7). "By the seven thousand years of temporal existence is meant the time of the earth's duration from the fall of Adam to the end of time, which will come after the Millennium" (Joseph Fielding Smith, in Smith and Sjodahl, p. 474).

The first five seals highlight, in two or three verses (Rev. 6:1–11), each of the first five thousand years (see also McConkie, 1973, Vol. 3, pp. 476–85). In the sixth seal, representing the sixth millennium, John saw four angels holding the judgments of God (Rev. 7:1; D&C 77:8) and another angel who represented the work of the RESTORATION (Rev. 7:2–3; D&C 77:9–11; McConkie, 1973, Vol. 3, pp. 489–94).

The seventh seal opens in chapter 8. But the prediction of Christ's return does not occur until chapter 19. Thus, a major portion of the book focuses on the time just prior to Jesus' second coming (cf. D&C 77:13). Peter declared that Christ would not come again "until the times of restitution of all things" (Acts 3:21). It is central to this latter-day restitution that angelic ministers (MORONI₂, John the Baptist, Peter, James, John, Moses, etc.) brought back not only the fulness of the everlasting gospel and its keys and ordinances but also the "sealing power," which is the power to bind things on earth and have them be binding in heaven (Matt. 16:19). The restoration of the gospel and the power of sealing are important conditions for Christ's coming. During this period three characteristics will prevail: judgments, the kingdom of Christ versus the kingdoms of the world, and the destruction of latter-day Babylon.

As trumpets sound and "vials" of destruction are poured out, one devastating scourge follows another, including vast pollutions, rampant wickedness, and the battle of Armageddon (Rev. 8–11, 16). In the midst of these judgments allowed by God, a voice declares that "the kingdoms of this world are become the kingdoms of our Lord, and of his Christ" (Rev. 11:15). Chapter 12 portrays the Church of Christ and the kingdom of God (JST Rev. 12:7; McConkie, 1973, Vol. 3, p. 516). In chapter 13, Satan's kingdoms oppose the Saints and the work of God. Chapter 14 then shows the triumph of Christ's kingdom and what leads to that victory. Christ comes to Mount Zion with his servants (14:1–5), and an angel, having the everlasting gospel to preach to the earth, flies through the heavens (14:6–7). (Verse 6 provides the inspiration for the well-known ANGEL MORONI STATUE placed atop some LDS temples.) Then the fall of Babylon is announced (14:8–11). Like the angel from the east (Rev. 7:2), this angel is interpreted to represent the work of the restoration (McConkie, 1973, Vol. 3, p. 530). It is this work, directed by Christ and his servants, which brings about the eventual destruction of all worldly kingdoms. The fall of Babylon (Rev. 16–18) is so dramatic that all the hosts of heaven spontaneously shout, "Alleluia" (Rev. 19:1–6).

After Christ's coming (Rev. 19:7–21), the vision concludes in quick succession with the Millennium (Rev. 20:1–6), the loosing of Satan for a "little season" (Rev. 20:7–10; D&C 88:111–15), the great Judgment (Rev. 20:11–15), and the celestialization of the earth (Rev. 21–22:5). Thus, the Revelation of John shows that in spite of all of Satan's efforts to the contrary, God's work will triumph and Christ will come again to reign with his Saints for a thousand years during the Millennium and throughout eternity.

BIBLIOGRAPHY

Lund, Gerald N. "Insights from the JST into the Book of Revelation." *The Joseph Smith Translation,* ed. M. Nyman and R. Millet. Provo, Utah, 1985.

McConkie, Bruce R. *Doctrinal New Testament Commentary,* Vol. 3, pp. 476–85, 489–94, 516, 530. Salt Lake City, 1973.

———. "Understanding the Book of Revelation." *Ensign* 5 (Sept. 1975):85–89.

———. *The Mortal Messiah,* Vol. 1, pp. 426–27. Salt Lake City, 1979.

Smith, Hyrum M., and Janne M. Sjodahl. *Doctrine and Covenants Commentary,* rev. ed. Salt Lake City, 1951.

GERALD N. LUND

JOHN THE BAPTIST

John the Baptist was born in Judea about six months before the Savior Jesus Christ. John's primary mortal mission was to prepare the way for, and baptize, Jesus. His later role in restoring the Aaronic Priesthood in 1829 is particularly significant to Latter-day Saints.

Biblical scholars discern subtle differences in the way each of the four New Testament Gospels presents information about John the Baptist. Mark seems to emphasize how John prefigured Jesus, in that both proclaimed the gospel and then were given over to death. Luke points to personal relationships between John and Jesus, along with important links that the Baptist provides between the Old Testament and the New. Matthew records several ways in which John's ministry parallels that of Jesus, yet at the same time makes it clear that John was subordinate to Jesus, who identifies John as "the Elias who is to come" (cf. Matt. 11:14). The Greek Gospel of John, on the other hand, seems to minimize John's apocalyptic teachings, quotes him as denying that he was that Elias (John 1:21), and never uses the title "the Baptist," apparently in order to emphasize John's role as the first person at that time to know by revelation, and to witness, that Jesus was the son of God (see J. Meier, "John the Baptist in Matthew's Gospel," *Journal of Biblical Literature* 99 [1980]:383–86).

For Latter-day Saints, these nuances are transcended by John's larger roles subsumed within the PLAN OF SALVATION. For example, his ministry illustrates the concept of the need for a prophet, for "God will do nothing, but he revealeth his secret unto his servants the prophets" (Amos 3:7); he came as a voice of warning, proclaiming the gospel of repentance, bearing testimony of Jesus Christ, baptizing by immersion, holding divine authority, promising the gift of the Holy Ghost, and enduring to the end, even by suffering martyrdom. He was the Elias who was "to prepare all things" (JST Matt. 11:15), but not the Elias "who was to restore all things" (JST John 1:22, 26).

Both of John's parents were descendants of Aaron: Zacharias was an officiating priest in the temple of Jerusalem, and Elisabeth, of the daughters of Aaron, was a relative of Mary the mother of Jesus (Luke 1:5, 36). His birth was promised by the angel Gabriel (*see* NOAH), who visited Zacharias while he was officiating in the temple. Although Zacharias and Elisabeth had fervently prayed for children, none had been born to them. In their old age, Gabriel's promise was received with some doubt by Zacharias. As a sign, Gabriel struck Zacharias deaf and evidently dumb until the naming of the baby eight days after John's birth, the day John was circumcised according to the law of Moses. Contrary to the custom, by previous direction of Gabriel, the baby was named John instead of Zacharias, after his father. Zacharias gave his son a blessing on this occasion, the words of which are known as the Benedictus in Roman Catholic and Protestant terminology (Luke 1:68–79).

Little is known of John's early life and training. When Mary visited Elisabeth during their pregnancies, John "leaped in her womb" (Luke 1:41). He was "filled with the Holy Ghost from his mother's womb" and "was ordained by the angel of God" when he was eight days old (D&C 84:27–28). Since his parents were elderly, some wonder if he was soon orphaned or associated with religious sects in the Judean desert. Somehow he was carefully reared in gospel principles, for he came forth from the desert preaching repentance (Matt. 3:2) and was well prepared. He knew his mission and the source of his authority.

Jesus said of him, "Among those that are born of women there is not a greater prophet" (Luke 7:28). John the Baptist was dearly loved by the Savior. John had unusual privileges: none other would proclaim the immediate coming of Jesus; none other would be privileged to baptize the Lamb of God; none other was the legal administrator in the affairs of the kingdom then on the earth and holder of the keys of power. "These three reasons constitute him the greatest prophet born of a woman" (*TPJS*, p. 276).

With these credentials John came forth vigorously preaching

repentance and many principles of the gospel in the wilderness of Judea near the river Jordan (Mark 1:4–5). He ate ritually clean foods, locusts (Lev. 11:22), and wild honey; he drank "neither wine nor strong drink" (Luke 1:15); and he wore the traditional clothing of a prophet, camel's hair and a leather girdle (Mark 1:6). He also fasted (Matt. 11:18). He attracted large crowds and came under the increasing condemnation of those Jewish leaders whom he challenged with his preaching.

After a time, the "One mightier than I," even Jesus, approached John and requested baptism. A humble and meek John initially resisted, declaring that he needed to be baptized by Jesus. Upon Jesus' insistence, John baptized Jesus, following which he witnessed the sign of the dove descending from heaven upon the Christ (John 1:32).

At this juncture John alone seemed to bear the responsibility of spanning two dispensations. He was a child of promise whose mission had been prophesied years before by Isaiah, LEHI, and NEPHI₁ (Isa. 40:3; 1 Ne. 10:7–10; 2 Ne. 31:4–8).

John had begun his preaching and baptizing near the river Jordan probably about a year before Jesus began his public ministry. He "had no intention of founding a new sect" (Scobie, p. 131); his calling was to prepare the way for Jesus; and many of his followers became Jesus' closest and earliest disciples. His intense preaching of repentance had deeply angered those in power. He denounced the marriage of Herod Antipas to his brother's wife, Herodias, which clearly violated Jewish law (Lev. 20:21; Josephus, *Antiquities* 18.5.1–2). Herodias wanted John killed, but Herod Antipas had concern for John's popularity with the people. He had John imprisoned (Mark 6:17), somewhat pacifying the Pharisees, as well as Herodias. During all of this, Jesus went to Galilee. While in prison, John sent two of his disciples to Jesus to confirm their faith in the Savior's identity, and Jesus supported and sustained him (Luke 7:24–28). Through shrewd plotting and the beguiling dance of her daughter Salome, Herodias eventually manipulated Herod into having John beheaded.

John the Baptist was among the prophets and saints who were with Christ in his resurrection (D&C 133:55). Approximately eighteen centuries later, on Friday, May 15, 1829, this forerunner of the

Savior again appeared, this time as an angel of the Lord preparing the world for the Savior's second coming, and conferred the keys of the Aaronic Priesthood. This occurred when Joseph Smith and Oliver Cowdery withdrew to a secluded place on the Susquehanna River near Harmony, Pennsylvania, and prayed for instruction. Hardly had they begun when a heavenly messenger appeared, introducing himself as John the Baptist. Placing his hands upon their heads, he conferred upon them the priesthood of Aaron (D&C 13). He then commanded the young men to baptize each other in the nearby Susquehanna River and then lay hands upon each other to reconfer the priesthood that he had bestowed upon them. The messenger promised that the Melchizedek Priesthood, or higher priesthood, would be given to them at a future time by the apostles Peter, James, and John (JS—H 1:72).

BIBLIOGRAPHY

Matthews, Robert J. *A Burning Light.* Provo, Utah, 1972.
Scobie, Charles H. *John the Baptist.* Philadelphia, 1964.

LOUI NOVAK

JOHN THE BELOVED

John the Beloved is the author of five New Testament writings—a Gospel, the Revelation (Apocalypse; *see* JOHN, REVELATIONS OF), and three letters. Although the author identifies himself as John in the Revelation (Rev. 1:1, 4, 9), he is known only as "the Elder" in the letters and as "the disciple whom Jesus loved" in the Gospel. Ancient tradition and elements of style have supported the common authorship of these writings, but some argue that "the Beloved" and "the Elder" were two different people.

John emphasizes spiritual qualities in his writings, including some contrasting pairs of qualities that illustrate the two opposing spiritual forces in the world. Examples include light and darkness, love and hate, truth and falsehood, and God and the devil. John also emphasizes such ideas as bearing true witness, knowing the Lord, enduring to the end, and being raised up by the Savior.

John and his brother, James, were sons of Zebedee (some feel that Salome was Zebedee's wife, basing their identification on Matt. 27:56 and Mark 15:40), and the men of the family were fishermen at the Sea of Galilee. Their business prospered to the extent that they employed servants (Mark 1:19–20) by the time Jesus called the brothers to the full-time ministry. Although the Gospels of Matthew and Luke list Peter, Andrew, James, and John at the beginning of their lists, Mark and Acts place Peter, James, and John at the beginning of the list of the Twelve. These three apostles were alone with Jesus on special occasions, such as at the raising of Jairus' daughter (Mark 5:37–43), on the Mount of Transfiguration (Matt. 17:1–9), and at Jesus' suffering in the garden of Gethsemane (Matt. 26:37–45). The Prophet Joseph Smith taught that these three ancient apostles received the keys of the priesthood during the transfiguration experience (*TPJS*, p. 158).

John is usually identified as one of the two disciples of John the Baptist mentioned in the Gospel of John who became disciples of Jesus after his baptism (John 1:35–40). James and John were called Boanerges ("Sons of Thunder") by Jesus, perhaps because of their strong and impulsive personalities. Either they (Mark 10:35–40) or their mother on their behalf (Matt. 20:20–23) asked Jesus to grant them places of honor in his heavenly kingdom. Although rebuked for their ambition, they averred their willingness to share in his trials and suffering, and Jesus affirmed that they would do so.

John describes himself as "leaning on Jesus' bosom" during the Last Supper (John 13:23); later, when Jesus was bound and taken to the high priest, John (who "was known unto the high priest") and Peter followed along (John 18:15). John continued to follow the Savior through the ensuing events and was the only one of the Twelve recorded as being present at the Crucifixion. Jesus asked him to take care of his mother, Mary, and John took her to his own home (John 19:26–27).

Following the resurrection of Christ, Peter and John ran to the tomb when told by Mary Magdalene that the covering stone had been removed. John ran faster and arrived first at the empty tomb (John 20:1–8). Later, the Lord told Peter that John would remain (on earth) until the Lord's second coming (John 21:20–23), giving rise to the early Christian tradition that John did not die. The Prophet Joseph Smith confirmed and corrected that tradition in a revelation that states that John, having been given "power over death," remains on earth "as flaming fire and a ministering angel . . . for those who shall be heirs of salvation" until the Savior returns (D&C 7; see TRANS-LATED BEINGS). The resurrected Christ also mentioned John's continued earthly ministry during his visit to the people of the Book of Mormon (3 Ne. 28:6–8).

Peter and John appear together in many events of the early chapters of Acts, and some time after James' death (Acts 12:1–2) these two apostles were joined by another James, the "brother of the Lord" (Gal. 1:19), in a presiding responsibility over the Church; James, Peter, and John were the recognized "pillars" (Gal. 2:9).

After Peter's death (traditionally dated about A.D. 67), John would have been the senior and presiding apostle. Many sources state that years later John lived at Ephesus, was exiled to Patmos (c. A.D. 90) by the Emperor Domitian, and returned to Ephesus during the reign of Nerva (A.D. 96–98), Domitian's successor. During his exile to Patmos, John received the Revelation, which he was directed to send with cover letters to seven churches of Asia Minor. The importance of the Revelation to the Latter-day Saints is underscored by the vision of NEPHI₁ in the Book of Mormon, where that prophet was told by an angel not to write all he had seen, for the record of the last days would be made for the world by John, an apostle of the Lord (1 Ne. 14:18–27; cf. Ether 4:16).

After returning to Ephesus, John wrote the three letters that bear his name in the New Testament. Some think he also wrote his Gospel in Ephesus at this late date, but others date it earlier. Other writings have been ascribed to John, including the apocryphal *Acts of John,* and various versions of the *Apocryphon* [secret writing] *of John,* but none of these has been generally considered an authentic writing of the apostle.

In May-June 1829 the three ancient apostles, Peter, James, and John, appeared to Joseph Smith and Oliver Cowdery, ordained them to the Melchizedek Priesthood, and gave to them the same keys they had received on the Mount of Transfiguration (see D&C 27:12–13). Joseph Smith later received a revelation, parts of which paralleled the prologue to the Gospel of John, and was told that "the fulness of John's record" would be given at some future date (D&C 93:6, 18).

BIBLIOGRAPHY

Brown, Raymond E. *The Gospel According to John,* 2 vols. Garden City, N.Y., 1966, 1970.

———. *The Epistles of John.* New York, 1982.

Charles, R. H. *Revelation,* 2 vols. Edinburgh, 1920; rep. 1970.

Ford, J. Massyngberde. *Revelation.* New York, 1975.

Morris, Leon. *Commentary on the Gospel of John.* Grand Rapids, Mich., 1971.

Schnackenburg, Rudolf. *The Gospel According to St. John,* 3 vols. English trans., London, 1968–1982.

C. WILFRED GRIGGS

JOSEPH OF EGYPT

[*This entry consists of three articles:*

Joseph, Son of Jacob
Writings of Joseph
Seed of Joseph

Latter-day Saint scripture portrays a broader interest in Joseph of Egypt than the Bible does. The article Joseph, Son of Jacob *deals with the resulting wide sweep of LDS interests in Joseph, including the promises of the Lord about the latter-day importance of Joseph's posterity and his ancestral relationship to the Prophet Joseph Smith. The article* Writings of Joseph *treats specifically the matter of the writings of Joseph preserved in LDS scripture. The article* Seed of Joseph *focuses on the ancestral connection between Book of Mormon peoples and Joseph, son of Jacob.*]

JOSEPH, SON OF JACOB

The Book of Mormon prophet NEPHI₁ said of Joseph, son of Jacob, "He truly prophesied concerning all his seed. And the prophecies which he wrote, there are not many greater" (2 Ne. 4:2). Latter-day Saints hold Joseph to be a progenitor of a branch of the house of Israel, including certain BOOK OF MORMON PEOPLES about whom he prophesied. Additionally, he is honored as an ancestor of the Prophet Joseph Smith and many Church members and as one who prophesied concerning the RESTORATION of the gospel of Jesus Christ through Joseph Smith.

The current Bible text preserves little scripture attributed to

Joseph of Egypt. However, some writings of Joseph were recorded on the PLATES of brass, a scriptural record brought to the Western Hemisphere from Jerusalem by the prophet LEHI, and known among the Book of Mormon people. Another prophecy, restored by Joseph Smith, is now found in the JOSEPH SMITH TRANSLATION (JST) Genesis 50. In this text, the ancient Joseph prophesied the bondage of his father's family in Egypt and their eventual deliverance by Moses, and specifically names him and his brother, Aaron. Moses was to deliver Israel from Egypt, have power over the Red Sea, receive commandments from God, and be assisted by Aaron as his spokesman (JST Gen. 50:24, 29, 34–35).

The same source indicates that the Lord visited Joseph, promising him a righteous posterity, a branch of which would be separated from their kindred and taken to a distant country (JST Gen. 50:25–26). According to the Bible, Jacob had already prophesied that Joseph's branches—Ephraim and Manasseh—would inherit the "utmost bound of the everlasting hills" (Gen. 49:26). Moses described the new land of their inheritance as containing riches of both heaven and earth (Deut. 33:13–15). The Book of Mormon records the partial fulfillment of these prophecies with the exodus of the families of Lehi, a descendant of Manasseh (Alma 10:3), and Ishmael, a descendant of Ephraim (*JD* 23:184), to the western continents. The Book of Mormon is called "the stick of Ephraim" in modern revelation (D&C 27:5) and both "the stick of Ephraim" and "the STICK OF JOSEPH" (Ezek. 37:15–28, esp. verses 16 and 19).

Notwithstanding Israel's anticipated deliverance from Egypt under the leadership of Moses, Joseph of Egypt also foresaw that the Israelites would eventually be scattered. Still he was assured that they would be remembered by the Lord and that he would bring their descendants out of "bondage" in the last days. A "choice seer" was to be raised up, a descendant of Joseph, who would bear his name and whose father would also bear the same name. The prophecy stated that this latter-day Joseph would be highly esteemed by Joseph's descendants and would bring them knowledge of their progenitors. Moreover, he would be like both Joseph and Moses. As the ancient Joseph gathered his father's family in Egypt and supplied them with bread during famine, so the latter-day Joseph would gather their descendants from the ends of the earth to feast upon the words of everlasting life. Like Moses, he would bring forth the word of God (the Book of Mormon and other revelations), which would testify of, and sustain, other words of God that had already gone forth (the Bible), thereby confounding false doctrines and laying contentions to rest. As Moses would liberate Israel from Egyptian bondage, the "choice seer" of the last days would liberate them from the bondage of false traditions; as Moses would reveal a new covenant and prepare Israel to enter the PROMISED LAND, so his latter-day counterpart would reveal a new and everlasting covenant and prepare modern Israel, the Church, for the day of Christ's millennial reign (JST Gen. 50:24–38; cf. 2 Ne. 3; JST Gen. 48:11).

When Joseph Smith's father, Joseph Smith, Sr., acting in his office of patriarch, gave his son a patriarchal blessing, he further illuminated what was known to the ancient Joseph.

> I bless thee with the blessings of thy fathers Abraham, Isaac and Jacob; and . . . thy father Joseph, the son of Jacob. Behold, he looked after his posterity in the last days, when they should be scattered and driven by the Gentiles, and wept before the Lord; he sought diligently to know from whence the Son should come who should bring forth the word of the Lord, by which they might be enlightened, and brought back to the true fold, and his eyes beheld thee, my son; . . . and he said, As my blessings are to extend to the utmost bounds of the everlasting hills; as my father's blessing prevailed, over the blessings of his progenitors, and as my branches are to run over the wall, and my seed are to inherit the choice land whereon the Zion of God shall stand in the last days, from among my seed, scattered with the Gentiles, shall a choice Seer arise, whose bowels shall be a fountain of truth, whose loins shall be girded with the girdle of righteousness, whose hands shall be lifted with acceptance before the God of Jacob to turn away his anger from his anointed, whose heart shall meditate great wisdom, whose intelligence shall circumscribe and comprehend the deep things of God, and whose mouth shall utter the law of the just . . . and he shall feed upon the heritage of Jacob his father [*Utah Genealogical and Historical Magazine* 23 (Oct. 1932):175].

A blessing pronounced by Joseph Smith on Oliver Cowdery (Dec. 18, 1833) notes that Joseph of Egypt had seen Oliver in vision and knew of his scribal role in the translation of the Book of Mormon. Oliver was also told that Joseph of Egypt knew that Oliver would be present when the Aaronic Priesthood, or lesser priesthood, was restored and again when the Melchizedek Priesthood, or higher priesthood, was restored by messengers who received it from Jesus during his earthly ministry (Joseph F. Smith, *IE* 7 [Oct. 1904]:943). With the restoration of these priesthoods in 1829 and the publication of the Book of Mormon in 1830, the stage was set for fulfilling Moses' promise that the posterity of Ephraim and Manasseh would "push" or gather scattered Israel from the four quarters of the earth (cf. Deut. 33:17).

BIBLIOGRAPHY

Horton, George A., Jr. "Joseph: A Legacy of Greatness." In *Studies in Scripture*, ed. K. Jackson and R. Millet, Vol. 3, pp. 63–92. Salt Lake City, 1985.
McConkie, Joseph Fielding. *His Name Shall Be Joseph.* Salt Lake City, 1980.

JOSEPH FIELDING MCCONKIE

WRITINGS OF JOSEPH

Certain prophecies of Joseph of Egypt were preserved on brass plates carried by NEPHI₁ from Jerusalem to the Americas in approximately 590 B.C. The Book of Mormon makes available some of these prophecies. Although it is not known when Joseph's prophetic texts were recorded, they are doubtless very ancient. By contrast, the *History of Joseph, Prayer of Joseph, Testament of Joseph,* and *Joseph and Asenath* are considered to be Hellenistic Jewish writings, dating between 200 B.C. and A.D. 200, and are of unknown authorship (see Charlesworth). Joseph Smith noted "writings of Joseph" on papyri that he owned (*HC* 2:236).

According to Alma 46:24, Jacob the patriarch saw that part of Joseph's coat would be preserved, symbolizing a remnant of Joseph's seed (cf. *CWHN* 6:211–21). In addition, two similar though not identical texts from Joseph are preserved in 2 Nephi 3 and JST Genesis 50. Both prophesy that Moses will arise, that writings from "the fruit of the loins of Judah shall grow together" with writings of Joseph's descendants, and that a seer named Joseph—whose father would also be named Joseph—would appear in the last days (2 Ne. 3:6–17; JST Gen. 50:24–35; for similar expectations in pseudepigraphic texts, see McConkie). Associates of Joseph Smith saw him as the predicted seer, as did Joseph Smith himself. For instance, President John Taylor affirmed:

God called [Joseph Smith] to occupy the position that he did. How long ago? Thousands of years ago . . . Prophets prophesied about his coming, that a man should arise whose name should be Joseph, and that his father's name should be Joseph, and also that he should be a descendant of that Joseph who was sold into Egypt [*JD* 26:106].

BIBLIOGRAPHY

Charlesworth, James H. *The Old Testament Pseudepigrapha*, 2 vols. Garden City, New York, 1983–1985.

McConkie, Joseph F. "Joseph Smith as Found in Ancient Manuscripts." In *Isaiah and the Prophets*, ed. M. Nyman. Provo, Utah, 1984.

JAMES R. CLARK

SEED OF JOSEPH

The Book of Mormon teaches that Joseph, son of Jacob, "obtained a promise of the Lord" that his seed would become a "righteous branch unto the house of Israel" (2 Ne. 3:5) and that a latter-day descendant also named Joseph would have a role in bringing Joseph's seed and all the house of Israel "unto salvation" (2 Ne. 3:15).

While many of Joseph's posterity were among the ten tribes of Israel taken into captivity about 722 B.C. (2 Kgs. 17:5–6), a few descendants had settled in Jerusalem some 200 years earlier (cf. 2 Chr. 15:9–10). From those came the Book of Mormon leaders LEHI and ISHMAEL, who, about 600 B.C., led their families to the Western Hemisphere. Their descendants were later called "a remnant of the seed of Joseph" (Alma 46:23–24). Lehi reported that Joseph's prophecies concerning his seed included the following: (1) they would become a righteous people; (2) the Messiah would manifest himself to them; (3) a latter-day seer like Moses, raised up by God from Joseph's seed, would himself be called Joseph (2 Ne. 3:1–25); and (4) the righteous seed of the ancient Joseph who accept the gospel will help in building the NEW JERUSALEM and will participate in events of the last days (3 Ne. 20:10–28; 21:2–26).

BIBLIOGRAPHY

Ludlow, Daniel H. *A Companion to Your Study of the Book of Mormon.* Salt Lake City, 1976.

Pratt, Orson. "The Blessings of Joseph." *JD* 14:7–11.

LIESEL C. MCBRIDE

JOSEPH SMITH—HISTORY

The account called Joseph Smith—History, as it appears in the Pearl of Great Price, tells of the Prophet's experiences from his early years through May 1829. Franklin D. Richards, an early apostle, extracted this part of Joseph Smith's history from the much longer history of the Church printed in the *Times and Seasons* (*T&S* 3:726), and published the extract in 1851. In the preface of the first edition of the Pearl of Great Price, Richards expressed a hope that this collection of precious truths would increase the members' ability to defend the faith. Joseph Smith—History, the name now given to the historical extract, became canonized scripture to the members of the Church when they accepted the Pearl of Great Price by vote at the October 10, 1880, general conference (*see* PEARL OF GREAT PRICE: CONTENTS AND PUBLICATION).

This account in the Pearl of Great Price was not the first attempt to record the Prophet's early experiences. From the organization of the Church in 1830, he understood the importance of keeping records but his efforts were hindered by lawsuits, imprisonments, poverty, and mobs. John Whitmer kept a history between 1830 and 1832 that was lost for many years but is now available again, and Oliver Cowdery wrote eight letters about Joseph Smith's early visions that were published in *Messenger and Advocate* in 1834–1835. Joseph Smith began work on a history between July and November 1832; it opened with the words "A History of the life of Joseph Smith, Jr., an account of his marvilous [sic] experience," and described his early visions. Various clerks and historians made three more beginnings between 1834 and 1836. In the trying years 1837 and 1838, Joseph Smith and the First Presidency worked on the history of the Church, sometimes taking a grammar lesson before the writing sessions. Finally, in June 1839, Joseph undertook the work again. Materials from the previous efforts were assimilated into this new history, which eventually was published in the *Times and Seasons*, beginning March 1, 1842 (*T&S* 3:706). Joseph Smith—History, as we now have it in the Pearl of Great Price, was part of this 1839 version of the history of the Church.

The history introduces Joseph by giving a brief record of his ancestry and his own birth on December 23, 1805, in the township of Sharon, Windsor County, Vermont, one of eleven children of Joseph Sr. and Lucy Mack Smith. It tells of the religious conditions that led to Joseph Smith's first vision and describes what he saw and heard when the Father and Son appeared, in a direct, first-person account that makes no effort to adorn the events it relates. Oliver Cowdery, Joseph's close associate in these early years, wrote a much more ornate narrative of the early experiences. Joseph Smith simply described what happened to him, from the First Vision, through the visitation of MORONI₂, the visits to the hill CUMORAH, the translation of the gold plates, and to the visit of John the Baptist to restore the Aaronic Priesthood.

For many years the Church published Joseph Smith—History as a pamphlet with the title *Joseph Smith's Own Story.* Missionaries carried it to all parts of the world to help explain Joseph Smith's part in the restoration of the gospel in modern times.

BIBLIOGRAPHY

Clark, James R. *Story of the Pearl of Great Price.* Salt Lake City, 1955.

Jessee, Dean C. "The Writing of Joseph Smith's History." *BYU Studies* 11 (1971):439–73.

———. "The Reliability of Joseph Smith's History." *Journal of Mormon History* 3 (1976):23–46.

JOSEPH GRANT STEVENSON

JOSEPH SMITH—MATTHEW

Joseph Smith—Matthew is an extract from the JOSEPH SMITH TRANSLATION OF THE BIBLE (JST), as revealed to the Prophet Joseph Smith in 1831, and comprises a revision of Jesus' discourse on the Mount of Olives recorded in Matthew 23:39 through chapter 24. First published in Ohio in the mid-1830s as a broadside, Joseph Smith—Matthew was republished in 1851 as part of the original PEARL OF GREAT PRICE (Matthews, p. 52).

On March 7, 1831, Joseph Smith was directed to begin a translation of the New Testament "that ye may be prepared for the things to come" (D&C 45:60–61). In Matthew 24, Jesus foretold the impending destruction of Jerusalem. He also spoke of his own SECOND COMING and the destruction of the wicked.

The following are some of the significant additions and clarifications of Joseph Smith—Matthew to the King James text:

1. Jesus' disciples clearly understood that he would come again in glory "in the clouds of heaven, and all the holy angels with him" (JS—M 1:1).

2. Verses 4–22 of the King James text refer to "things I have spoken unto you concerning the Jews" (JS—M 1:21).

3. Verses 6, 7, and 14 of KJV are repositioned from the early part of the chapter, which deals with the Jews of New Testament times, to the latter part of the chapter, which concerns the second coming.

4. The end of the world is not the end of the earth, but the "destruction of the wicked" (JS—M 1:4, 55).

5. The parable in KJV verse 28 is completed to read, "Wheresoever the carcass is, there will the eagles be gathered together; so likewise shall mine elect be gathered from the four quarters of the earth" (JS—M 1:27).

6. The "abomination of desolation, spoken of by Daniel the prophet," applies both to conditions at the destruction of Jerusalem and to Jesus' second coming (JS—M 1:12, 32).

The plainness and clarity of Joseph Smith—Matthew eliminate much of the confusion that has surrounded Matthew 24. It states that the gospel must be preached in all the world and the elect gathered before the second coming (JS—M 1:31). Finally, the elect will know the signs of the times and will be prepared and preserved during the events of the last days.

BIBLIOGRAPHY

Matthews, Robert J. "A Plainer Translation": Joseph Smith's Translation of the Bible. Provo, Utah, 1985.

DAVID T. GILES

JOSEPH SMITH TRANSLATION OF THE BIBLE (JST)

Joseph Smith, the first PROPHET of The Church of Jesus Christ of Latter-day Saints, made a "new translation" of the Bible, using the text of the King James Version (KJV). This work differs from the KJV in at least 3,410 verses and consists of additions, deletions, rearrangements, and other alterations that cause it to vary not only from the KJV but from other biblical texts. Changes range from minor details to fully reconstituted chapters. This article presents statements by Joseph Smith telling why he made a Bible translation, gives information relating to the development and production of the work, examines a number of the significant variants, and considers some doctrinal results and historical implications.

VIEW OF THE BIBLE.   The official position of the Church is stated in its eighth article of faith: "We believe the Bible to be the word of God as far as it is translated correctly." The message of the Bible is held to be true, while details of accuracy and completeness are accepted within certain limits. The Prophet Joseph Smith explained: "I believe the Bible as it read when it came from the pen of the original writers. Ignorant translators, careless transcribers, or designing and corrupt priests have committed many errors" (*TPJS*, p. 327). And again, "From sundry revelations which had been received, it was apparent that many points touching the salvation of men, had been taken from the Bible, or lost before it was compiled" (*TPJS*, pp. 9–10).

Joseph Smith often used the words "translated" and "translation," not in the narrow sense alone of rendering a text from one language into another, but in the wider senses of "transmission," having reference to copying, editing, adding to, taking from, rephrasing, and interpreting. This is substantially beyond the usual meaning of "translation." When he said the Bible was not translated correctly, he not only was referring to the difficulties of rendering the Bible into another language but he was also observing that the manuscripts containing the text of the Bible have suffered at the hands of editors, copyists, and revisionists through centuries of transmission. Thus, the available texts of the Bible are neither as complete nor as accurate as when first written.

The Book of Mormon presents an account of a vision in which an angel, looking to the future, describes the Bible as a "record of the Jews" containing writings of "the prophets" and of the "Twelve Apostles of the Lamb." The vision asserts (1) that the ancient authors wrote under the inspiration of the Holy Ghost, (2) that originally their words contained the fulness of the gospel and were plain and easy to understand, but (3) that many things which were plain and precious, and many covenants, would be "taken away" from the original manuscripts; as a result, afterward (4) a great many persons, even with a Bible, would not understand the fulness of the gospel, but (5) the lost material would be restored through "other records" that the Lord would bring forth (1 Ne. 13:21–41). A somewhat parallel statement came to Joseph Smith in June 1830 while he was restoring a revelation received by Moses, declaring that many things would be taken "from the book" which Moses would write, but that the missing information would be restored through another prophet and thus be "had again" among those who believe (Moses 1:41). Latter-day Saints believe that the "other records" referred to include the Book of Mormon, the Doctrine and Covenants, the Pearl of Great Price, the JST, and other records still to come forth, and that the prophet divinely raised up to begin restoring the lost material is Joseph Smith (*see* SCRIPTURE: FORTHCOMING SCRIPTURE). In light of the foregoing statements, it is worth observing that the principal difficulty in the Bible apparently has been omissions. The remaining text may be generally correct in itself, but many important doctrinal items (resulting from the loss of a single word, a verse, a longer passage, or even whole books in some instances) are now missing.

AUTHORITY TO TRANSLATE.   The Prophet Joseph Smith claimed a divine appointment to make an inspired rendition or, as he termed it, a "new translation" of the Bible. This appointment can be illustrated by excerpts from his writings. After laboring off and on for ten months on the early chapters of Genesis, Joseph Smith received a revelation from the Lord on March 7, 1831, directing him to begin work on the New Testament: "It shall not be given unto you to know any further concerning this chapter, until the New Testament be translated, and in it all these things shall be made known; wherefore I give unto you that ye may now translate it" (D&C 45:60–61). The manuscript of the JST shows that Joseph Smith began the translation of Matthew the next day. On December 1, 1831, the Prophet entered the following in his journal: "I resumed the translation of the Scriptures, and continued to labor in this branch of my calling with Elder Sidney Rigdon as my scribe" (*HC* 1:238–39). On February 16, 1832, he reported a revelation concerning the resurrection of the dead that includes the following reference to his divine commission to translate: "For while

we [Joseph Smith and Sidney Rigdon] were doing the work of translation, which the Lord had appointed unto us, we came to the twenty-
ninth verse of the fifth chapter of John" (D&C 76:15). On March 8,
1833, he reported the word of the Lord to him as follows: "And when
you have finished the translation of the [Old Testament] prophets, you
shall from thenceforth preside over the affairs of the church" (D&C
90:13). On May 6, 1833, Joseph Smith reported the following revelation: "It is my will that you should hasten to translate my scriptures" (D&C 93:53). Although not a complete list, the foregoing items
illustrate Joseph Smith's claim to a divine appointment to translate
the Old and New Testaments.

PROCEDURE AND TIME FRAME.   When he began his work in 1830,
Joseph Smith did not have a knowledge of biblical languages. His
translation was not done in the usual manner of a scholar, but was a
revelatory experience using only an English text. He did not leave a
description of the translating process, but it appears that he would
read from the KJV and dictate revisions to a scribe.

Joseph Smith was assisted by various scribes. The manuscript
shows that Oliver Cowdery was the first, serving between June and
October 1830; he recorded an introductory revelation (Moses 1) and
the translation of KJV Genesis 1:1 to Genesis 4:18. John Whitmer
served second, from October until December 1830, recording the
translation of KJV Genesis 4:19 to approximately Genesis 5:20.
Sidney Rigdon was next, becoming the main scribe from early
December 1830 until the translation was finished on July 2, 1833.
He recorded most of the translation from KJV Genesis 5:21 to the
end of the Bible, although others recorded small portions.

They used a large edition of the KJV (9 inches by 11 inches by 2
inches), printed in 1828 by H. and E. Phinney Company of
Cooperstown, New York, that included the Old Testament
Apocrypha. (A notation on the flyleaf, in what appears to be Joseph
Smith's handwriting, states that it had been purchased from the
Egbert B. Grandin Bookstore in Palmyra, New York, on October 8,
1829, for $3.75). In this copy of the Phinney Bible are hundreds of
pencil and ink notations consisting primarily of checks or crosses
marking off passages to be revised. Likewise, a number of italicized
words in the KJV text—which usually represent words implicitly
understood in the Greek or Hebrew—are lined out. Words of the

revision were not written on the pages of the Bible itself, but were recorded on sheets of paper and identified by the appropriate citation. The manuscript is written in full from Genesis 1:1 through Genesis 24 and from Matthew 1:1 through John 5, including entire chapters in which there are no corrections. A more rapid and efficient system was eventually used in which only the actual points of revision were written. These sometimes consisted of only one or two words. The markings in the Bible that designate verses to be translated appear only in those portions where the shorter method was used. The manuscript sheets, 17 inches by 14 inches folded to produce surfaces 8½ inches by 14 inches, were once sewn together at the fold in convenient thicknesses. The entire manuscript consists of 477 pages.

The exact date on which the translation was begun is not known, but it is closely associated with the June 1830 revelation that contains an account of visions given to Moses before he composed the book of Genesis (see Moses 1). The work proceeded from June 1830 until July 2, 1833. Genesis 1–17 was translated first, being done between June 1830 and March 7, 1831. On the latter date Joseph Smith received the revelation instructing him to "translate" the New Testament (D&C 45:60–62), which he began at Matthew 1:1. It appears that for a few days the translation may have continued in both Genesis and in Matthew, but the Old Testament was subsequently laid aside, possibly at the end of Genesis 24, in favor of working on the New Testament. The work then proceeded consecutively through the entire New Testament until February 2, 1833. The remainder of the Old Testament (Genesis 25 through Malachi) was then translated, being completed five months later. In response to prayer as to whether he should translate the Apocrypha, Joseph Smith reported a revelation dated March 9, 1833, to the effect that he need not attend to it: "It is mostly translated correctly," though there are some errors and "interpolations by the hands of men" (D&C 91:1–2).

The dates on the JST manuscripts, when compared with dates of related revelations in the Doctrine and Covenants and with dates and events entered in Joseph Smith's personal journal, indicate the movement back and forth between the Old and New Testaments, as explained above, rather than a straight-line progress from Genesis through Revelation. Likewise, the varying styles of handwriting in the manuscript reflect the known coming and going of those who served as scribes. Although the bulk of the translation was accomplished by July 2, 1833, that work represented a preliminary draft. As the manuscript was later reviewed and prepared for publication, further revisions, refinements, and alterations were made.

After Joseph Smith's death in June 1844, the marked Phinney Bible and the 477–page manuscript were kept by his widow, Emma Smith. She permitted Dr. John M. Bernhisel to examine the materials in the spring of 1845 at Nauvoo, Illinois. Bernhisel later reported that he made a complete copy of the markings in the Bible and an extensive but incomplete copy of the manuscript entries (Matthews, 1975, p. 118). The Bernhisel manuscript is in the Historian's Library of the LDS Church in Salt Lake City, but the location of the Bernhisel marked Bible is not known. Emma Smith gave the Phinney Bible and the original manuscript to a publication committee representing the Reorganized Church of Jesus Christ of Latter Day Saints (RLDS Church) in 1866. These are now in the custody of the RLDS Church at Independence, Missouri.

PUBLICATION.   Although excerpts from the JST were published in Church newspapers and as a broadside tract during the lifetime of Joseph Smith, the entire work was not published in his day, even though he had intended and had expended considerable effort to accomplish it. The distraction of persecution, the demands of Church business, and the lack of financial means prevented him from completing and authorizing a manuscript ready for the press (Matthews, pp. 57–63).

In 1867, after considerable effort and expense, the RLDS Church published a copyrighted edition of the Bible, under the title *Holy Scriptures,* which incorporated the Prophet's translation into the format of a King James text. This was followed by many subsequent printings, all from the same stereotype plates. In 1936 a teacher's edition containing study helps was published by the RLDS Church. At that time a subtitle, "Inspired Version," was added, although the text remained the same as the 1867 edition. In 1944 a "New Corrected Edition" was published by the RLDS Church in which at least 352 verses were amended to correct typographical and judgment errors in the 1867 edition. These corrections were matters of detail, although in a few instances they significantly affected the meaning of the passages and brought the printed text into closer harmony with the manuscript. In 1970 a parallel column edition consisting of the Inspired Version and the King James Version was issued by the RLDS Church publishing house.

The Church of Jesus Christ of Latter-day Saints has never published the entire Joseph Smith Translation of the Bible. Portions of Genesis and of Matthew, distributed during the time of Joseph Smith in Kirtland and in Nauvoo, are included in the Pearl of Great Price under the title BOOK OF MOSES (JST Gen. 1 through 8:18) and JOSEPH SMITH—MATTHEW (JST Matt. 24). Extensive portions of JST Genesis 1–5 and a single excerpt each from Romans and Hebrews were used in the LECTURES ON FAITH and are still published therein. In 1979 the LDS Church published an edition of the King James Version with hundreds of JST footnotes and a seventeen-page appendix containing JST excerpts (*see* BIBLE: LDS PUBLICATION OF THE BIBLE).

EXTENT OF THE CHANGES.   Joseph Smith made extensive corrections and additions to the books of Genesis, Exodus, Psalms, Isaiah, Matthew, Luke, Romans, 1 Corinthians, Galatians, Hebrews, James, 2 Peter, and Revelation. He also made many alterations in the writings of the Old Testament prophets and in Mark, John, Acts, and several of the epistles. He made no changes in Ruth, Ezra, Esther, Ecclesiastes, Lamentations, Obadiah, Micah, Habakkuk, Zephaniah, Haggai, Malachi, Philemon, 2 John, and 3 John. He made some corrections in all other books of the Bible, and rejected the Song of Solomon as not being inspired scripture.

TITLE.   Joseph Smith's work with the Bible has been known by various titles. The revelations in the Doctrine and Covenants call it a "translation" (D&C 37:1; 90:13). Joseph Smith called it the "new translation," and it is known by this title in the early literature of the Church. It was published by the RLDS Church under the title "Holy Scriptures," with the later subtitle, "Inspired Version." Many call it an "inspired revision." In 1978 the LDS Church officially labeled it the "Joseph Smith Translation," abbreviated JST.

CONTRIBUTIONS OF THE JST.   Assessing the contributions of the JST requires a differentiation between the process and the product. The translation process was revelatory and educational, and was a means of expanding the Prophet Joseph Smith's knowledge and doctrinal awareness (cf. D&C 45:60–61). The contributions, therefore, go beyond the particular biblical text that may have initiated the process. Among the doctrines of the LDS Church that arose from the JST translation process are the building of Zion, patterned after Enoch's city; the age of accountability of children, with baptism at eight years; the extensive revelation about the degrees of glory and plural marriage (including celestial, eternal marriage); and various items of priesthood organization and responsibility. These and other doctrines were often introduced during the translation process and later developed through subsequent revelations now contained in the Doctrine and Covenants. Revelations in the Doctrine and Covenants received during the translation process are sections 76, 77, 86, and 91, and parts of 107 and 132. In this way the JST has affected the spiritual life of every member of the Church, even though most of the members have not known of the JST.

The tangible product—the printed JST—consists of a Bible with thousands of unique corrections, additions, and readings. Although many Latter-day Saints regard this as the most correct version of the Bible now available, and therefore use it as a valuable source for biblical understanding, the wider contribution has probably been the enlightening effect that the process had upon Joseph Smith and the subsequent revelations through him that have shaped Church doctrine and practice. Most of the doctrinal and organizational revelations that have governed the Church, and that are now published in the Doctrine and Covenants, came to Joseph Smith during the period that he was translating the Bible (1830–1833).

Many items in the Doctrine and Covenants relate directly to the process of the JST. These gave direction to the Prophet concerning matters related to the translation, the selection of scribes, when to proceed with the translation, which portions of the Bible to do next, when to lay the work aside for other matters, and other such information, but do not contain *texts* of the JST. This type of related information is seen in the editorial headnotes to sections 35, 71, 76, 77, 86, and 91; and in the text of D&C 9:2; 35:20; 37:1; 41:7; 42:56–58; 45:60–62; 73:3; 76:15–18; 77:1–15; 86:1–11; 93:53; 94:10; 104:58; and 124:89. The Pearl of Great Price presents part of

the *product,* and contains two extracts from the text of the JST, the Book of Moses and Joseph Smith—Matthew.

MAIN DOCTRINAL THEMES.   Most of the passages revised or added by Joseph Smith are of doctrinal significance. While many individual topics are involved, some main themes are (1) an emphasis in both the Old and New Testaments on the mission and divinity of Jesus Christ; (2) the nature of God; (3) the innocence of children; (4) the plan of salvation; (5) premortal life; (6) the holy priesthood and credentials of the patriarchs; (7) the ministries of ENOCH and of Melchizedek; and (8) clarification of ambiguous passages, elimination of some contradictions between biblical texts, and explanations of terms and phrases.

Representative passages of the types of information found only in Joseph Smith's translation of the Bible constitute the remainder of this article.

The purpose of the JST is to provide knowledge not found in other Bibles. Thus it is by nature declarative and informative.

1. Emphasis on Jesus Christ. The JST emphasizes that the gospel of Jesus Christ was taught in the earliest ages of mankind. According to JST Genesis 1–8 (published as Moses 1–8 in the Pearl of Great Price), Adam, Enoch, Noah, and the other patriarchs were preachers of righteousness and taught the gospel of Jesus Christ, including faith, repentance, baptism, and receiving the Holy Ghost.

The JST states that Adam was taught by a heavenly angel to offer animal sacrifice as a type and symbol of the atoning sacrifice that the Son of God would accomplish. He was instructed to do all things in the name of the Son. Adam was taught the gospel, was baptized by immersion, received the Holy Ghost, and was born of the Spirit (Moses 5, 6).

Enoch likewise knew the gospel of Jesus Christ, was ordained to the same priesthood that Adam held, and he taught these principles to others. To Enoch was given a vision that included the spirit world and future events upon the earth from his day to the second coming of Jesus Christ. He presided in a city of righteous people called Zion, which was translated and taken into heaven (Moses 6–7; *see* TRANSLATED BEINGS).

Noah was also a preacher of righteousness, ordained to the same

priesthood held by Adam and Enoch, and taught the gospel of Jesus Christ to his contemporaries, including faith in Jesus Christ, baptism, and the reception of the Holy Ghost (Moses 8:12–25).

The New Testament JST portrays a slightly stronger image of Jesus than does the KJV. Examples include the following: In the KJV the wise men ask Herod about the birth of the "King of the Jews" (Matt. 2:2); in the JST they pose a more searching question: "Where is *the child* that is born, *the Messiah* of the Jews?" (JST Matt. 3:2). [JST variants here and hereafter are in italics.] When Herod inquires of the scribes, he is told that it is written that Christ should be born in Bethlehem, "For out of thee shall come a Governor, that shall rule my people Israel" (Matt. 2:6); the JST reads, "for out of thee shall come *the Messiah, who* shall *save* my people Israel" (JST Matt. 3:6).

In the JST a transitional passage without a KJV equivalent is inserted between the end of KJV Matthew chapter 2 and the beginning of Matthew chapter 3:

> *And it came to pass that Jesus grew up with his brethren, and waxed strong, and waited upon the Lord for the time of his ministry to come. And he served under his father, and he spake not as other men, neither could he be taught; for he needed not that any man should teach him. And after many years, the hour of his ministry drew nigh* [JST Matt. 3:24–26].

At age twelve, when Jesus was teaching in the temple, the KJV (Luke 2:46) records that Jesus was "sitting in the midst of the doctors, both hearing them, and asking them questions." The JST reads, "*they were* hearing *him,* and asking *him* questions" (JST Luke 2:46).

The KJV account of Jesus' forty days in the wilderness states that Jesus went there "to be tempted of the devil. And when he had fasted forty days and forty nights, he was afterward an hungered" (Matt. 4:1–2). The JST reads: "Then Jesus was led up of the Spirit, into the wilderness, to be *with God.* And when he had fasted forty days and forty nights, *and had communed with God,* he was afterwards an hungered, *and was left to be tempted of the devil*" (JST Matt. 4:1–2). Luke's record (KJV) says that Jesus was "forty days tempted of the devil" (Luke 4:2). The JST reads, "*And after forty days, the devil came unto him, to tempt him*" (JST Luke 4:2).

The KJV states that "the devil taketh" Jesus to a "pinnacle of the temple" and also to a "high mountain" (Matt. 4:5–8; Luke 4:5–9).

The JST says it was "the Spirit" who transported Jesus to these places (JST Matt. 4:5–8; Luke 4:5–9).

In the KJV John 3:23 states that Jesus performed baptisms, but John 4:2 largely negates Jesus' activity as a baptizer by stating: "Though Jesus himself baptized not, but his disciples." The JST reads, "Though *he himself baptized not so many as his disciples; For he suffered them for an example, preferring one another*" (JST John 4:3–4).

Jesus' parables are touched upon in many JST passages. One of the most important is a statement, presented as the words of Jesus himself, explaining why he used parables to veil the spiritual message when speaking to certain individuals: "Hear another parable; *for unto you that believe not, I speak in parables; that your unrighteousness may be rewarded unto you*" (JST Matt. 21:34).

In Mark 7:22–24 (KJV) Jesus enters a house "and would have no man know it: but he could not be hid." JST Mark 7:22–23 reads, "and would *that no* man *should come unto him. But he could not deny them; for he had compassion upon all men.*"

Luke reports that while Jesus was on the cross, he cried out, "Father, forgive them; for they know not what they do" (KJV Luke 23:34). The JST adds a parenthetical clarification: "*(meaning the soldiers who crucified him)*" (JST Luke 23:35).

2. God's Dealings with Mankind. JST passages bearing on God's dealings with mankind include the following: Genesis 6:6 (KJV) states that "It repented the Lord that he had made man on the earth, and it grieved him at his heart." JST Genesis 8:13 (Moses 8:25) renders this passage thus: "And it repented Noah, and *his heart was pained,* that the Lord had made man on the earth." Exodus 7:3, 13; 9:12; 10:1, 20 (KJV) all state that God will harden Pharaoh's heart. In each of these the JST reads that Pharaoh will harden his own heart:

Isaiah 63:17 (KJV) reads "O Lord, why hast thou made us to err from thy ways, and hardened our heart?" The JST reads, "O Lord, why hast thou suffered us to err, . . . and *to harden* our heart?"

Matthew 6:13 (KJV) reads, "And lead us not into temptation," whereas the JST reads "*suffer us not to be led* into temptation" (JST Matt. 6:14).

3. Innocence of Children. Many passages bear on man's nature in relation to the fall of Adam, his agency, and accountability to God. For instance, concerning the innocence of little children, the JST states that in the days of Adam the Lord revealed that "the Son of God hath atoned for original guilt, wherein the sins of the parents cannot be answered upon the heads of the children, for they are whole from the foundation of the world" (JST Gen. 6:56; Moses 6:54). To Abraham the Lord said, "Children are not accountable before me until they are eight years old" (JST Gen. 17:11). Matthew 18:11 in the KJV states with reference to children: "For the Son of man is come to save that which is lost." The JST adds, "and to call sinners to repentance; but these little ones have no need of repentance, and I will save them."

4. Paul's Writings. The JST offers many clarifications regarding teachings attributed to Paul in the New Testament. Some of these are as follows:

First Corinthians 14:35 (KJV) reports Paul writing "it is a shame for women to speak in the church." The JST reads "for women *to rule* in the church."

Hebrews 6:1 (KJV) reads "Therefore leaving the principles of the doctrine of Christ, let us go on unto perfection." The JST reads "*not* leaving . . . "

Hebrews 7:3 (KJV) gives the impression that the prophet Melchizedek was "without father, without mother, without descent, having neither beginning of days, nor end of life." The JST states that it was not Melchizedek the man, but his priesthood, that was without lineage or descent, being thus contrasted to the Levitical priesthood.

In 1 Timothy 3:15–16 (KJV) Paul is reported to have written that the church is the "pillar and ground of the truth." In the JST it is Jesus, as God manifested in the flesh, who is the "pillar and ground of the truth."

[*See also* other passages from the JST in the appendix.]

BIBLIOGRAPHY
Durham, Reed Connell, Jr. "A History of Joseph Smith's Revision of the Bible." Ph.D. diss., Brigham Young University, 1965.
Howard, Richard P. *Restoration Scriptures*. Independence, Mo., 1969.
Matthews, Robert J. *"A Plainer Translation:" Joseph Smith's Translation of the Bible*. Provo, Utah, 1975.

————. *A Bible! A Bible!* Salt Lake City, 1990.

————. "Joseph Smith's Efforts to Publish His Bible Translation." *Ensign* 13 [Jan. 1983]:57–63).

Nyman, Monte S., and Robert L. Millet, eds. *The Joseph Smith Translation.* Provo, Utah, 1985.

ROBERT J. MATTHEWS

L

LAMAN

Laman was the eldest of six sons of LEHI and Sariah. Lehi was the patriarchal head and prophet at the beginning of the Book of Mormon, and Laman opposed his father and his younger brother NEPHI₁. Unlike the family conflicts in the book of Genesis between Esau and Jacob and between Joseph and his jealous brothers, the hostilities between Laman and Nephi were never quieted or reconciled.

Laman's opposition to the things of God arose from a combination of conflicting spiritual values and a common reaction against the favor he perceived going to a younger brother. The record of Nephi portrays Laman as strong-willed, hard-hearted, impulsive, violent, judgmental, and lacking in faith. Though Laman followed his father in their journeyings, he never shared in the spiritual calling that inspired Lehi.

In his rebelliousness, Laman charged that Lehi was a visionary and foolish man (1 Ne. 2:11). Still Lehi continued to exhort him "with all the feeling of a tender parent," even though he feared from what he had seen in a vision that Laman and Lemuel would refuse to come into God's presence (1 Ne. 8:36–37).

Laman objected to leaving Jerusalem and the family's lands, possessions, and security, and to traveling to a new land (1 Ne. 2:11). Throughout their journey he complained of the hardships and was resentful that God had selected Nephi to become "a ruler and a teacher" ahead of him (1 Ne. 2:21–22; 16:36–38). Laman and Lemuel beat Nephi with a rod (1 Ne. 3:28), attempted to leave him tied up in the wilderness to die (1 Ne. 7:16), bound him on board ship, and treated him harshly (1 Ne. 18:11). On various occasions, Laman was rebuked by an angel, chastened by the voice of the Lord, or "shocked" by divine power. Still, he longed for the popular life of Jerusalem even though Lehi had prophesied the city would be destroyed.

Laman was supported in his stance by his wife and children, by Lemuel (the next eldest son) and his family, and by some of the sons of ISHMAEL and their families. Before he died, Lehi left his first blessing with Laman and Lemuel on the condition that they would "hearken unto the voice of Nephi" (2 Ne. 1:28–29), but they so opposed Nephi that he was instructed by God to lead the faithful to settle a new land away from Laman and Lemuel in order to preserve their lives and religious beliefs.

Laman and his followers became the LAMANITES, persistent enemies of the NEPHITES. Stemming from these early personal conflicts, the Lamanites insisted for many generations that Nephi had deprived them of their rights. Thus, the Lamanites taught their children "that they should hate [the Nephites] . . . and do all they could to destroy them" (Mosiah 10:17). When Laman's descendants were converted to faith in Christ, however, they were exemplary in righteousness; and Book of Mormon prophets foretold a noteworthy future for them in the latter days.

BIBLIOGRAPHY

Matthews, Robert J. *Who's Who in the Book of Mormon.* Salt Lake City, 1976.

McConkie, Joseph F., and Robert L. Millet. *Doctrinal Commentary on the Book of Mormon,* Vol. 1. Salt Lake City, 1987.

ALAN K. PARRISH

LAMANITES

The name Lamanite refers to an Israelite people spoken of in the Book of Mormon, who were descendants of LEHI and ISHMAEL, both of whom were descendants of JOSEPH OF EGYPT (1 Ne. 5:14). They were

part of the prophet Lehi's colony, which was commanded of the Lord
to leave Jerusalem and go to a new promised land (in the Western
Hemisphere). The Lamanite peoples in the Book of Mormon during
the first 600 years of their history are all linked in some way to LAMAN
and Lemuel, Lehi's oldest sons. At times the name refers to "the
people of Laman"; at other times it can identify unbelievers and
ignore ancestral lines, depending on contextual specifics regarding
peoples, time, and place.

LAMANITES IN THE BOOK OF MORMON. After the death of the prophet
Lehi (c. 582 B.C.), the colony divided into two main groups,
Lamanites and NEPHITES (2 Ne. 5), each taking the name from their
leader. These patronyms later evolved into royal titles (Mosiah 24:3;
cf. Jacob 1:11). The Book of Mormon, though a Nephite record,
focuses on both Lamanites and Nephites, by means of complex
contrasts between the two groups. In the text, other peoples are generally subsumed under one of these two main divisions:

> Now the people which were not Lamanites were Nephites; nevertheless,
> they were called Nephites, Jacobites, Josephites, Zoramites, Lamanites,
> Lemuelites, and Ishmaelites. But I, Jacob, shall not hereafter distin-
> guish them by these names, but I shall call them Lamanites that seek
> to destroy the people of Nephi, and those who are friendly to Nephi I
> shall call Nephites, or the people of Nephi, according to the reigns of
> the kings [Jacob 1:13–14].

In the beginning, political and religious disagreements arose
between the Lamanites and the Nephites. Subsequently, an increasing cultural differentiation of the Lamanite people from the Nephites
seems to have resulted from their different responses to Lehi's religious teachings. Social change quickly took place along many lines.
Consequently, the name Lamanite can refer to descendants of Laman
and his party; to an incipient nationality based upon an ideology, with
its own lineage history and religious beliefs (Mosiah 10:12–17); or to
one or more cultures. The Book of Mormon describes several
Lamanite cultures and lifestyles, including hunting-gathering (2 Ne.
5:24), commerce (Mosiah 24:7), sedentary herding, a city-state
pattern of governance (Alma 17), and nomadism (Alma 22:28). The
politicized nature of early Lamanite society is reflected in the way in
which dissenters from Nephite society sought refuge among

Lamanites, were accepted, and came to identify themselves with them, much as some Lamanites moved in the opposite direction.

Early in the sixth century of Lamanite history (c. 94–80 B.C.), large-scale Lamanite conversions further divided the Lamanite peoples as many embraced the messianic faith in Jesus Christ taught by Nephite missionaries (Alma 17–26). The Lamanite king Lamoni, a vassal; his father, the suzerain king; and many of their subjects accepted the prophesied Christ and rejected their former lifestyles. They took upon themselves a covenant of pacifism, burying their weapons and renouncing warfare, and moved into Nephite territory for their safety (Alma 27:21–26; 43:11–12). This pattern of Lamanite conversion lasted for at least eighty-four years and through several generations (cf. Alma 24:5–6, 15–19, 20–24; 26:31–34; 44:20; Hel. 5:51; 15:9). This major division of Lamanite society had significant political impact: the identity of some of these converts remained Lamanite, but distinct from those who rejected the religion; others chose to be numbered among the Nephites (3 Ne. 2:12, 14–16); and the unconverted Lamanites were strengthened by numerous dissenters from Nephite subgroups (Alma 43:13), some of whom chose explicitly to retain their former identities (3 Ne. 6:3).

After the destructions that occurred at the time of Christ's crucifixion and the subsequent conversions (3 Ne. 11–28), a new society was established in which ethnic as well as economic differences were overcome, and there were no "Lamanites, nor any manner of -ites; but they were in one, the children of Christ" (4 Ne. 1:17). This situation persisted until almost the end of the second century A.D., when those who rejected the Christian church, regardless of their ancestry, "had revolted from the church and taken upon them the name of Lamanites; therefore there began to be Lamanites again in the land" (4 Ne. 1:20). Divisions increased, so that by A.D. 231 "there arose a people who were called the Nephites, and they were true believers in Christ; and among them there were those who were called by the Lamanites—Jacobites, and Josephites, and Zoramites. . . . And . . . they who rejected the gospel were called Lamanites, and Lemuelites, and Ishmaelites" (4 Ne. 1:36, 38).

It had been prophesied that eventually only Lamanite peoples and those who joined them would remain of the original groups (Alma 45:13–14). After the final battles between Lamanites and Nephites, only those who accepted Lamanite rule survived in Book of Mormon lands (Morm. 6:15).

LAMANITES IN EARLY LDS HISTORY.   At the beginning of LDS Church history, one reason the Book of Mormon was published was so that it could be taken to the Lamanites (D&C 19:26–27). Within six months of the Church's organization, missionaries were sent to people thought to have Lamanite ancestry (D&C 28:8; 32:2).

[*See also* Book of Mormon Peoples; Native Americans.]

BIBLIOGRAPHY
"The Church and Descendants of Book of Mormon Peoples." *Ensign* 5 (Dec. 1975); the entire issue devoted to this topic.
De Hoyos, Arturo. *The Old and the Modern Lamanite.* Provo, Utah, 1970.
Sorenson, John L. *An Ancient American Setting for the Book of Mormon.* Salt Lake City, 1985.
Tyler, S. Lyman. *Modern Results of the Lamanite Dispersion: The Indians of the Americas.* Provo, Utah, 1965.
Widtsoe, John A., and Franklin S. Harris, Jr. *Seven Claims of the Book of Mormon.* Independence, Mo., 1935.

GORDON C. THOMASSON

LAW OF MOSES

Distinctive views concerning the law of Moses and its relationship to Christ and to the attainment of individual salvation are set forth in the Book of Mormon and Doctrine and Covenants. The Church of Jesus Christ of Latter-day Saints teaches that this law was given by God to MOSES, that it formed part of a peculiar covenant of obedience and favor between God and his people, that it symbolized and foreshadowed things to come, and that it was fulfilled in the atonement of Jesus Christ.

The law of Moses is best understood in a broad sense. It consists of "judgments," "statutes," "ordinances," and "commandments." The Book of Mormon refers to its also including various "performances," "sacrifices," and "burnt offerings." Nowhere in scripture is its full breadth, depth, diversity, and definition made explicit. On such matters, information can be drawn from the Pentateuch itself (the Torah) and from biblical scholarship, but one can only conjecture as to what these terms meant to Book of Mormon writers.

A narrow definition would confine the law of Moses to a body of prohibitions and commands set forth in separate, unrelated literary units within the first five books of the Bible. This view makes it difficult to speak of "biblical law," since these provisions are not drawn together as a unity by the Torah itself. The scattered codes and series include the Covenant Code (Ex. 20:23–23:19), Deuteronomic Law (Deut. 12–26), the Holiness Code (Lev. 17–26), purity laws (Lev. 11–15), festival rituals (Deut. 16), regulations pertaining to sacrifices (Num. 28–29), and the TEN COMMANDMENTS (Ex. 20:2–17; Deut. 5:6–21). While some biblical scholars conclude that "these were once independent units, subsisting in their own right, each having its own purpose and sphere of validity, and having been transmitted individually for its own sake in the first place" (Noth, p. 7), Latter-day Saints generally accept at face value statements in the Bible that attribute authorship to Moses, but the Church has taken no official stand concerning the collection and transmission of these legal texts in the Pentateuch. Scribes and copyists evidently made a few changes after the time of Moses (e.g., compare Moses 1–5 with Gen. 1–6).

Compounding the question of what was meant by the term "law of Moses" in the Book of Mormon is the fact that the "five books of Moses" that the Nephites possessed predated Ezra's redaction and canonization of the Pentateuch (444 B.C.). Quoted passages (e.g., Mosiah 13:12–24), however, indicate that the Nephite laws were substantially similar to the biblical texts that Jews and Christians have today.

As early as the third century A.D., the Jewish view held that the commandments numbered 613. Rabbi Simlai reportedly stated that "613 commandments were revealed to Moses at Sinai, 365 being prohibitions equal in number to the solar days, and 248 being mandates corresponding in number to the limbs [sic] of the human body" (Encyclopedia Judaica 5:760, quoting Talmud Bavli, Makkot 23b). About a third of these commandments have long been obsolete, such as those relating to the tabernacle and the conquest of Canaan. Others were directed to special classes, such as the Nazarites, judges, the king, or the high priest, or to circumstances that would rarely occur. Excluding these, about a hundred apply to the whole people and range from the spiritually sublime to the mundane. Examples of eternally relevant commandments of the law of Moses are the Ten Commandments and those relating to loving God, worshiping God, loving one's neighbor, loving the stranger, giving charity to the poor, dealing honestly, not seeking revenge, and not bearing a grudge. Other commandments cover a kaleidoscope of daily matters, including valuing houses and fields, laws of inheritance, paying wages, agriculture, animal husbandry, and forbidden foods. Jewish scholars classify these as commandments vis-à-vis God and commandments vis-à-vis fellow human beings (Mishnah *Yoma* 8:9).

Two other definitions should be mentioned. One identifies the law of Moses as coextensive with the Pentateuch. Around the time of Christ, New Testament writers sometimes called the Pentateuch "the law" (Luke 24:44; Gal. 4:21), even though the word "torah" has broader meaning (i.e., "teachings") and the Pentateuch contains poetry and narratives in addition to commandments, and some passages speak to all persons and nations (Gen. 9:1–7). The other defines the law as theologically synonymous with the doctrinal belief, whether mistaken or not, that salvation is dependent upon the keeping of commandments, thus distinguishing the law from grace, which for many Christians eliminates the task of sorting out which Mosaic laws are still in force.

Agreeing in some respects and departing in others from traditional Jewish or Christian views, the main lines of LDS belief about the law of Moses are as follows:

1. Jesus Christ was Jehovah, the God of the Old Testament who gave the law to Moses (3 Ne. 15:5; *TPJS*, p. 276). Jesus, speaking after his atonement and resurrection, stated, "The law is fulfilled that was given unto Moses. Behold, I am he that gave the law, and I am he who covenanted with my people Israel" (3 Ne. 15:4–9).

2. The entire law was in several senses fulfilled, completed, superseded, and enlivened by Jesus Christ. Jesus said, "In me it hath *all* been fulfilled" (3 Ne. 12:18; italics added). Its "great and eternal gospel truths" (*MD*, p. 398) are applicable through Jesus Christ in all dispensations as he continues to reveal his will to prophets "like unto Moses" (2 Ne. 3:9–11).

3. Latter-day Saints believe that the law of Moses was issued to the Israelites as a preparatory gospel to be a schoolmaster to bring them to Christ and the fulness of his gospel (Gal. 3:24; cf. Jacob 4:5; Alma 34:14). The authority to act in the name of God is embodied in two priesthoods, the Melchizedek, or higher, which embraces all divinely delegated authority and extends to the fulness of the law of the gospel, and Aaronic, or lesser, which extends only to lesser things, such as the law of carnal commandments and baptism (D&C 84:26–27). While Moses and his predecessors had the higher priesthood and the fulness of the gospel of Christ, both of which were to be given to the children of Israel, "they hardened their hearts and could not endure [God's] presence; therefore, the Lord in his wrath . . . took Moses out of their midst, and the Holy Priesthood also; and the lesser priesthood continued" (D&C 84:23–24; see Heb. 3:16–19; Mosiah 3:14; *TPJS*, p. 60).

4. Book of Mormon people brought the law of Moses with them from Jerusalem. Even though they endeavored to observe it strictly until the coming of Christ (e.g., 2 Ne. 5:10; Alma 30:3), they believed in Christ and knew that salvation did not come by the law alone but by Christ (2 Ne. 25:23–24) and understood that the law would be superseded by the Messiah (Mosiah 13:27–28; 2 Ne. 25:23–25).

5. For Latter-day Saints, all things are given of God to man as types and shadows of the redeeming and atoning acts of Christ (2 Ne. 11:4; Mosiah 13:31). Thus, the law of Moses typified various aspects of the atonement of Christ.

6. Covenant making, promises, and obedience to commandments are part of the fulness of the gospel of Christ: "Through the Atonement of Christ, all mankind may be saved, by obedience to the laws and ordinances of the Gospel" (A of F 3). Both for Latter-day Saints and regarding Jewish observance of the law of Moses, grace, faith, and works are all essential to salvation: "It is by grace that we are saved, after all we can do" (2 Ne. 25:23). No mortal's obedience to law will ever be perfect. By law alone, no one will be saved. The grace of God makes up the deficit. The Church does not subscribe to a doctrine of free-standing grace unrelated to instructions and expectations required of man. It does have commandments relating to diet, modesty, and chastity, as well as many ordinances,

such as baptism, laying on of hands, and WASHINGS AND ANOINT-
INGS. If man were perfect, salvation could come on that account;
walking in the way of the Lord would be perfectly observed. Since
man is mortal and imperfect, God in his love makes known the
way his children should walk, and extends grace "after all they
can do."

BIBLIOGRAPHY
Daube, David. *Studies in Biblical Law.* New York, 1969.
Falk, Ze'ev. *Hebrew Law in Biblical Times.* Jerusalem, 1964.
Jackson, Kent P. "The Law of Moses and the Atonement of Christ." In *Studies in
Scripture,* Vol. 3, pp. 153–72. Salt Lake City, 1985.
Noth, Martin. *The Laws in the Pentateuch and Other Studies.* Edinburgh, 1966.
Patrick, Dale. *Old Testament Law.* Atlanta, 1985.

DOUGLAS H. PARKER
ZE'EV W. FALK

LECTURES ON FAITH

Included under the title "Lectures on Faith" in the 1835 edition of
the Doctrine and Covenants, these seven "lectures on theology" (*HC*
2:176) were presented to the School for the Elders in the early winter
of 1834–1835 in Kirtland, Ohio. The school was organized to help
Church leaders and missionaries "[qualify] themselves as messengers of Jesus Christ, to be ready to do His will in carrying glad tidings to all that would open their eyes, ears, and hearts," by being
"more perfectly instructed in the great things of God" (*HC* 2:169–70).

The lectures address three major themes: "first, faith itself—
what it is; secondly, the object on which it rests; and thirdly, the
effects which flow from it" (Dahl and Tate, p. 31). The first lecture
explains what faith is; the second shows how the knowledge of God
first came into the world and traces this knowledge from Adam to
Abraham; the third and fourth discuss the necessary and unchanging attributes of God; the fifth deals with the nature of God the
Father, his son Jesus Christ, and the Holy Ghost; the sixth teaches
that acquiring faith unto salvation depends on knowing that one's life
is pleasing to God, which knowledge can be obtained only by the
willingness to sacrifice all earthly things; and the seventh treats the

fruits of faith—perspective, power, and ultimately perfection. In the 1835 edition of the Doctrine and Covenants the seven lectures comprised seventy-four pages. The lectures are organized in numbered paragraphs in which principles are stated and supporting scriptures quoted. Appended to the first five lectures are lists of questions and answers restating the principles discussed. These catechisms are about as long as the lectures themselves.

No clear evidence documents who actually wrote the lectures. Recent authorship studies ascribe the wording of the lectures "mainly to Sidney Rigdon," with Joseph Smith substantially involved, and others perhaps having some influence. Joseph Smith's close involvement with the lectures is suggested by Willard Richards's history, which reports that Joseph was "busily engaged" in November in making "preparations for the School for the Elders, wherein they might be more perfectly instructed in the great things of God" (HC 2:169–70). The same source indicates that in January 1835 Joseph was engaged in "preparing the lectures on theology for publication" (HC 2:180). From these references and other circumstances it seems evident that the lectures were prepared and published with Joseph Smith's approval (Dahl and Tate, pp. 7–10; 16, n. 8).

Until 1921 the "Lectures on Faith" were printed in almost all the English-language editions of the Doctrine and Covenants, and in many, but not all, non-English editions. An introductory statement in the 1921 edition of the Doctrine and Covenants explains that the lectures were deleted because "they were never presented to nor accepted by the Church as being otherwise than theological lectures or lessons" (see DOCTRINE AND COVENANTS EDITIONS). The decision may also have been influenced by what many readers have perceived as conflicts between statements about the Godhead in the fifth lecture and certain later revelations (D&C 130; Dahl and Tate, pp. 16–19). Others have found these conflicts to be more apparent than real and have attempted reconciliations (R. Millet, in Dahl and Tate, pp. 221–40).

The "Lectures on Faith" have been published separately from the Doctrine and Covenants for the LDS community four times: in 1840–1843, by Parley P. Pratt in England; in 1940, by compiler N. B. Lundwall in Salt Lake City; in 1985, by Deseret Book Company, Salt Lake City; and in 1990, by the Religious Studies Center at

Brigham Young University. They were published separately twice by schismatic groups: in 1845–1846, by Sidney Rigdon (in Pittsburgh, soon after he left the Church); and in 1952, by the Reorganized Church of Jesus Christ of Latter Day Saints. The Religious Studies Center publication includes a newly edited version of the lectures designed to make the text more readable. It provides textual comparison charts that identify all textual changes that have occurred in various printings of the lectures from 1835 to 1990. It also contains a summary of historical information, a doctrinal discussion of the topic of each lecture, and an extensive bibliography (Dahl and Tate).

Most members of The Church of Jesus Christ of Latter-day Saints are not acquainted with the text of the "Lectures on Faith," though many may recognize excerpts that are occasionally quoted in speeches and writings of leaders and scholars. A sampling of these quotations as printed in the 1990 edited edition follows:

Lecture One

1. Faith [is] the first principle in revealed religion, and the foundation of all righteousness.

9. Faith is the assurance which men have of the existence of things which they have not seen and . . . the principle of action in all intelligent beings.

12. As faith is the moving cause of all action in temporal concerns, so it is in spiritual.

13. But faith is not only the principle of action, but it is also the principle of power in all intelligent beings, whether in heaven or on earth.

15. The principle of power which existed in the bosom of God, by which he framed the worlds, was faith.

Lecture Two

55. Let us here observe that after any members of the human family are made acquainted with the important fact that there is a God who has created and does uphold all things, the extent of their knowledge respecting his character and glory will depend upon their diligence and faithfulness in seeking after him, until, like Enoch, the brother of Jared, and Moses, they shall obtain faith in God and power with him to behold him face to face.

Lecture Three

2–5. Let us here observe that three things are necessary for any rational and intelligent being to exercise faith in God unto life and salvation. First, the idea that he actually exists; Secondly, a *correct* idea of his character, perfections, and attributes; Thirdly, an actual knowledge that the course of life which one is pursuing is according to His will.

Lecture Four

11. Without the knowledge of all things God would not be able to save any portion of his creatures. For it is the knowledge which he has of all things from the beginning to the end that enables him to give that understanding to his creatures by which they are made partakers of eternal life. And if it were not for the idea existing in the minds of men that God has all knowledge, it would be impossible for them to exercise faith in him.

13. It is also necessary that men should have the idea of the existence of the attribute justice in God in order to exercise faith in him unto life and salvation. For without the idea of the existence of the attribute justice in the Deity, men could not have confidence sufficient to place themselves under his guidance and direction. For they would be filled with fear and doubt lest the Judge of all the earth would not do right, and thus fear or doubt existing in the mind would preclude the possibility of the exercise of faith in him for life and salvation. But when the idea of the existence of the attribute justice in the Deity is fairly planted in the mind, it leaves no room for doubt to get into the heart; and the mind is enabled to cast itself upon the Almighty without fear, and without doubt, and with the most unshaken confidence, believing that the Judge of all the earth will do right.

Lecture Five

2. There are two personages who constitute the great, matchless, governing, and supreme power over all things, by whom all things were created and made. . . . They are the Father and the Son: the Father being a personage of spirit, glory, and power, possessing all perfection and fulness. The Son, who was in the bosom of the Father, is a personage of tabernacle, made or fashioned like unto man, being in the form and likeness of man, or rather man was formed after his likeness and in his image. He is also the express image and likeness of the personage of the

Father, possessing all the fulness of the Father, or the same fulness with the Father; being begotten of him, and ordained from before the foundation of the world to be a propitiation for the sins of all those who should believe on his name. He is called the Son because of the flesh . . . possessing the same mind with the Father, which mind is the Holy Spirit that bears record of the Father and the Son. These three are one; or, in other words, these three constitute the great, matchless, governing and supreme power over all things.

Q & A 15. Do the Father, Son, and Holy Spirit constitute the Godhead? They do.

Lecture Six

2. It is essential for any person to have an actual knowledge that the course of life which he is pursuing is according to the will of God to enable him to have that confidence in God without which no person can obtain eternal life.

4. Such was and always will be the situation of the Saints of God. Unless they have an actual knowledge that the course they are pursuing is according to the will of God, they will grow weary in their minds and faint.

7. Let us here observe that a religion that does not require the sacrifice of all things never has power sufficient to produce the faith necessary unto life and salvation. For from the first existence of man, the faith necessary unto the enjoyment of life and salvation never could be obtained without the sacrifice of all earthly things. It is through this sacrifice, and this only, that God has ordained that men should enjoy eternal life. And it is through the medium of the sacrifice of all earthly things that men do actually know that they are doing the things that are well pleasing in the sight of God.

12. But those who have not made this sacrifice to God do not know that the course which they pursue is well pleasing in his sight. For whatever may be their belief or their opinion, it is a matter of doubt and uncertainty in their mind; and where doubt and uncertainty are, there faith is not, nor can it be. For doubt and faith do not exist in the same person at the same time. So persons whose minds are under doubts and fears cannot have unshaken confidence, and where unshaken confidence is not, there faith is weak. And where faith is weak, the persons will not be able to contend against all the opposition, tribulations, and afflictions

which they will have to encounter in order to be heirs of God and joint-heirs with Christ Jesus. But they will grow weary in their minds, and the adversary will have power over them and destroy them.

Lecture Seven

19. All things which pertain to life and godliness are the effects of faith.
20. When faith comes, it brings its train of attendants with it—apostles, prophets, evangelists, pastors, teachers, gifts, wisdom, knowledge, miracles, healings, tongues, interpretation of tongues, etc. All these appear when faith appears on the earth and disappear when it disappears from the earth. For these are the effects of faith and always have attended and always will attend it. For where faith is, there will the knowledge of God be, also, with all things which pertain thereto: revelations, visions, and dreams, as well as every other necessary thing, so the possessors of faith may be perfected and obtain salvation [Dahl and Tate, pp. 31–104].

The Prophet Joseph Smith, Oliver Cowdery, Sidney Rigdon, and Frederick G. Williams, who compiled the first edition of the Doctrine and Covenants, said in the "Lectures on Faith" preface "that it contains, in short, the leading items of the religion which we have professed to believe," and "we have . . . endeavored to present *our* belief, though in few words, and when we say this, we humbly trust that it is the faith and principles of this society as a body" (Dahl and Tate, pp. 29–30).

Although it is impossible to evaluate the long-term impact of the lectures on LDS belief and teaching, the process of producing the lectures led early Church leaders to articulate and synthesize some of what they had learned from the revelations of the Restoration with the understanding of the Bible that they inherited from American Christianity. Although these lectures have received limited attention from most Latter-day Saints, others have taken them quite seriously and praised their value. LDS scripturalist and apostle Bruce R. McConkie wrote regarding the lectures, "They were not themselves classed as revelations, but in them is to be found some of the best lesson material ever prepared on the Godhead; on the character, perfections, and attributes of God; on faith, miracles, and sacrifice. They can be studied with great profit by all gospel scholars" (*MD*, p. 439). The 1990 republication of the lectures signals the desire of some

LDS scholars to stimulate interest in their historical and doctrinal significance for the Church.

BIBLIOGRAPHY

Dahl, Larry E., and Charles D. Tate, eds. *The Lectures on Faith in Historical Perspective.* Provo, Utah, 1990.

Gentry, Leland H. "What of the Lectures on Faith?" *BYU Studies* 19 (Fall 1978):5–19.

Larsen, Wayne A.; Alvin C. Rencher; and Tim Layton. "Who Wrote the Book of Mormon? An Analysis of Wordprints." *BYU Studies* 20 (Spring 1980):249, app. E ("Lectures on Faith"); rev. repr. in *Book of Mormon Authorship,* ed. Noel B. Reynolds, pp. 183–84. Provo, Utah, 1982.

Phipps, Alan J. "The Lectures on Faith: An Authorship Study." Master's thesis, Brigham Young University, 1977.

Van Wagoner, Richard S.; Steven C. Walker; and Allen D. Roberts. "The 'Lectures on Faith': A Case Study in Decanonization." *Dialogue* 20 (Fall 1987):71–77.

LARRY E. DAHL

LEHI

The patriarch and prophet Lehi led his family from Jerusalem to the Western Hemisphere about 600 B.C. and was the progenitor of two major BOOK OF MORMON PEOPLES, the NEPHITES and the LAMANITES. His visions and prophecies were concerned chiefly with the pending destruction of Jerusalem, the mortal ministry of the coming Messiah—including the time of his coming and the prophet who would precede him—and future events among his own descendants in the promised land. His words provided spiritual guidance to both lines of his posterity during their mutual history (1 Ne. 1, 8, 10; 2 Ne. 1–3). Several of his prophecies concerning his posterity remain to be fulfilled. Although Lehi wrote much, only portions were preserved in the present Book of Mormon from the records of two of his sons NEPHI₁ and JACOB (cf. 1 Ne. 1:16–17; 19:1; Jacob 2:23–34; 3:5; see Brown).

At the time of his first known vision, Lehi lived near Jerusalem, was familiar with "the learning of the Jews," and possessed "gold and silver, and all manner of riches" (1 Ne. 1:2; 3:16). He knew the Egyptian language and was familiar with desert nomadic life. Some scholars have suggested that Lehi was a merchant or smith with ties to Egypt (*CWHN* 5:34–42; 6:58–92).

His life was dramatically changed when he beheld a "pillar of fire" and "saw and heard much" while praying about the predicted fall of Jerusalem (1 Ne. 1:6). In a vision he saw God and a radiant being—accompanied by twelve others—who gave him a book in which he read of the impending destruction of the city and of "the coming of a Messiah, and also the redemption of the world" (1 Ne. 1:19). Like the speeches of his contemporary JEREMIAH, Lehi's warnings to the people of Jerusalem roused strong opposition. Surrounded by growing hatred, he was warned by God that the people sought his life; therefore, he was to flee with his family, consisting of his wife, Sariah, his sons, LAMAN, Lemuel, Sam, and Nephi, and his daughters (1 Ne. 1:8–2:5).

Sariah once accused her husband of being a "visionary man" in a hard test of her faith (1 Ne. 5:2). The phrase aptly characterizes Lehi, for he dreamed dreams and saw visions through which God guided his family to the promised land. After fleeing Jerusalem, at divine behest Lehi twice sent his sons back: once to obtain written records (containing the holy scriptures, a record of the Jews from the beginning, the law, prophecies, and genealogical records) needed to preserve the family's history, language and religion; and a second time to invite ISHMAEL and his family—including marriageable daughters—to join the exodus (chaps. 3–4, 7).

Through revelation, Lehi instructed his sons where game could be hunted in the wilderness (16:30–31). In this he was assisted by a curious compasslike object (*see* LIAHONA) that operated according to the faith, diligence, and heed they gave it (16:10, 28–29).

One of Lehi's grandest visions was of the Tree of Life (1 Ne. 8). In a highly symbolic setting, Lehi saw the prospects for his family members measured against the plan of salvation. Nephi had the same vision opened to him and gave details and interpretation to what his father had seen (1 Ne. 11–14). Lehi first saw a man dressed in white who led him through a "dark and dreary waste." After traveling many hours, he prayed for divine help and found himself in a large field where there grew a tree whose fruit was white and desirable (symbolic of God's love). When he urged his family to come and partake, all did so except Laman and Lemuel. Lehi also saw a path, alongside which ran an iron rod (representing God's word) leading to the tree and extending along the bank of a river. Many people pressing forward to reach the path became lost in a mist of darkness (temptations); some reached the tree and partook, only to become ashamed and fall away; others, following the rod of iron, reached the tree and enjoyed the fruit. On the other side of the river Lehi saw a large building (the pride of the world) whose inhabitants ridiculed those eating the fruit. LDS scholars have pointed out that the features of Lehi's dream are quite at home in the desert in which Lehi was traveling (*CWHN* 6:253–64; cf. Griggs; Welch).

Lehi's prophecies concerned the future redemption of Israel. He spoke of the destruction of Jerusalem (587 B.C.), the taking of the Jews to Babylon, and their subsequent return to Jerusalem. He foretold the mission of JOHN THE BAPTIST and the Messiah's coming, death, and resurrection. Finally, Lehi compared Israel's eventual scattering to "an olive-tree, whose branches should be broken off and . . . scattered upon all the face of the earth" (1 Ne. 10:12; cf. ALLEGORY OF ZENOS).

In the wilderness Sariah bore two sons, Jacob and Joseph (1 Ne. 18:7). Apparently the journey was so difficult that she and Lehi aged substantially. During the transoceanic voyage, their grief—caused by the rebellion of their two eldest sons—brought them close to death (18:17–18).

In the New World, Lehi gathered his family before his death to give them final teachings and blessings (2 Ne. 1–4). He taught them that he had received a great promise regarding his descendants and the land they now possessed. This promise was conditioned upon their righteousness: "Inasmuch as ye shall keep my commandments ye shall prosper in the land; but inasmuch as ye will not keep my commandments ye shall be cut off from my presence" (2 Ne. 1:20; cf. Abr. 2:6).

Lehi addressed his son Jacob about the plan of salvation (2 Ne. 2). Instead of using imagery, he explained it plainly and logically. He taught that while all know good from evil, many have fallen short. However, the Messiah has paid the debt if men and women will accept his help with a contrite spirit. He further explained that a fundamental opposition in all things exists so that people must choose. He reasoned that, as freedom of choice allowed ADAM and EVE to fall, so it permits each to choose between "liberty and eternal life, through the great Mediator of all men, or to choose captivity and death, according to the captivity and power of the devil" (2 Ne. 2:27).

Before giving his final blessings to others in the family (2 Ne. 4:3–11), Lehi spoke to Joseph, his youngest (2 Ne. 3), mentioning two other Josephs: JOSEPH who was sold into Egypt, and another, of whom the first Joseph had prophesied—Joseph Smith. He then set forth Joseph Smith's mission of bringing forth the Book of Mormon, prophesying that a "cry from the dust" would summon Lehi's seed (2 Ne. 3:19–25), and he promised the sons and daughters of Laman and Lemuel, "in the end thy seed shall be blessed" (2 Ne. 4:9).

After Lehi's death, family dissentions forced Nephi and others who believed the revelations of God to separate from the group led by the two oldest brothers, causing a rupture in the colony. While Lehi lived, his family stayed together, a demonstration of his leadership abilities.

[*See also* Book of Mormon: First Book of Nephi.]

BIBLIOGRAPHY

Brown, S. Kent. "Lehi's Personal Record: Quest for a Missing Source." *BYU Studies* 24 (Winter 1984):19–42.

Griggs, C. Wilfred. "The Book of Mormon As an Ancient Book." *BYU Studies* 22 (Summer 1982):259–78.

Nibley, Hugh. *Lehi in the Desert, An Approach to the Book of Mormon,* and *Since Cumorah.* In *CWHN,* Vols. 5–7.

Welch, John W. "The Narrative of Zosimus and the Book of Mormon." *BYU Studies* 22 (Summer 1982):311–32.

S. KENT BROWN
TERRENCE L. SZINK

LIAHONA

The Liahona was a compass or director "prepared . . . by the hand of the Lord" for the Book of Mormon prophet LEHI as he and his family traveled in the wilderness (2 Ne. 5:12). It was shown to the Prophet Joseph Smith and the Three Witnesses in 1829 along with the Book of Mormon plates (D&C 17:1). The Liahona was also understood as a symbol for the words of Christ: "For just as surely as this [Liahona] did bring our fathers, by following its course, to the promised land, shall the words of Christ, if we follow their course, carry us . . . into a far better land of promise" (Alma 37:45).

Described as a ball made of fine brass and "of curious workmanship," it had two spindles, one pointing the direction Lehi's family should travel (1 Ne. 16:10). The term "Liahona" appears only once in the Book of Mormon (Alma 37:38). It was usually referred to as "the ball" (1 Ne. 16:16, 26–27; etc.), "compass" (1 Ne. 18:12; Alma 37:43–44; etc.), or "director" (Mosiah 1:16; cf. D&C 17:1).

Lehi found the Liahona, provided by the Lord (Alma 37:38), outside of his tent door while camping in the wilderness after leaving Jerusalem (1 Ne. 16:10). As his party traveled through the Arabian desert and across the ocean to the promised land, one of the spindles pointed the direction to travel. Moreover, the Liahona was a medium through which God communicated with Lehi's family. Written messages occasionally appeared on it, giving them specific directions (1 Ne. 16:26–29).

The instrument worked according to the faith and obedience of Lehi's family. When they lacked faith or disobeyed, it ceased to function. Passed down from generation to generation along with the sacred records, it was stored with the GOLD PLATES.

Liahona is the title of an international Spanish-language magazine published by the Church.

BIBLIOGRAPHY
Nibley, Hugh. *Since Cumorah.* 2nd ed. *CWHN* 7:251–63. Salt Lake City, 1988.

DOUGLAS KENT LUDLOW

LORD'S PRAYER

Latter-day Saints regard the Lord's Prayer, which appears twice in the New Testament and once in the Book of Mormon (Matt. 6:9–13; Luke 11:2–4; 3 Ne. 13:9–13), as a guide for all prayer, whether public or private. The three versions teach similar principles but are not identical. The JOSEPH SMITH TRANSLATION (JST) of the Bible clarifies some phrases in the biblical texts.

Luke gives a version of the Lord's Prayer after Jesus was asked by his disciples to "teach us to pray" (Luke 11:1). In the sermons recounted in Matthew and in the Book of Mormon, Jesus introduces the prayer by first cautioning his listeners to avoid "vain repetitions" and to pray "after this manner," indicating that the prayer is meant as a pattern.

All versions of the Lord's Prayer open with the salutation "Our Father," which implies a close and abiding relationship between God and human beings, his spirit children, and sets the pattern of addressing prayers to God the Father.

The salutation is followed by the phrase "hallowed be thy name," which exemplifies respect and a worshipful attitude appropriate to the holy nature of prayer. Then, after expressing hope for the divine kingdom to come, the Savior submits his will to God's with the words "thy will be done in earth, as it is in heaven" (Matt. 6:10), exemplifying another important component of prayer.

After setting a proper context for prayer, Christ makes his first request—for "daily bread." When regarded as a model for prayer, this phrase can be seen as supplication for both temporal necessities and spiritual food. Christ's second request, that God "forgive us our debts, as we forgive our debtors" (Matt. 6:12 and 3 Ne. 13:11), appears in Luke as "forgive us our sins; for we also forgive every one that is indebted to us" (Luke 11:4). An important element in personal prayer is acknowledging and asking forgiveness for one's sins, but always in conjunction with forgiving the offenses of others (cf. D&C 64:10).

The texts then include a phrase that is perhaps the most difficult to understand in most common translations of the Lord's Prayer—"lead us not into temptation," which could be read to imply that God might influence toward evil unless implored to do otherwise. This problem is resolved in the JST, which reads, "And suffer us not to be led into temptation" (JST Matt. 6:14; cf. the Syriac translation; see also James 1:13). Christ's purpose appears to be to inspire mortals to ask daily for God's help as they try to resist evil and to live purely.

In closing the prayer, Christ again acknowledges God's power and glory and then ends with "Amen," as do all LDS prayers. (On the long ending of the Lord's Prayer, cf. Welch, 1990, pp. 157–60).

By praying with their personal heartfelt feelings "after this manner," rather than reciting the Lord's Prayer as a memorized piece,

Latter-day Saints seek to find true communion with God the Father, through his Son Jesus Christ.

[*See also* Sermon on the Mount.]

BIBLIOGRAPHY
Welch, John W. "The Lord's Prayers." *Ensign* 6 (Jan. 1976):14–17.
———. *The Sermon at the Temple and the Sermon on the Mount.* Salt Lake City, 1990.

SUE BERGIN

LOST SCRIPTURE

Latter-day Saints recognize that many ancient scriptures have been lost. Some contents of these sacred records are known, but much remains obscure. Latter-day Saints look forward to a time when all things revealed from God will be restored and made known again.

The Bible is of inestimable worth; nevertheless, it testifies to its own incompleteness. It mentions sacred works that are no longer available (Josh. 10:13; 1 Kgs. 11:41; 1 Chr. 29:29; Eph. 3:3; Col. 4:16; Jude 1:14–15), and it refers to Old Testament prophecies presently missing (*see* Matt. 2:23; John 8:56).

Likewise, the Book of Mormon identifies several prophetic writings absent from the Bible, such as words of ZENOS, ZENOCK, NEUM, EZIAS, and JOSEPH OF EGYPT (see also *HC* 2:236), which were found on the brass PLATES. Their prophecies dealt with the future of Israel and the coming of Jesus Christ. Nephi's brother Jacob stated that all the prophets had testified of Jesus Christ (Jacob 4:4–6; 7:9–11; cf. John 5:39), a fact not readily apparent in the Old Testament as it now exists. The Prophet Joseph Smith wrote in 1832, "From sundry revelations which had been received, it was apparent that many important points touching the salvation of man, had been taken from the Bible, or lost before it was compiled" (*HC* 1:245; cf. 1 Ne. 13:26–42). Remedying this, in part, was one of the purposes of the JOSEPH SMITH TRANSLATION OF THE BIBLE (JST).

The Doctrine and Covenants speaks of lost writings of JOHN THE BELOVED (D&C 7:1–8; 93:5–18) and refers to a law of dealing with enemies given by God to Abraham, Isaac, Jacob, and Joseph, but not found in the Bible (D&C 98:28–37); the Pearl of Great Price restores a portion of the writings of Abraham, Moses, Enoch, and Adam, especially about the Creation and early history of God's dealings with man. Enoch mentioned an ancient BOOK OF REMEMBRANCE and a genealogy of Adam (Moses 6:5–8, 46), along with now-missing blessings and prophecies uttered by Adam and his descendants at the valley of Adam-ondi-Ahman before Adam's death (D&C 107:53–57).

Many Book of Mormon source materials are not now accessible. The GOLD PLATES given to Joseph Smith in 1827 mention a record of LEHI (1 Ne. 1:16–17) and other writings of NEPHI₁ (1 Ne. 9:1–6). JACOB, MORMON, and MORONI₂ note that they could scarcely include "the hundredth part" of what could have been written (Jacob 3:13; 3 Ne. 5:8; Ether 15:33). The Lord often commanded the Nephite record keepers not to write or circulate certain things (see 1 Ne. 14:25–28; 3 Ne. 26:11–12), and Joseph Smith was similarly commanded by the Lord not to translate a large sealed portion of the gold plates (D&C 17:6; see also Ether 4:1–7; 5:1–6).

In another, broader sense, much "scripture" was never written down by mortals at all. Whatever God's authorized servants say "when moved upon by the Holy Ghost" is scripture (D&C 68:1–6). If all the acts and words of the Savior had been recorded, John said "the world itself could not contain the books that should be written" (John 20:30–31; 21:25). Also not in written form are myriads of inspired utterances of prophets and apostles and of other men and women filled with the Holy Ghost. Such scripture is not lost to God. "All things are written by the Father," Jesus said (3 Ne. 27:26), and testimonies spoken on earth are recorded in heaven for the angels to look upon (D&C 62:3) and will be recalled at some future day.

BIBLIOGRAPHY

Matthews, Robert J. *A Bible! A Bible!* Salt Lake City, 1990.

McConkie, Joseph Fielding. *Prophets and Prophecy,* pp. 141–54. Salt Lake City, 1988.

ROBERT A. CLOWARD

MALACHI, PROPHECIES OF

The importance of Malachi's prophecies is reflected in their prominence in nonbiblical LDS scriptures. For example, the resurrected Jesus instructed hearers in the Western Hemisphere (c. A.D. 34) to include Malachi 3 and 4 with their records (3 Ne. 24–25), and references to Malachi's prophecies appear in the DOCTRINE AND COVENANTS and the PEARL OF GREAT PRICE. Those prophecies pertaining to the latter days concern (1) the Lord's latter-day advent; (2) the messenger sent to prepare his way; (3) the sons of Levi and their offering; (4) tithing; (5) the lot of the wicked; and (6) Elijah's mission. Some of his timeless teachings pertain to such matters as the fatherhood of God and brotherhood of man (Mal. 2:10), the problems of divorce (2:14–16), and problems of immorality (3:5–6).

Malachi prophesied that the Lord would come suddenly to his temple (Mal. 3:1). Latter-day Saints believe that one such appearance occurred in the Kirtland Temple when Jesus appeared there in 1836. Other messengers also restored keys (D&C 110), making possible the "complete salvation and exaltation of all who are willing to obey the gospel" (Smith 2:47).

The "messenger" sent to prepare the way (Mal. 3:1) can refer to all messengers whom God may send to restore blessings and authority lost through apostasy (*see* ELIAS). Most messengers who have assisted in establishing the latter-day kingdom of God have bestowed priesthood powers and keys vital to the authoritative performance of saving ordinances (D&C 1:17–18; 128:20–21).

The Lord promised that he will "purge" the Levites so that they will become worthy to function again (Mal. 3:3). When he has done this, he will direct the restoration of sacrifices (cf. D&C 13). Joseph Smith wrote that the "offering of [animal] sacrifice has ever been connected and forms a part of the duties of the Priesthood. It began with the Priesthood, and will be continued until after the coming of Christ . . . when the [Aaronic] Priesthood is restored with all its authority, power and blessings" (HC 4:211).

Malachi emphasizes tithing. Indicting those who have "gone away" by failing to pay tithes and offerings, the Lord promises that if they will return, "I will return" (Mal. 3:7). The principle of tithing, which was practiced as early as Abraham (cf. Gen. 14:20; 28:22), has been renewed in the latter days (D&C 119:4), and blessings are assured for those who give tithes and offerings. The "windows of heaven will be opened," including the pouring out of "revelations" as a reward for such sacrifice (Lee, p. 16).

In the last days, trouble awaits the wicked. "The day cometh, that shall burn as an oven; . . . and all that do wickedly, shall be stubble." They shall be burned, leaving neither "root [ancestors] nor branch [children]" (Mal. 4:1; cf. T. Burton, IE 70 [Dec. 1967]:80–82). This burning "is not a figure of speech" (Smith 1:238). "It may be . . . that nothing except the power of faith and the authority of the priesthood can save individuals" (McConkie, p. 93). But the "Sun of righteousness" (Mal. 4:2; cf. 3 Ne. 25:2) will bring the healing power of the resurrection and redemption (2 Ne. 25:13), and the righteous will be nourished "as calves of the stall" because of their obedience to the Lord (1 Ne. 22:24).

Malachi's prophecies climax with the mission of Elijah, which receives prominent attention in latter-day sacred writings. During the angel Moroni's visits to Joseph Smith in 1823, he quoted Malachi 4:5–6 with modifications: "Behold, I will reveal unto you the Priesthood, by the hand of Elijah the prophet, before the coming of the great and dreadful day of the Lord. And he shall plant in the hearts of the children the promises made to their fathers. . . . If it were not so, the whole earth would be utterly wasted at his coming" (JS—H 1:38–39). In fulfillment, Elijah appeared to Joseph Smith and

Oliver Cowdery in the Kirtland Temple on April 3, 1836 (Passover time), and restored the sealing powers (D&C 110:13–16).

Speaking of Malachi 4:5–6, Joseph Smith asked, "How is [this prophecy] to be fulfilled? The keys are to be delivered, the spirit of Elijah is to come, the Gospel to be established, the Saints of God gathered, Zion built up, and the Saints to come up as saviors on Mount Zion. But how? . . . By building their temples . . . and receiving all the ordinances, baptisms, confirmations, washings, anointings, ordinations and sealing powers upon their heads, in behalf of all their progenitors who are dead, and redeem them; . . . and herein is the chain that binds the hearts of the fathers to the children, and the children to the fathers, which fulfills the mission of Elijah" (*HC* 6:184). If this eternal goal could not be achieved, one of the major purposes of the plan of redemption would fail.

An integral part of this plan is to "further the work of turning the hearts of the children to the fathers by getting . . . sacred family records in order. These records, including especially the 'book containing the records of our dead' (D&C 128:24), are a portion of the 'offering in righteousness' referred to by Malachi (3:3), which we are to present in His holy temple, and without which we shall not abide the day of His coming" (Kimball, pp. 542–43).

BIBLIOGRAPHY

Kimball, Spencer W. *The Teachings of Spencer W. Kimball,* ed. Edward L. Kimball. Salt Lake City, 1982.

Lee, Harold B. "The Way to Eternal Life." *Ensign* 1 (Nov. 1971):9–17.

McConkie, Bruce R. "Stand Independent Above All Other Creatures." *Ensign* 9 (May 1979):92–94.

Smith, Joseph Fielding. *Church History and Modern Revelation,* 2 vols. Salt Lake City, 1953.

GEORGE A. HORTON, JR.

MAN OF HOLINESS

According to ENOCH's record, Man of Holiness is one NAME OF GOD: "In the language of Adam, Man of Holiness is his name, and the name of his Only Begotten is the Son of Man, even Jesus Christ" (Moses 6:57). God further declared in the revelation to Enoch:

"Behold, I am God; Man of Holiness is my name" (Moses 7:35). This name reinforces the observation that God the Father is an exalted man of flesh and bones (D&C 130:22) and that every aspect of his character is holy.

In almost a dozen instances, the pre-Christian Nag Hammadi text "Eugnostos the Blessed" uses similar terms—"Immortal Man," "First Man," and "Man"—for the Father (Robinson, pp. 229–31). Another Nag Hammadi tractate, "The Second Treatise of the Great Seth," refers to God as "the Man" and "Man of Greatness" (Robinson, p. 364). Thus, ancient authors likewise seem to have defined the Father as a glorified person with a body in whose image man was created.

BIBLIOGRAPHY

Brown, S. Kent. "Man and Son of Man." In *The Pearl of Great Price: Revelations From God,* ed. H. Donl Peterson and C. Tate. Provo, 1989.

Robinson, James M., ed. *The Nag Hammadi Library,* 3rd rev. ed. San Francisco, 1988.

GERALD E. JONES

MANUSCRIPT, LOST 116 PAGES

The first 116 pages of the original manuscript of Joseph Smith's translation of the Book of Mormon from the plates of Mormon are commonly known as "the 116 pages" or the "lost manuscript." These foolscap-size pages were hand-written in Harmony, Pennsylvania, between April and June 14, 1828. Although principally transcribed by Martin Harris from dictation by Joseph Smith, some of the pages may also have been transcribed by Joseph's wife, Emma Smith, or her brother, Reuben Hale.

The pages contained materials "from the Book of Lehi, which was an account abridged from the plates of Lehi, by the hand of Mormon," as Joseph explained in the preface to the first edition of the Book of Mormon (see also *HC* 1:56). LEHI's record is mentioned in 1 Nephi 1:17 and, today, is partially preserved through NEPHI's abridgment of it, primarily in 1 Nephi 1–10.

In June 1828 Martin Harris asked Joseph Smith repeatedly to allow him to show the 116 pages to family members to allay their skepticism and criticism of the translation. After prayerful inquiry of the Lord, Joseph Smith twice emphatically denied these requests. As Joseph's 1832 and 1839 histories indicate, a third request received divine permission for Harris to take the 116 manuscript pages to Palmyra, New York. The Prophet required Harris to solemnly covenant that he would show them only to his brother, his parents, his wife, and her sister.

Harris's failure to return to Harmony as promised caused Joseph great anxiety and necessitated a strenuous journey to Manchester. There, a reluctant Harris reported that someone had stolen the manuscript from his home after he had broken his covenant and indiscriminately showed it to persons outside his family. Grief-stricken, Joseph Smith readily shared responsibility for the loss. The most widespread rumor was that Harris's wife, irritated at having earlier been denied a glimpse of the ancient PLATES, had removed the manuscript translation from Martin's unlocked bureau and burned it. Not long afterward, she and Martin separated.

In consequence of this loss and of having wearied the Lord with the requests to let Harris take the pages, Joseph temporarily lost custody of the plates and the URIM AND THUMMIM to the angel MORONI (D&C 3). Lucy Mack Smith notes also that two-thirds of Harris's crop was oddly destroyed by a dense fog, which she interpreted as a sign of God's displeasure (Smith, p. 132). Following much humble and painful affliction of soul, Joseph Smith again received the plates as well as the Urim and Thummim, and his gifts were restored.

Joseph Smith was forbidden by the Lord to retranslate that part of the record previously translated because those who had stolen the manuscript planned to publish it in an altered form to discredit his ability to translate accurately (D&C 10:9–13). Instead, he was to translate the small plates of Nephi (1 Nephi–Omni) down to that which he had translated (D&C 10:41). Those plates covered approximately the same period as had the lost manuscript, or four centuries from Lehi to BENJAMIN. Mormon had been so impressed with the choice prophecies and sayings contained in the small plates that he had included them with his own abridgment of Nephite writings when told to by the Spirit for "a wise purpose" known only to the Lord (W of M 1:7).

The loss of the 116 pages taught Joseph Smith and his associates several lessons: that one should be satisfied with the first answers of the Lord, that keeping one's covenants is a serious matter, that God forgives the repentant in spite of human weakness, and that through his caring foresight and wisdom the Lord fulfills his purposes.

BIBLIOGRAPHY

Bushman, Richard L. *Joseph Smith and the Beginnings of Mormonism,* pp. 89–94. Urbana, Ill., 1984.

Jessee, Dean C., ed. *The Papers of Joseph Smith,* Vol. 1, pp. 9–10, 286–88. Salt Lake City, 1989.

Smith, Lucy Mack. *History of Joseph Smith,* pp. 124–32. Salt Lake City, 1958.

WILLIAM J. CRITCHLOW III

MARRIAGE SUPPER OF THE LAMB

According to ancient and modern scripture, Jesus Christ, the bridegroom (Matt. 25:1–13), will host a "marriage supper" at his second coming when he symbolically claims his bride, the faithful members of his Church (Rev. 19:5–9; D&C 109:73–74).

In Jesus' parable of the marriage of the king's son (Matt. 22:1–14), "the king" represents God, and "his son" is Jesus. The guests first "bidden to the wedding," are the house of Israel. Guests invited later from "the highways" are the GENTILES to whom the gospel went after most Jews rejected it in the MERIDIAN OF TIME (*JC,* pp. 536–40).

Latter-day Saints believe that by teaching and exemplifying the gospel of Jesus Christ throughout the world they are extending to all mankind the invitation to come to the marriage feast. "For this cause I have sent you . . . that the earth may know that . . . all nations shall be invited. First, the rich and the learned, the wise and the noble; . . . then shall the poor, the lame, and the blind, and the deaf, come in unto the marriage of the Lamb, and partake of the supper of the Lord" (D&C 58:6–11).

After partaking of the sacrament with his apostles, Jesus said, "I will not drink henceforth of this fruit of the vine, until that day when I drink it new with you in my Father's kingdom" (Matt. 26:29). In latter days, the Lord declared, "The hour cometh that I will drink of the fruit of the vine with you" (D&C 27:5–12). "There is to be a day when . . . those who have kept the faith will be . . . admitted to the marriage feast; . . . they will partake of the fruit of the vine," or the sacramental emblems of Christ's atoning sacrifice, and reign with him on the earth (*TPJS*, p. 66).

BIBLIOGRAPHY
McConkie, Bruce R. *The Millennial Messiah*, pp. 346–47. Salt Lake City, 1982.

JOHN M. MADSEN

MARTYRS

The term "martyr" (Greek *martys*, "a witness") in Christianity refers to a person who has suffered death because of his or her Christian witness or commitment and who subsequently has been accorded honors by a church. While Latter-day Saints honor Joseph and Hyrum Smith as martyrs, they do not venerate them in annual celebrations of their death dates, nor do they view them as heavenly intercessors for mortals.

The ancient use of the term "martyr" involves the legal environment—witnesses testifying in a legal proceeding. The basic idea relates to establishing facts or assertions that concern matters beyond the experience of the listeners. The meaning has reference to objective events or to personal testimonies. However, the usual scriptural use carries the additional meaning of revelation by the Holy Spirit, which would empower a witness to bear inspired testimony of religious truths.

OLD TESTAMENT.   In the ancient usage, the name of the Mosaic tabernacle was "tent of testimony" or "tabernacle of witness." The ark within the tabernacle contained the tablets of stone with the Lord's Ten Commandments, Aaron's rod that budded, and a pot of manna. These were tokens of the spiritual power of God.

While most references to "witness" and "testify" carry legal meanings, one sees the additional revelatory sense of a witness in Isaiah's revelation, in which he "saw" the Lord and heard the seraphim cry, gave him an understanding of bearing witness to prophetic matters that are beyond usual human experience (Isa. 6:1–7).

Isaiah also recorded a divine commission in which the Lord, the Holy One of Israel, promised to gather his sons and daughters from the ends of the earth. As a result, Israel would come to know the acts of God on their behalf: "Therefore, ye are my witnesses, saith the Lord, that I am God" (Isa. 43:1–12). Though afflicted and hated for their testimony, it would not be in vain: Generations to come would be blessed by it (Isa. 60:14–15). In another instance, the Lord instructed Jeremiah to purchase a plot of land from his cousin. He summoned legal witnesses, paid for the land with silver according to "law and custom," and wondered why he should buy land falling to Babylon. The Lord explained that his purchase of land by a deed foreshadowed that later the people of the city would buy and sell land, a prophetic or spiritual witness of their future return from Babylon (Jer. 32:6–44).

NEW TESTAMENT. The terms "record," "testimony," and "witness" are used more than two hundred times in the New Testament. In speaking to Pilate, Jesus asserted that he had been born into the world to "bear witness unto the truth" (John 18:37; cf. 1 Tim. 6:13). Further, one of Jesus' discourses illuminating the basis of witnessing identified six foundations for a testimony: Jesus himself, John the Baptist, Jesus' own works, the Father, the scriptures, and Moses (John 8:14; cf. 5:32–47). Just prior to his ascension, Jesus explained to the apostles that, after the Holy Ghost had come upon them, they would be "witnesses" to him in Jerusalem and the "uttermost part of the earth" (Acts 1:8). He had warned them they might be hated, afflicted, and killed for his name's sake (Matt. 5:10–12; 24:9). The apostles' association with Jesus during the post-Resurrection ministry satisfied the legal aspect of witnessing, but their testimony of his messianic character would be conferred and confirmed by the Holy Ghost. In a related vein, one's death could be viewed as a martyrdom for Christ, with eternal rewards to follow, as seen in Revelation 2:8–10; cf. 14:13. Certainly those true to the Savior, and redeemed by him, are his witnesses and are rewarded by him (Rev. 7:13–17).

LATTER-DAY SCRIPTURE. In the Book of Mormon, several persons die and are honored as martyrs. The prophet ABINADI is the most notable example (Mosiah 12:1–17:1). Others include the women and children of Ammonihah who were burned to death for their beliefs (Alma

14:1–10). At the death of those women and children, the prophet ALMA₂ assured his friend AMULEK that "the Lord receiveth them up unto himself, in glory" (Alma 14:11).

The Doctrine and Covenants teaches that "all they who have given their lives for [God's] name shall be crowned" (D&C 101:15) and that the blood of the innocent ascends to God "in testimony" (D&C 109:49; cf. 98:13). In this connection, members of the Church refer to the murder of Joseph and Hyrum Smith as "the martyrdom of Joseph Smith the Prophet, and Hyrum Smith the Patriarch" (D&C 135:1). The Lord spoke through Brigham Young that "it was needful that [Joseph Smith] should seal his testimony with his blood, that he might be honored and the wicked might be condemned" (D&C 136:39; cf. 135).

BIBLIOGRAPHY

Patch, Robert C. "The Spiritual Connotation in the Scriptural Concept of Witness." Ph.D. diss., Brigham Young University, 1964.

Trites, Allison A. *The New Testament Concept of Witness.* Cambridge, 1977.

ROBERT C. PATCH

MARY, MOTHER OF JESUS

Centuries before her birth, Book of Mormon prophets referred to Mary by name in prophecies of her vital mission (Mosiah 3:8). Describing her as "most beautiful and fair above all other virgins" (1 Ne. 11:13–20) and a "precious and chosen vessel" (Alma 7:10), they prophesied that Mary would bear the Son of God and was therefore blessed above all other women. "We cannot but think that the Father would choose the greatest female spirit to be the mother of his Son, even as he chose the male spirit like unto him to be the Savior" (McConkie, p. 327).

Mary's willingness to submit to the will of the Father was noted in the biblical account. When Gabriel announced that she would be the mother of the Savior, Mary was perplexed; yet she did not waver in her humble obedience and faith in God. Her response was unadorned: "Behold the handmaid of the Lord; be it unto me according to thy word" (Luke 1:38).

Had Judah been a free nation, Mary could have been recognized as a "princess of royal blood through descent from David" (*JC*, p. 90). Being of that earthly lineage, Jesus was correctly called a descendant of David.

As a faithful Jewish woman, she followed the customs of her day. At least forty-one days after giving birth to her first son, Mary went to the Court of the Women, where she became ceremonially clean in the purification rite, offering two turtledoves or two pigeons at the temple as a sacrifice (Luke 2:22–24). In the years that followed, Mary bore additional children by her earthly husband Joseph (Matt. 1:25; 13:55–56; Mark 6:3). One of them, "James the Lord's brother" (Gal. 1:19), became a Christian leader in Jerusalem.

In the New Testament, Mary is mentioned in conjunction with the accounts of the youthful Jesus teaching in the temple (Luke 2:41–51), his turning the water to wine at Cana (John 2:2–5), his crucifixion (John 19:25–26), and as mourning with the apostles after Jesus' ascension (Acts 1:14).

Doctrinally, Latter-day Saints do not view Mary as the intercessor with her son in behalf of those who pray and they do not pray to her. They affirm the VIRGIN BIRTH but reject the traditions of the immaculate conception, of Mary's perpetual virginity, and of her "assumption" (cf. McConkie, p. 327). Mary, like all mortals, returns to the Father only through the atonement of her son Jesus Christ.

BIBLIOGRAPHY
McConkie, Bruce R. *The Mortal Messiah*. Salt Lake City, 1981.

CAMILLE FRONK

MATTHEW, GOSPEL OF

Latter-day Saints consider the Gospel of Matthew as the preeminent introduction to the New Testament. The Gospel of Matthew is reproduced and revised in LDS scripture more than any other biblical text except the Genesis creation account. It is edited throughout in the Prophet Joseph Smith's inspired revision of the Bible (*see* JOSEPH SMITH TRANSLATION OF THE BIBLE [JST]), and the edited version of Matthew 24 is reproduced in the Pearl of Great Price (JS—M 1:1–55). The Sermon on the Mount is virtually repeated in the Book of Mormon by the resurrected Savior to his "other sheep" (John 10:16; 3 Ne. 15:21) in the Western Hemisphere (3 Ne. 12–14); but it is made explicit that it is the poor in spirit who come unto him who are blessed; and it is implied that blessedness comes to all other categories mentioned in the beatitudes by the same means (3 Ne. 12:2–12). The Doctrine and Covenants provides an explanation of the parable of the wheat and the tares in a latter-day context (D&C 86). Each rendition is easily recognized as basically the same sermon. However, the inspired changes are significant to Latter-day Saints, as they often establish or support major points of doctrine.

Latter-day Saints, like many others, equate Levi and Matthew, acknowledging the "publican" apostle as author of the gospel (Matt. 9:9). As a Jew, Matthew saw Christianity as the culmination of Judaism, with Jesus as the promised Messiah. In many details of Jesus' life, Matthew saw fulfillment of Old Testament prophecy, and the JST enriches the Matthean theme that all this was done "that it might be fulfilled which was spoken by the prophets" (Matt. 2:23; cf. Millet, 1985, pp. 152–54). Through a royal line, beginning with Abraham, Matthew establishes Jesus' Davidic ancestry (Matt. 1:1–17) and his right to reign as "king of the Jews" (Matt. 27:37); and he relates the nativity story from Joseph's viewpoint (Matt. 1:18–25; Matt. 2:1–25). The Prophet Joseph Smith adds that Jesus grew up with his brethren and waited for his ministry to come, serving under his "father," and "needed not that any man should teach him" (JST Matt. 3:24–25).

Many scriptures note that the Messiah will be "like unto Moses" (Deut. 18:15–19; Moses 1:6; 1 Ne. 22:20–21; Acts 7:37; JS—H 1:40), and in the Matthew account readers see parallels between some of the experiences of Moses and Jesus: There was a sovereign who slew children, a return from Egypt, forty days on a mountain, and the miraculous feeding of multitudes. Most of all, there was an enunciation of divine law by both. The promised similitude, however, may have established expectations in Jewish hearts that Jesus failed to satisfy.

To Latter-day Saints, the Sermon on the Mount is a concise summary of much of Jesus' teaching, emphasizing the spirit of the law and encouraging righteous acts for righteous reasons. They recognize it as a single discourse of Jesus in light of his complete repetition of it among the Nephites (3 Ne. 12–14). Both the JST and 3 Nephi versions include enriching details not found in extant biblical texts, including the setting of the sermon. For example, Jesus directed only his chosen twelve and other selected disciples to take no thought for their life or for the morrow (3 Ne. 13:25) and to teach from house to house, noting that while the world will persecute them, their Heavenly Father will provide for them (JST Matt. 6:2, 25–27). Then he turned to the multitude and warned of unrighteous judgment (3 Ne. 14:1). Latter-day Saints acknowledge the necessity of good judgment and seek to judge righteously (see JST Matt. 7:2; cf. Moro. 7:15–19).

The JST revision of Matthew is replete with subtle but meaningful differences from the King James text. It becomes clear, for instance, that Jesus entered the Judean wilderness primarily to commune with his Father, not merely to be tempted (JST Matt. 4:1–2), and, unswayed by any doubt of his divinity as the One foretold by the prophets, he called his apostles (JST Matt. 4:18). JST Matthew 17:14 introduces a latter-day Elias: "Then the disciples understood that he spake unto them of John the Baptist, and also of another who should come and restore all things, as it is written by the prophets." A doctrinal principle is strengthened when Jesus declares that he came to save the lost, but little children need no repentance (JST Matt. 18:2; 19:13; cf. Moro. 8:5–24).

Latter-day Saints recognize the importance of faith, good works, and ordinances, and do not stress one above the others, as all are essential for salvation. They draw support from Matthew's many references to faith and good works (e.g., Matt. 16:27), and they recognize the ordinances of baptism by immersion (Matt. 3:16; JST Matt. 3:44–45), ordination to the priesthood (Matt. 10:1), and healing of the sick (Matt. 9:18). In addition, they believe that Jesus established a formal church organization under the supervision of his ordained apostles, and they cite the Matthean text both for Jesus' intent to establish a church (Matt. 16:18) and for the existence of the Church (Matt. 18:17; cf. Millet, 1985, pp. 148–51). At Caesarea Philippi, when Peter declared Christ's divinity (Matt. 16:15), Jesus affirmed that he knew this only through revelation from the Father, noting, "Thou art Peter, and upon this rock I will build my church" (Matt. 16:17–18). While Mormons acknowledge Peter's primacy in the early Church, they quickly point out that Christ's Church—both in Peter's day and in the latter days—was and is founded upon the rock of revelation and that living prophets still look to that rock for guidance.

BIBLIOGRAPHY

Millet, Robert L. "The JST and the Synoptic Gospels: Literary Style." In *The Joseph Smith Translation*, ed. M. Nyman and R. Millet. Provo, Utah, 1985.

———. "The Testimony of Matthew." In *Studies in Scripture*, ed. K. Jackson and R. Millet, Vol. 5, pp. 38–60. Salt Lake City, 1986.

WM. REVELL PHILLIPS

MERIDIAN OF TIME

The meridian of time has been defined by one LDS apostle as "the middle or high point of that portion of eternity which is considered to be mortal time" (*MD*, 1966, p. 486). It is the dispensation in which Jesus Christ lived in mortality. The term does not occur in the Bible, but is found in the Doctrine and Covenants (20:26; 39:3) and in the Book of Moses (5:57; 6:57, 62; 7:46).

The word "meridian" suggests the middle. According to Old Testament genealogies, from the fall of Adam to the time of Jesus Christ was approximately 4,000 years. It has been nearly 2,000 years since Jesus' birth. The millennial reign will commence "in the beginning of the seventh thousand years" (D&C 77:12). After the Millennium there will be a "little season," the exact length of which is not revealed, but it could be several hundred years. In the context of these events, the Lord's mortal ministry took place near the meridian, or middle, of mortal time (*DS* 1:81).

The meridian of time may also be seen as the high point of mortal time. Latter-day revelation shows that all of the ancient prophets looked forward to the Messiah's coming (Jacob 4:4; Mosiah 13:33–35; 15:11). His coming fulfilled their prophecies, and he was prefigured in the LAW OF MOSES (Mosiah 13:29–32) and in ancient ceremonial ordinances (Moses 5:5–8). The meridian of time is the apex of all dispensations because of the birth, ministry, and atonement of Christ. Without him all prophetic writings and utterances would have had no efficacy, and the hopes of mankind today and forever would be but futile desires and yearnings without possibility of fulfillment.

MARSHALL T. BURTON

MILLENARIANISM

While the word "Millennium" simply means a thousand years, *the* Millennium is usually understood as a thousand-year period during which Christ will reign on earth. Latter-day Saints from the beginning anticipated the return of Christ and worked to prepare the world for his coming. The Bible mentions the thousand-year period only in Revelation 20:2–7, though many interpreters believe that various Old Testament prophecies, such as Isaiah's vision of the lamb and lion lying down together (Isa. 11), describe that time. "Millenarianism" refers to belief in and the study of the Millennium—how near it is and what life then will be like.

Not surprisingly, Christians have differed on these matters throughout history. Those who take a literal approach to prophecy anticipate a millennial world fundamentally distinct from the present age, an actual return to the paradisiacal conditions that prevailed in the GARDEN OF EDEN. For others, the millennial prophecies are mere metaphors for the better times ahead as the world is gradually Christianized. In nineteenth-century America, the latter interpretation was dominant. Most people believed that religious revivals and foreign missions, not the personal return of Jesus Christ, would be the means of ushering in the Millennium. They defined the Millennium in terms of the spiritual rather than the spiritual and physical transformation of the earth.

The Latter-day Saints rejected this figurative vision of the future. They believed that only the miraculous, divine intervention of Christ could fully destroy wickedness and re-create the New Eden. Mormons then and now literally expect the earth to be "renewed and receive its paradisiacal glory" (A of F 10). The extraordinary biological, geological, and social changes that will make the earth a paradise include the abolishment of infant mortality; the herbivorization of carnivores; the unification of continental landmasses; and the cessation of all enmity, strife, and warfare.

As the revelations unfolded during the early years of the Church, it was learned that Christ and those raised in the first resurrection at the beginning of the Millennium "will not probably dwell upon the earth, but will visit it when they please, or when it is necessary to govern it" (*TPJS*, p. 268). The Saints also came to realize that the destruction of the wicked accompanying Christ's second coming will not remove all unbelievers from the earth. Thus, missionary work will be a major millennial activity. Once the role of temples in the redemption of living and dead became clear, temple work was added to the list of anticipated millennial pursuits.

Since the first century, some Christians have felt that the second coming of Christ was near. Given the numerous revelations to Joseph Smith and the other dramatic developments of early Church history, many early Latter-day Saints also expected the promised day in their lifetimes. That feeling has been strong at other periods during the subsequent history of the Church, though not as sustained or pervasive as in its earliest years. While affirming the significance of the Millennium, modern Church leaders regularly make calming and qualifying statements as a counterpoint to undue anxiety about its proximity.

BIBLIOGRAPHY

Clouse, Robert G., ed. *The Meaning of the Millennium.* New York, 1974.

Gaustad, Edwin S., ed. *The Rise of Adventism.* New York, 1974.

Underwood, Grant. "The Millenarian World of Early Mormonism." Ph.D. diss., University of California at Los Angeles, 1988.

GRANT UNDERWOOD

MIRACLES

A miracle is a beneficial event brought about through divine power that mortals do not understand and of themselves cannot duplicate. Members of The Church of Jesus Christ of Latter-day Saints believe in the reality of miracles as a consequence of their belief in the existence of God and of his power and goodness.

Just as a shepherd tends his flocks, watches over them, and uses his power to help them, so Jesus Christ used his power and knowledge to help others when he was on earth. For instance, when the supply of wine was exhausted at the marriage feast at Cana, at his mother's request, Jesus miraculously provided wine (John 2:1–10). This act was consistent with his love and compassion, but the means by which he changed the water into wine is not understood, and of themselves people cannot duplicate it. Thus, it is called a miracle.

Numerous other examples of the beneficial results of miracles performed by Jesus include the raising from the dead of the widow's son at Nain (Luke 7:11–16), the cleansing of the ten lepers (Luke 17:12–19), and the restoration of the sight of the blind man at Bethsaida (Mark 8:22–26).

Latter-day Saints value miracles because of their beneficial character. As stated in the Book of Mormon, "God has provided a means that man, through faith, might work mighty miracles; therefore he becometh a great benefit to his fellow beings" (Mosiah 8:18). Although God brings about marvelous events to bless humankind, it is known that not every spiritual manifestation necessarily comes from God (*TPJS*, pp. 202–214; Rev. 13:13–14; *see also* SIGN SEEKING).

Faith is considered necessary to bring divine intervention in behalf of those in need. For example, as the Book of Mormon prophet ALMA₂ noted, LEHI and his group of emigrants were given the LIAHONA, a compasslike device to direct their travels toward a new and promised land. "And it did work for them according to their faith in God; therefore, if they had faith to believe that God could cause that those spindles [of the compass] should point the way they should go, behold it was done; therefore they had this miracle, and also many other miracles wrought by the power of God, day by day" (Alma 37:40).

God desires to bless his children and sometimes does so in ways that require the manifestation of extraordinary power. He is restrained only by their lack of faith. Thus, the absence of miracles is evidence of the lack of faith among his children, "for it is by faith that miracles are wrought; and it is by faith that angels appear and minister unto men; wherefore, if these things have ceased wo be unto the children of men, for it is because of unbelief, and all is vain" (Moro. 7:37). "For if there be no faith among the children of men God can do no miracle among them" (Ether 12:12).

When the faithful receive a blessing from God, especially one that requires a manifestation of his extraordinary power, the proper response is gratitude to God for the blessing (D&C 46:32). Manifestations of God's extraordinary power usually come only after faith and do not necessarily create faith (cf. Ether 12:7); it is appropriate, therefore, not to make a public show of such sacred experiences as a demonstration of religious belief. Seeking manifestations of the extraordinary power of the divine for the purpose of coming to believe is rejected as improper sign seeking.

Of the miraculous gifts of the spirit that come to the righteous, the Lord says, "For verily I say unto you, they are given for the benefit of those who love me and keep all my commandments, and him that seeketh so to do; that all may be benefited that seek or that ask of me, that ask and not for a sign that they may consume it upon their lusts. . . . And all these gifts come from God, for the benefit of the children of God" (D&C 46:9, 26).

A miraculous gift especially valued is the healing of the sick. However, not every faithful soul who ails will be raised, for the Lord has said, "And whosoever among you are sick, and have not faith to be healed, but believe, shall be nourished and with all tenderness, with herbs and mild food. . . . And the elders of the church, two or more, shall be called, and shall pray for and lay their hands upon them in my name; and if they die they shall die unto me, and if they live they shall live unto me" (D&C 42:43–44). Thus though the sick may be healed (D&C 46:19), if that does not occur, the sick are nourished by all prudent means, including those available in modern medical science. The elders of the Church perform this ordinance of administering to the sick, as the scriptures prescribe (cf. James 5:14–15; D&C 46:20), and the healing or other blessings are then in accordance with the will of God.

Personal experience with miracles might confirm the faith of the recipients. Further, personal experiences with miracles may give others increased confidence in scriptural accounts of miracles.

Of all the miraculous gifts of God given to his children, the one of greatest benefit is the atonement of Jesus Christ. By powers and means not understood by mere mortals, Jesus was able to take upon himself the sins of the world and make it possible for anyone, by repentance, to escape the otherwise inescapable suffering of sin and the doom of death, and thereby return to the presence of God. "For behold, I, God, have suffered these things for all, that they might not suffer if they would repent . . . which suffering caused myself, even God, the greatest of all, to tremble because of pain, and to bleed at every pore, and to suffer both body and spirit" (D&C 19:16, 18). The miracle of forgiveness and the marvel of resurrection are supreme indeed.

BIBLIOGRAPHY
Kimball, Spencer W. *Faith Precedes the Miracle*, chap. 1. Salt Lake City, 1972.

PAUL C. HEDENGREN

MORMON

Mormon was a PROPHET, an author, and the last NEPHITE military commander (c. A.D. 310–385). The Book of Mormon bears his name because he was the major abridger–writer of the GOLD PLATES from which it was translated. He was prepared by the experiences of his youth to become a prophet: he was taught "the learning of [his] people," was a "sober child" and "quick to observe," and in his fifteenth year was "visited of the Lord" (Morm. 1:2, 15). At sixteen he became the general of all the Nephite armies and largely succeeded in preserving his people from destruction until A.D. 385, when virtually all of them but his son MORONI$_2$ were destroyed in battles with the LAMANITES (6:8–15; 8:1–3). As keeper of the Nephite records, Mormon abridged the large PLATES of Nephi, bound with them the small plates of Nephi, and added his own short history (W of M 1:1–5; Morm. 1:1). Before his death, he hid the records entrusted to him in the hill CUMORAH, "save it were these few plates which I gave unto my son Moroni" (Morm. 6:6). The Prophet Joseph Smith received and translated Mormon's abridgment, the small plates of Nephi, and a few other documents, and published them in 1830 as the Book of Mormon.

First and foremost, Mormon was a prophet to his people, urging them to "repent, and be baptized in the name of Jesus, and lay hold upon the gospel of Christ" (Morm. 7:8). He taught that they were "a remnant of the seed of Jacob" (7:10) and could have the blessings of ISRAEL if they would live for them. He also underscored the supporting relationship of the Bible and the Book of Mormon: "For behold, this [record, the Book of Mormon] is written for the intent that ye may believe that [record, the Bible]; and if ye believe that ye will believe this also" (7:9).

Mormon's son Moroni₂ finished the record, including one of Mormon's addresses and two of Mormon's epistles in his own book of Moroni. Mormon's talk on faith, hope, and charity (Moro. 7) teaches that charity, the greatest of those three virtues, is "the pure love of Christ, and it endureth forever; and whoso is found possessed of it at the last day, it shall be well with him" (7:47). One of Mormon's letters (Moro. 8) condemns INFANT BAPTISM as a practice that denies the atonement of Jesus Christ, stating "it is solemn mockery before God, that ye should baptize little children" (8:9). Rather, little children need not repent, but "are alive in Christ, even from the foundation of the world" (8:12). In the other epistle (Moro. 9) Mormon notes that the destruction of the Nephites is just retribution for their wickedness, which is so bad that he "cannot recommend them unto God lest he should smite me" (9:21).

As abridger of Nephite records, Mormon had access to a veritable library of engraved documents and was commanded to make an abridgment of the large plates of Nephi so that Lamanites, Jews, and GENTILES of the latter days could know of the Lord's COVENANTS and what he had done for their ancestors and could thereby be convinced that Jesus is the Christ (see BOOK OF MORMON: TITLE PAGE). While making his abridgment, Mormon often noted that he could not include even a hundredth part of the source records (e.g., Hel. 3:14). He regularly sought opportunity to draw spiritual lessons from the course of events experienced by his people. The phrase "and thus we see" frequently introduces one of Mormon's interpretive observations (cf. Hel. 3:27–30). One of the most significant passages from his hand appears in Helaman 12, wherein he offers compelling views about the often vain and fickle character of human nature, especially in response to material prosperity.

As an author, Mormon expressed his feelings, sorrowing at living in a wicked society (Morm. 2:19), and confessing that he had loved and prayed for his people (3:12), but was at last without hope (5:2). He measured civility by how women and children fared (4:14, 21), seeking to unite them with husbands and fathers even when facing certain doom (6:2, 7). When the last Nephites fell, he penned a poignant lament in their memory (6:16–22).

As general of the Nephite armies (Morm. 2–6), Mormon helped to preserve his people from destruction by the Lamanites for some fifty-eight years but then began to lose them, first to sin and then to death (Morm. 2:11–15). Even so, he taught survivors that they would be spared if they would repent and obey the gospel of Jesus Christ, "but it was in vain; and they did not realize that it was the Lord that had spared them, and granted unto them a chance for repentance" (3:3). At one time the Nephites became so vicious and hardened that Mormon refused to lead them into battle (3:11). But he could not bear to watch them perish, and although he had no hope that they could survive, he relented (5:1) and led them into their last battle from which only he, his son Moroni$_2$, and a few others survived (8:2–3). Moroni$_2$ lived to complete his father's record (8:1).

BIBLIOGRAPHY
Holland, Jeffrey R. "Mormon: The Man and the Book." *Ensign* 8 (Mar. 1978):15–18; (Apr. 1978):57–59.

PHYLLIS ANN ROUNDY

MORONI, ANGEL

The angel Moroni is the heavenly messenger who first visited the Prophet Joseph Smith in 1823. As a mortal named MORONI$_2$, he had completed the compilation and writing of the Book of Mormon. He ministered to Joseph Smith as a resurrected being, in keeping with his responsibility for the Book of Mormon, inasmuch as "the keys of the record of the stick of Ephraim" had been committed to him by the Lord (D&C 27:5). Pursuant to this responsibility he first appeared to Joseph Smith on the night of September 21–22, 1823 (JS—H 1:29–49; D&C 128:20), and thereafter counseled with him in several reappearances until the book was published in 1830. During that time, he instructed Joseph Smith, testified to the Three Witnesses of the Book of Mormon, and otherwise assisted in the work of restoring the gospel.

Because of the angel Moroni's role in restoring the everlasting gospel to be preached to all the world (cf. Rev. 14:6–7; D&C 133:31–39), the Church placed a statue depicting him as a herald of the Restoration atop the Salt Lake Temple, and later on the hill CUMORAH near Palmyra, New York, where anciently he had buried the Book of Mormon plates. Copies of the statue have also been placed atop several other LDS temples.

[*See also* Angel Moroni Statue.]

BIBLIOGRAPHY

Peterson, H. Donl. *Moroni: Ancient Prophet, Modern Messenger.* Bountiful, Utah, 1983.

JOSEPH B. ROMNEY

MORONI₁

The first Moroni mentioned in the Book of Mormon (died c. 56 B.C.) was twenty-five years old when he was appointed captain of the NEPHITE armies (Alma 43:16). He upheld the liberty of the Nephites against threats posed by invading armies and by "kingmen," who tried to reestablish a monarchy by force after failing to win popular support. Moroni rallied his people for a seven-year struggle by raising "the title of liberty," a banner on which he wrote his reasons for defense, and by having his people covenant to defend their freedom and obey God's commandments (Alma 46:12–13, 20).

Despite many battles, Moroni did not become bloodthirsty. He operated within legal authority, and when he gained advantage over enemies, he offered them freedom if they would lay down their weapons and take an oath not to war again. He introduced new armor and fortifications and sought the direction of a prophet about what his armies should do (Alma 43:23; *see also* BOOK OF MORMON, HISTORY OF WARFARE IN). Five hundred years later, MORMON, the chief editor and compiler of the Book of Mormon, wrote, "If all men had been . . . like unto Moroni, behold, the very powers of hell would have been shaken forever" (Alma 48:17). Mormon even named his son, Moroni₂, after him.

BIBLIOGRAPHY

England, Eugene. "Moroni and His Captains." *Ensign* 7 (Sept. 1977):29–36.

MELVIN J. THORNE

MORONI₂

Moroni₂ is the last prophet and author of the last book in the Book of Mormon. His life spanned the latter part of the fourth century and the early fifth century. He led ten thousand troops in the last battle against the LAMANITES, serving under his father, MORMON, who was commander in chief. Prior to the final war, Mormon had abridged the PLATES of Nephi that covered a thousand years of his people's history. He commanded Moroni to conclude the Nephite record by writing "the sad tale of the destruction of [their] people" (Morm. 8:3) and to preserve all the sacred writings (Moro. 9:24).

After Moroni wrote the required postscript to his father's record and prophesied its future discovery (Morm. 8–9), he added an abridgment of ancient Jaredite engravings, a record of a nation that had inhabited the Western Hemisphere for approximately 1,700 years prior to the Nephites' arrival, or perhaps overlapping their arrival (the Book of Ether). "According to the will of the Lord," he then added ten concluding chapters on ordinances, principles, and church practices that he called the book of Moroni.

Moroni spoke with prophetic assurance of conditions in the last days because "Jesus Christ hath shown you unto me, and I know your doing" (Morm. 8:35). With fervor, he proclaimed Christ to be a God of miracles who is the same in all ages unless unbelief causes miracles to cease. He spoke with confidence of the divinity and teachings of Jesus Christ because "I have seen Jesus, and . . . he hath talked with me face to face, . . . even as a man telleth another in mine own language, concerning these things" (Ether 12:39).

Moroni also recorded prophecies of the BROTHER OF JARED, a Jaredite prophet, who helped lead his colony to the New World. These prophecies are "sealed" to come forth at a future day (Ether 4:1–7).

Moroni's last entry in the Book of Mormon was likely written about A.D. 421, thirty-six years after the final battle. He then finished writing the title page of the Book of Mormon and finally buried the Book of Mormon plates to preserve them for a future generation.

Fourteen hundred years later this same Moroni, then a resurrected being "sent from the presence of God," appeared to Joseph Smith, a seventeen-year-old youth, on the night of September 21,

1823, and told him of the sacred records deposited in a stone box in a nearby hill (the hill Cumorah) in what is now Ontario County, New York, within a few miles of Joseph's home in Manchester Township. Moroni appeared to Joseph more than twenty times during the next six years, tutoring him for his calling as a prophet and giving counsel and information concerning the acquisition, translation, and guardianship of the Book of Mormon plates (JS—H 1:27–54).

Moroni is frequently identified with the Church because portrayals of him blowing a trumpet, handling the gold plates, or instructing Joseph Smith are commonly displayed—for instance on LDS temple spires, on covers of several printings of the Book of Mormon, and in paintings. A depiction of Moroni with a trumpet is the official emblem on grave markers of American Mormon servicemen.

Moroni is commonly portrayed with a trumpet because of an interpretation of a prophecy of John the Revelator wherein he saw an angel heralding the return of the everlasting gospel to the earth in the last days:

> And I saw another angel fly in the midst of heaven, having the everlasting gospel to preach unto them that dwell on the earth, and to every nation, and kindred, and tongue, and people, saying with a loud voice, Fear God, and give glory to him; for the hour of his judgment is come: and worship him that made heaven, and earth, and the sea, and the fountains of waters [Rev. 14:6–7].

[*See also* Angel Moroni Statue.]

BIBLIOGRAPHY

Peterson, H. Donl. *Moroni: Ancient Prophet, Modern Messenger.* Bountiful, Utah, 1983.

H. DONL PETERSON

MOSES

Few PROPHETS are more revered in ancient and latter-day scripture than Moses, who serves as a model of prophetic leadership not only in the Bible but also in the Book of Mormon, Doctrine and Covenants, and Pearl of Great Price (see Luke 16:29–31; 24:27;

2 Ne. 3:9; D&C 28:2; 103:16; 107:91; Moses 1:41). Modern revelation confirms and amplifies the biblical accounts of Moses' intimate association with deity; his role as seer, liberator, lawgiver, and leader of ISRAEL; and his connection with the books of the Pentateuch.

God chose Moses for his earthly mission in premortal life (*TPJS,* p. 365). JOSEPH OF EGYPT, son of Jacob, prophesied that the Lord would raise up Moses to deliver Jacob's descendants from Egyptian bondage (2 Ne. 3:9–10; JST Gen. 50:29, 34–35). His preparation for his monumental task began in his youth. Raised in Pharaoh's court, Moses "was learned in all the wisdom of the Egyptians" and became "mighty in words and in deeds" (Acts 7:22). After fleeing from Egypt to Midian (Ex. 2:15), he married Zipporah. His father-in-law, Jethro, ordained him to the Melchizedek Priesthood, which had come down through generations of prophets (D&C 84:6–17). Known as "priest of Midian" (Ex. 3:1), Jethro descended from Midian, son of ABRAHAM and Keturah (Petersen, pp. 49–50).

Moses not only received instructions directly from God, as the Bible records, but he was also given inspiring revelations concerning God's many creations (Moses 1:4, 33–35) and the earth and its inhabitants (Moses 1:8, 27–28). An account of these VISIONS was revealed to the Prophet Joseph Smith in June 1830 as part of the JOSEPH SMITH TRANSLATION OF THE BIBLE (JST) and constitutes chapter one of the BOOK OF MOSES in the Pearl of Great Price. For Latter-day Saints, this stands as "the missing introduction not only to Genesis, but to the entire Bible" (Turner, p. 43).

The visions were given to Moses on a high mountain, "the name of which shall not be known among the children of men" (Moses 1:1, 42), after the event at the burning bush and before he led Israel from bondage (Moses 1:17, 26). Hence, they were received separately from the revelations of the Ten Commandments (Ex. 3–4; 19–20). The visions exhibit five themes: the greatness of God in comparison to humans (Moses 1:2–5, 8–11, 35–38); Jesus Christ as the Only Begotten Son and creator of "worlds without number" (1:32–34); Satan and his opposition to the divine plan (1:12–22); the spiritual stature of Moses (1:6, 25–28, 40–41); and God's purposes (1:30, 31, 39). Moses was able to endure God's presence because he was transfigured, meaning that during the visionary experience God's own glory quickened him (Moses 1:2, 11). He learned that he was created in the similitude of God's Only Begotten Son (Moses 1:6), and was told to write his revelations, even though much of what he recorded would be lost—due to wickedness—until another prophet, like himself, would bring forth his visions to believers of a later day (Moses 1:40–41).

Latter-day scripture attests to Moses' hand in the composition of the Pentateuch (1 Ne. 5:11; 19:23). He had access to, and edited, prior prophetic records, including those of ADAM and ENOCH, which were once apparently included in the works composing the earliest form of the Pentateuch, now found in Moses 2–8 (cf. 1 Ne. 13:20–40).

While in the wilderness, Moses taught the Israelites about the sanctifying power of the Melchizedek Priesthood, "that they might behold the face of God" (D&C 84:23). Unfortunately, they rejected his efforts, and because of their hardened hearts, Moses and the Melchizedek Priesthood were taken from their midst. The lesser or Aaronic Priesthood remained (D&C 84:24–27).

Moses' ministry extended beyond his mortal lifetime. Along with ELIJAH, he returned to the MOUNT OF TRANSFIGURATION, spoke with Christ, and bestowed certain keys of the priesthood upon the chief apostles (Matt. 17:1–4; D&C 138:45; HC 3:387). Because he needed a body of flesh and bones to perform this errand and because the Resurrection was yet forthcoming, Moses was translated and taken into heaven, like Enoch and Elijah, without experiencing the normal death portrayed in Deuteronomy 34:5–6 (cf. Alma 45:19).

Possessing the keys for gathering Israel (Petersen, p. 186), Moses appeared in the Kirtland Temple on April 3, 1836, and conferred those keys on the Prophet Joseph Smith and Oliver Cowdery (D&C 110:11) so that the full authority of the priesthood could operate in this dispensation. Latter-day scripture reminds all priesthood holders of Moses' significance by declaring that those who honor and magnify the priesthood become the adopted sons of Moses (D&C 84:33–34). Moses is also revered by other Christians and by Jews and Moslems.

BIBLIOGRAPHY

Jackson, Kent, and Robert Millet, eds. *Studies in Scripture*, Vol. 3, pp. 93–223. Salt Lake City, 1985.

Petersen, Mark E. *Moses: Man of Miracles.* Salt Lake City, 1977.

Sperry, Sidney B. "The Mission of Moses: Out of Bondage." *Ensign* 3 (Oct. 1973):30–35.
Turner, Rodney. "The Visions of Moses." In *Studies in Scripture*, ed. R. Millet and K. Jackson, Vol. 2, pp. 43–61. Salt Lake City, 1985.

ANDREW C. SKINNER

MOSIAH₁

The first Mosiah mentioned in the Book of Mormon, a king, saved those NEPHITES who "would hearken unto the voice of the Lord" by leading them away from their ancestral home, the land of Nephi, where they were threatened by LAMANITES about 200 B.C. (Omni 1:12). After they had wandered for an unknown period, Mosiah and his group "discovered a people, who were called the people of Zarahemla" (Omni 1:13–14; *see also* BOOK OF MORMON PEOPLES; MULEK). He taught them his language—their language having deteriorated because they lacked written records—and was chosen ruler over both groups (Omni 1:17–19). "By the gift and power of God" he interpreted "engravings" on a stone that the people of Zarahemla had discovered, telling of yet another and earlier migration (Omni 1:20–22; *see also* JAREDITES). Mosiah ruled for about four decades and was succeeded as king by his son BENJAMIN.

BIBLIOGRAPHY
Ludlow, Victor L. "Scribes and Scriptures." In *Studies in Scripture*, ed. K. Jackson, Vol. 7, pp. 196–204. Salt Lake City, 1987.

MELVIN J. THORNE

MOSIAH₂

Mosiah₂ (c. 153–91 B.C.) ruled as a Nephite king during almost thirty-three years of Book of Mormon history. His reign was marked by an innovative separation of religious and civic functions and a popular political reform, reflecting the increased pluralism of Nephite society during this historical period.

Mosiah's people consisted of two groups, Nephites and

Mulekites, who had voluntarily united under his grandfather, MOSIAH₁. They appear, to some extent, to have retained their separate identities (Mosiah 25:4). The Mulekites were the more numerous group, but the Nephite leaders were able to rule effectively, relying on covenant and commitment rather than force. The people entered into a sacred covenant by which they were promised deliverance and prosperity if they would keep their king's commandments, "or the commandments of God," which he would give them (Mosiah 2:31)—a commitment they honored during all of Mosiah's reign.

Mosiah learned the languages and regard for the sacred records of his ancestors from his father, BENJAMIN, and was a wise and patient man who knew the laws and prophecies contained in the Nephite records (Mosiah 1:2–3). Mosiah became king (c. 124 B.C.) three years before his aged father's death. The coronation, described in detail in Mosiah 1–6, exhibits several features similar to ancient Near Eastern coronations. The account of the coronation also provides valuable information about the religious and political patterns of the time (*see* BENJAMIN). Mosiah was in his thirtieth year when he began to reign. He walked "in the ways of the Lord," and like his father, he provided for his own temporal needs so that he would not become a burden to his people (Mosiah 6:6–7).

Challenges soon arose for Mosiah. Limhi's people arrived in Zarahemla and had to be assimilated into Nephite society. They brought with them the twenty-four PLATES of Ether, which Mosiah, being a seer, translated (Mosiah 28:10–19). This Jaredite record revealed an ominous lesson, for wickedness, oppression, and violence had led to the extinction of a people. In contrast, Mosiah promoted righteousness, equality, and harmony in his kingdom. When another group led by ALMA₁ arrived in Zarahemla, Mosiah authorized Alma to organize churches and gave him control over them, including the power to admit members to, or expel members from, that covenant community. The creation of this subgroup comprised of seven churches in Nephite society (Mosiah 25:23) allowed Alma's followers to live as they wished, but it also appears to have sowed seeds of civic tension.

At this time, an opposition group formed. Under a strident leader named Nehor, it rejected Alma's teachings and advocated the creation of a publicly supported priesthood. Mosiah's sons, Ammon, Aaron, Omner, and Himni, together with ALMA₂ and a rising generation that had been too young at the time of Mosiah's coronation to understand the words of King Benjamin (Mosiah 26:1), joined these dissenters. They engaged in systematic religious persecution of the church, wreaking havoc among the Nephite community and with Mosiah's family and reputation. Mosiah dealt with the problem by prohibiting acts of religious persecution (Mosiah 27:2). He also sought divine help through fervent prayer and fasting to reform his sons. Angelic intervention (Mosiah 27:10–32) led to the spiritual transformation of these rebellious souls. Deeming it better soon thereafter to proclaim the gospel than to rule over the kingdom, none of his four sons would accept the Nephite throne.

Under these circumstances and near the end of his life, Mosiah effected a political reform that abolished Nephite kingship. His final speech in 91 B.C. justified righteous monarchs such as his father and himself, but warned against the overriding threats posed by wicked rulers (Mosiah 29:13–21).

In place of kingship, Mosiah created a unique system of judges subject to the voice of the people. From what is known about this legal reform, it appears that each judge was chosen by popular voice, "that every man should have an equal chance"; higher judges judged the lower judges, and a selected body of lower judges judged the higher judges (Mosiah 29:25–29, 38). This law set new precedents by providing that judges should be paid; it also established an Egyptian-style system of measures for exchanging various grains and precious metals (Alma 11:1, 4–19), prohibited all forms of slavery (Alma 27:9), imposed a severe punishment on those who would not pay their debts (Alma 11:2), and granted liberty of belief (Mosiah 29:39; Alma 30:11). The people accepted the law of Mosiah and selected their judges, including Alma₂ as the first chief judge. The equity and justice of this prophet-king won for him the love of his people:

> And they did wax strong in love towards Mosiah; yea, they did esteem him more than any other man; for they did not look upon him as a tyrant who was seeking for gain, . . . for he had not exacted riches of them, neither had he delighted in the shedding of blood; but he had

established peace in the land, and he had granted unto his people that they should be delivered from all manner of bondage; therefore they did esteem him, yea, exceedingly, beyond measure [Mosiah 29:40].

BIBLIOGRAPHY
"The Coronation of Kings." *F.A.R.M.S. Update.* Provo, Utah, July 1989.
"The Law of Mosiah." *F.A.R.M.S. Update.* Provo, Utah, March 1987.

PAUL RYTTING

MOTHER IN ISRAEL

Every worthy woman who lives a virtuous life and who promotes righteousness in her family and in the Church is entitled both to the designation "mother in Israel" and to the promises given to Sarah and other biblical mothers in Israel (*see* ABRAHAM; ISRAEL; SARAH). These promises are open to all faithful women who teach others to love the Lord and keep his commandments. The title designates intelligent and faithful support of the Church and its leaders, and historically it has been applied most frequently to leaders among women. It is often found in patriarchal blessings and is a title and a promise with more than earthly significance. Motherhood is a God-given role vital to the exaltation of a woman and her family.

"Mother in Israel" first appears in the song of Deborah that describes the travail of the people under Jabin, the king of Canaan, until Deborah, a mother in Israel, arose to lead them out of bondage (Judg. 5:2–31; cf. 2 Sam. 20:19).

In Old Testament times, a woman's strength and authority were found in her mothering of faithful children, especially sons. Besides Eve, other outstanding examples of mothers who influenced Old Testament history include Sarah, Rebekah, Leah, Rachel, Hannah, and Naomi. Sarah, of course, figures indispensably in the blessing given to Abraham, and the Lord promised her explicitly that she would be "a mother of nations" (Gen. 17:16). That such a blessing was culturally significant is apparent in the admonition given to Rebekah by her family as she left to marry Isaac: "Be thou the mother of thousands of millions" (Gen. 24:60). Barrenness in biblical culture was often seen as a reproach to a woman and to her family, a matter of sorrow for a woman, and often a matter for sincere prayer to God, but not rejection (e.g., 1 Sam. 1:4–8).

In the Christian era, after the death of the apostles, a tradition developed that gave precedent honor to women who offered themselves celibate to religious service. However, as the Protestant reformation emerged, motherhood again became a crowning glory and "the home, not the convent, became the center of woman's highest religious vocation" (Madsen, p. 184).

The expression "mother in Israel" can be found in writings of post-Reformation England and more prominently in Puritan New England. Among Latter-day Saints, who consciously identify with biblical themes and ancient Israel, the appellation appeared early, but was applied infrequently and then only to such outstanding women as Lucy Mack Smith and Eliza R. Snow. At the October 1845 general conference of the Church, a year following the deaths of her sons Joseph, Hyrum, and Samuel, Lucy Mack Smith "wished to know of the congregation, whether they considered her a mother in Israel." President Brigham Young put her question to those assembled, who answered with a resounding, "Yes" (*CHC*, 2:538–39).

In 1916 the *Relief Society Magazine* published a series of articles entitled "Mothers in Israel." One prominent woman honored was Eliza R. Snow. Though childless, she was called a "mother of mothers in Israel" and praised for her leadership among women, for her intelligence, and for her faithful support of the Church and its leaders (Gates, pp. 183–90).

As in New England, the phrase "mother in Israel" appeared in early Utah history in the obituaries of many faithful women who succored the Church and their families. Sometimes they were older women with large families and sometimes notable women in other circumstances. For example, Mary Fielding Smith had only two children of her own, both young enough when she died that no claim could be made of their future significance, yet at her death, evidently in recognition of her character and commitment, she was called a mother in Israel. A son and a grandson later became Presidents of the Church.

Currently the term is most often found in patriarchal blessings when a woman is promised in substance that she will stand "as a mother in Israel." President Joseph Fielding Smith said, "To be a mother in Israel in the full gospel sense is the highest reward that can come into the life of a woman" (p. 883). It is a promise open to all faithful sisters who love and serve the Lord and keep his commandments, including those who do not have the opportunity to bear children in this life.

The Book of Mormon recounts the history of 2,000 righteous stripling warriors who were able to accomplish great things and receive great blessings because they believed in what they had "been taught by their mothers" (Alma 56:47–48; 57:21). Modern mothers in Israel also have a responsibility to teach their children—and others whom they are in a position to influence—to love the Lord and keep his commandments. The prophets of this dispensation have consistently stressed the importance of committed motherhood both by those who bear and those who care and have counseled that this is a divinely given role important to the salvation and exaltation of God's children.

BIBLIOGRAPHY

Benson, Ezra Taft. *To the Mothers in Zion.* Salt Lake City, 1987.

Gates, Susa Young. "Mothers in Israel." *Relief Society Magazine* 3 (Jan. 1916):538–39.

———. "The Mothers of Mothers in Israel." *Relief Society Magazine* 3 (Apr. 1916):183–90.

Madsen, Carol Cornwall. "Mothers in Israel: Sarah's Legacy." In *Women of Wisdom and Knowledge,* ed. M. Cornwall and S. Howe, pp. 179–201. Salt Lake City, 1990.

Reynolds, Sydney Smith. "Wife and Mother: A Valid Career Option for the College-Educated Woman." *Ensign* 9 (Oct. 1979):67–70.

Smith, Joseph Fielding. "Mothers in Israel." *Relief Society Magazine* 57 (Dec. 1970):883–86.

SYDNEY SMITH REYNOLDS

MOUNT OF TRANSFIGURATION

The Mount of Transfiguration was the scene of a transcendent New Testament event. It has been set in perspective by revelations to the Prophet Joseph Smith and portrayed with several related components. First, Jesus conversed with Moses and Elijah, who were then translated beings (Matt. 17:3–4). Second, a transfiguration of Jesus Christ himself occurred there, confirming his divine nature and calling to his three chief apostles: Peter, James, and John (Matt. 17:1–2). Third, those apostles were also temporarily transfigured during that experience (*TPJS*, p. 158). Fourth, in vision those apostles saw the earth in its future transfigured state as the inheritance of the faithful (D&C 63:20–21). Fifth, those same apostles received certain priesthood keys of the kingdom of God, which they utilized during their mortal ministries (*HC* 3:387). Sixth, Moses and Elijah, who were also on the Mount of Transfiguration, also conferred priesthood keys to Joseph Smith and Oliver Cowdery in the Kirtland Temple on April 3, 1836 (D&C 110:11–16).

The experience on the mount no doubt strengthened the Savior as he approached the last months before his atoning sacrifice. Moses and Elijah visited him as he prepared for the infinite sufferings in Gethsemane and the agonies of Golgotha (Luke 9:30–31; *JC*, p. 373).

Jesus' transfiguration before Peter, James, and John made them "eyewitnesses of his majesty" (2 Pet. 1:16). During their visit, the voice of the Father bore record of the Savior's mission, giving assurance to Peter, James, and John of the Father's love and his approval of Jesus (Matt. 17:5–8). Because these apostles would soon constitute the First Presidency of the early church (*MD*, pp. 571–72), the event was an unforgettable personal witness of the Father's acknowledgment of Jesus' redemptive mission. John later testified, "We beheld his glory, the glory as of the only begotten of the Father" (John 1:14).

The temporary transfiguration of Peter, James, and John allowed them to hear the voice of the Father and see the transfigured Son (cf. Moses 1:9–11). This extraordinary experience helped prepare them for the coming burden of Church leadership following Jesus' departure from his earthly ministry. Well did Peter declare, "Lord, it is good for us to be here" (Matt. 17:4).

Peter, James, and John also saw the millennial day when the earth will be transfigured, returning it to its condition prior to the fall of Adam (*TPJS*, pp. 12–13; cf. A of F 10). The earth's transfiguration will take place at the time of Christ's second coming (*MD*, pp. 795–96).

The bestowal of priesthood keys on the presiding apostles formed a fifth purpose of the transfiguration. During his ministry, Jesus conferred the Melchizedek Priesthood on the Twelve, authorizing them to act under his direction (Mark 3:14–15; John 15:16; cf. *JD* 25:207). But with the prospect of his departure, the Twelve needed independent authority to direct Church affairs. Fulfilling his promise that Peter would receive the keys of the kingdom (Matt. 16:13–20), Jesus took the chief apostles to the mount, where they received those keys.

After beholding the transfigured Jesus and undergoing transfiguration themselves, the apostles saw Moses and Elijah (and perhaps others; cf. McConkie, p. 400), who had been translated so that they could appear with physical bodies to bestow priesthood keys by the laying on of hands, which made possible, among other things, the preaching of the gospel throughout the world (Matt. 18:19–20) and performing saving ordinances for the living and the dead (cf. 1 Cor. 15:29).

The latter-day fulfillment of some of these events occurred in the Kirtland Temple. The Melchizedek Priesthood and the office and keys of apostleship had been conferred on Joseph Smith and Oliver Cowdery probably in late May or early June 1829 (cf. D&C 27:12), embracing the authority to establish the Church (D&C 128:20). On April 3, 1836, additional keys were given to Joseph and Oliver in the Kirtland Temple by Moses and Elijah—the same ancient ministrants who appeared on the mount—and an additional messenger named ELIAS, who conferred the "dispensation of the gospel of Abraham" (D&C 110:12). The restoration of these keys set in motion the latter-day mission of the Church, including missionary work and all ordinances for the living, as well as redemption of the dead through vicarious ordinance work in temples.

BIBLIOGRAPHY

Haight, David B. "'We Beheld His Glory.'" *Ensign* 7 (May 1977):7–10.

Matthews, Robert J. "Tradition, Testimony, Transfiguration, and Keys." In *Studies in Scripture*, ed. K. Jackson and R. Millet, Vol. 5, pp. 296–311. Salt Lake City, 1986.

McConkie, Bruce R. *Doctrinal New Testament Commentary*, Vol. 1, pp. 397–404. Salt Lake City, 1965.

DALE C. MOURITSEN

MULEK

Mulek, a Book of Mormon leader, son of Zedekiah, escaped the sack of Jerusalem (587 B.C.) and went with others to a place in the Western Hemisphere that they called the land of Mulek (Hel. 6:10). Later a region was named for Zarahemla, a descendant of Mulek (Mosiah 25:2). These people were eventually discovered by Nephite refugees from LAMANITE predations in the south. Mulek is important because he established one of the BOOK OF MORMON PEOPLES and because Bible students have assumed that Nebuchadnezzar executed all of Zedekiah's sons, an observation unsupported by ancient evidence and refuted by the Book of Mormon account of Mulek's survival.

According to the Book of Mormon, the NEPHITES and "Mulekites" formed a coalition, making MOSIAH₂ king over both groups. The Nephites discovered in Mulek's descendants an additional witness concerning the destruction of Jerusalem. The Mulekites were elated to have access to Nephite records, since their own language and traditions had been distorted in the absence of historical documents. The Mulekites lived thenceforth among the Nephites, enjoying separate-but-equal status and ultimately outnumbering the descendants of Nephi (Mosiah 25:1–4, 13).

Ancient Near Eastern sources affirm that during the Babylonian destruction of Jerusalem, Mulek's father, Zedekiah, who was deserted by all who escaped, was captured with members of his family and a few courtiers. Nebuchadnezzar slew Zedekiah's sons and courtiers, put his eyes out, and deported him to Babylon (Josephus, *Antiquities,* 10.8.2). But his daughters, and presumably his wives, stayed at Mizpah until Gedeliah, a former minister with Babylonizing tendencies in Zedekiah's cabinet, was murdered by Ishmael, who then tried to deport the Mizpah colony. When pursued, Ishmael abandoned his captives and fled with eight men to Ammon. The people of Mizpah, including Zedekiah's women, headed for Egypt, fearful of Chaldean reprisals (2 Kgs. 25; Jer. 41–43).

Mulek might have been away when the city fell; perhaps he eluded his captors at Jericho; the women could have hidden him (as Jehoshiba hid her nephew Joash of the royal line earlier [see 2 Kgs. 11:2–4]); he may even have been unborn, although he probably avoided captivity some other way. But nothing in the Bible or other known sources precludes the possibility of his escape from Jerusalem.

Concerning Mulek's existence, the Bible offers important evidence. Mulek is a nickname derived from *melek* (Hebrew, king), a diminutive term of endearment meaning "little king." Its longer form occurs in the Bible as *Malkiyahu* (in English, Malchiah), meaning "Jehovah is king." Malchiah is identified as "the son of Hammelech" in Jeremiah 38:6. But Hammelech is a translator's error, since *ben-hammelek* means "son of the king" and is not a proper name—a fact confirmed by the Septuagint (LXX Jer. 45:6). A fictive paternity thus obscures the lineage of Malchiah as the actual son of Zedekiah. It is also known that names ending in *-yahu* (in English, *-iah*) were common during the late First Temple period, that Zedekiah indeed had a son named Malkiyahu (Aharoni, p. 22), and that the familial forms of *yahu*-names were shorter than their "full" forms. The study of a seal owned by Jeremiah's scribe shows that his full name was Berekyahu (in English, Berechiah), although the biblical text uses only the shorter Baruch (Avigad). This is consistent with viewing the hypocoristic Mulek as the diminutive of Malkiyahu, since *a* is often assimilated to *o* or *u* in the vocalic structure of most Semitic languages. It is therefore possible that the Mulek of the Book of Mormon is "Malchiah, son of the king" mentioned in Jeremiah 38:6.

BIBLIOGRAPHY

Aharoni, Yohanan. "Three Hebrew Ostraca from Arad." *Bulletin of the American Schools of Oriental Research* 197 (Feb. 1970):16–42.

Avigad, Nahman. "Jerahmeel & Baruch." *Biblical Archeologist* 42:2 (Spring 1979):114–18.

"New Information About Mulek, Son of the King." *F.A.R.M.S. Update.* Provo, Utah, 1984.

Rainey, Anson. "The Prince and the Pauper." *Ugarit-Forschungen* 7 (1975):427–32.

H. CURTIS WRIGHT

N

NAME OF GOD

Latter-day Saints invoke the name of God in prayers, in ordinances such as baptism, in testimony bearing, and in sermons. In certain ceremonies, they take upon themselves God's sacred name in covenantal pledges to keep his commandments. They also employ the various names of God to distinguish between members of the Godhead. Consequently, the names of God are considered very sacred and are not to be taken in a vain way or spoken in profanity.

The word from the Hebrew Bible most commonly translated "God" or "gods" is *'elohim,* the plural of *'eloah* or *'el,* which means "lofty one" or "exalted one." The plural ending *-im* may indicate royal loftiness as well as plurality (*see* ELOHIM).

The formal name of God in the Old Testament is "Jehovah" or "YHWH" (Hebrew *yhwh*), which comes from a root suggesting "I was, am, and will be forever." Some consider *yhwh* to be a name too sacred to be spoken; consequently, in many Bible versions, *yhwh* is translated "Lord."

Joseph Smith's first vision and later revelations confirmed the separate identity of the Father and the Son. To distinguish them individually in some scriptures, however, is very difficult. For instance, Jesus Christ has spoken the words of the Father by divine investiture as if he were the person of the Father (cf. *MFP* 5:26–34; John 14:24). Jesus continually emphasized the "oneness" or unity of mind and purpose of the Godhead and set it forth as an example to disciples. The term "God," therefore, may apply equally to the Father and the Son. The prayer of Jesus to his Father after the Last Supper was that followers might be "one, even as we are" (John 17:1–26; cf. 3 Ne. 11:27, 32–36; D&C 132:12).

The principal name of the Eternal Father is not clearly stated in scripture although several names and titles appear. Where identification is appropriate, Latter-day Saints have designated the Father by the exalted name-title Elohim (*MFP* 5:26).

The use of sacred names plays an important part in LDS worship. For example, Latter-day Saints have been instructed to address God in prayer with the title "Our Father" and to offer prayers in the name of Jesus Christ (Matt. 6:9; 3 Ne. 13:9). In baptismal prayers and sacrament prayers, faithful members covenant to take upon themselves the name of Christ. The participants commit themselves to remember Christ, which means to be an example of him to the world, to love him, to have faith in him, and to walk in his way (cf. 2 Ne. 31:19–20; Mosiah 5:7–12).

Jesus Christ has specifically commanded that his Church should bear his name. He said, further, that his people will be called by that name at the last day (3 Ne. 27:1–12; Mosiah 5:7–14; D&C 115:4).

The Lord has also revealed that ordinances and blessings performed in his name by his authorized servants are binding in heaven as well as on earth (D&C 132:45–46; 128:9). Ordinances, such as baptism, marriage, and vicarious work in temples, are performed in the "name of the Father, and of the Son, and of the Holy Ghost."

In modern times, as in the past, the Lord has cautioned men and women not to utter his name in vain speech (Ex. 20:7; D&C 63:60–64) nor to defile it through improper conduct. He has directed his people to keep pledges and "keep yourselves from evil to take the name of the Lord in vain, for I am the Lord your God, even the God of your fathers" (D&C 136:21).

BIBLIOGRAPHY

Madsen, Truman G. "'Putting on the Names': A Jewish-Christian Legacy." In *By Study and Also by Faith*, ed. J. Lundquist and S. Ricks, Vol. 1, pp. 458–81. Salt Lake City, 1990.

Talmage, James E. *AF*. Salt Lake City, 1915.

GLADE L. BURGON

NATIVE AMERICANS

LDS BELIEFS.   The Book of Mormon, published in 1830, addresses a major message to Native Americans. Its title page states that one reason it was written was so that Native Americans today might know "what great things the Lord hath done for their fathers."

The Book of Mormon tells that a small band of Israelites under LEHI migrated from Jerusalem to the Western Hemisphere about 600 B.C. Upon Lehi's death his family divided into two opposing factions, one under Lehi's oldest son, LAMAN (*see* LAMANITES), and the other under a younger son, NEPHI₁ (*see* NEPHITES).

During the thousand-year history narrated in the Book of Mormon, Lehi's descendants went through several phases of splitting, warring, accommodating, merging, and splitting again. At first, just as God had prohibited the Israelites from intermarrying with the Canaanites in the ancient promised land (Ex. 34:16; Deut. 7:3), the Nephites were forbidden to marry the Lamanites with their dark skin (2 Ne. 5:23; Alma 3:8–9). But as large Lamanite populations accepted the gospel of Jesus Christ and were numbered among the Nephites in the first century B.C., skin color ceased to be a distinguishing characteristic. After the visitations of the resurrected Christ, there were no distinctions among any kind of "ites" for some two hundred years. But then unbelievers arose and called themselves Lamanites to distinguish themselves from the Nephites, or believers (4 Ne. 1:20).

The concluding chapters of the Book of Mormon describe a calamitous war. About A.D. 231, old enmities reemerged and two hostile populations formed (4 Ne. 1:35–39), eventually resulting in the annihilation of the Nephites. The Lamanites, from whom many present-day Native Americans descend, remained to inhabit the American continent. Peoples of other extractions also migrated there.

The Book of Mormon contains many promises and prophecies about the future directed to these survivors. For example, Lehi's grandson Enos prayed earnestly to God on behalf of his kinsmen, the Lamanites. He was promised by the Lord that Nephite records would be kept so that they could be "brought forth at some future day unto the Lamanites, that, perhaps, they might be brought unto salvation" (Enos 1:13).

The role of Native Americans in the events of the last days is noted by several Book of Mormon prophets. Nephi₁ prophesied that in the last days the Lamanites would accept the gospel and become a "pure and delightsome people" (2 Ne. 30:6). Likewise, it was revealed to the Prophet Joseph Smith that the Lamanites will at some future time "blossom as the rose" (D&C 49:24).

After Jesus' resurrection in Jerusalem, he appeared to the more righteous Lamanites and Nephites left after massive destruction and prophesied that their seed eventually "shall dwindle in unbelief because of iniquity" (3 Ne. 21:5). He also stated that if any people "will repent and hearken unto my words, and harden not their hearts, I will establish my church among them, and they shall come in unto the covenant and be numbered among this the remnant of Jacob [the descendants of the Book of Mormon peoples], unto whom I have given this land for their inheritance"; together with others of the house of Israel, they will build the NEW JERUSALEM (3 Ne. 21:22–23). The Book of Mormon teaches that the descendants of Lehi are heirs to the blessings of Abraham and will receive the blessings promised to the house of Israel.

THE LAMANITE MISSION (1830–1831).   Doctrine and a commandment from the Lord motivated the Latter-day Saints to introduce the Book of Mormon to the Native Americans and teach them of their heritage and the gospel of Jesus Christ. Just a few months after the organization of the Church, four elders were called to preach to Native Americans living on the frontier west of the Missouri River.

The missionaries visited the Cattaraugus in New York, the Wyandots in Ohio, and the Shawnees and Delawares in the unorganized territories (now Kansas). Members of these tribes were receptive to the story of the Restoration. Unfortunately, federal Indian agents worrying about Indian unrest feared that the missionaries were inciting the tribes to resist the government and ordered the missionaries to leave, alleging that they were "disturbers of the peace" (Arrington and Bitton, p. 146). LDS pro-Native American beliefs continued to be a factor in the tensions between Latter-day Saints and their neighbors in Ohio, Missouri, and Illinois, which eventually led to persecution and expulsion of the Latter-day Saints from Missouri in 1838–1839 and from Illinois in 1846.

RELATIONS IN THE GREAT BASIN.   When the Latter-day Saints arrived in the Great Salt Lake Valley in 1847, they found several Native

American tribal groups there and in adjacent valleys. The Church members soon had to weigh their need to put the limited arable land into production for the establishment of Zion against their obligation to accommodate their Native American neighbors and bring them the unique message in the Book of Mormon.

Brigham Young taught that kindness and fairness were the best means to coexist with Native Americans and, like many other white Americans at the time, he hoped eventually to assimilate the Indians entirely into the mainstream culture. He admonished settlers to extend friendship, trade fairly, teach white man's ways, and generously share what they had. Individuals and Church groups gave, where possible, from their limited supplies of food, clothing, and livestock. But the rapid expansion of LDS settlers along the Wasatch Range, their preoccupation with building Zion, and the spread of European diseases unfortunately contravened many of these conciliatory efforts.

A dominating factor leading to resentment and hostility was the extremely limited availability of life-sustaining resources in the Great Basin, which in the main was marginal desert and mountain terrain dotted with small valley oases of green. Although Native Americans had learned to survive, it was an extremely delicate balance that was destroyed by the arrival of the Latter-day Saints in 1847. The tribal chiefs who initially welcomed the Mormons soon found themselves and their people being dispossessed by what appeared to them to be a never-ending horde, and in time they responded by raiding LDS-owned stock and fields, which resources were all that remained in the oases which once supported plants and wildlife that were the staples of the Native American diet. The Latter-day Saints, like others invading the western frontier, concerned with survival in the wilderness, responded at times with force.

An important factor in the conflict was the vast cultural gap between the two peoples. Native Americans in the Great Basin concentrated on scratching for survival in a barren land. Their uncanny survival skills could have been used by the Mormons in 1848, when drought and pestilence nearly destroyed the pioneers' first crops and famine seriously threatened their survival.

The Utes, Shoshones, and other tribal groups in the basin had little interest in being farmers or cowherders, or living in stuffy sod or log houses. They preferred their hunter-gatherer way of life under the open sky and often resisted, sometimes even scoffed at, the acculturation proffered them. Nor did they have a concept of land ownership or the accumulation of property. They shared both the land and its bounty—a phenomenon that European Americans have never fully understood. The culture gap all but precluded any significant acculturation or accommodation.

Within a few years, LDS settlers inhabited most of the arable land in Utah. Native Americans, therefore, had few options: They could leave, they could give up their own culture and assimilate with the Mormons, they could beg, they could take what bounty they could get and pay the consequences, or they could fight. Conflict was inevitable. Conflict mixed with accommodation prevailed in Utah for many years. Violent clashes occurred between Mormons and Native Americans in 1849, 1850 (Chief Sowiette), 1853 (Chief Walkara), 1860, and 1865–1868 (Chief Black Hawk)—all for the same primary reasons and along similar lines. Conflict subsided, and finally disappeared, only when most of the surviving Native Americans were forced onto reservations by the United States government.

Still, the LDS hand of fellowship was continually extended. Leonard Arrington accurately comments that "the most prominent theme in Brigham's Indian policy in the 1850s was patience and forbearance. . . . He continued to emphasize always being ready, using all possible means to conciliate the Indians, and acting only on the defensive" (Arrington, p. 217). Farms for the Native Americans were established as early as 1851, both to raise crops for their use and to teach them how to farm; but most of the "Indian farms" failed owing to a lack of commitment on both sides as well as to insufficient funding. LDS emissaries (such as Jacob Hamblin, Dudley Leavitt, and Dimmick Huntington) continued, however, to serve Native American needs, and missionaries continued to approach them in Utah and in bordering states. Small numbers of Utes, Shoshones, Paiutes, Gosiutes, and Navajos assimilated into the mainstream culture, and some of that number became Latter-day Saints. But overall, reciprocal contact and accommodation were minimal. By the turn of the century, contact was almost nil because most Native Americans lived on reservations far removed from LDS communities. Their contact with whites was mainly limited to government soldiers and agency officials and to non-Mormon Christian missionaries.

RELATIONS IN RECENT TIMES. Beginning in the 1940s, the Church reemphasized reaching out to Native Americans. The Navajo-Zuni Mission, later named the Southwest Indian Mission, was created in 1943. It was followed by the Northern Indian Mission, headquartered in South Dakota. Eventually, missionaries were placed on many Indian reservations. The missionaries not only proselytize, but also assist Native Americans with their farming, ranching, and community development. Other Lamanite missions, including several in Central and South America and in Polynesia, have also been opened. Large numbers of North American Indians have migrated off reservations, and today over half of all Indians live in cities. In response, some formerly all-Indian missions have merged with those serving members of all racial and ethnic groups living in a given geographical area.

An Indian seminary program was initiated to teach the gospel to Native American children on reservations, in their own languages if necessary. Initially, Native American children of all ages were taught the principles of the gospel in schools adjacent to federal public schools on reservations and in remote Indian communities. The Indian seminary program has now been integrated within the regular seminary system, and Indian children in the ninth through twelfth grades attend seminary, just as non-Indian children do.

The Indian Student Placement Services (ISPS) seeks to improve the educational attainment of Native American children by placing member Indian children with LDS families during the school year. Foster families, selected because of their emotional, financial, and spiritual stability, pay all expenses of the Indian child, who lives with a foster family during the nine-month school year and spends the summer on the reservation with his or her natural family. Generally, the children enter the program at a fairly young age and return year after year to the same foster family until they graduate from high school.

From a small beginning in 1954, the program peaked in 1970 with an enrollment of nearly 5,000 students. The development of more adequate schools on reservations has since then reduced the need for the program and the number of participants has declined. In 1990, about 500 students participated. More than 70,000 Native American youngsters have participated in ISPS, and evaluations have shown that participation significantly increased their educational attainment.

In the 1950s, Elder Spencer W. Kimball, then an apostle, encouraged Brigham Young University to take an active interest in Native American education and to help solve economic and social problems. Scholarships were established, and a program to help Indian students adjust to university life was inaugurated. During the 1970s more than 500 Indian students, representing seventy-one tribes, were enrolled each year. But enrollment has declined, so a new program for Indian students is being developed that will increase the recruiting of Native American students to BYU and raise the percentage who receive a college degree. The Native American Educational Outreach Program at BYU presents educational seminars to tribal leaders and Indian youth across North America. It also offers scholarships. American Indian Services, another outreach program originally affiliated with BYU, provides adult education and technical and financial assistance to Indian communities. In 1989, American Indian Services was transferred from BYU to the Lehi Foundation, which continues this activity.

In 1975, George P. Lee, a full-blooded Navajo and an early ISPS participant, was appointed as a General Authority. He was the first Indian to achieve this status and served faithfully for more than ten years. Elder Lee became convinced that the Church was neglecting its mission to the Lamanites, and when he voiced strong disapproval of Church leaders, he was excommunicated in 1989.

The Church has always had a strong commitment to preaching the gospel to Native Americans and assisting individuals, families, communities, and tribes to improve their education, health, and religious well-being. Programs vary from time to time as conditions and needs change, but the underlying beliefs and goodwill of Latter-day Saints toward these people remain firm and vibrant.

BIBLIOGRAPHY

Arrington, Leonard J. *Brigham Young: American Moses.* New York, 1985.

———, and Davis Bitton. *The Mormon Experience: A History of the Latter-day Saints.* New York, 1979.

Chadwick, Bruce A., Stan L. Albrecht, and Howard M. Bahr. "Evaluation of an Indian Student Placement Program." *Social Casework* 67, no. 9 (1986):515–24.

Walker, Ronald W. "Toward a Reconstruction of Mormon and Indian Relations, 1847–1877." *BYU Studies* 29 (Fall 1989):23–42.

BRUCE A. CHADWICK
THOMAS GARROW

NATURAL MAN

The phrase "natural man" is understood by Latter-day Saints to be an unrepentant person; it does not imply that mortals are by nature depraved or evil, but only that they are in a fallen condition. "Natural man" describes persons who are "without God in the world, and they have gone contrary to the nature of God" (Alma 41:11). The Lord declared to Joseph Smith: "Every spirit of man was innocent in the beginning; and God having redeemed man from the fall, men became again, in their infant state, innocent before God" (D&C 93:38).

The atonement of Christ does not automatically free mankind from a fallen condition, although it does guarantee all a physical resurrection. Rather, it makes possible for men and women to escape the condition of natural man by accepting the Atonement and nurturing the light of Christ within them. King BENJAMIN was told by an angel that "the natural man is an enemy to God, and has been from the fall of Adam." But a person can "put off the natural man" by yielding to "the enticings of the Holy Spirit," and can become "a saint through the atonement of Christ the Lord, . . . [by becoming] as a child, submissive, meek, humble, patient, full of love" (Mosiah 3:19). The phrase "natural man," therefore, does not describe a condition that causes sin but a consequence of sin, of going against the commandments of God. As the prophet ABINADI taught, "he that persists in his own carnal nature, and goes on in the ways of sin and rebellion against God, remaineth in his fallen state" (Mosiah 16:5). In such rebellion, one is left without excuse. As explained by SAMUEL THE LAMANITE:

> Whosoever doeth iniquity, doeth it unto himself; for behold, ye are free; ye are permitted to act for yourselves; for behold, God hath given unto you a knowledge and he hath made you free. He hath given unto you that ye might know good from evil, and he hath given unto you that ye might choose life or death [Hel. 14:30–31].

The apostle PAUL speaks of the natural man as being in a state incapable of understanding spiritual truth. "But the natural man receiveth not the things of the Spirit of God: for they are foolishness unto him: neither can he know them, because they are spiritually discerned" (1 Cor. 2:14). Moreover, the natural man "walk[s] according to the course of this world, fulfilling the desires of the flesh and of the mind" (Eph. 2:2–3).

Because the natural man is unrepentant and indulgent, one must overcome this condition through repentance and submission to the Spirit of God. President Brigham Young stated that God "has placed us on the earth to prove ourselves, to govern, control, educate and sanctify ourselves, body and spirit" (*JD* 10:2, in *Discourses of Brigham Young*, ed. J. Widtsoe, p. 57, Salt Lake City, 1971). Parley P. Pratt, an apostle, explains how the Holy Ghost aids in the process:

> [It] increases, enlarges, expands and purifies all the natural passions and affections; and adapts them, by the gift of wisdom, to their lawful use. It inspires, develops, cultivates and matures all the fine-toned sympathies, joys, tastes, kindred feelings and affections of our nature [*Key to the Science of Theology*, 10th ed., p. 101, Salt Lake City, 1973].

Repentance is manifested as "[yielding] to the enticings of the Holy Spirit, . . . [being] willing to submit to all things which the Lord seeth fit to inflict upon him, even as a child doth submit to his father" (Mosiah 3:19). Neal A. Maxwell of the Quorum of the Twelve Apostles has pointed out that humility and selflessness develop a capacity for discipline and a control of natural appetites. This is a difficult process, which requires that "men and women of Christ magnify their callings without magnifying themselves" (p. 16).

BIBLIOGRAPHY
Maxwell, Neal A. "Put Off the Natural Man, and Come Off Conqueror." *Ensign* 20 (Nov. 1990):14–16.
Millet, Robert L. *Life in Christ*, pp. 23–35. Salt Lake City, 1990.

R. J. SNOW

NATURE, LAW OF

Rational inquiry into nature (*physis*) was for Greek philosophers the way to know reality. The natural was originally radically distinguished from law (*nomos*), which identified merely human conventions. Thus, for example, it is natural for humans to speak, but it is not natural to speak Greek. Hence, law was not initially thought of by such philosophers as natural, though it was natural for humans to be governed by such conventions. Later the terms "nature" and "law" began to be linked to describe a prepolitical golden age without rules, contracts, property, or marriage. Understood in this way, "natural law," after the decline from the golden age, did not provide the model for civil law, but instead identified a realm accessible to reason that transcends the world. Roman Catholic theologians eventually borrowed the expression "natural law" from pagan philosophy to ground a structured social ethic. Thomas Aquinas, in his Aristotelian restructuring of Christianity, distinguished four levels of law: eternal, divine, natural, and human. Eternal law, the mind of God and structure of reality, he held, is known both through revelation as divine law and through reason as natural law, and human law should strive to reflect the natural law.

Though Latter-day Saints sometimes speculate about the reasons for the positive law given through divine revelation and also about the moral sense of mankind, a moral natural law is not clearly delineated in the LDS canon. Some suggest that rough equivalents for a moral natural law might be elicited from scripture. But theology, grounded in philosophical speculation, is typically seen as a competitor to divine revelation. Such speculation remains tentative and problematic. Hence, there is little talk of a moral natural law among Latter-day Saints.

LDS scriptures, rather than relying upon notions of a moral natural law, speak of God's commandments, statutes, and ordinances; of God's will and plans and purposes; of the ordering of the world (including its metes and bounds); of law given by God; and so forth. The laws mentioned in the scriptures seem, instead, to be instances of divine positive law, though they are not arbitrary, since as moral prescriptions they form the terms of the covenant entered into in the hope that blessings will flow from obedience to God. It is assumed that God's commandments rest on reasons not fully accessible to human inquiry or explication.

There is, however, another strand of thought among Latter-day Saints, one that affirms what might be called the "laws of nature," where that term identifies the regularities found by the sciences. These laws are seen as descriptive, not prescriptive or normative. They are thought either to be set in place by God or to exist independently of God's will and hence function as conditions that must be managed as plans are worked out by man in cooperation with God. Such views are entertained by many Latter-day Saints, especially those trained in the natural sciences, but they have not been systematically set forth or integrated with the teachings in the scriptures.

It is the prophetic gift that makes available the terms of the covenant with God, and such covenants are accompanied by blessings and cursings. Latter-day Saints thus emphasize obedience to what amounts to divine positive law and not to the dictates of nature as known by human reason.

BIBLIOGRAPHY

d'Entreves, A. P. *Natural Law*. London, 1951.

Madsen, Truman G. "Joseph Smith and the Problems of Ethics." In *Perspectives in Mormon Ethics*, ed. Donald E. Hill, pp. 29–48. Salt Lake City, 1983.

LOUIS C. MIDGLEY

NEPHI₁

The first of several leaders named Nephi in the Book of Mormon, Nephi₁ was an influential prophet and the founder of the NEPHITE people. He was apparently well educated, faithful and obedient to God, courageous, and bold. An inspired prophet, he had visions of Jesus Christ and of the world's future; he also interpreted the prophecies of others, such as his father, LEHI, and Isaiah. He authored the first two books in the Book of Mormon, which provide virtually all known information about him. He was a skilled craftsman and leader, and succeeded Lehi as leader of the family (ahead of his three older brothers). Above all, he trusted in God: "My voice shall forever ascend up unto thee, my rock and mine everlasting God" (2 Ne. 4:35).

HISTORY.   Nephi was born c. 615 B.C. His father, the prophet Lehi, led his family group out of Jerusalem just after 600 B.C., through the Arabian desert, and across the ocean to the Western Hemisphere. While in the wilderness, Nephi saw a vision that was to shape many of his basic views; it is partially reported in 1 Nephi 11–14. In the promised land, he was designated by his father to succeed him as leader of the family (2 Ne. 1:28–29), but his older brothers LAMAN and Lemuel rebelled, and half the group associated with them. Nephi was inspired to flee with all who believed in the warnings and revelations of God (2 Ne. 5:6) and set up a new city, the city of Nephi.

Nephi established his people on sound political, legal, economic, and religious bases. They acclaimed him king, although he resisted this action initially. He taught them to be industrious and to provide for their needs, and he prepared them with training and weapons for defense against their enemies. He followed the LAW OF MOSES, built a temple like the temple of Solomon (though without "so many precious things"), and anointed his younger brothers Jacob and Joseph as priests and teachers to instruct the people and lead them in spiritual matters (2 Ne. 5:10, 16, 26). Before he died, he appointed a new king (called the "second Nephi"; Jacob 1:11) and appointed his brother Jacob as the caretaker of religious records (Jacob 1:1–4, 18).

VISIONS. Because of the great visions and revelations he received, Nephi shared a role with his father as a founding prophet. At a young age he was inspired by the Holy Spirit and believed his father's words. He heard the voice of the Lord telling him that he would become a ruler and teacher over his brothers (1 Ne. 2:22). He witnessed the vision of the TREE OF LIFE shown earlier to his father (1 Ne. 8), which showed him the future birth, baptism, and ministry of Jesus Christ, as well as the future rise and demise of his own people. He was shown also the future establishment of the Gentiles in the Western Hemisphere and the restoration of the gospel in their midst (1 Ne. 11–14). Because of these revelations, Nephi was able to teach his people the gospel, or "doctrine of Christ"—the means by which they could come unto Christ and be saved (2 Ne. 30:5; 31:2–32:6). His carefully formulated teaching of this doctrine provided a model that other Nephite prophets invoked repeatedly.

Because the Nephites had received the fulness of the gospel of Jesus Christ, their strict observance of the law of Moses was oriented toward its ultimate fulfillment in Jesus, and Nephi explained to his people that they should observe the law of Moses as a means of keeping Christ's future atonement always in their minds (2 Ne. 25:29–30). The law itself had become "dead" to those who were "made alive in Christ" and who knew that Jesus was the one to whom they could look directly "for a remission of their sins" (2 Ne. 25:25–27).

RECORD KEEPING AND LITERACY. Nephi founded the extensive Nephite tradition of record keeping (see BOOK OF MORMON PLATES AND RECORDS). He was inspired to keep two separate accounts, both of which were continued for hundreds of years. The official record kept by the kings, known as the large plates of Nephi, began with the book of Lehi and contained the historical chronicles of the Nephites for one thousand years. The GOLD PLATES given to Joseph Smith contained Mormon's abridged version of Nephi's large plates and provided most of the text for the Book of Mormon (from the book of Mosiah to the book of Mormon). However, thirty years after leaving Jerusalem, Nephi was instructed by God to compose a second record focusing on spiritual matters. Known as the small plates of Nephi, this record contains Nephi's retrospective account of the founding events and subsequent prophecies of a line of prophets and priests that descended from Jacob down to about 200 B.C. The opening books in today's printed Book of Mormon, 1 Nephi through Omni, come from this record. Nephi's revelations and inspired teachings shaped the religious understanding of his followers, the Nephites.

When Nephi began writing his small plates, he was a mature prophet-king. The record reveals his concern with helping his people and their descendants to understand the future atonement of Jesus Christ and the legitimacy of his own calling as their ruler and teacher. In composing this record, Nephi used his father's record and his own earlier and more comprehensive record, both unavailable today.

The exceptional literacy of the later Nephite leaders may have been due to the fact that Nephi was a man of letters. The text suggests that he was probably fluent in both Hebrew and Egyptian and states that he had been "taught somewhat in all the learning" of the Jews and of his father (1 Ne. 1:1–3).

Nephi displayed literary learning in the way he organized his writings and in the variety of literary forms and devices he employed, including those of narrative, rhetoric, and poetry, including a psalm. The techniques, stories, prophecies, and teachings of Nephi provided models and substance for his successors (*see* BOOK OF MORMON AS LITERATURE). He loved the writings of Isaiah and quoted them extensively (e.g., 1 Ne. 20–21; 2 Ne. 12–24), often providing interpretations.

THE MAN AND HIS MESSAGES.   Nephi constructed the book of 1 Nephi on a tightly balanced and interrelated set of founding stories and revelations, all designed to show "that the tender mercies of the Lord are over all those whom he hath chosen, because of their faith, to make them mighty even unto the power of deliverance" (1 Ne. 1:20). Nephi supports this thesis in 1 Nephi with stories of how God has intervened in human affairs to deliver his faithful followers, and Nephi in particular, from their enemies. But these are only types and shadows. Nephi's true proof is set forth in 2 Nephi, where he says that the atonement of Jesus Christ makes available to all who have faith in Christ a liberation from sin and spiritual redemption from hell and the devil, their greatest enemy. All men and women who follow the example of Christ and enter into his way through repentance and baptism will be blessed with a baptism of fire and the Holy Ghost—which brings individual guidance and a remission of sin—so that they might endure to the end in faith and receive eternal life (2 Ne. 31).

Into a more spiritual account on his small plates, Nephi also wove a vivid defense of his own political primacy by using allusions to MOSES and JOSEPH OF EGYPT (Reynolds, 1987). In defending his ruling position as a younger son, Nephi tells how the two oldest sons rejected their father and the Lord and how he (Nephi) was selected and blessed by the Lord and his father. He relates how, with the help of the Lord, he acquired the brass plates (1 Ne. 3–4), persuaded Ishmael and his family to join Lehi's group (1 Ne. 7), prevented starvation in the wilderness (1 Ne. 16), and constructed a ship and sailed it successfully across the ocean (1 Ne. 17–18). In these exploits, Nephi was consistently opposed and threatened, even with death, by Laman and Lemuel; but in each crisis, he was miraculously delivered by the power of the Lord and blessed to complete his task.

Though he was unable to bridge the gulf between himself and his brothers, Nephi's writings reveal that he was a man with an impressive range of human sensitivities, and he yearned for their welfare. He developed his enormous faith in his father and in the Lord at a young age and never faltered. Consequently, he obeyed without murmuring. He pondered his father's prophecies and repeatedly asked the Lord for personal understanding and direction. He had a deep love and sense of responsibility for his people: "I pray continually for them by day, and mine eyes water my pillow by night, because of them" (2 Ne. 33:3). He also had charity for all other people. Nephi gloried in plainness and in truth, and he knew that his words were harsh against unrepentant sinners (2 Ne. 33:5–9). He anguished deeply because of temptations and his own sins, and particularly because of his feelings of anger against his enemies (2 Ne. 4:26–29). His spiritual strength and depth were grounded in the knowledge that

Jesus Christ had heard his pleas and had redeemed his soul from hell (2 Ne. 33:6).

BIBLIOGRAPHY

Bergin, Allen E. "Nephi, A Universal Man." *Ensign* 6 (Sept. 1976):65–70.

Cannon, George Q. *The Life of Nephi.* Salt Lake City, 1883; repr. 1957.

Reynolds, Noel B. "Nephi's Outline." *BYU Studies* 20 (Winter 1980):131–49.

———. "The Political Dimension in Nephi's Small Plates." *BYU Studies* 27 (Fall 1987):15–37.

Sondrup, Steven P. "The Psalm of Nephi: A Lyric Reading." *BYU Studies* 21 (Summer 1981):357–72.

Turner, Rodney. "The Prophet Nephi." In *The Book of Mormon: First Nephi, the Doctrinal Foundation,* ed. M. Nyman and C. Tate, pp. 79–97. Provo, Utah, 1988.

NOEL B. REYNOLDS

NEPHI₂

Nephi₂ succeeded his father, HELAMAN₃, in 39 B.C. as the Nephite chief judge, evidently at a young age. Because of wickedness among the Nephites, he resigned the judgment seat in 30 B.C. and went with his younger brother Lehi to preach the gospel of Jesus Christ among the Lamanites. Although imprisoned and threatened with death, they were preserved by the power of God and converted thousands of Lamanites (Hel. 5).

Nephi returned thereafter to Zarahemla, boldly condemned the corrupt Nephite leaders, miraculously revealed the identity of a murderer, and exercised the power of God to invoke a famine on the Nephites. Although the Nephites repented occasionally, their conversion and the peace that followed did not last. When time was about to expire on the prophecy of SAMUEL THE LAMANITE regarding the birth of Christ, Nephi passed the records to his son NEPHI₃ and left, never to be heard of again (3 Ne. 1:3; 2:9).

BIBLIOGRAPHY

Welch, John W. "Longevity of Book of Mormon People and the Age of Man." *Journal of the Collegium Aesculapium* 3 (1985):34–42.

MELVIN J. THORNE

NEPHI₃

Nephi₃ was the eldest son of Nephi₂. He was given responsibility for all the Nephite records in 1 B.C. (3 Ne. 1:2). Because of his great faith and his concern for his people, he was told by the voice of Jesus the day before Jesus' birth that the Savior would be born "on the morrow." Later, he consolidated, led, and defended the righteous, moving them to the land Bountiful. He survived the destructions occurring in the Western Hemisphere at the Savior's death (3 Ne. 8–9) and was the first to whom the resurrected Christ gave the power to baptize (3 Ne. 11:18–22). He served as the leading disciple in the Church spoken of in this part of the Book of Mormon and saw his people enjoy years of peace and righteousness.

BIBLIOGRAPHY
Arnold, Marilyn. "The Nephi We Tend to Forget." *Ensign* 8 (Jan. 1978):68–71.

MELVIN J. THORNE

NEPHI₄

Nephi₄ was the son of NEPHI₃. Nephi₄ kept the Nephite records during the extraordinarily blessed era that followed the appearance of Jesus Christ to the Nephites. He saw his people live in love, unity (having all things in common), righteousness, and obedience because the love of God abounded in their hearts. A type of united order or law of consecration was practiced by them during this time. His people experienced the rebuilding of cities, prosperity, miracles, peace, and happiness. Little else is known about his life. He died sometime after A.D. 110 (see 4 Ne. 1:1–19).

MELVIN J. THORNE

NEPHITES

[*The Nephites are the primary group who kept the record known as the Book of Mormon. This complex population was initially descended from*

Lehi *through four of his sons (Sam,* Nephi₁, *Jacob, and Joseph) and their friend* Zoram, *although the descendants of other people also joined themselves to the Nephites from time to time (see* Book of Mormon Peoples*). The Nephites were distinguished by their belief in the gospel of Jesus Christ, as taught by Lehi and Nephi, as opposed to the lack of faith of the* Lamanites, *often their enemies but also descendants of Lehi.*

For an account of Nephite life, see Book of Mormon Economy and Technology. *Political and legal practices among the Nephites are described in* Book of Mormon, Government and Legal History in. *The traditions of record keeping among the Nephites are summarized in* Book of Mormon Plates and Records. *Nephite religious belief and culture are detailed in* Book of Mormon Religious Teachings and Practices. *Nephite women and their contributions are reported in* Women in the Book of Mormon.]

NEUM

Neum was an ancient Israelite PROPHET whose words were contained on the PLATES of brass, a record carried to the Western Hemisphere from JERUSALEM about 600 B.C. by the Book of Mormon prophet LEHI and his colony. Neum's work is not preserved in the Hebrew Bible or other known sources. Concerning the time of his writing, it is only definite that he predated Lehi's departure.

Neum is mentioned only once in the Book of Mormon. In writing to his future readers, Nephi₁ cited him along with other prophets who foretold aspects of the mortal mission of Jesus Christ. According to Neum's words, the God of ABRAHAM, Isaac, and Jacob (Jesus Christ) would be crucified (1 Ne. 19:10). This confirmed what Nephi himself had seen previously in a vision (1 Ne. 11:32–33).

KENT P. JACKSON

NEW HEAVEN AND NEW EARTH

This phrase depicts the earth's destiny of renewal, one cosmic aspect of the RESTORATION OF ALL THINGS. In LDS theology, "the earth will be renewed and receive its paradisiacal glory" (A of F 10). That renewal will include restoration of its former components—for example, the return of the city of ENOCH—and also its former purity and Edenic state.

Ancient biblical prophets taught that the beginnings of this fulfillment are to be associated with the coming of the Messiah and his millennial reign. The phrase reflects the vision of Isaiah (65:17; 66:22) and the revelation of JOHN (Rev. 2:17; 3:12; 5:9; 14:3; 21:1). Book of Mormon prophets likewise speak of a new heaven and a new earth (Ether 13:9) and of "all things" becoming new (3 Ne. 15:2). The Doctrine and Covenants contains prophecies that every corruptible "element shall melt with fervent heat; and all things shall become new, that [God's] knowledge and glory may dwell upon all the earth" (D&C 101:23; cf. 29:23–24; 42:35, 62, 67; 45:66; 84:2–4; 133:56).

The Hebrew root for "new" (*chadash*) points to a time of refreshing rather than replacement. Consistent with this understanding, Mormons expect that the earth will not be destroyed but glorified, not transcended but transformed, and that ultimately the polarization of earth and heaven will be overcome. Faithful Saints are promised the "fulness of the earth" (D&C 59:16) and "an inheritance upon the earth when the day of transfiguration shall come, when the earth shall be transfigured" (D&C 63:20–21).

The earth fills the "measure [the purpose] of its creation" (D&C 88:19, 25) and its biography follows typologically that of mankind. It has fallen from paradise, it has been baptized in water, and it will be baptized by fire. It will die (Isa. 51:6; D&C 45:22; 88:26) and be "quickened again," and will not only regain its pristine condition but a higher state still (D&C 88:25–26). "This earth will be Christ's" (D&C 130:9). It will have a one-thousand-year sabbatical and then become a veritable URIM AND THUMMIM in fulfillment of John's vision of its appearance as a "sea of glass" (D&C 130:7–9; Rev. 2:17), a habitation worthy of God. "It will be rolled back into the presence of God" and "crowned with celestial glory" (*TPJS*, p. 181; cf. *WJS*, p. 60). Then those who have been "quickened by a portion of the celestial glory shall then receive of the same, even a fulness" (D&C 88:29). God, "in whose bosom it is decreed that the poor and the meek of the earth shall inherit it" (D&C 88:17), will fulfill his promise "that bodies who are of the celestial kingdom may possess it forever and ever; for for this intent was it made and created, and for this intent are they sanctified" (D&C 88:20).

BIBLIOGRAPHY

Turner, Rodney. *Footstool of God: Earth in Scripture and Prophecy*. Orem, Utah, 1983.

THOMAS J. RISKAS, JR.

NEW JERUSALEM

For Latter-day Saints, the gathering of ISRAEL in the last days and the building of the city of ZION and of the New Jerusalem are closely related concepts.

The tenth article of faith, written by the Prophet Joseph Smith in 1842, declares that the New Jerusalem will be built upon the American continent. He learned this as he translated the Book of Mormon (3 Ne. 20:22; Ether 13:2–6). Additional revelation on this subject came in September 1830 and was further clarified in the subsequent months (D&C 28:9; 42:33–36, 62, 67; 57:3). In July 1831, Joseph Smith traveled to Jackson County, Missouri, at the command of the Lord, where it was announced that the long-awaited gathering of Israel would commence. The city of Zion (also called the New Jerusalem) and its temple would be built in Independence, Missouri (D&C 57:1–3).

Even as the ancient tribes of Israel were scattered north of the Holy Land and their identity was lost, their prophets foretold a gathering of Israel in the last days in a consecrated land (Jer. 31:1–12). Zion would be reestablished. This prophecy includes the promise that the "pure in heart" will receive the higher principles and truths of the full gospel of Jesus Christ (D&C 97:21; 100:16; 101:18). Both where and how they live will come about under divine influence. Since favorable spiritual conditions may exist anywhere in the world, cities of Zion and of Zion people, the "pure in heart," could be located anywhere in the world (D&C 97:21). However, there is to be a "center place," or capital city, of Zion. It is referred to both as "the city of Zion" and as "the city of New Jerusalem" (D&C 57:2; 84:2; cf. 45:66–67).

The writings of Ether, written prior to 125 B.C., abridged by MORONI$_2$ in the Book of Mormon, prophesy of the preparations for the coming of the Messiah and of a New Jerusalem in the Western Hemisphere. It is to be built by the remnant of the seed of JOSEPH OF EGYPT (Ether 13:3–10). Ether also speaks of the destruction of Jerusalem of old, adding that it will be rebuilt with a temple and become a holy city (Ether 13:11).

Also, the book of Revelation speaks of "the holy city, new Jerusalem, coming down from God out of heaven" (Rev. 21:2, 10). This may relate to the return of the city of Enoch, the Zion that in Enoch's day was caught up into heaven (Moses 7:12–21, 59–64).

The future rebuilding of the Holy Land for the house of Judah and the building of the New Jerusalem in the Western Hemisphere for the house of Joseph are associated with the return of the Messiah to the earth. Of this era, the 1845 Proclamation of the Twelve (*MFP* 1:252–66) says:

> He will assemble the Natives, the remnants of Joseph in America; and make them a great, and strong, and powerful nation: and he will civilize and enlighten them, and will establish a holy city, and temple and seat of government among them, which shall be called Zion.
>
> And there shall be his tabernacle, his sanctuary, his throne, and seat of government for the whole continent of North and South America for ever. In short, it will be to the western hemisphere what Jerusalem will be to the eastern. . . .
>
> The city of Zion, with its sanctuary and priesthood, and the glorious fulness of the gospel, will constitute a standard which will put an end to jarring creeds and political wranglings, by uniting the republics, states, provinces, territories, nations, tribes, kindred, tongues, people and sects of North and South America in one great and common bond of brotherhood. Truth and knowledge shall make them free, and love cement their union. The Lord also shall be their king and their lawgiver; while wars shall cease and peace prevail for a thousand years [pp. 259–60].

The prophet Isaiah declared that in a future time "out of Zion shall go forth the law, and the word of the Lord from Jerusalem" (Isa. 2:2–3; cf. Micah 4:1–2). Latter-day Saints believe this refers to the two Zion headquarters in the two hemispheres from which the Messiah, the returned Son of God, will reign triumphantly over the whole earth.

GRAHAM W. DOXEY

NEW TESTAMENT

During the early centuries of the Christian era, the New Testament gospels were the principal written witness of Jesus as the Christ. No other collection of writings carried the insight, the power of teaching, and, consequently, the spiritual appeal to Christians. The New Testament also stands as the foundation of the RESTORATION of the gospel in the latter days. It was while reading in the Epistle of JAMES (1:5) that the youthful Joseph Smith was inspired to pray to the Lord about his confusion over religious matters, leading to his first vision (JS—H 1:7–20). The New Testament is one of the STANDARD WORKS, or canonized scriptures, accepted by Latter-day Saints, who seek spiritual strength and enlightenment from its pages. Further, they accept the New Testament sketches as accurate portrayals of the life and ministry of Jesus Christ as well as the ministry of his apostles and their associates, that reveal much of the order and organization of the earliest New Testament Church. Moreover, the New Testament includes many of God's covenants and commandments given personally by Jesus and, after his ascension, through his apostles. Latter-day Saints also value the New Testament prophecies about the latter days.

The writings of the New Testament were likely all produced within the first century of the Christian era. Even so, its collection of texts went through three centuries of changes, and acceptance or rejection, before it acquired its recognized and current form, first listed in the Easter letter of Athanasius in Egypt in A.D. 367. The third synod of Carthage (A.D. 397) canonized the books of the New Testament as represented in the letter of Athanasius because each writing had three qualifications: apostolic authority, support of a major Christian community, and an absence of false teachings.

The rise of so-called heresies in the second century demonstrated the loss of prophetic revelation and thus marked the need for Christians to turn back to the apostles for authoritative writings. One of the heretics, Marcion (c. A.D. 130), limited his early collection of scripture to one gospel, Luke, and to the letters of Paul, which he freely edited.

THE GOSPELS.   For at least two reasons Latter-day Saints view the New Testament gospels as essentially accurate accounts of the life and ministry of Jesus Christ. First, many pre-Christian prophecies, especially in the Book of Mormon, detailed specific events in Jesus' life, including his mother's name, circumstances of his birth, his baptism, his selection of twelve apostles, the miracles he performed, his rejection and suffering, and his death and resurrection (e.g., 1 Ne. 11:13–36; Mosiah 3:5–11). Second, Joseph Smith's inspired work in the JOSEPH SMITH TRANSLATION OF THE BIBLE (JST) led him to add clarifying details to the setting and content of certain stories about Jesus and to view many of Jesus' PARABLES and teachings as applicable to the latter days.

The Gospel of Matthew is characterized by two distinct features: frequent use of Old Testament references and six of Jesus' discourses (*see* MATTHEW, GOSPEL OF). It is assumed that Matthew's frequent use of Old Testament references indicates both a Jewish audience and the view that Christianity was the fulfillment of prophetic Judaism.

Significantly for Latter-day Saints, portions of this gospel receive attention in extrabiblical scriptures. For instance, the Book of Mormon records that when the resurrected Jesus visited disciples in the Western Hemisphere (c. A.D. 34), he delivered a sermon almost identical to the SERMON ON THE MOUNT, underscoring the validity and universality of the sermon (3 Ne. 12–14; Matt. 5–7; *see also* BEATITUDES). Additionally, Joseph Smith's work on the JST led him to make inspired revisions, the most frequently noted being those in the Sermon on the Mount and in Jesus' discourse about the fate of Jerusalem and his second coming (Matt. 24; *see* JOSEPH SMITH—MATTHEW).

While only modest attention has been given to Mark's gospel in LDS scholarly writings, Church members have traditionally found great value in studying its pages. Its portrayal of Jesus may be the most dynamic, and may ultimately go back to the eyewitness recollections of PETER, the chief apostle.

The Gospel of Luke, called by some scholars "the most beautiful book" in the world, holds special interest for Latter-day Saints for several reasons, including its narrative of the Christmas story, its seventeen parables not recorded elsewhere, its strong emphases on remission of sin and Jesus' sympathy for all people, its account of the call and mission of the seventy disciples, and the distinct prominence it gives to women.

The Gospel of JOHN was written that "ye might believe that Jesus is the Christ" (John 20:31). Besides presenting a series of Jesus' discourses not contained in the other gospels, John uses a series of "Messianic metaphors" to disclose Jesus' divine nature and his mission: Word; Lamb; Living Water; I Am; Bread of Life; Living Bread; Light of the World; Good Shepherd; Resurrection; the Way, Truth and Life; and the True Vine. Many of these metaphors also appear in the Doctrine and Covenants, a latter-day scripture, where such language is expanded and applied to the restored Church. Further, Jesus' discussion of "other sheep," recorded only in John 10:14–16, was specifically referred to by the risen Jesus during his visit to disciples in the Western Hemisphere when he wanted to make a point about those to whom he was sent to minister (3 Ne. 15:12–24). During that same post-Resurrection visit, Jesus used several phrases and descriptions—particularly of himself and his work—that are characteristic of John's gospel (e.g., 3 Ne. 11:10–11, 14, 27, 32–36).

THE ACTS OF THE APOSTLES.   From the narrative of the ascension of Jesus through the account of the ministry of Paul, the book of Acts relates the spiritual ministry of apostolic witnesses during the early years of Christianity. Latter-day Saints are interested that, in replacing Judas, one apostle was chosen to complete the twelve and that Peter set the qualifications of apostles: They must know the ministry of Jesus, they must be ordained, and they must be witnesses of his resurrection (Acts 1:21–22). Latter-day apostles in the Church are also "special witnesses of the name of Christ in all the world" (D&C 107:23; cf. 27:12; 84:108). In addition, the book of Acts indicates the rich outpouring of the Holy Ghost in the early Church, both in the form of guiding revelation and in manifestations of the gifts of the Spirit, characteristics that Latter-day Saints experience and value. Further, certain prophetic statements have particular meaning. For example, Latter-day Saints understand Paul's prophecy to the elders of Ephesus concerning mutinous problems within the early Church to be an inspired declaration about the impending apostasy (Acts 20:29–30). Moreover, they view Peter's prediction of Jesus' return from heaven at "the times of restitution of all things" as commencing with the latter-day restoration of the gospel (3:19–21). Further, the book of Acts has a good deal to say about the organization, doctrines, and character of the preaching of the early Christian church.

THE EPISTLES. Letters in the New Testament are traditionally divided into two groups, the writings of Paul and the general epistles.

The style of Paul's writings varies from the almost formal exposition in Romans to the charming persuasion in Philemon. In addition to teachings valued by other Christians, Latter-day Saints exhibit particular interest in certain doctrines, ecclesiastical offices, and practices noted in Paul's works. For instance, the place of the Gentiles in the history of salvation (Rom. 9–11) is also addressed in the Book of Mormon (e.g., 1 Ne. 13:20–14:7; 22:6–11; 2 Ne. 10:8–18; see GENTILES, FULNESS OF); joint-heirship with Christ (Rom. 8:16–17) is taught in modern revelation (D&C 84:35–38); adoption into the covenant people of God (Rom. 8:14–15) is taught in the Book of Mormon (e.g., 2 Ne. 30:2); the value of spiritual gifts (1 Cor. 12; cf. 1 Thes. 5:19–20) is emphasized in modern scripture (D&C 46); the importance of charity, or love (1 Cor. 13), is underscored particularly by words of the prophet Mormon (Moro. 7:40–48); Paul's list of virtues to be sought (Philip. 4:8) is the base of Joseph Smith's thirteenth article of faith; the encroaching apostasy (Gal. 1:6–9) and disunity in the early church (1 Cor. 1:10–13), as well as Paul's prophecy about the inevitability of the apostasy (2 Thes. 2:1–4; cf. 1 Tim. 4:1–3), formed an important focus of the risen Jesus' words to Joseph Smith in the First Vision (JS—H 1:18–19); the fulfillment of the LAW OF MOSES in Christ (e.g., Gal. 3) is emphatically affirmed by the risen Jesus in the Book of Mormon (3 Ne. 15:3–10; cf. 9:19–20); and his literal physical resurrection, attended by many proofs (1 Cor. 15), is underlined and augmented by the appearances of the risen Jesus to disciples in the Western Hemisphere (c. A.D. 34; 3 Ne. 11–28) and in statements to Joseph Smith (cf. D&C 130:22). In matters of Church organization, Latter-day Saints find Paul's discussions of apostolic leadership (Gal. 1:18–19; 2:9–10) and his mention of priesthood offices such as apostles, prophets, Evangelists (Eph. 2:19–21; 4:11–13), and bishops and deacons (1 Tim. 3) to be significant for Church administration. In terms of practices or ordinances, Latter-day Saints value Paul's statements on the sacrament (1 Cor. 10:14–21; 11:23–30; cf. 3 Ne. 18:28–29; Moro. 4–5), his mention of baptism for the dead (1 Cor. 15:29), and his instructions on the laying on of hands (1 Tim. 4:14; 5:22). These things exist in the LDS

Church as a result of latter-day revelation, and the New Testament epistles attest to their presence in the early Church.

Concerning the general epistles, that of James stands out in the LDS view because of its influence on the young Joseph Smith. In addition to the passage that led him to pray for divine guidance (James 1:5), Latter-day Saints value both the teaching that the quality of one's faith in Christ is mirrored in one's daily actions (James 2:14–26) and the practice of blessing the sick (James 5:14–15). From the writings of Peter, perhaps the most frequently cited are those that speak of Jesus' mission among departed spirits while his body lay in the tomb (1 Pet. 3:18–20; 4:6), an important subject in latter-day revelation (D&C 138). In addition, passages that discuss the TRANSFIGURATION (2 Pet. 1:17–18) and the inspired means whereby prophecy is to be interpreted (2 Pet. 1:19–21) hold interest for Latter-day Saints. Because they are led by apostles and believe that an apostasy occurred from the early Christian church, Latter-day Saints have been drawn to the components of the apostolic witness in John's letters (1 Jn. 1:1) and to indications that a serious apostasy was already under way in the early Church (1 Jn. 4:1–3; 3 Jn. 1:9–10).

BOOK OF REVELATION.   Besides naming the apostle John as the author of this work (1 Ne. 14:18–28), latter-day scripture has focused both on issues mentioned in the book of Revelation (D&C 77) and on additional material written by John (D&C 7; see JOHN, REVELATIONS OF). Latter-day Saint interest has focused on matters that have to do with the latter days (cf. *TPJS*, pp. 287–94), including the discussions of the eventual demise of evil and the millennial reign of Christ and his righteous followers (Rev. 19–20), the anticipation of the NEW JERUSALEM (Rev. 21), and the vision of "another angel [flying] in the midst of heaven, having the everlasting gospel to preach unto them that dwell on the earth" (Rev. 14:6). This latter passage has usually been interpreted as referring to the angel MORONI, who visited Joseph Smith in 1823 and revealed to him the burial place of the GOLD PLATES. Moreover, Latter-day Saints understand the warning against adding to or taking away from the book (Rev. 22:18–19) as applying specifically to the book of Revelation rather than to an expanding canon of scripture that they value (cf. Deut. 4:2; 12:32; 2 Ne. 29:3–14).

BIBLIOGRAPHY

Anderson, Richard L. *Understanding Paul.* Salt Lake City, 1983.

Bruce, Frederick Fyvie. *New Testament History.* Garden City, N.Y., 1972.

Conybeare, W. J., and John S. Howson. *The Life and Epistles of St. Paul.* Grand Rapids, Mich., 1968 (reprint).

Edersheim, Alfred. *The Life and Times of Jesus the Messiah,* 2 vols. Grand Rapids, Mich., 1950 (reprint).

Jackson, Kent P., and Robert L. Millet, eds. *Studies in Scripture,* Vol. 5. Salt Lake City, 1986.

McConkie, Bruce R. *Doctrinal New Testament Commentary,* 3 vols. Salt Lake City, 1965–1973.

————. *The Promised Messiah: The First Coming of Christ.* Salt Lake City, 1978.

————. *The Mortal Messiah: From Bethlehem to Calvary,* 4 vols. Salt Lake City, 1979–1981.

Millet, Robert L., ed. *Studies in Scripture,* Vol. 6. Salt Lake City, 1987.

Sperry, Sidney B. *Paul's Life and Letters.* Salt Lake City, 1955.

Talmage, James E. *JC.* Salt Lake City, 1915.

ROBERT C. PATCH

NOAH

Noah is one of God's most notable prophets, patriarchs, and ministering messengers. He became a second father—with ADAM—of all mankind following the Flood and later returned to earth as the angel Gabriel to announce the births of JOHN THE BAPTIST and Jesus Christ (*HC* 3:386; *TPJS*, p. 157). LDS revelation has amplified what is known about Noah in the Bible.

Lamech, son of Methuselah and grandson of ENOCH, begat Noah, fulfilling COVENANTS that the Lord made with Enoch that a remnant of his posterity would always be found among all nations (Moses 7:52) and that Noah would be born of his lineage through Methuselah (Moses 8:2). Lamech chose the name Noah because of the "comfort" the child would bring to his family in their toil (8:9). Though Noah had brothers and sisters, nothing about them is known (8:10).

A promised child of noble ancestry, including Adam and other "preachers of righteousness" (Moses 6:22–23), Noah was ordained to the priesthood at age ten by Methuselah (D&C 107:52), an unusually young age when compared with the ages at which other antediluvian patriarchs were ordained (D&C 107:42–51).

Though Noah lived in times of wickedness (Moses 8:20–22,

28–30), Noah successfully raised three sons who "hearkened unto the Lord . . . and they were called the sons of God" (8:13). Unfortunately, his "fair" granddaughters "sold themselves" by marrying wicked husbands, losing the benefits of living in a righteous environment (8:14–15). He taught the gospel of the anticipated Savior Anointed (Jesus Christ), as Enoch had, including faith, repentance, baptism in the name of the Savior, and reception of the Holy Ghost (Moses 8:16, 19, 23–24). He warned that failure to heed his message would bring the floods upon his hearers (D&C 138:41; Moses 8:24).

Noah was "perfect in his generation; and he walked with God" (Moses 8:27). Like Adam, he received dominion over the earth and all living things (*HC* 3:386). Thus, Methuselah's PROPHECY "that from his [own] loins should spring all the kingdoms of the earth (through Noah)" was dramatically fulfilled (Moses 8:3).

Noah stands "next in authority to Adam in the Priesthood" (*HC* 3:386), and "in third position from the Lord" (Petersen, p. 2), and conferred the power of the priesthood on his righteous posterity (D&C 84:14–15).

Eighteen centuries after announcing Christ's birth, Noah—again as Gabriel—visited the Prophet Joseph Smith to restore priesthood keys (D&C 128:21). Noah is to return to earth after Christ's second coming to attend the MARRIAGE SUPPER OF THE LAMB (D&C 27:5–7).

BIBLIOGRAPHY

Parrish, Alan K. "The Days of Noah." In *Studies in Scripture*, ed. R. Millet and K. Jackson, Vol. 2, pp. 145–59. Salt Lake City, 1985.

Petersen, Mark E. *Noah and the Flood.* Salt Lake City, 1982.

ANDREW C. SKINNER

O

OATHS

Oaths are solemn declarations used to affirm a statement or strengthen a promise. Anciently, oath-swearing formed an important part of social, political, economic, and religious interaction. God himself uses an oath and promise in his covenants with man (cf. Jer. 22:5; Amos 6:8; D&C 97:20). In covenant-making, ritual oaths attest the fidelity of those entering into the covenant. Sometimes an oath is sworn that anticipates punishment in case of failure to perform a specified act, and in some cases the covenant process symbolically depicts specific punishments (Jer. 34:18–19).

Oath-swearing was common among the Book of Mormon peoples. NEPHI₁ swore an oath to Zoram assuring him full status in Lehi's family (1 Ne. 4:32–34), and Zoram swore to accompany Nephi and his brothers into the wilderness, after which their "fears did cease concerning him" (1 Ne. 4:37). Oaths of office were administered to judges (Alma 50:39). In a manner reminiscent of biblical and other Near Eastern peoples, the NEPHITES swore to support MORONI₁ in defensive war, and used their rent garments to represent the punishment they wished upon themselves should they fail (Alma 46:21–22).

Oaths were also used with evil intent. For sinister purposes, the Gadianton robbers and the JAREDITES swore secret oaths that had once been sworn by Cain (Hel. 6:21–26; Ether 8:15; Moses 5:29).

Oaths continue to play a role in Latter-day Saint religion and ritual. The higher priesthood is received through an "oath and covenant" (D&C 84:39–40; cf. Heb. 7:11–22) of faithfulness. Following a pattern similar to ancient covenant-making, Latter-day Saints make holy covenants in temples. In their worship and prayer they use the word amen, which in Hebrew means "verily," "truly," or "let it be affirmed," and is considered a form of an oath comparable to expressions used in ancient Israel (Deut. 27:14–26; cf. D&C 88:135). The raising of the right hand of the congregation in periodic conferences in approval for those called to Church positions is viewed as a silent oath signifying one's determination to sustain those persons in their callings.

Frequent and superficial use of oaths can become an abuse and may diminish their sincere and sacred functions, and oaths made "in vain" are profane and blasphemous. Christ admonished his followers to avoid oaths sworn without real intent and told them to make their commitments simply by saying "yes" or "no" (Matt. 5:33–37; 23:16–22).

BIBLIOGRAPHY
Johnson, Roy. "The Use of Oaths in the Old Testament and the Book of Mormon." *F.A.R.M.S.*, Provo, Utah, 1982.
Szink, Terrence. "An Oath of Allegiance in the Book of Mormon." In *Warfare in the Book of Mormon*, ed. S. Ricks and W. Hamblin. Salt Lake City, 1990.

TERRENCE L. SZINK

OIL, CONSECRATED

Olive oil is used by members of The Church of Jesus Christ of Latter-day Saints in blessing the sick and in performing initiatory ordinances in the temple. Before oil is used, it is consecrated in a short ceremony. An officiating Melchizedek Priesthood bearer, holding an open vessel containing pure olive oil, consecrates it by the authority of the priesthood and in the name of Jesus Christ for its intended purposes. The oil is then stored and used upon occasion as required.

The use of oil in religious rites can be seen in the record of Old Testament times, when it was used to anoint objects (Gen. 28:18–19; Lev. 8:10–12), as an offering (Ex. 25:1–6), and to anoint priests (Ex.

29:7; Lev. 21:10–12) and kings (1 Sam. 10:1; 16:3). In the New Testament, oil was used to anoint the sick (Mark 6:13; James 5:14).

Two New Testament PARABLES illustrate possible symbolisms of oil both as a therapeutic ointment and as a source of light. The good Samaritan, finding the injured traveler, "bound up his wounds, pouring in oil and wine" (Luke 10:34). In another parable wise virgins "took oil in their vessels with their lamps" and thus were in possession of material to provide light, to celebrate the coming of the bridegroom, Christ (Matt. 25:1–13).

The reason for using olive oil rather than any other kind of oil is never clearly stated in the scriptures. To say that olive oil is preferred because it is the oil indigenous to the Holy Land would be simplistic. A more likely explanation results from examining the wide range of meanings symbolized by the olive tree and the oil derived from the olive fruit, the only major culinary oil that is derived from a fruit. The olive branch has long been a token of peace. The olive tree is used in scripture as a symbol for the house of Israel (Hosea 14:6; Rom. 11:17; Jacob 5; D&C 101:43–62).

PAUL Y. HOSKISSON

OLD TESTAMENT

The Old Testament is one of the STANDARD WORKS, or SCRIPTURES, accepted by The Church of Jesus Christ of Latter-day Saints, which values it for its prophetic, historical, doctrinal, and moral teachings. The Old Testament recounts an epochal series of ancient dispensations during which people received periodic guidance through divine covenants and commandments, many of which remain basic and timeless. In relation to the Old Testament, it is significant for Latter-day Saints that in September 1823 the angel Moroni quoted a series of Old Testament PROPHECIES when he revealed the location of an ancient record written on GOLD PLATES to the Prophet Joseph Smith, whose translation yielded the Book of Mormon (JS—H 1:36–41). Moreover, Joseph Smith's extensive labors on the Old Testament and the accompanying revelations to him (June 1830–July 1833), which led to the JOSEPH SMITH TRANSLATION OF THE BIBLE (JST) and certain informative sections of the Doctrine and Covenants, underscore the importance of these scriptural texts. In addition, from the Book of Mormon it is clear that before 600 B.C. the prophet LEHI and his colony carried to the Western Hemisphere from Jerusalem a record on the PLATES of brass that included many Old Testament texts (1 Ne. 5:10–15), leading Lehi and his descendants to look forward to a redeemer (1 Ne. 19:22–23) and giving them a guide for their moral and spiritual development (Mosiah 1:3, 5).

The Old Testament, even by the name Old Covenant, is thus not outmoded in the LDS view. It contains narrative, wisdom, and prophetic literature from ancient epochs; and even though some "plain and precious" parts have been lost, many of these have been restored in LDS scripture (1 Ne. 13:40). It frames a series of ancient covenants with Jehovah (Jesus Christ) as distinguished from the higher covenants in the New Testament (e.g., Matt. 26:28; Luke 22:20; 1 Cor. 11:25; 2 Cor. 3:6; Heb. 7:22). Latter-day Saints view them all as elements in the same divine plan of salvation.

ETERNAL COVENANTS AND COMMANDMENTS.   Latter-day Saints feel a need to learn and practice the principles prescribed in all the divine covenants and commandments, which are eternally valid. To know and understand God's eternal purposes requires a study of the past eras documented in the Old Testament, together with those available in other ancient and modern scriptures. For example, Latter-day revelations help Latter-day Saints read the Old Testament with fuller appreciation for the continuity of the eternally significant concepts taught by the prophets in the scriptures.

From the beginning, the divine covenants associated with salvation have been taught through prophetic words, and some have been typified by sacrificial ordinances. A revelation to Moses, restored through Joseph Smith, states that animal sacrifice was required from the days of Adam and Eve (Moses 5:5) and that such sacrifices were "a similitude of the sacrifice of the Only Begotten of the Father" (Moses 5:7).

Another Old Testament covenant verified in modern revelation is the Abrahamic covenant. It pertains not alone to literal descendants of Abraham but also to those adopted into Abraham's family because of their faith in the true God and their baptism into the gospel of Christ (Gen. 12:1; Gal. 3:26–29). These "descendants" of Abraham are charged with bringing the blessings of this covenant to all nations, through teaching about the true and living God and making known his plan of salvation (Abr. 2:9–11). Responsibility for knowing and acting in accordance with the covenant of Abraham has been transmitted to latter-day heirs by revelation (D&C 110:12). Moreover, a promise by the resurrected Jesus is recorded in the Book of Mormon that descendants of his ancient covenant people Israel, who have been scattered abroad, shall "be gathered in from the east and from the west, and from the south and from the north; and they shall be brought to the knowledge of the Lord their God, who hath redeemed them" (3 Ne. 20:13). They are to be established in their lands of inheritance and will accomplish their ancient and culminating responsibility of building the kingdom of the Lord (3 Ne. 20:21–46; cf. Isa. 52:1–15). For Latter-day Saints the RESTORATION "of all things" (Acts 3:21) includes many Old Testament principles, doctrines, and ideals.

TEMPORARY AND ETERNAL LAWS.   Latter-day Saints do not believe that when Jesus fulfilled the LAW OF MOSES he thereby abrogated the law, the prophets, and the writings of the Old Testament (3 Ne. 15:5–8). Indeed, he fulfilled the law of sacrifice by allowing his own blood to be shed (Alma 34:13) and by replacing certain ancient worship performances (3 Ne. 12:18–20; 15:2–10). Thus, the feast of Passover became the commemorative sacrament of the Last Supper (Luke 22:1–20): The paschal lamb culminated in the Lamb of God (Ex. 12:5, 21; 1 Cor. 5:7; 1 Pet. 1:19; Rev. 5:6). Sacrifice of animals culminated in Jesus' ultimate sacrifice, of which they were mere types, but the sacrifice of "a broken heart and contrite spirit" continues (3 Ne. 9:19–20; cf. Rom. 12:1).

Jesus reiterated many moral and spiritual laws taught by Moses and the prophets. These include laws regarding REVERENCE for God, respect for parents, chastity in moral conduct, avoiding violence and murder, and practicing honesty with fellow beings (e.g., Matt. 5:17–48; cf. 3 Ne. 12:17–48; Luke 16:19–31; 24:13–47). The Book of Mormon prophet ABINADI reiterated the Ten Commandments and was adamant about the necessity of teaching and living according to their standards (Mosiah 12:33–37; 13:12–26). And latter-day revelation confirms the same necessity for any who would please the Lord (e.g., D&C 20:17–19; 42:18–29; 52:39).

For Latter-day Saints, all principles of morality and righteousness taught by Old Testament prophets remain valid. Micah, for instance, asks, "What doth the Lord require of thee, but to do justly, and to love mercy, and to walk humbly with thy God?" (Micah 6:8). The Lord taught through Habakkuk that divinely inspired visions will surely come to fulfillment, even if far off; therefore, "the just shall live by his faith" (Hab. 2:3–4). Moses urged the Israelites to live according to God's laws as good examples to others: "Keep therefore and do them [the laws and ordinances], for this is your wisdom and your understanding in the sight of the nations, which shall hear all these statutes, and say, Surely this great nation is a wise and understanding people" (Deut. 4:6). Jesus appealed to Deuteronomy and Leviticus concerning the first and second commandments, to love God and one's fellow beings (Deut. 6:4–5; Lev. 19:18, 33–34; Mark 12:28–34).

This, however, is not to say that all worship practices admonished in "the law and the prophets" were to be perpetuated eternally. About 150 B.C., the Book of Mormon prophet Abinadi explained, "I say unto you that it is expedient that ye should keep the law of Moses as yet; but I say unto you, that the time shall come when it shall no more be expedient to keep the law of Moses. And moreover, I say unto you, that salvation doth not come by the law alone; and were it not for the atonement, which God himself shall make for the sins and iniquities of his people, that they must unavoidably perish, notwithstanding the law of Moses" (Mosiah 13:27). The risen Jesus rehearsed teachings which he had fulfilled from the law and the prophets, the Psalms, and "all the scriptures" to the disciples on the road to Emmaus and to the eleven apostles gathered in Jerusalem (Luke 24:13, 27, 33, 44). Only certain things had an end in him (3 Ne. 15:8; Gal. 3:24).

Latter-day Saints therefore value those Old Testament laws and doctrines that are eternal, believing that they were "given by inspiration of God" and are "profitable for doctrine, for reproof, for correction, for instruction in righteousness" (2 Tim. 3:16).

PROPHETIC ANTICIPATION OF THE MESSIAH. More than five centuries before the time of Christ, JACOB, a Book of Mormon prophet, stated that his people knew of Christ through the teachings of Moses and the prophets, and thus had hope of his coming (Jacob 4:4–5). And NEPHI₁ added, "For this end hath the law of Moses been given; and all things which have been given of God from the beginning of the world, unto man, are the typifying of [Christ]" (2 Ne. 11:4). On another occasion, Jacob said that "all the holy prophets . . . believed in Christ," and that his people faithfully kept the law of Moses, "it pointing our souls to [Christ]." Indeed, they saw in Abraham's offering of Isaac "a similitude of God and his Only Begotten Son" (Jacob 4:4–5). Amulek, a later Book of Mormon teacher (c. 75 B.C.), when speaking of the "great and last sacrifice" of the Son of God, declared that "this is the whole meaning of the law, every whit pointing to that great and last sacrifice . . . [of] the Son of God" (Alma 34:13–14).

The relevance of prophetic teachings and ordinances for bringing people to Christ is shown by Jesus' own references to such rites and teachings. While coming down from the MOUNT OF TRANSFIGURATION, he spoke to Peter, James, and John about things "written of the Son of man, that he must suffer many things, and be set at nought" (Mark 9:12; cf. Isa. 53:3–7). In his hometown of Nazareth, he announced his fulfillment of Isaiah's prophecy of the Messiah's actions of healing and making people free (Luke 4:21; Isa. 61:1–2). After healing a man on the Sabbath, Jesus told those who would condemn him that the time was nigh that even the dead would hear his voice, alluding, no doubt, to prophecies of that event (John 5:25; cf. Isa. 24:22). His parting words to that same audience were, "Had ye believed Moses, you would have believed me: for he wrote of me" (John 5:46; cf. Deut. 18:15–19 and Acts 3:22–23; 1 Ne. 22:21; 3 Ne. 20:23). Even in his last mortal hour, as he suffered and fulfilled the promises of redemption, Jesus quoted the first line of Psalm 22—"My God, my God, why hast thou forsaken me?"—as if to point to the imminent fulfillment of the remaining lines of the Psalm (Matt. 27:46; cf. Ps. 22:7–8, 12–19).

Early Christian missionaries converted many to Christ among those who "searched the scriptures daily" (Acts 17:10–12). Those scriptures included what is now known as the Old Testament. Christian teachers succeeded in showing "by the scriptures that Jesus was Christ" (Acts 18:24–28). PAUL declared that scriptures "written aforetime were written for our learning, that we through patience and comfort of the scriptures might have hope" of salvation (Rom. 15:4).

Concerning Christ's future advent, more than a score of "royal" and "messianic" psalms anticipate the Lord's reign in the final age. Psalms 72 and 100 are typical (*see* PSALMS, MESSIANIC PROPHECIES IN). Moreover, in the prophetic books of the Old Testament more chapters look forward to his triumphant final reign than point toward his first advent and sacrifice (e.g., Isa. 40, 43, 45, 52, 60, 63, 65; Ezek. 37–48; Dan. 12; Zech. 12–14).

PROPHECIES FOR PRESENT AND FUTURE.   For Latter-day Saints, the present era of the gospel of Jesus Christ began not only with Joseph Smith's first vision but also with the visits of other divine messengers, who quoted Old Testament prophecies with the promise that they were about to be fulfilled. The angel Moroni quoted to Joseph Smith some of the eschatological prophecies of Malachi, Isaiah, Joel, and— according to Wilford Woodruff—Daniel, and promised their fulfillment (JS—H 1:29, 33, 36–41; *JD* 24:241).

Latter-day Saints use both ancient and modern prophecies to bring the gospel light to the GENTILES so that all can be mutually blessed (Isa. 49:5–22; D&C 86:11; 110:12; 124:9). In the last days the God of heaven will set up his kingdom to embrace all people, rolling forth until it fills the earth (Dan. 2:31–45; D&C 65). The Lord "shall bring again Zion" and, in doing so, will publish peace and salvation, proclaiming, "Thy God reigneth!" Then all nations will see the salvation of God (Isa. 52:7–10). All can be a part of ZION, "the pure in heart" (D&C 97:19–21). "Saviours shall come up on mount Zion," as Obadiah said, "and the kingdom shall be the Lord's" (Obad. 1:21; D&C 103:7–10).

BIBLIOGRAPHY

Ludlow, Daniel H. *A Companion to Your Study of the Old Testament.* Salt Lake City, 1981.

Ludlow, Victor L. *Unlocking the Old Testament.* Salt Lake City, 1981.

Matthews, Robert J. *"A Plainer Translation": Joseph Smith's Translation of the Bible.* Provo, Utah, 1975.

McConkie, Bruce R. *The Promised Messiah.* Salt Lake City, 1978.

Nyman, Monte S., ed. *Isaiah and the Prophets.* Provo, Utah, 1984.

Reynolds, Noel B. "The Brass Plates Version of Genesis." In *By Study and Also by Faith,* ed. J. Lundquist and S. Ricks, Vol. 2, pp. 136–73. Salt Lake City, 1990.

Sperry, Sidney B. *The Voice of Israel's Prophets.* Salt Lake City, 1965.

———. *The Spirit of the Old Testament.* Salt Lake City, 1970.

ELLIS T. RASMUSSEN

ORGANIZATION OF THE CHURCH IN NEW TESTAMENT TIMES

Latter-day Saints "believe in the same organization that existed in the Primitive Church, namely, apostles, prophets, pastors, teachers, evangelists, and so forth" (A of F 6). They believe that Jesus Christ bestowed his priesthood on those he called and appointed to positions of responsibility in the Church he organized. They believe that in the "Primitive Church" a person had to be "called of God, by prophecy, and by the laying on of hands, by those who [were] in authority, to preach the Gospel and administer in the ordinances thereof" (A of F 5; cf. John 15:16; 20:22–23; Acts 6:6; 13:1–3). The Church established by Christ provided for a general leadership composed of apostles and prophets, with each local congregation under the direction of an "overseer," a bishop. The apostles were charged to bear the good news of the gospel of Jesus Christ to all the world and to organize converts into churches, or mutually supportive communities of saints.

The latter-day restoration of this administrative structure is distinctive, but shares some features retained also by Protestant and Catholic traditions. It resembles Protestantism in its attempt to return to the basic doctrines and procedures of the early Church. However, it shares a more Catholic conviction of the need for authoritative church leadership and a centralized organization. The Church of Jesus Christ of Latter-day Saints is particularly distinctive in its belief in the leadership of living PROPHETS who guide it through revelation.

The LDS position is in agreement with the several allusions to Church structure in the NEW TESTAMENT. In 1 Corinthians 12:28, Paul describes the organization of the Church as "first apostles [apostoloi, "sent ones," i.e., representatives, agents], secondarily prophets." In Ephesians 2:20, the Church at Ephesus is said to be "built upon the foundation of the apostles and prophets, Jesus Christ himself being the chief corner stone." Three of the apostles—PETER, JAMES, and JOHN—are clearly a leading group (like a First Presidency), and Peter seems to lead this group in initiating authoritative action and receiving revelation (Matt. 16:18; Acts 1–5; 8–10). Latter-day Saints regard Peter as the prophet or president of the Church in New Testament times.

The early Church also had bishops (epískopoi, "overseers, supervisors," 1 Tim. 3:1), elders (presbúteroi, Acts 15:22; 16:4; 20:17, where a council of elders is grouped with the apostles), teachers (*didáskaloi*, 1 Cor. 12:28, here mentioned just after the apostles and prophets; Eph. 4:11), deacons (*diákonoi*, "servants, helpers," Philip. 1:1), and a group of seventy (Luke 10:1) who gave missionary service. All of these offices have LDS equivalents.

However, Latter-day Saints do not claim an exact, one-to-one correspondence between the primitive Church and the restored Church. Continuing revelation provides for continual adaptations of the basic ecclesiastical pattern. For instance, in the early New Testament Church the three leading apostles were part of the council of the twelve, while in the latter-day Church they generally are a separate quorum. In the early Church, elders appear to have been older members of a congregation, while in the LDS Church they are often, or usually, younger men. Deacons and teachers were adults in the primitive Church (1 Tim. 3:12) and in the early LDS Church. In the twentieth-century Church, however, young men ordinarily receive these priesthood offices at the ages of twelve and fourteen. The LDS Church has no officer entitled evangelist (*euaggelistēs*, "good message announcer") or pastor (*poimēn*, "shepherd," Eph. 4:11–14); but Joseph Smith taught that the evangelist was a patriarch, an official who gives revelatory "fatherly" blessings (see *TPJS*, p. 151); and a pastor, although not an ordained officer in the priesthood, could well be any leader who serves as a "shepherd of the flock" (*MD*, p. 557).

[*See also* Apostasy.]

BIBLIOGRAPHY

Dahl, Larry E., and Charles D. Tate, Jr., eds. *The Lectures on Faith in Historical Perspective*. Provo, Utah, 1990.

See Bruce R. McConkie, *Mormon Doctrine* (Salt Lake City, 1966), for articles on separate offices in The Church of Jesus Christ of Latter-day Saints; Thomas F. O'Dea, *The Mormons*, pp. 174–86 (Chicago, 1957); James Talmage, *The Articles of Faith*, chap. 11, pp. 198–216 (Salt Lake City, 1971); and D. Michael Quinn, "From Sacred Grove to Sacral Power Structure," *Dialogue* 17.2 (1984):9–34.

See *The Interpreter's Dictionary of the Bible* (Nashville, Tenn., 1962), for articles on separate offices from a non-Mormon perspective; F. Agnew, "The Origin of the New Testament Apostle Concept: A Review of Research," *Journal of Biblical Literature* 105 (1986):75–96; and A. Lemaire, "The Ministries in the New Testament: Recent Research," *Biblical Theology Bulletin* 3 (1973):133–66.

TODD COMPTON

P

PAPYRI, JOSEPH SMITH

The term "Joseph Smith papyri" refers narrowly to twelve extant pieces of the Egyptian papyrus that the Prophet Joseph Smith acquired from Michael H. Chandler in July 1835. Located in the Church Archives, these fragments range in size from 7.5 in. x 12.5 in. to 6.5 in. x 4.5 in. Facsimile No. 1 in the BOOK OF ABRAHAM came from one of these fragments. Broadly, the term also refers to Facsimiles Nos. 2 and 3 in the same book and to papers and all the Egyptian materials of the Kirtland period of Church history containing small sections of copied papyrus text. The discovery and transmission of the mummies and papyri are discussed in BOOK OF ABRAHAM: ORIGIN OF THE BOOK OF ABRAHAM.

The origin of the ancient writings is fascinating to trace. In 1798 Napoleon's Egyptian conquest reawakened Europe to Egypt's treasures. One Italian collector, Antonio Lebolo, excavated in Egypt between 1817 and 1821. In 1820 he worked at Thebes, near El Gourna; Chandler said that Lebolo's mummies came from there (Todd, pp. 45, 130). About 1822 Lebolo returned to Italy, where he died on February 19, 1830. In 1831 his son Pietro investigated why shipping merchant Albano Oblasser had not reimbursed him for eleven mummies. In 1833 Pietro authorized Francesco Bertola, in Philadelphia, to sell eleven mummies that Oblasser had sent to a partnership in New York (Peterson, pp. 145–47).

How Chandler obtained his possessions is not known. It is known that Lebolo's mummies and papyri were exhibited in Philadelphia (April–May 1833) and Baltimore. By September 1833, six had been shown in Harrisburg and one had been publicly dissected in Philadelphia. In June of 1835, four mummies and papyri were exhibited at Cleveland, twenty miles southwest of Kirtland (Todd, pp. 108–143).

In early July 1835, Chandler visited Kirtland, where he met Joseph Smith and inquired "if he had a power by which he could translate the ancient Egyptian. Mr. Smith replied that he had" (P. Pratt, *Millennial Star*, July 1842). Chandler presented some hieroglyphics, which others supposedly had interpreted. Joseph Smith left and returned with a written English translation corresponding to the interpretation Chandler had already received. The Prophet displayed interest in the papyri, but Chandler would not break up his exhibit. Shortly thereafter, Church members purchased for $2,400 "four human figures . . . with two or more rolls of papyrus" (*HC* 2:235). Oliver Cowdery remembered that it was "two rolls . . . [with] two or three other small pieces," the text written "with black, and a small part, red ink or paint" (*Messenger and Advocate*, Dec. 31, 1835). Within three days, Joseph Smith translated some "hieroglyphics, and much to our joy found that one of the rolls contained the writings of ABRAHAM, another, writings of JOSEPH OF EGYPT." Joseph Smith spent from July 17 to 31 "continually . . . translating an alphabet . . . and arranging a grammar" of Egyptian (*HC* 2:236–38). On October 1, while he worked on the alphabet, the "principles of astronomy as understood by Father Abraham . . . unfolded" (*HC* 2:286). On November 17 he "exhibited the alphabet" (*HC* 2:316). He recorded "translating the Egyptian records" on October 7, November 19–20 (20th: "made rapid progress"), and November 24–26 (*HC* 2:289, 318, 320). LDS Church Archives contain Book of Abraham texts (Abr. 1:1–2:18) from this period.

In 1837 a visitor wrote: "These records were torn, . . . some parts entirely lost, but Smith is to translate the whole by divine inspiration and that which is lost, like Nebuchadnezzar's dream, can be interpreted as well as that which is preserved." Joseph Smith let the mummies and papyri be moved to nearby towns, and in 1836 they were in the Kirtland Temple. Despite care, the papyri had been damaged. Consequently, they were cut into pieces, and some were pasted on paper for preservation. By January 4, 1838, there were at least "two undivided thirds." During 1838–1839, the papyri and mummies spent the winter in Quincy, Illinois, where they were exhibited, a practice that continued until 1856 (Todd, pp. 197–203).

In 1842 Joseph Smith worked to prepare the facsimiles for publication and, likely, wrote his "Explanations," which are printed with them; on February 23, he instructed the printer on making the plate for Facsimile No. 1, which with its "Explanation" was printed in the March 1 issue of the *Times and Seasons,* with Abraham 1:1–2:18. On March 4 he instructed the printer on Facsimiles Nos. 2 and 3; on March 8–9 he did "translating" and "revising" (*HC* 4:518, 543–48). The final installment of the book of Abraham (2:19–5:21) and Facsimile No. 2 with its "Explanation" were printed in the March 15 issue; Facsimile No. 3 and its "Explanation" were printed May 16.

Although the papyrus rolls had been shortened, a visitor in February 1843 saw "a long roll of manuscript, [being told] it was the 'writing of Abraham'" and was shown "another roll" (Todd, p. 245). After Joseph Smith's death, the Egyptian artifacts were held principally by his mother, and then by Emma Smith after Lucy's death on May 14, 1856. On May 25, 1856, Emma sold "four Egyptian mummies with the records with them" to Mr. Abel Combs (*IE,* Jan. 1968, pp. 12–16). (Pioneers brought one fragment west.) Combs then sold two mummies with some papyri, which were sent to the St. Louis Museum (1856); they ended up in the Chicago Museum (1863), where they apparently burned in 1871. The fate of Combs's two other mummies and papyri is unknown, but some papyri remained, for in 1918 Mrs. Alice Heusser of Brooklyn, a daughter of Combs's housekeeper, approached the New York Metropolitan Museum of Art (MMA) with papyri once owned by Joseph Smith. In 1947 MMA acquired papyri from her widower. In May 1966 Aziz S. Atiya of the University of Utah saw eleven Heusser fragments at MMA. He informed Church leaders, and on November 27, 1967, the Church acquired the fragments; one of them is Facsimile No. 1.

Egyptologists who have studied the fragments in recent years generally identify them as religious texts, some from the *Book of the Dead* dating from 500–300 B.C., and some from the *Book of Breathings* dating from about A.D. 100. Since the rediscovery of the fragments, researchers have sought to learn if any of them, other than Facsimile No. 1, is related to the book of Abraham.

[*See also* Book of Abraham: Facsimiles from the Book of Abraham.]

BIBLIOGRAPHY
Nibley, Hugh. *The Message of the Joseph Smith Papyri.* Salt Lake City, 1975.
Peterson, H. Donl. "Sacred Writings from the Tombs of Egypt." In *The Pearl of Great Price: Revelations from God,* ed. D. Peterson and C. Tate. Provo, Utah, 1989.
Todd, Jay M. *Saga of the Book of Abraham.* Salt Lake City, 1969.

JAY M. TODD

PARABLES

Parables are short didactic narratives that make use of characters, situations, and customs familiar to their audience. They are meant to convey a spiritual message, but the reader usually must infer the message from the story, which generally is a presentation of some aspect of daily life. Because they are stories, parables are sometimes more memorable and more interesting than direct exhortation. Parables are seen to have several layers of meaning and may be understood differently, depending on the sensitivity and spiritual preparation of the hearer. For Latter-day Saints, it is significant that through the Prophet Joseph Smith the Lord offered some additional parables and used those given during Jesus' ministry to enrich that part of the message of the RESTORATION of the gospel that points to events of the latter days.

In the JOSEPH SMITH TRANSLATION OF THE BIBLE (JST), Joseph Smith reworked some of the parables of Christ recorded in the synoptic gospels. In addition, he often referred to Christ's parables in discourses and articles. In revelations from the Lord, he received at least three original parables not in the New Testament (D&C 38:26–27; 88:51–61; 101:43–62). For those in the New Testament that he reworked, because he recognized that the meaning of a parable is in its relevance to the original audience, he used as a key for interpretation the situation that drew the parable from Christ (*TPJS*, pp. 276–77). Then under inspiration he interpreted virtually all the parables of Matthew 13 to apply to the latter days or to the mission of the restored Church of helping to prepare people for the SECOND COMING of Christ (cf. D&C 45:56; 63:53–54; *TPJS*, pp. 94–99).

Joseph Smith showed many of Christ's parables to be relevant to the mission of the latter-day Church. For example, Doctrine and Covenants section 86 interprets the parable of the wheat and the tares (cf. Matt. 13:24–30, 36–43) as portraying the Apostasy and the restoration of Christ's true gospel: "The apostles were the sowers of the seed," but "after they have fallen asleep . . . the tares choke the wheat and drive the church into the wilderness" (D&C 86:2–3). However, the wheat, or Christ's true church, resprouts: "In the last days, . . . the Lord is beginning to bring forth the word, and the blade is springing up and is yet tender" (D&C 86:4). The JST applies this parable to the latter days: "In that day, before the Son of Man shall come, he shall send forth his angels and messengers of heaven" (JST Matt. 13:42). These angels and messengers are called to strengthen the wheat in the last days before the wicked will be destroyed. The focus of this parable thus becomes the time just before the end of the world (cf. D&C 101:65–66).

Other references further link Christ's parables to the latter-day Church. The JST version of the parable of the ten virgins (Matt. 25:1–13) begins, "At that day, before the Son of man comes, the kingdom of heaven shall be likened unto ten virgins" (JST Matt. 25:1). The Doctrine and Covenants also refers to this parable: At "the coming of the Son of Man . . . there will be foolish virgins among the wise; and at that hour cometh an entire separation of the righteous and the wicked" (D&C 63:53–54; cf. 45:56–57). Of the parable of the mustard seed (Matt. 13:31–32), "the least of all seeds: but when it is grown, it is the greatest among herbs" (Matt. 13:32), Joseph Smith wrote, "Now we can discover plainly that this figure is given to represent the Church as it shall come forth in the last days" (*TPJS*, p. 98). He also saw a comparison with the Book of Mormon:

> Let us take the Book of Mormon, which a man took and hid in his field . . . to spring up in the last days, or in due time; let us behold it coming forth out of the ground, . . . even towering, with lofty branches, and God-like majesty, until it, like the mustard seed, becomes the greatest of all herbs. And it is truth, and it has sprouted and come forth out of the earth, and righteousness begins to look down from heaven, and God is

sending down His powers, gifts and angels, to lodge in the branches thereof [*TPJS*, p. 98].

In discussing other parables, Joseph Smith compared the three measures of meal in which a woman hid leaven (Matt. 13:33) to the three witnesses to the Book of Mormon (*TPJS*, p. 100). The treasure hidden in a field for which a man "selleth all that he hath, and buyeth that field" (Matt. 13:44) is likened to the Saints' "selling all that they have, and gathering themselves together unto a place that they may purchase for an inheritance" (*TPJS*, p. 101). To the "householder, which bringeth forth out of his treasure things that are new and old" (Matt. 13:52), the Prophet Joseph Smith compared "the Book of Mormon coming forth out of the treasure of the heart, . . . the covenants given to the Latter-day Saints, [and] the translation of the Bible—thus bringing forth out of the heart things new and old" (*TPJS*, p. 102).

Other parables were used in the Doctrine and Covenants to offer counsel for particular incidents. In 1833, Latter-day Saints in Jackson County, Missouri, were driven from their homes by armed mobs. In a revelation received by Joseph Smith on December 16, 1833, two parables suggested appropriate action. The first parable (D&C 101:43–62) is original, although it echoes Christ's parable of the wicked husbandmen (cf. Matt. 21:33–44). A nobleman sends servants to his vineyard to plant twelve olive trees and then to protect the vineyard by raising a hedge, setting watchmen, and erecting a tower. His servants at first obey but then become slothful. An enemy comes at night, breaks down the hedge and the olive trees, and takes over the vineyard. The nobleman calls the servants to task and then asks all the men of his house to go "straightway unto the land of [his] vineyard, and redeem [his] vineyard" (D&C 101:56). This parable, interpreted two months later in a subsequent revelation (D&C 103), served as the basis of Zion's Camp, a militia of LDS men called to March from Ohio to Missouri for the purpose of recovering the land of their fellow Saints.

The other parable cited in the December 1833 revelation (D&C 101:81–91) is that of the woman and the unjust judge (Luke 18:1–8). The judge grants the woman's suit because her continual pleading annoys him. Likewise the displaced Saints of the time were urged to "importune at the feet of the judge," then the governor, then the president of the United States, until they obtained redress (D&C 101:85–89).

These parables, as well as others he employed (cf. D&C 35:16; 38:24–27; 45:36–38; 88:51–61), add a richness to Joseph Smith's teachings.

BIBLIOGRAPHY

Brooks, Melvin R. *Parables of the Kingdom.* Salt Lake City, 1965.

Burton, Alma P., ed. *Discourses of the Prophet Joseph Smith,* pp. 196–204. Salt Lake City, 1965.

Jeremias, Joachim. *The Parables of Jesus.* London, 1954.

SUSAN HOWE

PAUL

The Church recognizes Paul as a true apostle of Jesus Christ. No other early apostle has had the impact on subsequent believers through both his personal example and his written words that Paul has. The early Christian apostle to the Gentiles, in his New Testament letters, produced a rich source of Christian doctrine and the single most important doctrinal influence upon many of the denominations of modern Christendom. Without Paul, the doctrine of justification by faith in Christ would be largely missing from the Bible, and considerably less would be known about grace, the Lord's Supper, church structure, the Apostasy, or the role of gifts of the Spirit in the Church.

BIOGRAPHICAL SKETCH.   Details of Paul's life are found in his letters and in the book of Acts. Born in Tarsus of Cilicia (modern southeastern Turkey), Paul was multicultural. As a Jew, he was known by the name of Saul and was educated in Jerusalem as a Pharisee under the famous rabbi Gamaliel. He was also a Roman citizen by birth, a rare privilege for a Jew at that time. Finally, he was familiar with Greek language and culture through his early environment in the Hellenistic city of Tarsus. Thus, he was able to deal with Jews, Romans, and Greeks on their own cultural terms—a great advantage for his later missionary work.

As a Pharisee working for the Jewish high priest, Saul was an early and zealous persecutor of Christians and personally assented to the execution of Stephen (Acts 7:58–8:3). However, as Saul traveled toward

Damascus to arrest Christians there, the resurrected Christ appeared to him in a vision. As a result of this experience, Saul embraced the cause of Christ and spent the rest of his life in his service.

After baptism, Saul "went into Arabia, and returned again unto Damascus" (Gal. 1:17). He was so effective in preaching Christ that he provoked much Jewish opposition and was eventually compelled to flee for his life. Returning to Jerusalem after three years, he met briefly with Peter and James, the Lord's brother, and then went to Cilicia and Syria, where he spent approximately the next decade preaching the gospel.

Barnabas brought Saul to Antioch, whence they left on their first missionary journey. On this journey, Saul began using his Roman name, Paul, and established his basic strategy for missionary work. Whenever he entered a city, Paul went first to the Jews, preaching Christ in their synagogues. Usually they would reject his message, but Gentiles associated with the synagogues would frequently be converted; Paul would then turn his attention to teaching the Gentiles of that city and would establish a branch of the Church made up of Gentiles and perhaps a few Jewish converts.

Two more missionary journeys of over three years each are described in Acts, and Paul was successful in teaching the gospel and establishing churches throughout much of present-day Turkey and Greece. Returning to Jerusalem after his third missionary journey, Paul met with such intense Jewish opposition to his presence in the temple that he was put into custody by the Romans and held in prison in Caesarea for two years before being sent to Rome for trial. Though shipwrecked on the way, he was eventually imprisoned in Rome and was executed around A.D. 64, during the reign of the emperor Nero.

The Prophet Joseph Smith gave a description of Paul: about five feet tall, dark hair, penetrating eyes, and a powerful orator (*TPJS*, p. 180; *WJS*, p. 59). He also indicated that Paul was acquainted with ENOCH (*TPJS*, p. 170) and that Abel "was sent down from heaven unto Paul to minister consoling words, and to commit unto him a knowledge of the mysteries of godliness" (*TPJS*, p. 169).

PAUL'S TEACHINGS.   One of Paul's greatest contributions to the New Testament is his forceful statement of justification (that is, being absolved of guilt) by faith in Christ (cf. Gal. 2–3; Rom. 2–5). Early on, Paul had taught his Gentile converts that they did not need to live the LAW OF MOSES in order to be justified before God. It was sufficient to make and keep the gospel covenant, the covenant of faith, to do this, while outward observance of the law of Moses was not (Gal. 2:16). In particular, after Christ's atonement, there was no longer any necessity of observing the earlier law and covenant of Moses, which were rendered obsolete by the law and covenant of the gospel (cf. Heb. 8:6–13; 3 Ne. 9:17–20). Thus, Paul's Gentile converts did not need to become Jews in order to become Christians (cf. Acts 15:5–29), for human beings are "justified by faith without the deeds of the law" (Rom. 3:28). A complete commitment to the gospel of Jesus Christ, the covenant of faith, automatically fulfills all previous obligations before God, including the obligations of the law of Moses.

Paul also taught the related doctrine of salvation by grace. Latter-day Saints recognize at least four ways in which Paul spoke of salvation as an operation of the grace of God. First, through the atonement of Christ, a free gift, Adam's posterity is not accountable for the transgression of Adam (Rom. 5:18–21). Second, it naturally follows that death—a consequence of Adam's transgression—will be done away by the gift of resurrection that will be graciously given to all human beings (1 Cor. 15:21–22). Third, the fact that God has offered a new covenant of faith in place of the old rules of performances and ordinances, which mankind then was not able to live perfectly, is in itself an act of grace. And fourth, that the Savior volunteered to suffer and die for the sake of others is the greatest expression of the grace of God. Thus, salvation is accessible to mankind only through the gracious acts and gifts of God. As Paul said, "We have access by faith into this grace wherein we stand, and rejoice in hope of the glory of God" (Rom. 5:2). However, in Paul's theology, the doctrines of salvation by grace and justification by faith do not eliminate but require the absolute necessity for high personal standards of conduct (1 Cor. 6:9–11; Gal. 5:19–21).

Paul also taught that God's knowledge is unlimited and that God's plan has anticipated all future events and cannot be thwarted. God knows the end from the beginning and has already prepared the inheritance of those who choose to keep his will (Eph. 1:4–14). Though the King James Version of the Bible uses the problematic word "predestinated" (Greek, *proorizō*), Latter-day Saints do not understand it to mean that some are saved and some are damned according to a prior decision by God. Latter-day Saints prefer the term foreordination to "predestination" and insist that the foreknowledge of God does not impinge upon the free agency of human beings.

Not all, or possibly not even most, of Paul's letters have been preserved. Latter-day Saints believe that if a more complete collection of Paul's letters had survived, it would reflect a theology much like that of the restored gospel of latter days. They see support for this in the number of references in Paul to doctrines that are now peculiar to the Latter-day Saints, such as baptism for the dead (1 Cor. 15:29), the three degrees of glory (1 Cor. 15:39–41; 2 Cor. 12:2), the premortal life (Eph. 1:4), and the necessity of an ecclesiastical organization that includes apostles and prophets (Eph. 2:19–20; 4:11–13). Latter-day Saints assume that Paul did not expand on these topics in his extant writings because they were written to people who already knew about them.

Paul is a major source of predictions of the apostasy of the early Christian church. He is quoted in Acts 20:29–30 as warning the elders from Ephesus and Miletus that grievous wolves would descend after his departure, "not sparing the flock," and that disaffected members would tear up the Church from within. He warned the Thessalonians not to expect the coming of Christ before the Apostasy had taken place (2 Thes. 2:2–3). Significantly, he reminded both groups that this warning had been part of his preaching from the first (2 Thes. 2:5; Acts 20:31).

Latter-day Saints do not see in Paul an opposition to women, sex, or marriage. Rather, Paul's general statement of principle on marriage is "Let every man have his own wife, and let every woman have her own husband" (1 Cor. 7:2; cf. Heb. 13:4). Paul goes on to address special circumstances (1 Cor. 7:8–16) and admonishes all people to care first for the things of God (verses 25–38), but his advice regarding particular situations should not be confused with his general policy. Husbands are to love their wives, and vice versa (Eph. 5:28), for "neither is the man without the woman, neither the woman without the man, in the Lord" (1 Cor. 11:11). It is clear that women were valued associates and held positions of responsibility in Paul's congregations (cf. Rom. 16:1–4).

Paul's influence upon Joseph Smith and the Latter-day Saints is seen at many points. Joseph Smith referred to "the admonition of Paul" (cf. Philip. 4:8) in describing the highest moral aspirations of the Latter-day Saints (A of F 13). The language of Paul is discernible in most of the Articles of Faith (e.g., in A of F 4 on the first principles of the gospel [cf. Heb. 6:1–2]; in A of F 5 on ordination to the priesthood [cf. 1 Tim. 4:14]; in A of F 6 on the officers of the Primitive Church [cf. Eph. 4:11]; and in A of F 7 on the gifts of the Spirit [cf. 1 Cor. 12:8–12]), and part of the sublime hymn to charity (1 Cor. 13:4–8) is also found in the Book of Mormon (Moro. 7:45–46). These are taken as indications that Jesus was the ultimate source of all of these teachings.

Of Paul's life, the Prophet Joseph Smith observed:

Follow the labors of this Apostle from the time of his conversion to the time of his death, and you will have a fair sample of industry and patience in promulgating the Gospel of Christ. Derided, whipped, and stoned, the moment he escaped the hands of his persecutors he as zealously as ever proclaimed the doctrine of the Savior. . . . Paul rested his hope in Christ, because he had kept the faith, and loved His appearing and from His hand he had a promise of receiving a crown of righteousness [*TPJS*, pp. 63–64].

[*See also* Joseph Smith Translation of the Bible (JST); New Testament.]

BIBLIOGRAPHY
Anderson, Richard Lloyd. *Understanding Paul.* Salt Lake City, 1983.
McConkie, Bruce R. *Doctrinal New Testament Commentary,* Vols. 2–3. Salt Lake City, 1970–1973.
Sperry, Sidney B. *Paul's Life and Letters.* Salt Lake City, 1955.

J. PHILIP SCHAELLING

PEARL OF GREAT PRICE

[*The Pearl of Great Price consists of a diverse collection of sacred works that are accepted as scripture by Latter-day Saints. The article* Contents and Publication *offers an overview of the individual texts in the collection as well as details about the history of how the documents were brought together and were then received as scripture by Church members. The article titled* Literature *briefly treats the variety of literary features that characterize the Pearl of Great Price.*]

CONTENTS AND PUBLICATION

One of the four STANDARD WORKS accepted as scripture by The Church of Jesus Christ of Latter-day Saints, the Pearl of Great Price includes various documents known as "Selections from the Book of Moses," "The Book of Abraham," "Joseph Smith—Matthew," "Joseph Smith—History," and "The Articles of Faith."

It was first published at Liverpool, England, in 1851 by Franklin D. Richards, then president of the British Mission and a member of the Quorum of the Twelve Apostles, in response to requests from converts for further information about their new church. In addition to selected revelations from Genesis in the JOSEPH SMITH TRANSLATION OF THE BIBLE (JST) and the BOOK OF ABRAHAM, the 1851 edition contained Matthew 24 as revealed to the Prophet Joseph Smith in 1831 (currently titled JOSEPH SMITH—MATTHEW); "A Key to the Revelations of St. John" (now D&C 77), a revelation received by Joseph Smith on December 25, 1832 (now D&C 87); and Joseph Smith's 1838 account of his early VISIONS and translation of the Book of Mormon (now JOSEPH SMITH—HISTORY). It also incorporated certain extracts from the Doctrine and Covenants (sections 20, 107, and 27), thirteen untitled statements previously published in the *Times and Seasons* in March 1842 and now known as the Articles of Faith, and a poem titled "Truth" that later became the LDS hymn "Oh Say, What Is Truth?"

The book of Moses originally consisted of several revelations given to Joseph Smith as he was revising the Bible under inspiration, beginning in June 1830. In the 1851 edition of the Pearl of Great Price, these excerpts were untitled. The 1878 edition added the titles "Visions of Moses" (chap. 1) and "Writings of Moses" (chaps. 2–8). These revelations were first printed in Church newspapers between 1832 and 1851 (Clark, pp. 9–17).

The book of Abraham is linked to Joseph Smith's work on rolls of papyri that the Church obtained in 1835. Soon after he began studying the rolls, he produced a record of the life of the patriarch Abraham and a description of the creation of the world similar to that in Genesis and the book of Moses. In 1842 the Nauvoo *Times and Seasons* and the *Millennial Star* in England printed the available text and facsimiles. It is certain that the materials incorporated into the books of Moses and Abraham were extracts and that more information was available than has ever been included in the printed editions of the Pearl of Great Price.

The second edition of the Pearl of Great Price, the first American edition, was published at Salt Lake City in 1878 and added "A Revelation on the Eternity of the Marriage Covenant, Including Plurality of Wives," which is now known as Doctrine and Covenants section 132. On October 10, 1880, in general conference at Salt Lake City, the membership of the Church accepted the Pearl of Great Price as a standard work. When additional changes were made—including page size and format—another vote in 1890 reaffirmed the acceptance of the Pearl of Great Price as scripture.

James E. Talmage, later a member of the Quorum of the Twelve Apostles, under assignment of the First Presidency, divided the work into chapters and verses, added some titles (such as "The Book of Moses"), and eliminated some portions, such as the materials also published in the Doctrine and Covenants. These changes were formally approved by Church membership at the October conference of 1902.

At general conference on April 3, 1976, Joseph Smith's vision of the celestial kingdom received in the Kirtland Temple on January 21, 1836, and President Joseph F. Smith's vision of the redemption of the dead (October 3, 1918) were added to the Pearl of Great Price. In 1979 these two revelations were transferred to the Doctrine and Covenants as sections 137 and 138.

BIBLIOGRAPHY

Clark, James R. *The Story of the Pearl of Great Price.* Salt Lake City, 1955.

Millet, Robert L., and Kent P. Jackson, eds. *Studies in Scripture,* Vol. 2. Salt Lake City, 1985.

Peterson, H. Donl, and Charles D. Tate, Jr., eds. *The Pearl of Great Price: Revelations from God.* Provo, Utah, 1989.

KENNETH W. BALDRIDGE

LITERATURE

Drawing the effective metaphor of its title from the literary treasures of the Savior's parables (Matt. 13:45), this book of scripture—despite its diversity of sections—consistently sustains a grandeur of language enriched throughout with vivid word pictures and the subtle touches of diverse literary techniques.

For example, Enoch hears and describes the personified soul of the earth alliteratively as the "*m*other of *m*en" agonizing from the bowels of the earth that she is "*w*eary" of "*w*ickedness." The tension of the drama resolves itself as the voice uses assonance in pleading for "r*i*ghteousness" to "ab*i*de" for a season (Moses 7:48).

Also remarkable is the artistic control of tone throughout the narrative of JOSEPH SMITH—HISTORY. Despite his having been the victim of severe persecution, Joseph objectively selects connotative words that allow the readers to discover for themselves the abuse he had suffered. In describing the deep schisms among the sects in his village, he skillfully calls into question the "great love" and "great zeal" of the clergy in their efforts to have everybody "converted," as they were "pleased to call it." The irony of tone remains dignified but becomes incrementally more poignant as he next refers to their "seemingly good feelings" being "more pretended than real"; he finalizes his deep disappointment by leaving no doubt regarding the irony: "So that all their good feelings one for another, if they ever had any, were entirely lost in a strife of words and a contest about opinions" (JS—H 1:6).

The final verse in the Pearl of Great Price addresses the value of artistry not only in writing but also in all aspects of life. Referring to the literarily beautiful writings of Paul, it affirms Joseph Smith's conviction that the Latter-day Saints must search the handiwork of God for all that is "virtuous, lovely, or of good report" (A of F 13).

O. GLADE HUNSAKER

"PECULIAR" PEOPLE

Latter-day Saints consider themselves a peculiar people in the biblical sense of being a covenant people with the Lord. Their lifestyle, stemming from the doctrines and practices of the Church, also makes them a different or peculiar people. In any dispensation, followers of Jesus Christ produce a distinct culture:

> Is there a gospel culture? . . . Is there a gospel community or society?
> . . . Zion has always been described as a city, an organized society, set
> apart from the world. If the community preserves its integrity for any

length of time, it is bound to emerge as a separate culture. The earliest reference to the culture I have in mind is Israel as the "peculiar people." Moses and Aaron disengaged the children of Israel from the culture of Egypt, the most distinctive culture of its time. The Lord tells them: "Ye have seen what I did unto the Egyptians, and how I bare you on eagles' wings, and brought you unto myself. Now therefore, if ye will obey my voice indeed, and keep my covenant, then ye shall be a peculiar treasure unto me above all people" [Ex. 19:4–5; Nibley, pp. 22–23].

But to the extent that a covenant people do not honor their allegiance to God, they become more like the cultures they are raised in and are indistinguishable from those who know not God (see Smith, W., 1959). Nevertheless, when a people honor their commitment to God, there are evidences that distinguish them and make them peculiar to the population at large. "By their fruits ye shall know them" (Matt. 7:20; see also 1 Jn. 3:10–18; Moro. 7:5–17).

Large comparisons of LDS behavior patterns with those of the general population are not extensive in the research literature, but because Latter-day Saints comprise 70 percent of the population of Utah, comparisons of Utah data with regional and national samples give a reliable estimate of how Latter-day Saints differ from the general population. And demographers who have compared Utah Latter-day Saints with those living elsewhere in the United States find more similarities than differences, and conclude that "Utah Mormons are not distinctive compared to Mormons elsewhere" (Heaton, "Demography," p. 193).

Latter-day Saints are taught to live by a health code requiring abstention from alcohol, tobacco, tea, and coffee. Utah ranks lowest of the fifty states in the consumption of all types of alcoholic beverages. Utah's mortality rate from diseases related to alcohol and tobacco use (heart disease/stroke and cancer) is very low (Smith, James E., p. 69).

Latter-day Saints value education highly, and the percentage of the Utah population completing up to three years of high school ranks first in the nation (93 percent), and Utah is seventh in the nation in both graduation rates from high school (80 percent) and from four-year colleges (20 percent) (Van Mondfrans, Smith, and Moss, pp. 198–99). Moreover, the relationship between education and religiosity among Latter-day Saints is the opposite of the national trend, with the most educated Mormons being the most actively involved in the Church (Albrecht).

For Latter-day Saints married in a temple, family commitments are not only for mortality but for eternity, and divorce rates among temple-married Latter-day Saints have traditionally been much lower than for those who marry by civil authority or marry non-Latter-day Saints (Thomas, p. 49). Also, premarital sexual involvement is a sin in LDS doctrine, and Utah unmarried teenagers report substantially lower rates of sexual intercourse than either the regional or national averages. Moreover, higher rates of sexual abstinence among unmarried adolescents in Utah are positively correlated with religious affiliation and attendance (especially LDS membership) and with the following characteristics, which reflect LDS counsel: living with both biological parents, educational aspirations, the avoidance of early and steady dating, abstention from drug and alcohol use, and personal belief in premarital abstinence (Governor's Task Force on Teenage Pregnancy Prevention, "Preventing Teenage Pregnancy in Utah," Oct. 3, 1988, p. 39; see also Miller, McCoy, and Olson).

Many of the "peculiar" features of LDS lives reflect faith in the counsel of modern prophets who offer revelation about how followers of Jesus Christ should operate in the world without becoming of the world. This counsel has included among many other things encouraging the observance of family home evening, keeping journals, planting gardens, avoiding debt, not dating until the age of sixteen, and preparing food and resources to meet emergencies.

BIBLIOGRAPHY

Albrecht, Stan L. "The Consequential Dimension of Mormon Religiosity." *BYU Studies* 29 (Spring 1989):57–108.

Chadwick, Bruce A. "Teenage Pregnancy and Out-of-Wedlock Births." In *Utah in Demographic Perspective.* ed. T. Martin, T. Heaton, and S. Bahr, pp. 23–36. Salt Lake City, 1986.

Heaton, Tim B. "The Demography of Utah Mormons." In *Utah in Demographic Perspective*, ed. T. Martin, T. Heaton, and S. Bahr, pp. 181–93. Salt Lake City, 1986.

————. "Four C's of the Mormon Family: Chastity, Conjugality, Children, and Chauvinism." In *The Religion and Family Connection: Social Science Perspectives*, ed. Darwin L. Thomas, pp. 107–24. Provo, Utah, 1988.

Miller, Brent C.; J. Kelly McCoy; and Terrance D. Olson. "Dating Age and Stage as Correlates of Adolescent Sexual Attitudes and Behavior." *Journal of Adolescent Research* 1 No. 3 (1986):361–71.

Nibley, Hugh. "Comments, Hugh [W.] Nibley." In *Mormonism: A Faith for All Cultures,* ed. F. LaMond Tullis, pp. 22–28. Provo, Utah, 1978.

Smith, James E. "Mortality." In *Utah in Demographic Perspective,* ed. T. Martin, T. Heaton, and S. Bahr, pp. 59–69. Salt Lake City, 1986.

Smith, Wilford E. "The Urban Threat to Mormon Norms." *Rural Sociology* 24 (1959):355–61.

———. "Mormon Sex Standards on College Campuses, or Deal Us Out of the Sexual Revolution!" *Dialogue* 10 (1976):76–81.

Thomas, Darwin L. "Do Early Marriages Tend to End in Disaster?" *New Era* 3 (Mar. 1973):48–50.

Van Mondfrans, Adrian; Ralph B. Smith; and Vanessa Moss. "Education." In *Utah in Demographic Perspective,* ed. T. Martin, T. Heaton, and S. Bahr, pp. 195–215. Salt Lake City, 1986.

WILFORD E. SMITH

PETER

Simon bar-Jona, later known as Cephas or Peter, became the senior and chief apostle of Jesus Christ. He was evidently the presiding officer over the ancient Church after Christ's death. In the present dispensation, as a resurrected being, he restored apostolic authority to the Prophet Joseph Smith and Oliver Cowdery.

The New Testament contains more information about Peter than about any of the other apostles. This provides some indication of his ministry, his character, and his relationship to the Savior. In contrast to the sometimes impetuous younger Peter portrayed in the Gospels, the apostle's later ministry and epistles bespeak a mature leader of patient faith whose sincere concern is for the spiritual well-being of the flock that Jesus entrusted to him (John 21:15–17). Differences persist, however, in the portraits of Peter derived from the various biblical accounts, and these are extrapolated in scholarly analyses of the role and theology of Peter. Recourse to later Christian writings from the second and third centuries reveals other views about Peter's position in the pristine Church. It cannot be presumed, therefore, that all that is written about him is clearly factual.

Originally from Bethsaida, a small fishing port somewhere on the north shore of the Sea of Galilee, Peter resided in the town of Capernaum with his wife and mother-in-law at the time of his apostolic call. Peter's given name was Simon and his patronymic, bar-Jona, identifies him as the son of Jonah (Matt. 16:17). The name

Simon *(Simon)* and that of his brother Andrew *(Andreas)* are derived from the Greek renditions of their names. Living in a region where, in addition to the native Aramaic, Greek was widely used as a language of business and trade, Peter may have been conversant with the tongue in which his scriptural writings were later penned. Although Peter was a fisherman by occupation, and despite the description of Peter and John by the elders of the Sanhedrin as being "without learning" (Acts 4:13), the Galilean apostles were literate men, probably without normal rabbinical training but with broad general understanding and capability.

Peter was among the first of Jesus' disciples. To him, then called Simon, was extended a special call, marked by the reception of a new name, which in Jewish tradition "denoted the conferring of a special divine mission" (Winter, p. 5). John describes Christ's bestowal upon Simon bar-Jona of the title "Cephas, which is by interpretation, A stone" (John 1:42). The Aramaic *kepha* and its Greek equivalent, *petros,* are common nouns and prior to that time were unused as proper names. A dispute of long duration continues among Catholic and Protestant scholars (Winter, pp. 6–25; Horsley, pp. 29–41) concerning the definition of *petros,* "a rock or stone," and *petra,* "a large mass of rock," as these words pertain to Peter's name and its connection to Christ's wordplay "Thou art Peter, and upon this rock I will build my church" (Matt. 16:18). LDS doctrine holds that revelation was the rock denoted by Jesus and that Peter's call to become the prophet to lead the early Church is here foretold. Relevant to this passage, Joseph Smith applied the term "seer" to define *cephas* (JST John 1:42), and Bruce R. McConkie (pp. 133, 380–83) relates this to the seership, or power of continuing revelation, which he further connects to the keys of the kingdom (Matt. 16:19) bestowed on Peter, the chief apostle, upon the MOUNT OF TRANSFIGURATION, an account of which immediately follows in Matt. 17:1–13.

Peter's primacy in the ancient Church derived from apostolic authority. His first place among the twelve apostles is clear in a number of contexts: all New Testament lists of the apostles mention Peter first; the phrase "Peter and they that are with him" describes the apostles (e.g., Luke 8:45); and Peter acts as their spokesman in posing questions to Jesus (e.g., Luke 12:41). Miracles, teaching incidents, and special events (e.g., Matt. 14:25–31; Mark 14:26–42; Luke 5:1–10) center around Peter alone or on him as the key apostle involved (Muren, p. 150). After the trial of Jesus before Caiaphas, Peter stayed nearby in the dark and the cold. Although during Jesus' trial he denied certain allegations about association or affiliations with the disciples, and acquaintance with Jesus, Peter was the first apostle to whom the resurrected Christ appeared (Luke 24:33–35; 1 Cor. 15:5).

Peter's leading position is perceived by Latter-day Saints as one of presidency. Two LDS Church Presidents have likened Peter's office to that of the President of the Quorum of the Twelve Apostles (McKay, p. 20; Kimball).

The apostles JAMES and JOHN occupied a position second to that of Peter. Together these three were privileged to attend Jesus on three most sacred occasions: at Jesus' raising of Jairus' daughter from the dead (Mark 5:35–43), at his glorification on the Mount of Transfiguration (Matt. 17:1–13; Mark 9:2–9), and at his suffering in the garden of Gethsemane (Mark 14:26–42). Latter-day Saints attribute the presence of Peter, James, and John on these occasions to the priesthood office that they held among the apostles. Joseph Smith taught that the Savior, Moses, and Elias, when transfigured before them, gave the keys of the Melchizedek Priesthood to Peter, James, and John (*TPJS*, p. 158; *see* MOUNT OF TRANSFIGURATION).

Through this authority, Peter, James, and John directed the Church in the name of Jesus Christ after his death. Peter presided over the selection of a new apostle to replace Judas (Acts 1:15–26) and over the ministry on the day of Pentecost (Acts 2). Peter confronted the Sanhedrin, performed miracles, and preached the gospel of Christ (Acts 3–4). In many of these activities John was Peter's companion, but Peter took the lead. Through important revelations pertaining to the extension of the gospel to the Gentiles (Acts 10), Peter's calling as prophet, seer, and revelator is evident (Muren, pp. 150–52). Although modern revelation provides much clarification of information in this regard, Peter's role of presiding over Church councils and directing the general apostolic effort is patently demonstrable through examination of the New Testament and other early Christian sources (Brown, pp. 9–16, 1973).

Because of his ancient office, it was Peter who, with the assistance of James and John, was commissioned to restore apostolic authority to a new gospel dispensation and to endow Joseph Smith with the same priesthood keys that Christ had given to Peter, thereby reauthorizing the performance of the ordinances of salvation by the authority of the priesthood.

Peter's two epistles in the New Testament contain an abundance of inspired and inspiring teachings and exhortations. Throughout 1 and 2 Peter, concern is expressed for the salvation and sanctification of the flock, reminding the faithful that this can be obtained only through knowledge of Jesus Christ and performance of the ordinances of the priesthood (cf. *TPJS*, pp. 297, 303–305; Muren, pp. 153–56). Peter also provides information about the salvation of the dead (1 Pet. 3:18–22; 4:6), and he exhorts all members of the Church to be holy, to feed the flock, to be humble, and to secure salvation through making their calling and election sure (1 Pet. 4–5; 2 Pet. 1). A final concern is expressed for the spiritual welfare of the Church, which Peter warns will soon experience the teaching of false doctrines that will threaten individual salvation (2 Pet. 2–3). Of these epistles Joseph Smith remarked, "Peter penned the most sublime language of any of the apostles" (*TPJS*, p. 301).

BIBLIOGRAPHY

Brown, Raymond E.; Karl Donfried; and John Reumann, eds. *Peter in the New Testament*. Minneapolis, Minn., 1973.

Brown, S. Kent. "James the Just and the Question of Peter's Leadership in the Light of New Sources." In *Sperry Lecture Series*, pp. 9–16. Provo, Utah, 1973.

Horsley, A. Burt. *Peter and the Popes*. Salt Lake City, 1989.

Kimball, Spencer W. "Peter, My Brother." In *BYU Speeches of the Year*. Provo, Utah, 1971.

McConkie, Bruce R. *Doctrinal New Testament Commentary*, Vol. 1. Salt Lake City, 1978.

McKay, David O. *Ancient Apostles*. Salt Lake City, 1964.

Muren, Joseph C. "Peter." In *A Symposium on the New Testament*. Salt Lake City, 1980.

Winter, Michael M. *Saint Peter and the Popes*. Westport, Conn., 1960.

JOHN FRANKLIN HALL

PLATES, METAL

[*The Book of Mormon mentions several records, most of which were inscribed on metal plates. The text of the Book of Mormon was inscribed on metal plates; see* Book of Mormon Plates and Records;

Book of Mormon: the Words of Mormon; *and* Gold Plates. *In addi-*
tion, the scriptural record possessed by the Book of Mormon colony that
fled Jerusalem and came to the Americas under the leadership of the
prophet Lehi was engraved on plates of brass; see Book of Mormon: An
Overview. *This colony continued to prepare metal plates, which were*
then used to inscribe records both sacred and secular; see Book of
Mormon Economy and Technology. *It is also known that a prophet*
named Ether inscribed on metal leaves the record of his people, the ear-
liest Book of Mormon group to migrate to the Western Hemisphere; see
Book of Mormon: Book of Ether *and* Jaredites. *The final set of plates*
abridged by Mormon were seen by the Book of Mormon Witnesses.
For information about the major writers or abridgers of these plates,
see Mormon; Moroni$_2$; Mosiah$_2$; *and* Nephi$_1$.]

PREDESTINATION

The Church of Jesus Christ of Latter-day Saints rejects the belief in
predestination—that God predetermines the salvation or the damnation of every individual. The gospel teaches that genuine human freedom and genuine responsibility—individual agency in both thought
and action—are crucial in both the development and the outcome of
a person's life. Church doctrine rejects the strict dual option providing only heaven or hell as an outcome, since people vary widely in
their levels of spiritual attainment. At the same time, Latter-day
Saints recognize both the indispensable need for the grace of God
manifested through Jesus Christ and the effective spiritual guidance
that comes through divine foreordination.

The LDS position is based in part on the teachings of Paul that
God "will render to every man according to his deeds" and that
"there is no respect of persons with God" (Rom. 2:6, 11). These two
principles provide a basis for understanding Paul's use of the term
"predestination." The term apparently connoted "to be ordained
beforehand for godly labor." In the sense that one's potential or calling has been recognized and declared, this interpretation conforms
with the Greek term Paul used, *proorizō*, and does not denote an irre-
versible or irresistible predetermination.

Latter-day Saints are to "look unto God in every thought" (D&C

6:36), because no person can save himself. But neither can God redeem anyone without that person's effort and collaboration. All are free to accept or reject God's help and powers of redemption. It is clearly taught in scripture that with his help both justification and sanctification will be "just and true" (D&C 20:30). "But there is a possibility that man may fall from grace and depart from the living God; therefore let the church take heed, and pray always, lest they fall into temptation; yea, and even let those who are sanctified take heed also" (D&C 20:32, 33).

RICHARD D. DRAPER

PRIESTCRAFT

The Book of Mormon says, "Priestcrafts are that men preach and set themselves up for a light unto the world, that they may get gain and praise of the world; but they seek not the welfare of Zion. . . . But the laborer in Zion shall labor for Zion; for if they labor for money they shall perish" (2 Ne. 26:29, 31). Inherent in this definition is the concern that Church leaders must labor to build ZION into the hearts of the people, and not for their personal aggrandizement or reward. When leaders "make merchandise" of men's souls (2 Pet. 2:3), they turn religion into a business, and pride, materialism, and unrighteous dominion follow.

Both in scripture and in literature priestcraft is condemned. Peter cursed Simon the sorcerer, who wanted to purchase the priesthood for money (Acts 8:14–24). Dante's Peter castigates several popes and priests for not serving freely and for making a sewer of the sepulcher of Peter by selling priesthood appointment (*Paradiso* 27:22–57). Chaucer observed that greed for personal gain and glory often replaced genuine priesthood service ("General Prologue" and "Introduction to the Pardoner's Tale," *Canterbury Tales*). Milton's lines from *Lycidas* condemning a clergy who "for their bellies' sake, / Creep and intrude, and climb into the fold" (ll. 114–15) sum up the evil of priestcraft: "The hungry sheep look up, and are not fed, / But swoln with wind and the rank mist they draw, / Rot inwardly, and foul contagion spread" (ll. 125–27).

CHARLES D. TATE, JR.

PROMISED LAND, CONCEPT OF A

In the Book of Mormon, the prophet LEHI spoke of a particular promised land as "choice above all other lands; a land which the Lord God hath covenanted with me should be a land for the inheritance of my seed" (2 Ne. 1:5). Because the earth belongs to the Lord (Ps. 24:1), those who inherit a promised land must covenant to "serve the God of the land," who will then keep them "free from bondage, and from captivity" (Ether 2:12); otherwise they will "be swept off" (Ether 2:10; cf. Deut. 27–28).

From the beginning, the Lord has reserved choice lands for righteous followers. They include the GARDEN OF EDEN for Adam and Eve (Gen. 2:9), a "land of promise" for Enos (Moses 6:17), and Zion for Enoch and his people (Moses 7:19). Notably, God received up Zion's inhabitants (Moses 7:69), who will return to earth to the NEW JERUSALEM during the last days (Moses 7:62–64; Rev. 21:2). Moreover, God gave the land of Canaan "unto [Abraham's] seed . . . for an everlasting possession" if "they hearken to [God's] voice" (Abr. 2:6). This promise was partially fulfilled when Moses led the Israelites out of Egypt to Canaan.

The BOOK OF MORMON PEOPLES, including the family of Lehi and the JAREDITES, were given a promised land in the hemisphere now called the Americas, on condition of keeping God's commandments (1 Ne. 2:20; Ether 1:42–43). The prophet MORONI$_2$ warned future inhabitants of this land: "Behold, this is a choice land, and whatsoever nation shall possess it shall be free . . . if they will but serve the God of the land, who is Jesus Christ" (Ether 2:12). This admonition applies to all lands that the Lord has promised to any of his peoples.

Latter-day Zion, a "promised land" for members of The Church of Jesus Christ of Latter-day Saints, includes the city New Jerusalem that will be built in the Americas (A of F 10) and, in another sense, the stakes of the Church in all the world. Members also believe that the New Jerusalem is where the "lost ten tribes" will first come (D&C 133:26).

Through the Prophet Joseph Smith, the Lord promised in 1831 to lead the Saints to a "land of promise" (D&C 38:18; cf. Ex. 3:8). Because of persecution by enemies and sin among Church members, Joseph Smith was unsuccessful in establishing a permanent community (D&C 101:1–8). After his death, the Saints migrated to the Rocky Mountains, "a land of peace" (D&C 136:16), and still anticipate fulfillment of the Lord's promises to open the way for building New Jerusalem in the designated place (D&C 42:9; 57:1–5; 101:9–22).

BIBLIOGRAPHY
Davies, William D. "Israel, the Mormons, and the Land." In *Reflections on Mormonism*, ed. T. Madsen, pp. 79–87. Provo, Utah, 1978.

CLARISSA KATHERINE COLE

PROPHECY

Latter-day Saints believe in both ancient and modern prophecy; indeed, continuing prophetic guidance is held to be a characteristic or sign of the true church. These concepts were an integral part of the LDS Church's origin and restoration, and they continue to distinguish the Church from many other religious movements.

The term "prophecy" encompasses the entire range of divinely inspired utterances of a PROPHET, both as a "forth-teller" and as a "fore-teller." The predominant assumption by many readers is that this term in the scriptures refers usually to foretelling—the prophetic power to reveal events in the future—but it is not so limited. Prophecy is a diverse spiritual gift bestowed by the Holy Ghost (2 Pet. 1:21; 1 Ne. 22:2; Moro. 10:8; D&C 20:26; 68:4). Prophecy is firmly grounded in history, and prophets as spokespersons for the Lord have the power to reveal things relevant to the past, present, and future. The gift of prophecy, as demonstrated by Miriam, Deborah, Huldah, and others, is not limited to any special ordination in the priesthood (*AF*, pp. 228–29) but can be given to all as Moses understood when he cried: "Would God that all the Lord's people were prophets, and that the Lord would put his spirit upon them!" (Num. 11:29; cf. 1 Cor. 14:1–5, 29, 31, 39). In the restored Church all are baptized, confirmed, and provided with the gift of the Holy Ghost, through which all can enjoy prophetic gifts pertinent to their stewardships.

The possession of spiritual gifts, including the gift of prophecy, is one of the vital means of guiding the true Church (A of F 7). Paul elaborated upon the gift of prophecy in the early Church (1 Cor. 12, 14). Moroni₂ similarly explained, "All these gifts of which I have spoken, which are spiritual, never will be done away, even as long as the world shall stand, only according to the unbelief of the children of men" (Moro. 10:8–19); and the Lord included the gift of prophecy among the spiritual gifts in the restored Church as declared in a revelation to Joseph Smith (D&C 46:7–29).

Through his prophets the Lord reveals the plan of salvation and the gospel, full appreciation of which requires a correct understanding of significant events from the past as well as the present and future. Thus, prophetic guidance provides the eternal perspective necessary for individuals to understand their roles in the time in which they live and urges all to repent and prepare for what lies ahead. It is when people need hope that prophets become predictive.

Because knowledge of God's gracious plan of redemption has been so helpful to all mortals, all of the prophets have spoken about the coming of Christ (Luke 24:44–48; Jacob 4:4; Mosiah 13:33; D&C 20:26), and ancient prophecies demonstrate that people before his advent had a detailed knowledge of the events of the mission of Christ as well as a profound doctrinal understanding of his Atonement (2 Ne. 2, 9; Mosiah 3; Alma 34). Enoch, for example, foresaw the coming of the Messiah, his death on the cross, and his resurrection and ascension into heaven (Moses 7:53–59); Isaiah described Christ as a suffering servant (Isa. 53; cf. Abinadi's explanation in Mosiah 14–15); Lehi saw Christ's coming and noted the meaning of his baptism (1 Ne. 10:4–11); Nephi₁ prophesied that Christ's mother would be a virgin from Nazareth (1 Ne. 11:13–20); and both King Benjamin and Alma₂ noted that her name would be Mary (Mosiah 3:7; Alma 7:10). In addition, Nephi cited prophecies of Zenos, Zenock, and Neum, ancient prophets whose works are not extant in the Old Testament, giving details of the Crucifixion and Resurrection and the events that would accompany his death along with a foretaste of the atoning benefits to humankind wrought thereby (1 Ne. 19:10–21).

Many biblical prophets, including Isaiah, Jeremiah, Ezekiel, Malachi, and Christ himself, foresaw events in fulfillment of the Lord's plan for the latter days. The Pearl of Great Price and the Book of Mormon contain prophecies from the biblical and Book of Mormon periods specifically preserved to give hope and guidance in later times. For example, "The Lord showed Enoch all things, even unto the end of the world" (Moses 7:67), including the restoration of the gospel, the building of Zion, the coming of Christ, and the ushering in of the Millennium (Moses 7:62–66); Nephi and Moroni foresaw the spiritual conditions of pride, wickedness, unbelief, and false doctrine prevalent in the world at a time propitious to the restoration of the gospel, with the coming forth of the Book of Mormon as an instrument in the ensuing conversion and gathering of Israel (2 Ne. 26–30; Morm. 8–9).

The Doctrine and Covenants, like the ancient scriptures, contains divine admonitions, instructions, and reproofs, and also gives guidance through many prophetic predictions of events yet to transpire. A prophecy of civil war in the United States and of ultimate worldwide strife has already been partly fulfilled (D&C 87; 130:12–13; *see also* CIVIL WAR PROPHECY). Other prophecies still to be fulfilled include predictions of the signs of ultimate times (D&C 29:14–21; 45:16–47; 88:86–93), the preparatory preaching of the gospel to all nations, the latter-day gathering of Israel (D&C 133), the building of Zion (D&C 84:1–5), the second coming of Christ (D&C 45:48–53; 133:17–25), the Millennium (D&C 63:49–52; 101:22–31), and the resurrection of the dead and final judgment (D&C 29:22–30; 76; 88:95–116). The stated purposes of such prophecies are to warn and inform the inhabitants of the earth of the urgent need to repent and to share the gospel in all the earth and thus: "Be prepared in all things against the day when tribulation and desolation are sent forth" (D&C 29:8); therefore, "labor ye, labor ye in my vineyard for the last time—for the last time call upon the inhabitants of the earth" (D&C 43:28–29; cf. 133:4–5).

The scriptures address the problem of distinguishing true and false prophecies (Matt. 7:15–20; *TPJS*, p. 365). The Old Testament criterion, "If the thing follow not, nor come to pass, that is the thing which the Lord hath not spoken" (Deut. 18:22), is of course not always a practicable test for the prophet's contemporaries to discern the validity of the call and message.

Joseph Smith noted that "a prophet [is] a prophet only when he [is] acting as such" (*TPJS*, p. 278), and Brigham Young taught that the responsibility of discernment lies with individual members of the Church (*JD* 9:150). When Nephi's brothers wanted to know the truth of his prophecies, he told them that the Lord says, "If ye will not harden your hearts, and ask me in faith, believing that ye shall receive, with diligence in keeping my commandments, surely these things shall be made known unto you" (1 Ne. 15:11). These modes of evaluating a prophet's teachings are still valid. Jesus promised his disciples, "When he, the Spirit of truth, is come, he will guide you into all truth . . . and he will shew you things to come" (John 16:13). These prophetic gifts of the Holy Ghost have been restored and are available to all worthy individuals. Paul wrote to the Corinthians, "No man can say that Jesus is the Lord, but by the Holy Ghost" (1 Cor. 12:3). Indeed, the spirit of prophecy was, and is, "the testimony of Jesus" (Rev. 19:10). Moroni$_2$ promised all who will believe and partake of the spiritual gifts available that the truthfulness of spiritual things can be ascertained through serious intent, study, reflection, and prayer: "And by the power of the Holy Ghost ye may know the truth of all things" (Moro. 10:3–5; 1 Ne. 10:17–19; Moro. 7:12–18; D&C 9). The validity and value of prophetic teachings, past and present, may thus be known.

BIBLIOGRAPHY

Heschel, Abraham J. *The Prophets*. New York, 1962.
McConkie, Joseph F. *Prophets and Prophecy*. Salt Lake City, 1988.
Nibley, Hugh. *The World and the Prophets*. *CWHN*, Vol. 3.
Wilson, Robert R. *Prophecy and Society in Ancient Israel*. Philadelphia, 1980.

DAVID R. SEELY

PROPHECY IN BIBLICAL TIMES

From Adam (Moses 6:8) to John the Revelator, the Lord has revealed his word to prophets: "The Lord God will do nothing, but he revealeth his secret unto his servants the prophets" (Amos 3:7; cf. Num. 12:6–8; Jer. 23:18). Prophecy refers to God's word received by prophets acting as authorized intermediaries between God and humans.

The Lord called men from the course of their normal lives to be prophets and revealed his word in various ways: by face-to-face encounters, his voice alone, divine messengers, dreams, and inspiration. Often prophets received the Lord's word through symbolic object lessons, visions of councils in heaven and scenes of judgment, and views of past, present, and future events, and hence, they were also called "foretellers" and "forth-tellers." Occasionally expressed poetically, biblical prophecy is rich in imagery, metaphor, symbolism, allusion, and other literary figures. Besides the prophecies in the Bible, others from the biblical period are preserved in the Pearl of Great Price, the Book of Mormon, and the Doctrine and Covenants.

Biblical prophets acted frequently as mediators of covenants. Prophets such as Adam, Enoch, Noah, the BROTHER OF JARED, Abraham, and Moses acted as agents through whom the Lord established his covenants among men and women. These prophets proclaimed the gospel and called their contemporaries to repent and join in a covenantal relationship with the Lord, providing inspired descriptions of future blessings and cursings that depended on obedience to the conditions of the covenants. Prophets who followed, such as Lehi, Ether, Isaiah, Jeremiah, King Benjamin, and John the Baptist, renewed the covenant and warned the covenant people, in varying states of apostasy, that they must repent and keep their covenantal obligations or face the consequences of disobedience—judgment, destruction, and scattering.

Biblical prophets often addressed the present by looking into the future, and prophecies of destruction were balanced by those of hope. Prophets foresaw apostasy and RESTORATION, the scattering and gathering of Israel, the coming of Jesus Christ and his atonement (Jacob 4:4; Mosiah 13:33; D&C 20:26), and times of tribulation preceding his return (Acts 3:21). Along with their indictments of covenant Israel, many prophets delivered oracles directed to foreign nations, affirming the universal scope of their message (Amos 9:7). Most prophets in biblical times directed their unpopular message of repentance toward individuals or the community, thus placing the prophet in opposition to the prevailing social, political, and religious values, practices, and institutions of his time and place. Some prophets were killed or persecuted by those whose beliefs and behavior they condemned.

From the beginning, the Lord has set no limit on his ability to send prophets at his discretion. "And I do this that I may prove unto many that I am the same yesterday, today, and forever; . . . and because that I have spoken one word ye need not suppose that I cannot speak another; for my work is not yet finished; neither shall it be until the end of man, neither from that time henceforth and forever" (2 Ne. 29:9). Biblical prophecy did not end with MALACHI but continued with the coming of John the Baptist (Matt. 13:57; Luke 7:39; 1 Ne. 10:4). In addition, the prophetic tradition continued in the Western Hemisphere until the destruction of the NEPHITES around A.D. 400. Joel prophesied the future restoration of prophecy: "I will pour out my spirit upon all flesh; and your sons and your daughters shall prophesy, your old men shall dream dreams, your young men shall see visions" (Joel 2:28). The fulfillment of this prophecy was acknowledged by PETER on the day of Pentecost (Acts 2:16–18) and again by the angel MORONI to the Prophet Joseph Smith (JS—H 1:41).

Latter-day scriptures cite, interpret, and allude to ancient prophecy, emphasizing its relevance to the restored Church. For example, important prophecies not in the biblical canon, such as those of JOSEPH OF EGYPT (2 Ne. 3) and ZENOS (Jacob 5), are preserved in the Book of Mormon. NEPHI$_1$ (e.g., 1 Ne. 20–22; 2 Ne. 11–24), JACOB (2 Ne. 7–8), ABINADI (Mosiah 14–15), and Christ (3 Ne. 20–25) cite Isaiah extensively and provide inspired interpretation (*see* ISAIAH: TEXTS IN THE BOOK OF MORMON). In the Doctrine and Covenants, Joseph Smith addressed specific questions about Isaiah 11 (D&C 113) and the book of Revelation (D&C 77) and through revelation confirmed the fulfillment of several biblical prophecies in the latter days, including Daniel's vision of "the stone which is cut out of the mountain without hands" as the restoration of the gospel (D&C 65:2) and the coming of ELIJAH in Malachi 4:5–6 by his appearance in the Kirtland Temple in 1836 (D&C 110).

BIBLIOGRAPHY

Jackson, Kent, ed. *Studies in Scripture*, Vol. 4. Salt Lake City, 1991.
Lindblom, Johannes. *Prophecy in Ancient Israel*, 2nd ed. Oxford, 1978.
Sperry, Sidney B. *The Voice of Israel's Prophets*. Salt Lake City, 1952.

DAVID R. SEELY

PROPHECY IN THE BOOK OF MORMON

The Book of Mormon reports prophecies made during a thousand-year period concerning the future of the NEPHITES and LAMANITES, the earthly ministry of Jesus Christ, his visit to the Western Hemisphere, the future RESTORATION of the gospel to the GENTILES, and related events of the last days. While this record includes the fulfillment of some prophecies, Latter-day Saints see fulfillment of other prophecies in the restoration of the gospel through the Prophet Joseph Smith and expect yet others to be fulfilled in the future.

Messianic prophecies include the number of years until Jesus' birth (1 Ne. 10:4; Hel. 14:2), conditions surrounding his birth (1 Ne. 11:13–21), his mother's identity (Mosiah 3:8), the manner and location of his baptism by John the Baptist (1 Ne. 10:7–10), his miracles and teachings (1 Ne. 11:28–31), and his atonement, resurrection, and second coming. PROPHETS foretold details concerning Christ's crucifixion and his atoning sacrifice, one stating that "blood cometh from every pore, so great shall be his anguish for the wickedness and the abominations of his people" (Mosiah 3:7). Furthermore, he would rise on the third day (2 Ne. 25:13) and appear to many (Alma 16:20). SAMUEL THE LAMANITE prophesied specific signs of Christ's birth and death to be experienced among BOOK OF MORMON PEOPLES (Hel. 14).

During his visit to the Americas, the risen Jesus attested to the authenticity of these prophecies by stating that "the scriptures concerning my coming are fulfilled" (3 Ne. 9:16). Later, he reminded NEPHI$_3$ of a prophecy of his resurrection, the fulfillment of which had not been recorded. The details were promptly added to Nephite records (3 Ne. 23:6–13; cf. Hel. 14:25).

The Book of Mormon relates the fulfillment of other prophecies foretelling events among Book of Mormon peoples. Besides many Messianic prophecies, examples include ALMA$_2$ prophesying that the Nephites, dwindling in unbelief, would eventually become extinct (Alma 45:9–14; Morm. 6:11–15) and ABINADI forecasting the destiny of his captors and their descendants (Mosiah 11:20–25; 17:15–18). Other prophecies anticipated more immediate events. For example, on the eve of Jesus' birth, when lives of believers were threatened by unbelievers, Nephi$_3$ received divine assurance that "on the morrow" the signs of Christ's birth would be seen (3 Ne. 1:9–15).

Book of Mormon prophets also forecast events of the latter days. They foretold the European exploration of America (1 Ne. 13:12–15), the American Revolution (1 Ne. 13:16–19), and the gathering of Israel (1 Ne. 22; 3 Ne. 20–22). They warned of deceptive practices among religionists, including priestcraft, secret combinations, and neglect of the poor. They foretold the impact of the Book of Mormon on latter-day people and the destruction of the wicked. The prophecies of MORONI$_2$ included admonitions addressed to those who would live in the last days: "Behold, I speak unto you as if ye were present, . . . behold, Jesus Christ hath shown you unto me, and I know your doing" (Morm. 8:35).

Under inspiration, prophets in the Book of Mormon frequently quoted previous prophets in support of their teachings. They warned that in rejecting the living prophet's witness, their hearers were rejecting the testimonies of such revered prophets as Isaiah, Moses, and ZENOS (Hel. 8:11–20).

Prophesying falsely was viewed as a crime among the Nephites (W of M 1:15–16). Agreement with past prophets was a test of a prophet's authenticity. For instance, during a debate, JACOB exposed Sherem as a false prophet by showing that his testimony contradicted previous prophecy. Jacob then demonstrated that his own teachings agreed with former prophets, thus sealing Sherem's conviction as a false prophet (Jacob 7:9–12).

Prophecy sometimes came in dreams or visions after pondering and prayer. Lehi and NEPHI$_1$ were caught up in the Spirit (1 Ne. 1:7–8, 11:1). King BENJAMIN and Samuel the Lamanite were visited by angels (Mosiah 3:2; Hel. 13:7). Prophecy was delivered variously, as in a psalm by Nephi$_1$ (2 Ne. 4:20–35), in Zenos' allegory (Jacob 5), or in Jacob's chastisements (2 Ne. 9:30–38).

Besides their service to God, as his messengers, prophets served as religious leaders (ALMA$_1$), kings (Benjamin; MOSIAH$_2$), military leaders (Helaman$_1$), and historians (Nephi$_3$). They were also social and moral critics of their society. Jacob denounced wickedness among his people not only because of its effects on that generation but also for wounds inflicted on the next (Jacob 2–3). Samuel the Lamanite foretold dire future consequences of the Nephites' lifestyle, criticizing their state of degradation (Hel. 13).

The presence of prophets and of contemporary prophecies were important to the Book of Mormon people. MORMON testified, "I also know that as many things as have been prophesied concerning us . . . have been fulfilled, and as many as go beyond this day must surely come to pass" (W of M 1:4).

BIBLIOGRAPHY

Nibley, Hugh. *The Prophetic Book of Mormon.* In *CWHN* 8. Salt Lake City, 1989.

Parsons, Robert E. "The Prophecies of the Prophets." In *First Nephi, the Doctrinal Foundation*, ed. M. Nyman and C. Tate. Provo, Utah, 1988.

CAMILLE FRONK

PROPHET

[*This entry consists of two articles:* Prophets *presents the LDS belief in prophets, both past and present, as an integral part of the Church, and* Biblical Prophets *discusses the phenomenon of prophets and prophecy as a distinctive feature of biblical religion.*]

PROPHETS

A belief in prophets and their messages lies at the heart of LDS doctrine (A of F 4, 5, 6, 7, 9). Latter-day Saints recognize the biblical and Book of Mormon prophets, as well as latter-day prophets, as servants of Jesus Christ and accept as scripture the Bible, the Book of Mormon, the Pearl of Great Price, and the Doctrine and Covenants. They believe that Joseph Smith and all subsequent Presidents of the Church were and are prophets and representatives of Jesus Christ.

The word "prophet" comes from the Greek *prophetes*, which means "inspired teacher." Although neither the Greek term nor its Hebrew equivalent, *nabi*, initially required the function of foretelling (Smith, p. 3), all prophecy looks to the future. Since the Lord has chosen some of his servants to be foretellers—to disclose, sometimes in specific terms, momentous events that are to occur—the predictive element often overshadows other implications of the word in the minds of some.

But the gift of prophecy is not restricted to those whose words have been recorded in scripture. By scriptural definition, a prophet is anyone who has a testimony of Jesus Christ and is moved by the Holy Ghost (Rev. 19:10; cf. *TPJS*, pp. 119, 160). Moses, voicing his approval of two men who had prophesied, exclaimed, "Would God that all the Lord's people were prophets, and that the Lord would put his spirit upon them!" (Num. 11:26–29). Schools of prophets and "sons" (followers) of prophets, some false and some true, existed in large numbers in Old Testament times. In modern times, speaking of Brigham Young, Elder Wilford Woodruff said, "He is a prophet, I am a prophet, you are, and anybody is a prophet who has the testimony of Jesus Christ, for that is the spirit of prophecy" (*JD* 13:165). It follows that this spirit does not operate in every utterance of its possessor. The Prophet Joseph Smith explained that "a prophet [is] a prophet only when he [is] acting as such" (*HC* 5:265).

In 1820 a passage in James (1:5) led to Joseph Smith's first vision (JS—H 1:11–20). Three years later the angel-prophet-messenger MORONI$_2$, while instructing Joseph Smith, quoted from the prophets Malachi, Joel, and Isaiah, who told of the forthcoming mission of the Messiah and of the role of prophets, including Elijah, in the latter-day restoration of the gospel. Subsequent revelations given to Joseph Smith make frequent reference to the prophets of the Old and New Testaments. Most frequently cited, in addition to those mentioned above, are Enoch, Noah, Abraham, Isaac, Jacob, Moses, Peter, James, John, and John the Baptist. In April 1836, the prophets Moses, Elias, and Elijah appeared to Joseph Smith and Oliver Cowdery and committed to them the keys of the priesthood (see D&C 110:11–16). Other angelic messengers, all prophets, had been instrumental in restoring the Aaronic and Melchizedek priesthoods, beginning in 1829 (JS—H 1:68–73).

Joseph Smith had the spirit of prophecy after he and Oliver Cowdery were baptized in May 1829 (JS—H 1:73–74), and his prophetic office was officially recognized when the Church was organized on April 6, 1830. A revelation to him says, "Thou shalt be called a seer, a translator, a prophet, an apostle of Jesus Christ, an elder of the church . . . being inspired of the Holy Ghost to lay the foundation thereof" (D&C 21:1–2). In March 1836, under the prophetic leadership of Joseph Smith, the membership of the Church sustained the First Presidency and the Quorum of the Twelve Apostles as prophets, seers, and revelators (*HC* 2:417). Their successors have been similarly sustained.

An unbroken series of prophets have led the Church since the death of Joseph Smith in 1844: Brigham Young (1844–1877); John Taylor (1877–1887); Wilford Woodruff (1887–1898); Lorenzo Snow (1898–1901); Joseph F. Smith (1901–1918); Heber J. Grant (1918–1945); George Albert Smith (1945–1951); David O. McKay (1951–1970); Joseph Fielding Smith (1970–1972); Harold B. Lee (1972–1973); Spencer W. Kimball (1973–1985); Ezra Taft Benson (1985–1994); and Howard W. Hunter (1994–). Since 1847, these prophets have administered the affairs of the Church from Church headquarters in Salt Lake City. They have dedicated themselves to their appointed mission of helping the people of the world prepare for eternal life, and for the second coming of Jesus Christ. They have provided leadership for the international missionary program of the Church and for the building of temples. The living prophet continues to receive revelations, select and ordain leaders by the spirit of prophecy, and serve as the principal teacher of the Church, instructing its members in doctrine and in righteous living.

Prophets and their messages have occupied a central place in God's dealings with his children from the beginning. Elder Bruce R. McConkie, an apostle, has written that a foreordained prophet has stood at the head of God's church in all dispensations of the gospel from the time of Adam (see Moses 5:9, 10) to the present, including, for example, Noah, Abraham, Moses, Peter, and Joseph Smith (*A New Witness for the Articles of Faith*, Salt Lake City, 1985, p. 2).

Prophets are always witnesses of Jesus Christ, a fact that is particularly evident in the Book of Mormon. The experience common to all its prophets is the witness they bore of Jesus Christ, the Messiah—of his divine sonship and his earthly mission. A number of them, including Lehi, Nephi$_1$, Jacob, Benjamin, Abinadi, Alma$_2$, and Samuel the Lamanite, foretold his coming (1 Ne. 1:19; 10:4; 19:7–8; Jacob 4:4–5; Mosiah 3:5–8). They foresaw his atoning sacrifice and his resurrection (Mosiah 3:10–11; 15). Nephi wrote earlier of ancient prophets, Zenos, Neum, and Zenock (1 Ne. 19:10; 3 Ne. 10:14–16), who also foretold the visitation of Jesus Christ to the Americas after his resurrection (3 Ne. 11–26). Because Latter-day Saints identify Jesus Christ as Jehovah, they recognize that Old Testament prophets bore this same witness.

The Book of Mormon, apart from its function as history, is essentially a record of the dealings of God with a long series of prophets, from Lehi, in the sixth century before Christ, to Moroni$_2$, a thousand years later. As witnesses of Jesus Christ, all were called to be teachers of righteousness. Though their teachings were all based in the gospel of Jesus Christ and they taught the same essential things, the record we have preserves some individual points of emphasis: Abinadi stressed living the Mosaic law with the proper spirit (Mosiah 12, 13); Nephi$_1$ and Alma$_2$ preached baptism and repentance (2 Ne. 31; Mosiah 18), as did Alma's sons (Alma 17–29). Many, including Nephi$_1$, Enos, Ether, and Moroni, were prompted to write and speak of faith and the gift of the Holy Ghost (e.g., 2 Ne. 26:13; 32:2–3). In counsel to his son Jacob, Lehi taught the principles of "opposition in all things" and of agency (2 Ne. 2). King Benjamin urged his people to serve God by serving one another (Mosiah 2:17). He and other Book of Mormon prophets, like their Old Testament counterparts, warned against vanity, greed, sexual immorality, materialism, and similar sins; but they also counseled love, kindness, patience, humility, and all peaceable things.

The Hebrew prophets spoke for God for many centuries until the post-apostolic era, from the second to the nineteenth centuries, when faith in continuing prophecy had vanished in that part of the world and when people assumed, even as did some in Jesus' day, that the prophets were dead (John 8:53) and their offices abolished. To believe that God had spoken to people of one's own time was "the test that Christ's generation could not pass" (*CWHN* 3:7).

"He that prophesieth," wrote Paul, "speaketh unto men to edification, and exhortation, and comfort" (1 Cor. 14:3)—such a person teaches, admonishes, and gives assurance of God's love. The prophets have proclaimed those God-given messages in many ways and with varying emphases. Their messages, though timeless in import, have been relevant to the immediate life of communities and nations. Some have combined their functions as prophets with other activities, such as being judges, military leaders, historians, poets, and church and civic administrators.

Some prophets have been popular figures and charismatic leaders—Moses, Samuel, and Alma$_2$, for instance. But many have suffered abuse and betrayal. For every prophet who has been honored during earth life, many have suffered persecution and even martyrdom (2 Chr. 36:15–16; Matt. 5:11–12; Mosiah 17:20; D&C 135). Clearly, prophetic messages have not been designed to gain popular favor. A fundamental, common theme in all these messages is the call to repentance. Though prophets have counseled mercy, brotherhood, and humility, and though they have promised life and joy to those who have sought to love God and to receive his love, they have foreseen sorrow and despair as the unavoidable consequences of immorality, greed, idolatry, malice, pride, and other sins. They have yearned for peace, but they have condemned false prophets who have cried, "Peace, peace; when there is no peace" (Jer. 6:14). Unwarranted complacency, obsessive materialism, and the worship of other gods were main attributes of false prophets and their followers.

The messages of the prophets have taken many forms. Foremost are direct instructions and commandments from God to his children, as in much of the Pentateuch and the Doctrine and Covenants. Many have come as sermons and covenant renewal ceremonies, such as those of Moses and Joshua (Deut. 4–11; Josh. 24). Important truths are found in the counsel of the prophets to their own families, as in the words of Lehi and Alma$_2$ to their children (2 Ne. 1–4; Alma 36–42). Some prophetic messages have been recorded in letters, such as the epistles of Paul, James, Peter, and John in the New Testament and those of Joseph Smith in Doctrine and Covenants 127 and 128. Some are expressed as prayer—such as David's prayer of thanksgiving (2 Sam. 7:18–29)—and some are couched in symbol and poetry: the symbolism of Ezekiel and John the Revelator, the songs of David, the poetic passages of Isaiah and Jeremiah, the figurative language of Paul (Eph. 6:10–18), and such poetic utterances as the "new song" in Doctrine and Covenants 84:98–102.

No true prophets, ancient or modern, have ever called themselves to their positions. Some, such as Moses, Amos, and Jeremiah, have even accepted the calling reluctantly. Some, including John the Baptist, Samuel, Nephi$_1$, and Joseph Smith, were called in childhood or youth.

The calls made to individual prophets and God's further communications with and through them have been accomplished in various ways: through the ministering of angels; in dreams; in day or night visions; by prophetic inspiration, an intense conviction verified by subsequent events; by the literal voice of God; and in face-to-face visitations such as those experienced by Moses (Ex. 33:11), Enoch

(Moses 7:4), and Joseph Smith (JS—H 1:17). Sometimes the call has come with blinding intensity, as in those of Paul and Alma$_2$; sometimes, as with Elijah, the prophet has heard "a still small voice" (1 Kgs. 19:12). God has often spoken to his prophets in answer to prayer, but true prophets have not been mystics who try to make contact with the unseen by self-induced trances or similar means.

The calling of a prophet has always been made, and his messages have been written or spoken, through the power of the Holy Ghost, sometimes called the Spirit of the Lord (Acts 2:1–4, 37–42). Ananias put his hands on Paul that he might receive his sight and be filled with the Holy Ghost. "And straightway he preached Christ . . . that he is the Son of God" (Acts 9:17–20). So, too, did the prophets before Paul, and so have all of them since. In close conjunction with the gift of the Holy Ghost is the priesthood power that has been exercised by God's representatives throughout all dispensations.

BIBLIOGRAPHY
Madsen, Truman G. *Joseph Smith the Prophet*. Salt Lake City, 1989.
Nibley, Hugh. *The World and the Prophets*. Vol. 3 of *CWHN*.
Smith, J. M. Powis. *The Prophets and Their Times*. Chicago, 1925.
Welch, John W. "The Calling of a Prophet." In *The Book of Mormon: First Nephi, The Doctrinal Foundation*, ed. M. Nyman and C. Tate, pp. 35–54. Provo, Utah, 1988.

RALPH A. BRITSCH
TODD A. BRITSCH

BIBLICAL PROPHETS

The phenomenon of PROPHECY is a distinctive feature of biblical religion. In its fully developed character, it sets biblical religion apart from other religions of the ancient Near East. As in other related matters, such as worship, sacrifice, ethical principles, and practices, ISRAEL shared much with its neighbors. But often, and specifically in matters of religion, the people of the Bible formed and forged something distinctive and different from all that came before or continued side by side. And this is particularly true of biblical prophecy.

With few exceptions the surviving materials of pagan antiquity command now only marginal academic interest—quaint reminders of a distant past—whereas the prophets of the Bible speak across the centuries with words, and out of experiences, that have direct bearing on modern lives and meaning for modern civilization.

Prophets in the Bible claim to be both foretellers and forth-tellers and base their claims upon their private access to the God of Israel, who is the ruler of history—past, present, and future. Prophecy as an essential part of Israel's theopolitical structure and the prophetic movement as an actual historical phenomenon had their beginnings with Samuel and his band of followers in the eleventh century B.C., at the point of transition from the era of the judges to the beginnings of the monarchy with the installation of Saul as royal head of the Israelite Confederation, or League of Tribes. Prophets, beginning with Samuel, played a significant, if not deci-sive, part in establishing but also censuring the monarchy and remained an integral part of Israelite society as long as the monar-chy survived, and even beyond, when there was still thought or hope of restoring the kingship of the house of David. While God generally speaks to prophets through VISIONS, auditions, and even dreams, with MOSES he spoke face to face (Deut. 34) or mouth to mouth (Ex. 33). And whereas other prophets often only sense the presence of deity, Moses saw his actual form and person (Num. 12; cf. Ex. 33–34).

From the biblical records of the prophets and their experiences, one can piece together a picture of prophets and their calling.

THE CALL. The divine call and commission mark the beginning of the prophet's career. In all recorded cases, the details are striking and distinctive; no two prophetic situations are exactly the same, although all share important elements. We have sufficient data for people like Moses, Samuel, Elisha (but not ELIJAH), and the great lit-erary prophets such as Amos, Hosea, ISAIAH, JEREMIAH, and EZEKIEL to fill out a composite picture. But we lack information about the call of such prophets as Nathan and Ahijah. Typically, the call is initi-ated by God and is often accompanied by one or more visions, along with some unusual or miraculous occurrence (e.g., the burning bush). It is the combination of circumstances that persuades the prophet (or prophetess) that he (or she) is not hallucinating but is having contact with the living God.

THE COMMISSION. The call is always accompanied by a commission. The purpose is to enlist or draft the prophet to carry out a mission or duty—to do something in response to the call. Some prophets are reluctant to take on such responsibility, and therefore make excuses or otherwise try to evade their calling (e.g., Moses, Jeremiah, and, above all, Jonah). Other prophets are eager to carry out their task and hasten to do so (e.g., Isaiah, Ezekiel, perhaps Hosea). The basic rules for the prophet—the marching orders, as it were—are given succinctly and eloquently in the book of Jeremiah: "Wherever I send you, you shall go, and what I tell you, you shall say" (Jer. 1:7 [author translation]). In brief, the prophet is the ambassador or messenger of God, and his (or her) sole duty is to deliver the message as given.

THE MESSAGE.   In most cases, the message is for others and especially for the nation, its leaders, and the people generally. Often it contains warnings and threats, sometimes promises and encouragement. Inevitably there is a predictive element, as messages are mostly oriented to the future but rooted in the past. For the most part, predictions are morally conditioned, based upon the covenant between God and Israel, offering the choice between life and death, with success as the result of obedience and failure as the consequence of disobedience and defiance. Occasionally the oracles are pronounced absolutely, guaranteeing the future, whether of destruction or restoration. Occasionally they are timebound—that is, within a specified period the events described will occur, but often no time frame is specified. Even when moral or temporal conditions are not articulated, they may be implied by the speaker or inferred by the hearers. A notable case is the flat prediction by Micah (Micah 3:12) that Jerusalem will be destroyed. A century later, Jeremiah quotes the passage not to show that the prophecy was unfulfilled (Jerusalem had not been destroyed and was still standing), or much less to indict Micah as a false prophet, but rather to argue that as a result of the prophecy, the king (Hezekiah) and the people repented, and hence Yahweh (Jehovah) forgave them and spared the city (Jer. 26:16–19). It was the prophet's message that produced the result, and therefore both he and his message were vindicated as coming from God.

THE PROPHET AS WONDER-WORKER.   MIRACLES are clearly and strongly associated with prophets such as Moses, Samuel, and especially Elijah and Elisha—as well as Isaiah among the so-called writing prophets—but there are many prophets with little or no such connection (e.g., Jeremiah, Amos, Hosea, Micah, etc.). Miracles seem to be attached to unusual charismatic individuals who were also prophets but not necessarily to the role or office of prophet. In the case of Moses, they were designed to strengthen and confirm his claims to have received an authentic and authoritative message from God, and they served to augment the function and purpose of visions and similar experiences of other prophets.

SUCCESS AND FAILURE.   On the whole, the results of the prophetic experience are themselves unpredictable, and success or failure on the part of individual prophets hardly affects their status as true prophets of God. Prophets such as Samuel and Elisha are reported to have met with much success in carrying out their missions. With Elijah and perhaps Isaiah, the results are mixed, as also with Amos, Hosea, and Micah. Ultimately, they were all recognized as true prophets, not because the leaders and the people heeded their words (often they did not), but because they faithfully reported what they heard from the mouth of God, regardless of consequences for themselves or the people to whom they delivered the message. The survival of the nation was seen to be at stake, and it was of the greatest importance to distinguish true from false prophets. This was no mere academic exercise, but required the best judgment of leaders and people alike.

TESTS OF TRUE PROPHETS.   The book of DEUTERONOMY offers rules of procedure to decide the issue of truth and falsehood. There are two basic principles, both practical and applicable: (1) if the prophet speaks in the name of, and delivers messages from, another God or other gods, then he is automatically condemned for apostasy and must be put to death (Deut. 13:1–5); (2) if the prophet makes a prediction and in due course the prediction is not fulfilled—that is, what is predicted does not come to pass—then the prophet is judged to be false and is to be executed (Deut. 18:20–22).

But the Deuteronomic rules will not work in many situations, and the jury is thrown back on other resources. In the end, the decision cannot wait until all the evidence is in, and must be based on other factors. The chief factor (after the basic test of orthodoxy: in the name of which God does the prophet speak?) must be the impact the prophet makes on his audience: his honesty, his courage, his reliability—the ability to make real to the listeners the experience of God and his messages to the prophet and through him to the people. Later there can be confirmation and vindication.

THE PROPHET AS CUSTODIAN OF COVENANT AND COMMUNITY. From beginning to end, the emphasis in prophetic utterance is on the ethical dimension of biblical religion and how it affects the well-being of the nation and its individual members. In contrast to the cultic concerns of the priests, the prophets stress the moral demands of deity and the ethical requirements of the covenant. The survival and success of the community depend more on the righteousness of the nation than on either the cultic activities of the priests or the military, political, social, and economic exploits of the king and his coterie. The battle against idolatry and apostasy was waged unremittingly through the whole biblical period, and the leaders in the struggle were the prophets. Second to that and equally difficult and important was the obligation to one's neighbor and to the community as a whole. On these two foundations, the prophetic message was constructed, and the prophets never ceased to propound the elementary and basic truths about biblical religion and the relationship of God to his people.

PROPHETS AND UNIVERSALISM. With the great prophets of the eighth and following centuries B.C., there was an important shift, although the basic truths remained untouched. The same requirements and the same standards were upheld and applied even more sharply to an Israel prone to defection and default. With the appearance of the great world powers—Assyria in the eighth and seventh centuries B.C. and Babylonia toward the end of the seventh and on into the sixth— the question of the survival of the little kingdoms of Israel and Judah (and their neighbors) became acute. The prophets raise the issue sharply and in a new way for the first time since the time of the patriarchs, with a larger perspective on the world scene and the role of Yahweh in ruling over the nations. The place of Israel and Judah in the larger picture is defined, and a theory of world order and time frame is foreshadowed. The implications of a single God ruling the universe but with special ties to one small nation (or two kingdoms) are developed. The danger and threats to the people of God are defined more sharply, but so also are the hopes and promises of the future. Ultimately, the God of the world, who is also the God of his particular way, and a restored and revealed Israel will take their place among the nations in a harmonious resolution of conflicts—to form the Peaceable Kingdom. The ultimate vision encompasses all nations and peoples, with a special place for Israel, still obligated by essential covenant stipulations, but a leader and model for all the others. Personal faith and morality are at the core of prophetic religion, but the implications and ramifications are social, national, and ultimately worldwide.

THE PROPHET AS SPOKESMAN FOR THE PEOPLE OF GOD.   Normally one thinks of the priests as offering up prayers and sacrifices to God in behalf of the people, and especially of the role of the High Priest on the Day of Atonement. In the same manner, prophets may exercise the role of intercessor, but in a different context. Jeremiah mentions two intercessors, Moses and Samuel, while confirming that God himself has denied that role to Jeremiah. The most dramatic case is that of Moses in the episode of the golden calf (Ex. 32). Only Moses has the audacity and the closeness to God to demand a change of heart and mind on the part of the deity. Only Moses can command repentance on the part of God (but see JST Ex. 32:14). And he succeeds, as the text reports. Israel is spared. A different poetic version of the same event is Psalm 90:13. It is not accidental or incidental that this is the only psalm in the Bible directly attributed to Moses.

Moses remains the unique model of a prophet of Israel because of his inspiration, his leadership, and ultimately his intercessory powers. The closing words of the book of Deuteronomy reflect this singularity: "Not has arisen a prophet in Israel like Moses, whom God knew face to face" (Deut. 34:10 [author translation]; cf. Ex. 33:11). And Yahweh would talk to Moses face to face, as men and women talk to their companions (cf. also Num. 12:8): "Mouth to mouth I speak to him . . . and the shape of Yahweh he beholds" (author translation).

BIBLIOGRAPHY
Friedrich, Gerhard, ed., and Geoffrey W. Bromiley, ed. and trans. *Theological Dictionary of the New Testament*, Vol. 6, pp. 781–861. Grand Rapids, Mich., 1964–1974.
Nibley, Hugh. *The World and the Prophets. CWHN 3.*
Sawyer, John F. A. *Prophecy and the Prophets of the Old Testament*. Oxford, 1987.

DAVID NOEL FREEDMAN

PSALMS, MESSIANIC PROPHECIES IN

The Psalms are a rich source of messianic prophecy; indeed Psalms 2, 22, 69, and 110 are cited or partially quoted as messianic prophecies in the NEW TESTAMENT. The Prophet Joseph Smith appreciated the messianic and prophetic nature of the Psalms, revising under inspiration several verses to make them even more emphatically prophetic of the messianic message (*see* JOSEPH SMITH TRANSLATION OF THE BIBLE [JST]). Included in the revisions are Psalms 10, 11, 12, and 24.

Citations from Psalms contribute 116 of the 283 Old Testament quotations in the New Testament. Of these, a number are clearly messianic. For instance, Psalm 2:7 is referred to in Acts 13:33; and Hebrews 1:5 and 5:5 specifically apply the affirmation "Thou art my Son" to Jesus. Nearing death on the cross, Jesus himself quoted Psalm 22:1 (Matt. 27:46) and much of the rest of that Psalm characterizes his suffering. His disciples recalled the zeal mentioned in Psalm 69:9 during Jesus' cleansing of the temple (John 2:17); and the same verse is applied to Christ by Paul in Romans 15:3. Jesus credits the Holy Ghost with inspiring David in Psalm 110:1, and applies the passage to himself (Mark 12:35–37; Luke 20:41–44). Hebrews 5:6 quotes Psalm 110:4 concerning Christ and the Melchizedek Priesthood.

The JST revision of Psalm 10:15–16 alludes to the kingly role of the Messiah: "O Lord, thou wilt break the arm of the wicked. . . . And the Lord shall be king . . . for the wicked shall perish out of his land."

Psalm 11:1–5 similarly becomes more messianic by specifying the last days rather than a contemporary Davidic event: "In that day thou shalt come, O Lord; and I will put my trust in thee. Thou shalt say unto thy people . . . " (JST Psalm 11:1). Referring to the Messiah's overcoming of evil, verse 3 is changed to read, "But the foundations of the wicked shall be destroyed, and what can they do?" The JST also casts verse 4 into the future, emphasizing a future deliverance from evil and speaking of the Lord "when he shall come into his holy temple." Verse 5 is doubled in length and adds a key messianic clause, "and he shall redeem the righteous."

JST Psalm 12:1–8 begins with a sentence not found in the King James Version—that underscores divine assistance: "In that day thou shalt help, O Lord, the poor and the meek of the earth." Other verses—2, 4, 5, 6, and 8—have been recast into the future tense. Verse 5 (JST) is messianic, beginning, "Therefore, thus saith the Lord, I will arise in that day, I will stand upon the earth and I will judge the earth for the oppression of the poor."

JST Psalm 24:7–10 proclaims a future redeemer. Verse 8 reads, "And he will roll away the heavens; and will come down to redeem his people; to make you an everlasting name; to establish you upon his everlasting rock." The future redeemer is also noted in verse 10: "Even the king of glory shall come unto you; and shall redeem his people, and shall establish them in righteousness."

Latter-day Saints may thus see more messianic prophecies in the Psalms because Joseph Smith revealed a more messianically oriented Psalter than was found in his King James text. They also accept a tradition of prophecy during the Israelite period and its fulfillment either with the coming of Christ or with the latter-day RESTORATION of the gospel in preparation for the Messiah's millennial reign.

BIBLIOGRAPHY

McConkie, Joseph F. "Joseph Smith and the Poetic Writings." In *The Joseph Smith Translation*, ed. M. Nyman and R. Millet. Provo, Utah, 1985.

GERALD E. JONES

R

RAISING THE DEAD

God has the power to raise the dead. This truth is confirmed by ancient scripture and reaffirmed by revelations in the RESTORATION OF THE GOSPEL in this dispensation. When asked if the "Mormons" could raise the dead, the Prophet Joseph Smith replied, "No, . . . but God can raise the dead, through man as an instrument" (*TPJS*, p. 120).

Raising the dead is the act of restoring to life one whose eternal spirit has departed from its mortal body. Restoration to mortal life, however, is not to be equated or confused with resurrection of the body from death to immortality. A person raised from the dead is not thereby made immortal; in such cases, the individual becomes mortal a second time and must die again before being raised in the resurrection to immortality (Bruce R. McConkie, *Doctrinal New Testament Commentary*, Vol. 1, p. 256, Salt Lake City, 1965).

The scriptures report that on three separate occasions during his mortal ministry Jesus raised individuals from the dead. The daughter of Jairus was called back to life within hours of her death (Mark 5:22–43). The lifeless body of the widow's son in the village of Nain was being carried to the cemetery when Jesus intervened and commanded him to arise, "and he that was dead sat up, and began to speak" (Luke 7:11–17). The body of Lazarus had been dead four days, prepared for burial, and entombed when Jesus commanded,

"Lazarus, come forth. And he that was dead came forth" (John 11:1–46). During his ministry in the Western Hemisphere, the resurrected Jesus again performed many miracles, including raising a man from the dead (3 Ne. 26:15).

Jesus gave his twelve apostles power to raise the dead (Matt. 10:8). He also gave this power to his disciples in the Western Hemisphere, and they "did heal the sick, and raise the dead" (4 Ne. 1:5).

Elijah raised the widow's son (1 Kgs. 17:17–24). Elisha restored to life the son of a Shunammite woman (2 Kgs. 4:18–37). Peter raised Tabitha and "presented her alive to her friends" (Acts 9:36–42). Paul raised Eutychus (Acts 20:7–12). Nephi₃ restored his brother Timothy to life after he had suffered a violent death (3 Ne. 7:19; 19:4).

The priesthood authority by which miracles were performed in ancient times by the servants of God has been restored and is functional in the latter days. The power to raise the dead, if the Lord wills, is inherent in the exercise of priesthood authority by righteous priesthood holders and in the restoration of the gospel of Jesus Christ.

BIBLIOGRAPHY
Cowley, Matthew. *Matthew Cowley Speaks*, p. 247. Salt Lake City, 1971.
Romney, Thomas C. *The Life of Lorenzo Snow*, pp. 406–419. Salt Lake City, 1955.

DENNIS D. FLAKE

REASON AND REVELATION

LDS teaching affirms the supreme authority of divine revelation. However, revelation is not understood as an impediment to rational inquiry but as the framework within which the natural human desire to know can most vigorously and fruitfully be exercised. In traditional Judaism and Islam, revelation is mainly seen as law, and the orthodox life of pious obedience is incompatible with the questioning spirit of philosophic life. The Christian view of religion as belief or faith and of revelation as teachings or doctrine has encouraged a perennial interest in reconciling the authority of revealed religion with that of reason. Thus, among revealed religions, Christianity has been the most open—and the most vulnerable—to the claims of reason.

The theological tradition of medieval Christianity viewed the Gospels as a supernatural fulfillment of the brilliant but partial insights of natural reason as represented by Greek philosophers, especially Plato and Aristotle. The Christian philosophers Augustine and Aquinas agreed with their pagan predecessors that reason is the noblest natural human faculty, but argued that it cannot reach God, its true end, without the aid of revelation. Thus, revelation was held to be superior, but even this superiority was to some extent defined by a view of the good inherited from pre-Christian philosophy.

The founders of the Protestant tradition attacked this alliance between classical philosophy and the gospel, and tended to limit reason to an instrumental status. So limited, however, the Protestants viewed the exercise of reason as redounding to the glory of God. In this way, the Reformation laid the foundation for the later alliance between faith and technological science.

The LDS understanding of this issue rests upon foundations equally distinct from Protestant and Catholic traditions. LDS doctrine emphasizes the continuity between the natural and the divine realms, a continuity founded in part on the eternal importance of human understanding. But Latter-day Saints do not see the dignity of the mind as the sole basis of this continuity. Rather, they look to the exaltation of the whole person—not only as a knower of truth but also as a servant of the Lord and a source of blessings to one's fellow beings and one's posterity. In contrast to other Christian and Jewish traditions, moreover, LDS teaching emphasizes the necessity of present and future revelation, both to the individual and to the Church, in the pursuit of all these ends.

Warnings against the arrogance of human reason are common and founded in scripture. Thus, the Book of Mormon prophet Jacob decries "the vainness, and the frailties, and the foolishness of men! When they are learned they think they are wise, and they hearken not unto the counsel of God, for they set it aside, supposing they know of themselves, wherefore, their wisdom is foolishness and it profiteth them not. And they shall perish. But to be learned is good if they hearken unto the counsels of God" (2 Ne. 9:28–29). He thus announces a theme—the goodness of learning—that is almost as prominent in LDS teaching as the necessity of revelation, especially in the Doctrine and Covenants, where the Saints are enjoined to pursue learning of all kinds by "study" as well as by "faith" (D&C 88:78–79, 118).

Though one purpose of rational inquiry is to enhance missionary work (D&C 88:80), the goodness of learning transcends any practical applications. Indeed, this intellectual goodness is linked directly and intrinsically with the exaltation of the individual, whose nature must conform to the "conditions" or "law" of the kingdom he or she attains: "For intelligence cleaveth unto intelligence; wisdom receiveth wisdom; truth embraceth truth; virtue loveth virtue; light cleaveth unto light" (D&C 88:38–40). Such perfections also pertain to natural human faculties, directed and aided by general and personal revelation, for ultimately the light that "enlighteneth your eyes" and "quickeneth your understandings" is the "light of Christ," the "light of truth . . . which is in all things" (D&C 88:6, 7, 11, 13; cf. Moro. 7:16–25).

Revealed light and natural light are not completely distinct categories. Revelation engages natural reason and indeed may build upon it. It is sometimes described in LDS teaching as "a still voice of perfect mildness" able to "pierce unto the very soul" (Hel. 5:21–31) or as a spirit that resonates with the mind to produce a feeling of "pure intelligence" or "sudden strokes of ideas" (*TPJS*, p. 151). It is thus appropriate to seek and prepare for revelation by the effort of reason: "You must study it out in your mind; then you must ask me if it be right" (D&C 9:8).

LDS teaching encourages a distinct openness to the intrinsic as well as instrumental goodness of the life of the mind, an openness founded on the continuity between the human and divine realms. The full exercise of human reason under the direction of revelation holds a high place among the virtuous and praiseworthy ends to be sought by the Saints (A of F 13), for the scripture promises that "whatever principle of intelligence we attain unto in this life, it will rise with us in the resurrection," and the more "knowledge and intelligence" one gains through "diligence and obedience," the greater "the advantage in the world to come" (D&C 130:18–19). This emphasis on intellectual development in human progress toward godhood accords with the fundamental doctrine that is the official motto of Brigham Young University—namely, that "the glory of God is intelligence" (D&C 93:36).

Equated with "light and truth," such intelligence by nature "forsake[s] that evil one" (D&C 93:37). It cannot be simply identified with conventional measures of "intelligence" or with the Greek philosophic idea of a pure, immaterial, and self-directed intelligence, a concept that was very influential in medieval theology. For Latter-day Saints, the attainment of intelligence must be integrated with the labor of shaping the material world and binding together families and generations, for "the elements are eternal, and spirit and element, inseparably connected, receive a fulness of joy" (D&C 93:33). To the doctrine that "the glory of God is intelligence," one must add God's statement to Moses that "this is my work and my glory—to bring to pass the immortality and eternal life of man" (Moses 1:39).

BIBLIOGRAPHY

Etienne Gilson's *Reason and Revelation in the Middle Ages* (New York, 1938) provides an excellent discussion from a Thomistic standpoint. Hugh W. Nibley, in "Educating the Saints" (in *Nibley on the Timely and the Timeless*, edited by T. Madsen, Provo, Utah, 1978), cites quotations from former Church President Brigham Young to praise intellectual improvement as essential both to individual salvation and to building the kingdom of God. For an interesting attempt to set forth LDS revelation as harmonious with the evidence of reason, see Parley P. Pratt's *Key to the Science of Theology* (Salt Lake City, 1973). Though somewhat confined by the categories of nineteenth-century science, Pratt exhibits much of the distinctive potential of Mormon belief for engagement with scientific cosmology. Leo Strauss, in "Jerusalem and Athens: Some Preliminary Reflections" (in *Studies in Platonic Political Philosophy*, ed. T. Pangle, pp. 147–73, Chicago, 1983), emphasizes the difference between the life of rational inquiry and the life of pious obedience.

RALPH C. HANCOCK

RESTORATION OF ALL THINGS

The concept of a restoration of all things is biblical and is frequently spoken of in The Church of Jesus Christ of Latter-day Saints. Peter spoke of the anticipated "times of restitution of all things, which God hath spoken by the mouth of all his holy prophets since the world began" (Acts 3:21). Latter-day Saints understand this as a prophetic anticipation of a full and final restoration of the gospel in the development and fulfillment of the purposes of God in the last days. The current era is therefore called the Dispensation of the Fulness of Times in which all things will be gathered together in Christ (Eph. 1:10; D&C 27:13). The Church teaches that every gospel truth and blessing, and all priesthood authority, keys, ordinances, and covenants necessary for mankind's eternal salvation have been, or will be, restored in this dispensation. In this manner, the blessings of dispensations past will "flow into the most glorious and greatest of dispensations, like clear streams flowing into a mighty river" (*DS* 1:168).

The restoration spoken of in the scriptures involves more than a reestablishment of the Church and the function of saving ordinances. Scattered Israel will be gathered, the SECOND COMING OF CHRIST will occur, the Millennium will begin, the kingdom of God will be established worldwide, and "the earth will be renewed and receive its paradisiacal glory" (A of F 10).

The Prophet Joseph Smith testified that he was visited by divine messengers from former dispensations who conferred upon him priesthood powers and restored ordinances, doctrines, and blessings that existed in their dispensations. A brief outline follows:

1. God the Father and his Son Jesus Christ initiated the restoration when they appeared to Joseph Smith in the spring of 1820. He was told to join none of the churches of the day, and he was also taught important truths about the nature of the Godhead.

2. The angel MORONI visited Joseph Smith, revealing the plates of the Book of Mormon, which Joseph Smith translated, restoring gospel knowledge that had been lost to the earth in the centuries since biblical times. Latter-day Saints believe that the canon of scripture is not closed and that God "will yet reveal many great and important things pertaining to the Kingdom of God" (A of F 9), including additional volumes of holy scripture.

3. On May 15, 1829, Joseph Smith and Oliver Cowdery were ordained to the Aaronic Priesthood under the hands of John the Baptist (D&C 13:1).

4. In 1829 or 1830, three New Testament apostles—Peter, James, and John—conferred the Melchizedek Priesthood, including the power of laying on of hands for the gift of the Holy Ghost, upon Joseph and Oliver and ordained them "apostles and special witnesses" of Jesus Christ. This ordination restored to earth the same authority that existed in the Church during the Savior's ministry.

5. The restoration includes reestablishment of an organization to teach the gospel and administer its ordinances. The sixth Article of Faith states, "We believe in the same organization that existed in the Primitive Church, namely, apostles, prophets, pastors, teachers, evangelists, and so forth." Formal organization of the Church occurred on April 6, 1830, in Fayette, New York.

6. On April 3, 1836, the prophet MOSES came to Joseph Smith and Oliver Cowdery in the Kirtland Temple in Ohio and conferred the "keys of the gathering of Israel from the four parts of the earth" (D&C 110:11).

7. The prophet ELIAS conferred the keys of the dispensation of the gospel of Abraham (D&C 110:12), restoring the patriarchal order of marriage and the gifts and blessings given to Abraham and his posterity (*DS* 3:127; *MD*, p. 203).

8. ELIJAH restored authority to bind and seal on earth and in heaven, including the power to seal husbands and wives to each other, and children to their parents (Smith, p. 252). This fulfilled Malachi's prophecy that Elijah should be sent to "turn the hearts of the fathers to the children, and the children to the fathers, lest the whole earth be smitten with a curse" (Mal. 4:5–6; D&C 110:15). The genealogical research of the LDS Church and the temple ordinances performed on behalf of the dead are integral parts of this process.

The restoration will result in the culmination of all of God's purposes on the earth. The scriptures even speak of a reshaping of the land surfaces, with a coming together of the continents (D&C 133:23–24; cf. Gen. 10:25).

The fundamental purpose of the Restoration is to prepare the Church and the world to receive their King, the Lord Jesus Christ. Latter-day Saints view the restoration of all things as the work of God preparatory to the time when all old things shall become new, with a new heaven and a new earth. The restoration will include resurrection, regeneration, and renewal to all life upon the earth and the glorification of the earth itself, when it becomes a celestial sphere (Isa. 65:17; Matt. 19:28; Rev. 21:1; D&C 29:22–25; 88:17–20, 25–26). As explained by Alma, referring in particular to the Resurrection, "the plan of restoration is requisite with the justice of God; . . . that all things should be restored to their proper order" (Alma 41:2).

BIBLIOGRAPHY
Hinckley, Gordon B. *Truth Restored.* Salt Lake City, 1947.
Matthews, Robert J. "The Fulness of Times." *Ensign* 19 (Dec. 1989):46–51.
Smith, Joseph Fielding. *The Restoration of All Things.* Salt Lake City, 1945.

CORY H. MAXWELL

RESTORATION OF THE GOSPEL OF JESUS CHRIST

When Latter-day Saints speak of the "restoration of the gospel of Jesus Christ" they refer primarily to the restoration that has occurred in the latter days, establishing the Dispensation of the Fulness of Times (Eph. 1:10; D&C 27:13). However, there have been a number of restorations of the gospel over the history of the earth.

"Restoration" means to bring back that which was once present but which has been lost. The introduction of the gospel of Jesus Christ on this earth began with Adam and Eve. In the GARDEN OF EDEN they partook of the fruit of the tree of knowledge of good and evil (Moses 4:12), and as a result they became fallen and mortal and were expelled from the garden. God then revealed to them that they could be redeemed through the Only Begotten (Moses 5:1–12) and gave Adam the Priesthood after the Order of the Son of God (cf. Abr. 1:3; Fac. 3, Fig. 3, Book of Abraham). Thereafter, they received the various ordinances of the gospel, including a ceremonial endowment, and entered into covenants of obedience to all of God's command-ments (Fac. 3, Fig. 3, Book of Abraham).

After Adam and Eve became parents, they taught their children the gospel of Jesus Christ. But many of their posterity loved Satan more than God and from that time forth began to be "carnal, sensual, and devilish" (Moses 5:12–13). Eventually mankind substituted worldly interests in place of the commandments of God, and in time the gospel was distorted, fragmented, and lost from the earth.

Prophets have been called by God from time to time to *restore* the true covenants and gospel of Jesus Christ. One of the prophets was ABRAHAM (Abr. 3:22–25), who, having proved his faithfulness in numerous ways, was given a special covenant for himself, his descendants, and all who accept the gospel. This covenant extended to all future generations and nations of the earth. Another was MOSES, through whom the Lord restored the gospel for a short time, but because of the unwillingness of the people, the Lord instituted a preparatory law to help the people turn their hearts from idolatry to God (*see* LAW OF MOSES). Later God revealed his gospel to ELIJAH, ISAIAH, JEREMIAH, and EZEKIEL, among others, who urged the people to repentance and faithfulness. Many ancient prophets testified of a coming Messiah and of his crucifixion and resurrection. They also spoke of a subsequent long period of apostasy, but promised that there would be a restoration in the latter days, prior to the second coming of the Lord (cf. Amos 8–9).

The same gospel, covenants, and ordinances that had once been given to Adam, ENOCH, NOAH, Abraham, Moses, and the other ancient prophets, were restored to the earth during the MERIDIAN OF TIME when Jesus Christ lived on the earth. However, the Church that Jesus established in New Testament times was short-lived because of apostasy, which resulted in part from persecution and the eventual dispersion and death of the apostles. Hence, the authority of the priesthood, much of the gospel of Christ, and the ordinances and covenants were again lost to the earth. PETER, JOHN, and PAUL each spoke of this apostasy, which was already starting in their day, and prophesied that there would also be a restoration.

In the spring of 1820 a vision was given to Joseph Smith, near Palmyra, New York, in response to his fervent prayer to know the truth concerning religion. In this experience, Joseph Smith was visited by God the Father and his Son Jesus Christ (JS—H 1:17). In subsequent visits, holy angels instructed, ordained, and prepared him to become a latter-day prophet and an instrument in God's hands in restoring the gospel of Jesus Christ for the last time and setting up the kingdom spoken of by Daniel (Dan. 2; D&C 27:13; 65:1–6).

As part of this restoration, The Church of Jesus Christ of Latter-day Saints was organized by revelation on April 6, 1830, "it being regularly organized and established agreeable to the laws of our country, by the will and commandments of God" (D&C 20:1). It has the same priesthood, doctrines, and ordinances, and the same "organization that existed in the Primitive Church, namely, apostles, prophets, pastors, teachers, evangelists, and so forth" (A of F 6).

Eventually, all of the keys of the priesthood, which had been given to man from Adam's time onward, were restored. Prophets who held priesthood keys anciently came to Joseph Smith and conferred those keys upon him (D&C 128:18). These included JOHN THE BAPTIST (D&C 13), Peter, JAMES, and John (D&C 27:12), and Moses, ELIAS, and Elijah (D&C 110:11–16).

Thus, through the latter-day Prophet there has been a restoration of the gospel of Jesus Christ on the earth with the powers, authority, and ordinances as in ancient times. Other aspects of the restoration to occur are the gathering of Israel, the SECOND COMING OF CHRIST, and the Millennium.

[*See also* Restoration of All Things.]

BIBLIOGRAPHY
Smith, Joseph Fielding. *The Restoration of All Things.* Salt Lake City, 1945.

R. WAYNE SHUTE

REVELATIONS, UNPUBLISHED

Not all revelations of God to his latter-day PROPHETS have been formally published, let alone accepted by the common consent of the Church as canonized scripture. Just as the compilers of the Bible had to decide which texts to include, similar decisions have been made in this dispensation with respect to modern revelations. Initially this process was carried out by those assigned by the Prophet Joseph Smith to gather the revealed materials, organize them, and, under his supervision, print the Book of Commandments (1833) and the Doctrine and Covenants (1835). They included those revelations that were relevant "for the establishment and regulation of the kingdom of God on the earth in the last days" (D&C [1981], "Explanatory Introduction"). Latter-day Saints believe that divine inspiration played a role in guiding these selections (*DS* 3:202).

Many revelations are not included in the STANDARD WORKS, however; for example, those given to specific individuals under particular circumstances containing personal instructions rather than doctrine for the Church. Many are published in the *History of the Church* or are found in collections of Church documents. Examples include a revelation calling John E. Page to go to Washington, D.C. (*HC* 6:82), and a revelation about the division of the United Firm (*Kirtland Revelation Book,* p. 111). Also excluded are temple ordinances and other sacred matters not published to the world.

The Church of Jesus Christ of Latter-day Saints regards its canon of scripture as open, and two earlier revelations were added to the canon in 1979 (D&C 137 and 138). Latter-day Saints believe that God "will yet reveal many great and important things pertaining to the Kingdom of God" (A of F 9).

Another example of revelation received but not published is the revelation underlying the announcement by the First Presidency in June 1978 extending the priesthood to all worthy male members of the Church. Only an official statement concerning that revelation was published (*see* DOCTRINE AND COVENANTS: OFFICIAL DECLARATION—2). Other changes in the Church, such as the recent expanding of the role of the Seventy, accelerating temple building, and expanding missionary activity, are viewed by Latter-day Saints as manifestations of divine direction. The revealed basis of these changes is not always published, as it more often was in the early years of the Church. As Elder James E. Faust declared, "In our time God has revealed how to administer the Church with a membership of over six million differently than when there were just six members of the Church" (Faust, p. 8).

A few writers have attempted to collect and publish revelations that are attributed to prophets but not published in the scriptures. Some of these texts are based on credible sources; others come from sources that are suspect, if not invalid. When a so-called revelation contains statements and declarations that are clearly out of harmony with the standard works and official statements of the First Presidency, such materials are considered to be spurious.

In biblical times, false prophets sometimes spoke and wrote in the names of others and claimed revelations from God (cf. Deut. 18:20–22; Matt. 7:15). Today, some people similarly find journals or produce documents containing alleged revelations. The main guideline used for assessing these is as follows: "No one shall be appointed to receive commandments and revelations in this church excepting my servant Joseph Smith, Jun., for he receiveth them even as Moses . . . until I shall appoint . . . another in his stead" (D&C 28:2, 7).

Latter-day Saints believe that the right to receive revelation for the entire Church is reserved for the President of the Church.

BIBLIOGRAPHY

Cook, Lyndon W. *The Revelations of the Prophet Joseph Smith.* Provo, 1981.

Faust, James E. "Continuous Revelation." *Ensign* 19 (Nov. 1989):8–11.

C. MAX CALDWELL

REVERENCE

Latter-day Saints share with other religious people an inner yearning or inclination to venerate that which is holy. President David O. McKay emphasized this principle by saying, "The greatest manifestation of spirituality is reverence; indeed, reverence is spirituality. Reverence is profound respect mingled with love" (*Instructor* 101 [Oct. 1966]:371). The supreme object of reverence is God the Father; his son Jesus Christ did the will of the Father by effecting the infinite atonement; and Latter-day Saints also equally revere him. They revere not only his personage but his name as well, for as Peter said, "there is none other name under heaven given among men, whereby we must be saved" (Acts 4:12; cf. 2 Ne. 25:20). Taking the name of the Lord, or of the Father, in vain is therefore a serious form of irreverence.

While taking pains to avoid any semblance of idolatry, Latter-day Saints revere or venerate all that proceeds from God. Knowledge that "the earth is the Lord's, and the fulness thereof" (Ps. 24:1) and his "very handiwork" (D&C 104:14) impels the Latter-day Saint to respect it. The meek, or the reverent, shall inherit it (Ps. 37:11; Matt. 5:5; D&C 88:17–18).

Certain buildings are set apart as places of worship, and in those places the attitude of reverence is particularly fostered. Written on the eastern facade of the most important of these edifices, the temples, are the words "Holiness to the Lord—The House of the Lord." Howard W. Hunter, an apostle, noted that "the temple where Jesus taught and worshipped in Jerusalem was built in such a way as to establish respect for and devotion to the Father. Its very architecture taught a silent but constant lesson of reverence. . . . It was intended to be a place of solace for men's woes and troubles, the very gate of heaven" (*Ensign* 7 [Nov. 1977]:52–53). Within the temple are revealed sacred symbols that intimately tie the Latter-day Saint to Christ and his atonement. Because of these vital links, the temple ordinances are valued and revered and become treasures to be discussed only within the sacred walls. Indeed, only Latter-day Saints who are faithful may participate in temple worship.

Reverence is expected to pervade public places of worship as well. Because Latter-day Saints tend to be vibrant and sociable and because they often worship with their children, the Church leaders periodically emphasize the importance of reverence. Addressing the issue, President Gordon B. Hinckley stated, "We encourage the cultivation of friends with happy conversations among our people. However, these should take place in the foyer, and when we enter the chapel we should understand that we are in sacred precincts. . . . All who come into the Lord's house should have a feeling they are walking and standing on holy ground" (*Ensign* 17 [May 1987]:45).

Latter-day Saints hold as inimical to reverence the tendency of modern society to cynicism and lightmindedness. They believe that honoring the sacred is necessary to ensure a stable relationship with God.

BIBLIOGRAPHY

Handy, Linda Lee. "Helping Children Listen." *Ensign* 12 (Mar. 1982):46–47.
"Reverence." *Seek to Obtain My Word* (Melchizedek Priesthood Personal Study Guide), pp. 139–44. Salt Lake City, 1989.
Romney, Marion G. "Reverence." *Ensign* 12 (Sept. 1982):3–5.

LYNN A. MCKINLAY

RICHES OF ETERNITY

Eternal riches come from God and are associated with wisdom and eternal life: "Seek not for riches but for wisdom; and behold, the mysteries of God shall be unfolded unto you, and then shall you be made rich. Behold, he that hath eternal life is rich" (D&C 11:7). Latter-day Saints believe that the "voice of glory and honor and the riches of eternal life" is one of the voices used by Jesus to gather his people

(D&C 43:25) and that God adversely judges those who fail to seek earnestly the riches of eternity (D&C 68:31).

Although the phrase "the riches of eternity" occurs in scripture only in the Doctrine and Covenants (D&C 38:39; 67:2; 68:31; 78:18), the distinction between earthly and heavenly rewards is also biblical. The Psalms, for example, point out: "A little that a righteous man hath is better than the riches of many wicked" (Ps. 37:16). In the SERMON ON THE MOUNT, Jesus admonished his followers to "lay not up for yourselves treasures upon earth, . . . but lay up for yourselves treasures in heaven" (Matt. 6:19–20). In this life and in the world to come, the richest spiritual blessings come only from the eternal God.

These spiritual blessings include tangible as well as intangible gifts, for in the Lord's eyes "all things" are spiritual (D&C 29:34). As Orson Pratt stated, "Heavenly riches and earthly riches are of the same nature, only one is glorified and made immortal, while the other is in a fallen, unglorified state. If we are not willing to be governed by the law of equality in regard to that which is of the least value, who shall entrust us with all the riches of eternity?" (pp. 596–97).

Obtaining eternal riches can be equated with receiving and enjoying eternal life. "There is that maketh himself rich, yet hath nothing: there is that maketh himself poor, yet hath great riches. The ransom of a man's life are his riches" (Prov. 13:7–8). The word "ransom" (Hebrew *kofer*) refers to a payment made to redeem a person, suggesting to Latter-day Saints and other Christians that genuine riches are found in Christ's atoning redemption. Thus, Paul relates the winning of God's riches with repentance and eternal reward (Rom. 2:4–11), as well as with wisdom and knowledge (Rom. 11:33; Eph. 1:17–19). In Ephesians, Paul links them specifically to Christ: "Unto me . . . is this grace given, that I should preach among the Gentiles the unsearchable riches of Christ" (Eph. 3:8).

BIBLIOGRAPHY

Nibley, Hugh. "How to Get Rich" and "But What Kind of Work?" In *CWHN* 9:178–201, 252–89.

Pratt, Orson. *Masterful Discourses and Writings of Orson Pratt.* Salt Lake City, 1946.

CATHERINE CORMAN PARRY

RUTH

The heroine of the biblical book of Ruth has been both a formal and an informal model of ideal womanhood for members of The Church of Jesus Christ of Latter-day Saints: loyal, hard-working, converted, courageous, she makes the best of what is available and, not incidentally, is pleasing and desirable.

Individual Latter-day Saints and Church instructional manuals frequently cite as exemplary Ruth's departure from her Moabite customs, gods, and people in order to accompany her mother-in-law, Naomi, worshiping Jehovah in his land and adopting the ways of his people. While members have not traditionally emphasized cultural details of the story, they have considered important Ruth's obedience to Naomi and the resulting marriage to Boaz by which she—the foreigner and Moabite convert—becomes a great-grandmother of David, and therefore an ancestress of Jesus Christ.

From 1928 to 1972, Ruth and her gleaning were official models for Church women eighteen years and older in Gleaner classes of the Young Women's Mutual Improvement Association and its successor, the Young Women organization. By achieving spiritual, cultural, homemaking, and service goals, a woman could earn the Golden Gleaner award, counterpart of the Master M Man award for men. The names of these honors express historical conceptions of admirable female and male roles in the Church. Sheaves of wheat, the Gleaners' emblem, were represented on instructional manuals and cards, and on metal pins.

FRANCINE R. BENNION

S

SABBATH DAY

The Sabbath is a day set apart for rest and spiritual renewal. The importance of Sabbath observance, taught from the Creation and throughout religious history, is reconfirmed in modern scripture and in the teachings of LDS leaders. Fundamentals of Sabbath observance include prayer, gospel study, worship at Sabbath meetings, uplifting family activities, and service to others.

God set the pattern when, after six days of creation labors, he rested on the seventh (Gen. 2:2; Moses 3:2). Following the Exodus, Moses instructed the Israelites to gather double portions of manna on the day preceding "the rest of the holy sabbath unto the Lord" (Ex. 16:23). Indeed, the word "Sabbath" is derived from the Hebrew *shabbath,* meaning "to break off," "to desist," or "to rest." The Ten Commandments included the command, "Remember the sabbath day, to keep it holy. Six days shalt thou labour, and do all thy work: But the seventh day is the sabbath of the Lord thy God: in it thou shalt not do any work" (Ex. 20:8–10).

The New Testament is replete with references to the Sabbath. By then, some had lost the spirit of the law and hedged it in inflexible obedience. The Savior reproved them: "The Sabbath was made for man, and not man for the Sabbath. Wherefore the Sabbath was given unto man for a day of rest; and also that man should glorify God, . . . For the Son of Man made the Sabbath day, therefore the Son of Man

556

is Lord also of the Sabbath" (JST Mark 2:25–27). Following Jesus' earthly ministry, the early Christians gathered on the Lord's day, the first day of the week, in observance of his resurrection (cf. Acts 20:7; Rev. 1:10).

Since its beginning, the LDS Church has observed the Sabbath on the first, rather than the seventh, day of the week (for some exceptions in the Middle East, *see* SUNDAY). The key revelation giving the pattern, scope, and purpose of Sabbath observance came to Joseph Smith on August 7, 1831, a Sunday:

> And that thou mayest more fully keep thyself unspotted from the world, thou shalt go to the house of prayer and offer up thy sacraments upon my holy day;
>
> For verily this is a day appointed unto you to rest from your labors, and to pay thy devotions unto the Most High; . . .
>
> But remember that on this, the Lord's day . . . thou shalt do none other thing, only let thy food be prepared with singleness of heart that thy fasting may be perfect, or, in other words, that thy joy may be full [D&C 59:9–13].

Throughout LDS history, leaders have emphasized the importance of Sabbath observance, teaching that the Sabbath is a holy day of worship, on which the faithful renew their covenants with the Lord, meet and teach each other the things of the Spirit, visit and strengthen the weak and afflicted, and study and contemplate the word of the Lord. While they have avoided arbitrarily specific prohibitions, Church leaders have given clear guidelines, as in this instruction from President Spencer W. Kimball:

> The purpose of the commandment is not to deprive man of something. Every commandment that God has given to his servants is for the benefit of those who receive and obey it. . . .
>
> The Sabbath is not a day for indolent lounging about the house or puttering around in the garden, but is a day for consistent attendance at meetings for the worship of the Lord, drinking at the fountain of knowledge and instruction, enjoying the family, and finding uplift in music and song.
>
> The Sabbath is a holy day in which to do worthy and holy things. Abstinence from work and recreation is important, but insufficient. The Sabbath calls for constructive thoughts and acts, and if one merely

lounges about doing nothing on the Sabbath, he is breaking it. To observe it, one will be on his knees in prayer, preparing lessons, studying the gospel, meditating, visiting the ill and distressed, writing letters to missionaries, taking a nap, reading wholesome material, and attending all the meetings of that day at which he is expected. . . .

It is true that some people must work on the Sabbath. And, in fact, some of the work that is truly necessary—caring for the sick, for example—may actually serve to hallow the Sabbath. However, in such activities our motives are a most important consideration.

When men and women are willing to work on the Sabbath to increase their wealth, they are breaking the commandments; for money taken in on the Sabbath, if the work is unnecessary, is unclean money. . . .

Sabbath-breakers too are those who buy commodities or entertainment on the Sabbath, thus encouraging pleasure palaces and business establishments to remain open—which they otherwise would not do. If we buy, sell, trade, or support such on the Lord's day we are as rebellious as the children of Israel ["The Sabbath—A Delight," *Ensign* 8 (Jan. 1978):4–5].

The form of LDS Sabbath observance has evolved through the years, but the principles have remained the same. Of the Church's first conference meeting, on June 9, 1830, Joseph Smith wrote, "Having opened by singing and prayer, we partook together of the emblems of the body and blood of our Lord Jesus Christ. We then proceeded to confirm several who had lately been baptized, after which we called out and ordained several to the various offices of the Priesthood. Much exhortation and instruction was given" (*HC* 1:84). Singing, prayer, SACRAMENT, and teaching—those have remained the fundamentals of Latter-day Saint Sabbath meetings.

For many years, following the organization of the Sunday School in 1849, Sabbath services consisted of Sunday School in the morning and sacrament meeting in the afternoon or early evening. Weekly ward priesthood meetings were held on Monday evenings, and fast and testimony meeting on the first Thursday of each month. In 1896, fast day was changed to the first Sunday to make attendance more convenient and less disruptive to members in their employment; in the 1930s, priesthood meeting was changed to Sunday mornings.

Another major change came in 1980 with consolidation of all

Sunday meetings into a single time block—generally three hours, including Relief Society, young women, and primary meetings that formerly were held midweek. The change was instituted to save time, travel, and expense; to allow several wards to meet more conveniently in a single building; to strengthen the home by allowing families to spend more time together during the week; and to provide more time for Church members to devote to community service.

In announcing the change, the First Presidency reemphasized the Church's fundamental principles regarding the Sabbath: "A greater responsibility will be placed upon the individual members and families for properly observing the Sabbath day." They suggested that each family participate in a Sunday gospel study hour and in "other appropriate Sabbath activities, such as strengthening family ties, visiting the sick and homebound, giving service to others, writing personal and family histories, genealogical work, and missionary work" (*Church News*, Feb. 2, 1980, p. 3).

The Lord has promised blessings to those who observe the Sabbath as a holy day. In ancient times, he promised to send them rain in due season, help them overcome their enemies, give them peace, multiply them, and establish his covenant with them (Lev. 26:2–9). "And I will walk among you; and will be your God, and ye shall be my people" (v. 12; cf. Isa. 58:13–14). In modern times, he has reaffirmed these promises: "Inasmuch as ye do this, the fulness of the earth is yours" (D&C 59:16).

BIBLIOGRAPHY

For a collection of articles treating LDS Sabbath observance, including perspectives on both doctrine and historical practice, see *Ensign* 8 (Jan. 1978).

WILLIAM B. SMART

SACRAMENT

[*This entry is in two parts:* Sacrament *and* Sacrament Prayers. *The first part explains the practice of partaking of the sacrament in The Church of Jesus Christ of Latter-day Saints, and the second part gives the history and contents of the sacrament prayers used in the administering of the sacrament.*]

SACRAMENT

The word "sacrament" is used by The Church of Jesus Christ of Latter-day Saints to refer almost exclusively to the Lord's Supper. The English word "sacrament" derives from the Old French *sacrement* by way of Middle English; the Old French noun in turn is based on the Latin *sacramentum,* which denotes a sum deposited by the two parties to a suit (so named probably from being deposited in a sacred place) binding an agreement, oath of allegiance, or obligation. Though the word never occurs in the Bible, the sacrament has come to have a major role in the practices of nearly all Christian denominations. In traditional Catholic and Protestant Christianity, the "sacrament of the Lord's Supper" is regarded as one of a group of sacraments, whose purpose is to serve both as conveyors of God's grace and as the outward signs that such grace has been bestowed. The definition of seven sacraments for the Roman Catholic church came at the Fourth Lateran Council, convened by Pope Innocent III in 1215. Protestant reformers, while rejecting most of the sacramental doctrines of the medieval church, retained the notion of sacraments with respect to baptism and the Eucharist.

In Latter-day Saint usage, sacrament designates that ordinance instituted by Jesus Christ as a means by which worthy Saints may renew their covenants with their Redeemer and with God the Father (cf. Mosiah 18:8–10; *JC*, pp. 596–97; *AF*, p. 175). On the eve of his trial and crucifixion in Jerusalem and surrounded by his closest associates, the twelve apostles, Jesus took bread, which he blessed and broke and then gave to them, saying, "Take, eat; this is my body." Jesus likewise took the cup, blessed it, and then gave it to them, "Drink ye all of it; For this is my blood of the new testament, which is shed for many for the remission of sins" (Matt. 26:26–28). The Book of Mormon records that the resurrected Jesus instituted this same ordinance in memory of his body and blood as he showed himself to the righteous of the Western Hemisphere after his ascension from Jerusalem (3 Ne. 18:7; 20:3; 26:13).

Paul notes that the Savior gave a commandment to perform this ordinance regularly, "As often as ye eat this bread, and drink this cup, ye do shew [i.e., testify of] the Lord's death till he come" (1 Cor. 11:26). The New Testament indicates that the injunction was observed in the early Christian Church (cf. Acts 2:42; 20:7). To the

Saints at Corinth, Paul wrote in plainness of the simple ordinance which he had received from the Lord, stressing that it was done "in remembrance of [Jesus Christ]" (1 Cor. 11:19–26; cf. Luke 22:19; 3 Ne. 18:7).

The time and setting chosen by Jesus for administering the Sacrament among his Jerusalem disciples tie this ordinance to the older observances of the Passover, including the bread and wine he used, and to which he gave new symbolism (Matt. 26:26–28; Luke 22:15–20). Through his atonement Christ fulfilled the purpose of the ordinance of animal sacrifice found in the Old Testament, which was to prefigure the ultimate sacrifice of the Son of God. The new ordinance replaced the need for animal sacrifice with the sacrifice on the part of Christ's followers of a broken heart and contrite spirit (3 Ne. 9:18–20).

The sermon that Jesus delivered on the topic of the "bread of life" in the Gospel of John draws on the symbolism of the Lord himself as "the living bread which came down from heaven." It also prefigures the ordinance of the sacrament that he initiated later as a reminder to all that salvation comes only through "the living bread" and the "living water" (cf. John 6:48–58). In the postapostolic age, however, theologians transformed the symbolic nature of the sacrament of the Lord's Supper into the dogma of transubstantiation, thereby introducing the notion that those who partake of the bread and wine miraculously ingest the literal body and blood of Christ, although the outward appearance of the emblems (i.e., the accidentals) remain the same. The LDS Church rejects this dogma and holds that the sacrament is to help the Saints remember Jesus and that the transformation envisioned is a renovation of the human soul by the Spirit (D&C 20:75–79).

The sacrament in LDS belief does not serve primarily as a means of securing remission of sins. It does, however, focus attention on the sacrifice for sin wrought by the Savior and on the need for all those who have been baptized to maintain their lives constantly in harmony with his teachings and commandments. For this reason, there are numerous scriptural injunctions concerning the need for compliance with God's commandments by those who partake of the sacrament (1 Cor. 11:22–23; 3 Ne. 18:28–29; D&C 46:4). Unbaptized children, however, being without sin, are entitled and expected to partake of the sacrament to prefigure the covenant they themselves will make at the age of accountability, age eight. In administering the sacrament, Christ himself used emblems readily at hand at the Last Supper—bread and wine. To Joseph Smith the Lord declared "that it mattereth not what ye shall eat or what ye shall drink when ye partake of the sacrament, if it so be that ye do it with an eye single to my glory—remembering unto the Father my body which was laid down for you, and my blood which was shed for the remission of your sins" (D&C 27:2). In typical LDS practice, bread and water are used.

The ordinance of the sacrament is administered by "those having authority"—that is, by priesthood bearers. According to modern revelation, priests in the Aaronic Priesthood and any Melchizedek Priesthood holder may officiate at the sacrament table; in general practice, the table is prepared by teachers in the Aaronic Priesthood, and the bread and water are blessed by priests and passed to the members of the Church by deacons in the same priesthood.

The prayers spoken over these emblems are among the few that are scripturally prescribed exactly. Those who partake of the sacrament place themselves under covenant with the Lord to take upon them the name of Christ, to always remember him, and to keep his commandments. The Lord in turn covenants that they may always have his Spirit to be with them (D&C 20: 75–79; Moro. 4–5; John 6:54).

BIBLIOGRAPHY

Madsen, Truman G. "Christ and the Sacrament" and "The Sacramental Life." *Christ and the Inner Life*, pp. 39–42. Salt Lake City, 1981.

PAUL B. PIXTON

SACRAMENT PRAYERS

The sacrament prayers, which were revealed by the Lord to the Prophet Joseph Smith, are among the few set prayers in the Church, and the only ones members are commanded to offer "often" (D&C 20:75). They are offered regularly during the administration of the ordinance of the sacrament in sacrament meeting, occupying a central place in the religious lives of Latter-day Saints. They originate in ancient practice and, with one exception (the current use of water instead of wine), preserve the wording of NEPHITE sacramental prayers:

O God, the Eternal Father, we ask thee in the name of thy Son, Jesus Christ, to bless and sanctify this bread to the souls of all those who partake of it; that they may eat in remembrance of the body of thy Son, and witness unto thee, O God, the Eternal Father, that they are willing to take upon them the name of thy Son, and always remember him, and keep his commandments which he hath given them, that they may always have his Spirit to be with them. Amen [Moroni 4:3].

O God, the Eternal Father, we ask thee, in the name of thy Son, Jesus Christ, to bless and sanctify this wine to the souls of all those who drink of it, that they may do it in remembrance of the blood of thy Son, which was shed for them; that they may witness unto thee, O God, the Eternal Father, that they do always remember him, that they may have his Spirit to be with them. Amen [Moroni 5:2].

The prayers, in turn, formalize language used by the resurrected Savior when he visited the Americas (3 Ne. 18:5–11; cf. D&C 20:75–79). Subsequent to a revelation in August 1830 (D&C 27) water has been used instead of wine.

No such exact wording of the prayers is included in the New Testament. However, one scholar has detected parallels between Latter-day Saint sacrament prayers and ancient eucharistic formulas (Barker, pp. 53–56). The JOSEPH SMITH TRANSLATION OF THE BIBLE (JST) confirms that key elements of the sacrament prayers were part of the original Last Supper: Jesus included covenantal obligations similar to those in the prayers (JST Matt. 26:25) and made clear that his action introduced a formal "ordinance" that they were to repeat often (JST Mark 14:24). Further, in the JST, Jesus does not say, "This is my body," and "This is my blood"—metaphors whose interpretation has historically divided Christians on the matter of "transubstantiation." He said instead, "This is in remembrance of my body," and "This is in remembrance of my blood" (JST Matt. 26:22, 24; cf. JST Mark 14:21, 23).

The sacrament prayers invite personal introspection, repentance, and rededication, yet they are also communal, binding individuals into congregations who jointly and publicly attest to their willingness to remember Christ. This shared commitment to become like Christ, repeated weekly, defines the supreme aspiration of Latter-day Saint life.

BIBLIOGRAPHY
Barker, James L. *The Protestors of Christendom.* Independence, Mo., 1946.
Tanner, John S. "Reflections on the Sacrament Prayers." *Ensign* 16 (Apr. 1986):7–11.
Welch, John W. "The Nephite Sacrament Prayers." *F.A.R.M.S. Update.* Provo, Utah, 1986.

JOHN S. TANNER

SACRIFICE IN BIBLICAL TIMES

The first commandments received by Adam and Eve after being driven from the Garden of Eden were to worship God and to offer the firstlings of their flocks and herds (Moses 5:5–6). Adam and Eve obeyed. Later, an angel explained to them the purpose for the law of sacrifice: it was made in similitude of the offering that the Son of God would make of his own life for all mankind (Moses 5:7). Each offering was to point to the necessity of the Savior's sacrifice. Thus, Adam and Eve knew that a future atonement was to be made by Jesus Christ and that only through him could fallen man be reconciled to God.

Latter-day Saints believe that to perform any ordinance, a man must hold the priesthood, which includes the authority from God necessary to offer sacrifices after the pattern that Adam received. But because of an unwillingness to follow God, historically many turned away, worshiped falsely, and followed selfish practices for personal aggrandizement, as did Cain (Moses 5:18–31). For the faithful, because sacrifice promoted faith in the Lord and reliance on him, selfishness was superseded, for the best was not to be used for self but for God. Men and women could thus recognize that it was not the earth, sun, or idols that supplied necessities, but God.

From Seth to Jacob, God's people renewed their covenant relationship with him, apparently by offering two kinds of sacrifice: the burnt offering and slain offering. Through Moses, Israel received and practiced further ordinances to remind them daily of their duty toward God (Lev. 1–7; Mosiah 13:30). Types and symbols which were woven into the LAW OF MOSES taught God's people of the Savior's atoning sacrifice (2 Ne. 11:4; Mosiah 13:31; Alma 25:16).

The Book of Mormon prophet LEHI and his family brought the Mosaic sacrificial system to the Western Hemisphere. NEPHITES continued those sacrificial practices until the resurrected Savior appeared to them (3 Ne. 9:19–20).

The Lord specifically forbade human sacrifice (Lev. 18:21; Jer. 19:5; Morm. 4:14, 21). Thus, when God commanded Abraham to sacrifice Isaac, he was testing Abraham's faith and teaching him of the Redeemer to come (Gen. 22; Heb. 11:17–19; Jacob 4:5; John 3:16; Gal. 3:8). The trial proved that Abraham loved God unconditionally; therefore, he could be blessed unconditionally.

The Bible prophet MALACHI predicted a time when Levites would again offer sacrifice in righteousness (Mal. 3:3). Such offerings will not be of the Mosaic type, which were fulfilled in Christ. However, the sacrificial system that antedated Moses was not fulfilled in Jesus. The Prophet Joseph Smith, taught that blood sacrifices similar to those revealed to Adam will once again be performed prior to Christ's second coming in order to complete the RESTORATION OF ALL THINGS (*TPJS*, pp. 172–73; *DS* 3:94–95). These may be undertaken for only a brief period and perhaps only by a selected group. In a very different sense sacrifice continues in modern LDS temples (D&C 124:38–39), for those laboring therein are modern equivalents of Levites, and performance of temple ordinances in behalf of the dead constitutes an offering of righteousness (D&C 128:24).

BIBLIOGRAPHY

DeVaux, Roland. *Ancient Israel*, Vol. 2, pp. 415–56. New York, 1965.

Draper, Richard D. "Sacrifices and Offerings: Foreshadowings of Christ." *Ensign* 10 (Sept. 1980):20–26.

McMullin, Phillip W. "Sacrifice in the Law of Moses: Parallels in the Law of the Gospel." *Ensign* 20 (Mar. 1990):37–41.

RICHARD D. DRAPER

SAMUEL THE LAMANITE

Samuel the LAMANITE was the only Book of Mormon prophet identified as a Lamanite. Apart from his sermon at Zarahemla (Hel. 13–15), no other record of his life or ministry is preserved. Noted chiefly for his prophecies about the birth of Jesus Christ, his prophetic words, which were later examined, commended, and updated by the risen Jesus (3 Ne. 23:9–13), were recorded by persons who accepted him as a true PROPHET and even faced losing their lives for believing his message (3 Ne. 1:9).

Approximately five years before Jesus' birth, Samuel began to preach repentance in Zarahemla. After the incensed Nephite inhabitants expelled him, the voice of the Lord directed him to return. Climbing to the top of the city wall, he delivered his message unharmed, even though certain citizens sought his life (Hel. 16:2). Thereafter, he fled and "was never heard of more among the Nephites" (Hel. 16:8).

Samuel prophesied that Jesus would be born in no more than five years' time, with two heavenly signs indicating his birth. First, "one day and a night and a day" of continual light would occur (Hel. 14:4; cf. Zech. 14:7). Second, among celestial wonders, a new star would arise (Hel. 14:5–6). Then speaking of mankind's need of the Atonement and Resurrection, he prophesied signs of Jesus' death: three days of darkness among the Nephites would signal his crucifixion, accompanied by storms and earthquakes (14:14–27).

Samuel framed these prophecies by pronouncing judgments of God upon his hearers. He spoke of a final devastation—four hundred years distant—that would end Nephite civilization because of its rebellion against God. This desolation would come through "the sword and with famine and with pestilence" (13:9; cf. Morm. 1:19). He spoke of curses from God on the land (13:17–20, 23, 30, 35–36), on property (13:18–19, 21, 31), and on the people themselves (13:19, 21, 32, 38). Such afflictions would arise because the Nephites would knowingly reject true prophets while accepting false ones, clamor for wealth, and refuse to acknowledge the blessings of God (13:19–34). Samuel reiterated the judgments of God against the Nephites (15:1–3, 17) and then emphasized the divine promises extended to the Lamanites—including assurances for "the latter times" of "restoration" (15:4–16).

S. MICHAEL WILCOX

SARAH

Sarah was the wife of ABRAHAM. Originally named Sarai (which possibly meant "contentions"), she was renamed Sarah ("princess") when, in her old age, God promised Abraham that she would bear a son. The fragmentary information available about her paints a picture of great faith manifested in sacrifices not easily made. Sarah shared equally in Abraham's trials; her experience permits a feminine perspective on the universal obligations of faith, hope, and sacrifice.

Childless until late in life, Sarah suffered years of travail. Barrenness was a heavy burden for any woman in Near Eastern cultures but would have been felt as a particularly searing inadequacy by a woman whose husband had received divine promises of endless posterity.

Against this backdrop, Sarah was twice thrust into situations where she had to feign being unmarried in order to protect Abraham—first with Pharaoh (Gen. 12) and then with Abimelech (Gen. 20). The book of Abraham makes it clear that this was not mere cowardice or prevarication on Abraham's part; it was obedience to divine direction (Abr. 2:22–25). But this did not simplify Sarah's dilemma. Already torn between commitment to sacred marriage vows and the apparent certainty of death if she did not play the allotted role, she was required to rely on God for protection during the very hours when his instructions seemed to place her in the jaws of destruction. As in the ultimate trial with Isaac, it was the joint faith of Sarah and Abraham that ultimately opened the path of deliverance.

In her old age, Sarah gave Hagar, her maid, to Abraham. Modern revelation indicates that Sarah thereby "administered unto Abraham according to the law" (D&C 132:65), and more recent scholarship has confirmed the widespread legal obligation of the childless wife in the ancient Near East to provide her husband with a second wife (Claus Westermann, *Genesis 12–36*, p. 239, Minneapolis, 1985). Tensions flared with Hagar and later Ishmael (Gen. 16:4–16; 21:8–10). In both cases, Hagar was driven away, first temporarily when pregnant, and then permanently, with her teenage son Ishmael. Significantly, in both cases, the Lord had Abraham place the resolution of these conflicts in Sarah's hands: "In all that Sarah hath said unto thee, hearken unto her voice" (Gen. 21:12; cf. Gen. 16:4–6).

The promise that she would bear a son, which had caused Sarah to "laugh . . . within herself" (Gen. 18:12), was fulfilled in the birth of Isaac. The scriptures do not indicate whether Sarah knew beforehand of the call to take Isaac to Moriah, but she had been prepared. Her experiences had carved out in her a reservoir of patient faith, and she was capable of complete trust in God. Sarah was human and real and sometimes even imperfect in wrestling with the burdens of obedience. Yet she endured. Ultimately, she entered with Abraham into the exaltation that her motherhood helped prepare for all the house of Israel (see D&C 132:37).

BIBLIOGRAPHY

Nibley, Hugh. "A New Look at the Pearl of Great Price, Part 11: The Sacrifice of Sarah." *IE* 73 (Apr. 1970):79–95.

LOUISE GARDINER DURHAM

SCRIPTURE

[This entry consists of four articles:

Scriptures
Authority of Scripture
Words of Living Prophets
Forthcoming Scripture

The origin and history of the Latter-day Saints is closely tied to scripture, ancient and modern. The article Scriptures *sets out the LDS view of scripture and the differences between it and other scriptural traditions and concepts.* Authority of Scripture *deals with the role of scripture in the beliefs and practices of Latter-day Saints. The essay* Words of Living Prophets *focuses on one of the distinctive features of LDS belief, that of divine revelation through modern prophets. The article* Forthcoming Scripture *treats the LDS expectation, rooted primarily in latter-day scripture, that other scriptures are yet to be revealed by God.]*

SCRIPTURES

Although "scripture" usually denotes written documents, in LDS sources it is also defined as "whatsoever [God's representatives] shall speak when moved upon by the Holy Ghost" (D&C 68:2–4; cf. 1:38; 2 Pet. 2:21; 2 Tim. 3:16). This broader understanding of the term is at once a comprehensive principle and a functional definition, taking into account both written and spoken modes of inspiration.

Roberts, an authoritative second-generation historian and a General Authority, wrote of the corpus of scripture:

It fixes permanently the general truths which God has revealed. It preserves, for all time and for all generations of men, the great frame-work of the plan of salvation—the Gospel. There are certain truths that are not affected by ever-changing circumstances; truths which are always the same, no matter how often they may be revealed; truths which are elementary, permanent, fixed; from which there must not be, and cannot be, any departure without condemnation. The written word of God preserves the people of God from vain and foolish traditions, which, as they float down the stream of time, are subject to changes by distortion, by addition or subtraction, or by the fitful play of fancy in fantastic and unreliable minds. It forms a standard by which even the living oracles of God may instruct themselves, measure themselves, and correct themselves. It places within the reach of the people, the power to confirm the oral words, and the ministry of the living oracles, and thus to add faith to faith, and knowledge to knowledge [*IE* 3 (May 1900):576–77].

In contrast, in Judaism the replacement of prophets by rabbis or scholars as custodians and interpreters of scripture was taken to the extreme: "Even if they [the sages] tell you that left is right and right is left—hearken unto their words" (*Midrash Siphre on Deut.* 17:10–11; cf. Jerusalem Talmud tractate *Horayoth* 1:1, 45d). Reassurance against error, even community error, was given on the ground that even the errors made in decisions of law are binding. In a dramatic case, Rabbi Eliezer claimed that a heavenly voice sanctioned his minority opinion. But Rabbi Joshua insisted that the Torah, or text of scripture, is not in heaven but on earth and that the majority view must prevail (*see also* Davies, *Paul and Rabbinic Judaism*, 1980, pp. 374, 212n). In traditional Christianity, ecclesiastical councils have sometimes assumed similar prerogatives.

In their doctrine of scripture, Latter-day Saints have reduced these and other tensions, such as those that exist between biblical and Talmudic Judaism (i.e., between the written and the oral law) or, as in the Roman and Eastern Christian traditions, between the biblical heritage and the claims of both tradition and the pronouncements of the creeds, or, as in Protestantism, between the original intent, coupled with the spirit of scripture, and the claim that individual interpretation is valid.

The idea of an open canon has meant historically a certain openness to other historical, apocryphal, and pseudepigraphical sources. Modern scripture assures Latter-day Saints that important records will yet come to light (cf. 2 Ne. 29:10–14; A of F 9). The Old Testament Apocrypha contains many things "that are true" but also many interpolations (D&C 91); "To those who desire it, should be given by the Spirit to know the true from the false" (*HC* 1:363). By analogy, other documents recently recovered (e.g., the Dead Sea Scrolls, the Nag Hammadi library, and related inscriptions and fragments) are viewed as instructive, though not canonical. In some cases, their teachings anticipate and echo authentic scriptural materials.

The importance of linguistic, contextual, historical, and literary approaches to scripture has been emphasized in the LDS Church in several ways: a School of the Prophets was organized in the very infancy of the Church where Hebrew, Greek, and German were studied as biblical aids; the alternative Bible translations, including the revisions of the JOSEPH SMITH TRANSLATION OF THE BIBLE (JST), were used; official preference was given for the King James Version on the grounds of its literary style and its availability to other Christian groups, and others; various editions of biblical and latter-day scriptures, including critical texts, Bible dictionaries, and selective utilization of burgeoning efforts of worldwide biblical scholarship were utilized (*see* BIBLE SCHOLARSHIP).

A whole constellation of meanings attends the concept of the living word coming from a living prophetic voice. Moreover, the living voice is generally richer than any writing, which is at best a cryptosynopsis. On these grounds, Joseph Smith said, in effect, that one should never trust a letter to say what could be said in person. "No matter how pure your intentions may be; no matter how high your standing is, you cannot touch man's heart when absent as when present" (*Woman's Exponent* 3 [April 1, 1875]:162). The range of possible misunderstanding is significantly increased when one has only the written word.

In the history of canon, various stages or periods have witnessed exegesis, expansion, and the glosses and stylistic alterations that also change substance. One can argue that over the centuries this process has worked in the direction of textual improvement and power; but one can maintain equally that there have been departure and dilution and textual corruption. Latter-day Saints see both processes at work. "Ignorant translators, careless transcribers, or designing and corrupt priests have committed many errors" (*TPJS*, p. 327). On the other hand, the Bible and other texts are impressively preserved, with sufficient light to bless and condemn. For their part, Latter-day Saints ultimately trust the inspiration of the Spirit.

Latter-day Saints are not alone in this position. For instance, H. J. Schoeps shows that Jewish criticism of the ideas of temple and sacrifice were changed when the Bible was assembled (Davies, p. 61). And over the centuries, changes have often led away from, rather than toward, a refinement of original Christian norms and practices.

The revelatory power of scripture depends in part on its adaptive quality. Of modern scripture and, by implication, all earlier scripture the word of the Lord says, "These commandments are of me, and were given unto my servants in their weakness, after the manner of their language, that they might come to understanding" (D&C 1:24).

Plain meaning has also been a leading principle in LDS exegesis. "My soul delighteth in plainness," said the Book of Mormon prophet NEPHI₁ (2 Ne. 31:3). Nothing can override the plain meaning of the text (cf. Talmudic tractate *Shabbath* 63a). This position is neither a refusal to see subtle and layered meanings in the text nor a theologically a priori position that permits allegorical excess, as in the teachings of some early rabbis and Christian schoolmen. Deeper meanings cannot be superimposed on a text of scripture, but are to be found by divine aid in the intent and spirit of the original author (cf. 2 Pet. 1:20–21). For all their complexity and diversity, the scriptures are written in ordinary language; for instance, the working vocabulary of the Book of Mormon comprises fewer than 2,300 basic words.

In practice, Latter-day Saints view certain other texts with special respect, based on their use, each with its own measure of authority. For example, exact prayers are specified for baptism and for the sacrament. Other authoritative texts and words—with differing levels of authority—include messages of the First Presidency, temple ordinances and covenants, patriarchal blessings, the hymnal, handbooks for priesthood and auxiliary organizations, and manuals for teaching in the various ward organizations.

A unity of the faith, often seen as remarkable, arises both from a unique openness to further revelation and from the Church's system of checks and balances. The Church's lay participation, which entails the sharing of responsibility, and the law of common consent operate together in the process of presenting, confirming, and accepting the inspired word.

For Latter-day Saints, the scriptures are not reducible to scientific history, sociology, or folklore; a simple set of fundamentals, commandments, and legal apparatus; charming parabolic accounts; esoteric and hidden names with mystical connections that have a power and life of their own. The scriptures are the result of an outpouring from on high whose present meaning and relevance to a person require painstaking study and direct inspiration.

Objecting to the views of the Torah as a closed world, Martin Buber wrote, "To you God is one who created once and not again; but to us God is He who 'renews the work of creation every day.' To you God is One who revealed Himself once and no more; but to us He speaks out of the burning thornbush of the present . . . in the revelations of our innermost hearts—greater than words" (p. 204). This statement captures much of the spirit of the LDS approach to scripture. Meaning and power rise against "hardening" traditions and sponsor trust in the living witness of the Spirit to illumine, clarify, and sanctify scripture as the "present truth."

BIBLIOGRAPHY

Buber, Martin. *Great Jewish Thinkers of the Twentieth Century*, ed. S. Noveck. Clinton, Mass., 1963.

Clark, J. Reuben, Jr. "When Are Church Leaders' Words Entitled to Claim of Scripture?" *Church News*, July 31, 1954, pp. 9–11.

Davies, W. D. "Reflections on the Mormon Canon." *Harvard Theological Review* 79 (1986):44–66. Reprinted in *Christians Among Jews and Gentiles*, ed. G. W. E. Nicklesburg and George W. MacRae, S.V., pp. 44–66. Philadelphia, 1986.

Osborne, D. *Juvenile Instructor* 27 (Mar. 15, 1892):173.

Stendahl, Krister. "The Sermon on the Mount and Third Nephi in the Book of Mormon." In *Meanings*, p. 100. Philadelphia, 1984.

Welch, John W., and David J. Whittaker. "Mormonism's Open Canon: Some Historical Perspectives on Its Religious Limits and Potentials." *F.A.R.M.S. Paper*. Provo, Utah, 1986.

W. D. DAVIES
TRUMAN G. MADSEN

AUTHORITY OF SCRIPTURE

For Latter-day Saints, the concept of scripture entails two comple-
mentary definitions—a broad definition that embraces all revelation
from God as "scripture," and a narrower view that includes only the
STANDARD WORKS as "the scriptures." Both categories are authoritative, since both are viewed as coming from God.

The first definition uses "scripture" as synonymous with such
terms as "inspired" or "divinely revealed." Concerning those who
have been called and ordained to proclaim God's word, a revelation
in the DOCTRINE AND COVENANTS provides the foundation: "Whatsoever they shall speak when moved upon by the Holy Ghost shall be
scripture, shall be the will of the Lord, shall be the mind of the Lord,
shall be the word of the Lord, shall be the voice of the Lord, and the
power of God unto salvation" (D&C 68:4). In this light, Latter-day
Saints hold in high regard the words of Church leaders at all levels.
Especially authoritative are the official pronouncements of the First
Presidency and the Quorum of the Twelve Apostles, who are sustained by Church members as "prophets, seers, and revelators."
Their writings and addresses—particularly in general conference—
are cited frequently as guides for living and for authoritative interpretation of doctrine. Statements issued by the First Presidency
represent the official position and policy of the Church.

Joseph Smith taught that "a prophet was a prophet only when he
was acting as such" (*HC* 5:265). Thus, the words of prophets carry
the force of scripture only when they are uttered under the influence
of the Holy Ghost. Latter-day Saints freely acknowledge this divine
influence in the teachings and counsel of leaders and deem it a privilege to be instructed by them. They consider this inspired direction
to be "scripture" in the broad definition and endeavor to harmonize
their lives with it.

The more restrictive view of what constitutes scripture would
include only what is called "the scriptures"—that is, the four standard works: the Bible, the Book of Mormon, the Doctrine and
Covenants, and the Pearl of Great Price. These constitute the canonized, authoritative corpus of revealed writings against which all else
is measured. President Joseph Fielding Smith taught, "My words,
and the teachings of any other member of the Church, high or low, if
they do not square with the revelations, we need not accept them. . . .

We have accepted the four standard works as the measuring yardsticks, or balances, by which we measure every man's doctrine" (*DS* 3:203).

While the Church views its scriptures as a canon in a strict sense, they are not viewed as closed. The doctrine of continuing revelation is one of the fundamental beliefs of the Church. As was expressed by Joseph Smith, "We believe all that God has revealed, all that He does now reveal, and we believe that He will yet reveal many great and important things pertaining to the Kingdom of God" (A of F 9). While accepting "all that God has revealed," whether canonized in the scriptures or not, Latter-day Saints also believe that revelation continues to enlighten their leaders. Moreover, additional divine guidance is anticipated because God "will yet reveal many great and important things." Those future revelations will be scripture, according to the broad definition, and it is likely that some of them will be added to the scriptures in due time.

BIBLIOGRAPHY

Jackson, Kent P. "Latter-day Saints: A Dynamic Scriptural Process." In *The Holy Book in Comparative Perspective*, ed. F. Denny and R. Taylor, pp. 63–83. Columbia, S.C., 1985.

———. "The Sacred Literature of the Latter-day Saints." In *The Bible and Bibles in America*, ed. E. Frerichs, pp. 163–91. Atlanta, Ga., 1988.

Talmage, James E. *AF*, pp. 236–313.

KENT P. JACKSON

WORDS OF LIVING PROPHETS

Any message that comes from God to man by the power of the Holy Ghost is scripture to the one who receives it, whether in written or spoken form (*MD*, p. 682; cf. 2 Ne. 32:3). PAUL wrote to Timothy that "all [written] scripture is given by inspiration of God, and is profitable for doctrine, for reproof, for correction, for instruction in righteousness" (2 Tim. 3:16). Further, every person may receive personal revelation for his or her own benefit. God, however, has always designated prophets to speak for him, thus resulting in holy writ or scripture. When Aaron was called as a spokesman for Moses, the Lord said, "And he shall be thy spokesman unto the people: and he shall be . . . to thee instead of a mouth, and thou shalt be to him instead of God" (Ex. 4:15–16).

Members of The Church of Jesus Christ of Latter-day Saints

believe in continuous revelation, especially to prophets who direct the Church. This doctrine was announced in a revelation received through the Prophet Joseph Smith in November 1831: "And whatsoever [the Lord's servants] shall speak when moved upon by the Holy Ghost shall be scripture, shall be the will of the Lord, shall be the mind of the Lord, shall be the word of the Lord, shall be the voice of the Lord, and the power of God unto salvation" (D&C 68:4). Inspired utterances of the prophet and President of the Church have been and may in the future be added to the STANDARD WORKS by the common consent of the Church.

Latter-day Saints sustain the First Presidency and the Quorum of the Twelve Apostles as prophets, seers, and revelators. Since the prophet and President of the Church is sustained as *the* prophet, seer, and revelator, he is the official spokesman who speaks on behalf of the Lord to the Church (D&C 21:4–5; 28:2). These other prophets, seers, and revelators have the right, power, and authority to declare the mind and will of God to his people, subject to the presiding authority of the President (D&C 132:7).

The inspired utterances of the President of the Church become binding upon members of the Church whether formally accepted as part of the written CANON or not. The living prophet's inspired words supersede and become more important to Latter-day Saints than the written canon or previous prophetic statements (D&C 5:10). The salvation and exaltation of members of the Church depend upon their adherence to this divine INSPIRATION through the living prophet, which comes as a VOICE OF WARNING to the world (D&C 1:4–5).

This doctrine appears in the Old Testament. For example, people could be saved from the flood only by listening to the voice of God through his prophet NOAH. Likewise, the Israelites were expected to accept and be responsibly obedient to words of Moses as if the Lord himself had spoken them (Deut. 18:18–22). The Lord also taught that "if there be a prophet among you, I the Lord will make myself known unto him in a vision, and will speak unto him in a dream" (Num. 12:6).

Early Christian emphasis on the "living voice" can be found in the writings of Papias (c. A.D. 130): "If anyone chanced to come who had actually been a follower of the elders, I would enquire as to the discourses of the elders, what Andrew or Peter said, or what Philip or Thomas or James, or what John or Matthew or any other of the Lord's disciples . . . say. For I supposed that things out of books did not profit me so much as the utterances of a living and abiding voice" (Eusebius, *Ecclesiastical History* 3.39.4).

Latter-day Saints accept the doctrine that what God declares, "whether by [his] own voice or by the voice of [his] servants, it is the same" (D&C 1:38). On the other hand, prophets have the right to personal opinions; not every word they speak is therefore regarded as an official pronouncement or interpretation of scripture. Only when they are inspired to speak to the Church by the Holy Ghost do they speak scripture. In order for a hearer to determine whether a prophet speaks thus, the power of the Holy Ghost must testify to the individual that the message is divinely inspired. The Holy Ghost is given to all to know the truth of all things (Moro. 10:5).

BIBLIOGRAPHY

Benson, Ezra Taft. "Fourteen Fundamentals in Following the Prophet." *BYU Speeches of the Year, 1977–80*, pp. 26–30. Feb. 26, 1980.

Church Educational System. *Teachings of the Living Prophets*, pp. 6–22. Salt Lake City, 1982.

Clark, J. Reuben, Jr. "When Are Church Leaders' Words Entitled to Claim of Scripture?" *Church News* (July 31, 1954):9–11.

Horton, George A., Jr. *Keys to Successful Scripture Study*, pp. 2–11. Salt Lake City, 1989.

A. GARY ANDERSON

FORTHCOMING SCRIPTURE

Latter-day Saints believe that God "will yet reveal many great and important things" (A of F 9), that the heavens are not closed, and that God continues to "pour down knowledge from heaven upon [their] heads" (D&C 121:23). Forthcoming revelations are expected to include both ancient truths restored and new truths uncovered.

The scriptures specifically foretell the restoration of many books that will make known plain and precious things taken away from the world (1 Ne. 13:39–40). These include the BOOK OF ENOCH (D&C 107:57); an additional account of the events on the Mount of Transfiguration (D&C 63:20–21); the fulness of the record of John and of visions about the end of the world (1 Ne. 14:18–27; Ether 4:16; D&C 93:6, 18); the sealed portion of the Book of Mormon, which includes the vision of the BROTHER OF JARED (2 Ne. 27:7–11;

Ether 3:25–27; 4:7); the brass plates (Alma 37:4–5; *see also* BOOK OF MORMON PLATES AND RECORDS); a more complete record of the teachings of Jesus Christ to the Nephites (3 Ne. 26:6–11); and records of the lost tribes of Israel (2 Ne. 29:12–13).

How or when these scriptures will come forth is unknown, beyond the general belief that further revelations will come in the Lord's time when people repent, exercise faith, and are prepared to receive them (2 Ne. 28:30; Ether 4:1–12). Latter-day Saints believe that the world has seen only the beginning of the great doctrinal and scriptural restoration whereby God will "gather together in one all things in Christ" (Eph. 1:10). Heavenly and earthly records of all dispensations are to be gathered together (1 Ne. 13:41), and "nothing shall be withheld" (D&C 121:28).

BIBLIOGRAPHY

Maxwell, Neal A. "God Will Yet Reveal." *Ensign* 16 (Nov. 1986):52–59.
McConkie, Bruce R. "The Doctrinal Restoration." In *The Joseph Smith Translation*, ed. M. Nyman and R. Millet, pp. 1–22. Provo, Utah, 1985.

ROBERT A. CLOWARD

SCRIPTURE, INTERPRETATION WITHIN SCRIPTURE

The key to interpreting scriptural passages often lies in the body of scripture itself. For example, some passages from the Old Testament receive commentary and interpretation in the New Testament. Jesus Christ frequently taught from the Old Testament, not only giving interpretation—as in David's need to eat the temple shew bread (1 Sam. 21:1–6) as justification for his disciples plucking wheat on the Sabbath (Mark 2:23–26)—but also often emphasizing that the scriptures testify of himself as Messiah (Luke 4:18–21; John 5:39). The additional scriptures that Latter-day Saints accept—the BOOK OF MORMON, the DOCTRINE AND COVENANTS, and the PEARL OF GREAT PRICE—also cite and interpret the Bible. In fact, many of the clearest explications of doctrine arise from modern revelations or restored scripture.

In the Pearl of Great Price, the BOOK OF MOSES and the BOOK OF ABRAHAM augment the Old Testament Genesis account of the

Creation (Moses 2–3; Abr. 4–5), affirm human agency (Moses 3:17; 7:32), clarify the fall of Adam (Moses 4; Abr. 5), and explain the resulting need for a redeemer (Moses 6:59; cf. 4:1–2; 5:7–8). In addition, these two books add information on the claims of Satan and the choosing of Christ in the premortal world (Moses 4:1–4; Abr. 3:27–28) where all the spirits of mankind lived before their advent on the earth.

In JOSEPH SMITH—MATTHEW, the Prophet Joseph Smith received clarification of the Savior's discussion in Matthew 24 of the events to precede the fall of Jerusalem and those to precede Jesus' latter-day coming. According to the JOSEPH SMITH—HISTORY, MORONI$_2$ quoted Malachi 4:6 to Joseph Smith differently from the Old Testament version, suggesting that the phrase "the fathers" refers to the Patriarchs, especially ABRAHAM, with whom God made covenants pertaining to Abraham's posterity, who would bear priesthood ordinances to the world for the exaltation of the human family (JS—H 1:39; D&C 27:9–10).

The Book of Mormon clarifies many of the writings of Old Testament prophets. The prophet NEPHI$_1$ quoted Isaiah 48–49 (1 Ne. 20–21) and then gave a plain commentary on the major points of those chapters in 1 Nephi 22, emphasizing that the NEPHITES were a remnant of scattered Israel, who would eventually be gathered with the aid of the GENTILES. In another example, about 148 B.C. the Nephite prophet ABINADI identified the "suffering servant" of Isaiah 53 as Jesus Christ (Mosiah 15:2–5) and enlarged on Isaiah's discussion of the Messiah's Atonement (Mosiah 14–15).

The Book of Mormon also illuminates the SERMON ON THE MOUNT (Matt. 5–7). In a similar sermon given in the Western Hemisphere (3 Ne. 12–14), the resurrected Jesus said, "Blessed are the poor in spirit *who come unto me*" (3 Ne. 12:3; italics added). Such added words, plus the context of Jesus' address, indicate that one must come to the Savior through baptism and righteousness to receive the blessings promised in the BEATITUDES.

The Doctrine and Covenants offers explication on several obscure points in the book of Revelation that pertain to events of the Last Days, such as the gathering of Israel and their receiving priesthood ordinances (D&C 77:8–9, 11). Elucidation of biblical passages that focus on latter-day signs to precede Jesus' second coming are found especially in Doctrine and Covenants 45 and 86. While pondering 1 Peter 3:18–20, President Joseph F. Smith received a vision of the redemption of the dead (now D&C 138) that clarified and enlarged the Savior's redemptive work in the spirit world following his crucifixion.

Much modern revelation came to the Prophet Joseph Smith in response to questions arising from his work on the JOSEPH SMITH TRANSLATION OF THE BIBLE (JST). For example, while meditating on the resurrection to life or damnation mentioned in John 5:29, Joseph Smith and Sidney Rigdon received the revelation on the degrees of glory in the resurrection (D&C 76). Joseph Smith recorded several instances in which, while pondering a passage of scripture (e.g., James 1:5, an invitation to ask the Lord for wisdom), he prayed and received additional scripture from the Lord that made the first more plain or confirmed its reality (JS—H 1:11–20). While translating from the Book of Mormon PLATES, Joseph Smith and Oliver Cowdery prayed after reading about baptism. In answer, JOHN THE BAPTIST came with authority and instructions on baptism (JS—H 1:68–72). After their baptisms, the Prophet described their being filled with the Holy Ghost: "Our minds being now enlightened, we began to have the scriptures laid open to our understandings, and the true meaning and intention of their more mysterious passages revealed unto us in a manner which we never could attain to previously, nor ever before had thought of" (JS—H 1:74).

Nephi observed that having the spirit of prophecy is essential to grasping the correct understanding of scripture. He mentioned in particular Isaiah, "for because the words of Isaiah are not plain unto you, nevertheless they are plain unto all those that are filled with the spirit of prophecy" (2 Ne. 25:4). In chapters 25–30, Nephi provided prophetic insight into the teachings of Isaiah.

Modern revelation and restored scripture offer indispensable interpretations of the Bible, helping Latter-day Saints to understand the Bible more fully. Jesus rebuked those who had taken away the "key of knowledge" or the means whereby the biblical scriptures could be understood (JST Luke 11:53), thereby causing confusion in the interpretation of scripture. The Lord said, "Because that ye have a Bible ye need not suppose that it contains all my words; neither need ye suppose that I have not caused more to be written. . . . I shall speak unto the Jews and they shall write it; and I shall also speak unto the Nephites and they shall write it; and I shall also speak unto the other tribes of the house of Israel . . . and they shall write it. . . . And my word also shall be gathered in one" (2 Ne. 29:10, 12, 14; cf. Ezek. 37:16–20). Latter-day Saints interpret the Bible in the light of restored scripture and modern revelation because these have reestablished the lost key of knowledge.

BIBLIOGRAPHY

Gileadi, Avraham. "Isaiah: Four Latter-day Keys to an Ancient Book." In *Isaiah and the Prophets*, ed. M. Nyman. Provo, Utah, 1984.

McConkie, Bruce R. "The Bible, a Sealed Book." In *Supplement to a Symposium on the New Testament*, Church Educational System, pp. 1–7. Salt Lake City, 1984.

Rust, Richard Dilworth. "'All Things Which Have Been Given of God . . . Are the Typifying of Him': Typology in the Book of Mormon." In *Literature of Belief*, ed. N. Lambert. Provo, Utah, 1981.

M. CATHERINE THOMAS

SCRIPTURE STUDY

From childhood, Latter-day Saints are taught to read and study the scriptures in order to know Jesus Christ and his teachings. Those having faith will be able to read by the power of the Lord and hear the Lord's voice (D&C 18:35–36). They will be given power to expound scripture (D&C 25:7; 97:3–5; 100:11), which includes reasoning with people (D&C 68:1), unfolding and laying open the scriptures to them (Alma 12:1; 21:9; JS—H 1:74), responding to their questions (Alma 12:8–10), explaining what prompted the passage (*TPJS*, pp. 276–77), and likening the messages of the scriptures to their needs (1 Ne. 19:23). Latter-day Saints are to avoid disputation regarding the scriptures and are told particularly to avoid doctrinal contention (D&C 10:62–68; 19:31; 3 Ne. 11:28–40; *HC* 5:340). Missionaries are to read and preach from the scriptures (Alma 18:36; D&C 22:12–13). The resurrected Jesus read chapters of scripture and expounded all things, both great and small, to hearers in the Western Hemisphere (3 Ne. 23:6,14; 26:1).

Scripture study is central to the teaching activities of the Church and plays a major role in strengthening the spiritual life of the members and in helping them to acquire a testimony. Members are urged to read and examine the scriptures daily, both individually and as families (Kimball, pp. 2–5). They are instructed to ponder the messages of the scriptures, to pray concerning them, and to relate the teachings to their own lives. Members are cautioned that unless they teach their children the scriptures, they will "dwindle in unbelief"; hence, the Book of Mormon prophets treasured their scriptures and made great effort to obtain them and safeguard them in their travels (1 Ne. 4:5–18; Mosiah 1:4–5).

The current Church curriculum is based on the scriptures, and manuals include scriptural references to aid teachers, provide weekly reading assignments, and anchor learning on a scriptural foundation. The study of the scriptures is also enhanced by articles published in Church magazines, written by lay members, leaders, and scholars. Courses on the Bible, the Book of Mormon, the Doctrine and Covenants, and the Pearl of Great Price are offered through the Church Educational System, and Brigham Young University helps coordinate scripture research and makes research reports available to the Church membership.

The 1979–1981 published edition of the scriptures aids readers in their scriptural study, making available extensive cross-references, maps, an index, a topical guide, and a Bible dictionary. Members may also examine alternative English or other translations in their study. Joseph Smith once expressed appreciation for the Martin Luther German translation (*WJS*, p. 351) and the Greek and Hebrew versions: "My soul delights in reading the word of the Lord in the original" (*PWJS*, p. 161). In addition to the editions of the scriptures published by the Church in many languages, tape recordings of the scriptures and computer word-search programs are available as further study aids.

Religious research studies indicate that the more education Latter-day Saints receive, the more likely they are to study the gospel. Nearly half of the LDS college graduates surveyed in the United States and Canada regularly study gospel principles.

In Latter-day Saint scripture, the Lord urges all people to open their hearts and give ear to his word, to lay hold of it, to cling to it (1 Ne. 8:1–38), to ponder it, to search it, to feast upon it, and to treasure it (2 Ne. 32:3; 3 Ne. 23:1; D&C 84:85). With such receptiveness, one understands the word of the Lord in one's heart and mind, does not rebel against the Lord, lets go of prejudice, and is compassionate and caring (Mosiah 2:9; 3 Ne. 19:33; 2 Ne. 7:5; D&C 31:7; 75:25; 101:92; 109:56; 124:9). Those who study the scriptures with an open heart are promised that their tongues will be loosened and they will learn what to say with the convincing power of God (D&C 11:21–22; 23:2–3; 84:85; cf. Alma 17:2–3).

BIBLIOGRAPHY

Albrecht, Stan L., and Tim B. Heaton. "Secularization, Higher Education, and Religiosity." *Review of Religious Research* 26 (1984):42–58.

"Catalogue—A Scripture Research Library." F.A.R.M.S. Provo, Utah, published yearly.

Kimball, Spencer W. "How Rare a Possession—the Scriptures!" *Ensign* 15 (July 1985):2–5.

Packard, Dennis J., and Sandra Packard. *Feasting upon the Word.* Salt Lake City, 1981.

DENNIS J. PACKARD

SECOND COMING OF JESUS CHRIST

[*The second coming of Jesus Christ refers to his return to the earth in glory to reign as King of Kings, as contrasted to his first coming as an infant in Bethlehem. Articles relevant to this topic are* David, Prophetic Figure of Last Days; Marriage Supper of the Lamb; Parables; Restoration of All Things.

Both the first and second appearances were foretold in the scriptures, with the second advent to be accompanied by earthshaking events of worldwide consequence. See Armageddon; Joseph Smith—Matthew; Malachi, Prophecies of.]

SECRET COMBINATIONS

In latter-day scriptures, secret combinations are groups of conspirators who plot and initiate "works of darkness" for evil and selfish purposes. Secret combinations have existed since the days of Cain (Moses 5:51). Satan is their author (2 Ne. 26:22), power and gain are their motives (Ether 8:15, 25), and conspiracy is their method of operation

(Hel. 6:22–24). Secret combinations may be brotherhoods, groups, societies, or governments. They operate in secrecy to perform evil acts for the purpose of gaining power over the minds and actions of people.

As the enemies of honest men and women governed by the rule of law, such secret combinations seek to subvert public virtue and legally constituted authority. They defile, defraud, murder, deceive, and destroy the elements of good government, religious or secular. Their goal is to seize power and to rule over all the people (3 Ne. 6:27–30), which results in the destruction of human freedom and agency and the paralysis of peaceful and just communities.

Secret combinations and their practices have a scriptural and historic tradition that extends from the days of Cain's secret covenant with Satan to modern times. Members of these Satanic combinations are bound by secret oaths and covenants. The devil proclaims, initiates, and sustains these combinations and their conspiratorial practices (Moses 5:29–33, 47–52).

In the Book of Mormon, several secret combinations challenged governments ruled by the "voice of the people" or by righteous kings. They were a continuing threat to the Jaredites, who succumbed eventually to their power. Later, they were a threat to the Nephite and Lamanite nations when the Gadianton combinations, over a period of many years, challenged the constituted authorities and eventually seized power. The concerted effort of the whole populace later defeated the Gadiantons, but others rose in their place. The Book of Mormon details the tactics and strategies of the Gadiantons, mentions a variety of countermeasures, and shows that a secret combination was responsible for the final downfall of the Nephites (Hel. 2:13–14; Ether 8:21; *see also* BOOK OF MORMON: HELAMAN *and* BOOK OF MORMON: 3 NEPHI).

In the contemporary world, secret combinations take various forms and operate at different levels of society. They are expressed in organized crime and in religious, economic, and political conspiracies. The Lord has warned that secret combinations will be present in modern society (D&C 38:29; Ether 8:20–25). They threaten freedom everywhere. However, Latter-day Saints believe that secret combinations and their practices can be overcome, but only through righteous living and full support of honest government.

Secret combinations are often referred to in latter-day scripture, particularly in the book of Moses and the Book of Mormon. In the

Doctrine and Covenants, this term describes those who have conspired against the Saints (D&C 42:64). It does not appear in the
Bible, but the equivalent "conspiracy" is used at least ten times.

BIBLIOGRAPHY

Hillam, Ray C. "The Gadianton Robbers and Protracted War." *BYU Studies* 15
(Winter 1975):215–24.

Meservy, Keith H. "'Gadiantonism' and the Destruction of Jerusalem." In *The Pearl
of Great Price: Revelations from God*, ed. H. D. Peterson and C. Tate, pp. 171–95.
Provo, Utah, 1989.

Peterson, Daniel C. "The Gadianton Robbers as Guerrilla Warriors." In *Warfare in
the Book of Mormon*, ed. S. Ricks and W. Hamblin, pp. 146–73. Salt Lake City,
1990.

"Secret Combinations." *F.A.R.M.S. Update* (Oct. 1989).

RAY C. HILLAM

SEED OF ABRAHAM

The "seed of Abraham" are those who, through righteousness, inherit
the blessings promised Abraham through the covenant he made with
the Lord and who themselves are a promised blessing to Abraham
(Gen. 12:1–5; 13:16; 17; Abr. 2:6–11). The phrase also has messianic overtones: Abraham saw the days of the Messiah and rejoiced
(John 8:56). Jesus Christ is of the seed of Abraham (Gal. 3:16).

In a lineal sense, two groups are called the "seed of Abraham" in
scripture. The first comprises the literal descendants of Abraham
through Isaac (Gen. 26:1–4) and Jacob (Gen. 28; 35:9–13), who are
thus the twelve tribes of Israel. The second comprises the descendants of Ishmael and the many other children of Abraham.

In addition to those who are of lineal descent, all who are not of
Abrahamic lineage but who become adopted by their acceptance of
the gospel of Jesus Christ and continued obedience to God's commandments are heirs of all the blessings of the Abrahamic covenant
(*TPJS*, pp. 149–50). Adoption is completed by the gospel ordinances, including baptism and confirmation; ordination to the priesthood, and magnifying one's calling in the priesthood; the temple
endowment; and eternal marriage, through which husbands, wives,
and families share "all the blessings of Abraham, Isaac, and Jacob."
Modern revelation assures that these people will have a fulness of

blessings, even "all that [the] Father hath" (D&C 84:38). They are "sanctified by the Spirit unto the renewing of their bodies," and they become "the seed of Abraham" (D&C 84:34).

ALLEN C. OSTERGAR, JR.

SEER STONES

Joseph Smith wrote that in 1823 an angel told him about "two stones in silver bows . . . fastened to a breastplate . . . the possession and use of [which] constituted 'seers' in ancient or former times" (JS—H 1:35). Joseph used these and other seer stones that he found in various ways (occasionally referred to by the biblical term URIM AND THUMMIM) for several purposes, primarily in translating the Book of Mormon and receiving revelations (see *HC* 1:21–23, 33, 36, 45, 49; 3:28; 5:xxxii; *CHC* 6:230–31).

Historical sources suggest that effective use of the instruments required Joseph to be at peace with God and his fellowmen, to exercise faith in God, and to exert mental effort (*CHC* 1:128–33). Otherwise, little is said authoritatively about their operation. Occasionally, people have been deceived by trying to use stones to receive revelation, the best-known latter-day example in the Church being Hiram Page (D&C 28:11–12).

While useful in translating and receiving revelation, seer stones are not essential to those processes. Elder Orson Pratt reported that Joseph Smith told him that the Lord gave him the Urim and Thummim when he was inexperienced as a translator but that he later progressed to the point that he no longer needed the instrument ("Two Days' Meeting at Brigham City," *Millennial Star* 36 [1874]:498–99).

RICHARD E. TURLEY, JR.

SERMON ON THE MOUNT

The Sermon on the Mount (Matt. 5–7) is for Latter-day Saints, as well as for all other Christians, a key source for the teachings of Jesus and of Christian behavior ethics. The fact that parallel accounts appear

in the BOOK OF MORMON (3 Ne. 12–14) and the JOSEPH SMITH TRANS-
LATION OF THE BIBLE (JST Matt. 5–7) offers both the opportunity for a
better understanding of the Sermon and the obligation to refute
notions of mere plagiarism by the Prophet Joseph Smith. A careful
comparison of the texts reveals significant differences that are attributable primarily to the specific setting of the Book of Mormon sermon.

In the Book of Mormon account, the resurrected Jesus appeared
to the more righteous survivors of a fierce storm and major earthquake in the Western Hemisphere who had gathered at the temple in
the land called Bountiful. The setting includes the performance of
ordinances, for the people prepared for baptism, first that of water by
twelve men whom Jesus had ordained, followed by that of fire from
the Lord himself (3 Ne. 12:1). The sermon at the temple thus provides the assembled multitude with an understanding of their duties
and obligations. It also introduces them to the fulness of the gospel
that Jesus established among them because he had fulfilled the law
"that was given unto Moses" (3 Ne. 15:4–10) under which they had
lived. Obedience to Jesus' gospel gave the Book of Mormon people
two hundred years of peace and harmony as it became established
throughout their lands (4 Ne. 1:17–23). Since Jesus himself observes
that he had given a similar sermon in Palestine before he ascended to
his Father (3 Ne. 15:1), Latter-day Saints have no doubt that the
Sermon on the Mount reflects a unified presentation that the Savior
possibly gave on several occasions (JST Matt. 7:1–2, 9, 11) and not
merely a collection brought together by Matthew or his sources. As
in many speaking situations, a speaker can repeat the basic message
with appropriate alterations to fit the specific audience.

SETTING OF THE SERMONS.   While much of the text in 3 Nephi 12–14
is identical to Matthew 5–7, there are numerous and significant differences. Most of the differences stem from the specific setting of the
Book of Mormon sermon. First, the risen Jesus opened his Book of
Mormon sermon with three additional BEATITUDES that underscore its
purpose as an address to believers: "Blessed are ye if ye shall give
heed unto the words of these twelve whom I have chosen; . . . blessed
are ye if ye shall believe in me and be baptized; . . . more blessed are
they who shall believe in your words . . . and be baptized . . . [and]
receive a remission of their sins" (3 Ne. 12:1–2). Further, the Book of

Mormon account is post-Resurrection, and the emphasis is on the fact that the Lord has completely fulfilled his mission of salvation. Thus, Jesus can summarize the series of antitheses recorded in 3 Nephi 12:21–45: "Those things which were of old time, which were under the law, in me are all fulfilled" (3 Ne. 12:46). Furthermore, rather than instructing the people "Be ye therefore perfect, even as your Father which is in heaven is perfect" (Matt. 5:48), Jesus in meaningfully modified words told them, "I would that ye should be perfect even as I, or your Father who is in heaven is perfect" (3 Ne. 12:48). In place of the open-ended "one jot or one tittle shall in no wise pass away from the law, till all be fulfilled" (Matt. 5:18), the Book of Mormon passage replaced the phrase "till all be fulfilled" with "but in me it hath all been fulfilled" (3 Ne. 12:18).

Other changes reflect both the Book of Mormon setting and the absence of antipharisaic statements that figure prominently in Matthew's account. Two examples of the former are the replacement of the "farthing" (Matt. 5:26) with the "senine" (3 Ne. 12:26), which was the smallest Nephite measure of gold (Alma 11:3, 15–19), and the lack of reference to the swearing "by Jerusalem . . . the city of the great King" (Matt. 5:35). Similarly, the sermon at the temple in Bountiful does not mention surpassing the righteousness of the scribes and Pharisees, as in Matthew 5:20, or that of the publicans who are loved by their friends (Matt. 5:46–47). In place of the references to the scribes and Pharisees (Matt. 5:20), the Lord told the Nephites: "Except ye shall keep my commandments, which I have commanded you at this time, ye shall in no case enter into the kingdom of heaven" (3 Ne. 12:20). Also, the Book of Mormon account does not contain the references to self-mutilation found in Matthew 5:29–30, or the qualifying phrase "without a cause" in Matthew 5:22 (cf. 3 Ne. 12:22).

CLARIFICATIONS.   A further type of difference consists of additions to the Sermon on the Mount text that often provide sensible clarifications. Several examples are found in the Beatitudes. The Book of Mormon version noted that it is "the poor in spirit *who come unto me*" who inherit the kingdom of heaven (3 Ne. 12:3; Matt. 5:3; emphasis added). At the end of 3 Nephi 12:6 (cf. Matt. 5:6), one finds "blessed are all they who do hunger and thirst after righteousness, for they shall be filled *with the Holy Ghost*" (emphasis added). While these

might seem to be small changes, they nonetheless enhance understanding of Jesus' meaning.

For Latter-day Saints, the message of the Sermon on the Mount
centers on its normative value. As a covenant-making people, they
take upon themselves the obligation to emulate the Savior in their
personal lives and to work toward the ultimate goal of becoming like
him. Although the demands are substantial, they are provided an
incentive to strive to become like their divine model (cf. 2 Ne.
31:7–10, 16; 3 Ne. 27:27). The simple words and teachings that
Jesus gave to his followers in Palestine and to the Book of Mormon
survivors are still applicable to his Saints today.

[*See also* Lord's Prayer.]

BIBLIOGRAPHY

Stendahl, Krister. "The Sermon on the Mount and Third Nephi." In *Reflections on Mormonism,* ed. T. Madsen, pp. 139–54. Provo, Utah, 1978.

Thomas, Catherine. "The Sermon on the Mount: The Sacrifice of the Human Heart." In *Studies in Scripture,* ed. K. Jackson and R. Millet, Vol. 5, pp. 236–50. Salt Lake City, 1986.

Welch, John W. *The Sermon at the Temple and the Sermon on the Mount.* Salt Lake City, 1990.

ROBERT TIMOTHY UPDEGRAFF

SETH

Seth was the son of Adam and Eve, a high priest, a patriarch, and
one chosen to fill the birthright promise of the covenant seed. While
the Bible devotes only seven verses to Seth (Gen. 4:25–26; 5:3–4,
6–8), Latter-day scripture adds substantial detail, underscoring his
importance in a manner reminiscent of other ancient texts. According
to LDS sources, Seth was born after numerous other children (Moses
5:2–3), was ordained at age sixty-nine by Adam, and became patriarchal leader after the death of his father (D&C 107:41–42).

Following the murder of ABEL, Seth inherited the birthright of the
patriarchal order of the high priesthood because of his righteousness
(D&C 107:40–43), taking Abel's place (Gen. 4:25; Moses 6:2). "The
order of this priesthood was confirmed to be handed down from father
to son, and rightly belongs to the literal descendants of [Seth's] cho-

sen seed, to whom the promises were made . . . in the days of Adam, and came down by lineage . . . from Adam to Seth, who . . . received the promise of God by his father, that his posterity should be the chosen of the Lord, and that they should be preserved unto the end of the earth" (D&C 107:40–42). At Adam-ondi-Ahman, before his death, Adam bestowed a "blessing upon seven of his [descendants]—Seth, Enos, Jared, Canaan, Mahalaleel, Enoch, and Methuselah" (Durham, p. 64).

Seth was obedient and righteous under the tutelage of Adam so that "he seemed . . . like unto his father in all things," and was called "a perfect man" (D&C 107:43), as were NOAH and others (Gen. 6:9; Job 1:1). He "offered an acceptable sacrifice, like unto his brother Abel," with the result that "God revealed himself unto Seth" (Moses 6:3). Apocryphal texts, seeking patterns for the ministry of the expected Messiah, focus on notions of Seth's leadership in the premortal life, his complete obedience, and his role as father and patriarch of the covenant race (Brown, p. 278).

BIBLIOGRAPHY

Brown, S. Kent. "The Nag Hammadi Library: A Mormon Perspective." In *Apocryphal Writings and the Latter-day Saints*, ed. C.W. Griggs. Provo, Utah, 1986.

Charlesworth, James H. *The Old Testament Pseudepigrapha*, 2 vols. Garden City, N.Y., 1983–1985.

Woodruff, Wilford. *Discourses of Wilford Woodruff*, comp. G. Homer Durham. Salt Lake City, 1969.

L. LAMAR ADAMS

SIGN SEEKING

Signs are greeted by the faithful with reverence and appreciation (*see* SIGNS AS DIVINE WITNESS). On the other hand, a sign can become a condemnation to an unbeliever (D&C 63:7–11). Skeptics may rationalize the signs as aberrations of nature, harden their heart, and not recognize or acknowledge God's "hand in all things" (D&C 59:21). When an unbeliever seeks for a sign he is tempting God and subjects himself to possible condemnation and the WRATH OF GOD. Two vivid Book of Mormon cases illustrating the consequences of unholy sign seeking are Sherem (Jacob 7:13–14) and Korihor (Alma 30:43–56).

Furthermore, Jesus said to the Jewish rulers, "a wicked and adulterous generation seeketh after a sign" (Matt. 16:4). And in the latter days, Jesus explained that "he that seeketh signs shall see signs, but not unto salvation" (D&C 63:7). There is a great difference between signs to confirm or reward faith and the seeking of signs as an excuse for not exercising faith or as a substitute for faith.

BIBLIOGRAPHY

Smith, Joseph. *TPJS*, pp. 157, 278.

Smith, Joseph Fielding. *Church History and Modern Revelation*, p. 4. Salt Lake City, 1948.

R. WAYNE SHUTE

SIGNS

[*Signs mark, indicate, represent, symbolize, give direction, or point to other things beyond themselves, and are sometimes miraculous or extraordinary in nature. The scriptures speak of God's "signs and wonders" by which his work, power, and wisdom are made known or recognized by people in the earth (Ex. 7:3–5). True signs provide objective evidence that an event can reasonably be expected, such as the new star in the east being a sign of Christ's birth (Matt. 2:1, 2) or certain dark clouds heralding a storm (Matt. 16:1–4). False or counterfeit signs are deceptive and give a false hope of security if accepted (Ex. 7:11–12; 8:7; D&C 63:7–9.*

Articles pertaining directly to this subject are Sign Seeking; Signs as Divine Witness; Signs of the Times. *Related articles are* Miracles *and* Second Coming of Jesus Christ.]

SIGNS AS DIVINE WITNESS

Signs have been given by the Lord to manifest his power "both in heaven and in earth" (Jacob 7:14); to witness that Jesus Christ shall come (Jacob 7:14; D&C 39:23; 68:10); to strengthen the faith of believers (D&C 35:8; 58:64; 84:65); and to ratify the condemnation of unbelievers (D&C 63:11).

In revealing his power in the heavens and on earth, God has used numerous signs and wonders. He "hath given a law unto all things, by which they move in their times and their seasons; and their courses are fixed, even the courses of the heavens and the earth, which comprehend the earth and all the planets, . . . and any man who hath seen any or the least of these hath seen God moving in his majesty and power" (D&C 88:42–47). Miracles performed by the power of God are signs of his might and majesty (cf. Ex. 7:3). He parted the Red Sea for the children of Israel after bringing the ten plagues upon the Egyptians (Ex. 7–12; 14:1–31). He confirmed Gideon's divine call by several signs (Judg. 6:17–23, 36–40).

During his mortal ministry the Lord filled empty nets with fish after the disciples had fished all night but caught nothing (Luke 5:6). He healed the sick, raised the dead, caused the lame to walk and the blind to see, and calmed the storm (*see* MIRACLES). The foregoing, and with hundreds of other instances, attest to the power and might of God, both in heaven and on earth.

Signs strengthen the faith of believers and therefore are beheld by those who already believe in Christ as confirmations of their belief. Jesus Christ revealed to the Prophet Joseph Smith, "I will show miracles, signs, and wonders, unto all those who believe on my name" (D&C 35:8) and "he that believeth shall be blest with signs following, even as it is written" (D&C 68:10). Signs that follow faithful believers are many. They "shall heal the sick, . . . cast out devils, and shall be delivered from those who would administer . . . deadly poison," and if occasion warrants, they could even "raise the dead" (D&C 124:98–100; cf. Mark 16:17–18). In addition, faithful Saints have a comforting assurance, which comes to those who recognize the signs, that God's plans will not be frustrated (D&C 3:1; 10:43).

In addition to manifesting God's power, signs have been given as a witness of the coming of Christ to earth. Latter-day Saints believe that signs were given to prepare the people for his coming in the MERIDIAN OF TIME. King BENJAMIN declared, "And many signs, and wonders, and types, and shadows showed he unto them, concerning his coming" (Mosiah 3:15). MORMON reports that among the Book of Mormon people, signs and wonders abounded prior to the birth of Christ in the Holy Land (3 Ne. 1:4–22) and before his visit to the Western Hemisphere (3 Ne. 8–10).

Of particular interest in the present Dispensation of the Fulness of Times are signs pertaining to the second coming of Christ (*see* SECOND COMING OF JESUS CHRIST). The Lord has revealed the SIGNS OF THE TIMES (1 Thes. 5:1–2) to guide the faithful in their preparation for the "great and dreadful day of the Lord" (D&C 110:14)—that is, for Christ's second coming to the earth. Thus, the faithful watch for the signs so that when the hour comes, it will be great, but not dreadful to them (cf. 1 Thes. 5:2–4).

Elder Bruce R. McConkie noted at least fifty-one different signs, many of which pertain to natural phenomena, that have been foretold, pointing to the second coming of Christ. These include earthquakes, famines, depressions, economic turmoil, strikes, anarchy, violence, disasters, calamities, disease, plague, and pestilence. At the same time, both worldly knowledge and gospel knowledge increase, holy temples are built throughout the earth, Israel is gathered, and the true gospel is preached in all the world (*MD*, pp. 715–34).

BIBLIOGRAPHY

Smith, Joseph. *TPJS*, pp. 160, 198, 224, 262.

R. WAYNE SHUTE

SIGNS OF THE TIMES

The phrase "signs of the times" was used by Jesus Christ when he reproved certain antagonists for not recognizing earlier prophecies relative to his second advent. He said they understood signs pertaining to the weather, but did not understand the "signs of the times" (Matt. 16:3). Recognizing such signs will enable discerning individuals to understand the unfolding of prophetic events in the final phase of the earth's history. Prophets before and after Christ have prophesied that there would be signs pertaining to events occurring prior to Christ's second coming (Joel 2:30–31; Amos 8:11–12; 2 Thes. 2:1–3; *TPJS*, pp. 286–87).

These signs include the coming of false Christs and false prophets and the deception of many who believe in them (Matt. 24:11, 23–24). Included also are wars, rumors of wars, famines, earthquakes, pestilence, and other natural calamities (Matt. 24:6, 27; Mark 13:5–8). Latter-day revelation provides additional insights concerning these eschatological catastrophes and the consequences of them for those who are unprepared (D&C 29:13–21; 45:25–45). The gospel of Jesus Christ will be preached throughout the earth as a sign that the Lord's coming draws near (JS—M 1:31), and for those who believe and obey, his coming will be glorious. Even though no one on earth knows the exact time of Jesus' return (D&C 49:7), those who recognize the signs and prepare themselves by "treasuring up [his] word, shall not be deceived" (JS—M 1:37). These shall be as the "wise virgins" of Jesus' parable and shall profit from the signs of the times (Matt. 25:1–13; D&C 45:56; 53:54).

DAVID F. BOONE

SIN

Sin is willful wrongdoing. James indicates that it can also be the willful failure to do right: "Therefore to him that knoweth to do good, and doeth it not, to him it is sin" (4:17). Sin is transgression of the law (1 Jn. 3:4), but one is not held responsible for sins against a law that one has not had opportunity to know. Orson F. Whitney, an apostle, explained:

> Sin is the transgression of divine law, as made known through the conscience or by revelation. A man sins when he violates his conscience, going contrary to light and knowledge—not the light and knowledge that has come to his neighbor, but that which has come to himself. He sins when he does the opposite of what he knows to be right. Up to that point he only blunders. One may suffer painful consequences for only blundering, but he cannot commit sin unless he knows better than to do the thing in which the sin consists. One must have a conscience before he can violate it [pp. 241–42].

God does not hold one responsible for wrong done in ignorance or harm done to others unintentionally, because such actions do not constitute sin. One's ignorance, immaturity, or even recklessness may injure others, and individuals may be accountable for the consequences they help to bring about. But in such situations, where there is no ill intent, there is no sin. This does not mean that people who do wrong in ignorance do not suffer, perhaps physically or in their relationships with others. Moreover, when one becomes aware of having contributed to problems, it usually would be considered sin to avoid making amends or to refuse to help correct the difficulties created.

The Greek verb used in the New Testament meaning "to sin" is *hamartanein*. This word invokes the imagery of the archer, and can mean "to miss the mark." When people sin, they look "beyond the mark" toward inferior or selfish goals. The scriptures define mankind's high mark or calling as "that they might have joy" (2 Ne. 2:25). God, who experiences a fulness of joy (cf. 3 Ne. 28:10), may be trusted to know the proper way to bliss. He offers to his children all that he has. He sent his Son to "save his people from their sins" (Matt. 1:21). To sin knowingly is to transgress or overstep the borders of the way to peace and happiness, and to reject the mission of the Savior.

All mortals inherently possess hearts that can be attuned to depths of love, peace, and purity (cf. Moro. 7:14–18). But through sin (intentionally doing wrong), humans obliterate joy and foster hatred, violence, and misery (see 2 Ne. 2:26–27; Mosiah 3:19; Hel. 14:30–31). Sin wastes, corrupts, saddens, and destroys. It extinguishes the "perfect brightness of hope" offered by Christ (2 Ne. 31:20) and replaces it with despair (Moro. 10:22). Its sting does not enliven or gladden the heart, but awakens "a lively sense of . . . guilt" (Mosiah 2:38), which is an unwished-for but inescapable consequence for the unrepentant.

The first taste of sin is bitter. As children mature, "sin conceiveth in their hearts, and they taste the bitter" (Moses 6:55). However, experimentation with sin is deceptively addictive. Even as a person's spiritual sensitivities dim; the sting may seem to diminish in time. Things are not as they seem to one in sin. It is as though one sleeps. The repetition of sin (known in the scriptures as wickedness) clouds one's view, and the effects of sin are more bitter with the progressive passing of life. Isaiah compares it to "when an hungry man dreameth, and, behold, he eateth; but he awaketh, and his soul is empty" (Isa. 29:8). And PAUL noted, sinners "being past feeling have given themselves over unto lasciviousness, to work all uncleanness with greediness" (Eph. 4:19).

Sin includes the willful breaking of covenants with God. It ruptures family and social relationships, creates disorder and mistrust, and encourages the selfish pursuit of one's own ends to the detriment of the community. Covenants give a sense of stability and permanence—they signal what to expect from one another. But sin creates uncertainty and instability. It never leads to the happiness expected, but to disappointment. As Jacob testified, breaking covenants creates suffering for the innocent: "Ye have broken the hearts of your tender wives . . . ; and the sobbings of their hearts ascend up to God against you. . . . Many hearts died, pierced with deep wounds" (Jacob 2:35).

Sins are expressions of living in resistance to God and the things of the spirit. "A man being evil cannot do that which is good" (Moro. 7:10), because his behavior springs from a hard or bitter heart. One can quit "being" evil only through a change of heart; it is not just a modification or control of external actions (cf. Mosiah 5:2–15). The truth is either received or resisted. When the woman of Samaria who talked with the Savior at the well reported her conversation to others, she said, "Come, see a man, which told me all things that ever I did" (John 4:29). What the Savior told her included her current sins—"and he whom thou now hast is not thy husband" (John 4:18). Yet, she received his declarations; she accepted his testimony that he was the Christ and invited her friends to see for themselves (John 4:25–26, 29). Had she been hard-hearted, or had she clung to her sins, she would not have accepted his statements about her, or his testimony of his own divinity. She would not have come to the road of repentance and forgiveness.

To escape the effects of sin, mankind must both accept the Atonement and repent. AMULEK, a Book of Mormon prophet, explains that the Atonement saves men *from* their sins, not *in* them (Alma 11:37). It is in large measure one's own sins that produce feelings of affliction and despair, perhaps more than what one suffers from the wrongs received from others. Mortals are punished *by* their sins rather than *for* them. This condition is described in the scriptures as the "bondage of sin" (D&C 84:49–51; Morm. 8:31).

Those in this bondage live in opposition to the two great commandments upon which hang all the law and the prophets: "Thou shalt love the Lord thy God with all thy heart, and with all thy soul, and with all thy mind," and "thou shalt love thy neighbor as thyself" (Matt. 22:37, 39). If these are the greatest of commandments, then perhaps the most debilitating sin is a refusal to love. Selfishness, greed, envy, pride, self-righteousness, resentment, hostility, smugness, self-pity, and lust are all ways of refusing to love. The allowance often asked for by sinners regarding these may contribute more to negative family relationships or even the level of crime in a society than supposed. Discourtesy can escalate to hostility, which in turn can escalate to violence.

Sinners are offended by the truth and find it a burden, as when LAMAN and Lemuel, after having the plan of salvation rehearsed to them by their brother NEPHI₁, complained, "Thou hast declared unto us hard things, more than we are able to bear" (1 Ne. 16:1). Those refusing to live the truth rationalize and justify their wrongdoing. Cain, already having committed murder, responded to the Lord's inquiry about Abel's whereabouts by lying ("I know not"), and then hypocritically challenging God: "Am I my brother's keeper?" (Gen. 4:9; Moses 5:34).

Sin blinds one to the truth in any given situation. Nathan the prophet told king David a story of a man who possessed many flocks of sheep, but who, nevertheless, slaughtered the pet ewe lamb of a poor family to feed a guest. David was incensed. He judged that such a man should restore to the wronged family fourfold and be executed. Nathan declared: "Thou art the man" (2 Sam. 12:7). Spiritually blinded by his adultery with Bathsheba and the murder of her husband Uriah (2 Sam. 11), David no longer saw himself as he was seen by the prophet or, apparently, by anyone willing to examine the situation on the basis of the Lord's commandments.

"If we say that we have fellowship with him [Christ], and walk in darkness, we lie, and do not the truth: . . . If we say that we have no sin, we deceive ourselves, and the truth is not in us" (1 Jn. 1:6, 8). When a truth is not lived, it is seen falsely. Even personal guilt for sin is seen by the unrepentant as having been placed on them by someone else, and not as a symptom of their own hardness against the truth. Whether the sin be "great," such as murder, adultery, or embezzlement, or "small," as in pride, harshness, or jealousy, its effects are manifest in predictable patterns of behavior. These patterns commonly include being burdened by, blind to, or excusing oneself from, what one knows to be true.

Rarely do the scriptures give a detailed catalog of sins. Usually they give illustrative examples (cf. Alma 1:32; 16:18; Hel. 4:12). President Ezra Taft Benson described the attitudes associated with the universal sin of pride: "Our enmity toward God takes on many labels, such as rebellion, hard-heartedness, stiff-neckedness, unrepentant, puffed up, easily offended, and sign seekers" (Benson, p. 4). King Benjamin noted, "I cannot tell you all the things whereby ye may commit sin; for there are divers ways and means, even so many that I cannot number them. But this much I can tell you, that if ye do not . . . continue in the faith of what ye have heard concerning the coming of our Lord, even unto the end of your lives, ye must perish. And now, O man, remember, and perish not" (Mosiah 4:29–30).

To be spiritually born of God is to be awakened, to be released from the burdens of sin (*see* NATURAL MAN). The Book of Mormon records the history of a people who, for a time, overcame the bondage of sin. Of them it says, "And it came to pass that there was no contention in the land, because of the love of God which did dwell in the hearts of the people. And there were no envyings, nor strifes, nor tumults, nor whoredoms, nor lyings, nor murders, nor any manner of lasciviousness; and surely there could not be a happier people among all the people who had been created by the hand of God" (4 Ne. 1:15–16).

To overcome sin and be forgiven are to forsake ungodliness, to acknowledge dependence on God, and to seek to do his will. God's help is indispensable to abandoning sin: "He changed their hearts; . . . he awakened them out of a deep sleep, and they awoke unto God" (Alma 5:6). Those who abandon sin have "received his image in [their] countenances" and exercise faith in the redemption of Christ (cf. Alma 5:14–19); they are full of love (Mosiah 3:19; John 13:35; 15:10).

From an eternal perspective, there is no tragedy except in sin. Mortals are not on earth to prove themselves to one another but to God. This earth life is a probationary time, a test to see whether mankind will "do all things whatsoever the Lord their God shall command them" (Abr. 3:25; cf. Alma 34:34). Those whose "hearts are set . . . upon the things of this world, and aspire to the honors of men," or who cover their sins, gratify their pride, nurture vain ambition, or seek to control and dominate others "in any degree of unrighteousness" grieve the Spirit of the Lord (D&C 121:35, 37).

Escaping sin is a simple but not an easy matter. Repentance requires deep suffering, the uttermost farthing, all that one is capable of doing: "none but the truly penitent are saved" (Alma 42:24; cf. D&C 19). "We are saved [by grace] after all we can do" (2 Ne. 25:23). Those who abandon sin are characterized by going "forward with a steadfastness in Christ, having a perfect brightness of hope, and a love of God and of all men" (2 Ne. 31:20).

BIBLIOGRAPHY

Benson, Ezra Taft. "Beware of Pride." *Ensign* 19 (May 1989):4–6.

Kimball, Spencer W. *The Miracle of Forgiveness.* Salt Lake City, 1969.

———. *The Teachings of Spencer W. Kimball,* ed. Edward L. Kimball, pp. 80–114. Salt Lake City, 1982.

Whitney, Orson F. *Saturday Night Thoughts.* Salt Lake City, 1927.

BRUCE L. BROWN
TERRANCE D. OLSON

SONS OF PERDITION

In LDS scripture Lucifer and CAIN are called Perdition, meaning "destruction" (D&C 76:26; Moses 5:24). The unembodied spirits who supported Lucifer in the WAR IN HEAVEN and were cast out (Moses 4:1–4) and mortals who commit the UNPARDONABLE SIN against the Holy Ghost will inherit the same condition as Lucifer and Cain, and thus are called "sons of perdition."

Perdition is both a place and a spiritual condition. As a place, it is synonymous with that hell to which both unembodied and resurrected sons of perdition will be consigned following the last judgment (2 Ne. 28:23; D&C 29:38; *TPJS*, p. 361). This future kingdom of the devil will be devoid of any of the Spirit and glory of God. (D&C 88:24).

The spiritual condition of those in this realm is described metaphorically as a lake of unquenchable fire and brimstone and as "a worm [that] dieth not" (Jacob 6:10; D&C 76:44). They will be "vessels of wrath, doomed to suffer the wrath of God" (D&C 76:33). God's wrath will originate within them when they contrast his holiness and majesty with their own filthiness and ignominy (2 Ne. 9:14; Alma 12:14–17; Morm. 9:4–5; *TPJS*, p. 361). The Prophet Joseph Smith explained, "A man is his own tormentor and his own condemner. . . . The torment of disappointment in the mind of man is as exquisite as a lake burning with fire and brimstone" (*TPJS*, p. 357). Fire and brimstone characterize the person, not the place.

The awful realization that they are truly damned, have lost all favor with God, have rejected all that he represents, and have lost the opportunity for repentance will be compounded by their subjection to Lucifer and Cain, who are consumed with like misery and frustration (2 Ne. 2:27; Moses 1:22). Such is the ultimate "damnation of hell" (*TPJS*, p. 198).

Perdition is the second death: total banishment not only from God's literal presence but also from the influence of his Spirit (2 Ne. 9:15–16; Hel. 14:18; D&C 88:32). Those who sin against the Holy Ghost commit the unpardonable sin and will suffer the fulness of the second death (Alma 39:6; Hel. 14:16–19). All others will be saved eventually in one of the degrees of glory (D&C 76:40–43; *JD* 8:154).

Sons of perdition are not merely wicked; they are incorrigibly evil. In sinning against the revelations of the Holy Ghost, they have sinned against the greater light and knowledge of God. They willfully and utterly pervert principles of righteousness and truth with which they were once endowed, and transform them into principles of evil and deception. Joseph Smith declared, "You cannot save such persons; you cannot bring them to repentance" (*TPJS*, p. 358). No divine principle can cleanse the sons of perdition; following the last judgment, they will remain "filthy still" (D&C 29:44; 88:35). It is revealed that "it had been better for them never to have been born" (D&C 76:32).

Those who become sons of perdition while in mortality will be resurrected with unglorified physical bodies and "rise to the damnation of their own filthiness" (*TPJS*, p. 361). Cain, thus resurrected, will then rule over the unembodied Lucifer (Moses 5:23; *MD*, p. 109).

It has been suggested that in the absence of the life-sustaining powers of God's Spirit, sons of perdition will eventually become disorganized and return to "native element" (*JD* 1:349–52; 5:271; 7:358–59). However, scripture declares that "the soul can never die" (Alma 12:20) and that in the Resurrection the spirit and the body are united "never to be divided" (Alma 11:45; cf. 12:18; D&C 93:33). The ultimate fate of sons of perdition will be made known only to those who are partakers thereof and will not be definitely revealed until the last judgment (D&C 29:27–30; 43:33; 76:43–48; *TPJS*, p. 24).

Few individuals have been identified as sons of perdition. Although Judas is often so regarded, there is a question whether he had received the Holy Ghost sufficiently to sin against it at the time of his betrayal of Christ (John 17:12; Smith, pp. 433–34).

BIBLIOGRAPHY

Smith, Joseph F. *Gospel Doctrine.* Salt Lake City, 1946.

RODNEY TURNER

SPAULDING MANUSCRIPT

The Spaulding Manuscript is a fictional story about a group of Romans who, while sailing to England early in the fourth century A.D., were blown off course and landed in eastern North America. One of them kept a record of their experiences among eastern and midwestern American Indian tribes. The 175-page manuscript was first published as a 115-page monograph in 1885, some seventy years after the death of its author, Solomon Spaulding (sometimes spelled Spalding). The only known manuscript was lost from 1839 until its discovery in Honolulu, Hawaii, in 1884. It was promptly published by both the Latter-day Saints and Reorganized Latter Day Saint churches to refute the theory of some critics that it had served as an original source document for the Book of Mormon, supposedly supplied to Joseph Smith by Sidney Rigdon.

Spaulding was born in Ashford, Connecticut, on February 21, 1761. He served in the American Revolution, later graduated from Dartmouth College, and became a clergyman. He subsequently lost his faith in the Bible, left the ministry, and worked unsuccessfully at a variety of occupations in New York, Ohio, and Pennsylvania until his death near Pittsburgh in 1816. About 1812 he wrote *Manuscript Found,* which he attempted to publish to relieve pressing debts.

There are similarities in the explanation for the origins of both *Manuscript Found* and the Book of Mormon. The introduction to the Spaulding work claims that its author was walking near Conneaut, Ohio (about 150 miles west of the place in New York where Joseph Smith obtained the gold plates), when he discovered an inscribed, flat stone. This he raised with a lever, uncovering a cave in which lay a stone box containing twenty-eight rolls of parchment. The writing was in Latin. The story is primarily a secular one, having virtually no religious content. A character in the novel possessed a seerstone, similar to objects used by Joseph Smith. However, none of the many names found in either volume matches any of those in the other, nor is there the remotest similarity in literary styles.

The first to assert that a direct connection existed between the Book of Mormon and *Manuscript Found* was Doctor Philastus Hurlbut, who was excommunicated from the Church in June 1833. Desiring to discredit his former coreligionists, Hurlbut set out in the ensuing months to refute Joseph Smith's claims for the origins of the Book of Mormon. He interviewed members of Spaulding's family, who swore that there were precise similarities between Spaulding's work and the Book of Mormon. He also located the neglected manuscript, but must have been disappointed to discover that it had no demonstrable connection with the Book of Mormon.

In 1834, Hurlbut was involved with Eber D. Howe in preparing a significant anti-Mormon publication, *Mormonism Unvailed.* Its final chapter dealt with the Spaulding theory of the origin of the Book of Mormon. Howe admitted in the book that the only document known to have been authored by Spaulding had been found, but he asserted that this was not *Manuscript Found.* The title penciled on the brown paper cover was *Manuscript Story—Conneaut Creek.* Howe speculated that Spaulding must have composed another manuscript that served as the source of the Book of Mormon, but no additional writings of Spaulding have ever surfaced. By the 1840s, the so-called

Spaulding theory had become the main anti-Mormon explanation for the Book of Mormon.

Spaulding's manuscript, lost for forty-five years, was among items shipped from the office of the Ohio *Painesville Telegraph,* owned by Eber D. Howe, when that office was purchased in 1839 by L. L. Rice, who subsequently moved to Honolulu. Rice discovered the manuscript in 1884 while searching his collection for abolitionist materials for his friend James H. Fairchild, president of Oberlin College. Believers in the Book of Mormon felt vindicated by this discovery, and they published Spaulding's work to show the world it was not the source for the Book of Mormon.

Since 1946, no serious student of Mormonism has given the Spaulding Manuscript theory much credibility. In that year, Fawn Brodie published *No Man Knows My History.* This biography of Joseph Smith, hostile to his prophetic claims, dismissed the idea of any connection between Spaulding and Smith or their writings. Rigdon first met Joseph Smith in December 1830 after the Book of Mormon was published.

Nevertheless, some have continued to promote the Spaulding theory (e.g., see Holley). In 1977, graphologists claimed to have detected similarities between the handwriting of Spaulding and of one of the scribes who transcribed some of the Book of Mormon from Joseph Smith's dictation. After considerable media attention and further scrutiny, anti-Mormon spokespersons acknowledged that they had been too hasty. The handwriting evidence did not support a connection between Solomon Spaulding and Joseph Smith.

BIBLIOGRAPHY

Bush, Lester E., Jr. "The Spaulding Theory Then and Now." *Dialogue* 4 (Autumn 1977):40–69.

Bushman, Richard L. *Joseph Smith and the Beginnings of Mormonism.* Urbana, Ill., 1985.

Fairchild, James H. "Manuscript of Solomon Spaulding and the Book of Mormon." *Bibliotheca Sacra*, pp. 173–74. Cleveland, Ohio, 1885.

Holley, Vernal. "Book of Mormon Authorship: A Closer Look." Ogden, Utah, 1983; this booklet is reviewed by A. Norwood, *Review of Books on the Book of Mormon* 1 (1989):80–88.

LANCE D. CHASE

STANDARD WORKS

Standard works are the books accepted by Latter-day Saints as SCRIP-TURE: the BIBLE, BOOK OF MORMON, DOCTRINE AND COVENANTS, and PEARL OF GREAT PRICE. In early Latter-day Saint usage, the term apparently included more writings than the scriptures. In 1874 George A. Smith described "standard works" as the scriptures and other works published by the Church that illustrate "the principles of life and salvation made known in the gospel of Jesus Christ" (*JD* 17:161; cf. 11:364). By 1900, however, the phrase "standard works" came to refer only to the scriptures (Smith, pp. 363–65; *AF,* p. 7).

Anciently, the Lord declared to the prophet NEPHI₁ that the words of his seed, joined with the Lord's words, would be declared "unto the ends of the earth, for a standard unto my people" (2 Ne. 29:2). In this sense, a standard is a rule for measuring or a model to be followed. The scriptures contain the doctrine and principles that serve as the rules and models by which Latter-day Saints are to live. Hence, they become the standard by which spiritual and other matters are to be judged or measured.

The standard works are different from other writings in the Church, for they have been formally accepted by the Church as revelation and are viewed as containing the word of God. It is his voice that has given them through his PROPHETS (see D&C 18:34–36). Latter-day Saints accept the Bible as the word of God, but recognize that some errors and omissions have occurred in the processes of transmission and translation (A of F 8). The Book of Mormon, Doctrine and Covenants, and Pearl of Great Price, brought forth in modern times by the Prophet Joseph Smith, are likewise accepted as the word of God (see *MD,* p. 364).

Although The Church of Jesus Christ of Latter-day Saints accepts the present scriptures as "standard works," the canon of scripture is not closed. "We believe all that God has revealed, all that He does now reveal, and we believe that He will yet reveal many great and important things pertaining to the Kingdom of God" (A of F 9). Latter-day Saints also esteem the words of the living prophets of God as scripture, for when they "speak as they are moved upon by the Holy Ghost," they speak the will, mind, and word of the Lord (D&C 68:3–4). Latter-day Saints are encouraged to study and ponder all these in connection with the standard works and to apply them to their own lives, that all "might be for our profit and learning" (1 Ne. 19:23).

BIBLIOGRAPHY
Smith, Joseph F. *GD*.

CLYDE J. WILLIAMS

STICK OF JOSEPH

[*For Latter-day Saints, the "Stick of Joseph" and the "Stick of Ephraim" refer to the Book of Mormon. Both phrases appear in the book of the prophet Ezekiel (37:16, 19). The view that the Stick of Joseph consists of a scriptural record receives support from the Book of Mormon and the Doctrine and Covenants (1 Ne. 13:35–40; 2 Ne. 3:11–12, 18–21; D&C 27:5). Articles that deal with this subject are* Book of Mormon, Biblical Prophecies about; Ezekiel, Prophecies of; Joseph of Egypt: Writings of Joseph; *and* "Voice from the Dust."]

STICK OF JUDAH

[*In LDS terminology, the "Stick of Judah" refers to the Bible. The phrase appears in the book of the prophet Ezekiel (37:19). The belief that the Stick of Judah consists of a scriptural record is stated in the Book of Mormon (1 Ne. 3:9–12; 5:5–6, 10–13; 13:20–29; 2 Ne. 3:11–12; cf. D&C 27:5). Articles that discuss this subject are* Book of Mormon, Biblical Prophecies about *and* Ezekiel, Prophecies of.]

STRAIT AND NARROW

Latter-day Saints speak of following the "strait and narrow" path to eternal life. These words are found in both ancient and modern scripture. For them as for other Christians, probably the best-known passage in which these words are conjoined is Matthew 7:13–14: "Enter ye in at the strait gate: . . . because strait is the gate, and narrow is the way, which leadeth unto life, and few there be that find it."

"Strait" and "narrow" mean approximately the same: constricted, tight. The juxtaposition of synonyms is a typical Hebrew literary parallelism. The terms thus translated reveal diverse nuances, enhancing the implications of the metaphors. The Greek word *stene(s)*, translated "strait" in the King James Bible, is defined as "narrow." The word for "narrow" is the perfect passive participle of *thlibo*, meaning "pressed together, made narrow, oppressed." Several Hebrew words exhibit similar meanings. Jesus Christ and a number of prophets utilized such terms in constructing an image with diverse applications, but with the ultimate end of portraying the strict path to God's presence.

In the Book of Mormon, LEHI uses especially vivid imagery in recounting his vision of the TREE OF LIFE: "And I beheld a rod of iron, and it extended along the bank of the river. . . . And I also beheld a strait and narrow path, which came along by the rod of iron" (1 Ne. 8:19–20). Near the end of his record, NEPHI₁, son of Lehi, offers the clearest explanation of the images in this vision, pointing out that the gate to the strait and narrow path consists of repentance, baptism, and remission of sins. The gospel, then, is the good news that there exists such a path, which men and women can follow to eternal life by "press[ing] forward, feasting upon the word of Christ, and endur[ing] to the end" (2 Ne. 31:17–20). This emphasis on Christ is in harmony with the observation that the strait and narrow path is the "way." One may compare Jesus' response to Thomas in John 14:6: "I am the way, the truth, and the life: no man cometh unto the Father, but by me."

The connotations of the Hebrew and Greek words for "strait" and "narrow" suggest that the path is not easy. One's journey on the path is to be a challenge, but not so strenuous a one that it is hopeless. Jesus affirmed, "My yoke is easy, and my burden is light" (Matt. 11:30). A related concept is found in a homophone of "strait," with different etymological roots. It is expressed in a poignant psalm wherein Nephi prayed to the Lord, "Wilt thou make my path straight before me! Wilt thou not place a stumbling block in my way—but that thou wouldst clear my way before me, and hedge not up my way" (2 Ne. 4:33).

BIBLIOGRAPHY

Stapley, Delbert L. "The Straight Gate—Repentance and Baptism." *IE* 58 (June 1955):416–18.

Wirthlin, Joseph B. "The Straight and Narrow Way." *Ensign* 20 (Nov. 1990):64–66.

DANIEL B. MCKINLAY

SUNDAY

Whereas the seventh or SABBATH DAY was established as a day of rest and worship and a commemoration of the Creation (Ex. 20:10–11), the "first day of the week," Sunday, or the Lord's Day, was consecrated to remember the atonement and resurrection of Jesus Christ (Acts 20:7; 1 Cor. 16:2; Rev. 1:10). Moreover, a new ordinance, the SACRAMENT, was introduced so that Christian worshipers on that day might venerate Jesus' atoning sacrifice. For Latter-day Saints, modern revelation fixes the day of weekly worship and holy rest as "the Lord's day," which is Sunday, the first day of the week (see D&C 59:9–12).

Jesus' fulfillment of the LAW OF MOSES brought several changes, including the practice of meeting on the first day of the week to commemorate Jesus' resurrection. That the Lord intended a change in the day of worship is suggested by certain events of his postmortal ministry. For instance, it was on the first day of the week (Sunday) that he initially appeared to the apostles (John 20:19). It was also on the first day of the week that he reappeared to these same apostles, then in company with Thomas (John 20:26). After Jesus' resurrection, it was on the day of Pentecost, a festival on the first day of the week observed by ancient Israel fifty days after Passover (cf. Lev. 23:15–16), that the assembled Saints and others received their most essential guide to eternal life, the Holy Ghost (Acts 2:1–12). On that day of Pentecost the apostolic ministry began with the conversion of three thousand souls through the preaching of PETER (Acts 2:37–41).

The early Christians understood the significance of this change in the day of their worship, as can be seen by their continued practice of congregating on the first day of the week: "And upon the first day of the week, when the disciples came together to break bread, Paul preached unto them" (Acts 20:7; 1 Cor. 16:2; cf. Col. 2:16). Early Christian writers confirm the continued use of the first day of the week as the accepted new day of worship, only noting exceptions (e.g., Eusebius, *Ecclesiastical History* 3.27.5). By A.D. 321, Constantine had officially designated the first day of the week as a day of rest. The word "Sunday" for the first day came from the weekly pagan worship of the sun god in Rome.

In a revelation received on August 7, 1831, a Sunday, the Lord confirmed his prescribed design in changing the day of public worship: "But remember that on this, the Lord's day [Sunday], thou shalt offer thine oblations and thy sacraments unto the Most High" (D&C 59:12).

For members of The Church of Jesus Christ of Latter-day Saints, the day of the week on which they gather to pay devotion to God and his Son matters less than receiving the edification and enlightenment that may be gained from worship. This observation is confirmed, for example, by the Church's custom of worshiping weekly in countries in the Middle East on a day other than Sunday.

As President Joseph F. Smith explained, Latter-day Saints are to gather on a day to "mingle with the saints that their moral and spiritual influence may help to correct our false impressions and restore us to that life which the duties and obligations of our conscience and true religion impose upon us" (Smith, p. 243; see D&C 59:9–19).

BIBLIOGRAPHY

Kittel, Gerhard, ed. *Theological Dictionary of the New Testament*, Vol. 8, pp. 1–34. Grand Rapids, Mich., 1964–1974.

Smith, Joseph F. *GD*, pp. 241–47. Salt Lake City, 1939.

GLEN E. BARKSDALE

SWORD OF LABAN

Laban, a Book of Mormon contemporary of NEPHI₁ in JERUSALEM (c. 600 B.C.), possessed a unique sword. "The hilt thereof was of pure gold, and the workmanship thereof was exceedingly fine, and the blade thereof was of the most precious steel" (1 Ne. 4:9). Nephi was "constrained by the Spirit" to kill Laban (1 Ne. 4:10). Among other things he had opposed the Lord's imperative to relinquish the plates and had "sought to take away" Nephi's life (1 Ne. 4:11). Using Laban's "own sword," Nephi slew him (1 Ne. 4:18), retained the sword, and brought it to the Western Hemisphere.

Nephi made many swords "after the manner" of the sword of Laban (2 Ne. 5:14) and used the sword in "defence" of his people (Jacob 1:10), as did King BENJAMIN (W of M 1:13). Benjamin later delivered the sword to his son MOSIAH₂ (Mosiah 1:16). The sword of Laban seems to have been preserved as a sacred object among the Nephites, as was Goliath's sword in ancient Israel (1 Sam. 21:9).

In June 1829 the three witnesses to the Book of Mormon plates were promised a view of the sword (D&C 17:1). According to David Whitmer's report, that promise was fulfilled "in the latter part of the month" (Andrew Jenson, *Historical Record*, nos. 3–5, May 1882, Vol. VI, Salt Lake City, p. 208).

President Brigham Young also reported that the Prophet Joseph Smith and Oliver Cowdery saw the sword of Laban when they entered a cave in the hill Cumorah with a large room containing many plates. "The first time they went there the sword of Laban hung upon the wall; but when they went again it had been taken down and laid upon the table across the gold plates; it was unsheathed, and on it was written these words: 'This sword will never be sheathed again until The Kingdoms of this world become the Kingdom of our God and his Christ'" (*JD* 19:38).

BIBLIOGRAPHY

Alan R. Millard. "King Og's Bed." *Bible Review*, VI, no. 2 (Apr. 1990):19. Contains a description of a sword or dagger discovered in Pharaoh Tutankhamen's tomb in 1922 that is remarkably similar to the sword of Laban.

REED A. BENSON

SYMBOLISM

The word "symbol" derives from the Greek word *súmbolon*, which means literally "something thrown together"; this word can be translated "token." Contracting parties would break a *súmbolon*, a bone or tally stick, into two pieces, then fit them together again later. Each piece would represent its owner; the halves "thrown together" represent two separated identities merging into one. Thus this concept of "symbol" (unity; separation; restoration) provides a model for love, the Atonement, separation and reunification, our original unity with God, our earthly separation, our eventual return to the divine presence and renewed perfect unity with God. Furthermore, this meaning of symbol shows that understanding any symbol requires the "throwing together" of an earthly, concrete dimension and a transcendent, spiritual dimension. Plato's idea that knowledge is remembrance (of a premortal existence) (*Meno* 81c–d) has relevance here.

Symbolism plays a significant role in LDS life. The overriding theme is that all things bear record of Christ, "both things which are temporal, and things which are spiritual; things which are in the heavens above, and things which are on the earth, and things which are in the earth, and things which are under the earth, both above and beneath: all things bear record of me" (Moses 6:63). The use of symbols among the Latter-day Saints expresses religious roots, cultural connections, and modes of life. More connected to Hebrew traditions than most Christian churches and at the same time eschewing many traditional Christian symbols, LDS symbolism is unique among modern religions.

Since LDS worship services are nonliturgical and, except for Christmas, Easter, and the Sunday Sabbath, do not adhere to the usual Christian calendar, many Christian symbols are absent from LDS religious practices. Thus, although the atonement and crucifixion of Jesus Christ are at the heart of their scriptures and theology, traditional symbols such as the cross and the chalice are not prominent. Nor are the rich iconographic materials associated with the traditional churches, especially the emblems, signs, colors, patterns, and symbols that developed during the Middle Ages and during the Renaissance.

The Church embraces biblical symbolic rituals such as baptism (with its attendant associations with death, burial, and rebirth), the sacrament of the Lord's Supper (with its connection to the blood and body of Christ), and marriage (which signifies both human and divine unity).

Some LDS symbols derive from the Book of Mormon. For example, the iron rod (1 Ne. 8:19) symbolizes the word of God as man approaches the Tree of Life (1 Ne. 11:25); the Liahona, the compass or pointer used by the Nephites in their travels (1 Ne. 16:10; Alma 37:38–39), symbolizes guidance through sensitivity to the Spirit; the large and spacious building stands for the corruption of worldly values (1 Ne. 8:31); though the cosmic tree is a universal symbol, the Book of Mormon describes it uniquely as the love of God (1 Ne. 11:21–23).

The Church's history, especially the period of the exodus from the Midwest and the settlement of the Intermountain West, has been a fountainhead of symbols. The covered wagon and the handcart symbolize the faith, courage, and sacrifice of the pioneers; the seagull, the miraculous delivery from a natural disaster; the tabernacle, the quest for sanctuary; and the beehive, the industry and ingenuity required of true disciples.

The architecture of most LDS meetinghouses is plain and uniform. There are spires, but no crosses; few buildings have cruciform design; and very few have stained-glass windows. Again, reflecting plain, New England-style origins, the interiors of LDS churches contain no crosses or other religious symbols. The sacrament or communion table is plain and adorned only with white tablecloths. It usually rests at the same level with, and is generally adjacent to, the pews, reflecting emphasis on a lay ministry and congregational principles.

LDS temples, both in their structure and ordinances, reflect the glory of God. Their entrances are inscribed, "The House of the Lord/Holiness to the Lord," symbolizing both a sanctuary from the world and heaven itself. The Nauvoo Temple had a frieze consisting of sun stones, moon stones, and star stones, symbolizing degrees of glory. Temples built in pioneer Utah had elaborate spires and pinnacles, bas-relief, and stained-glass windows, most of which contained symbolic materials. Often temples are built on a hill and near water to suggest not only their elevation from the world, but also their separateness from it and the beauty of the living water of Christ's redemption and exaltation.

The interiors of the temples, too, are highly symbolic, suggestive of the progressive stages of the plan of salvation. By the use of films and murals, symbolic presentations are given of the creation of the world, the Garden of Eden, the telestial or present world, the postmortal terrestrial world, and the celestial kingdom where God dwells. Also associated with the temples are the symbols of the all-seeing eye and the handclasp. Like many Mormon symbols, these have Masonic parallels, though they are by no means original to Masonry, and have different meanings in an LDS context.

Temples contain baptismal fonts that rest on the backs of twelve oxen symbolizing the twelve tribes of Israel. The rooms where marriages and family sealings are solemnized contain altars and mirrored walls in which participants can see their reflections multiplied to infinity, symbolizing the eternal nature of marital love and the family unit. At the conclusion of the temple service, those participating in the endowment ceremony pass from the terrestrial room to the celestial room through a veil, which symbolizes the transition from time into eternity.

The temple ceremony is richly symbolic, with sacred symbolism in the signs, tokens, clothing, covenants, dramatic enactment, and prayer circle. The unifying connection of this symbolic material is the idea of centering. Everything in the temple is suggestive of centering oneself on Christ. The enactment of this privilege precedes the symbolic entrance into the celestial world and the presence of God.

Because it has some unique scriptures and theology and because it has both correspondence with, and independence from, its Judeo-Christian roots, The Church of Jesus Christ of Latter-day Saints will continue to have its own unique symbolic system.

BIBLIOGRAPHY

Andrew, Laurel B. *The Early Temples of the Mormons.* New York, 1977.

Eliade, Mircea. *Patterns in Comparative Religion.* Cleveland and New York, 1958.

————. *The Sacred and the Profane.* New York, 1959.

Hamilton, C. Mark. *The Salt Lake Temple: A Monument to a People.* Salt Lake City, 1983.

Lundquist, John, and Stephen Ricks, eds. *By Study and Also by Faith,* Vol. 1. Salt Lake City, 1990. See esp. Hamblin, pp. 202–21; Parry, pp. 482–500; Porter and Ricks, pp. 501–22; Compton, pp. 611–42.

Madsen, Truman G., ed. *The Temple in Antiquity.* Provo, Utah, 1984.

Nibley, Hugh. *The Message of the Joseph Smith Papyri.* Salt Lake City, 1976.

————. "Treasures in the Heavens." *Nibley on the Timely and the Timeless,* pp. 49–84. Provo, Utah, 1978.

Paulsen, Richard. *The Pure Experience of Order,* pp. 45–55. Albuquerque, N.M., 1982.

TODD COMPTON

T

TEN COMMANDMENTS

The Ten Commandments, or "decalogue," literally "ten words" (Ex. 34:28; Deut. 4:13; 10:4), are usually understood to be the divine injunctions revealed to Moses and recorded in Exodus 20:1–17 and Deuteronomy 5:6–21. These basic standards of behavior, part of the covenant made on Sinai between the Lord and the children of ISRAEL, have relevance transcending the dispensation of MOSES, and have been quoted (Mosiah 12:34–35; 13:12–24) and elaborated throughout later scripture (Matt. 5:21–37; D&C 42:18–28; 59:6).

The Ten Commandments encapsulate the basic tenets of the Torah, or LAW OF MOSES. Refugees from Egyptian bondage, the Israelites agreed to keep the law (Ex. 19:8), and in return the Lord promised to make them "a peculiar treasure . . . a kingdom of priests, and an holy nation" (Ex. 19:5–6). Moses, realizing that keeping this covenant was essential to Israel's successful establishment in Canaan, used the decalogue to remind his people of their covenant as they prepared to enter the PROMISED LAND (Deut. 5:6–21).

In response to the Israelites' worship of the golden calf, Moses shattered the original tablets on which the commandments were engraved (Ex. 32:19). Though a second set was produced (Ex. 34:1), the JOSEPH SMITH TRANSLATION OF THE BIBLE (JST) indicates that the accompanying law was diminished. The second law was "not . . .

according to the first . . . [but] after the law of a carnal commandment" (JST Ex. 34:1–2; JST Deut. 10:1–2).

Each set was made up of two stone "tables of testimony" (Ex. 31:18), reflecting the two classes of instructions they contained. The first group, or "table," consists of commandments dealing with the relationship between God and his children. They forbid the worship of other gods and of idols, the misuse of the Lord's name, and the desecration of the SABBATH DAY. These are elaborated with explanations and consequences. The second table, written in short, direct statements, deals with relationships among God's children, containing commands to honor parents, and not to kill, commit adultery, steal, bear false witness, or covet.

These standards have been known in all dispensations (*MD*, p. 782), but in the form received by Moses they were an important influence on later scripture. In the Book of Mormon, ABINADI, in his defense before King Noah, quotes the entire decalogue from Exodus (Mosiah 12:34–35; 13:12–24). Christ, who fulfills the law, expands upon the terse second table in the SERMON ON THE MOUNT (Matt. 5:21–37; 3 Ne. 12:21–37). He warns of attitudes that lead to misdeeds, forbidding not only adultery, but lust, not only killing, but anger. The second table is likewise expanded in latter-day revelation. The Doctrine and Covenants forbids stealing, adultery, killing, or "anything like unto it" (59:6), while D&C 42:18–28 details the consequences of such actions.

Finally, Christ not only expands upon applications of the commandments, but reduces the two principal focuses of the decalogue to their essence. Each of the two great commandments, to love the Lord (Matt. 22:37; Deut. 6:5) and to love one's neighbor (Matt. 22:39; Lev. 19:18; Rom. 13:9), encapsulates one of the two tables of the Ten Commandments.

BIBLIOGRAPHY

Fuller, Reginald H. "The Decalogue in the New Testament." In *Interpretation: A Journal of Bible and Theology* 43 (1989):43–55.

Wells, Robert E. "We Are Christians Because. . . ." *Ensign* 14 (Jan. 1984):16–19.

BRUCE T. VERHAAREN

THEOLOGY

The traditional task of theology (from the Greek *theos*, God, and *logos*, study of) is to seek understanding of God's reality, to describe divine things rationally, and to elaborate the present meaning of past manifestations of God, whether theoretically, practically, descriptively, or critically. Since scriptures and specific revelations supply Latter-day Saints with authoritative answers to many of the traditional concerns of faith, members of the Church tend to devote little energy to theoretical, speculative, or systematic theology. For Latter-day Saints, faith is anchored in revelations that occurred in history. From the perspective of the restored gospel, what can be known about divine things must be revealed by God. Though rationally structured, coherent, and ordered, the content of Latter-day Saint faith is not the fruit of speculation, nor has it been deduced from premises or derived from philosophical or scientific inquiries into the nature of things.

The word "theology" and much of what it describes originated with Plato, Aristotle, and the Orphics. The word is not found in the Bible or other LDS scriptures. What is typically understood as theology within Christianity was introduced by Origen (A.D. 185–254) and developed by Augustine (A.D. 354–430). Latter-day Saints have little interest in theology in the sense of trying to discover divine things with the unaided resources of the human mind. Even when theology is seen as essentially descriptive or apologetic, it is not entirely at home in the LDS community.

Not having what has traditionally been understood as theology, Latter-day Saints instead have texts that describe theophanies and special revelations and contain inspired teachings, along with several accounts of God's establishing his covenant people, usually coupled with accounts of a dialectic of obedience and disobedience that followed such events. These accounts may be said to contain "theology," but not in the sense that their meaning is discovered by human ingenuity instead of disclosed through the proclaimed word and will of God.

The core of faith is not a confession to a creed but a personal witness that Jesus of Nazareth is the Christ. Events such as the Prophet Joseph Smith's first vision and belief in continuing contact between God and his prophets anchor Latter-day Saint beliefs, allowing those beliefs to be both clearly identified and adapted to changing circumstances. This leaves little room for systematic treatises intended to fix, order, and settle the understanding of the believers, though it does allow room for reason as a tool for attaining coherence and for working out implications in the revelations (*see* REASON AND REVELATION).

Nor is the Book of Mormon a theological treatise. Instead, it is a long and tragic history, filled with prophetic warnings about deviations from covenants with God. In this sacred text, the gospel of Jesus Christ—beginning with faith, repentance, baptism, and the gift of the Holy Ghost—provides the foundation for all other beliefs. According to the plan of God, those who genuinely comply and endure to the end will eventually be saved in the kingdom of God. As both ground and substance of LDS faith, these points of doctrine are understood as realities, not as matters of conjecture. It is a mistake to see them (or what is built upon them "line by line" through additional divine revelation) as "theology," as that term is generally understood among Christians. Since the texts setting forth the gospel or doctrine of Jesus Christ are rooted in events that Latter-day Saints believe actually happened, it is in exegetical and historical work that both the explication and the defense of the faith usually take place.

Latter-day Saints can scarcely be said to have much in the way of a dogmatic theology, though they sometimes informally borrow a Christian tendency to designate the whole of their beliefs and dogma by the label "theology." Some of the early leaders, coming as they did from sectarian backgrounds, seem to have felt a need for something approaching an orderly and authoritative setting forth of their beliefs. What they produced were initially called theological lectures (*see* LECTURES ON FAITH), and they seem to have been modeled after formal treatises like those by Charles G. Finney (1792–1875) or Alexander Campbell (1788–1866). But the formal methodology of these seven lectures has not been much adopted by other LDS writers.

The early Latter-day Saints were fond of the word "theology," and it turns up conspicuously in some of their writings. A well-known example is Parley P. Pratt's *A Key to the Science of Theology* (1855), in which he defined theology as "the science of communication, or of correspondence, between God, angels, spirits, and men, by means of visions, dreams, interpretations, conversations, inspirations, or the spirit of prophecy and revelation." For Pratt, theology embraced all principles and powers upon which the worlds are organized, sustained, reformed, and redeemed: "It is the science of all other sciences and useful arts" (pp. 1–2). Such books have filled a need for a seemingly orderly explication of what was believed to have been revealed through Joseph Smith and for an indication of how to apply those revelations "in the duties of life" (*AF*, p. 5). To some extent, such works approach systematic theology, in that they are concerned with identifying truth, its structure, correspondences, and unity. These volumes have dogmatic dimensions with respect to the attributes and roles of God, his government, the creation, redemption, eschatology, and the like. They are also concerned with scrutinizing moral aspects of human life, free actions, suffering, ignorance, and sin. But their authors do not approach these topics by the use of reason unaided by revelation, nor are they considered officially authoritative by Latter-day Saints.

The desire for definitive answers to a host of vexing and unsettled questions has been satisfied in the present era by books like Bruce R. McConkie's *Mormon Doctrine*. This book did not derive from a philosophical culture, as did much of traditional Christian theology. It is more nearly an instance of what those outside of Mormon circles would label as dogmatic, rather than formal or systematic, theology. Such compendia have no official standing and represent the opinions of their authors. Their pronouncements, however, are popular among some in the Church.

Some LDS teachings have been set forth in a seemingly philosophical framework by Sterling M. McMurrin, who has attempted to show how classical philosophy and Christian theology might be accommodated to what he defines as the metaphysics inherent in LDS teachings. Still, he discounts divine revelation, does not take the LDS approach to epistemology seriously, and looks instead for signs of naturalism and humanism. Thus, his views are incomprehensible to many Latter-day Saints, since he diverts attention away from historical matters and the crucial prophetic claims upon which the Latter-day Saint faith rests.

Elements of McMurrin's stance have been appropriated by a few historians interested in trying to show that there has been a radical reconstruction of Mormon theology in its first 150 years, and that it has shifted from a pessimistic orthodoxy to an optimistic liberalism and back again toward a pessimistic neo-orthodoxy. Such explicitly theological literature seems selective, if not contrived or forced, and it has had virtually no impact on the life of believers. Instead, the influential scholarly works among Latter-day Saints tend to be either strictly historical or exegetical, though these works also have no official standing.

BIBLIOGRAPHY

For an elaboration of some of the themes addressed above, see Louis Midgley, "Prophetic Messages or Dogmatic Theology?" *Review of Books on the Book of Mormon* 1 (1989):92–113. For investigations from a Latter-day Saint perspective of the differences between the prophetic and theological approaches to matters of faith, see Hugh W. Nibley, *The World and the Prophets*, in *CWHN* 3; likewise, M. Gerald Bradford, "On Doing Theology," *BYU Studies* 14 (Spring 1974):345–58. For an attempt to cast LDS beliefs in traditional theological terminology and then to compare and contrast those formulations with the views of various philosophers and theologians, see Sterling M. McMurrin, *The Theological Foundations of the Mormon Religion* (Salt Lake City, 1965). The historical grounds and tendencies of early Latter-day Saints to eschew systematic treatises and formal theology are discussed by Richard L. Bushman, *Joseph Smith and the Beginnings of Mormonism* (Urbana, Ill., 1984).

For a fine brief introduction to theology, see Yves Congar, "Christian Theology," in *Encyclopedia of Religion*, Vol. 14, pp. 455–64 (New York, 1987). For more detailed treatments, see Brian Hebblethwaite, *The Problems of Theology* (Cambridge, 1980); Theodore W. Jennings, Jr., *Introduction to Theology* (Philadelphia, 1976); and Wolfhart Pannenberg, *Theology and the Philosophy of Science* (Philadelphia, 1976).

LOUIS C. MIDGLEY

THREE NEPHITES

LDS stories of the Three Nephites comprise one of the most striking religious legend cycles in the United States. Bearing some resemblance to stories of the prophet Elijah in Jewish lore, or of the Christian saints in the Catholic tradition, Three Nephite accounts are nevertheless distinctly Mormon. Part of a much larger body of LDS traditional narratives, these stories are not official doctrine and are not published in official literature. They are based on the Book of Mormon account of Christ's granting to three Nephite disciples, during his visit to the New World following his death and resurrection, the same wish he had earlier granted to JOHN THE BELOVED—to "tarry in the flesh" in order to bring souls to him until his second coming (John 21:22; 3 Ne. 28:4–9). The Book of Mormon account states:

"And they [the Three Nephites] are as the angels of God, and . . . can show themselves unto whatsoever man it seemeth them good. Therefore, great and marvelous works shall be wrought by them, before the great and coming day [of judgment]" (3 Ne. 28:30–31; *see also* BOOK OF MORMON: THIRD NEPHI).

As the newly founded Church grew in numbers, an ever-increasing body of stories began circulating among the people, telling of kindly old men, usually thought to be these ancient Nephite disciples, who had appeared to individuals in physical or spiritual distress, helped them solve their problems, and then suddenly disappeared.

Because they span a century and a half of LDS history, these narratives mirror well the changing physical and social environments in which Latter-day Saints have met their tests of faith. For example, in pre–World War II agrarian society, the stories told of Nephites' guiding pioneer trains to water holes, saving a rancher from a blizzard, providing herbal remedies for illnesses, plowing a farmer's field so that he could attend to Church duties, or delivering food to starving missionaries. In the contemporary world, the stories tell of Nephites' leading LDS genealogists to difficult library resources, pulling a young man from a lake after a canoeing accident and administering artificial respiration, stopping to fix a widow's furnace, guiding motorists lost in blizzards, comforting a woman who has lost her husband and daughter in an airplane crash, and pulling missionaries from a flaming freeway crash.

Even though the settings of the newer stories have moved from pioneer villages with a country road winding past to urban settings with freeways sounding noisily in the background, some circumstances have remained constant. In the stories, the Three Nephites continue to bless people and, in telling these stories, Latter-day Saints continue to testify to the validity of Church teachings and to encourage obedience to them. The stories continue to provide the faithful with a sense of security in an unsure world, persuading them that just as God helped righteous pioneers overcome a hostile physical world, so will he help the faithful endure the evils of urban society. Taken as a whole, then, the stories continue to provide understanding of the hearts and minds of Latter-day Saints and of the beliefs that move them to action.

BIBLIOGRAPHY

Lee, Hector. *The Three Nephites: The Substance and Significance of the Legend in Folklore.* University of New Mexico Publication in Language and Literature, no. 2. Albuquerque, N.M., 1949.

Wilson, William A. "Freeways, Parking Lots, and Ice Cream Stands: The Three Nephites in Contemporary Society." *Dialogue* 21 (Fall 1988):13–26.

WILLIAM A. WILSON

TOPICAL GUIDE

The Latter-day Saint edition of the Bible, first published in 1979, includes a 598-page "Topical Guide with Selected Concordance and Index." It is designed to aid SCRIPTURE STUDY and is considered by Latter-day Saints to be a major, unique reference tool.

The Topical Guide provides 3,495 categories citing about 50,000 verses from the Bible, the Book of Mormon, the Doctrine and Covenants, and the Pearl of Great Price. By bringing together references from all four STANDARD WORKS, the Topical Guide enables readers to see the unity and harmony of all these scriptures. It also shows how latter-day revelations bring greater clarity to the understanding of the word of God.

A preliminary topical guide, listing the main supporting scriptures for over 600 topics, which were selected initially with seminary students and young missionaries in mind, was published in 1977. Scripture references at first were gathered by about one hundred teachers in the Church Educational System, along with the same number of returned missionaries at Brigham Young University, who were called to render this Church service. The original number of scriptural topics grew to about 750, and over 2,500 other concordance or index categories were also added. Several committees then collated, evaluated, and selected entries to be included in the current version.

All entries are arranged alphabetically. Parenthetical cross-references to related entries and to the BIBLE DICTIONARY follow the heading in many entries.

Citations within entries are listed in the following order: Bible, Book of Mormon, Doctrine and Covenants, Pearl of Great Price. Each citation gives the specific chapter and verse and a brief excerpt from the passage, with the key word italicized. If the key word is identical to the entry heading, only the initial letter appears. Each citation refers to a single verse, but readers are also alerted that surrounding verses may contribute to understanding.

After certain references, cross-references to other passages containing similar wording may appear in parentheses. This allows students to see relationships among similarly worded passages. If a student cannot find a citation in its expected sequence, it may be necessary to look back through earlier references for parenthetical cross-references. Some entries conclude with a brief list of additional passages.

As a concordance and index, the Topical Guide helps readers to locate specific verses on subjects of interest. (For people and places, the Topical Guide generally refers students to the Bible Dictionary). The Topical Guide goes beyond standard concordances with its topical dimension, bringing together pertinent references on common topics of interest to Latter-day Saints (such as "Faith," "Resurrection," or "Jesus Christ, Atonement through"), whether or not the relevant passages share the same specific key word. For example, the entry "Prayer, Pray" contains 176 references not only to verses with variations of *prayer* and *pray* but also to passages with such words as *call upon, inquire, ask,* and *seek*; in addition, cross-references are given to entries on "Communication," "Faith," "God, Access to," "Meditation," and "Supplication," as well as to the Bible Dictionary entry on prayer.

The Topical Guide is not exhaustive, however, either as a concordance or as a listing of all passages on given topics. Although by necessity it is selective and somewhat interpretive, its purpose is not to define or limit thinking but to stimulate scripture study and suggest profitable directions that study may take. It strives to offer not only a quick path to specific destinations but also a gateway to deeper acquaintance with the word of God.

The combined edition of the Book of Mormon, Doctrine and Covenants, and Pearl of Great Price published in 1981 also contains an expanded index, constructed on principles similar to those governing the Topical Guide.

BIBLIOGRAPHY
Anderson, Lavina Fielding. "Church Publishes First LDS Edition of the Bible." *Ensign* 9 (Oct. 1979):9–18.
Horton, George A. "I Have a Question." *Ensign* 16 (Apr. 1986):41.
Ludlow, Daniel H. *Marking the Scriptures,* pp. 41–43. Salt Lake City, 1980.

BRUCE T. HARPER

TRANSFIGURATION

Transfiguration for mortals consists of a temporary physical and spiritual change, allowing them not only to behold the glory of God but to enter his presence. It is characterized by illumination of countenance such as MOSES experienced (Moses 1:11; Ex. 34:29–35) and comes about by an infusion of God's power (*MD*, p. 725). Because God is a being of transcendent glory, it is impossible for men and women to enter his presence without their physical bodies being spiritually "quickened." The Prophet Joseph Smith explained that God "dwells in eternal fire; flesh and blood cannot go there, for all corruption is devoured by the fire. 'Our God is a consuming fire'" (*TPJS*, p. 367; cf. Heb. 12:29; Deut. 4:24). Transfiguration bestows on individuals a temporary condition compatible to that of deity and allows them to see God face-to-face.

Modern revelation says that "no man has seen God at any time in the flesh, except quickened by the Spirit of God" (D&C 67:11). Soon after Moses' call, for example, he was transfigured so that he could withstand God's power; he later wrote: "His glory was upon me; and I beheld his face, for I was transfigured before him" (Moses 1:11). After God's spirit withdrew, Moses returned to his normal mortal condition and testified that he had beheld God with his own eyes, not however with his natural but with his spiritual or transfigured eyes. He explained that his "natural eyes could not have beheld; for I should have withered and died in [God's] presence" (Moses 1:10–11).

From time to time, other worthy persons have been transfigured. Jesus was transfigured before PETER, JAMES, and JOHN on the MOUNT OF TRANSFIGURATION so that "his face did shine as the sun, and his raiment was white as the light" (Matt. 17:2). On the same occasion, the apostles were similarly changed, enabling them to remain in his transfigured presence (*TPJS*, p. 158). At the opening of the present dispensation, Joseph Smith was spiritually quickened so that he could see both God the Father and his Son Jesus Christ and receive instruction from them. After seeing a transcendent brilliance descend upon him, the Prophet wrote: "When the light rested upon me I saw two Personages, whose brightness and glory defy all description, standing above me in the air" (JS—H 1:16–17). When the VISION of the three degrees of glory was received, he and Sidney Rigdon were "in the Spirit," with the result that they "were enlightened, so as to see and understand the things of God" (D&C 76:11–12, 113–119; cf. D&C 110:1–4).

Transfiguration should not be confused with translation of the body, though both possibly affect the body in similar ways. Transfiguration describes a momentary change, whereas TRANSLATED BEINGS experience a long-term change that ends only when they pass from mortality to immortality (3 Ne. 28:8). Among those translated are ENOCH and the city ZION (Moses 7:18–23, 27; *MD*, p. 727), ELIJAH, the apostle JOHN (D&C 7), and the three Nephite disciples (3 Ne. 28:4–11, 15–40).

The earth itself will be transfigured at Christ's second coming. While on the Mount of Transfiguration the three apostles saw not only God's divine glory but also the earth in its transfigured state (cf. D&C 63:21; *TPJS*, p. 13). Modern revelation says that, through obedience and enduring to the end, faithful Saints will receive an inheritance upon the transformed earth when the millennial day arrives (D&C 63:20–21).

BIBLIOGRAPHY

McConkie, Bruce R. *The Mortal Messiah*, Vol. 4, pp. 392–96. Salt Lake City, 1981.
Turner, Rodney. "The Visions of Moses." In *Studies in Scripture*, ed. K. Jackson and R. Millet, Vol. 2, pp. 43–61. Salt Lake City, 1985.

DALE C. MOURITSEN

TRANSLATED BEINGS

Latter-day Saint scriptures speak of a unique class of beings, persons whom the Lord has "translated" or changed from a mortal state to one in which they are temporarily not subject to death, and in which they experience neither pain nor sorrow except for the sins of the world. Such beings appear to have much greater power than mortals. All translated beings will eventually experience physical death and resurrection (*MD*, p. 807–808). Translation is a necessary condition in special instances to further the work of the Lord.

Translated beings are not resurrected beings, though all translated beings either have since been or yet will be resurrected or "changed in the twinkling of an eye" to a resurrected state (3 Ne.

28:8). In effect, this last change is their death, and they therefore receive what amounts to an instantaneous death and resurrection. Resurrection is a step beyond translation, and persons translated prior to the resurrection of Christ were resurrected with him (cf. D&C 133:54–55); it is expected that those translated since Christ's resurrection will be resurrected at his second coming.

During the period from Adam to MELCHIZEDEK, many faithful persons were translated. Enoch and the righteous residents of his city of Zion were translated not many years after Adam's death (Moses 7:18–21, 31, 63, 69; D&C 38:4; 45:11–14; 84:99–100; Gen. 5:22–24; Heb. 11:5). During the period from Enoch to Noah, it appears that faithful members of the Church were translated, for "the Holy Ghost fell on many, and they were caught up by the powers of heaven into Zion" (Moses 7:27).

After the Flood, others were also translated. In his inspired rendition of the Bible, Joseph Smith tells of many who "were translated and taken up into heaven" (JST Gen. 14:32–34). Fewer translations apparently occurred in the New Testament era, though JOHN THE BELOVED (John 21:20–23; D&C 7) and the THREE NEPHITES were translated (3 Ne. 28).

Translated beings are assigned special ministries, some to remain among mortals, as seems to be the case of John and the Three Nephites, or for other purposes, as in the case of MOSES and ELIJAH, who were translated in order to appear with physical bodies hundreds of years later on the MOUNT OF TRANSFIGURATION prior to the resurrection of Christ. Had they been spirits only, they could not have laid hands on the mortal Peter, James, and John (cf. D&C 129:3–8). Why those of Enoch's city were translated, we are not specifically informed, although the Prophet Joseph Smith explained the role of translated beings thus: "Many have supposed that the doctrine of translation was a doctrine whereby men were taken immediately into the presence of God, and into an eternal fullness, but this is a mistaken idea. Their place of habitation is that of the terrestrial order, and a place prepared for such characters He held in reserve to be ministering angels unto many planets, and who as yet have not entered into so great a fullness as those who are resurrected from the dead" (*TPJS*, p. 170).

The scriptures do not define differences between TRANSFIGURATION and translation, but it appears that transfiguration is more temporary, as in Matthew 17:1–9 and Moses 1:11, occurring primarily to permit one to behold spiritual things not possible in the mortal condition.

BIBLIOGRAPHY
Pratt, Orson. "The Doctrine of Translation." *JD* 17:146–49.

MARK L. MCCONKIE

TREE OF LIFE

Four images of the Tree of Life are significant for Latter-day Saints: in the GARDEN OF EDEN; in LEHI's vision (1 Ne. 8); the parable of ALMA₂ comparing the word to a seed that can grow to be "a tree springing up unto everlasting life" (Alma 32:28–43); and the so-called Tree of Life Stone from pre-Hispanic Mexico.

From earliest times, people in many cultures have venerated trees because they are majestic and, compared to a person's life span, seemingly immortal. Groves were among the first places used for sacred rites, and many cultures envisioned the heavens supported by the branches of a giant tree whose roots led to the underworld and whose sturdy trunk formed the link between the two realms. The most important attribute ascribed to the Tree of Life by those for whom such a symbol existed was its ability to provide immortality to those who ate its fruit. The Tree of Life was present in the Garden of Eden (Gen. 2:9) and is a standard symbol in ancient temples, as well as in temples of The Church of Jesus Christ of Latter-day Saints. It will be present at the end and its fruit available to eat "for him that overcometh" (Rev. 2:7).

Lehi's vision conveys an unforgettable message of the need to "give heed to the word of God and remember to keep his commandments always in all things" (1 Ne. 15:25). In his vision, Lehi saw by a fountain of living waters a tree "whose fruit was desirable to make one happy" (1 Ne. 8:10). The tree represented "the love of God" (1 Ne. 11:25). A path led to the tree, and great numbers of people walked the path, but many became lost in a mist of darkness. A "rod of iron" ran along the path, and only those in the multitude who pressed "their way forward, continually holding fast to the rod" (1 Ne. 8:30), reached the tree and partook of the desired fruit.

Alma used the Tree of Life image to teach about the acquisition of faith in the word of God, which he compared to a seed. When planted in one's heart and "nourished with much care," it would grow in the believer to yield the same sweet and pure fruit described by Lehi. By diligence and patience, one can "feast upon [this fruit] even until ye are filled, that ye hunger not, neither shall ye thirst" (Alma 32:42). Other ancient texts also describe the faithful as trees in God's paradise (Ps. 1:3; Odes of Solomon 11).

Interest was generated among Latter-day Saints in the 1950s by the discovery of a pre-Columbian sculpture that bore a complex Tree of Life scene similar to those found in the ancient Near East. Izapa Stela 5, carved sometime between 100 B.C. and A.D. 100, portrays a large tree in full leaf, laden with fruit, and surrounded by several persons and objects, including water. Some investigators are convinced that the scene is a depiction of Lehi's vision; others are less certain, since the scene also contains items that are difficult to understand, such as triangles and U-shaped elements. The elaborate clothing and headdresses worn by the people, the various objects they hold, and an array of other elements make this carving, which is one of the most complex from this period in Mexico, exceptionally difficult to interpret.

Another intricate Tree of Life carving discovered in Mexico is the beautiful sarcophagus lid from the tomb in the Temple of the Inscriptions at Palenque. Once thought to depict a deity, it is now thought to portray a king named Pacal (meaning "shield") at the moment of his death. As he falls to the earth (represented by the monster face), the sacred ceiba tree rises toward the heavens, topped by the divine serpent-bird, and flanked by two oval cartouches emblematic of the sun.

Whether or not such artworks are related to the Book of Mormon, the remains of cultures from the Near East (*CWHN* 6:254–55; 7:189–92) and Mesoamerica show that the Tree of Life was a significant image in many areas of the world.

BIBLIOGRAPHY
Christensen, Ross, ed. *The Tree of Life in Ancient America.* Provo, Utah, 1968; on Izapa Stela 5 research up to 1965.
James, E. O. *The Tree of Life: An Archaeological Study.* Leiden, 1966.
Norman, V. Garth. *Izapa Sculpture.* Provo, Utah, 1973; for the most complete description of Izapa Stela 5.
Robertson, Merle G. *The Sculpture of Palenque,* Vol. 1, fig. 99. Princeton, 1983.

MARTIN RAISH

U

UNPARDONABLE SIN

The gravest of all sins is blasphemy against the Holy Ghost. One may speak even against Jesus Christ in ignorance and, upon repentance, be forgiven, but knowingly to sin against the Holy Ghost by denying its influence after having received it is unpardonable (Matt. 12:31–32; Jacob 7:19; Alma 39:6), and the consequences are inescapable. Such denial dooms the perpetrator to the hell of the second spiritual death (*TPJS*, p. 361). This extreme judgment comes because the person sins knowingly against the light, thereby severing himself from the redeeming grace of Christ. He is numbered with the SONS OF PERDITION (D&C 76:43).

The Prophet Joseph Smith explained, "No man can commit the unpardonable sin after the dissolution of the body, nor in this life, until he receives the Holy Ghost" (*TPJS*, p. 357). To commit the unpardonable sin, a person "must receive the Holy Ghost, have the heavens opened unto him, and know God, and then sin against Him. After a man has sinned against the Holy Ghost, there is no repentance for him. . . . he has got to deny Jesus Christ when the heavens have been opened to him, and to deny the plan of salvation with his eyes open to the truth of it" (*TPJS*, p. 358; cf. Heb. 10:26–29).

If people have such knowledge and willfully turn altogether away, it is a sin against light, a sin against the Holy Ghost, and figuratively "they crucify to themselves the Son of God afresh, and put him to an open shame" (Heb. 6:4–6; D&C 76:35). Such remain as though there were no Atonement, except that they shall be resurrected from the dead (Alma 11:41).

RODNEY TURNER

URIM AND THUMMIM

The Urim and Thummim is mentioned in the Bible and, with added details about its use and significance, in latter-day scriptures. It is an instrument prepared by God through which revelation may be received. Abraham learned about the universe through the Urim and Thummim (Abr. 3:1–4). The Prophet Joseph Smith "through the medium of the Urim and Thummim . . . translated the [Book of Mormon] by the gift and power of God" (*HC* 4:537; D&C 10:1; JS—H 1:62). Servants of God who are allowed to use the Urim and Thummim have been known as seers (Mosiah 8:13), among whom were Abraham, Moses, the brother of Jared, Mosiah$_2$, Alma$_1$, Helaman$_1$, Moroni$_2$, and Joseph Smith.

In antiquity at least two different Urim and Thummim existed, and possibly three. Chronologically, the brother of Jared received the first known one (D&C 17:1). This same set came into the hands of Mosiah$_2$ and other Book of Mormon prophets, subsequently being deposited with the GOLD PLATES (JS—H 1:35). The fate of the second set, given to Abraham (Abr. 3:1), remains unknown. Unless Abraham's Urim and Thummim had been passed down, Moses received a third set mentioned first in Exodus 28:30. The Urim noted in 1 Samuel 28:6, probably an abbreviated form of Urim and Thummim, was most likely the one possessed by Moses (cf. Num. 27:18–21). What happened to this one is also unknown, though certainly by postexilic times the Urim and Thummim were no longer extant (Ezra 2:63; Neh. 7:65).

Joseph Smith described the Urim and Thummim as "two transparent stones set in the rim of a [silver] bow fastened to a breast plate" (*HC* 4:537; JS—H 1:35). Biblical evidence allows no conclusive description, except that it was placed in a breastplate over the heart (Ex. 28:30; Lev. 8:8).

Urim and Thummim is the transliteration of two Hebrew words

meaning, respectively, "light(s)" and "wholeness(es)" or "perfection(s)." While it is usually assumed that the -*im* ending on both words represents the Hebrew masculine plural suffix, other explanations are possible.

The Urim and Thummim to be used during and after the Millennium will have a functional similarity to the Urim and Thummim mentioned above. God's dwelling place is called a Urim and Thummim; and the white stone of Revelation 2:17 is to become a Urim and Thummim for inheritors of the celestial kingdom (D&C 130:8–10).

PAUL Y. HOSKISSON

V

VIEW OF THE HEBREWS

Ethan Smith's *View of the Hebrews* (Poultney, Vt., 1823; second enlarged edition, 1825) combines scriptural citations and reports from various observers among American Indians and Jews to support the claim that the Indians were the descendants of the lost ten tribes of Israel. It is one of several books reflecting the popular fascination at the time of Joseph Smith with the question of Indian origins. While some have claimed it to be a source for the Book of Mormon, no direct connections between this book and the Book of Mormon have been demonstrated.

The full title of the 1825 edition is *View of the Hebrews; or the Tribes of Israel in America. Exhibiting the Destruction of Jerusalem; the Certain Restoration of Judah and Israel; the Present State of Judah and Israel; and an Address of the Prophet Isaiah to the United States Relative to Their Restoration.* The author, Ethan Smith (no relation to Joseph Smith), was pastor of the Congregational church in Poultney, Vermont.

The first chapter deals with the destruction of Jerusalem in A.D. 70 by the Romans, as referred to in scriptural prophecy and historical sources. The second chapter tells of the literal expulsion of the ten tribes of Israel in 721 B.C. and the establishment of the kingdom of Judah; it also maintains that their restoration will be literal, and it quotes heavily from Isaiah. The third chapter summarizes the outcast condition of Israel in 1823; it also argues that the natives of America are "the descendants of Israel" and propounds that all pre-Columbian Americans had one origin, that their language appears originally to have been Hebrew, that they had an ark of the covenant, that they practiced circumcision, that they acknowledged one and only one God, that their tribal structure was similar to Hebrew organization, that they had cities of refuge, and that they manifest a variety of Hebraic traits of prophetic character and tradition. These claims are supported by citations from James Adair and Alexander von Humboldt. The fourth chapter emphasizes the restoration of Israel, quoting from Isaiah and using Isaiah chapter 18 to create an "Address" to the United States to save Israel. In conclusion, Ethan Smith pleads that the "suppliants of God in the West" be faithful and helpful in bringing scattered Israel "to the place of the name of the Lord of hosts, the Mount Zion."

Alleged relationships of *View of the Hebrews* to the Book of Mormon have attracted interest periodically through the years. Ethan Smith's book was published in the adjoining county west of Windsor County, where Joseph Smith was born and lived from 1805 to 1811. Nevertheless, there is no evidence that Joseph Smith ever knew anything about this book. Detractors have pointed to several "parallels" between the two books, but others point to numerous "unparallels"; as two of many examples, the Book of Mormon never mentions an ark of the covenant or cities of refuge.

I. Woodbridge Riley in 1902 was the first author to suggest a relationship between *View of the Hebrews* and the Book of Mormon (*The Founder of Mormonism*, New York, 1902, pp. 124–26). In 1921, LDS Church authorities were asked to reply to questions posed by a Mr. Couch of Washington, D.C., regarding Native American origins, linguistics, technology, and archaeology. B. H. Roberts, a member of the First Quorum of Seventy, undertook a study of Couch's issues; he received some assistance from a committee of other General Authorities. Roberts's first report, in December 1921, was a 141-page paper entitled "Book of Mormon Difficulties." However, he was not satisfied with that work and later delved more deeply into other critical questions about Book of Mormon origins, which led him to a major analysis of *View of the Hebrews*.

Around March–May 1922, Roberts wrote a 291-page document,

"A Book of Mormon Study," and an eighteen-point summary entitled "A Parallel." In the "Study" Roberts looked candidly at the possibility that Joseph Smith could have been acquainted with Ethan Smith's book and could have used it as a source of the structure and some ideas in the Book of Mormon. He cited some twenty-six similarities between the two books. In all his writings, Roberts did not draw any conclusions that Joseph Smith used Ethan Smith's work to write the Book of Mormon, but rather posed questions that believers in the Book of Mormon should be aware of and continue to find answers for. Roberts's faith in the Book of Mormon as divinely revealed scripture was unshaken by his studies.

Roberts's papers were published in 1985. This again stirred an interest in the relationship of *View of the Hebrews* and the Book of Mormon, especially since the editorial "Introduction" concluded that "the record is mixed" as to whether Roberts kept his faith in the authenticity of the Book of Mormon after making his studies (B. D. Madsen, p. 29). Subsequent research, however, strongly indicates that Roberts remained committed to the full claims of the origin and doctrine of the Book of Mormon to the end of his life (Welch, pp. 59–60), and substantial evidence favors the position that there is little in common between the ideas and statements in *View of the Hebrews* and the Book of Mormon.

BIBLIOGRAPHY

Madsen, Brigham D., ed. *B. H. Roberts: Studies of the Book of Mormon.* Urbana, Ill., 1985.

Madsen, Truman G., comp. *B. H. Roberts: His Final Decade.* Provo, Utah, 1985.

Welch, John W. "B. H. Roberts: Seeker After Truth." *Ensign* 16 (Mar. 1986):56–62.

RICHARD C. ROBERTS

VIRGIN BIRTH

Mary, mother of Jesus Christ, was a virgin at the time of Jesus' birth. Of Old Testament prophets, ISAIAH alone foretold this circumstance (Isaiah 7:14), but Book of Mormon prophets also foresaw the virgin birth. NEPHI₁ described Mary as "a virgin, most beautiful and fair" and "mother of the son of God, after the manner of the flesh" (1 Ne. 11:15, 18). ALMA declared that Christ "shall be born of Mary . . . a virgin . . . who shall . . . conceive by the power of the Holy Ghost and bring forth a son, yea, even the Son of God" (Alma 7:10).

In fulfillment of these prophecies, Gabriel "was sent from God . . . to a virgin . . . and the virgin's name was Mary," and Gabriel announced to her that she would "bring forth a son, and . . . call his name Jesus." To her question, "How shall this be?" Gabriel answered, "The Holy Ghost shall come upon thee . . . therefore [the child] . . . born of thee shall be called the Son of God" (Luke 1:26–35). Thereafter, Joseph married Mary but "knew her not till she had brought forth her firstborn son" (Matt. 1:25). Thus, Jesus was born of a mortal mother who was a virgin.

[*See also* Mary, Mother of Jesus.]

BIBLIOGRAPHY
McConkie, Bruce R. *The Promised Messiah*, pp. 465–66. Salt Lake City, 1978.

ELEANOR COLTON

VISIONS

A vision from God is a form of revelation whereby God discloses himself and his will. It is a visual mode of divine communication, in contrast with hearing words spoken or receiving impressions to the mind. LDS experience is consistent with biblical precedent in affirming that visions constitute a mark of divine approval. Such heavenly manifestations informed and directed Old Testament prophets (e.g., Daniel, Isaiah) and New Testament apostles (e.g., Peter, Paul). They have similarly been part of the foundation of revelation upon which Latter-day Saint prophets and apostles have asserted their testimony of the Lord. The visions of Joseph Smith and of the Book of Mormon prophets are comparable with those of the other testamental epochs. These historic periods of testimony—the Old, the New, the Book of Mormon, and the Latter-day—show similar patterns of revelation from God. Each of these dispensations of the gospel has included visions that communicated the mind and will of the Lord for that time.

An experience of a vision in Old Testament times is "The Lord spake unto Moses face to face, as a man speaketh with his friend"

(Ex. 33:11). Similarly, Moses "saw God face to face, and he talked with him, and the glory of God was upon Moses; therefore Moses could endure his presence" (Moses 1:2). The vision of Stephen in Acts 7:55–56 is no less vivid: "He, being full of the Holy Ghost . . . said, Behold, I see the heavens opened, and the Son of man standing on the right hand of God." Comparable is the vision of Joseph Smith and Sidney Rigdon recorded in D&C 76:19: "The Lord touched the eyes of our understandings and they were opened. . . . And we beheld the glory of the Son, on the right hand of the Father." Each vision is unequivocal and is accompanied by the Spirit of the Lord.

These distinctive testimonies anchor all the rest of God's communion by a visual link with an ordinarily unseen world that directs the destiny of humankind. They provide a vivid sense of the nature of God and his design for the world that gives coherence to all other scripture and inspiration. Spiritual illumination, visual and otherwise, is contingent upon faith and trust in the Lord and obedience to him. When people reject or stray from the will of the Lord, they withdraw from his spirit (Mosiah 2:36), and visions cease. And, as declared in Proverbs 29:18: "Where there is no vision, the people perish."

In LDS doctrine visions are perceptions, aided by the Spirit, of something ordinarily invisible to human beings. The things disclosed are viewed as part of general reality. This process is according to natural law and is not "supernatural," in the usual sense of that term. It is analogous to the fact that some physically real phenomena, such as X rays and atomic particles, are not discerned by the ordinary senses but may be detected by scientific instruments. In the case of visions, the instrument is the person, and the mechanism of observation is faith aided by the Spirit of God.

It is vital to distinguish authentically revealed visions from self-induced imaginings, wish-fulfilling dreams, errors of perception, satanic deceptions, and pathological hallucinating, all of which have been abundant in human history. Spurious visions result from seeking "signs"; authentic visions usually come unbidden. "He that seeketh signs shall see signs, but not unto salvation. . . . Faith cometh not by signs, but signs follow those that believe" (D&C 67:7, 9).

Certain criteria assist in judging the authenticity of any revelation, including a vision:

- It strengthens faith in Jesus Christ, the Son of God, and in his divine mission and doctrine.

- It is confirmed by the witness of the Holy Ghost to the sincere seeker.

- It is usually experienced and reported by an ordained servant of the Lord, often in the name of the Lord. It is declared clearly and unequivocally, and has general application for a people or a time, or for all people and all time. Inspired visions may be experienced by others, but they have specific application to those persons or situations.

- The witness is usually supported by additional testimony, such as accompaniment of the Spirit of God, other manifestations, or the word of additional testators.

- It is consistent with scriptural principles and established doctrine.

- The one receiving and conveying the message is morally upright, honest, and humbly obedient to the commandments of God.

- The content revealed and the behavior admonished are comprehensible as good and true.

- The consequences of following the information or direction are beneficial to the individual and to others, except in cases where the vision contains a rebuke of iniquity or a prophecy of destruction.

- Feelings of enlightenment, edification, and peace, rather than of anxiety or confusion, follow the receiving or awareness of the vision.

- It is not induced by drugs, eroticism, violent or hyperemotional ritual, or worship of false spirits.

While it is often asserted that visions are merely the natural outcome of psychology, biology, culture, or drugs, this viewpoint has never been adequately supported. Such interpretations are helpful for a narrow range of explainable phenomena but do not reach the transcendent and inspirational realm of true visions. Theories from the time of Freudian psychoanalysis to the modern psychobiology of dreams and altered states of consciousness fall short of comprehending divinely given concepts.

BIBLIOGRAPHY

Flusser, David. "Visions." In *Encyclopaedia Judaica*, Vol. 16, pp. 166–68. Jerusalem, 1972.

Nibley, Hugh. *Enoch the Prophet.* In *CWHN*, Vol. 2.

ALLEN E. BERGIN

"VOICE FROM THE DUST"

For Latter-day Saints, the phrase "voice from the dust" speaks of the coming-forth of the BOOK OF MORMON (cf. 2 Ne. 25:18; 26:16), which was translated from metal PLATES buried in the ground for fourteen centuries. As early as Joseph Smith, LDS leaders have consistently indicated that this phrase applies to the Book of Mormon (*PJS*, p. 307; Hinckley, p. 10). This distinctive phrase and others like it usually appear in a context that speaks of the need for repentance and of an accompanying VOICE OF WARNING that will "whisper out of the dust" (Isa. 29:4).

Latter-day Saints believe prophets foresaw that in the latter days a book, a companion to the Bible, would come forth as another testament of Jesus Christ (Ezek. 37:15–19; 2 Ne. 29:1–14). This other testament is the Book of Mormon. The Lord foretold the coming-forth of such a record to ENOCH: "And righteousness will I send down out of heaven; and truth will I send forth out of the earth, to bear testimony of mine Only Begotten" (Moses 7:62; cf. Ps. 85:11; *TPJS*, p. 98). According to the Book of Mormon, JOSEPH OF EGYPT also prophesied that one of his descendants would write words from the Lord that "shall cry from the dust; yea, even repentance unto their brethren, even after many generations have gone by them" (2 Ne. 3:18–20; cf. 33:13; Morm. 8:16, 23, 26; Moro. 10:27).

BIBLIOGRAPHY

Hinckley, Gordon B. *Faith, The Essence of True Religion.* Salt Lake City, 1989.

WILLIAM SHEFFIELD

VOICE OF WARNING

The concept of a divine warning is part of the Judeo-Christian tradition and is a primary focus in The Church of Jesus Christ of Latter-day Saints. Section 1 of the Doctrine and Covenants, which by revelation is designated as a preface (verse 6), proclaims the voice of warning to be an essential thrust of the restored gospel of Jesus Christ: "And the voice of warning shall be unto all people, by the mouths of my disciples, whom I have chosen in these last days" (verse 4). The gospel of Jesus Christ is by nature a voice of warning because it calls people to repentance.

In LDS theology the voice of warning has four components: (1) deity, who originates the message; (2) the message, which is the gospel of Jesus Christ; (3) an authorized messenger, who delivers the message; and (4) mankind, to whom the message is delivered.

The voice is the voice of God, whether by his Spirit (D&C 88:66), his servants (D&C 1:38), or inspired writings (2 Ne. 33:13–15). The warning is for mankind to prepare by repentance for the great day of the Lord (D&C 1:11–12). The warning voice is a proclamation of revealed truth to the inhabitants of the earth so "that all that will hear may hear" (D&C 1:11). Eventually all will be persuaded or left without just excuse (D&C 88:81–82; 101:91–93; 124:3–10).

In modern time as in antiquity, a solemn responsibility envelops both the messengers and those to whom the message is delivered. The Lord informed Ezekiel, "I have made thee a watchman unto the house of Israel: therefore hear the word at my mouth and give them warning from me" (Ezek. 3:17). Only those who hearken to the warning are spared the punishments and receive the blessings. The messengers who deliver the message also save their own souls; if they fail to deliver the message they acquire responsibility for those whom they failed to warn—"[their] blood will I require at thine hand" (Ezek. 3:18–21).

It is a covenant obligation of all who are baptized into the Church of Jesus Christ to "stand as witnesses of God at all times, and in all things, and in all places" (Mosiah 18:9). Once warned, "it becometh every man . . . to warn his neighbor" (D&C 88:81). The messengers who deliver the warning will be present at the day of judgment as witnesses (D&C 75:21; 2 Ne. 33:11; Moro. 10:34). The essence of missionary work is for each member of the Church to become a voice of warning to those who have not been warned (see *DS* 1:307–311).

NEIL J. FLINDERS

WAR IN HEAVEN

When Latter-day Saints speak of the "war in heaven," they generally mean the conflict in the premortal life that began when Lucifer, in a rebellion against God the Father and his Son Jesus Christ, sought to overthrow them. The result was that Lucifer and his followers were cast out of heaven. The prophet Isaiah (Isa. 14:12–15) and John the Revelator (Rev. 12:4–9) both referred to the war, and Jesus himself spoke of having "beheld Satan as lightning fall from heaven" (Luke 10:17–18). Latter-day revelation gives additional insight, which is supplemented by the teachings of latter-day prophets.

To "bring to pass the immortality and eternal life of man" (Moses 1:39), God the Father instituted the eternal plan of salvation, which centered on mankind's agency, anticipated the fall of man, and provided a savior. Although previously known in the heavenly realm, the plan was formally presented to the spirit children of God at a council in heaven. "Whom shall I send?" (Abr. 3:27) was the Father's call for someone to be the Redeemer. His eldest Son (D&C 93:21; Col. 1:15), known also as Jehovah, one "like unto God" (Abr. 3:24), and chosen from the beginning (Moses 4:2), officially accepted this role and responded, "Here am I, send me" (Abr. 3:27). He also stated, "Father, thy will be done, and the glory be thine forever" (Moses 4:2). With this formal acceptance and selection of the future

Messiah, the spirit children of God "shouted for joy" (Job 38:7). It was also a time to signify individual commitment to the Father's plan.

Not all accepted, however. The scriptures state that Lucifer, an "angel of God who was in authority in the presence of God" (D&C 76:25), rebelled and offered himself as the proposed redeemer, saying to the Father, "Behold, here am I, send me" (Moses 4:1). His offer was not well-intentioned and was a defiance of the Father and his Only Begotten Son. Lucifer's proposal was couched in his own interests: "I will be thy son, and I will redeem all mankind, that one soul shall not be lost, and surely I will do it; wherefore give me thine honor" (Moses 4:1). His proposal, if accepted, would have destroyed mankind's agency (Moses 4:3). Lucifer possessed character flaws, which finally manifested themselves in jealousy of the Christ and rejection of the Father's plan. Just how he proposed to save every soul is not explained but it apparently allowed either no opportunity for sin or, if sin did occur, no condemnation for sin. As his reward for saving everyone, Lucifer demanded that God surrender his honor and power to Lucifer (Isa. 14:13; D&C 29:36; Moses 4:3).

Although Lucifer made a false offer of salvation without individual responsibility, he gained many followers, and "war in heaven" ensued. Michael, the archangel (who later was Adam), led the "forces" of Jehovah in a battle for the loyalties of the Father's spirit children. The exact nature of this war is not detailed in the scriptures, but there can be little doubt that it involved the principles of the gospel of Jesus Christ and how mankind was to be saved. The Prophet Joseph Smith explained, "The contention in heaven was—Jesus said there would be certain souls that would not be saved; and the devil said he could save them all, and laid his plans before the grand council, who gave their vote in favor of Jesus Christ. So the devil rose up in rebellion against God, and was cast down, with all who put up their heads for him" (*TPJS*, p. 357).

Lucifer and his followers, who were "a third part of the hosts of heaven" (Rev. 12:4; D&C 29:36), made open warfare against the Father, the Son, the Holy Ghost, and the eternal plan of salvation and were cast down to earth (cf. Jude 1:6), eternally deprived of being born into mortality with physical bodies, and never to have salvation (*TPJS,* pp. 181, 297–98). So tragic was the fall of Lucifer that "the heavens wept over him" (D&C 76:26).

Known on earth as Satan or the devil, Lucifer and his followers still continue the war against the work and the people of God, being permitted to do so to give people opportunity to exercise agency, being "enticed by the one or the other" (2 Ne. 2:16–25). They will persist until the day of judgment, when Michael, the archangel, and his armies will ultimately prevail and cast them out forever (D&C 88:111–15).

BIBLIOGRAPHY

McConkie, Bruce R. *Doctrinal New Testament Commentary,* Vol. 3, pp. 513–19. Salt Lake City, 1973.

Top, Brent L. "The War in Heaven." In *The Life Before.* Salt Lake City, 1988.

BRENT L. TOP

WASHING OF FEET

The ordinance of washing of feet performed by Jesus Christ after the Last Supper with his apostles was a gesture of humility. Amidst discussion of who would be the greatest in the kingdom, Jesus, demonstrating what he had taught, removed his outer robe and performed this menial task, teaching that one who would be a leader must be a servant (John 13:1–8; cf. D&C 88:141). The Joseph Smith Translation adds this explanation about this incident: "Now this was the custom of the Jews under their law; wherefore, Jesus did this that the law might be fulfilled" (JST John 13:10). By this clarification it appears that the washing of feet was an ordinance of the law of Moses.

There is no clear explanation of the washing of feet in the Old Testament, although it is evident that it was a social custom for administering kindness to a guest. The washing of feet is not mentioned in the Book of Mormon, and it is spoken of only briefly in the Doctrine and Covenants in 88:138–41.

DOUGLAS A. WANGSGARD

WASHINGS AND ANOINTINGS

Ritual anointings were a prominent part of religious rites in the biblical world. Recipients of the anointing included temple officiants (Ex. 28:41), prophets (1 Kgs. 19:16), and kings (1 Sam. 16:3; 1 Kgs. 1:39). In addition, sacral objects associated with the Israelite sanctuary were anointed (Ex. 30:22–29). Of equal importance in the religion of the Israelites were ablutions or ceremonial washings (Ex. 29:4–7). To ensure religious purity, Mosaic law required that designated individuals receive a ritual washing, sometimes in preparation for entering the temple (Ex. 30:17–21; Lev. 14:7–8; 15:5–27).

The washings and anointings of the biblical period have a parallel today in The Church of Jesus Christ of Latter-day Saints. In response to a commandment to gather the saints and to build a house "to prepare them for the ordinances and endowments, washings, and anointings" (*TPJS*, p. 308), these ordinances were introduced in the Kirtland Temple on January 21, 1836 (*HC* 2:379–83). In many respects similar in purpose to ancient Israelite practice and to the washing of feet by Jesus among his disciples, these modern LDS rites are performed only in temples set apart and dedicated for sacred purposes (D&C 124:37–38; *HC* 6:318–19).

Many symbolic meanings of washings and anointings are traceable in the scriptures. Ritual washings (Heb. 9:10; D&C 124:37) symbolize the cleansing of the soul from sins and iniquities. They signify the washing-away of the pollutions of the Lord's people (Isa. 4:4). Psalm 51:2 expresses the human longing and divine promise: "Wash me thoroughly from mine iniquity, and cleanse me from my sin" (cf. Ps. 73:13; Isa. 1:16).

The anointing of a person or object with sacred ointment represents sanctification (Lev. 8:10–12) and consecration (Ex. 28:41), so that both become "most holy" (Ex. 30:29) unto the Lord. In this manner, profane persons and things are sanctified in similitude of the Messiah (Hebrew, "anointed one"), who is Christ (Greek, "anointed one").

BIBLIOGRAPHY

McConkie, Joseph Fielding, and Donald W. Parry. *A Guide to Scriptural Symbols.* Salt Lake City, 1990.

DONALD W. PARRY

WITNESSES, LAW OF

The scriptural law of witnesses requires that in the mouth of two or three individuals shall every word be established (Deut. 19:15; 2 Cor. 13:1; 1 Tim. 5:19). This law applies in divine as well as human relations, for members of the Godhead bear witness of one another (John 5:31–37; 3 Ne. 11:32), and books of holy writ give multiple witness to the work of God in the earth (2 Ne. 29:8–13). The law of witnesses is prominent in the history and practice of The Church of Jesus Christ of Latter-day Saints.

A witness gives personal verification of, or attests to the reality of, an event. To "witness" in the scriptural sense is much the same as in the legal sense: to give personal testimony based on firsthand evidence or experience. To bear false witness is a very serious offense (Deut. 5:20; 19:16–21). When prophets have an experience with the Lord, often he commands them to "bear record" of him and of the truths that have been revealed (1 Ne. 10:10; 11:7; D&C 58:59; 112:4; 138:60). In legal affairs, testimony is usually related to what a person knows by the physical senses. In spiritual matters there is additional knowledge or information received through the Holy Spirit.

The Bible illustrates that God often works with mankind through two or more witnesses (Num. 35:30; Deut. 17:6; 19:15; Matt. 18:15–16). Likewise, latter-day scripture teaches the need for witnesses (D&C 6:28; 42:80–81; 128:3). One person's word alone, even though it may be true, may not be sufficient to establish and bind the hearer to the truth. Witnesses provide the means of establishing faith in the minds of people, for faith comes by hearing the word of God through the power of human testimony accompanied by the Holy Ghost (Rom. 10:17; *TPJS*, p. 148; *Lectures on Faith*, 2). In the BOOK OF MORMON, the prophet NEPHI₁ combined his brother Jacob's testimony with Isaiah's testimony to reinforce and verify his own witness of the divine sonship of the Redeemer (2 Ne. 11:2–3). Likewise, Alma₂ called upon the words of ZENOS, ZENOCK, and MOSES to corroborate his own testimony of the Son of God (Alma 33:2–23).

When the keys of the priesthood were restored to the Prophet Joseph Smith and often when visions were received, the Prophet was accompanied by a witness. This is the case with the restoration of the

Aaronic Priesthood, the Melchizedek Priesthood, the keys given in the Kirtland Temple (Ohio), and the vision of the degrees of glory (D&C 13; 76; 110). Subsequent to the translation of the Book of Mormon and prior to its publication, three men on one occasion, and eight men on a separate occasion, in addition to Joseph Smith, became witnesses of the Book of Mormon PLATES (*see* BOOK OF MORMON WITNESSES). The Prophet Joseph was likewise accompanied in his martyr's death by his brother Hyrum, a second martyr or witness, making their testimony valid forever (D&C 135:3; 136:39). The meaning of the Greek word *martyr* is "witness."

The scriptures also indicate other ways in which the law of witnesses applies:

THE DIVINITY OF JESUS CHRIST.   JOHN THE BAPTIST testified of the divinity of Jesus (John 1:15; 3:26; 5:32–39), the Father testified of Christ (Matt. 3:17; 17:5; John 8:18), and Christ himself bore record of his own divinity as the Son of God (Matt. 26:63–64; John 11:4; 13:31). The theme of John 5–8 illustrates the principle of witnesses. When Jesus spoke in his own behalf, some Jews, referring to the law of witnesses, said, "Thou bearest record of thyself; thy record is not true" (John 8:13). Jesus had earlier explained that both John the Baptist and the Father in Heaven had borne record of him (John 5:31–39; 8:18) and his testimony was therefore valid and binding. He declared that his works testified that he was the Son of God (John 5:31–38). Peter also bore testimony that Jesus was the Son of God, a fact he had learned by revelation (Matt. 16:16).

JESUS' RESURRECTION FROM THE DEAD.   Witnesses to the resurrection of Christ included groups of women, two disciples on the road to Emmaus, and the apostles (Matt. 28; Luke 24; Acts 4:33; 5:32). Paul records that there were in Galilee over 500 witnesses to Jesus' resurrected body (1 Cor. 15:6). The Book of Mormon reports that about 2,500 people in America witnessed the resurrected body of Jesus Christ by seeing and touching it, and did "bear record" of it (3 Ne. 11:14–16; 17:25).

AUTHENTICATION OF RITES AND CEREMONIES.   In the Church, witnesses are officially present for all baptisms and marriages. Witnesses also confirm proxy baptisms, endowments, marriages, and sealings in the temples on behalf of the dead (D&C 127:6).

Missionaries travel in pairs as witnesses for one another (Mark 6:7; Luke 10:1; D&C 42:6; 52:10; 61:35; 62:5).

ON JUDGMENT DAY.   In the final judgment that God will render to all mankind, the fact of the gospel having been taught on the earth by multiple witnesses will be important. Nephi₁ has written, "Wherefore, by the words of three, God hath said, I will establish my word. Nevertheless, God sendeth more witnesses, and he proveth all his words" (2 Ne. 11:3; cf. 27:14).

In a very fundamental way, the Bible and the Book of Mormon are witnesses to each other. Each record establishes the truth found in the other, and the DOCTRINE AND COVENANTS establishes the truth of them both (1 Ne. 13:20–40; 2 Ne. 3:12; 29:8–14; Morm. 7:8–9; D&C 17:6; 20:11–12; 42:12). The written testimony of two nations, the Jews and the Nephites, is a witness to the world that there is a God (2 Ne. 29:8).

BIBLIOGRAPHY

McConkie, Bruce R. *A New Witness for the Articles of Faith*, pp. 446–47. Salt Lake City, 1985.

Trites, Allison A. *The New Testament Concept of Witness*. Cambridge, 1977.

Van Orden, Bruce A. "The Law of Witnesses in 2 Nephi." In *The Book of Mormon: Second Nephi, The Doctrinal Structure*, ed. M. Nyman and C. Tate, pp. 307–21. Provo, Utah, 1989.

ROBERT L. MARROTT

WOMEN IN THE BOOK OF MORMON

Some general conclusions about Book of Mormon women can be drawn from the book's fragmentary material about marriage, family, and religious organization. Six women are mentioned by name: Sariah, Isabel, Abish, EVE, SARAH, and MARY. Since no women are mentioned as religious or military leaders and only a few as political leaders, it appears that males held virtually all leadership positions in this society. Also, since the Book of Mormon was written primarily to remind future readers of the goodness of God and to persuade them to believe in Christ, it contains no law books and little intellectual or social history discussing the meshing of familial and religious practices. It is reasonable to assume, however, that these people began with many customs similar to their ancestral Semitic cultures and that their practices changed somewhat over the years.

In Nephite society, marriage and childbearing were expected, carrying religious significance and responsibilities (1 Ne. 7:1; Mosiah 4:14–15; 4 Ne. 1:11). Marriages may have been arranged within ethnic groups (1 Ne. 16:7; Alma 17:24) and were restricted outside certain groups (Alma 3:8). Polygamy and concubinage were prohibited and scorned; monogamy was expected, except as the Lord might command otherwise to "raise up seed" unto himself (Jacob 2:27–30).

Husbands and wives were expected to be faithful and loyal to each other (Jacob 3:7). One case shows that a wife was valued, even if unable to conceive. The righteous Jaredite king Coriantum remained with his barren wife until her death at age 102. He then married a young maid and fathered sons and daughters (Ether 9:23–24). It was, likewise, a sign of great wickedness that the priests of king Noah deserted their families. While in hiding, they abducted twenty-four Lamanite women for wives. When Lamanite kinsmen discovered and sought to kill the priests several years later, however, these women faithfully pleaded for the lives of their husbands (Mosiah 23:33).

Men were expected to support their wives and children, as well as the widows and children of men killed in war (Mosiah 21:17). Men were to pray for their households (Alma 34:21), and many took up arms to defend their families.

Both parents were concerned about their offspring (1 Ne. 5:1–7; 8:37). LEHI blessed and counseled his granddaughters and grandsons (2 Ne. 4:3–9). Children were taught to honor their mother and father. HELAMAN₁ and his 2,000 young warriors credited their Ammonite mothers with instilling in them the faith that "if they did not doubt, God would deliver them" (Alma 56:47).

In religious life, women participated in assemblies at the temple (Jacob 2:7; Mosiah 2:5–8), in teaching their children about God (Alma 56:46–47), and in offering sacrifice (1 Ne. 5:9). Evidently they were not excluded from, or segregated during, worship (2 Ne. 26:28–33); nor is there any indication that they were considered ritually unclean during menstruation. The gospel taught by the NEPHITES and Christ in the Book of Mormon is addressed to all, regardless of gender, age, or descent (2 Ne. 26:33; Mosiah 27:25; Alma 11:44; 32:23; 3 Ne. 17:25). Baptism was offered to all men and women who believed (Mosiah 18:16; Moro. 9:10). Women demonstrated profound faith and were tested by great sacrifice. In Ammonihah, women were burned to death with their children for refusing to renounce their faith in Christ (Alma 14:7–11). Apparently the LIAHONA responded to the collective faith and diligence of the entire group, men and women (1 Ne. 16:28).

During the years in the wilderness, the Lehite women toiled and were strong, but little is known about their activities, other than pregnancy and childbirth. Spinning is the only work specifically attributed to women (Mosiah 10:5; Hel. 6:13). Women's dancing is associated with leisure and sometimes with wickedness (1 Ne. 18:9; Mosiah 20:1; Ether 8:10–11). Harlots provided immoral sexual activity in return for sustenance (Mosiah 11:14).

Politically, women had rights of succession to the Lamanite throne, for when Amalickiah murdered a Lamanite king, rule passed to the queen, whom Amalickiah then married to gain the throne (Alma 47:32–35). In extreme crises women took up arms in war alongside their men (Alma 54:12; 55:17; Ether 15:15).

Assignment of tasks in the family or in the whole economy—trade, planting and harvesting crops, and tending animals—is not apparent. Cycles of colonization, agriculture, urbanization, war, destruction, and renewal, as well as differing belief systems, certainly affected family and work patterns.

The Book of Mormon women Sariah, Abish, and Isabel can be viewed not only as historical figures but also as archetypal figures of, respectively, the righteous mother, the godly servant, and the attractive but sexually impure outsider.

Sariah was the faithful mother of the Nephite and Lamanite nations. She left a comfortable home near Jerusalem with Lehi and their family to suffer the rigors of desert and ocean travel, bearing two more sons, JACOB and JOSEPH, late in life while in the wilderness (1 Ne. 18:7, 17–19). She complained against Lehi when she thought their sons were dead, but affirmed his calling and the power of God when they returned unharmed (1 Ne. 5:2–8). With Lehi she gave sacrifice in thanksgiving. She was the mother of six sons and at least two daughters (2 Ne. 5:6).

Abish, a Lamanite convert of surpassing faith, servant to the queen of king Lamoni, recognized that the power of God had overcome

the king, queen, and Ammon when they fell to the ground uncon-
scious; she gathered people to witness the event and then raised the
queen with her touch when the confusion of the crowd led to contention. Many believed the testimonies of the revived queen, who then
raised the king, who also testified of Jesus (Alma 19:16–36).

Isabel, according to ALMA$_2$ (Alma 39:3–4), was a harlot who stole
the hearts of many, including that of Alma's son Corianton, who for a
time forsook the ministry to go after her (Alma 39:3).

The other three named women are biblical figures: Eve (e.g., 2 Ne.
2:15–20; cf. several references to "our first parents," e.g., 2 Ne. 9:9);
Sarah (2 Ne. 8:2); and Mary, the mother of Jesus (e.g., Mosiah 3:8).
Eve is mentioned in the context of an explication of the doctrine of the
fall of Adam as the precursor of the salvation of mankind. Sarah is recognized as the faithful mother of nations. Mary is called "a virgin, most
beautiful and fair above all other virgins" (1 Ne. 11:15).

Other women are known in the Book of Mormon only by their
individual deeds: the wife of NEPHI$_1$, a daughter of Ishmael, tried to
soften wicked hearts with her tears (1 Ne. 7:19; 18:19); Ishmael's
wife and three of their daughters supported Nephi (1 Ne. 7:6); a
maidservant fled from Morianton's camp, after being severely beaten
by him, to warn MORONI$_1$ of the plans of her rebel master (Alma
50:30–31); a daughter of Jared originated a plot to regain the kingdom for her father through enticement, violence, and deceit (Ether
8–9); two Lamanite queens were converted by the sons of Mosiah$_2$
(Alma 19:29–30; 22:19–24). Perhaps, as in some Semitic cultures
today, the formal or more polite way of referring to a woman was not
by her given name, but by describing her position in the family, such
as "the daughter of Jared." Others so designated include Ishmael's
wife, Ishmael's daughters, Ishmael's eldest daughter and wife of
Zoram, Lehi's daughters and Nephi's sisters, Lamoni's daughter; and
Coriantumr's unrepentant daughters.

The behavior and treatment of women were seen as an index of
social and spiritual health. Many references to women concern their
suffering during war, captivity, and hardship. Nephi and his brothers
measure the difficulty of their travels in terms of the suffering of their
wives, though Nephi emphasizes that the women were made strong
like the men, while his brothers describe their wives' sufferings as
being worse than death (1 Ne. 17:1, 20). Jacob sharply contrasts male

infidelity with the tenderness of the women (Jacob 2–3); immorality is described as precipitating the collapse of both family and society. The inhumanity and depravity of dying civilizations are also described in terms of the suffering of women: Lamanites fed to women and children the flesh of their dead husbands and fathers (Moro. 9:8); Nephite women were sacrificed to idols (Morm. 4:15, 21); Nephites raped captured Lamanite women, tortured them to death, and then ate their flesh as a token of their bravery (Moro. 9:9–10).

Much of the imagery involving women in the Book of Mormon parallels that in the Bible. For example, Christ compares his gathering of the repentant to a mother hen gathering her chicks under her wing. As in Proverbs 3:13–20, wisdom is female (Mosiah 8:20), as is mercy (Alma 42:24). Sometimes female imagery is applied to the Lord, as when the mother nursing her child is the image used of the Lord comforting and remembering his covenant children (1 Ne. 21:15).

In a sense, the woman is the image of God's people. The biblical imagery of God as husband and his people as wife is continued in the Book of Mormon, mostly from the writings of Isaiah. Decadent Israel is described as devoid of honorable men, in that they valued women as decorative sex objects (2 Ne. 13:16–26; Isa. 3:16–26). When God's people become unfaithful to him, they are called "the whore of all the earth" (2 Ne. 10:16). When he calls his people to repentance, the Lord asks rhetorically, "Have I put thee away? . . . Where is the bill of your mother's divorcement?" (2 Ne. 7:1; Isa. 50:1). The images of a mother too weak to nurse her child and a pregnant woman so near term she is unable to flee destruction are used to motivate the Nephites to repent (Hel. 15:1–2); the woman whose children are lost is the image of desolation (1 Ne. 21:20–21). Those who accept "marriage" with the Lord are to experience joy as abundant as that of a barren woman who becomes a mother of many children, and the Lord consoles his people by saying, "For thy maker, thy husband, the Lord of Hosts is his name; . . . For a small moment have I forsaken thee, but with great mercies will I gather thee" (3 Ne. 22:1, 5–8; Isa. 54:1, 5–8).

BIBLIOGRAPHY

Spencer, Majorie Meads. "My Book of Mormon Sisters." *Ensign* 7 (Sept. 1977):66–71.

DONNA LEE BOWEN
CAMILLE S. WILLIAMS

WRATH OF GOD

The "wrath of God" is a term usually indicating his disapproval of the deeds of the wicked and justifying the inevitable punishments that will befall them if they do not repent. Latter-day Saints believe that his response is a natural application of the law of justice (Mosiah 3:26), which requires that punishments be exacted when God's laws have been violated or the blood of innocent Saints has been shed (Morm. 8:21–41; D&C 77:8). The scriptures state that God sends cursings, judgments, and destruction upon the unbelieving and the rebellious, including all who reject the Savior or his prophets and are not willing to confess his hand in all things (D&C 1:6–13; 59:21; 63:6; 88:85; 104:8; 124:48, 52; Moses 7:1). The scriptures assert that those who attempt to destroy the righteous can expect to give an account to an offended God (1 Ne. 22:16). The Lord has sometimes chastened his disobedient children through war, plague, famine, and earthquake (1 Ne. 14:15–16; D&C 63:33; 87:1–6; 112:24–26). Not all natural calamities, however, are the direct result of the wrath of God, although the scriptures clearly indicate that God has used these for his purposes.

God's wrath may come upon individuals or nations or civilizations when they have "ripened in iniquity" (Gen. 15:16; Deut. 9:4–5; 1 Ne. 17:35; Ether 2:9). His wrath manifests itself most completely when a majority of the people desire that which is contrary to the laws of God and have already chosen iniquity for themselves (Mosiah 29:25–27). The people of NOAH's day (Gen. 6–8), the people of Ammonihah (Alma 16:9–11), the JAREDITES (Ether 14–15), the NEPHITES (3 Ne. 8–9; Morm. 6), and, to a small degree, the Latter-day Saints in Missouri (D&C 105:2–9; 124:48) all experienced God's wrath in their time (see *MD*, p. 771).

The severest form of punishment will be dealt to the SONS OF PERDITION, who are known as "vessels of wrath" (D&C 76:33). These will suffer God's rejection and exclusion throughout eternity (D&C 76:31–37), for they have committed an UNPARDONABLE SIN against the light and knowledge obtained through the Holy Ghost.

While the Lord may chasten his people in mortality, chastisement will be tempered with his mercy and compassion as his children heed and obey him (D&C 101:2–9; 3 Ne. 22:8–10). Those who escape the wrath of God will include all persons who repent and keep the commandments, and prepare themselves for the hour of judgment that is to come, gathering "together upon the land of Zion, and upon her stakes" as a place of refuge (D&C 115:6; cf. Alma 12:33–37; 13:30; D&C 88:76–88; 98:22). Even God's wrath is intended to be beneficent, for whom he loves, he chastens (D&C 95:1; cf. Heb. 12:6–11).

BIBLIOGRAPHY

McConkie, Bruce R. *The Millennial Messiah,* pp. 500–505. Salt Lake City, 1982.

DONALD B. GILCHRIST

Z

ZENOCK

Zenock was a preexilic Israelite prophet whose words were found on the PLATES of brass, a record carried from Jerusalem to the new promised land in the Western Hemisphere by the Book of Mormon prophet LEHI c. 600 B.C. Zenock is not known from the Hebrew Bible or other sources and is noted in only five passages in the Book of Mormon. It is possible that he was of the lineage of JOSEPH OF EGYPT and an ancestor of the NEPHITES (3 Ne. 10:16).

Each reference to Zenock refers to his teaching of either the coming or redemptive mission of Jesus Christ. NEPHI₁, son of Lehi, in teaching from the words of previous prophets, stated that the God of Abraham, Isaac, and Jacob (Jesus Christ) would be "lifted up, according to the words of Zenock" (1 Ne. 19:10), referring to his crucifixion. Alma 33:16 contains the only direct quotation of Zenock's words, citing him as one of many Israelite prophets who foretold the mission of the Son of God (Alma 33:14–17; cf. 34:7) and quoting him on the mercies that God grants because of his Son. ALMA₂ noted, however, that because the people "would not understand" Zenock's words, they "stoned him to death" (Alma 33:17). NEPHI₂ cited Zenock and others who testified of the coming of the Son of God (Hel. 8:20). In the last reference to his work, MORMON wrote that ZENOS and Zenock foretold the destruction that preceded the coming of Christ to the remnant of their posterity (3 Ne. 10:16).

KENT P. JACKSON

ZENOS

Zenos is one of four Israelite prophets of Old Testament times cited in the BOOK OF MORMON whose writings appeared on the PLATES of brass but who are not mentioned in the Old Testament (*see also* ZENOCK; NEUM; and EZIAS). Zenos is quoted or mentioned by NEPHI₁ (1 Ne. 19:10–17), JACOB (Jacob 5:1–77; 6:1), ALMA₂ (Alma 33:3–11, 13, 15), AMULEK (Alma 34:7), NEPHI₂ (Hel. 8:19–20), and MORMON (3 Ne. 10:14–17).

Although specific dates and details of Zenos' life and ministry are not known, the Book of Mormon provides considerable information about him from his teachings and related facts. Evidently he lived sometime between 1600 and 600 B.C. because he was apparently a descendant of JOSEPH OF EGYPT and his writings were on the plates of brass taken from JERUSALEM to the Americas by Nephi₁ about 600 B.C. He may also have been a progenitor of the Book of Mormon prophet LEHI (cf. 3 Ne. 10:16). Zenos spent time "in the wilderness" (Alma 33:4), but also preached "in the midst" of the "congregations" of God (Alma 33:9). Some of his enemies became reconciled to him through the power of God, but others were visited "with speedy destruction" (Alma 33:4, 10). Finally, he was slain because of his bold testimony of the coming of the "Son of God" (Hel. 8:13–19).

A major theme in the teachings of Zenos was the destiny of the house of Israel. His allegory or parable comparing the house of Israel to a tame olive tree and the Gentiles to a wild olive tree constitutes the longest single chapter in the Book of Mormon, Jacob chapter 5 (*see* BOOK OF MORMON: BOOK OF JACOB). The allegory refers to major events in the scattering and gathering of the house of Israel (*see* ALLEGORY OF ZENOS; ISRAEL: GATHERING OF ISRAEL; ISRAEL: SCATTERING OF ISRAEL).

The second-longest quotation from Zenos in the Book of Mormon is his hymn of thanksgiving and praise recorded in Alma 33:3–11, which emphasizes prayer, worship, and the mercies of God. A careful comparison of the style and contents of this hymn with *Hymn* H (or 8) and *Hymn* J (or 10) of the *Thanksgiving Hymns* of the Dead Sea Scrolls, noting certain striking similarities, suggests that the three may have been written by the same person. Further, the life situations of the author (or authors) are very similar (*CWHN* 7:276–83). Some LDS scholars anticipate that other evidences of Zenos' writings may appear as additional ancient manuscripts come to light.

Book of Mormon prophets frequently quoted Zenos because of his plain and powerful testimony of the future life, mission, atonement, death, and resurrection of the Son of God. Alma$_2$ recorded part of Zenos' prayer to God, recounting that "it is because of thy Son that thou hast been thus merciful unto me, therefore I will cry unto thee in all mine afflictions, for in thee is my joy; for thou hast turned thy judgments away from me, because of thy Son" (Alma 33:11). Nephi$_1$ recalled Zenos' knowledge that after the Son of God was crucified, he would "be buried in a sepulchre" for three days, and a sign of darkness should be "given of his death unto those who should inhabit the isles of the sea, more especially given unto those who are of the house of Israel" (1 Ne. 19:10). Amulek quoted Zenos' words to show "that redemption cometh through the Son of God" (Alma 34:7). Mormon included Zenos as one of the prophets who spoke of events associated with "the coming of Christ" (3 Ne. 10:15), as did Nephi$_2$, who stated, "Yea, behold, the prophet Zenos did testify boldly; for the which he was slain" (Hel. 8:19).

Elder Bruce R. McConkie of the Quorum of the Twelve Apostles summarized some of the teachings of Zenos and evaluated his contributions as follows:

> It was Zenos who wrote of the visit of the Lord God to Israel after his resurrection; of the joy and salvation that would come to the righteous among them; of the desolations and destructions that awaited the wicked among them; of the fires, and tempests, and earthquakes that would occur in the Americas; of the scourging and crucifying of the God of Israel by those in Jerusalem; of the scattering of the Jews among all nations; and of their gathering again in the last days "from the four quarters of the earth" (1 Ne. 19:11–17). I do not think I overstate the matter when I say that next to Isaiah himself—who is the prototype, pattern,

and model for all the prophets—there was not a greater prophet in all Israel than Zenos [p. 17].

BIBLIOGRAPHY

McConkie, Bruce R. "The Doctrinal Restoration." In *The Joseph Smith Translation, The Restoration of Plain and Precious Things*, ed. M. Nyman and R. Millet. Provo, Utah, 1985.

Nibley, Hugh. "Prophets in the Wilderness." *CWHN* 7:264–90.

DANIEL H. LUDLOW

ZION

Latter-day Saints use the name Zion to signify a group of God's followers or a place where such a group lives. Latter-day scriptures define Zion as the "pure in heart" (D&C 97:21). Other uses of the name in scripture reflect this one. For example, Zion refers to the place or land appointed by the Lord for the gathering of those who accept his gospel (D&C 101:16–22; 3 Ne. 20–22). The purpose of this gathering is to raise up a committed society of "pure people" who will "serve [God] in righteousness" (D&C 100:13, 16). Hence, the lands of Zion are places where the pure in heart live together in righteousness. Geographical Church units are called "stakes . . . of Zion" (D&C 101:21–22). The Church and its stakes are called Zion because they are for gathering and purifying a people of God (D&C 43:8–11; Eph. 4:11–13). Scripture also refers to Zion as a "City of Holiness" (Moses 7:19), because the "sanctified" or "pure" live there (Moro. 10:31–33; Alma 13:11–12), and a "city of refuge" where the Lord protects them from the peril of the world (D&C 45:66–67).

"Pure in heart" may be explained in terms of the gospel of Jesus Christ. Jesus said that to be saved a person must believe in him, repent of sins, and be born of water and of the Spirit (John 3:5, 16; 3 Ne. 27:20). Scripture describes the rebirth to which Jesus refers as a "mighty change in your hearts" or being "born of God" (Alma 5:13, 14). It means that the person puts off the "natural man" and puts on a new nature that has "no more disposition to do evil, but to do good continually" (Mosiah 5:2; 3:19). A person pure of heart is one who has died to evil and awakened to good. Thus "pure people," being alive to good, dwell together in righteousness and are called Zion

(Moses 7:18). Zion, then, is the way of life of a people who live the gospel of Jesus Christ.

Since love comprehends all righteousness (Matt. 22:36–40), the people of Zion live together in love as equals (D&C 38:24–27). They have "all things common" (4 Ne. 1:3). They labor together as equals, each contributing to the good of all and to the work of salvation according to their individual talents (D&C 82:3; Alma 1:26). As equals, all receive the things that are necessary for survival and well-being, according to their circumstances, wants, and needs (D&C 51:3, 9). Consequently, among a people of Zion there are no rich or poor (4 Ne. 1:3). It is written of the ancient people of Enoch that "the Lord called his people Zion, because they were of one heart and one mind, and dwelt in righteousness; and there was no poor among them" (Moses 7:18).

People of Zion enjoy fulness of life, or happiness, in the highest degree possible in this world and, if they remain faithful, in the world to come (4 Ne. 1:3, 16; Mosiah 16:11). According to LDS belief, persons may attain different degrees of "fulness" of life, ranging from "celestial" to "telestial," depending on the level of "law" they "abide" (D&C 88:22–35; 76). By living the principles of Zion, the people live together according to the celestial law that governs the highest order of heaven and partake of the life it promises (D&C 105:4–5). Fulness of life in the celestial degree consists in being filled with God's love, or being alive to all that is good—a state of happiness that reaches full fruition only in eternity (Eph. 3:17–19; Moro. 7:16–25, 44–48). The capacity of people to live celestial law and enjoy life in its fulness results from the purifying rebirth already mentioned.

The prophets always labor to prepare people to become a people of Zion. Sometimes people embrace Zion; most often they do not. For example, the followers of Enoch (the son of Jared and father of Methuselah; Gen. 5:18–24; Luke 3:37) built Zion, and because of their righteousness, "God received [them] up into his own bosom" (Moses 7:69; Heb. 11:5). Later, Noah declared the word of life unto "the children of men, even as it was given unto Enoch" (Moses 8:19). Still later, Moses "sought diligently" that his people might be purified and enter the rest of God, as did Enoch's people (D&C 84:23–45). But the people of Noah and, to a lesser degree, the people of Moses "hardened their hearts" (D&C 84:24) and refused to accept the ways of Zion. On the other hand, "the people in the days of Melchizedek" were "made pure and entered into the rest of the Lord their God" (Alma 13:10–14). Before 125 B.C. in ancient America, King BENJAMIN's people and the Nephites who followed the prophet ALMA₁ underwent that mighty change of heart that makes a people pure (Mosiah 2–5; Alma 5:3–14). When Jesus Christ visited his "other sheep" in ancient America after his crucifixion (John 10:16; 3 Ne. 15:21), he established Zion among them. It is said of them that "there was no contention in the land, because of the love of God which did dwell in the hearts of the people. . . . Surely there could not be a happier people among all the people who had been created by the hand of God" (4 Ne. 1:3, 15–16). The Bible also describes early Christians who experienced purification and lived the order of Zion (Acts 2:44; 4:32; 15:9).

In the RESTORATION, Joseph Smith taught his people that they can, and must, become people of Zion. That vision inspires the labors and programs of the Church to this day. In establishing Zion, Latter-day Saints believe they may be a light to humankind (D&C 115:4–6) and usher in the millennial reign of Christ (Moses 7:60–65; D&C 43:29–30). During the Millennium, Zion will have two great centers—JERUSALEM of old and a NEW JERUSALEM in America—from which "the law" and the "word of the Lord" will go forth to the world (Isa. 2:3; Ether 13:2–11).

BIBLIOGRAPHY

Zion as explained here is much more detailed than, but bears certain social similarities to, the idea of Zion found in the work of Martin Buber in *On Zion: The History of an Idea* (New York, 1973). An LDS work that applies the idea of Zion to contemporary life is Hugh W. Nibley's *Approaching Zion* (*CWHN* 9).

A. D. SORENSEN

ZIONISM

Zion (Hebrew, early the Jerusalem mountain on which the City of David was built) is employed in LDS scripture both geographically and spiritually: the land of Zion and "the pure in heart" (D&C 84:99; 97:21; 100:16; cf. Moses 7:18–21). The declaration that "we believe in the literal gathering of Israel and the restoration of the ten tribes" refers to a new Zion in America as well as a renewed Jerusalem in the Old World. Latter-day scripture declares that Jerusalem will become the spiritual-temporal capital of the whole Eastern Hemisphere, "One Great Centre, and one mighty Sovereign" (*MFP* 1:259), while Zion will be the place of refuge and divine direction in the Western Hemisphere.

In 1831, less than two years after the organization of the Church, Joseph Smith received a revelation that included the imperative "Let them who be of Judah flee unto Jerusalem, unto the mountains of the Lord's house" (D&C 133:13). In 1833 he wrote that the tribe of Judah would return and obtain deliverance at Jerusalem, citing Joel, Isaiah, Jeremiah, Psalms, and Ezekiel (cf. *TPJS*, p. 17).

In March 1836, the dedicatory prayer given by Joseph Smith at the Kirtland Temple—since canonized and used as a pattern in later LDS temple dedications—pleaded that "Jerusalem, from this hour, may begin to be redeemed; and the yoke of bondage may begin to be broken off from the house of David" (D&C 109:62–63). In 1840–1841, Orson Hyde, an apostle, was commissioned by the Prophet to go to Jerusalem and dedicate the land. His prayer petitioned for the gathering home of the exiles, the fruitfulness of the earth, the establishing of an independent government, the rebuilding of Jerusalem, and "rearing a Temple in honor of thy name" (Heschel, p. 18). Two years later, Joseph Smith prophesied that the gathering and rebuilding would occur "before the Son of Man will make his appearance" (*TPJS*, p. 286). These prayers and prophecies have been frequently reiterated by other apostolic authorities, both on the Mount of Olives and on Mount Carmel in the Holy Land and in official convocations of the Saints throughout the world.

Jewish tradition warns that commitment to "sacred soil" without faith in the living God is a form of idolatry. Early in the twentieth century the Zionist movement advocated a compromise between secular Zionists, who envisioned a state without traditional Judaism, and religious Zionists, who argued that the state must be grounded in traditional Judaism. History in the modern political state of Israel has thus far implemented that compromise.

Spiritual Zionism among Latter-day Saints is advocated in the setting of concern for all of the children of God. It does not pronounce on specific geopolitical struggles or endorse speculations on the exact "when" and "how" of the fulfillment of ancient and modern prophecy. Many LDS leaders see events of the past 160 years as a preface. They continue to plead for peace and for coexistence with all the peoples who lay claim to old Jerusalem and the Holy Land: Jewish, Christian, Islamic, and others.

The term Zion, pertaining to a spiritually significant New Jerusalem in America, is one of the central themes of the Doctrine and Covenants (*see* NEW JERUSALEM).

BIBLIOGRAPHY
Davis, Moshe, ed. *With Eyes Toward Zion*, Vol. 2. New York, 1986.
Heschel, Abraham J. *Israel, an Echo of Eternity*. New York, 1968.
Madsen, Truman G. *The Mormon Attitude Toward Zionism*, ed. Yaakov Goldstein. Haifa, 1980.

TRUMAN G. MADSEN

ZORAM

Three men named Zoram are noted in the Book of Mormon. The first Zoram was the servant of Laban, a Jewish commander in Jerusalem about 600 B.C. (1 Ne. 3:31). This Zoram gave the disguised NEPHI₁ the plates of brass thinking he was Laban. Offered freedom if he would become part of Nephi's group in the wilderness, Zoram accepted Nephi's offer and made an oath to stay with them from that time on (1 Ne. 4:20–38). He married one of the daughters of Ishmael (1 Ne. 16:7), was a true friend to Nephi, was blessed by Nephi's father, Lehi, (2 Ne. 1:30–32), and went with Nephi when the Nephite colony separated after Lehi's death (2 Ne. 5:5–6). His descendants were called Zoramites.

A second Zoram was the chief captain over the armies of the Nephites in 81 B.C. He consulted with Alma₂, the high priest over the church, regarding his military actions (Alma 16:5–8).

The third Zoram was the leader of a group called Zoramites who separated themselves from the Nephites about 24 B.C. and apostatized from the established church. These Zoramites killed Korihor, the antichrist (Alma 30:59). Alma₂ led a missionary contingent among them to try to reclaim them from their apostasy and to prevent them from entering into an alliance with the Lamanites. While several of their poor were reconverted, the majority continued in their wicked ways (Alma 31:35), eventually joining the Lamanites and becoming antagonists to the Nephites. Some Zoramites served as Lamanite military commanders and even as kings (Alma 43:4–44; 48:5; 3 Ne. 1:29).

BIBLIOGRAPHY
Nibley, Hugh. *CWHN* 6:127–30; 8:543–44.

MONTE S. NYMAN

APPENDIX
JOSEPH SMITH TRANSLATION OF THE BIBLE
(SELECTIONS)

The Joseph Smith Translation of the Bible (JST) contains several thousand verses that are different from the King James Version. As space limitations prevent a complete presentation in this Appendix, the texts below were selected for their doctrinal value; variations from the King James Version are shown in italics. Extracts of the Joseph Smith Translation published in the PEARL OF GREAT PRICE (Book of Moses and Joseph Smith—Matthew) are readily available; therefore, the texts of these extracts are not included here, although reference is made to them. Also, excerpts that are used in the *Encyclopedia* article JOSEPH SMITH TRANSLATION OF THE BIBLE are not repeated here. The excerpts included here are used by permission of the Reorganized Church of Jesus Christ of Latter Day Saints.

VISIONS OF MOSES 1:1–42
(No equivalent in KJV.) The full text can be found in Moses chapter 1 of the Pearl of Great Price.

GENESIS 1:1–8:18 (KJV 1:1–6:13)
This material is not included here because it is reproduced in Moses chapters 2–8 of the Pearl of Great Price. It is greatly expanded over the King James text.

GENESIS 9:21–25
21 And the bow shall be in the cloud; and I will look upon it, that I may remember the everlasting covenant, *which I made unto thy father Enoch; that, when men should keep all my commandments, Zion should again come on the earth, the city of Enoch which I have caught up unto myself.*
22 *And this is mine everlasting covenant, that when thy posterity shall*

embrace the truth, and look upward, then shall Zion look downward, and all the heavens shall shake with gladness, and the earth shall tremble with joy;

23 *And the general assembly of the church of the first-born shall come down out of heaven, and possess the earth, and shall have place until the end come. And this is mine everlasting covenant, which I made with thy father Enoch.*

24 *And the bow shall be in the cloud, and I will establish my covenant unto thee, which I have made* between *me* and *thee,* for every living creature of all flesh that *shall be* upon the earth.

25 And God said unto Noah, This is the token of the covenant which I have established between me and *thee; for* all flesh that *shall be* upon the earth.

GENESIS 14:17–18 (KJV 14:18–19)

17 And Melchizedek, king of Salem, brought forth bread and wine; and he *break bread and blest it; and he blest the wine, he being* the priest of the most high God,

18 *And he gave to Abram,* and he blessed him, and said, Blessed Abram, *thou art a man* of the most high God, possessor of heaven and *of* earth.

GENESIS 14:25–40

25 *And Melchizedek lifted up his voice and blessed Abram.*

26 *Now Melchizedek was a man of faith, who wrought righteousness; and when a child he feared God, and stopped the mouths of lions, and quenched the violence of fire.*

27 *And thus, having been approved of God, he was ordained an high priest after the order of the covenant which God made with Enoch,*

28 *It being after the order of the Son of God; which order came, not by man, nor the will of man; neither by father nor mother; neither by beginning of days nor end of years; but of God;*

29 *And it was delivered unto men by the calling of his own voice, according to his own will, unto as many as believed on his name.*

30 *For God having sworn unto Enoch and unto his seed with an oath by himself; that every one being ordained after this order and calling should have power, by faith, to break mountains, to divide the seas, to dry up waters, to turn them out of their course;*

31 *To put at defiance the armies of nations, to divide the earth, to*

break every band, to stand in the presence of God; to do all things according to his will, according to his command, subdue principalities and powers; and this by the will of the Son of God which was from before the foundation of the world.

32 *And men having this faith, coming up unto this order of God, were translated and taken up into heaven.*

33 *And now, Melchizedek was a priest of this order; therefore he obtained peace in Salem, and was called the Prince of peace.*

34 *And his people wrought righteousness, and obtained heaven, and sought for the city of Enoch which God had before taken, separating it from the earth, having reserved it unto the latter days, or the end of the world;*

35 *And hath said, and sworn with an oath, that the heavens and the earth should come together; and the sons of God should be tried so as by fire.*

36 *And this Melchizedek, having thus established righteousness, was called the king of heaven by his people, or, in other words, the King of peace.*

37 *And he lifted up his voice, and he blessed Abram, being the high priest, and the keeper of the storehouse of God;*

38 *Him whom God had appointed to receive tithes for the poor.*

39 *Wherefore, Abram paid unto him tithes of all that he had, of all the riches which he possessed, which God had given him more than that which he had need.*

40 *And it came to pass, that God blessed Abram, and gave unto him riches, and honor, and lands for an everlasting possession; according to the covenant which he had made, and according to the blessing wherewith Melchizedek had blessed him.*

GENESIS 15:9–12

9 *And Abram said, Lord God, how wilt thou give me this land for an everlasting inheritance?*

10 *And the Lord said, Though thou wast dead, yet am I not able to give it thee?*

11 *And if thou shalt die, yet thou shalt possess it, for the day cometh, that the Son of Man shall live; but how can he live if he be not dead? he must first be quickened.*

12 *And it came to pass, that Abram looked forth and saw the days of the Son of Man, and was glad, and his soul found rest,* and he

believed in the Lord; and *the Lord* counted it unto him for righteousness.

GENESIS 17:3–7

3 And *it came to pass, that* Abram fell on his face, *and called upon the name of the Lord.*

4 And God talked with him, saying, *My people have gone astray from my precepts, and have not kept mine ordinances, which I gave unto their fathers;*

5 *And they have not observed mine anointing, and the burial, or baptism wherewith I commanded them;*

6 *But have turned from the commandment and taken unto themselves the washing of children, and the blood of sprinkling;*

7 *And have said that the blood of the righteous Abel was shed for sins; and have not known wherein they are accountable before me.*

GENESIS 17:11–12

11 And I will establish *a covenant of circumcision with thee, and it shall be* my covenant between me and thee, and thy seed after thee, in their generations; *that thou mayest know for ever that children are not accountable before me until they are eight years old.*

12 *And thou shalt observe to keep all my covenants wherein I covenanted with thy fathers; and thou shalt keep the commandments which I have given thee with mine own mouth, and I will be a God unto thee and thy seed after thee.*

GENESIS 19:9–15

9 *And they said unto him, Stand back. And they were angry with him.*

10 *And they said among themselves, This one man came in to sojourn among us, and he will needs now make himself to be a judge; now we will deal worse with him than with them.*

11 *Wherefore they said unto the man, We will have the men, and thy daughters also; and we will do with them as seemeth us good.*

12 *Now this was after the wickedness of Sodom.*

13 And Lot said, Behold now, I have two daughters which have not known man; let me, I pray you, *plead with my brethren that I may not* bring them out unto you; and ye shall *not* do unto them as seemeth good in your eyes;

14 *For God will not justify his servant in this thing; wherefore, let me plead with my brethren, this once only, that* unto these men ye do

nothing, *that they may have peace in my house;* for therefore came they under the shadow of my roof.

15 *And they were angry with Lot* and came near to break the door, but the *angels of God, which were holy men,* put forth their hand and pulled Lot into the house unto them, and shut the door.

GENESIS 21:5 (KJV 21:6)

5 And Sarah said, God has made me to *rejoice; and also* all that *know me* will *rejoice* with me.

GENESIS 48:5–11

5 And now, of thy two sons, Ephraim and Manasseh, which were born unto thee in the land of Egypt, before I came unto thee into Egypt; *behold, they* are mine, *and the God of my fathers shall bless them; even* as Reuben and Simeon they *shall be blessed, for they are* mine; *wherefore they shall be called after my name. (Therefore they were called Israel.)*

6 And thy issue which thou begettest after them, shall be thine, and shall be called after the name of their brethren in their inheritance, *in the tribes; therefore they were called the tribes of Manasseh and of Ephraim.*

7 *And Jacob said unto Joseph when the God of my fathers appeared unto me in Luz, in the land of Canaan; he sware unto me that he would give unto me, and unto my seed, the land for an everlasting possession.*

8 *Therefore, O my son, he hath blessed me in raising thee up to be a servant unto me, in saving my house from death;*

9 *In delivering my people, thy brethren, from famine which was sore in the land; wherefore the God of thy fathers shall bless thee, and the fruit of thy loins, that they shall be blessed above thy brethren, and above thy father's house;*

10 *For thou hast prevailed, and thy father's house hath bowed down unto thee, even as it was shown unto thee, before thou wast sold into Egypt by the hands of thy brethren; wherefore thy brethren shall bow down unto thee, from generation to generation, unto the fruit of thy loins for ever;*

11 *For thou shalt be a light unto my people, to deliver them in the days of their captivity, from bondage; and to bring salvation unto them, when they are altogether bowed down under sin.*

GENESIS 50:24–38

24 And Joseph said unto his brethren, I die, *and go unto my fathers; and I go down to my grave with joy. The God of my father Jacob be with you, to deliver you out of affliction in the days of your bondage; for the Lord hath visited me, and I have obtained a promise of the Lord, that out of the fruit of my loins, the Lord God will raise up a righteous branch out of my loins; and unto thee, whom my father Jacob hath named Israel, a prophet; (not the Messiah who is called Shilo;) and this prophet shall deliver my people out of Egypt in the days of thy bondage.*

25 *And it shall come to pass that they shall be scattered again; and a branch shall be broken off, and shall be carried into a far country; nevertheless they shall be remembered in the covenants of the Lord, when the Messiah cometh; for he shall be made manifest unto them in the latter days, in the Spirit of power; and shall bring them out of darkness into light; out of hidden darkness, and out of captivity unto freedom.*

26 *A seer shall the Lord my God raise up, who shall be a choice seer unto the fruit of my loins.*

27 *Thus saith the Lord God of my fathers unto me, A choice seer will I raise up out of the fruit of thy loins, and he shall be esteemed highly among the fruit of thy loins; and unto him will I give commandment that he shall do a work for the fruit of thy loins, his brethren.*

28 *And he shall bring them to the knowledge of the covenants which I have made with thy fathers; and he shall do whatsoever work I shall command him.*

29 *And I will make him great in mine eyes, for he shall do my work; and he shall be great like unto him whom I have said I would raise up unto you, to deliver my people, O house of Israel, out of the land of Egypt; for a seer will I raise up to deliver my people out of the land of Egypt; and he shall be called Moses. And by this name he shall know that he is of thy house; for he shall be nursed by the king's daughter, and shall be called her son.*

30 *And again, a seer will I raise up out of the fruit of thy loins, and unto him will I give power to bring forth my word unto the seed of thy loins; and not to the bringing forth of my word only, saith the Lord, but to the convincing them of my word, which shall have already gone forth among them in the last days;*

31 *Wherefore the fruit of thy loins shall write, and the fruit of the loins*

*of Judah shall write; and that which shall be written by the fruit of thy
loins, and also that which shall be written by the fruit of the loins of
Judah, shall grow together unto the confounding of false doctrines, and
laying down of contentions, and establishing peace among the fruit of
thy loins, and bringing them to a knowledge of their fathers in the latter
days; and also to the knowledge of my covenants, saith the Lord.*

32 *And out of weakness shall he be made strong, in that day when my
work shall go forth among all my people, which shall restore them,
who are of the house of Israel, in the last days.*

33 *And that seer will I bless, and they that seek to destroy him shall be
confounded; for this promise I give unto you; for I will remember you
from generation to generation; and his name shall be called Joseph,
and it shall be after the name of his father; and he shall be like unto
you; for the thing which the Lord shall bring forth by his hand shall
bring my people unto salvation.*

34 *And the Lord sware unto Joseph that he would preserve his seed
forever, saying, I will raise up Moses, and a rod shall be in his hand,
and he shall gather together my people, and he shall lead them as a
flock, and he shall smite the waters of the Red Sea with his rod.*

35 *And he shall have judgment, and shall write the word of the Lord.
And he shall not speak many words, for I will write unto him my law
by the finger of mine own hand. And I will make a spokesman for him,
and his name shall be called Aaron.*

36 *And it shall be done unto thee in the last days also, even as I have
sworn. Therefore,* Joseph said unto his brethren, God will surely visit
you, and bring you out of this land, unto the land which he sware
unto Abraham, and unto Isaac, and to Jacob.

37 And Joseph *confirmed many other things unto his brethren,* and
took an oath of the children of Israel, saying unto them, God will
surely visit you, and ye shall carry up my bones from hence.

38 So Joseph died *when he was* an hundred and ten years old; and
they embalmed him, and *they* put him in a coffin in Egypt; *and he
was kept from burial by the children of Israel, that he might be carried up and laid in the sepulchre with his father. And thus they remembered the oath which they sware unto him.*

EXODUS 6:2–3

2 And God spake unto Moses, and said unto him, I am the Lord;

3 And I appeared unto Abraham, unto Isaac, and unto Jacob. *I am*

the Lord God Almighty; *the Lord* JEHOVAH. *And was not my name* known unto them?

EXODUS 18:1
1 When Jethro, the *high* priest of Midian, Moses' father-in-law, heard . . .

EXODUS 22:28
28 Thou shalt not revile *against God,* nor curse the ruler of thy people.

EXODUS 23:3
3 Neither shalt thou countenance a *wicked* man in his cause.

EXODUS 32:14
14 And the Lord *said unto Moses, If they will repent of the evil which they have done, I will spare them, and turn away my fierce wrath; but, behold, thou shalt execute judgment upon all that will not repent of this evil this day. Therefore, see thou do this thing that I have com-manded thee, or I will execute all that which I had* thought to do unto *my* people.

EXODUS 33:20
20 And he said *unto Moses,* Thou canst not see my face *at this time, lest mine anger be kindled against thee also, and I destroy thee, and thy people;* for there shall no man *among them* see me *at this time,* and live, *for they are exceeding sinful. And no sinful man hath at any time, neither shall there be any sinful man at any time, that shall see my face and live.*

EXODUS 34:1–2
1 And the Lord said unto Moses, Hew thee two *other* tables of stone, like unto the first, and I will write upon *them* also, the words *of the law, according as they were written at the first on the* tables which thou brakest; *but it shall not be according to the first, for I will take away the priesthood out of their midst; therefore my holy order, and the ordinances thereof, shall not go before them; for my presence shall not go up in their midst, lest I destroy them.*
2 *But I will give unto them the law as at the first, but it shall be after the law of a carnal commandment; for I have sworn in my wrath, that they shall not enter into my presence, into my rest, in the days of their*

pilgrimage. Therefore do as I have commanded thee, and be ready in the morning, and come up in the morning unto mount Sinai, . . .

LEVITICUS 22:9

9 They shall therefore keep mine ordinance, lest they bear sin for it, and die; therefore, if they profane *not mine ordinances,* I the Lord *will* sanctify them.

NUMBERS 16:10

10 And he hath brought thee near to him, and all thy brethren the sons of Levi with thee; and seek ye the *high* priesthood also?

DEUTERONOMY 10:1–2

1 At that time the Lord said unto me, Hew thee two *other* tables of stone like unto the first, and come up unto me *upon* the mount, and make thee an ark of wood.

2 And I will write on the tables the words that were *on* the first tables, which thou breakest, *save the words of the everlasting covenant of the holy priesthood,* and thou shalt put them in the ark.

DEUTERONOMY 34:6

6 *For the Lord took him unto his fathers,* in a valley in the land of Moab, over against Beth-peor; *therefore* no man knoweth of his sepulcher unto this day.

1 SAMUEL 16:14–16, 23

14 But the Spirit of the Lord departed from Saul, and an evil spirit *which was not of* the Lord troubled him.

15 And Saul's servants said unto him, Behold now, an evil spirit *which is not of* God troubleth thee.

16 Let our lord now command thy servants, which are before thee, to seek out a man, who is a cunning player on a harp; and it shall come to pass, when the evil spirit, *which is not of* God, is upon thee, that he shall play with his hand, and thou shalt be well.

. . .

23 And it came to pass, when the evil spirit, *which was not of* God, was upon Saul, that David took a harp and played with his hand; so Saul was refreshed, and was well, and the evil spirit departed from him.

1 SAMUEL 19:9

9 And the evil spirit *which was not of* the Lord was upon Saul . . .

2 SAMUEL 12:13

13 And David said unto Nathan, I have sinned against the Lord. And Nathan said unto David, The Lord also hath *not* put away thy sin *that* thou shalt not die.

1 KINGS 3:14

14 And if thou wilt walk in my ways to keep my statutes, and my commandments, then I will lengthen thy days, *and thou shalt not walk in unrighteousness,* as did thy father David.

1 KINGS 14:8

8 And rent the kingdom away from the house of David and gave it thee, *because he kept not my commandments. But* thou hast not been as my servant David, *when he* followed me with all his heart only to do right in mine eyes.

2 CHRONICLES 18:20–22

20 Then there came out a *lying* spirit and stood before *them,* and said, I will entice him. And the Lord said unto him, Wherewith?
21 And he said, I will go out, and be a lying spirit in the mouth of all his prophets. And the Lord said, Thou shalt entice him, and thou shalt also prevail; go out, and do even so; *for all these have sinned against me.*
22 Now therefore, behold, the Lord hath *found* a lying spirit in the mouth of these thy prophets, and the Lord hath spoken evil against thee.

PSALM 11:1–5

1 *In that day thou shalt come, O Lord; and* I will put my trust *in thee. Thou shalt say unto thy people, for mine ear hath heard thy voice; thou shalt say unto every* soul, Flee unto *my* mountain; *and the righteous shall flee like* a bird *that is let go from the snare of the fowler.*
2 For the wicked bend their bow; lo, they make ready their arrow upon the string, that they may privily shoot at the upright in heart, *to destroy their foundation.*
3 *But the foundations of the wicked shall be destroyed, and what can they do?*
4 *For* the Lord, *when he shall come into* his holy temple, *sitting upon God's* throne in heaven, his *eyes shall pierce the wicked.*
5 Behold his eyelids *shall* try the children of men, *and he shall*

redeem the righteous, and they shall be tried. The Lord *loveth* the righteous, but the wicked, and him that loveth violence, his soul hateth.

PSALM 14:1–7

1 The fool hath said in his heart, *There is no man that hath seen God. Because he showeth himself not unto us, therefore* there is no God. *Behold,* they are corrupt; they have done abominable works, *and none of them* doeth good.

2 *For* the Lord looked down from heaven upon the children of men, *and by his voice said unto his servant, Seek ye among the children of men,* to see if there *are* any that *do* understand God. *And he opened his mouth unto the Lord, and said, Behold, all these who say they are thine.*

3 *The Lord answered and said,* They are all gone aside, they are together become filthy, *thou canst behold* none of them that *are doing* good, no, not one.

4 *All they have for their teachers are* workers of iniquity, *and there is* no knowledge *in them. They are they* who eat up my people. They eat bread and call not upon the Lord.

5 They are in great fear, for God *dwells* in the generation of the righteous. *He is the counsel of the poor, because they are ashamed of the wicked, and flee unto the Lord, for their refuge.*

6 *They are ashamed* of the counsel of the poor because the Lord is his refuge.

7 Oh that *Zion were established out of heaven,* the salvation of Israel. *O Lord, when wilt thou establish Zion?* When the Lord bringeth back the captivity of his people, Jacob shall rejoice, Israel shall be glad.

PSALM 22:12

12 Many *armies* have compassed me; strong *armies* of Bashan have beset me around.

PSALM 24:7–10

7 Lift up your heads, O ye *generations of Jacob;* and be ye lifted up; and the Lord strong and mighty; the Lord mighty in battle, who is the king of glory, *shall establish you forever.*

8 *And he will roll away the heavens; and will come down to redeem his people; to make you an everlasting name; to establish you upon his everlasting rock.*

9 Lift up your heads, O ye *generations of Jacob*; lift up your *heads*, ye everlasting *generations*, and the *Lord of hosts, the king of kings;*
10 *Even* the king of glory shall come *unto you; and shall redeem his people, and shall establish them in righteousness.* Selah.

PSALM 30:5, 9
5 For his anger *kindleth against the wicked; they repent, and in* a moment *it is turned away, and they are* in his favor, *and he giveth them* life; *therefore,* weeping may endure for a night, but joy cometh in the morning.

. . .

9 When I go down to the pit, *my* blood *shall return to* the dust. *I will* praise thee; *my soul* shall declare thy truth; *for what profit am I, if I do it not?*

PSALM 32:1
Blessed *are they* whose transgressions *are* forgiven, and who have *no* sins *to be* covered.

PSALM 36:1
The wicked, *who live in* transgression, saith in *their* hearts, *There is no condemnation; for* there is no fear of God before *their* eyes.

PSALM 138:8
8 The Lord will perfect me *in knowledge, concerning his kingdom. I will praise thee* O Lord, forever; *for thou art merciful, and wilt* not forsake the works of thine own hands.

PSALM 141:5
5 *When* the righteous smite me *with the word of the Lord* it is a kindness; and *when they* reprove me, it shall be an excellent oil, *and* shall not *destroy* my *faith*; for yet my prayer also shall be *for them. I delight not* in their calamities.

ISAIAH 42:19–23
19 *For I will send my servant unto you who are blind; yea, a messenger to open the eyes of the blind, and unstop the ears of the deaf;*
20 *And they shall be made perfect notwithstanding their blindness, if they will hearken unto the messenger, the Lord's servant.*
21 *Thou art a people,* seeing many things, but thou observest not; opening the ears *to hear, but thou* hearest not.

22 The Lord is *not* well pleased *with such a people, but* for his righteousness' sake he will magnify the law and make it honorable.

23 *Thou art* a people robbed and spoiled; *thine enemies*, all of them, *have snared thee* in holes, and they have hid thee in prison houses; they have taken thee for a prey, and none delivereth; for a spoil, and none saith, Restore.

ISAIAH 52:15
15 So shall he *gather* many nations . . .

AMOS 3:6–7
6 . . . shall there be evil in a city, and the Lord hath not *known* it?
7 Surely the Lord God will do nothing, *until* he revealeth *the* secret unto his servants the prophets.

MATTHEW 3:45–46 (KJV 3:16–17)
45 And Jesus, when he was baptized, went up straightway out of the water; *and John saw*, and lo, the heavens were opened unto him, and he saw the Spirit of God descending like a dove and lighting upon *Jesus.*
46 And lo, *he heard* a voice from heaven, saying, This is my beloved Son, in whom I am well pleased. *Hear ye him.*

MATTHEW 5:21 (KJV 5:19)
21 Whosoever, therefore, shall break one of these least commandments, and shall teach men so *to do, he shall in no wise be saved in the kingdom of heaven;* but whosoever shall do and teach *these commandments of the law until it be fulfilled,* the same shall be called great, *and shall be saved* in the kingdom of heaven.

MATTHEW 6:38 (KJV 6:33)
38 *Wherefore, seek not the things of this world but* seek ye first *to build up* the kingdom of God, and *to establish* his righteousness, and all these things shall be added unto you.

MATTHEW 7:4–11
4 *And again, ye shall say unto them, Why is it that thou* beholdest the mote that is in thy brother's eye, but considerest not the beam that is in thine own eye?
5 Or how wilt thou say to thy brother, Let me pull out the mote out of thine eye; *and canst not behold* a beam in thine own eye?
6 *And Jesus said unto his disciples, Beholdest thou the Scribes, and*

the Pharisees, and the Priests, and the Levites? They teach in their
synagogues, but do not observe the law, nor the commandments; and
all have gone out of the way, and are under sin.

7 *Go thou and say unto them, Why teach ye men the law and the*
commandments, when ye yourselves are the children of corruption?

8 *Say unto them,* Ye hypocrites, first cast out the beam out of thine
own eye; and then shalt thou see clearly to cast out the mote out of
thy brother's eye.

9 *Go ye into the world, saying unto all, Repent, for the kingdom of*
heaven has come nigh unto you.

10 *And the mysteries of the kingdom ye shall keep within yourselves;*
for it is not meet to give that which is holy unto the dogs; neither cast
ye your pearls *unto* swine, lest they trample them under their feet.

11 *For the world cannot receive that which ye, yourselves, are not able*
to bear; wherefore ye shall not give your pearls unto them, lest they
turn again and rend you.

MATTHEW 9:18–21

18 *Then said the Pharisees unto him, Why will ye not receive us with*
our baptism, seeing we keep the whole law?

19 *But Jesus said unto them, Ye keep not the law. If ye had kept the*
law, ye would have received me, for I am he who gave the law.

20 *I receive not you with your baptism, because it profiteth you noth-*
ing.

21 *For when that which is new is come, the old is ready to be put*
away.

MATTHEW 13:10–11, 29, 49–50 (KJV 13:12, 30, 49)

10 For whosoever *receiveth*, to him shall be given, and he shall have
more abundance;

11 But whosoever *continueth* not *to receive*, from him shall be taken
away even that he hath.

. . .

29 Let both grow together until the harvest, and in the time of harvest, I will say to the reapers, Gather ye together first the *wheat into*
my barn; and the tares are *bound* in bundles to *be burned.*

. . .

49 So shall it be at the end of the world.

50 *And the world is the children of the wicked.*

MATTHEW 16:26–29

26 *And now for a man to take up his cross, is to deny himself all ungodliness, and every worldly lust, and keep my commandments.*

27 *Break not my commandments for to save your lives;* for whosoever will save his life *in this world*, shall lose it *in the world to come.*

28 And whosoever will lose his life *in this world*, for my sake, shall find it *in the world to come.*

29 *Therefore, forsake the world, and save your souls;* for what is a man profited, if he shall gain the whole world, and lose his own soul? Or what shall a man give in exchange for his soul?

MATTHEW 17:10–14

10 And Jesus answered and said unto them, Elias truly shall first come, and restore all things, *as the prophets have written.*

11 *And again* I say unto you that Elias has come already, *concerning whom it is written, Behold, I will send my messenger, and he shall prepare the way before me;* and they knew him not, and have done unto him, whatsoever they listed.

12 Likewise shall also the Son of Man suffer of them.

13 *But I say unto you, Who is Elias? Behold, this is Elias, whom I send to prepare the way before me.*

14 Then the disciples understood that he spake unto them of John the Baptist, *and also of another who should come and restore all things, as it is written by the prophets.*

MATTHEW 21:47–56

47 And when the chief priests and Pharisees had heard his parables, they perceived that he spake of them.

48 *And they said among themselves, Shall this man think that he alone can spoil this great kingdom? And they were angry with him.*

49 But when they sought to lay hands on him, they feared the multitude, because they learned that the multitude took him for a prophet.

50 *And now his disciples came to him, and Jesus said unto them, Marvel ye at the words of the parable which I spake unto them?*

51 *Verily, I say unto you, I am the stone, and those wicked ones reject me.*

52 *I am the head of the corner. These Jews shall fall upon me, and shall be broken.*

53 *And the kingdom of God shall be taken from them, and shall be*

given to a nation bringing forth the fruits thereof; (meaning the Gentiles.)

54 *Wherefore, on whomsoever this stone shall fall, it shall grind him to powder.*

55 *And when the Lord therefore of the vineyard cometh, he will destroy those miserable, wicked men, and will let again his vineyard unto other husbandmen, even in the last days, who shall render him the fruits in their seasons.*

56 *And then understood they the parable which he spake unto them, that the Gentiles should be destroyed also, when the Lord should descend out of heaven to reign in his vineyard, which is the earth and the inhabitants thereof.*

MATTHEW 24:1–56 (KJV 24:1–51)

This expanded text is reproduced in Joseph Smith—Matthew 1:1–55 in the Pearl of Great Price.

MATTHEW 25:11 (KJV 25:12)

11 But he answered and said, Verily I say unto you, *Ye* know *me* not.

MARK 2:26–27

26 *Wherefore the Sabbath was given unto man for a day of rest; and also that man should glorify God, and not that man should not eat;*

27 *For the Son of Man made the Sabbath day,* therefore the Son of Man is Lord also of the Sabbath.

MARK 8:37–38

37 For whosoever will save his life, shall lose it; *or whosoever will save his life, shall be willing to lay it down for my sake; and if he is not willing to lay it down for my sake, he shall lose it.*

38 But whosoever shall *be willing to* lose his life for my sake, and the *gospel*, the same shall save it.

MARK 9:40–48

40 *Therefore,* if thy hand offend thee, cut it off; *or if thy brother offend thee and confess not and forsake not, he shall be cut off.* It is better for thee to enter into life maimed, than having two hands, to go into hell.

41 *For it is better for thee to enter into life without thy brother, than for thee and thy brother to be cast into hell;* into the fire that never shall be quenched, where their worm dieth not, and the fire is not quenched.

42 *And again,* if thy foot offend thee, cut it off; *for he that is thy standard, by whom thou walkest, if he become a transgressor, he shall be cut off.*

43 It is better for thee, to enter halt into life, than having two feet to be cast into hell; into the fire that never shall be quenched.

44 *Therefore, let every man stand or fall, by himself, and not for another; or not trusting another.*

45 *Seek unto my Father, and it shall be done in that very moment what ye shall ask, if ye ask in faith, believing that ye shall receive.*

46 And if thine eye *which seeth for thee, him that is appointed to watch over thee to show thee light, become a transgressor and offend thee, pluck him out.*

47 It is better for thee to enter into the kingdom of God, with one eye, than having two eyes to be cast into hell fire.

48 *For it is better that thyself should be saved, than to be cast into hell with thy brother,* where their worm dieth not, and where the fire is not quenched.

MARK 14:20–25

20 And as they did eat, Jesus took bread and blessed it, and brake, and gave to them, and said, *Take it, and eat.*

21 *Behold, this is for you to do in remembrance of my body; for as oft as ye do this ye will remember this hour that I was with you.*

22 And he took the cup, and when he had given thanks, he gave it to them; and they all drank of it.

23 *And he said unto them, This is in remembrance of my blood which is shed for many, and the new testament which I give unto you; for of me ye shall bear record unto all the world.*

24 *And as oft as ye do this ordinance, ye will remember me in this hour that I was with you and drank with you of this cup, even the last time in my ministry.*

25 Verily I say unto you, *Of this ye shall bear record; for* I will no more drink of the fruit of the vine *with you,* until that day that I drink it new in the kingdom of God.

MARK 14:36–38 (KJV 14:32–34)

36 And they came to a place which was named Gethsemane, *which was a garden; and the disciples began to be sore amazed, and to be*

very heavy, and to complain in their hearts, wondering if this be the Messiah.

37 *And Jesus knowing their hearts, said* to his disciples, Sit ye here, while I shall pray.

38 And he taketh with him Peter, and James, and John, *and rebuked them,* and said unto them, My soul is exceeding sorrowful, *even* unto death; tarry ye here and watch.

LUKE 3:4–10

4 As it is written in the book of the *prophet* Esaias; *and these are the words,* saying, The voice of one crying in the wilderness, Prepare ye the way of the Lord, and make his paths straight.

5 *For behold, and lo, he shall come, as it is written in the book of the prophets, to take away the sins of the world, and to bring salvation unto the heathen nations, to gather together those who are lost, who are of the sheepfold of Israel;*

6 *Yea, even the dispersed and afflicted; and also to prepare the way, and make possible the preaching of the gospel unto the Gentiles;*

7 *And to be a light unto all who sit in darkness, unto the uttermost parts of the earth; to bring to pass the resurrection from the dead, and to ascend up on high, to dwell on the right hand of the Father,*

8 *Until the fulness of time, and the law and the testimony shall be sealed, and the keys of the kingdom shall be delivered up again unto the Father;*

9 *To administer justice unto all; to come down in judgment upon all, and to convince all the ungodly of their ungodly deeds, which they have committed; and all this in the day that he shall come;*

10 *For it is a day of power; yea,* every valley shall be filled, and every mountain and hill shall be brought low; . . .

LUKE 5:23

23 *Does it require more power to* forgive sins *than to make the sick* rise up and walk?

LUKE 6:29–30

29 And unto him who smiteth thee on the cheek, offer also the other; *or, in other words, it is better to offer the other, than to revile again.* And him who taketh away thy cloak, forbid not to take thy coat also.

30 *For it is better that thou suffer thine enemy to take these things,*

than to contend with him. Verily I say unto you, Your heavenly Father who seeth in secret, shall bring that wicked one into judgment.

LUKE 8:23

23 But as they sailed he fell asleep; and there came down a storm of wind on the lake; and they were filled with *fear*, and were in *danger*.

LUKE 9:31

31 Who appeared in glory, and spake of his *death, and also his resurrection*, which he should accomplish at Jerusalem.

LUKE 10:22 (KJV 10:21)

22 In that hour Jesus rejoiced in spirit, and said, I thank thee, O Father, Lord of heaven and earth, that thou hast hid these things from *them who think they are* wise and prudent, and hast revealed them unto babes; even so, Father; for so it seemed good in thy sight.

LUKE 11:53 (KJV 11:52)

53 Woe unto you, lawyers! For ye have taken away the key of knowledge, *the fulness of the scriptures*; ye enter not in yourselves *into the kingdom*; and *those who* were entering in, ye hindered.

LUKE 12:9–12

9 But he *who* denieth me before men, shall be denied before the angels of God.

10 *Now his disciples knew that he said this, because they had spoken evil against him before the people; for they were afraid to confess him before men.*

11 *And they reasoned among themselves, saying, He knoweth our hearts, and he speaketh to our condemnation, and we shall not be forgiven. But he answered them, and said unto them,*

12 Whosoever shall speak a word against the Son of Man, *and repenteth*, it shall be forgiven him; but unto him *who* blasphemeth against the Holy Ghost, it shall not be forgiven him.

LUKE 12:34 (KJV 12:31)

34 *Therefore* seek ye to *bring forth* the kingdom of God, and all these things shall be added unto you.

LUKE 12:41–57

41 *For, behold, he cometh in the first watch of the night, and he shall*

also come in the second watch, and again he shall come in the third watch.

42 *And verily I say unto you, He hath already come, as it is written of him; and again when* he shall come in the second watch, or come in the third watch, *blessed are those servants when he cometh,* that he shall find so *doing;*

43 *For the Lord of those servants shall gird himself, and make them to sit down to meat, and will come forth and serve them.*

44 *And now, verily I say these things unto you, that ye may know this, that the coming of the Lord is as a thief in the night.*

45 *And it is like unto a man who is an householder, who, if he watcheth not his goods, the thief cometh in an hour of which he is not aware, and taketh his goods, and divideth them among his fellows.*

46 *And they said among themselves,* If the good man of the house had known what hour the thief would come, he would have watched, and not have suffered his house to be broken through *and the loss of his goods.*

47 *And he said unto them, Verily I say unto you,* be ye therefore ready also; for the Son of Man cometh at an hour when ye think not.

48 Then Peter said unto him, Lord, speaketh thou this parable unto us, or unto all?

49 And the Lord said, *I speak unto those whom the Lord shall make rulers* over his household, to give *his children* their portion of meat in due season.

50 *And they said, Who then is that faithful and wise servant?*

51 *And the Lord said unto them, It is that servant who watcheth, to impart his portion of meat in due season.*

52 Blessed *be* that servant whom his Lord *shall find,* when he cometh, so doing.

53 Of a truth I say unto you, that he will make him ruler over all that he hath.

54 *But the evil servant is he who is not found watching. And if that servant is not found watching, he will say* in his heart, My Lord delayeth his coming; and shall begin to beat the menservants, and the maidens, and to eat, and drink, and to be drunken.

55 The *Lord* of that servant will come in a day he looketh not for, and at an hour when he is not aware, and will cut him *down*, and will appoint him his portion with the unbelievers.

56 And that servant who knew his Lord's will, and prepared not *for his Lord's coming*, neither did according to his will, shall be beaten with many stripes.

57 But he that knew not *his Lord's will*, and did commit things worthy of stripes, shall be beaten with few. For unto whomsoever much is given, of him shall much be required; and to whom *the Lord* has committed much, of him *will men* ask the more.

LUKE 13:36 (KJV 13:35)

36 Behold, your house is left unto you desolate. And verily I say unto you, Ye shall not *know* me, *until ye have received from the hand of the Lord a just recompense for all your sins*; until the time come when ye shall say, Blessed is he who cometh in the name of the Lord.

LUKE 14:35–37

35 *Then certain of them came to him, saying, Good Master, we have Moses and the prophets, and whosoever shall live by them, shall he not have life?*

36 *And Jesus answered, saying, Ye know not Moses, neither the prophets; for if ye had known them, ye would have believed on me; for to this intent they were written. For I am sent that ye might have life. Therefore I will liken it unto salt* which is good;

37 But if the salt *has* lost *its* savor, wherewith shall it be seasoned?

LUKE 16:16–23

16 *And they said unto him, We have the law, and the prophets; but as for this man we will not receive him to be our ruler; for he maketh himself to be a judge over us.*

17 *Then said Jesus unto them,* The law and the prophets *testify of me; yea, and all the prophets who have written, even* until John, *have foretold of these days.*

18 Since that time, the kingdom of God is preached, and every man *who seeketh truth* presseth into it.

19 And it is easier for heaven and earth to pass, than for one tittle of the law to fail.

20 *And why teach ye the law, and deny that which is written; and condemn him whom the Father hath sent to fulfil the law, that ye might all be redeemed?*

21 *O fools! for you have said in your hearts, There is no God. And you pervert the right way; and the kingdom of heaven suffereth*

violence of you; and you persecute the meek; and in your violence you seek to destroy the kingdom; and ye take the children of the kingdom by force. Woe unto you, ye adulterers!

22 *And they reviled him again, being angry for the saying, that they were adulterers.*

23 *But he continued, saying,* Whosoever putteth away his wife, and marrieth another, committeth adultery; and whosoever marrieth her who is put away from her husband, committeth adultery. *Verily I say unto you, I will liken you unto the rich man.*

LUKE 17:36–40

36 And they answered and said unto him, Where, Lord, *shall they be taken.*

37 And he said unto them, Wheresoever the body is *gathered; or, in other words, whithersoever the saints are gathered,* thither will the eagles be gathered together; *or, thither will the remainder be gathered together.*

38 *This he spake, signifying the gathering of his saints; and of angels descending and gathering the remainder unto them; the one from the bed, the other from the grinding, and the other from the field, whithersoever he listeth.*

39 *For verily there shall be new heavens, and a new earth, wherein dwelleth righteousness.*

40 *And there shall be no unclean thing; for the earth becoming old, even as a garment, having waxed in corruption, wherefore it vanisheth away, and the footstool remaineth sanctified, cleansed from all sin.*

LUKE 21:24–25

24 *And then his disciples asked him, saying, Master, tell us concerning thy coming?*

25 *And he answered them, and said, In the generation in which the times of the Gentiles shall be fulfilled,* there shall be signs in the sun, and in the moon, and in the stars; and upon the earth distress of nations with perplexity, *like* the sea and the waves roaring. *The earth also shall be troubled, and the waters of the great deep;*

JOHN 1:1–34

1 In the beginning was the *gospel preached through the Son. And the gospel was the word, and the word was with the Son, and the Son was with God, and the Son was of God.*

2 The same was in the beginning with God.

3 All things were made by him; and without him was not anything made which was made.

4 In him was *the gospel*, and *the gospel was the life*, and the life was the light of men;

5 And the light shineth *in the world*, and the *world perceiveth* it not.

6 There was a man sent from God, whose name was John.

7 The same came *into the world* for a witness, to bear witness of the light, *to bear record of the gospel through the Son, unto all*, that through him *men* might believe.

8 He was not that light, but *came* to bear witness of that light,

9 *Which* was the true light, which lighteth every man *who* cometh into the world;

10 *Even the Son of God.* He *who* was in the world, and the world was made by him, and the world knew him not.

11 He came unto his own, and his own received him not.

12 But as many as received him, to them gave he power to become the sons of God; *only* to them *who* believe on his name.

13 *He was* born, not of blood, nor of the will of the flesh, nor of the will of man, but of God.

14 And the *same* word was made flesh, and dwelt among us, and we beheld his glory, the glory as of the Only Begotten of the Father, full of grace and truth.

15 John *bear* witness of him, and cried, saying, This *is* he of whom I spake; He *who* cometh after me, is preferred before me; for he was before me.

16 *For in the beginning was the Word, even the Son, who is made flesh, and sent unto us by the will of the Father, And as many as believe on his name shall receive of his fulness.* And of his fulness have all we received, *even immortality and eternal life, through his grace.*

17 For the law was given *through* Moses, but *life* and truth came *through* Jesus Christ.

18 *For the law was after a carnal commandment, to the administration of death; but the gospel was after the power of an endless life, through Jesus Christ, the Only Begotten Son, who is in the bosom of the Father.*

19 *And* no man hath seen God at any time, *except he hath borne record of the Son; for except it is through him no man can be saved.*

20 And this is the record of John, when the Jews sent priests and Levites from Jerusalem, to ask him; Who art thou?

21 And he confessed, and denied not *that he was Elias*; but confessed, *saying*; I am not the Christ.

22 And they asked him, saying; *How then art thou Elias? And he said, I am not that Elias who was to restore all things. And they asked him, saying,* Art thou that prophet? And he answered, No.

23 Then said they unto him, Who art thou? that we may give an answer to them that sent us. What sayest thou of thyself?

24 He said, I am the voice of one crying in the wilderness, Make straight the way of the Lord, as saith the prophet Esaias.

25 And they who were sent were of the Pharisees.

26 And they asked him, and said unto him; Why baptizest thou then, if thou be not the Christ, nor Elias *who was to restore all things*, neither that prophet?

27 John answered them, saying; I baptize with water, but there standeth one among you, whom ye know not;

28 *He it is of whom I bear record. He is that prophet, even Elias,* who, coming after me, is preferred before me, whose shoe's latchet I am not worthy to unloose, *or whose place I am not able to fill; for he shall baptize, not only with water, but with fire, and with the Holy Ghost.*

29 The next day John seeth Jesus coming unto him, and said; Behold the Lamb of God, who taketh away the sin of the world!

30 *And John bare record of him unto the people, saying,* This is he of whom I said; After me cometh a man who is preferred before me; for he was before me, and I knew him, *and* that he should be made manifest to Israel; therefore am I come baptizing with water.

31 And John bare record, saying; *When he was baptized of me*, I saw the Spirit descending from heaven like a dove, and it abode upon him.

32 And I knew him; *for* he *who* sent me to baptize with water, the same said unto me; Upon whom thou shalt see the Spirit descending, and remaining on him, the same is he who baptizeth with the Holy Ghost.

33 And I saw, and bare record that this is the Son of God.

34 *These things were done in Bethabara, beyond Jordan, where John was baptizing.*

JOHN 4:26 (KJV 4:24)

26 *For unto such hath God promised his* Spirit. And they *who* worship him, must worship in spirit and in truth.

JOHN 6:44

44 No man can come unto me, except *he doeth the will of my Father who hath sent me. And this is the will of him who hath sent me, that ye receive the Son; for the Father beareth record of him; and he who receiveth the testimony, and doeth the will of him who sent me,* I will raise up *in the resurrection of the just.*

JOHN 9:32

32 Since the world began was it not heard that any man opened the eyes of one that was born blind, *except he be of God.*

JOHN 10:8

8 All that ever came before me *who testified not of me* are thieves and robbers; but the sheep did not hear them.

JOHN 13:8–10

8 Peter saith unto him, *Thou needest not to* wash my feet. Jesus answered him, If I wash thee not, thou hast no part with me.

9 Simon Peter saith unto him, Lord, not my feet only, but also my hands and my head.

10 Jesus saith to him, He that *has* washed *his hands and his head,* needeth not save to wash his feet, but is clean every whit; and ye are clean, but not all. *Now this was the custom of the Jews under their law; wherefore, Jesus did this that the law might be fulfilled.*

ROMANS 3:24

24 *Therefore* being justified *only* by his grace through the redemption that is in Christ Jesus;

ROMANS 7:5–27

5 For when we were in the flesh, the motions of sins, which were *not according to* the law, did work in our members to bring forth fruit unto death.

6 But now we are delivered from the law wherein we were held, *being dead to the law,* that we should serve in newness of spirit, and not in the oldness of the letter.

7 What shall we say then? Is the law sin? God forbid. Nay, I had not

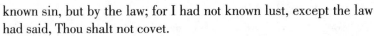

known sin, but by the law; for I had not known lust, except the law had said, Thou shalt not covet.

8 But sin, taking occasion by the commandment, wrought in me all manner of concupiscence. For without the law sin was dead.

9 For *once* I was alive without *transgression of* the law, but when the commandment *of Christ* came, sin revived, and I died.

10 And *when I believed not* the commandment *of Christ which came,* which was ordained to life, I found *it condemned me* unto death.

11 For sin, taking occasion, *denied* the commandment, *and* deceived me and by it *I was slain.*

12 *Nevertheless, I found* the law *to be* holy, and the commandment *to be* holy, and just, and good.

13 Was then that which is good made death unto me? God forbid. But sin, that it might appear sin by that which is good *working death in me*; that sin, by the commandment, might become exceeding sinful.

14 For we know that the *commandment* is spiritual; but *when I was under the law,* I was yet carnal, sold under sin.

15 *But now I am spiritual*; for that which *I am commanded to do, I do; and that which I am commanded not to allow,* I allow not.

16 *For what I know is not right I would* not *do; for that which is sin,* I hate.

17 If then I do *not* that which I would not *allow,* I consent unto the law, that it is good; *and I am not condemned.*

18 Now then, it is no more I that do *sin*; but I *seek to subdue that* sin *which* dwelleth in me.

19 For I know that in me, that is, in my flesh, dwelleth no good thing; for to will is present with me, but to perform that which is good I find not, *only in Christ.*

20 For the good that I would *have done when under the law, I find not to be good; therefore,* I do it not.

21 But the evil which I would not *do under the law, I find to be good*; that, I do.

22 Now if I do that, *through the assistance of Christ,* I would not *do under the law, I am not under the law; and* it is no more *that I seek to do wrong,* but to *subdue* sin that dwelleth in me.

23 I find then that *under the* law, that when I would do good evil *was* present with me; for I delight in the law of God after the inward man.

24 *And now I see another law, even the commandment of Christ, and it is imprinted in my mind.*

25 *But* my members *are* warring against the law of my mind, and bringing me into captivity to the law of sin which is in my members.

26 *And if I subdue not the sin which is in me, but with the flesh serve the law of sin;* O wretched man that I am! who shall deliver me from the body of this death?

27 I thank God through Jesus Christ our Lord, then, that so with the mind I myself serve the law of God.

ROMANS 8:8–10, 13

8 So then they that are *after* the flesh cannot please God.

9 But ye are not *after* the flesh, but *after* the Spirit, if so be that the Spirit of God dwell in you. Now if any man have not the Spirit of Christ, he is none of his.

10 And if Christ be in you, *though* the body *shall die* because of sin, *yet* the Spirit is life, because of righteousness.

. . .

13 For if ye live after the flesh, *unto sin*, ye shall die; but if ye through the Spirit do mortify the deeds of the body, ye shall live *unto Christ*.

1 CORINTHIANS 7:1, 5, 9, 29–33

1 Now concerning the things whereof ye wrote unto me, *saying*, It is good for a man not to touch a woman.

. . .

5 *Depart* ye not one *from* the other, except it be with consent for a time, that ye may give yourselves to fasting and prayer.

. . .

9 But if they cannot *abide*, let them marry; for it is better to marry than *that any should commit sin.*

. . .

29 But *I speak unto you who are called unto the ministry. For* this I say, brethren, the time that remaineth is but short, *that ye shall be sent forth unto the ministry.* Even they who have wives, shall be as though they had none; *for ye are called and chosen to do the Lord's work.*

30 And it shall be with them who weep, as though they wept not; and

them who rejoice, as though they rejoiced not, and them who buy, as though they possessed not;

31 And *them who* use this world, as not using it; for the fashion of this world passeth away.

32 But *I would, brethren, that ye magnify your calling.* I would have you without carefulness. For he who is unmarried, careth for the things that belong to the Lord, how he may please the Lord; *therefore he prevaileth.*

33 But he who is married, careth for the things that are of the world, how he may please his wife; *therefore there is a difference, for he is hindered.*

2 THESSALONIANS 2:7–9

7 For the mystery of iniquity doth already work, *and he it is who now worketh, and Christ suffereth him to work, until the time is fulfilled that he shall* be taken out of the way.

8 And then shall that wicked *one* be revealed, whom the Lord shall consume with the spirit of his mouth, and shall destroy with the brightness of his coming.

9 *Yea, the Lord, even Jesus,* whose coming is *not until* after *there cometh a falling away, by* the working of Satan with all power, and signs and lying wonders . . .

2 TIMOTHY 4:2

2 Preach the word; be instant in season; *those who are* out of season, reprove, rebuke, exhort with all long-suffering and doctrine.

HEBREWS 7:19–20, 25–26

19 For the law *was administered without an oath* and made nothing perfect, but *was only* the bringing in of a better hope; by the which we draw nigh unto God.

20 Inasmuch as *this high priest* was not without an oath, *by so much was Jesus made the surety of a better testament.*

. . .

25 For such an high priest became us, who is holy, harmless, unde-filed, separate from sinners, and made *ruler over* the heavens;

26 *And not* as those high priests *who* offered up sacrifice *daily,* first for *their* own sins, and then for the *sins of the people;* for *he needeth not offer sacrifice for his own sins, for he knew no sins; but for the sins of the people. And* this he did once, when he offered up himself.

HEBREWS 11:1

1 Now faith is the *assurance* of things hoped for, the evidence of things not seen.

1 PETER 4:2

2 For *you who have* suffered in the flesh *should cease* from sin, that *you* no longer the rest of *your* time in the flesh, should live to the lusts of men, but to the will of God.

1 JOHN 4:12

12 No man hath seen God at any time, *except them who believe.*

REVELATION 1:1–8

1 The Revelation of *John, a servant of God,* which *was given* unto him *of Jesus Christ,* to show unto his servants things which must shortly come to pass, *that* he sent and signified by his angel unto his servant John,

2 Who *bore* record of the word of God, and of the testimony of Jesus Christ, and of all things that he saw.

3 Blessed *are they* who read, and they who hear *and understand* the words of this prophecy, and keep those things which are written therein, for the time *of the coming of the Lord draweth nigh.*

4 *Now this is the testimony of* John to *the seven servants who are over* the seven churches in Asia. Grace unto you, and peace from him *who* is, and *who* was, and *who* is to come; *who hath sent forth his angel from* before his throne, *to testify unto those who are the seven servants over the seven churches.*

5 *Therefore, I, John,* the faithful witness, *bear record of the things which were delivered me of the angel,* and from Jesus Christ the first begotten of the dead, and the Prince of the kings of the earth.

6 *And* unto him *who* loved us, *be glory*; who washed us from our sins in his own blood, and hath made us kings and priests unto God, his Father. To him be glory and dominion, forever and ever. Amen.

7 *For* behold, he cometh *in the* clouds *with ten thousands of his saints in the kingdom, clothed with the glory of his Father.* And every eye shall see him; and they *who* pierced him, and all kindreds of the earth shall wail because of him. Even so, Amen.

8 *For he saith,* I am Alpha and Omega, the beginning and the ending, the Lord, who is, and who was, and who is to come, the Almighty.

REVELATION 2:26–27

26 And *to him who* overcometh, and keepeth my *commandments* unto the end, will I give power over *many kingdoms*;

27 And he shall rule them with *the word of God; and they shall be in his hands* as the vessels *of clay in the hands of* a potter; *and he shall govern them by faith, with equity and justice,* even as I received of my Father.

REVELATION 12:1–8

1 And there appeared a great *sign* in heaven, *in the likeness of things on the earth*; a woman clothed with the sun, and the moon under her feet, and upon her head a crown of twelve stars.

2 And *the woman* being with child, cried, travailing in birth, and pained to be delivered.

3 *And she brought forth a man child, who was to rule all nations with a rod of iron; and her child was caught up unto God and his throne.*

4 And there appeared another *sign* in heaven; and behold, a great red dragon, having seven heads and ten horns, and seven crowns upon his heads. And his tail drew the third part of the stars of heaven, and did cast them to the earth. And the dragon stood before the woman which was delivered, ready to devour her child *after* it was born.

5 And the woman fled into the wilderness, where she *had* a place prepared of God, that they should feed her there a thousand two hundred and threescore *years*.

6 And there was war in heaven; Michael and his angels fought against the dragon; and the dragon and his angels *fought against Michael*;

7 And *the dragon* prevailed not *against Michael, neither the child, nor the woman which was the church of God, who had been delivered of her pains, and brought forth the kingdom of our God and his Christ.*

8 Neither was *there* place found in heaven *for* the great dragon, *who* was cast out; that old serpent called the devil, and *also called* Satan, which deceiveth the whole world; he was cast out into the earth; and his angels were cast out with him.

INDEX

Aaron, brother of Moses, 1–2, 383, 576.

Aaron, son of Mosiah, 92–93, 451. *See also* Alma, book of

Aaronic Priesthood: named after Aaron, 1; Nephites held the, 190; restoration of the, 204, 546; role of the, 251, 259; functions of the, 267; restored by John the Baptist, 360, 376, 379; sacrifices and the, 425; Israelites held the, 448; may prepare sacrament, 562. *See also* Melchizedek Priesthood; Priesthood

Abel, 2–3; birth of, 12; murder of, 219, 590; ministers to Paul, 504

Abimelech, 567

Abinadi, 3–6; Alma₁ writes teachings of, 19; as a martyr, 89, 431–32; and the law, 113; wars verify words of, 121; quotes Isaiah, 334–35; on the natural man, 467; quotes Ten Commandments, 491, 615; on law of Moses, 492; prophecies of, 526

Abinadom, 88, 183

Abish, 648–49

Abraham, 6–10; promises to, 223–24, 318; vision of, 275; descendants of, 301; went to Jerusalem, 370; restored writings of, 423; practiced tithing, 425; restored gospel, 548–49; testing of, 565; and Sarah, 567; seed of, 586–87; and the Urim and Thummim, 629. *See also* Book of Abraham; Seed of Abraham

Abrahamic covenant: in the book of Abraham, 63–64; and circumcision, 220; in LDS teachings, 223–24; Elias restores keys of the, 287; fulfillment of the, 323; in the Old Testament, 490–91

Acts of John, 381

Acts of the apostles, 482, 503. *See also* New Testament

Adair, James, 632

Adam, 10–15; obedience of, 2–3; in the book of Moses, 213–14; and Cain, 218–19; covenants began with, 222–23; agency and, 226–27; vision of, 275; as an Elias, 286; blesses Enoch, 295, 299; Eve as companion to, 301–3; in the Garden of Eden, 308; in the JST, 397–98; restored writings of, 423; taught gospel, 548; practiced sacrifice, 564; led battle in premortal life, 641–42. *See also* Adamic